W9-BNV-427

20th CENTURY®
Bookkeeping & Accounting

TWENTY-SECOND EDITION

PAUL A. CARLSON
Professor Emeritus
Formerly Director, Division of Business Education
Wisconsin State College
Whitewater, Wisconsin

HAMDEN L. FORKNER
Professor Emeritus
Formerly Chairman, Department of Business Education
Teachers College, Columbia University
New York, New York

LEWIS D. BOYNTON
Chairman, Department of Business Education
Central Connecticut State College
New Britain, Connecticut

South-Western Publishing Company

Cincinnati 27 | Chicago 44 | Dallas 2 | Burlingame, Calif. | New Rochelle, N. Y.

B75

Copyright ©, 1962

Philippine Copyright, 1962

By South-Western Publishing Company

Cincinnati, Ohio

ALL RIGHTS RESERVED

The text of this publication, or any part thereof, may not be reproduced in any manner whatsoever without permission in writing from the publisher.

Library of Congress Catalog Card No.: 62-11536

K262

Printed in the United States of America

Preface

Why study bookkeeping and accounting?

Bookkeeping for economic understandings

Individuals, businesses, and governments are constantly compelled to make economic decisions. The individual makes economic decisions about how he will allot his income to his various needs and desires. A business makes economic decisions about expanding or contracting the activities of the business. A local, state, or national government makes economic decisions about its budget and the tax revenues that are needed to meet the budget. Each of these economic decisions can be arrived at soundly only when bookkeeping makes financial facts available to the decision maker.

Bookkeeping as general education

General education should include an understanding of all aspects of life. If it fails to do so, it does not achieve its purpose.

Business activities touch the lives of everyone. Everyone who earns an income is responsible for keeping records that can be checked by income tax authorities. Everyone is faced with the problem of trying to balance his expenses with his income and of providing a future for himself and his dependents. Virtually everyone who is employed contributes to social security and in many cases participates in pension plans. Many persons put their savings to work for them by purchasing savings bonds, by having savings accounts, by buying a home, and by investing in American business. Almost everyone has business dealings with banks, merchants, utility companies, insurance companies, and those with whom he works.

In each case the individual who does not know the basic principles of bookkeeping lacks the general education that will help him to understand these problems and how to meet them. The study of bookkeeping provides definite and specific opportunities for everyone, regardless of his future occupational goal, to learn the language and the problems of business and how to read intelligently the daily news reports about business and economic conditions. Bookkeeping also serves the important general education need of helping the student to discover whether he has an interest in and an aptitude for accounting as a profession.

Bookkeeping as vocational education

The study of bookkeeping prepares people for employment in business. A knowledge of bookkeeping is useful to many kinds of workers in business. A typist prepares statements and other reports dealing with bookkeeping work. A secretary takes dictation dealing with bookkeeping terms, transactions, and records. She may also keep bookkeeping records for her employer. A salesperson records cash and charge transactions, and is often required to assist in inventory work. Bookkeeping helps executives understand the problems of business.

The full-time bookkeeper is an important member of the office workers of the country. Experience as a bookkeeper with additional education often qualifies a person for the profession of accountancy. Accountancy is one of the highest paid professions. Accountants in business positions often become the top executives of corporations.

Features of this text

Reasons for this revision

New business practices, new business terms, and new methods of recording and reporting business records do not change the basic principles of bookkeeping. But a textbook that does not take into account the most recent new developments does not fulfill its obligation to students and teachers.

The purpose of the 22nd Edition of *20th Century Bookkeeping and Accounting* is to retain the general pattern of the eminently popular previous editions and at the same time to bring the book up to date by including modern terminology, modern methods of data processing, new forms, and new methods for developing a course in bookkeeping and accounting.

Stronger emphasis on the analysis of transactions into their debit and credit parts

Unless the student gets an early and a thorough grounding in the basic principles of debit and credit and how transactions are analyzed into their debit and credit parts, he tends to follow ritual rather than to learn to reason. The chapter entitled "Analyzing Transactions to Determine Debits and Credits" (Chapter 4) is studied before the student is asked to do the routine of recording the transaction. Through the use of T-accounts the student learns to analyze each bookkeeping transaction. Also the drills for understanding at the end of the early chapters give ample practice in debit and credit analysis.

New end-of-chapter materials challenge able students

The general pattern of vocabulary, questions, cases, and problems used in the preceding edition has been followed in this revision. But in the problem division, a new and important feature has been added. Two optional problems, that is, a supplementary problem and a bonus problem, have been provided to aid teachers in varying the assignments according to the needs of the students.

The problems at the end of the chapters in the new edition are of three types: (1) an Application Problem (or Problems) that reinforces learnings and gives practice in applying what the text has presented; (2) a Supplementary Problem that is designed for students who need to repeat a similar problem in order to understand better what has been learned; and (3) a Bonus Problem for students who need to be challenged to go beyond the mere repetition of a problem similar to the one they have already done.

Every student in the class will ordinarily do the Application Problems. Then according to the needs of the students, the teacher suggests the use of the Supplementary Problem or the Bonus Problem.

Application of modern practices

Extensive surveys were made among practicing accountants regarding what might be done to bring this edition of the text up to date. Among the suggestions received and followed were the following:

1. The work sheet. The work sheet has been modernized by listing on the work sheet all of the accounts in the ledger in the order in which they appear in the ledger regardless of whether they have account balances. It is now unnecessary to teach the student that he must write below the total of the trial balance the titles of accounts that are adjusted but that do not appear in the trial balance. This plan also makes it easier to prepare the financial reports directly from the work sheet because the accounts appear on the work sheet in the order in which they are to appear in the reports.

2. New terminology. The terminology of the text has been brought up to date by: (a) substituting the term "income statement" for the term "profit and loss statement"; (b) changing the account title "Profit and Loss Summary" to the title "Income and Expense Summary"; (c) changing "net profit" to the modern term "net income."

3. New forms. A modern form of balance sheet has been adopted by eliminating the details of increase and decrease of capital because of net income, net loss, and withdrawals. The new form shows the present capital of a sole proprietorship in one amount on one line. In the partnership chapter, a capital statement and a distribution of net income statement are presented so that the balance sheet and the income statement may be kept as simple as possible.

4. Automation and data processing. Attention to the effects of automated office equipment upon bookkeeping and accounting is given in this edition in two important ways:

(a) At the end of many chapters reference is made to automation and how it applies to the discussion of the chapter. In each of these chapters where a brief discussion of automation is included, it is pointed out that, regardless of whether records are kept by hand, by machines, or by automated equipment, the same principles of debits, credits, costs, income, expenses, assets, liabilities, and proprietorship apply. To operate any automated part of a bookkeeping system, a complete understanding of bookkeeping and accounting as taught in this textbook is essential.

(b) An appendix on automation gives the student a complete summary of the basic principles of automation in its simplest form.

5. Sales taxes. Sales taxes and the accounting for them have been included because of the wide use of sales taxes by local and state governments.

Acknowledgments

There have been many people who have contributed to the continual improvement of *20th Century Bookkeeping and Accounting* in each new edition. Innumerable students and teachers who have used the previous editions have been helpful by criticizing the editions they were using and by suggesting methods of making the textbook more teachable. Professional accountants as well as teachers of accounting have given freely of their professional knowledge. Finally, a number of teachers read the manuscript and indicated where further revisions would make the book more modern and useful. To all of these, the authors wish to express their sincere thanks.

PAUL A. CARLSON
HAMDEN L. FORKNER
LEWIS D. BOYNTON

Contents

vii

THE BOOKKEEPING PROCESS

Each business transaction is first recorded on a receipt, a cash register slip, a sales slip, or some other business paper.

No. 1   *October 1* 1962
RECEIVED FROM *R. A. Miller*
Forty-five 00/100 ——————— DOLLARS
FOR *Used typewriter desk*
$45.00   WOOD REALTY AGENCY
             BY *M. W. Wood*

From the business papers, transactions are recorded in books known as journals.

The entries in journals are sorted and summarized in a ledger.

From the figures in the ledger, statements are prepared to guide the owners in managing the business.

Chapter 1

Starting a bookkeeping system

What bookkeeping records show

Every well-managed business keeps accurate bookkeeping records. Whether the records are kept by hand or by machine, they always show what a business owns and what it owes. These records also show the income and the expenses of the business. Many business failures could be avoided if accurate records were kept.

Everyone who has good management of his personal affairs keeps bookkeeping records that show what he owns, what he owes, and what his income and his expenses are.

What a bookkeeper does

A bookkeeper records every change in what is owned and what is owed. He also records income and expenses. At regular times throughout the year he makes a summary of the records. This summary provides the business or the individual with important facts for use in managing business affairs.

Beginning a personal bookkeeping system

James Miller decides to keep records of his personal business affairs. His first step in starting a bookkeeping system is to find out how much he is worth. He does this by listing in one column what he owns and in another column what he owes. These facts are shown below.

What is owned:		*What is owed:*	
Cash on hand..........	$ 350.00	To Auto Finance Company...........$	525.00
Government bonds.....	1,500.00	To Benner's Garage....	42.00
Automobile...........	1,800.00	To Best Paint Company.	97.00
Furniture.............	4,500.00	To City Building and	
House................	19,000.00	Loan Company......	8,000.00
Total owned...........	$27,150.00	Total owed.............$	8,664.00

James Miller can now find what he is worth by subtracting what he owes from what he owns.

Total owned...........................	$27,150.00
Total owed............................	8,664.00
What he is worth......................	$18,486.00

The balance sheet

In bookkeeping, a business form showing what is owned, what is owed, and what the proprietor is worth on a specific date is called a *balance sheet*. The balance sheet of James Miller prepared from the information on page 1 is as follows:

Assets			Liabilities		
			James Miller		
			Balance Sheet		
			December 31, 1962		
Cash	350	00	Auto Finance Company	525	00
Government Bonds	1500	00	Benner's Garage	42	00
Automobile	1800	00	Best Paint Company	97	00
Furniture	4500	00	City Bldg. and Loan Co.	8000	00
House	19000	00	Total Liabilities	8664	00
			Proprietorship		
			James Miller, Capital	18486	00
Total Assets	27150	00	Total Liab. and Prop.	27150	00

Balance sheet of an individual

Heading of a balance sheet

Every balance sheet has a three-line heading. Each of the three lines of the heading of Mr. Miller's balance sheet gives important information:

Line 1. Who? — The name of the person: *James Miller*
Line 2. What? — The name of the business form: *Balance Sheet*
Line 3. When? — The date of the business form: *December 31, 1962*

Body of a balance sheet

The body of a balance sheet has three sections: (1) Assets, (2) Liabilities, and (3) Proprietorship. The Assets section is placed on the left-hand side of the balance sheet; the Liabilities section and the Proprietorship section are placed on the right-hand side of the balance sheet.

Balance Sheet	
Assets	Liabilities and Proprietorship
(Left-hand side)	(Right-hand side)

1. Assets. Anything of value that is owned is called an *asset*. James Miller's assets are: Cash, Government Bonds, Automobile, Furniture, and House. Each asset is given the briefest title possible that will describe it. For example, cash on hand and in the bank is listed as *Cash*.

2

2. Liabilities.   An amount owed is called a *liability*.   The one to whom an amount is owed is called a *creditor*.   Each liability is given the briefest title possible that will identify it.   For example, the amount owed to the Best Paint Company is listed on the liabilities side of the balance sheet as *Best Paint Company*.

3. Proprietorship.   The amount that would remain if all the liabilities were paid is known as *proprietorship*.   The amount of the proprietorship is shown on the right-hand side of the balance sheet. The name of the owner, the word *Capital*, and the amount of his proprietorship are all written on one line.

> In some bookkeeping systems the word written after the proprietor's name on the balance sheet may be *Investment*, or *Net Worth*, or *Proprietor*.   In this textbook the word *Capital* will be used.

Why does a balance sheet have two sides?

The balance sheet has two sides in order to separate the assets from the claims against these assets.   The left-hand side of the balance sheet is used to list the assets. The right-hand side of the balance sheet is used to list the claims against these assets.

Any Balance Sheet	
Assets	Claims Against the Assets

The claims listed on the right-hand side of the balance sheet are of two kinds: (a) the claims of the creditors (listed as liabilities) and (b) the claim of the owner (listed as proprietorship).

Any Balance Sheet	
Assets	Liabilities and Proprietorship

How to find how much the proprietor is worth

The amount of the proprietorship shown on the balance sheet is obtained by subtracting the total liabilities from the total assets.   For example:

Total assets on James Miller's balance sheet...............	$27,150.00
Less total liabilities on his balance sheet..................	8,664.00
Equals the amount of his net worth or capital..............	$18,486.00

Total of each side of the balance sheet

Note that the total of the left-hand side of James Miller's balance sheet, $27,150.00, is equal to the total of its right-hand side, $27,150.00.   When a balance sheet is complete and accurate, the total of the left-hand side of the balance sheet is always equal to the total of its right-hand side.   When the two final totals of the balance sheet are not equal, the error or errors should be located and corrected.

Beginning a bookkeeping system for a business

M. W. Wood is the proprietor of a real estate business known as the Wood Realty Agency. He has decided to install a new bookkeeping system that will give him complete information about the operation of his business. Before he can start his new bookkeeping system, he needs to know:

1. What the business *owns* — a list of the *assets* of the business.
2. What the business *owes* — a list of the *liabilities* of the business.
3. What his *net worth* is   — his *proprietorship*.

Everyone who owns and operates a business has personal assets as well as business assets. He may also have personal liabilities as well as business liabilities. When he makes a personal balance sheet, he includes only personal assets and personal liabilities. When he makes a business balance sheet, he includes only the assets and the liabilities of the business.

The balance sheet of the Wood Realty Agency

After M. W. Wood has listed the needed information, he prepares a balance sheet as the first step in starting a new bookkeeping system. The beginning balance sheet of the Wood Realty Agency is shown below.

Balance sheet of a business

Steps in preparing a balance sheet

In preparing a balance sheet, follow the steps listed on the next page.

As you study these steps, check each one with the illustration of the balance sheet of the Wood Realty Agency given above.

4

Step 1.   Write the heading on three lines; center each line.

Step 2.   Write the word *Assets* in the center of the first line of the wide column on the left-hand side of the balance sheet. Then list the name and the amount of each asset on the left-hand side of the balance sheet.

> When amounts are written in ruled columns of bookkeeping forms, dollar signs and decimal points are not written. The vertical red ruling in the amount column separates dollars from cents and serves as the decimal point. When an amount is in even dollars, two zeros are written in the cents column.

Step 3.   Write the word *Liabilities* in the center of the first line of the wide column on the right-hand side of the balance sheet. Then list the name of each creditor and the amount owed to each creditor on the right-hand side of the balance sheet.

Step 4.   Rule a single line across the amount column under the last liability amount, add the column, and write the amount of the total on the next line. Write the words *Total Liabilities* on the same line as the amount.

Step 5.   Skip one line after *Total Liabilities* and write the word *Proprietorship* as a heading in the center of the wide column. (A line is skipped in order to separate the Proprietorship section from the Liabilities section.) Then write the *name of the proprietor* and the word *Capital* on the next line under the heading *Proprietorship*. On a separate sheet of paper, find the amount of the proprietorship by subtracting the total liabilities from the total assets. Write the amount of the proprietorship in the amount column after the name of the proprietor.

Step 6.   Rule a single line across the amount column on the right-hand side of the balance sheet under the amount of the proprietorship. Add the total liabilities and the amount of the proprietorship and write the new total immediately below this line. Write the words *Total Liabilities and Proprietorship* on the same line as the total.

> If necessary, the words on this line may be abbreviated to *Total Liab. and Prop.*

Step 7.   Rule a single line across the amount column on the left-hand side of the balance sheet on the *same* line as the last single line on the right-hand side of the balance sheet. Add the assets amount column and write the total immediately below the single line. Write the words *Total Assets* on the same line as the amount of the total.

Step 8.   Compare the total of the left-hand side of the balance sheet with the total of the right-hand side. The two totals should be the same. If the two final totals are the same, rule double lines across the amount columns immediately under the total on each side of the balance sheet. If the final totals are not the same, find and correct the error or errors before ruling double lines

Beginning a bookkeeping system for a social organization

On August 1, the head of the athletic department of a high school decides to start a new bookkeeping system for his department. Before the system can be started, it is necessary to find what the athletic department owns, what it owes, and what it is worth. This information in balance sheet form is shown below.

High School Athletic Department Balance Sheet August 1, 1962				
Assets			**Liabilities**	
Cash	234 00	Abel Supply Company	325 00
Baseball Equipment	638 00	Coe Printing Company	47 00
Basketball Equipment	985 00	Martin Drug Company	79 00
Football Equipment	2137 00	Total Liabilities	451 00
Track Equipment	475 00		
		Proprietorship	
		H.S. Athletic Dept., Capital	4018 00
Total Assets	4469 00	Total Liab. and Prop.	4469 00

Balance sheet of a school organization

Analyzing the balance sheet of a school organization

This balance sheet is similar to the balance sheets illustrated on pages 2 and 4. Note that:

1. The heading has three lines showing the name of the organization, the name of the form, and the date.
2. The assets are all listed on the left-hand side of the balance sheet.
3. The liabilities are all listed on the right-hand side of the balance sheet.
4. The proprietorship is shown on the right-hand side of the balance sheet. The amount of the proprietorship is given the title *H. S. Athletic Dept., Capital.*
5. The total of the left-hand side of the balance sheet is equal to the total of the right-hand side: Assets equal Liabilities plus Proprietorship.

Use of dollar signs in bookkeeping

When amounts are written in ruled columns of bookkeeping forms, dollar signs and decimal points are not written. The vertical red ruling in the amount column separates dollars from cents and serves as the decimal point.

Use of zeros for no cents

When an amount is in even dollars, two zeros are written in the cents column. Because of the widespread use of accounting machines in copying handwritten records, many business firms require the writing of zeros for even dollars in all records.

Ruling single and double lines in bookkeeping

A single line is ruled across an amount column of a bookkeeping form to indicate either addition or subtraction. Double lines are ruled in bookkeeping to show completion of all work above the double lines including proof of accuracy.

Double lines are ruled under the final totals of the balance sheet to show that all work has been completed and that the balance sheet is believed to be accurate.

Equities

The claims against assets are sometimes referred to as *equities*. There are, therefore, two types of equities shown on every balance sheet: (1) the equity of the creditors and (2) the equity of the owner.

The term "equity" is often applied to the ownership of a single asset such as a house, or household goods, or an automobile. For example, if the owner of a house worth $25,000.00 owes $10,000.00 on a mortgage on the house, the owner's equity in the house is $15,000.00.

When the term "equity of the owner" is applied to an entire balance sheet, the meaning of equity is the same as net worth of the proprietor.

The fundamental bookkeeping equation

The total of the left-hand side of every balance sheet should equal the total of the right-hand side. The total amount of the assets is equal to the total amount of the liabilities plus the amount of the proprietorship. This important principle of bookkeeping may be stated in the form of the following simple equation:

$$\text{ASSETS} = \text{LIABILITIES} + \text{PROPRIETORSHIP}$$

This bookkeeping equation is true of all balance sheets and is therefore known as the *fundamental bookkeeping equation*. For example, the bookkeeping equation for the balance sheet illustrated on page 6 is:

Assets $4,469.00 = Liabilities $451.00 + Proprietorship $4,018.00

A similar bookkeeping equation may be stated for every balance sheet to summarize the three parts of a balance sheet and the relationship of the parts.

Increasing your business vocabulary

What is the meaning of each of the following:

(a) balance sheet   (c) liability   (e) proprietorship

(b) asset   (d) creditor   (f) equities

Chapter questions

1. How did James Miller find out how much he was worth?
2. What word did James Miller write immediately after his name in the proprietorship section of the balance sheet?
3. What is the heading of the section on the left-hand side of each of the balance sheets illustrated in this chapter?
4. What are the headings of the two sections on the right-hand side of each of the balance sheets in this chapter?
5. Why are double lines ruled under the final totals of a balance sheet?
6. State the fundamental bookkeeping equation that summarizes the contents of any balance sheet.

Cases for discussion

1. The Future Business Leaders of America chapter of your high school has a bank balance of $132.58 but no other assets and no unpaid bills. What is the amount of the proprietorship of this organization? Why?
2. Barty's Department Store has assets totaling $35,000.00. The amount of liabilities is $14,000.00. What is the net worth of the business? Why?

Drill for understanding

Drill 1-A. Personal assets, liabilities, and proprietorship

This drill is planned to give you additional skill in classifying items as assets, liabilities, and proprietorship before placing them on a balance sheet.

If you do not have a workbook, prepare a form similar to the one illustrated below at the right. If you have the workbook that correlates with this textbook, use the form in the workbook.

Instructions: 1. Classify each item as follows:

In the Answers column, print a capital *A* for asset, a capital *L* for liability, and a capital *P* for proprietorship. The first item, cash on hand, is given as an example.

Instructions: 2. Now cover your answers and see how rapidly you can do this drill mentally without looking at your answers. Repeat this mental drill several times for increased speed and accuracy.

ITEMS TO BE CLASSIFIED	ANSWERS
1. Cash on hand..............	A 1.
2. Owed to furniture store.......	_____ 2.
3. Automobile we own..........	_____ 3.
4. Owed to department store....	_____ 4.
5. Furniture we own............	_____ 5.
6. Owed to auto agency.........	_____ 6.
7. House we own..............	_____ 7.
8. Amount we are worth........	_____ 8.
9. Government bonds on hand...	_____ 9.
10. Any amount owed...........	_____ 10.
11. Any amount owned..........	_____ 11.
12. Difference between total assets and total liabilities.........	_____ 12.

8

Application problems

Problem 1-1. Balance sheet for an individual

Paul Larson plans to set up a personal bookkeeping system. He has prepared the following list of things owned and amounts owed:

Things owned:		Amounts owed:	
Cash on hand.............	$ 146.00	Owed to Cummings Garage	$ 172.00
Government bonds........	3,000.00	Owed to Oak Building and	
Automobile valued at......	1,700.00	Loan Co...............	7,600.00
Furniture valued at........	4,500.00	Owed to Thorp Finance Co.	630.00
House valued at..........	18,000.00		
Total value of items owned.	$27,346.00	Total amount owed........	$ 8,402.00

Instructions: Prepare a balance sheet for Paul Larson dated August 31 of the current year. Follow the steps for preparing a balance sheet given on page 5. Use the illustration of the balance sheet on page 2 as your model. Strive for accuracy and neatness.

Self-checking: Check the accuracy and the completeness of your work by comparing it with the balance sheet on page 2.

(a) Did you use three lines for the heading of your balance sheet?

(b) Did you center each of the three lines of the heading of your balance sheet?

(c) Did you center each of the three sectional headings within the body of your balance sheet: Assets, Liabilities, and Proprietorship?

(d) Did you leave a blank line between the Liabilities section and the Proprietorship section to separate these two sections?

(e) Is the amount of the total assets at the bottom of the left-hand side of your balance sheet on the same line as the amount of the total liabilities and proprietorship at the bottom of the right-hand side?

(f) Are the two totals at the bottom of your balance sheet the same amount?

(g) Did you draw single and double lines across the amount columns only?

Problem 1-2. Balance sheet for a small business

The following are the assets and the liabilities of the Quality Laundry, owned and operated by Frank Lane:

Assets		Liabilities	
Cash....................	$ 496.00	Madison Machine Co......	$ 678.00
Office Equipment..........	540.00	National Equipment Co....	531.00
Delivery Equipment.......	2,300.00		
Machinery...............	7,968.00		

Instructions: Prepare a balance sheet for the Quality Laundry dated September 30 of the current year. Use as your model the balance sheet illustrated on page 4.

Self-checking: Check your work with the questions that are listed under Problem 1-1.

Optional problems

Ordinarily each student will be expected to solve no more than one of the optional problems at the end of the chapter. Your teacher will indicate which of the two problems is your assignment.

★Supplementary Problem 1-S. Balance sheet for a small theater

The following are the assets and the liabilities of the Valley Theater, of which J. L. Tweedy is the proprietor.

Assets		Liabilities	
Cash....................	$ 1,495.00	City Light Company......	$ 62.00
Furniture...............	1,675.00	Films, Incorporated........	610.00
Equipment..............	5,125.00		
Building................	10,000.00		

Instructions: Prepare a balance sheet for the Valley Theater dated June 30 of the current year. Use the illustration of the balance sheet on page 4 as your model.

Self-checking: Check your work with the questions that are listed under Problem 1-1.

★Bonus Problem 1-B. Balance sheet for a school organization

The Palmyra High School Athletic Department decides on September 1 of the current year to start a bookkeeping system. As a first step it is necessary to prepare a balance sheet. The following information is supplied by the head of the Athletic Department:

Cash on hand is $216.00.

The football equipment on hand is worth $1,965.00, but $965.00 of the cost of this equipment is owed to the Athletic Supply Company.

The basketball equipment on hand is worth $700.00, but $200.00 of the cost of this equipment is owed to the Athletic Supply Company.

The baseball equipment on hand is worth $750.00, but $150.00 of the cost of this equipment is owed to the Palmyra Sporting Goods Company.

The track equipment on hand is worth $250.00, all of which is paid for.

The Athletic Department owes the Coe Printing Company $46.00 and the Martin Pharmacy $52.00.

Instructions: Prepare a balance sheet for the Palmyra High School Athletic Department dated September 1 of the current year. Use as your model the illustration of the balance sheet on page 6. Enter the entire amount owed to one creditor in one amount. Write "H. S. Athletic Dept., Capital" in the proprietorship section of your balance sheet.

Self-checking: Check your work with the questions that are listed under Problem 1-1.

Chapter 2

The opening entry

Recording the beginning balance sheet

The beginning balance sheet of the Wood Realty Agency was prepared on a sheet of paper. The information on the beginning balance sheet should be made a part of the permanent records of the business by recording it in one of the books of the business.

The journal

A book in which any of the records of a business are first written is called a *journal*. There are many different kinds of journals. Some journals have only one amount column, some have two amount columns, and others have many amount columns. A journal with two amount columns is commonly called a *general journal*.

The opening entry of the Wood Realty Agency

Each record in a journal is called an *entry*. An entry that records a beginning balance sheet is called an *opening entry*. The opening entry of the Wood Realty Agency was made in a general journal from the information on the following beginning balance sheet.

Wood Realty Agency Balance Sheet October 1, 1962					
Assets			**Liabilities**		
Cash	491	00	Adams Company	275	00
Automobile	2 180	00	McIntyre Company	342	00
Office Furniture	745	00	Triangle Motors	780	00
Office Machines	236	00	Total Liabilities	1 397	00
			Proprietorship		
			M. W. Wood, Capital	2 255	00
Total Assets	3 652	00	Total Liab. and Prop.	3 652	00

Beginning balance sheet of Wood Realty Agency

The amounts on the left-hand side of the balance sheet are recorded in the left-hand amount column of the two-column general journal. The amounts on the right-hand side of the balance sheet are recorded in the right-hand amount column of this journal. (See the diagram at the right.)

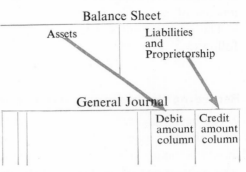

The left-hand amount column of the general journal is called the *Debit amount column*. The right-hand amount column of the general journal is called the *Credit amount column*. As will be shown in the journal entries in this chapter, every journal entry has two parts: (1) a debit part and (2) a credit part.

Steps in recording the opening entry in the general journal

The steps used in making the opening entry in the general journal of the Wood Realty Agency are as follows:

Step 1. *Date of entry.* Write the date of the opening entry in the Date column of the general journal as shown below.

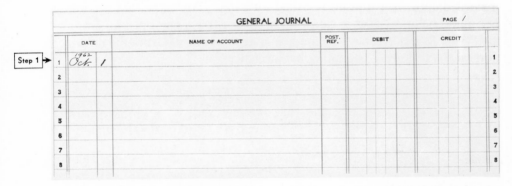

The date of the opening entry is written in the Date column on the first numbered line of the general journal. It consists of:

1. The *year*, written in small figures at the top of the first column.
2. The *month*, written immediately below the year on the first line in the first column.
3. The *day* of the month, written on the first line in the second column.

The date is written once and only once for each entry, regardless of how many lines are used for the entry.

12

Step 2. *Debit part of entry.* Write the *name* of each asset at the extreme left edge of the Name of Account column of the general journal. Write the *amount* of each asset in the Debit amount column.

The opening entry after all the assets have been recorded appears as follows:

		GENERAL JOURNAL			PAGE /	
	DATE	NAME OF ACCOUNT	POST. REF.	DEBIT	CREDIT	
1	1962 Oct. 1	Cash		49 1 00		1
2		Automobile		2 1 8 0 00		2
3		Office Furniture		74 5 00		3
4		Office Machines		23 6 00		4
5						5
6						6

Step 2 → (rows 3)

Step 3. *Credit part of entry.* Write the *name* of each liability in the Name of Account column of the general journal. Also write the *name* of the proprietor followed by the word *Capital* in that column. Indent each account title about one-half inch from the left edge of the column. Write the *amount* of each liability and the *amount* of the proprietorship in the Credit amount column.

The opening entry after the liabilities and the proprietorship have been recorded appears as follows:

		GENERAL JOURNAL			PAGE /	
	DATE	NAME OF ACCOUNT	POST. REF.	DEBIT	CREDIT	
1	1962 Oct. 1	Cash		49 1 00		1
2		Automobile		2 1 8 0 00		2
3		Office Furniture		74 5 00		3
4		Office Machines		23 6 00		4
5		Adams Company			27 5 00	5
6		McIntyre Company			34 2 00	6
7		Triangle Motors			78 0 00	7
8		M. W. Wood, Capital			2 2 5 5 00	8
9						9

Step 3 → (rows 6)

Step 4. *Explanation of entry.* Write a brief explanation of the complete journal entry in the Name of Account column immediately below the last credit item. Indent each line of the explanation one inch from the left edge of the Name of Account column. If more than one line is needed for the explanation, each line of the explanation begins with the same indention as the first line.

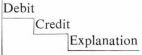

Debit
 Credit
  Explanation

The purpose of the journal explanation is to make the journal entry clear whenever reference is made to it. The explanation should therefore add any desirable information that is not indicated in the debit and the credit lines of the general journal. The explanation should be brief.

The complete opening entry in the general journal with the explanation written as the final step is shown below.

Opening entry of the Wood Realty Agency

Post. Ref. column

The heading of the Post. Ref. column is an abbreviation of "Posting Reference." The use of this column will be explained in Chapter 3.

Equality of debits and credits in every journal entry

In every journal entry, the total of the debit amounts must equal the total of the credit amounts. In the opening entry of the Wood Realty Agency, the total of the debit amounts, $3,652.00, is equal to the total of the credit amounts, $3,652.00.

Whenever the total debits of a general journal entry do not equal the total credits, the error or errors should be located and corrected.

14

Increasing your business vocabulary

What is the meaning of each of the following:

(a) journal   (c) entry   (e) debit amount column

(b) general journal   (d) opening entry   (f) credit amount column

Chapter questions

1. Why should the information on the beginning balance sheet be recorded in a journal?

2. What is the heading of the left-hand amount column of the general journal illustrated in this chapter?

3. What is the heading of the right-hand amount column of the general journal illustrated in this chapter?

4. Where is the date of the opening entry written in a general journal?

5. What kind of balance sheet items have amounts that are written in the Debit amount column in the general journal illustrated on page 14?

6. Where are the names of the debit amount items written in the general journal illustrated on page 14?

7. What two kinds of balance sheet items have amounts that are written in the Credit amount column in the general journal illustrated on page 14?

8. Where are the names of the credit amount items written in the general journal illustrated on page 14?

9. How far should the name of each credit entry be indented?

10. How far should the first word of each line of the explanation of the general journal entry be indented?

11. What is the purpose of the explanation in the general journal?

Cases for discussion

1. Ralph Brown desires to start a new bookkeeping system for the business that he operates. His assets consist of cash and office furniture. His only liability is to the Hickey Furniture Company.
   (a) What two items will be listed as debits in the opening entry in the journal?
   (b) What two items will be listed as credits in the opening entry?

2. The bookkeeper for the Chapman Insurance Agency finds the following items on the beginning balance sheet: Cash, Automobile, Office Furniture, Culver Company (a creditor), and Herbert W. Chapman, Capital.
   (a) Name the items that will be recorded in the journal as debits.
   (b) Name the items that will be recorded in the journal as credits.

Drill 2-A. *Debits and credits*

This drill is planned to give you skill in classifying balance sheet items as either debits or credits when recorded in a journal.

Instructions: 1. A list of balance sheet items to be classified is provided in your workbook for this drill. As you read each item, make a check mark in the proper column. If the amount of the item will be written as a debit in the opening entry in the journal, make a check mark in the Debit column of the form; if the amount of the item will be written as a credit in the opening entry, make a check mark in the Credit column. The first item, Automobile, is given as an example.

BALANCE SHEET ITEMS	DEBIT	CREDIT
1. Automobile	✓	

If you do not have a workbook, copy the above form on a sheet of paper and use the following list of balance sheet items: Automobile, Cash, Daniels Company (creditor); M. W. Wood, Capital; Office Furniture; Office Machines; Star Garage (creditor).

Instructions: 2. Now cover your answers and see how rapidly you can do this drill mentally without looking at your check marks. Repeat this mental drill several times for increased speed and accuracy.

Problem 2-1. *Opening entry for an individual*

Instructions: Prepare an opening entry in a general journal from the balance sheet at the top of page 17. Use September 1 of the current year as the date of the entry.

Self-checking: Compare your general journal entry with the illustration on page 14 and check the accuracy of your work by asking yourself the following questions:

(a) Did you write the date at the top of the Date column of the general journal, showing the year, the month, and the day?

(b) Does the first letter of each debit item in the Name of Account column touch the vertical red line?

(c) Is each credit item in the Name of Account column indented the same distance?

(d) Did you write the explanation so that the first word of the explanation is indented about twice as much as the credit items?

```
                        Henry Rinn
                      Balance Sheet
                    September 1, 19—
```

Assets			Liabilities		
Cash................	758	00	Star Building		
Government Bonds....	3,500	00	& Loan Co.........	2,500	00
Automobile..........	2,400	00	Winchester		
Furniture..........	3,250	00	Hardware Store....	145	00
House..............	18,500	00	Total Liabilities...	2,645	00
			Proprietorship		
			Henry Rinn, Capital.	25,763	00
Total Assets........	28,408	00	Total Liab. & Prop..	28,408	00

Problem 2-2. *Opening entry for a beauty shop*

Instructions: Prepare an opening entry in a general journal from the following balance sheet. Use October 1 of the current year as the date of this entry.

```
                   Uptown Beauty Shop
                      Balance Sheet
                    October 1, 19—
```

Assets			Liabilities		
Cash................	175	00	Beauty Supply Co.....	236	00
Supplies...........	136	00	Coburn Equipment Co..	447	00
Furniture..........	1,800	00	Total Liabilities....	683	00
Equipment..........	2,500	00			
			Proprietorship		
			Jane Hake, Capital...	3,928	00
Total Assets........	4,611	00	Total Liab. & Prop...	4,611	00

Self-checking: Check the accuracy of your general journal entry by asking yourself the questions given at the end of Problem 2-1.

★Supplementary Problem 2-S. Balance sheet and opening entry for a small service business

The Scott Garage is owned and operated by Robert Scott. His records show the following assets: Cash, $497.00; Garage Equipment, $3,250.00; Office Equipment, $1,275.00. He owes Clark Motor Company $985.00 and Marsh Equipment Company $312.00. The amount of his proprietorship is $3,725.00.

Instructions: 1. Prepare a balance sheet for the Scott Garage dated August 1 of the current year.

2. Record the opening entry in a general journal.

Self-checking: Check your work with the questions that are listed under Problem 1-1 on page 9 and Problem 2-1 on page 16.

★Bonus Problem 2-B. Balance sheet and opening entry separating business records from personal records

The Eastwood Parking Lot is owned and operated by L. P. Mason. He has asked you to prepare a balance sheet and an opening entry for his business records. He gives you the following information, which you will note is a mixture of business items and personal items:

Cash in the checking account of the Eastwood Parking Lot, $400.00; cash in his personal checking account, $290.00; furniture in his home, $3,000.00; equipment in the parking lot office, $350.00; building on parking lot, $500.00; house in which he lives, $18,900.00; family automobile, $2,100.00; parking lot land, $20,000.00.

Amounts owed are: to the Dolan Lumber Company, $80.00 for lumber purchased to make repairs on the parking lot building; to the Alcorn Furniture Company, $350.00 for furniture purchased for Mr. Mason's home; to the Webster Equipment Company, $100.00 for office equipment in the parking lot office.

Instructions: 1. Prepare a balance sheet for the Eastwood Parking Lot, L. P. Mason, proprietor. Use November 1 of the current year as the date. Be careful that you separate personal items from business items and list business items only on the balance sheet for the Eastwood Parking Lot.

2. Record the opening entry in a general journal.

Self-checking: Check your work with the questions that are listed under Problem 1-1 on page 9 and Problem 2-1 on page 16.

Chapter 3

Posting the opening entry

Need for ledger accounts

The opening entry in a general journal is a complete record of the assets, the liabilities, and the proprietorship of the business *at the time that the new bookkeeping system is installed.* As business is transacted from day to day, there will be changes in some of hese items. Some will be increased, some will be decreased, and some will remain unchanged.

The bookkeeping forms that are used to sort and summarize the changes caused by transactions are called *accounts.* A group of accounts is known as a *ledger.*

Each account in the ledger gives the proprietor a picture of what changes are taking place in that item. The complete collection of these "pictures" (ledger accounts) shows the proprietor what is happening to his entire business.

A ledger is often a loose-leaf book. It may also be a group of ledger sheets or ledger cards kept in a tray or filed in a filing cabinet.

Form of the ledger account

Several different forms of ledger accounts are used in business. The one most commonly used is the standard ledger account shown below.

DATE	ITEMS	POST. REF.	DEBIT		DATE	ITEMS	POST. REF.	CREDIT
	(Debit Side)					*(Credit Side)*		

(Account Title)   ACCOUNT NO.

Standard form of account

The name given to an account is known as the *account title.* The account title written at the top of the account indicates the nature of the items that are entered in the account. For example, the first account title in the ledger of the Wood Realty Agency is *Cash.* This cash account will show the changes in the amount of cash on hand because of cash received and cash paid.

19

The number given to an account to show its location in the ledger is known as the *account number*.

The position of debits and credits in the ledger account

The standard form of the ledger account is divided into a left half and a right half. The left half is called the *debit side;* the right half is called the *credit side.*

The amount column on the left-hand side has the heading *Debit.* The amount column on the right-hand side has the heading *Credit.* The headings of all the other columns are the same on each side of the account.

Opening accounts to form a ledger

Getting an account ready for use is known as *opening an account.* Getting a complete ledger ready for use is referred to as *opening a ledger.*

An account needs to be opened in the ledger for each item listed in the opening entry in the journal. Additional accounts will be opened in the ledger as they are needed.

The opening entry that will be used in this chapter is the entry that was developed in Chapter 2. The entry below is the same opening entry that was illustrated on page 14.

	DATE		NAME OF ACCOUNT	POST. REF.	DEBIT	CREDIT	
1	1962 Oct.	1	Cash		491 00		1
2			Automobile		2180 00		2
3			Office Furniture		745 00		3
4			Office Machines		236 00		4
5			Adams Company			275 00	5
6			McIntyre Company			342 00	6
7			Triangle Motors			780 00	7
8			M. W. Wood, Capital			2255 00	8
9			To record October 1				9
10			balance sheet.				10
11							11

GENERAL JOURNAL — PAGE 1

Opening entry of the Wood Realty Agency

Preparing a chart of accounts

A list of accounts that shows the arrangement of the accounts in the ledger and the number assigned to each account is called a *chart of accounts.* The chart of accounts used by the Wood Realty Agency is shown on page 62. The part of this chart that will be needed for the work of this chapter is shown at the top of the next page.

20

```
                    Wood Realty Agency
                    Chart of Accounts

                 Account                          Account
      Assets     Number      Liabilities         Number
Cash............    11    Adams Company.......      21
Automobile......    12    McIntyre Company....      22
Office Furniture.   13    Triangle Motors.....      23
Office Machines.    14
                              Proprietorship
                         M. W. Wood, Capital.      31
```

Partial chart of accounts for Wood Realty Agency

In the list of accounts given above, all asset accounts begin with the number 1; all liability accounts begin with the number 2; and the proprietorship account begins with the number 3.

The first digit of each account number tells in which *division* of the ledger the account is placed. The second digit of each account number tells the *position* of the account within its *division*. For example, the account number for Triangle Motors is 23. This number shows that the Triangle Motors account is in the *second* division of the ledger, the liability division, and is the *third* account in that division.

Steps used in opening each account in the ledger

The first account to be opened in the ledger is the first account listed on the chart of accounts. This account is Cash, account number 11. The steps used in opening the cash account are as follows:

Step 1. Write the name of the account, *Cash,* at the center of the first line of the first page in the ledger.

Step 2. Write the account number of the cash account, *11,* in the upper right-hand corner of the ledger page.

The heading of the cash account after the account has been opened appears in the ledger as follows:

Step 1 ▶

Cash

ACCOUNT NO. *11*   ◀ Step 2

DATE	ITEMS	POST. REF.	DEBIT	DATE	ITEMS	POST. REF.	CREDIT

An account is opened for each account title listed on the chart of accounts using the same steps as are used in opening the cash account.

Posting the first debit of the opening entry

Transferring entries in a journal to accounts in a ledger is called *posting*. The first item in the opening entry in the general journal of the Wood Realty Agency on page 20 is a debit to Cash. This debit item will be transferred to the debit side of the cash account in the ledger.

The steps used in posting this debit item from the general journal to the proper account in the ledger are as follows:

Step 1. Write the amount of the cash debit, $491.00, in the Debit amount column of the cash account as shown below.

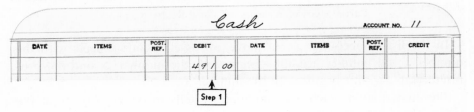

The amount is posted first because it is the most important part of the entry and the part in which an error is most likely to be made.

Step 2. Write the *date* of the journal entry in the Date column of the ledger account as shown below.

The date of the first entry in every ledger account consists of three parts: the year, the month, and the day. Write the date in the Date column as follows:

1. Write the year at the top of the Date column. The year is not written on the side of the account that has no entries.
2. Write the month in the first column under the heading *Date* on the same line as the amount. If the name of the month is long, such as October, it may be abbreviated. The name of the month is written only once on each side of the account that is used. The month is not written on a side of the account that has no entries.
3. Write the day of the month in the second column under the heading *Date*.

Step 3. Write in the Items column any special information that may be of value to anyone who later examines this account.

Bookkeepers distinguish between the beginning amounts in an account and the amounts recorded later as a result of business transactions. The beginning balance in the cash account is, therefore, labeled with a single word *Balance* in the Items column.

Step 4. Write *J1* in the column headed *Post. Ref.* in the cash account in the ledger. *J1* shows that this posting came from page 1 of the general journal. (Post Ref. is the abbreviation for Posting Reference.)

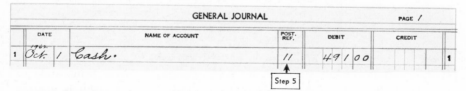

Step 5. Return to the journal and write in the Post. Ref. column of the journal the account number of the account to which the item was posted.

The account number, 11, is written in the Post. Ref. column of the general journal on the same line as the cash item. This number, 11, in the Post. Ref. column of the general journal shows that all the details of the posting of this line have been completed. For this reason the Post. Ref. figure in the journal is always written as the *last* step in posting.

The general journal with the account number of the cash account, 11, written in the Post. Ref. column is shown below.

	DATE		NAME OF ACCOUNT	POST. REF.	DEBIT	CREDIT	
1	Oct.	1	Cash	11	491 00		1

GENERAL JOURNAL   PAGE 1

Posting the remaining debits of the opening entry

The steps used in posting the first debit are followed in posting the remaining debits in the opening entry. The ledger accounts with debit amounts posted are shown on page 24. Each account is a separate page.

23

Cash — ACCOUNT NO. 11

DATE	ITEMS	POST. REF.	DEBIT	DATE	ITEMS	POST. REF.	CREDIT
1962 Oct 1	Balance	J1	491 00				

Automobile — ACCOUNT NO. 12

DATE	ITEMS	POST. REF.	DEBIT	DATE	ITEMS	POST. REF.	CREDIT
1962 Oct 1	Balance	J1	2180 00				

Office Furniture — ACCOUNT NO. 13

DATE	ITEMS	POST. REF.	DEBIT	DATE	ITEMS	POST. REF.	CREDIT
1962 Oct 1	Balance	J1	745 00				

Office Machines — ACCOUNT NO. 14

DATE	ITEMS	POST. REF.	DEBIT	DATE	ITEMS	POST. REF.	CREDIT
1962 Oct 1	Balance	J1	236 00				

Posting the credit items of the opening entry

The credits in the general journal are posted in the same manner as the debits, except that the credits are posted to the *right-hand* or *credit side* of the ledger accounts. After the credits in the general journal have been posted, the accounts affected appear as follows:

Adams Company — ACCOUNT NO. 21

DATE	ITEMS	POST. REF.	DEBIT	DATE	ITEMS	POST. REF.	CREDIT
				1962 Oct 1	Balance	J1	275 00

McIntyre Company — ACCOUNT NO. 22

DATE	ITEMS	POST. REF.	DEBIT	DATE	ITEMS	POST. REF.	CREDIT
				1962 Oct 1	Balance	J1	342 00

Triangle Motors — ACCOUNT NO. 23

DATE	ITEMS	POST. REF.	DEBIT	DATE	ITEMS	POST. REF.	CREDIT
				1962 Oct 1	Balance	J1	780 00

M. W. Wood, Capital — ACCOUNT NO. 31

DATE	ITEMS	POST. REF.	DEBIT	DATE	ITEMS	POST. REF.	CREDIT
				1962 Oct 1	Balance	J1	2255 00

Post. Ref. column of the general journal after posting

After all the posting of the opening entry has been completed, the Post. Ref. column in the general journal appears as follows:

	DATE		NAME OF ACCOUNT	POST. REF.	DEBIT	CREDIT	
			GENERAL JOURNAL			PAGE 1	
1	1962 Oct.	1	Cash	11	491 00		1
2			Automobile	12	2 180 00		2
3			Office Furniture	13	745 00		3
4			Office Machines	14	236 00		4
5			Adams Company	21		275 00	5
6			McIntyre Company	22		342 00	6
7			Triangle Motors	23		780 00	7
8			M. W. Wood, Capital	31		2 255 00	8
9			To record October 1				9
10			balance sheet.				10

Use of Post. Ref. numbers

The numbers in the posting reference columns in the journal and in the ledger are useful for cross reference. Anyone looking at any entry in the journal can find the number of the account in the ledger to which a specific item was posted. Similarly, anyone looking at an item in the ledger can find the page number of the journal from which the posting was made. This cross-reference information is useful if the accuracy of the posting is being checked or if additional information is desired.

The nature of account balances

The difference between the two sides of an account is known as the *account balance.* When an account contains only one entry, this single amount is the account balance. A balance on the left-hand side of an account is called a *debit balance.* A balance on the right-hand side of an account is called a *credit balance.* Note on page 24 that the balance of each asset account is a *debit balance.* Note on page 24 that the balance of each liability account is a *credit balance* and that the balance of the proprietor's capital account is also a *credit balance.*

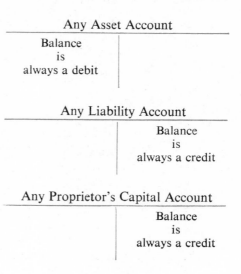

Any Asset Account

Balance is always a debit	

Any Liability Account

	Balance is always a credit

Any Proprietor's Capital Account

	Balance is always a credit

25

A beginning balance sheet, the opening entry, and the ledger

The chart at the right shows:

(1) The balance sheet is a sheet of paper that lists the assets, the liabilities, and the proprietorship of the business at the time the balance sheet is prepared.

(2) In starting a new book-keeping system, the information on the balance sheet is recorded in a book called a general journal. The assets on the balance sheet are recorded in the journal as debits; the liabilities and the proprietorship are recorded as credits.

(3) The items recorded in the opening entry in the general journal are posted to a book called a ledger. The ledger is made up of accounts, each of which is on a separate page.

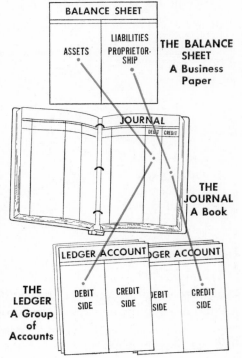

Increasing your business vocabulary

What is the meaning of each of the following:

(a) accounts	(f) credit side	(j) posting
(b) ledger	(g) opening an account	(k) account balance
(c) account title	(h) opening a ledger	(l) debit balance
(d) account number	(i) chart of accounts	(m) credit balance
(e) debit side		

Chapter questions

1. What are the printed headings on the debit side of the standard form of ledger account illustrated on page 19?
2. To what extent are the printed headings of the two sides of the standard form of ledger account different?
3. In the chart of accounts shown on page 21, what is the first digit of (a) all asset account numbers, (b) all liability account numbers, (c) the proprietorship account number?
4. What are the two steps used in opening an account in the ledger?
5. What are the three parts of the date in the first entry in every ledger account?

6. Why is the word *Balance* written in the Items column of the ledger account when posting each item of the opening entry?

7. What is the purpose of writing a journal page number in the Post. Ref. column in the ledger account?

8. What are the two purposes of writing a ledger account number in the Post. Ref. column in the general journal?

9. How does posting a credit item from the general journal differ from posting a debit item?

Cases for discussion

1. Edward Mitchell has several hundred accounts in his ledger and several hundred pages in his general journal. He is interested in checking an item in the ledger by tracing it back to the journal entry from which it was posted. How can he determine quickly the exact page of the journal where the item can be located?

2. Charles Coe is interrupted by a telephone call while in the midst of posting his general journal. If he has been following correct bookkeeping procedure in his posting, how can he tell quickly where he left off in the journal at the time his work was interrupted?

Drills for understanding

Drill 3-A. Classification of accounts in the ledger

This drill will give you additional skill in classifying accounts quickly as assets, liabilities, and proprietorship. You need this skill in all of your bookkeeping work.

Instructions: 1. A list of accounts for you to classify is given in your workbook. Classify each account by printing in the Answers column a capital *A* if the account is an asset, a capital *L* if the account is a liability, and a capital *P* if the account is a proprietorship. The first account title, Cash, is given at the right as an example.

Account Titles	Answers
(1) Cash	A

If you do not have a workbook, prepare your own form on a sheet of paper. Use a form similar to the illustration above. The account titles to be classified are:

(1) Cash
(2) Automobile
(3) Office Furniture
(4) Office Machines

(5) Adams Company (creditor)
(6) McIntyre Company (creditor)
(7) Triangle Motors (creditor)
(8) M. W. Wood, Capital

Instructions: 2. Now cover your Answers column and see how rapidly you can mentally classify the accounts without looking at your answers. Repeat this mental drill several times to see if you can increase your speed.

Drill 3-B. Debit balances and credit balances

A skeleton outline of a ledger account, as illustrated at the right, may be used for drill purposes. This form is commonly called a T account because it looks like a capital T.

```
              Cash
   _____
                |
                |
                |
```

Instructions: A list of eight accounts in T-account form is provided in your workbook. Write the word *Balance* on the proper side of each account to show where the balance will always appear in the account. The first account in the list, Cash, is given at the right as an example.

```
              Cash
   _____
   Balance      |
                |
```

If you do not have a workbook, prepare your own form on a sheet of paper. Prepare separate T accounts for the following accounts:

(1) Cash
(2) Automobile
(3) Office Furniture
(4) Office Machines
(5) Adams Company (creditor)
(6) McIntyre Company (creditor)
(7) Triangle Motors (creditor)
(8) M. W. Wood, Capital

Application problem

Problem 3-1. Recording and posting the opening entry for a laundry

The balance sheet of the Shorewood Laundry is shown below. The owner, L. P. Hermsen, has employed you to set up a new bookkeeping system for him.

Shorewood Laundry
Balance Sheet
August 1, 19—

Assets			Liabilities		
Cash.................	486	00	Allied Machinery Co...	711	00
Office Equipment......	363	00	National Equip. Co....	252	00
Delivery Equipment....	1,792	00	Total Liabilities.....	963	00
Machinery...........	5,630	00	Proprietorship		
			L. P. Hermsen, Cap....	7,308	00
Total Assets.........	8,271	00	Total Liab. & Prop....	8,271	00

Instructions: 1. Record the opening entry for the Shorewood Laundry on page 1 of a general journal. Use August 1 of the current year as the date.

2. Open accounts in a ledger for all of the account titles listed on the balance sheet. Allow one fourth of a page in your ledger for each account. Number the accounts as follows: asset accounts, 11 to 14; liability accounts, 21 and 22; and the proprietor's capital account, 31.

3. Post the opening entry.

Self-checking: Compare your ledger accounts with the models on page 24. Check the accuracy of your posting by asking yourself the following questions:

(a) Did you write the year, the month, and the day in each ledger account on the first line of the side of the account that was used?

(b) Are all of your postings of debits from the journal placed on the left-hand side of the four asset accounts?

(c) Are all of your postings of credits from the journal placed on the right-hand side of the liability and proprietorship accounts?

(d) Did you write in the Post. Ref. column of each ledger account the number of the journal page?

(e) Did you write in the Post. Ref. column of your journal the account number of the account in the ledger to which each line in the journal was posted? Did you make this your last step in posting?

Optional problems

★*Supplementary Problem 3-S. Chart of accounts, opening entry, and posting*

The balance sheet of Don's TV Service Shop is shown below. The owner, Donald C. Fisher, has employed you to set up a new bookkeeping system for him.

Don's TV Service Shop
Balance Sheet
September 1, 19—

Assets		Liabilities	
Cash................	635 00	Edison Supply Co......	462 00
Parts...............	1,274 00	Shaw and Co..........	250 00
Office Equipment......	489 00	Total Liabilities.....	712 00
Shop Equipment........	7,538 00		
		Proprietorship	
		Donald C. Fisher,	
		Capital............	9,224 00
Total Assets.........	9,936 00	Total Liab. & Prop....	9,936 00

Instructions: 1. Record the opening entry on page 1 of a general journal. Use September 1 of the current year as the date.

2. Prepare a partial chart of accounts similar to the one illustrated on page 21.

3. Open a ledger for the account titles listed on your chart. Allow one fourth of a page in your ledger for each account. Number each account.

4. Post the opening entry.

Self-checking: Check the completeness of your work by using the questions that are listed under Problem 3-1.

★Bonus Problem 3-B. *Chart of accounts, beginning balance sheet, opening entry, and posting*

Mr. William Wilson owns and operates the Wilson Insurance Agency. He has decided to install a new bookkeeping system. The account titles and the balances of all asset and liability accounts are listed below in alphabetic order:

Automobile	Debit	$2,300.00	Office Furniture	Debit	$600.00
Cash	Debit	1,800.00	Office Machines	Debit	800.00
Dalton Motors Co.	Credit	200.00	Polson Company	Credit	400.00
Merton Supply Co.	Credit	300.00	Rio Service Station	Credit	50.00

Instructions: 1. Prepare a partial chart of accounts with account numbers for the Wilson Insurance Agency. Use the illustration on page 21 as a model. List the cash account first in the assets division. List the liability accounts in alphabetic order. Place the capital account, William Wilson, Capital, last in this partial chart of accounts.

2. Prepare a balance sheet dated May 1 of the current year.

3. Record the opening entry on page 1 of a general journal.

4. Open a ledger for the account titles listed in your partial chart of accounts. Allow one fourth of a page in your ledger for each account. Number the accounts as shown on your chart.

5. Post the opening entry.

Self-checking: Check the completeness of your work by using the questions that are listed under Problem 3-1.

Chapter 4

Analyzing transactions
to determine debits and credits

What is a business transaction?

In business, any exchange of one value for another is known as a *business transaction*. Examples of business transactions are:

Transaction No. 1. Received cash, $45.00, for the sale of old office furniture.
Transaction No. 2. Paid cash, $100.00, to the Adams Company in part payment of the amount owed.

Transactions change account balances

Every business transaction increases or decreases the balance in each of two or more accounts in the ledger.

In some transactions, the balance of one account is *increased* while the balance of another account is *decreased* by the same amount. For example, in Transaction No. 1, $45.00 in cash was received when old office furniture was sold. Since cash was received, the asset Cash was *increased* by $45.00. Since office furniture was sold, the asset Office Furniture was *decreased* by the same amount, $45.00.

In some transactions, the balances of two accounts are *decreased* by the same amount. For example, in Transaction No. 2, $100.00 in cash was paid to the Adams Company in part payment of the amount owed that company. Since cash was paid out, the asset Cash was *decreased* by $100.00. Since part of the amount owed to the Adams Company was paid, the liability Adams Company was *decreased* by the same amount.

Examples will be given later of transactions that increase two or more accounts by the same amount and of transactions that affect more than two accounts.

Why does a ledger account have two sides?

A ledger account has two sides in order to make it easier to show additions to or subtractions from account balances. The illustration at the left on page 32 shows how increases and decreases in cash would be recorded if they were listed in one column. The illustration at the right on page 32 shows how increases and decreases in cash are recorded in the cash account when it has two sides.

Cash			Cash		
Beginning balance	5,000.00		Balance	5,000.00	500.00
Increase	1,000.00 +			1,000.00	1,200.00
Decrease	500.00 −			800.00	100.00
Decrease	1,200.00 −			200.00	
Increase	800.00 +				
Decrease	100.00 −				
Increase	200.00 +				

An account as it would appear if it had only one column   **An account with two amount columns**

In the cash account shown with two sides, one side of the account is used to record the beginning balance and the increases; the opposite side is used to record the decreases. This arrangement makes it easy to find the total of each column and to make the subtraction to find the new balance of the cash account.

Increases in assets, liabilities, and proprietorship

Why are increases in assets recorded as debits? The balance of each asset account is recorded on the left-hand side of the account as a *debit*. An *increase* in an asset is also recorded as a *debit* so that it can be added conveniently to the balance in the asset account. (See the diagram at the right.)

Any Asset Account	
Debit side is balance side and increase side	

Why are increases in liabilities and increases in proprietorship recorded as credits? The balance of each liability account is recorded on the *right-hand* side of the account as a *credit*. An *increase* in a liability is also recorded as a *credit* so that it can be added conveniently to the balance in the liability account. (See the diagram at the right.)

Any Liability Account	
	Credit side is balance side and increase side

The balance of each proprietorship account is recorded on the *right-hand* side of the account as a *credit*. An *increase* in proprietorship is also recorded as a *credit* so that it can be added conveniently to the *balance* in the proprietorship account. (See the diagram at the right.)

Any Proprietorship Account	
	Credit side is balance side and increase side

Summary. The *beginning balance* and the *increases* are always on the same side of the account. Every *asset* account has its balance and its increases on the *debit side*. Every *liability* and *proprietorship* account has its balance and its increases on the *credit side*.

Decreases in assets, liabilities, and proprietorship

Why are decreases in assets recorded as credits? All decreases in any account are recorded on the side opposite that used for the beginning balance. In an asset account, the beginning balance and the increases are recorded on the *left-hand* or *debit side*. Decreases in any asset account are therefore recorded on the *right-hand* or *credit side* of the account.

Any Asset Account	
Debit side is balance side and increase side	Credit side is decrease side

Why are decreases in liabilities and decreases in proprietorship recorded as debits? The beginning balance and the increases in liability and proprietorship accounts are recorded on the *right-hand* or *credit side* of the account.

Decreases in any liability or proprietorship account are recorded on the side opposite that used for the beginning balance. Decreases in liability and proprietorship accounts are therefore recorded on the *left-hand* or *debit side* of the account.

Any Liability Account	
Debit side is decrease side	Credit side is balance side and increase side

Any Proprietorship Account	
Debit side is decrease side	Credit side is balance side and increase side

How to analyze transactions

Every business transaction is recorded in a journal before it is posted to ledger accounts. Before a bookkeeper records a transaction in a journal, he needs to decide (a) what accounts are affected by the transaction and (b) what account or accounts will be debited and what account or accounts will be credited.

In the following paragraphs several transactions are analyzed into their debit and credit parts. In doing so, use is made of a skeleton form of ledger account that shows only the account title and the debit and the credit sides. A form of ledger account that shows only the account title and the debit and the credit sides is called a *T account*.

Transaction No. 1

Received cash, $45.00, for the sale of old office furniture.

In this transaction one asset is increased and another asset is decreased.

Step 1.   What two accounts are affected by this transaction?

The two accounts affected by this transaction are Cash and Office Furniture.

Step 2.   What kind of account is Cash and how is its balance changed by this transaction?

Cash is an asset account. The balance of the cash account is increased $45.00. The *increase side* of the cash account is the *debit side* because the balance of every asset account is on the *debit side*. The cash account is therefore *debited* for the amount of the increase, $45.00. (See the T account at the right.)

Cash	
45.00	
Debit side is balance side and increase side	

Step 3.   What kind of account is Office Furniture and how is its balance changed by this transaction?

Office Furniture is an asset account. In this transaction, the balance of the office furniture account is *decreased* $45.00. Decreases in any account are recorded on the side *opposite* the balance side. The office furniture account is therefore *credited* for the amount of the decrease, $45.00. (See the T account at the right.)

Office Furniture	
	45.00
Debit side is balance side	Credit side is decrease side

Equality of the debit and the credit in Transaction No. 1. Every transaction has two parts: (1) a debit part and (2) a credit part. The two parts are always equal.

In this transaction one asset account, Cash, is debited for $45.00 and another asset account, Office Furniture, is credited for $45.00. The debit part of the transaction equals the credit part as shown below.

Debit part (Cash $45.00) EQUALS credit part (Office Furniture $45.00)

Cash		Office Furniture	
45.00			45.00

Transaction No. 2

Paid cash, $100.00, to Adams Company in part payment of the amount owed to them.

In this transaction an asset is decreased and a liability is also decreased the same amount.

Step 1.   What two accounts are affected by this transaction?

The two accounts affected are Adams Company and Cash.

Step 2.   What kind of account is Adams Company and how is its balance affected by this transaction?

The Adams Company account is a liability account. In this transaction the balance of the Adams Company account is *decreased* $100.00. Since the balance of a liability account is always on the credit side of the account, this decrease in the Adams Company account must be recorded on the *opposite* side, the *debit* side. The Adams Company account is therefore debited for the amount of the decrease, $100.00.

Adams Company	
100.00	
Debit side is decrease side	Credit side is balance side

Step 3.   What kind of account is the cash account and how is its balance affected by this transaction?

Cash is an asset account. The balance of the cash account is decreased $100.00. Since the balance of an asset account is always on the debit side of the account, this decrease in the balance of the cash account must be recorded on the *opposite* side, the *credit* side.   The cash account is therefore credited for the amount of the decrease, $100.00.

Cash	
	100.00
Debit side is balance side	Credit side is decrease side

Equality of the debit and the credit in Transaction No. 2.   In this transaction, a liability account, Adams Company, is debited, and an asset account, Cash, is credited. The debit part of the transaction equals the credit part of the transaction as shown below.

Debit part (Adams Company $100.00) EQUALS credit part (Cash $100.00)

Adams Company		Cash	
100.00			100.00

Income transactions and income accounts

Increases in proprietorship. All businesses complete some transactions that increase an asset and increase proprietorship. For example, a real estate business receives cash as a commission for the sale of property; a physician receives fees for services performed; and an accountant receives fees for work done.

An increase in proprietorship that results from the operation of the business is called *income*. Income might be recorded in the proprietor's capital account. But a business may have several kinds of income. In order to have a clear picture in the ledger of each kind of income, it is desirable to have income accounts separate from the proprietor's capital account. Some examples of income accounts are Commissions Income, Rent Income, and Fees Income.

Transaction No. 3

Received cash, $725.00, as commission for the sale of a house.

In this transaction an asset is increased and proprietorship is also increased the same amount.

Step 1.   What two accounts are affected by this transaction?

The two accounts affected are Cash and Commissions Income.

Step 2.   What kind of account is Cash and how is it affected by this income transaction?

Cash is an asset account. When an asset account is *increased*, the asset is *debited* because increases are recorded on the same side as the *balance* of the account. Therefore Cash is debited for the amount of the cash received, $725.00. (See the T account at the right.)

Cash	
725.00	
Debit side is balance side and increase side	

Step 3.   What kind of account is Commissions Income and how is it affected?

Commissions Income is an income account. All income accounts are increases in proprietorship. The balances of all income accounts are *credit* balances, and all increases in income accounts are recorded on the *credit* side of the income account. Therefore in this transaction Commissions Income is credited for $725.00. (See the T account at the right.)

Commissions Income	
	725.00
	Credit side is increase side

Equality of the debit and the credit in Transaction No. 3. In this transaction, Cash is debited because the asset Cash is increased. Commissions Income is credited for the same amount because the income increases proprietorship. The debit part of the transaction equals the credit part of the transaction as shown below.

Debit part (Cash $725.00) EQUALS credit part (Commissions Income $725.00)

Cash	Commissions Income
725.00	725.00

Expense transactions and expense accounts

Decreases in proprietorship. Every business has to make payments for such items as rent, advertising, telephone, and other costs of operating a business. Each payment of this kind results in a decrease in the proprietorship. A decrease in proprietorship as a result of a business transaction is called an *expense*. A few examples of expense accounts are Rent Expense, Advertising Expense, and Miscellaneous Expense.

Each expense might be recorded as a debit in the proprietor's capital account. But a business usually has many different kinds of expenses. In order to have a clear picture in the ledger of each kind of expense, it is desirable to have the different expense accounts separate from the proprietor's capital account.

Transaction No. 4

Paid cash, $135.00, for rent of office for October.

In this transaction the proprietorship is decreased and an asset is also decreased the same amount.

Step 1.   What two accounts are affected by this transaction?

The two accounts affected are Rent Expense and Cash.

Step 2.   What kind of account is Rent Expense and how is it affected by this transaction?

Rent Expense is an expense account. All expenses *decrease* proprietorship. Therefore expenses are always *debits*. Rent Expense is *debited* for the amount paid for rent, $135.00.

Rent Expense	
135.00 Debit side is decrease in proprietorship side	

Step 3. What kind of account is Cash and how is it affected by this expense transaction?

Cash is an asset account. When an asset account is decreased, the asset account is credited. In this transaction, the balance of the Cash account is decreased. Since the balance of the cash account is on the debit side of the account, this decrease is recorded on the side opposite the balance. The cash account is therefore credited for the amount of the decrease, $135.00.

Cash	
	135.00
Debit side is balance side	Credit side is decrease side

Equality of the debit and the credit in Transaction No. 4. In this transaction an expense account, Rent Expense, is debited for $135.00 and an asset account, Cash, is credited for $135.00.

Debit part (Rent Expense $135.00) EQUALS Credit part (Cash $135.00)

Rent Expense		Cash	
135.00			135.00

Summary of the principles of debit and credit

Asset accounts always have *debit* balances. Therefore, an increase in an asset is always recorded on the *debit* side of the asset account. Decreases are recorded on the opposite side, the *credit* side.

Any Asset Account	
Debit side is balance side and increase side	Credit side is decrease side

Liability accounts always have *credit* balances. Therefore, an increase in a liability is always recorded on the *credit* side of the liability account. Decreases are recorded on the opposite side, the *debit* side.

Any Liability Account	
Debit side is decrease side	Credit side is balance side and increase side

A proprietorship account always has a *credit* balance. Therefore, an increase in proprietorship is always recorded on the *credit* side of the proprietorship account. Decreases are recorded on the opposite side, the *debit* side.

Any Proprietorship Account	
Debit side is decrease side	Credit side is balance side and increase side

Income increases proprietorship. Therefore, each income is recorded as a *credit* in an income account.

Any Income Account	
	Credit side is for increases in proprietorship from income transactions

Expenses decrease proprietorship. Therefore, each expense is recorded as a *debit* in an expense account.

Any Expense Account	
Debit side is for decreases in proprietorship from expense transactions	

Each transaction has a debit part and a credit part. The debit part should always equal the credit part.

Increasing your business vocabulary

What is the meaning of each of the following:

(a) business transaction

(b) T account

(c) income

(d) expense

Chapter questions

1. Why does a ledger account have two sides?
2. Why is an increase in an asset account recorded on the debit side of the account?
3. Why is an increase in a liability account recorded on the credit side of the account?
4. Why is an increase in a proprietorship account recorded on the credit side of the account?
5. Why is a decrease in an asset account recorded on the credit side of the account?
6. Why is a decrease in a liability account recorded on the debit side of the account?
7. Why is a decrease in a proprietorship account recorded on the debit side of the account?
8. In what book are business transactions recorded before they are posted to the ledger?
9. Why should a transaction be analyzed before it is recorded in a journal?
10. What are the two parts of every business transaction?
11. What effect does an income transaction have on proprietorship?
12. What effect does an expense transaction have on proprietorship?
13. Which side of an income account is used to record income?
14. Which side of an expense account is used to record expenses?

Cases for discussion

1. Mr. Anderson employs an inexperienced bookkeeper. To assist the bookkeeper, he prepares a list of the accounts in his ledger. After each account he indicates whether the balance of the account is normally a debit or a credit. What value is this information to the bookkeeper as he analyzes transactions into their debit and credit parts?

2. Mr. Aiken recorded all expenses and income directly in his capital account. Mr. Bolton recorded his expenses in separate expense accounts and his income in a separate income account. What are the advantages of Mr. Bolton's method of recording expenses and income as compared to Mr. Aiken's plan?

Drills for understanding

Drill 4-A. Account balances

Instructions: 1. Make a T account for each of the account titles listed below and write the proper account title on each account. The cash account is shown at the right as an example.

Cash

Automobile	J. R. Jones (Creditor)
Building	Land
Cash	Office Equipment
Commissions Income	Office Furniture
Frank Freeman, Capital	Rent Expense

Instructions: 2. Place a check mark (√) on the debit side of the T account if the balance of the account is usually a debit balance. Place a check mark on the credit side of the T account if the balance of the account is usually a credit balance. The cash account is shown as an example.

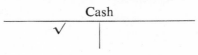

Drill 4-B. Increases and decreases in account balances

Instructions: 1. Make a T account for each of the account titles listed below and write the proper account title on each account.

Cash	W. R. Collins (Creditor)
Automobile	J. C. Thomas (Creditor)
Building	E. L. Cooper, Capital
Office Equipment	Commissions Income
Office Furniture	Rent Expense

Instructions: 2. In each T account make a plus sign (+) on the side of the account that is the increase side and a minus sign (−) on the side that is the decrease side.

Application problem

Problem 4-1. Analyzing transactions

Mr. A. B. Worden operates an accounting business. His ledger contains the following accounts:

Cash	Olsen Equipment Company (Creditor)
Office Furniture	A. B. Worden, Capital
Office Machines	Fees Income
Office Supplies	Advertising Expense
Burns Garage (Creditor)	Miscellaneous Expense
Craig Finance Company (Creditor)	Rent Expense
Davis Supply Company (Creditor)	Travel Expense

Note: The miscellaneous expense account is used to record all expenses that are not clearly advertising, rent, or travel expenses.

Instructions: 1. Before employing you to record transactions in his journal, Mr. Worden has asked you to fill out a form with the headings shown below as a test of your present knowledge of debits and credits.

Trans. No.	Account to be Debited	Debited because the account is	Account to be Credited	Credited because the account is
1	Cash	Increased	Fees Income	Increased

Instructions: 2. For each of the following transactions, (a) write the title of the account to be debited and indicate the reason for the debit by writing either "Increased" or "Decreased" in the proper column, and (b) write the title of the account to be credited and indicate the reason for the credit by writing either "Increased" or "Decreased" in the proper column. Transaction No. 1 is given as an example on the form above.

TRANSACTION
NUMBER

1. Received cash, $35.00, for accounting services rendered.
2. Paid cash, $300.00, for an electric typewriter.
3. Paid cash, $75.00, for office supplies.
4. Received cash, $60.00, for accounting services rendered.
5. Paid cash, $125.00, for rent of office.
6. Paid cash, $12.00, for telephone service.
7. Paid cash, $26.00, for advertising.
8. Received cash, $240.00, for accounting services rendered.
9. Paid cash, $100.00, to Burns Garage in part payment of amount owed.
10. Paid cash, $25.00, for membership in an accounting association.
11. Received cash, $380.00, for accounting services rendered.
12. Paid cash, $225.00, for a new office desk.
13. Received cash, $35.00, for sale of an old office desk.

14. Paid cash, $60.00, to Davis Supply Company in payment of amount owed.
15. Received cash, $50.00, for sale of old adding machine.
16. Paid cash, $375.00, for a new adding machine.
17. Paid cash, $80.00, to Olsen Equipment Company in payment of amount owed.
18. Paid cash, $15.00, for transportation to Asheville and return.
19. Paid cash, $24.00, for advertising.
20. Paid cash, $200.00, to Craig Finance Company in part payment of amount owed.

Optional problems

★Supplementary Problem 4-S. *Analyzing transactions into debit and credit parts*

Instructions: 1. Analyze each of the transactions given in Problem 4-1 into its debit part and its credit part. Use a form similar to the one illustrated below. Transaction No. 1 is given as an example.

TRANS. No.	DEBIT PART		CREDIT PART	
	ACCOUNT	AMOUNT	ACCOUNT	AMOUNT
1	Cash	35.00	Fees Income	35.00

★Bonus Problem 4-B. *Debit and credit analysis of ledger accounts*

Mr. J. C. Jackson owns and operates a dry-cleaning business. He maintains the following accounts in his ledger:

Cash
Automobile
Office Furniture
Office Machines
Parker Equipment Co. (creditor)

J. C. Jackson, Capital
Sales
Advertising Expense
Miscellaneous Expense
Rent Expense

Mr. Jackson has asked you to give him a better understanding of when an account is debited and when it is credited. You have decided to give him this information in T-account form.

Instructions: 1. Prepare a T account with account title for each account in his ledger.

2. On each side of each T account, give Mr. Jackson information similar to the following example:

Cash

Debited for balance and increases	Credited for decreases

Chapter 5

Journalizing business transactions

Immediate records of business transactions

At the time a business transaction occurs, a business paper that describes the transaction in detail should be prepared. In bookkeeping, a business paper prepared at the time of a transaction that describes a transaction is called an *immediate record.*

For example, when a business makes a cash payment, a check stub is filled out and a check is written. The check stub is the immediate record for the business that issues the check. When a merchant receives cash for a sale, the amount is rung up on the cash register, which prints the amount of the sale on a tape. This paper tape record is the immediate record of all cash sales. When a business issues receipts for all cash received, a carbon copy of the receipt is the immediate record.

Business transactions are recorded in a journal

In the previous chapter, business transactions were analyzed into their debit and credit parts. After each transaction is analyzed into its debit and credit parts, it is recorded in a journal. Separating a transaction into its debit and credit parts and recording it in a journal is called *journalizing.* All the information needed to journalize a transaction is obtained from the immediate record.

Journalizing business transactions increases accuracy

When a transaction is journalized, both the debit part and the credit part are recorded in the same place. Then any omission in recording part of the transaction can be seen readily and the error can be corrected immediately. Having the debit and the credit parts together also helps to make certain that the debit part equals the credit part.

Journalizing each business transaction also helps the bookkeeper to make certain that both the debit part and the credit part are posted to the proper accounts in the ledger. If transactions were recorded directly in accounts, interruption in the work might cause the bookkeeper to record only part of the transaction and to forget to record the other part. An error of this kind would be very difficult to locate.

The cash journal used by the Wood Realty Agency

All the transactions of a business might be recorded in a general journal similar to the journal that Mr. Wood used for his opening entry. If Mr. Wood continued to use this general journal for cash transactions, entries for cash receipts and cash payments might appear as follows:

	DATE		NAME OF ACCOUNT	POST. REF.	DEBIT	CREDIT	
1	1962 Oct.	1	Cash		4500		1
2			Office Furniture			4500	2
3			Sale of old office furniture				3
4		1	Adams Company		10000		4
5			Cash			10000	5
6			In part payment of amount owed.				6
7		3	Cash		72500		7
8			Commissions Income			72500	8
9			For sale of Wilson's house.				9
10		3	Rent Expense		13500		10
11			Cash			13500	11
12			For October rent.				12
13							13
14							14

GENERAL JOURNAL — PAGE 2

Cash transactions recorded in a general journal

Mr. Wood finds that he can journalize and post cash transactions more easily if he uses a special journal for cash transactions. A journal in which all cash transactions and only cash transactions are recorded is called a *cash journal*.

The two-column general journal was once commonly used by small businesses for recording all business transactions. Today it is generally used only for special entries such as the opening entry illustrated in Chapter 2. The use of the two-column journal for other special entries will be presented in later chapters.

The cash journal used by Mr. Wood is shown below. The transactions recorded in it are the same as the transactions illustrated above.

CASH JOURNAL — PAGE 1

	CASH DEBIT	GENERAL DEBIT	DATE	NAME OF ACCOUNT	NO.	POST. REF.	GENERAL CREDIT	COMMISSIONS INCOME CREDIT	CASH CREDIT	
1	4500		1962 Oct. 1	Office Furniture	R 1	13	4500			1
2		10000	1	Adams Company	Ck 1	21			10000	2
3	72500		3	Commissions Income	R 2	✓		72500		3
4		13500	3	Rent Expense	Ck 2	55			13500	4

Cash transactions recorded in a cash journal

Analyzing the cash journal of the Wood Realty Agency

The advantages of the cash journal with special amount columns for Cash Debit, Cash Credit, and Commissions Income Credit are:

1. In the general journal shown on page 44, three lines were used to record each transaction. In Mr. Wood's cash journal, each transaction is recorded on a single line.
2. Every transaction recorded in the cash journal is a cash receipt or a cash payment. Therefore, the account title Cash need not be written for each transaction. Only the name of the other account affected is written in the Name of Account column.
3. Special columns are provided for Cash Debit, Commissions Income Credit, and Cash Credit. The amounts entered in these columns are not posted separately. Only the total of each of these columns is posted. Posting only the total of a special column is much easier and faster than posting each item in the column separately.
4. A General Debit column and a General Credit column are provided for all accounts for which special columns are not provided. The two General columns of the cash journal are posted in the same manner as the two columns of the general journal.
5. The number of the receipt for each cash receipt and the number of the check for each cash payment are entered in the No. column. This makes it unnecessary to use a separate line for an explanation.

Transaction No. 1 — a cash received transaction

October 1, 1962. Received cash, $45.00, for the sale of old office furniture. Issued Receipt No. 1.

The immediate record of cash received. Each time Mr. Wood receives cash, he writes a receipt with a carbon copy. The original copy is given to the person from whom the cash is received. The carbon copy is kept in the receipt book as the immediate record of the transaction. The carbon copy of the first receipt issued by Mr. Wood is shown below.

Carbon copy of a receipt

No. 1 _____ *October 1* 19 62

RECEIVED FROM *R. G. Miller*

Forty-five ⁰⁰⁄₁₀₀ ——————— DOLLARS

FOR *Used typewriter desk*

$45.⁰⁰ ____ WOOD REALTY AGENCY

BY *M. W. Wood*

Entry for Transaction No. 1. Mr. Wood analyzed this transaction into its debit and credit parts. He then made the following entry on Line 1 of his cash journal:

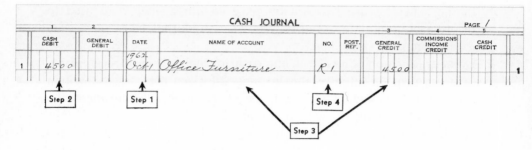

Mr. Wood used the following steps in recording this entry:

Step 1. *Date of Entry No. 1.* The year, month, and day — *1962, Oct. 1* — were written at the top of the Date column.

Step 2. *Debit part of Entry No. 1.* The cash account was debited by writing *$45.00* in the Cash Debit amount column on Line 1. The cash account was identified by the heading of the column, *Cash Debit.* It was not necessary to write the account title *Cash* because every transaction recorded in the cash journal affects cash. The cash account was debited because the asset Cash was increased.

> Note that the debit amount columns are at the left of the Name of Account column and that the credit amount columns are at the right.

Step 3. *Credit part of Entry No. 1.* The office furniture account was credited (a) by writing *$45.00* in the General Credit amount column and (b) by writing the words *Office Furniture* in the Name of Account column. The office furniture account was credited because the sale of some of the office furniture decreased the asset Office Furniture.

> The General amount columns in the journal are used to record amounts for which there are no special columns. When an amount is recorded in a General amount column, the name of the account debited or credited is written in the Name of Account column.

Step 4. *Explanation of Entry No. 1.* *R1* was written in the No. column to show that Receipt No. 1 was issued in this transaction. The letter *R* in the No. column stands for *receipt* and is followed by the number of the receipt. The number is obtained from the carbon copy of the receipt.

> At a later date, some information not shown in the cash journal may be desired. For example, a journal entry does not show what item of office furniture was sold or to whom it was sold. *R1* in the No. column of the cash journal shows that detailed information about this transaction may be obtained quickly from the carbon copy of the receipt in the receipt book. Therefore it is not necessary to repeat all these details in the cash journal.

46

Transaction No. 2 — a cash payment transaction

October 1, 1962. Paid cash, $100.00, to Adams Company in part payment of the amount owed. Issued Check No. 1.

The immediate record of a cash payment. Each time that cash is paid by Mr. Wood, he writes a check for the amount paid. Before writing the check, he fills out the stub of the check. The check stub shown below is the immediate record of this cash payment.

Check stub for
Transaction No. 2

Entry for Transaction No. 2. Mr. Wood analyzed this transaction into its debit and credit parts. He then made the following entry on Line 2 of his cash journal:

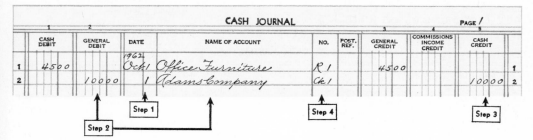

Mr. Wood used the following steps in recording this entry:

Step 1. *Date of Entry No. 2.* The day of the month, *1,* was written in the day column of the Date section of the cash journal. (The year and the month are written only once on each page of the cash journal, but the *day* of the month is recorded for each transaction.)

Step 2. *Debit part of Entry No. 2.* The Adams Company account was debited (a) by writing *$100.00* in the General Debit amount column and (b) by writing the words *Adams Company* in the Name of Account column — all on Line 2 of the journal. The Adams Company account was debited because the liability Adams Company was decreased.

47

Credit part of Entry No. 2. The cash account was credited by writing *$100.00* in the Cash Credit amount column. The cash account was credited because this cash payment transaction decreased the asset Cash.

Step 4. *Explanation of Entry No. 2. Ck1* was written in the No. column of the cash journal to show that Check No. 1 was issued in this transaction. The letters *Ck* in the No. column stand for *check* and are followed by the number of the check. The check number is obtained from the check stub.

The check number in the No. column of the cash journal shows which check stub has the additional details about this transaction. Since this information can be located quickly when needed, it is not necessary to record any of these details in the cash journal.

Transaction No. 3 — an income transaction

October 3, 1962. Received cash, $725.00, as commission for the sale of a house. Issued Receipt No. 2.

The immediate record. The carbon copy of Receipt No. 2 gave Mr. Wood all the information he needed for his journal entry for Transaction No. 3.

Entry for Transaction No. 3. Mr. Wood analyzed this transaction into its debit and credit parts. He then made the following entry on Line 3 of the cash journal:

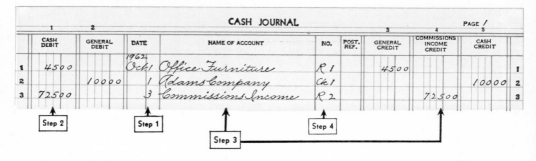

Mr. Wood used the following steps in recording the above entry in his cash journal:

Step 1. *Date of Entry No. 3.* The day of the month, *3*, was written on Line 3 in the day column of the Date section of the cash journal.

Step 2. *Debit part of Entry No. 3.* The cash account was debited by writing *$725.00* in the Cash Debit amount column. The cash account was debited because this cash received transaction increased the asset Cash.

Step 3. *Credit part of Entry No. 3.* The commissions income account was credited (a) by writing *$725.00* in the Commissions Income Credit column and (b) by writing the words *Commissions Income* in the Name of Account column. The commissions income account was credited because this cash received transaction increased proprietorship. If incomes were recorded directly in the proprietor's capital account, they would be recorded as credits. Therefore, when a separate account is kept for income transactions, an income account is credited.

Step 4. *Explanation of Entry No. 3.* R2 was written in the No. column to show that Receipt No. 2 was the immediate record for this entry.

Transaction No. 4 — an expense transaction

October 3, 1962. Paid cash, $135.00, for rent of office for October.

The immediate record. The stub of Check No. 2 gave Mr. Wood all the information he needed for his cash journal entry for this transaction.

Entry for Transaction No. 4. Mr. Wood analyzed this transaction into its debit and credit parts. He then made the following entry on Line 4 of the cash journal:

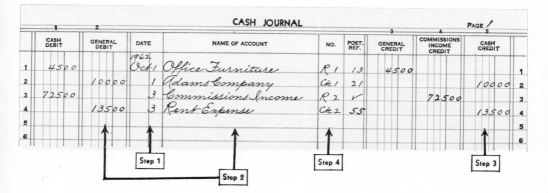

Mr. Wood used the following steps in recording the above entry in his cash journal:

Step 1. *Date of Entry No. 4.* The day of the month, *3*, was written on Line 4 in the day column of the Date section of the cash journal.

Step 2. *Debit part of Entry No. 4.* The rent expense account was debited by (a) writing *$135.00* in the General Debit amount column and (b) writing the words *Rent Expense* in the Name of Account column. The rent expense account was debited because all expenses decrease proprietorship.

Step 3. *Credit part of Entry No. 4.* The cash account was credited by writing *$135.00* in the Cash Credit amount column. The cash account was credited because this cash payment decreased the asset Cash.

Step 4. *Explanation of Entry No. 4. Ck2* was written in the No. column of the journal to show that Check No. 2 was issued in this transaction.

Recording Transactions Nos. 5 through 26

The transactions for the remainder of October were similar to those that have been discussed. The complete cash journal of the Wood Realty Agency for October is shown on page 51.

The Wood Realty Agency maintains five expense accounts: Advertising Expense, Automobile Expense, Entertainment Expense, Miscellaneous Expense, and Rent Expense. The account Miscellaneous Expense is debited for all expenses that cannot be charged to any of the other expense accounts.

Summary of journalizing in a cash journal

1. The complete record of each transaction is written on a single line of the cash journal.
2. For each amount in a *debit* amount column there is an equal amount in a *credit* amount column.
3. All cash receipts are increases in the asset Cash and are recorded as *debits* in the *Cash Debit* amount column.
4. All cash payments are decreases in the asset Cash and are recorded as *credits* in the *Cash Credit* amount column.
5. Each time Cash is *debited* in the Cash Debit amount column, the title of the account to be *credited* is written in the Name of Account column.
6. Each time Cash is *credited* in the Cash Credit column, the name of the account to be *debited* is written in the Name of Account column.

Double-entry bookkeeping

The recording of the two parts of each transaction, the debit part and the credit part, is called *double-entry bookkeeping.* Complete bookkeeping, then, is double-entry bookkeeping.

Double-entry bookkeeping is used in practically all well-organized businesses because it is the only method that provides a complete record of the effect of each transaction on ledger accounts. Recording only the debit part or only the credit part of a transaction is called *single-entry bookkeeping.*

CASH JOURNAL

PAGE 1

	CASH DEBIT	GENERAL DEBIT	DATE	NAME OF ACCOUNT	NO.	POST. REF.	GENERAL CREDIT	COMMISSIONS INCOME CREDIT	CASH CREDIT	
			1962							
1	4500		Oct 1	Office Furniture	R 1		4500			1
2		10000	1	Adams Company	Ck 1				10000	2
3	72500		3	Commissions Income	R 2			72500		3
4		13500	3	Rent Expense	Ck 2				13500	4
5		3000	3	Office Furniture	Ck 3				3000	5
6	20000		4	Commissions Income	R 3			20000		6
7		2300	5	Automobile Expense	Ck 4				2300	7
8	8000		8	Commissions Income	R 4			8000		8
9		12500	9	Triangle Motors	Ck 5				12500	9
10		5000	9	Advertising Expense	Ck 6				5000	10
11	9000		11	Commissions Income	R 5			9000		11
12		7500	12	McIntyre Company	Ck 7				7500	12
13		37500	15	Office Machines	Ck 8				37500	13
14	40000		16	Commissions Income	R 6			40000		14
15		600	17	Entertainment Expense	Ck 9				600	15
16	3900		17	Commissions Income	R 7			3900		16
17		7200	19	Advertising Expense	Ck 10				7200	17
18	29500		22	Commissions Income	R 8			29500		18
19		5000	23	Adams Company	Ck 11				5000	19
20	11300		24	Office Machines	R 9		11300			20
21	6500		25	Commissions Income	R 10			6500		21
22		900	25	Miscellaneous Expense	Ck 12				900	22
23		700	26	Entertainment Expense	Ck 13				700	23
24		1300	30	Automobile Expense	Ck 14				1300	24
25	11800		31	Commissions Income	R 11			11800		25
26		500	31	Miscellaneous Expense	Ck 15				500	26
27	217000 / 217000	107500 / 107500	31	Totals			15800 / 15800	201200 / 201200	107500 / 107500	27

Cash journal of Wood Realty Agency for October

Footing the cash journal

At the end of the month all amount columns of the journal were added. The total of each amount column was written in small pencil figures immediately under the last entry. Pencil totals written in small figures are commonly called *footings*.

Special columns in a cash journal

Each kind of business plans its cash journal to fit its needs. The Wood Realty Agency planned its journal with special columns for Cash Debit, Cash Credit, and Commissions Income Credit because transactions affecting these accounts occurred often.

Another type of business might have special columns for those expense items that occur frequently such as Advertising Expense Debit, Automobile Expense Debit, and Miscellaneous Expense Debit. Examples of cash journals with additional special columns are given in later chapters.

Proving cash on hand

Determining that the amount of cash on hand agrees with the book-keeping records is known as *proving cash*. Cash on hand is the bank balance plus all cash not deposited. Cash should always be proved when the cash journal is footed.

After the cash journal was footed, Mr. Wood made the following calculations to prove cash:

Cash balance at the beginning of the month as shown by the cash account in the ledger..............................	$ 491.00
Plus cash received during the month (footing of Cash Debit column).........	2,170.00
Total of beginning balance plus cash received...............	$2,661.00
Less cash paid during the month (footing of Cash Credit column)...	1,075.00
Amount of cash that should be on hand	$1,586.00

Mr. Wood had deposited all cash as it was received. His last check stub showed a balance of $1,586.00. This proved that the cash on hand agreed with the cash journal record.

Proving the equality of debits and credits

On a separate sheet of paper the footings of the debit columns were listed and added. The footings of the credit columns were also listed and added. The calculations are shown below.

Cash Debit footing........	$2,170.00	General Credit footing....	$ 158.00
General Debit footing.....	1,075.00	Commissions Income Credit footing................	2,012.00
		Cash Credit footing.......	1,075.00
Total debits.............	$3,245.00	Total credits............	$3,245.00

The sum of the totals of the *two debit* columns should equal the sum of the totals of the *three credit* columns. If the sum of the debits does not equal the sum of the credits, one or more errors have been made. The error or errors should be located and corrected.

Ruling the journal

After the equality of debits and credits was proved, a single line was drawn across all amount columns under the last entry. The totals of the columns were then entered in ink. The last day of the month was written in the Date column on the line with the totals. The word *Totals* was written in the Name of Account column. A double line was drawn across all columns except the Name of Account column. A ruler should always be used in drawing lines. Either red or black ink may be used.

The foregoing instructions apply to situations such as the one illustrated on page 51, where the journal page is not filled at the end of the month.

When a page that is filled is totaled, the printed rulings at the bottom of the page are used and ruling with a pen is unnecessary. If a page that is almost full is totaled, the printed rulings at the bottom of the page may also be used. In this case the spaces between the last entry and the printed rulings are canceled with a diagonal line drawn across the Name of Account column from the Date column to the No. column.

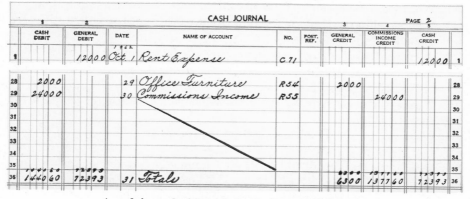

A cash journal with totals at the bottom of the page

Correcting errors in the journal

An error may be made in recording a transaction in the journal. If an error is in the amount, the incorrect amount should be canceled by drawing a line through it. The correct amount should then be written immediately above the canceled amount.

An error in an account title is corrected by drawing a line through the incorrect title and writing the correct title immediately above the canceled title.

Corrections of an error in an amount and of an error in an account title are shown in the illustration below.

Correcting errors in a journal

Increasing your business vocabulary

What is the meaning of each of the following:

(a) immediate record

(b) journalizing

(c) cash journal

(d) double-entry bookkeeping

(e) single-entry bookkeeping

(f) footings

(g) proving cash

Chapter questions

1. What are some examples of immediate records of business transactions?
2. Why should every transaction be journalized before it is posted to ledger accounts?
3. What are the advantages of special amount columns in the journal?
4. What business paper does Mr. Wood use for the immediate record of each cash received transaction?
5. What is the meaning of *R1* in the No. column on Line 1 in the cash journal on page 51?
6. What business paper does Mr. Wood use for the immediate record of each cash payment transaction?
7. What is the meaning of *Ck1* in the No. column on Line 2 in the cash journal on page 51?
8. Why is it necessary to write the name of the expense account in the Name of Account column each time an expense account is debited?
9. When should cash be proved?
10. How is cash proved?
11. If an error is made in recording an amount in the cash journal, how is the error corrected?
12. If an error is made in recording an account title in the cash journal, how is the error corrected?

Cases for discussion

1. Kenneth Cook uses a receipt book that has a receipt stub record for each receipt issued. Thomas Lewis uses a receipt book that has a carbon copy for each receipt issued and no stub record. What are the advantages of Lewis's plan of using a carbon copy of each receipt issued instead of a receipt stub record?
2. George Brooks is very particular about writing the stub of each check before he writes the check. As Dean Johnson is often in a hurry, he writes the check first and fills in the stub later. Why is Johnson's check-writing habit of sometimes writing the check before he fills in the stub not a good habit?
3. Both Paul Walters and Conrad Hill use columnar journals similar to the one illustrated on page 51. When Paul Walters records Commissions Income, he records the debit in the Cash Debit column and the credit in the Commissions Income Credit column and makes a check mark in the Name of Ac-

count column. Conrad Hill follows the same procedure except that he writes the account title, Commissions Income, in the Name of Account column. Which person do you believe follows the better plan? Why?

4. Conrad Hill refers to all of his cash payments as "my expenses." Paul Walters tells him that some cash payments increase the value of assets and that others decrease the amount of liabilities. Refer to the journal on page 51 and indicate which of the cash payments are not payments of expenses.

Drills for understanding

The following drills are planned to give you additional skill, accuracy, and speed in selecting proper account titles for business transactions and in analyzing the effect of the transaction.

Drill 5-A. *Debits and credits in journalizing*

Instructions: 1. Turn to the completed cash journal illustrated on page 51. On a form similar to the one shown below, copy the analysis of Line 1 of that cash journal.

LINE No.	TITLE OF ACCOUNT DEBITED	TITLE OF ACCOUNT CREDITED
1	Cash	Office Furniture

Instructions: 2. Write a similar analysis of each of the remaining entries of the cash journal on page 51, Lines 2 to 26.

Drill 5-B. *Analyzing the effect of debits and credits*

For each of the entries on Lines 1 to 26 in the cash journal illustrated on page 51 you are to tell whether an asset, a liability, or the proprietorship was increased or decreased.

Instructions: 1. On a form similar to the one shown below, copy the analysis of line 1 of the cash journal on page 51. The first analysis is given you as an example of what you are to do.

LINE No.	EFFECT OF DEBIT ENTRY	EFFECT OF CREDIT ENTRY
1	Increased an asset	Decreased an asset

Instructions: 2. Write a similar analysis of each of the remaining lines (Lines 2 to 26) of the journal illustrated on page 51. If an expense account was debited, write: *Decreased proprietorship.* If an income account was credited, write: *Increased proprietorship.*

55

Drill 5-C. *Analyzing transactions — debit, credit, and effect*

For each of the transactions listed below in this drill you are to write: (a) the title of the account debited and the title of the account credited, and (b) the effect of each debit and each credit in terms of increases and decreases.

Instructions: 1. On a form similar to the one shown below, copy the analysis of Transaction 1, which is given as an example.

1	2	3	4	5
TRANS. NO.	TITLE OF ACCOUNT DEBITED	EFFECT OF THE DEBIT	TITLE OF ACCOUNT CREDITED	EFFECT OF THE CREDIT
1	*Cash*	*Increased an asset*	*Commissions Income*	*Increased proprietor-ship*

Instructions: 2. Write a similar analysis of Transactions 2 to 15, using the following account titles in Columns 2 and 4 of your analysis form.

LIST OF ACCOUNT TITLES

Cash	Advertising Expense
Automobile	Automobile Expense
Office Furniture	Electricity Expense
Office Machines	Rent Expense
Atlas Company	Stationery Expense
Thompson Garage	Telephone Expense
Commissions Income	

TRANSACTIONS

1. Received cash as commission from sale of a house. (You copied this answer when you completed Instruction 1.)
2. Received cash from sale of old office furniture.
3. Paid cash for rent of office for October.
4. Paid cash for gas and oil used in operating the automobile.
5. Received cash from sale of old office machine.
6. Paid cash to Atlas Company in partial payment of amount owed.
7. Paid cash for purchase of new office furniture.
8. Paid cash to Thompson Garage in partial payment of amount owed.
9. Paid cash for purchase of new office machine.
10. Received cash as commission from sale of a house.
11. Paid cash for office stationery.
12. Paid cash for advertising.
13. Received cash as commission for renting a house.
14. Paid cash for telephone bill.
15. Paid cash for electric bill.

Application problems

Problem 5-1. *Journalizing cash transactions of a real estate business*

Instructions: 1. Record the following transactions of the Benson Realty Agency on page 3 of a five-column cash journal. Use as your model the five-column cash journal form illustrated on page 51. In the Name of Account column of your journal, use the account titles listed in Drill 5-C, Instruction 2.

TRANSACTIONS

Mar. 1. Received cash, $200.00, as commission from sale of a house. (Receipt No. 1)
2. Received cash, $16.00, from sale of old office furniture. (Receipt No. 2)
2. Paid cash, $75.00, for rent of office for March. (Check No. 1)
4. Paid cash, $5.50, for gas and oil for automobile. (Check No. 2)
5. Received cash, $90.00, as commission from renting a house. (Receipt No. 3)
7. Paid cash, $95.50, to Atlas Company in part payment of account. (Check No. 3)
10. Paid cash, $114.00, for new office furniture. (Check No. 4)
12. Paid cash, $32.50, to Thompson Garage in part payment of amount owed them. (Check No. 5)
15. Paid cash, $125.00, for a new office machine. (Check No. 6)
17. Received cash, $120.00, as commission from sale of a house. (Receipt No. 4)
19. Paid cash, $6.00, for office stationery. (Check No. 7)
23. Paid cash, $2.50, for advertisement in paper. (Check No. 8)
25. Received cash, $55.00, as commission from renting a house. (Receipt No. 5)
29. Paid cash, $10.00, for telephone bill. (Check No. 9)
29. Paid cash, $8.50, for electric bill. (Check No. 10)

Instructions: 2. Foot each of the five columns of your cash journal, using small pencil figures. Place these tiny pencil figures close to the line above so that they seem to hang from it. Study the model journal on page 51.

3. Prove cash. The balance on hand at the beginning of the month was $368.50. The balance on hand at the end of the month is $375.00.

4. Prove the equality of debits and credits in your cash journal by finding the sum of all the debit totals and then the sum of all the credit totals. The sum of the totals of the two debit columns should equal the sum of the totals of the three credit columns.

5. If the sum of the totals of the debits in your cash journal is equal to the sum of the totals of the credits, rule a single line across all amount columns of your cash journal. Compare your work with the cash journal on page 51.

6. Write the totals of each column in ink. Label these totals by writing the word *Totals* in the Name of Account column. All of these totals should be on the same line. Write the date on the line with the totals. Compare your work with the cash journal on page 51.

7. Rule double lines across all columns except the Name of Account column immediately below the totals. Use as your model the cash journal on page 51.

Problem 5-2. *Journalizing cash transactions of a certified public accountant*

Gordon Riley is a certified public accountant and obtains his income from fees for professional accounting services. The title he uses for his income account is Fees Income.

Instructions: 1. Record on page 10 of a five-column cash journal the selected transactions given below. Use the following account titles:

ASSETS	LIABILITIES	INCOME
Cash	Edison Company	Fees Income
Automobile	Shaw Company	EXPENSES
Office Furniture	PROPRIETORSHIP	Automobile Expense
Professional Library	Gordon Riley, Capital	Miscellaneous Expense
		Rent Expense

TRANSACTIONS

Oct. 1. Paid cash, $100.00, for rent of the office for October. (Check No. 1)
   1. Paid cash, $12.00, for parking space for the automobile for October. This is automobile expense. (Check No. 2)
   2. Received cash, $15.00, from sale of old office desk. This is office furniture. (Receipt No. 1)
   2. Received cash, $185.00, for accounting services. This is fees income. (Receipt No. 2)
   2. Paid cash, $5.85, for gas and oil for automobile. (Check No. 3)
   3. Paid cash, $240.00, for a new desk and a bookcase. (Check No. 4)
   4. Received cash, $270.00, for accounting services. (Receipt No. 3)
   10. Received cash, $175.00, for accounting services. (Receipt No. 4)
   14. Paid cash, $8.50, for a new book on accounting. This is professional library. (Check No. 5)
   15. Received cash, $250.00, for accounting services. (Receipt No. 5)
   19. Received cash, $110.00, for accounting services. (Receipt No. 6)
   22. Paid cash, $160.00, to the Shaw Company for amount owed on account. (Check No. 6)
   25. Paid cash, $31.25, to the Edison Company for amount owed on account. (Check No. 7)
   29. Received cash, $190.00, for accounting services. (Receipt No. 7)
   31. Paid cash, $15.20, for the electric bill for October. This is miscellaneous expense. (Check No. 8)
   31. Paid cash, $9.50, for the telephone bill for October. This is miscellaneous expense. (Check No. 9)

Instructions: 2. Foot each of the five columns of your cash journal. Use small pencil figures.

3. Prove cash. The balance on hand at the beginning of the month was $213.80. The balance on hand at the end of the month is $826.50.

4. Prove the equality of debits and credits in your cash journal.

5. Write the column totals. Write the word "Totals" in the Name of Account column.

6. Rule the cash journal.

This problem will be continued in the next chapter. If it is collected by your teacher at this time, it will be returned to you before it is needed in Problem 6-1.

Optional problems

★*Supplementary Problem 5-S. Journalizing cash transactions of an attorney*

David Wright is an attorney and obtains his income from legal fees for his professional services. The title he uses for his income account is *Fees Income*.

Instructions: 1. Use a five-column journal that has the same columnar headings as the journal shown on page 51, except substitute the heading Fees Income Credit for Commissions Income Credit.

2. Use the following account titles in journalizing the selected transactions given below the account titles:

Cash	Miscellaneous Expense
Office Furniture	Rent Expense
Anderson Publishing Company	Salary Expense
Fees Income	Stationery Expense

TRANSACTIONS

July 1. Paid cash, $125.00, for rent of the office for July. Issued Check No. 35.
    3. Received cash, $50.00, for legal services. Issued Receipt No. 21.
    5. Paid cash, $125.00, to the Anderson Publishing Company for amount owed on account. Issued Check No. 36.
    6. Received cash, $150.00, for legal services. Issued Receipt No. 22.
    9. Paid cash, $15.00, for stationery. Issued Check No. 37.
    12. Paid cash, $195.00 for a new desk. Issued Check No. 38.
    15. Received cash, $100.00, for legal services. Issued Receipt No. 23.
    17. Received cash, $75.00, for legal services. Issued Receipt No. 24.
    24. Paid cash, $12.50, for the telephone bill for July. Issued Check No. 39.
    27. Received cash, $145.00, for legal services. Issued Receipt No. 25.
    31. Paid cash, $250.00, for salary of the law clerk for month. Issued Check No. 40.

Instructions: 3. Foot each of the amount columns of your cash journal. Use small pencil figures.

4. Prove cash. The balance on hand at the beginning of the month was $438.66. The balance on hand at the end of the month is $236.16.

5. Prove the equality of debits and credits in your cash journal.

6. Write the column totals on the Totals line of your cash journal.

7. Rule the cash journal.

★*Bonus Problem 5-B. Journalizing cash transactions of a realtor*

The Mills Realty Agency is owned and operated by K. H. Mills. Some of the account titles in his ledger are listed below. These are not all of the accounts in his ledger, but they are all of the accounts that you will need in this problem.

Cash	Advertising Expense
Office Equipment	Automobile Expense
Office Furniture	Miscellaneous Expense
Commissions Income	Rent Expense

Mr. Mills uses a cash journal that has the same columnar headings as the cash journal illustrated in this chapter, but the arrangement of the columns is not the same. The amount columns in Mr. Mills's cash journal are as follows:

| CASH | | DATE | NAME OF | No. | P. | GENERAL | | COMMISSIONS INCOME |
DR.	CR.		ACCOUNT		R.	DR.	CR.	CR.

Instructions: 1. Record the following selected transactions in a cash journal ruled like the form above. Use the current year in recording the date. Use the account titles listed on page 59.

TRANSACTIONS

Dec. 1. Received $231.75 as commission on sale of a vacant lot. (Receipt No. 62)
 1. Paid $87.50 for repairs to his automobile. The damage came from an automobile accident. (Check No. 51)
 2. Paid $145.00 for rent for December. (Check No. 52)
 4. Received $200.00 as commission for renting property. (Receipt No. 63)
 5. Received $5.00 as refund from Lamont Equipment Company for overcharge on office equipment bought from them last month. This refund decreases the cost of our equipment. (Receipt No. 64)
 5. Paid $15.00 as a refund to a customer of a part of the commission received from him last month. (Check No. 53)
 6. Received $87.50 from Ohio Insurance Company to reimburse him for the automobile accident repair bill that he paid on December 1. (Receipt No. 65)
 7. Paid $7.75 for advertising. (Check No. 54)
 9. Paid $10.00 to have the office cleaned. (Check No. 55)
 11. Paid $8.35 for gas and oil used in operating the automobile on business. (Check No. 56)
 15. Received $475.00 as commission on the sale of a house. (Receipt No. 66)
 18. Received $45.00 as commission for renting a house. (Receipt No. 67)
 19. Received $23.00 for sale of old furniture. (Receipt No. 68)
 22. Paid $6.50 for entertaining a customer. (Check No. 57)
 25. Paid $10.50 for advertising. (Check No. 58)
 28. Received $2,500.00 as commission for sale of a farm. (Receipt No. 69)

Instructions: 2. Foot each of the amount columns of your cash journal. Use small pencil figures.

3. Prove cash. The balance on hand at the beginning of the month was $335.00. The balance on hand at the end of the month is $3,611.65.

4. Prove the equality of debits and credits in your cash journal.

5. Write the column totals on the Totals line of your cash journal.

6. Rule the cash journal.

Chapter 6

Posting

Need for posting the journal record of transactions

The cash journal on page 51 is a record of all transactions completed by the Wood Realty Agency during the month of October. Each entry in the cash journal will affect the balances of two accounts in the ledger.

In order that Mr. Wood may have a clear picture of what has happened to each account in his ledger, it is now necessary to post the cash journal. The process of posting will sort the journal entries into accounts and transfer each debit and each credit from the journal to the proper account in the ledger.

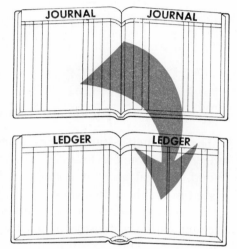

How the accounts in the ledger are arranged

In getting ready to post the cash journal to a new ledger, the first step is to plan a convenient arrangement of the accounts in the ledger. It is customary to have separate groups for assets, liabilities, proprietorship, income, and expenses. Each of these groups is called a division of the ledger. Mr. Wood arranged his ledger accounts in five divisions as shown at the right.

Some businesses have more than five divisions in the ledger. These variations will be developed in later chapters. For example, the ledger on page 263 has six divisions.

(1) Assets
(2) Liabilities
(3) Proprietorship
(4) Income
(5) Expenses

Chart of accounts of the Wood Realty Agency

The chart of accounts shows the plan of the ledger. It serves also as a guide in journalizing by showing the exact account titles that must be used for each journal entry. The chart of accounts of the Wood Realty Agency is shown on the following page.

```
┌─────────────────────────────────────────────────────────────────┐
│                    Wood Realty Agency                            │
│                    Chart of Accounts                             │
├─────────────────────────────────────────────────────────────────┤
│                     Account                         Account      │
│     (1) Assets      Number      (4) Income          Number       │
│  Cash..............  11      Commissions Income..  41             │
│  Automobile........  12                                          │
│  Office Furniture...  13         (5) Expenses                    │
│  Office Machines....  14      Advertising Expense..  51          │
│                               Automobile Expense...  52          │
│     (2) Liabilities           Entertainment                     │
│  Adams Company......  21      Expense.............  53           │
│  McIntyre Company...  22      Miscellaneous Expense  54          │
│  Triangle Motors....  23      Rent Expense.........  55          │
│                                                                  │
│  (3) Proprietorship                                             │
│  M. W. Wood, Capital  31                                        │
└─────────────────────────────────────────────────────────────────┘
```

Chart of accounts with five divisions

The first digit of an account number shows in which division of the ledger the account is located. For example, the first digit of the M. W. Wood, Capital account number is 3. This shows that this account is placed in the third division of the ledger, the proprietorship division.

The second digit of an account number shows the placement of the account within a division of the ledger. For example, the second digit of the Automobile Expense account number is 2. This shows that this account is the second account in this division, the expenses division.

Posting a columnar cash journal

A portion of the cash journal of the Wood Realty Agency, ready for posting, is shown below. (The complete page of this cash journal is shown on page 51.)

CASH DEBIT	GENERAL DEBIT	DATE	NAME OF ACCOUNT	NO.	POST. REF.	GENERAL CREDIT	COMMISSIONS INCOME CREDIT	CASH CREDIT	
			CASH JOURNAL					PAGE 1	
4500		1962 Oct. 1	Office Furniture	R 1		4500			1
									2

The special columns in the cash journal of the Wood Realty Agency are Cash Debit, Commissions Income Credit, and Cash Credit. Only the totals of these three special columns are posted. This plan saves much time and labor in posting. For example, all debits in the Cash Debit column of the cash journal are transferred to the cash account in the ledger in a single posting.

Each individual amount in the General Debit amount column of the cash journal must be posted separately to the *debit* side of the account named in the Name of Account column. Each individual amount in the General Credit amount column must be posted separately to the *credit* side of the account named in the Name of Account column.

Steps in posting Line 1 of the cash journal

The entry on Line 1 of the cash journal shows a debit to Cash and a credit to Office Furniture. The debit to Cash is not posted separately because it will be included when the total of this column is posted to the cash account. The credit to Office Furniture, since it is in a General column, is posted as follows:

Step 1. Write the amount of the credit, $45.00, in the Credit amount column of the office furniture account.

Step 2. Write the date of this journal entry in the Date column on the credit side of the office furniture account.

Since this is the first entry on the credit side of the office furniture account, it is necessary to write the complete date: 1962, Oct. 1.

Step 3. Write *C1* in the Post. Ref. column of the account in the ledger to show that this entry was posted from page 1 of the cash journal.

Step 4. Return to the cash journal and write in the Post. Ref. column of the cash journal the number of the ledger account, 13, to which this General Credit amount was posted. The cash journal now appears as follows:

A figure in the Post. Ref. column of the cash journal shows that all details of posting this line have been completed. For this reason the Post. Ref. figure is always written in the cash journal as the last step in posting.

Steps in posting Line 2 of the cash journal

The entry on Line 2 of the cash journal shows a debit to Adams Company and a credit to Cash. The credit to Cash is not posted separately because it will be included when the total of the Cash Credit column is posted to the cash account.

The steps in posting the debit to the Adams Company account are as follows:

Step 1. Write the amount of the debit, $100.00, in the Debit amount column of the Adams Company account.

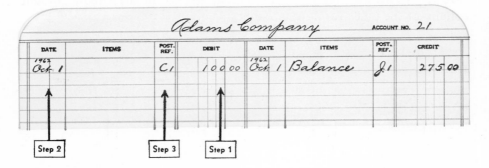

Step 2. Write the date of this journal entry in the Date column on the debit side of the Adams Company account.

Since this is the first entry on the debit side of the Adams Company account, it is necessary to write the complete date: 1962, Oct. 1.

Step 3. Write *C1* in the Post. Ref. column of the account in the ledger to show that this entry was posted from page 1 of the cash journal.

Step 4. Return to the cash journal and write in the Post. Ref. column of the cash journal the number of the ledger account, 21, to which the entry was posted. The cash journal then appears as follows:

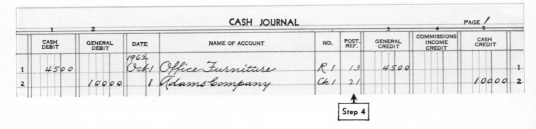

Completing the posting of the two General columns

Each amount in the General Debit column of the cash journal is posted to the debit side of the account named in the Name of Account column. Each amount in the General Credit column of the cash journal is posted to the credit side of the account named in the Name of Account column.

The amounts recorded in the General Debit and the General Credit columns of the cash journal are usually posted at frequent intervals during the month so that there will not be too much work at the end of the month.

Totals of the General columns of the cash journal are not posted

Since the individual amounts that make up the total of each General column are posted separately, the total itself is not posted. (The total of a column is posted only when the heading of the column is the name of an account and the items in it have not been posted separately.)

A check mark in parentheses is placed below the totals of each of the two General columns to show that these totals are not posted.

Posting the totals of special columns of the cash journal

In the cash journal of the Wood Realty Agency, the two Cash columns and the Commissions Income column are special columns. There is no posting from a special column until the end of the month; then only the total of the column is posted.

The total of each special column is posted to the account named in the heading of the column. For example, the total of the Cash Debit column of the cash journal is posted to the debit side of the cash account. The total of the Cash Credit column is posted to the credit side of the cash account. The total of the Commissions Income Credit column is posted to the credit side of the commissions income account.

Posting the total of the Cash Debit column

The steps used in posting the total of the Cash Debit column of the cash journal are as follows:

Step 1. Write the amount of the debit, $2,170.00, in the Debit amount column of the cash account in the ledger.

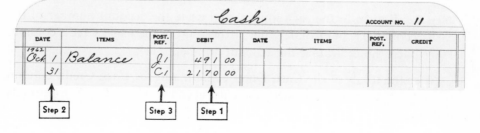

Step 2. Write the day found on the total line of the cash journal, 31, in the day column on the debit side of the cash account.

This is the second entry on the debit side of the cash account. The date of the first entry in the cash account is 1962, Oct. 1. The date of the second entry is also the same year and the same month; therefore, it is not necessary to repeat 1962 and Oct. on the debit side of the cash account.

Step 3. Write *C1* in the Post. Ref. column of the cash account in the ledger to show that this entry was posted from page 1 of the cash journal.

Step 4. Return to the cash journal and write the account number of the cash account, 11, immediately under the total of the Cash Debit column. Place parentheses around the account number: (11).

	CASH JOURNAL								PAGE *1*
CASH DEBIT	GENERAL DEBIT	DATE	NAME OF ACCOUNT	NO.	POST. REF.	GENERAL CREDIT	COMMISSIONS INCOME CREDIT	CASH CREDIT	
25	11800		31 Commissions Income	R 11	✓		11800		25
26		500	31 Miscellaneous Expense	Ck15	54			500	26
27	2 17000 1 07500	1 07500	31 Totals			1 58 00 2 01 200 1 07500	1 58 00 2 01 200	1 07500	27
28	(")								28

Step 4

Posting the total of the Cash Credit column

The steps used in posting the total of the Cash Credit column of the cash journal are as follows:

Step 1. Write the amount of the total, $1,075.00, in the Credit amount column of the cash account in the ledger.

Step 2. Write the day found on the total line of the cash journal in the day column on the credit side of the cash account. Since this is the first entry on the credit side of the cash account, it is necessary to write the complete date, 1962, Oct. 31.

Step 3. Write *C1* in the Post. Ref. column of the cash account in the ledger to show that this entry was posted from page 1 of the cash journal.

Step 4. Return to the cash journal and write the account number of the cash account, 11, immediately under the total of the Cash Credit column. Place parentheses around the account number: (11).

After the totals of the Cash Debit column and the Cash Credit column of the cash journal are posted, the cash account in the ledger appears as follows:

66

DATE	ITEMS	POST. REF.	DEBIT	DATE	ITEMS	POST. REF.	CREDIT
1962 Oct 1	Balance	J1	491 00	*1962* Oct 31		C1	1075 00
31		C1	2170 00				

Step 2   Step 3   Step 1

Posting the total of the Commissions Income Credit column

The steps used in posting the total of the Commissions Income Credit column of the cash journal are as follows:

Step 1.   Write the amount of the total, $2,012.00, in the Credit amount column of the commissions income account in the ledger.

Step 2.   Write the day found on the total line of the cash journal in the day column on the credit side of the commissions income account. Since this is the first entry on the credit side of the commissions income account, it is necessary to write the complete date, 1962, Oct. 31.

Step 3.   Write *C1* in the Post. Ref. column of the commissions income account in the ledger to show that this entry was posted from page 1 of the cash journal.

Step 4.   Return to the cash journal and write the account number of the commissions income account, 41, immediately under the total of the Commissions Income Credit column. Place parentheses around the account number: (41).

The commissions income account in the ledger after posting appears as follows:

Commissions Income   ACCOUNT NO. 41

DATE	ITEMS	POST. REF.	DEBIT	DATE	ITEMS	POST. REF.	CREDIT
				1962 Oct 31		C1	2012 00

Step 2   Step 3   Step 1

A check mark is placed in the Post. Ref. column of the cash journal for each entry in the Commissions Income Credit column to show that no more posting is required for the item on this line. (See illustration on page 68.) Many experienced bookkeepers prefer to insert a check mark in the Post. Ref. column at the time each amount in the Commissions Income Credit column is recorded. Such a procedure indicates in advance of posting that each of these amounts will not be posted individually.

	CASH DEBIT	GENERAL DEBIT	DATE	NAME OF ACCOUNT	NO.	POST. REF.	GENERAL CREDIT	COMMISSIONS INCOME CREDIT	CASH CREDIT	
1	4500		1962 Oct 1 Office Furniture	R1	13	4500			1
2		10000	1 Adams Company	Ck1	21			10000	2
3	72500		3 Commissions Income	R2	✓		72500		3
4		13500	3 Rent Expense	Ck2	55			13500	4
5		3000	3 Office Furniture	Ck3	13			3000	5
6	20000		4 Commissions Income	R3	✓		20000		6
7		2300	5 Automobile Expense	Ck4	52			2300	7
8	8000		8 Commissions Income	R4	✓		8000		8
9		12500	9 Triangle Motors	Ck5	23			12500	9
10		5000	9 Advertising Expense	Ck6	51			5000	10
11	9000		11 Commissions Income	R5	✓		9000		11
12		7500	12 McIntyre Company	Ck7	22			7500	12
13		37500	15 Office Machines	Ck8	14			37500	13
14	40000		16 Commissions Income	R6	✓		40000		14
15		600	17 Entertainment Expense	Ck9	53			600	15
16	3900		17 Commissions Income	R7	✓		3900		16
17		7200	19 Advertising Expense	Ck10	51			7200	17
18	29500		22 Commissions Income	R8	✓		29500		18
19		5000	23 Adams Company	Ck11	21			5000	19
20	11300		24 Office Machines	R9	14	11300			20
21	6500		25 Commissions Income	R10	✓		6500		21
22		900	25 Miscellaneous Expense	Ck12	54			900	22
23		700	26 Entertainment Expense	Ck13	53			700	23
24		1300	30 Automobile Expense	Ck14	52			1300	24
25	11800		31 Commissions Income	R11	✓		11800		25
26		500	31 Miscellaneous Expense	Ck15	54			500	26
27	2 17000	1 07500	31 Totals			15800	201200	107500	27
28	(")	(✓)				(✓)	(41)	(")	28
29									29

Cash journal of Wood Realty Agency for October after posting

The cash journal and the ledger after posting

The cash journal of the Wood Realty Agency after posting has been completed is shown above. The Post. Ref. column of the cash journal contains an account number or a check mark on each line except the totals line. Each account number in the Post. Ref. column shows that the amount on that line was posted individually. Each check mark in the Post. Ref. column shows that the amount was not posted individually.

An account number appears below each special column total. This shows that the total of each of these special columns was posted. A check mark below the General Debit and the General Credit totals shows that the totals of these columns were not posted.

The ledger of the Wood Realty Agency after all posting of this cash journal has been completed is shown on pages 69 and 70.

Cash ACCOUNT NO. 11

DATE	ITEMS	POST. REF.	DEBIT	DATE	ITEMS	POST. REF.	CREDIT
1962 Oct 1	Balance	J1	491 00	1962 Oct 31		C1	1075 00
31		C1	2170 00				

Automobile ACCOUNT NO. 12

DATE	ITEMS	POST. REF.	DEBIT	DATE	ITEMS	POST. REF.	CREDIT
1962 Oct 1	Balance	J1	2180 00				

Office Furniture ACCOUNT NO. 13

DATE	ITEMS	POST. REF.	DEBIT	DATE	ITEMS	POST. REF.	CREDIT
1962 Oct 1	Balance	J1	745 00	1962 Oct 1		C1	45 00
3		C1	30 00				

Office Machines ACCOUNT NO. 14

DATE	ITEMS	POST. REF.	DEBIT	DATE	ITEMS	POST. REF.	CREDIT
1962 Oct 1	Balance	J1	236 00	1962 Oct 24		C1	113 00
15		C1	375 00				

Adams Company ACCOUNT NO. 21

DATE	ITEMS	POST. REF.	DEBIT	DATE	ITEMS	POST. REF.	CREDIT
1962 Oct 1		C1	100 00	1962 Oct 1	Balance	J1	275 00
23		C1	50 00				

McIntyre Company ACCOUNT NO. 22

DATE	ITEMS	POST. REF.	DEBIT	DATE	ITEMS	POST. REF.	CREDIT
1962 Oct 12		C1	75 00	1962 Oct 1	Balance	J1	342 00

Triangle Motors ACCOUNT NO. 23

DATE	ITEMS	POST. REF.	DEBIT	DATE	ITEMS	POST. REF.	CREDIT
1962 Oct 9		C1	125 00	1962 Oct 1	Balance	J1	780 00

Ledger of Wood Realty Agency after posting all transactions for October

M. W. Wood, Capital ACCOUNT NO. 31

DATE	ITEMS	POST. REF.	DEBIT	DATE	ITEMS	POST. REF.	CREDIT
				1962 Oct. 1	Balance	J1	2 255 00

Commissions Income ACCOUNT NO. 41

DATE	ITEMS	POST. REF.	DEBIT	DATE	ITEMS	POST. REF.	CREDIT
				1962 Oct. 31		C1	2 012 00

Advertising Expense ACCOUNT NO. 51

DATE	ITEMS	POST. REF.	DEBIT	DATE	ITEMS	POST. REF.	CREDIT
1962 Oct. 9		C1	50 00				
19		C1	72 00				

Automobile Expense ACCOUNT NO. 52

DATE	ITEMS	POST. REF.	DEBIT	DATE	ITEMS	POST. REF.	CREDIT
1962 Oct. 5		C1	23 00				
30		C1	13 00				

Entertainment Expense ACCOUNT NO. 53

DATE	ITEMS	POST. REF.	DEBIT	DATE	ITEMS	POST. REF.	CREDIT
1962 Oct. 17		C1	6 00				
26		C1	7 00				

Miscellaneous Expense ACCOUNT NO. 54

DATE	ITEMS	POST. REF.	DEBIT	DATE	ITEMS	POST. REF.	CREDIT
1962 Oct. 25		C1	9 00				
31		C1	5 00				

Rent Expense ACCOUNT NO. 55

DATE	ITEMS	POST. REF.	DEBIT	DATE	ITEMS	POST. REF.	CREDIT
1962 Oct. 3		C.1	135 00				

Ledger of Wood Realty Agency after posting all transactions for October (concluded)

Recording increases in account balances

Assets are placed on the left-hand side of the balance sheet; therefore, when an asset is increased, the entry is made in a *debit* column of the journal and is posted to the *debit* side of the asset account.

Any Asset Account	
Debit side Balance side Increase side	

Liabilities are placed on the right-hand side of the balance sheet; therefore, when a liability is increased, the entry is made in a *credit* column of the journal and is posted to the *credit* side of the liability account.

Any Liability Account	
	Credit side Balance side Increase side

Proprietorship is placed on the right-hand side of the balance sheet; therefore, when proprietorship is increased by an additional investment, the entry is made in a *credit* column of the journal and is posted to the *credit* side of a proprietorship account.

Any Proprietorship Account	
	Credit side Balance side Increase side

Incomes increase proprietorship and are always recorded in the journal in a *credit* column. Income amounts are always posted to the *credit* side of an income account in the ledger.

Any Income Account	
	Credit side Balance side Increase side

Expenses decrease proprietorship and are always recorded in the journal in a *debit* column. Expense amounts are always debits and are posted to the *debit* side of an expense account in the ledger.

Any Expense Account	
Debit side Balance side Increase side	

Note that the balance of each asset account and each expense account always appears on the *debit* side of the account. Note also that the balance of each liability account, each proprietorship account, and each income account always appears on the *credit* side of the accounts.

Since the balance side of any account is always its increase side, note that the *debit* side of any asset account and of any expense account is its increase side. The *credit* side of any liability account, of any proprietorship account, and of any income account is its increase side.

71

Recording decreases in account balances

In bookkeeping, the amount to be *subtracted* in an account is always placed on the side of the account that is *opposite* the balance side. For example, if an amount is to be subtracted from an asset account balance, the amount to be subtracted is placed on the *credit* side of the asset account.

If an amount is to be subtracted from a liability account balance, the amount to be subtracted is placed on the *debit* side of the liability account. If an amount is to be subtracted from a proprietorship account balance, the amount to be subtracted is placed on the *debit* side of the proprietorship account.

The balance of an asset account is always a *debit*. Therefore the amount of a decrease in an asset is always placed in a *credit* column in the journal and is posted to the *credit* side of an asset account in the ledger.

The balance of a liability account is always a *credit*. Therefore the amount of a decrease in a liability is always placed in a *debit* column in the journal and is posted to the *debit* side of a liability account in the ledger.

The balance of a proprietor's capital account is always a *credit*. Therefore the amount of a decrease in proprietorship is always placed in a *debit* column in the journal and is posted to the *debit* side of a proprietorship account in the ledger.

Any Account That Has a Debit Balance	
Balance side	Subtraction side

Any Account That Has a Credit Balance	
Subtraction side	Balance side

Any Asset Account	
Debit side Balance side	Credit side Decrease side

Any Liability Account	
Debit side Decrease side	Credit side Balance side

Any Proprietorship Account	
Debit side Decrease side	Credit side Balance side

72

Chapter questions

1. What are the five divisions of the chart of accounts of the Wood Realty Agency?
2. What is shown by the number 53 that is assigned to the entertainment expense account in the chart of accounts on page 62?
3. Why is the amount in the Cash Debit column on Line 1 of the cash journal not posted as a separate amount to the cash account?
4. Why is the amount in the General Credit column on Line 1 of the cash journal posted separately to the office furniture account?
5. What are the four steps used in posting the first amount in the General Debit column of the cash journal on page 64?
6. How can you tell if the posting of a specific line in the cash journal has been completed?
7. What are the four steps used in posting the first amount in the General Credit column of the cash journal on page 62?
8. How do you show in the cash journal that the total of each of the two General columns does not need to be posted?
9. What are the four steps used in posting the total of the Cash Debit column of the cash journal?
10. What are the four steps used in posting the total of the Cash Credit column of the cash journal?
11. What are the four steps used in posting the total of the Commissions Income Credit column of the cash journal?

Cases for discussion

1. Mr. Leslie Babcock posts from both General columns of the cash journal in the order in which the transactions appear. Mr. John Devine posts all the amounts in the General Debit column first and then posts all the amounts in the General Credit column.
   (a) What are the advantages of the procedure used by Mr. Babcock?
   (b) What are the advantages of the procedure used by Mr. Devine?

2. Mr. Neels writes the account number of the ledger account to which the cash journal entry was transferred as the last step in the process of posting. Mr. Kissinger reverses this procedure and begins the posting process by writing the ledger account number in the Post. Ref. column of the cash journal as the first step in posting. What are the advantages of Mr. Neel's procedure?

3. J. R. Gammon has dozens of accounts in his ledger and numerous pages in his cash journal. While examining one of his ledger accounts, he becomes interested in getting some additional information about one of the amounts. He wants to trace this ledger entry back to the journal entry from which it was posted. How can he quickly determine the exact page of the cash journal to which to refer?

Drill 6-A. Analyzing transactions

Instructions: 1. Read Transaction No. 1 given below. Draw two T accounts and write the proper account titles for each, one for the debit part of the transaction and one for the credit part. Then indicate the amount of the debit in one T account and the amount of the credit in the other T account.

2. Record the additional transactions in T accounts. Use two T accounts for each transaction.

If these were complete accounts, they would have beginning balances; but it is not necessary to show balances in T accounts that are used merely for planning the debit and the credit for each entry.

TRANSACTIONS

1. Received cash, $20.00, from the sale of old office furniture.
2. Paid cash, $25.00, to Adams Company in part payment of the amount owed.
3. Paid cash, $37.50, for purchase of new office desk.
4. Received cash, $15.00, from sale of office machine.
5. Paid cash, $42.00, to Star Garage in part payment of the amount owed.

Drill 6-B. Analyzing transactions

Instructions: Plan the recording of the following transactions by the use of T accounts as you did in Drill 6-A.

TRANSACTIONS

1. Received cash, $600.00, as commission from sale of a house.
2. Paid cash, $76.00, for purchase of office machine.
3. Paid cash, $39.00, for purchase of office furniture.
4. Paid cash, $100.00, to Daniels Company in part payment of the amount owed.
5. Received cash, $18.00, from sale of office furniture.

Drill 6-C. Analyzing transactions

Instructions: Plan the recording of the following transactions by the use of T accounts as you did in Drill 6-A.

TRANSACTIONS

1. Received cash, $500.00, as commission from sale of a house.
2. Paid cash, $120.00, for rent for October.
3. Paid cash, $5.00, for gas and oil for automobile.
4. Received cash, $240.00, as commission from sale of a house.
5. Paid cash, $4.50, for telephone bill. (Miscellaneous Expense)
6. Paid cash, $20.00, for repairs on automobile.
7. Paid cash, $7.52, for electric bill. (Miscellaneous Expense)

Application problem

Problem 6-1. *Posting the cash journal of a certified public accountant*

The cash journal completed in Problem 5-2 of Chapter 5 is required for this problem. If Problem 5-2 has not been returned to you, complete Exercise 6-A in the Appendix.

Instructions: 1. Prepare the Riley ledger by opening the accounts listed on the chart of accounts below. Place six accounts on each page of the ledger. Use the account numbers shown in the following chart of accounts.

CHART OF ACCOUNTS			
(1) ASSETS	ACCT. NO.	(4) INCOME	ACCT. NO.
Cash	11	Fees Income	41
Automobile	12	(5) EXPENSES	
Office Furniture	13	Automobile Expense	51
Professional Library	14	Miscellaneous Expense	52
(2) LIABILITIES		Rent Expense	53
Edison Company	21		
Shaw Company	22		
(3) PROPRIETORSHIP			
Gordon Riley, Capital	31		

Instructions: 2. The asset accounts have *debit* balances as follows:

Cash	$ 213.80	Office Furniture	$560.00
Automobile	$2,750.00	Professional Library	$240.00

Copy these balances in the ledger that you have just prepared. Use the date October 1 of the current year.

Whenever a balance is copied in a ledger account, place a check mark in the posting reference column.

Instructions: 3. The liability and proprietorship accounts have *credit* balances as follows:

Edison Company	$ 31.25	Gordon Riley, Capital	$3,572.55
Shaw Company	$160.00		

Copy these balances in the ledger. Use the date October 1 of the current year.

Instructions: 4. Turn to the cash journal you completed for Problem 5-2. Post each amount recorded in the General Debit and the General Credit columns.

5. Place a check mark in the Post Ref. column for each entry crediting Fees Income. This check mark shows that this entry is not posted individually.

6. Post the totals of the three special columns of your cash journal to the proper accounts in your ledger. Place a check mark under the General Debit and General Credit columns to indicate that these totals are not posted.

Optional problems

★Supplementary Problem 6-S. Journalizing and posting the transactions of a theater

Gene Olson is the owner and operator of the Wilmot Theater. You will need to prepare his ledger before you can do the work in this problem.

Instructions: 1. Open the twelve accounts in the ledger that will be needed for this problem. Place six accounts on each page of your ledger. A chart of accounts showing the account titles with account numbers is given below.

CHART OF ACCOUNTS			
(1) ASSETS	ACCT. No.	(4) INCOME	ACCT. No.
Cash	11	Admissions Income	41
Equipment	12	(5) EXPENSES	
(2) LIABILITIES		Advertising Expense	51
Jones Optical Company	21	Film Rental Expense	52
Smith Sound Service	22	Miscellaneous Expense	53
		Rent Expense	54
(3) PROPRIETORSHIP		Salary Expense	55
Gene Olson, Capital	31	Utilities Expense	56

Instructions: 2. Copy the following balances in the proper accounts in your ledger, using July 1 of the current year as the date.

	DEBIT BALANCES	CREDIT BALANCES
Cash...	1,224.32	
Equipment.....................................	10,250.00	
Jones Optical Company....................................		345.00
Smith Sound Service.....................................		180.00
Gene Olson, Capital......................................		10,949.32

Instructions: 3. On page 7 of a cash journal similar to the model journal on page 68, journalize the transactions for July given below.

July 2. Paid cash, $150.00, for rent for July. (Check No. 183)
   3. Paid cash, $54.85, for advertising. (Check No. 184)
   5. Paid cash, $155.00, for projection equipment. (Check No. 185)
   7. Received cash, $475.00, from admissions income for the week. (Receipt No. 24)
   11. Paid cash, $165.00, to Jones Optical Company on account. (Check No. 186)
   12. Received cash, $25.00, from sale of old equipment. (Receipt No. 25)
   13. Received cash, $481.50, from admissions income for the week. (Receipt No. 26)
   14. Paid cash, $18.50, for admission tickets. This is miscellaneous expense. (Check No. 187)

July 16. Paid cash, $100.00, to Smith Sound Service on account. (Check No. 188)
   18. Paid cash, $8.75, for telephone bill. This is miscellaneous expense. (Check No. 189)
   20. Received cash, $503.20, from admissions income for the week. (Receipt No. 27)
   24. Paid cash, $47.50, for advertising. (Check No. 190)
   27. Received cash, $488.00, from admissions income for the week. (Receipt No. 28)
   30. Paid cash, $1,000.00, for film rentals. (Check No. 191)
   31. Paid cash, $522.50, for salaries. (Check No. 192)
   31. Paid cash, $101.85, for utilities expenses. (Check No. 193)
   31. Received cash, $281.50, from admissions income. (Receipt No. 29)

Instructions: 4. Post the individual amounts in the General Debit and General Credit columns to the accounts in the ledger.

5. Place a check mark in the Post. Ref. column for each entry crediting Admissions Income to show that this entry is not posted individually.

6. Foot each amount column with small pencil figures.

7. Prove cash. The cash on hand is $1,154.57.

8. Prove the equality of debits and credits in your cash journal.

9. Total and rule the cash journal.

10. Post the totals of the three special columns. Place a check mark under the General Debit and General Credit columns to indicate that these totals are not posted.

★ *Bonus Problem 6-B. Journalizing and posting the transactions of a lawyer*

You will need to prepare the ledger of James N. Henderson, a lawyer, before you can do the work in this problem.

Instructions: 1. Open the twelve accounts in the ledger that will be needed for this problem. Place six accounts on each page of your ledger. A chart of accounts showing the account titles with account numbers is given below.

CHART OF ACCOUNTS			
	ACCT. NO.		ACCT. NO.
(1) ASSETS		(4) INCOME	
Cash	11	Fees Income	41
Automobile	12		
Office Furniture	13	(5) EXPENSES	
Professional Library	14	Automobile Expense	51
		Miscellaneous Expense	52
(2) LIABILITIES		Rent Expense	53
Cummings Garage	21	Stationery Expense	54
Hoffman Company	22		
(3) PROPRIETORSHIP			
James M. Henderson, Capital	31		

Instructions: 2. Copy the following balances in the proper accounts in your ledger, using October 1 of the current year as the date.

	DEBIT BALANCES	CREDIT BALANCES
Cash...	1,313.00	
Automobile...	2,800.00	
Office Furniture....................................	450.00	
Professional Library................................	645.00	
Cummings Garage...................................		1,139.00
Hoffman Company..................................		184.50
James N. Henderson, Capital.........................		3,884.50

Instructions: 3. On page 10 of a cash journal like the one illustrated in Bonus Problem 5-B on page 60, journalize the transactions for October given below. The income column should be headed "Fees Income Credit."

Oct. 1. Paid cash, $125.00, for rent for October. (Check No. 116)
2. Received cash, $50.00, for legal services. (Receipt No. 81)
3. Paid cash, $45.00, for office furniture. (Check No. 117)
4. Paid cash, $14.88, for stationery. (Check No. 118)
9. Received cash, $32.50, for legal services. (Receipt No. 82)
10. Paid cash, $184.50, to Hoffman Company on account. (Check No. 119)
11. Received cash, $94.00, from sale of old office furniture. (Receipt No. 83)
15. Paid cash, $5.00, for automobile expense. (Check No. 120)
17. Paid cash, $7.50, for taking a client to dinner. This is miscellaneous expense. (Check No. 121)
18. Paid cash, $21.50, for repairs to automobile. (Check No. 122)
22. Paid cash, $4.50, for stationery. (Check No. 123)
24. Received cash, $244.00, for legal services. (Receipt No. 84)
25. Paid cash, $250.00, to Cummings Garage on account. (Check No. 124)
26. Received cash, $125.00, for legal services. (Receipt No. 85)
29. Received cash, $80.00, for legal services. (Receipt No. 86)
30. Paid cash, $14.00, for telephone bill. (Check No. 125)
31. Paid cash, $24.60, for utilities expense. (Check No. 126)

Instructions: 4. Post the individual amounts in the General Debit and General Credit columns to the accounts in the ledger.

5. Place a check mark in the Post. Ref. column for each entry crediting Fees Income to show that this entry is not posted individually.

6. Foot each amount column with small pencil figures.

7. Prove cash. The cash on hand is $1,242.02.

8. Prove the equality of debits and credits in your cash journal.

9. Total and rule the cash journal.

10. Post the totals of the three special columns. Place a check mark under the General Debit and General Credit columns to indicate that these totals are not posted.

Chapter 7

Proving the accuracy of posting

Need for accuracy in bookkeeping

Bookkeeping records are valuable only to the extent that they are completely accurate. The bookkeeper should use methods of proving accuracy that will help him to detect every error promptly. He should be careful to avoid errors and he should correct errors immediately when they are detected.

Two methods of checking the accuracy of bookkeeping records will be presented in this chapter:

1. Proving the accuracy of the cash account in the ledger by comparing its balance with the amount of cash on hand.
2. Taking a trial balance to test whether the debits in the ledger equal the credits in the ledger.

Finding the balance of the cash account

The cash account of the Wood Realty Agency after the balance has been found and recorded appears as follows:

				Cash				ACCOUNT NO. *11*	
DATE	ITEMS	POST. REF.	DEBIT		DATE	ITEMS	POST. REF.	CREDIT	
1962 *Oct. 1*	*Balance*	*J1*	*491*	*00*	*1962* *Oct. 31*		*C1*	*1075*	*00*
31		*C1* *1586.00*	*2170*	*00*					
			2661	*00*					

The steps used in finding the balance of the cash account are as follows:

Step 1. Add the amounts in the Debit column; write the total in small figures immediately under the last amount in that column. Use a sharp, firm pencil. This footing is written very small so that the next line can be used for another entry.

If there were several entries in the Credit column, you should add them and record the footing the same as you did in the Debit column. Since there is only one entry on the credit side of the cash account, it is not necessary to make a pencil footing on the credit side of this account.

Step 2. Subtract the total of the credit side from the total of the debit side as follows:

Total of debit side of cash account.........	$2,661.00
Total of credit side of cash account........	1,075.00
Difference between two sides of account....	$1,586.00

The difference between the two sides of an account is known as the *account balance*. Therefore the balance of the cash account is $1,586.00.

Step 3. Write the amount of the balance, $1,586.00, in the Items column in small pencil figures on the debit side of the cash account. Write this amount in line with the small pencil footing of the debit column.

The pencil balance of any account is written very small in the Items column of the account on the side with the larger total.

Proving the accuracy of the cash account

On October 31, the last check stub of the Wood Realty Agency shows a balance of $1,586.00. Since all cash receipts have been deposited, the balance shown on the check stub is the actual amount of cash on hand. The balance of the cash account in the ledger is also $1,586.00. When the cash on hand is found to agree with the balance of the cash account, the cash account is said to be proved.

A disagreement between the cash account and the amount of cash on hand may indicate that one or more errors have been made either in posting to the cash account or in calculating its balance.

The trial balance

The sum of the debits in the cash journal in Chapter 5 was found to be equal to the sum of the credits. It follows then that if no errors are made in posting, the total of the debit amounts in the ledger should equal the total of the credit amounts in the ledger. Therefore, a method of testing the accuracy of posting is to prove the equality of the debits and the credits in the ledger.

The proof of the equality of the debits and the credits in the ledger is called a *trial balance*. It consists of a list of account titles with the balances arranged in a debit amount column and a credit amount column and each amount column totaled. (See the illustration of a trial balance on page 84.)

Footing the accounts

Since account balances are recorded on the trial balance, the accounts should be footed before the preparation of the trial balance is started. The cash account was footed in connection with the proving of cash.

When an account has only one entry, it is not necessary to write a footing or a balance. The one amount in the account serves as the footing and the balance. Such an account is Account No. 12, Automobile, illustrated in the ledger below.

When an account has several entries on each side, both the Debit column and the Credit column are footed. The footing of the smaller side is subtracted from that of the larger side. The difference between the two footings is written in the Items column on the side of the account that has the larger total. This amount is the balance of the account. Account No. 13, Office Furniture, in the ledger below shows this method of footing.

When an account has only one debit entry and one credit entry, footings are not needed in the Debit and the Credit columns. The balance is written in the Items column on the side that has the larger amount. Account No. 22, McIntyre Company, illustrates this method.

When an account has two or more entries on one side only, that side is footed, but the balance is not written in the Items column because the footing is the balance. Account No. 51, Advertising Expense, illustrates this method of footing.

A complete ledger containing the necessary footings for all accounts is illustrated below and on pages 82 and 83.

A ledger with the accounts footed

Office Furniture — ACCOUNT NO. 13

DATE	ITEMS	POST. REF.	DEBIT	DATE	ITEMS	POST. REF.	CREDIT
1962 Oct 1	Balance	J1	745 00	1962 Oct 1		C1	45 00
3		C1	30 00				
	730.00		775 00				

Office Machines — ACCOUNT NO. 14

DATE	ITEMS	POST. REF.	DEBIT	DATE	ITEMS	POST. REF.	CREDIT
1962 Oct 1	Balance	J1	236 00	1962 Oct 24		C1	113 00
15		C1	375 00				
	498.00		611 00				

Adams Company — ACCOUNT NO. 21

DATE	ITEMS	POST. REF.	DEBIT	DATE	ITEMS	POST. REF.	CREDIT
1962 Oct 1		C1	100 00	1962 Oct 1	Balance	J1	275 00
23		C1	50 00		125.00		
			150 00				

McIntyre Company — ACCOUNT NO. 22

DATE	ITEMS	POST. REF.	DEBIT	DATE	ITEMS	POST. REF.	CREDIT
1962 Oct 12		C1	75 00	1962 Oct 1	Balance	J1	342 00
					267.00		

Triangle Motors — ACCOUNT NO. 23

DATE	ITEMS	POST. REF.	DEBIT	DATE	ITEMS	POST. REF.	CREDIT
1962 Oct 9		C1	125 00	1962 Oct 1	Balance	J1	780 00
					655.00		

M. W. Wood, Capital — ACCOUNT NO. 31

DATE	ITEMS	POST. REF.	DEBIT	DATE	ITEMS	POST. REF.	CREDIT
				1962 Oct 1	Balance	J1	2255 00

A ledger with the accounts footed (continued)

Commissions Income   ACCOUNT NO. 41

DATE	ITEMS	POST. REF.	DEBIT	DATE	ITEMS	POST. REF.	CREDIT
				1962 Oct. 31		C1	2012 00

Advertising Expense   ACCOUNT NO. 51

DATE	ITEMS	POST. REF.	DEBIT	DATE	ITEMS	POST. REF.	CREDIT
1962 Oct. 9		C1	50 00				
19		C1	72 00				
			1 2 2 0 0				

Automobile Expense   ACCOUNT NO. 52

DATE	ITEMS	POST. REF.	DEBIT	DATE	ITEMS	POST. REF.	CREDIT
1962 Oct. 5		C1	23 00				
30		C1	13 00				
			3 6 0 0				

Entertainment Expense   ACCOUNT NO. 53

DATE	ITEMS	POST. REF.	DEBIT	DATE	ITEMS	POST. REF.	CREDIT
1962 Oct. 17		C1	6 00				
26		C1	7 00				
			1 3 0 0				

Miscellaneous Expense   ACCOUNT NO. 54

DATE	ITEMS	POST. REF.	DEBIT	DATE	ITEMS	POST. REF.	CREDIT
1962 Oct. 25		C1	9 00				
31		C1	5 00				
			1 4 0 0				

Rent Expense   ACCOUNT NO. 55

DATE	ITEMS	POST. REF.	DEBIT	DATE	ITEMS	POST. REF.	CREDIT
1962 Oct. 3		C1	135 00				

A ledger with the accounts footed (concluded)

83

Wood Realty Agency
Trial Balance
October 31, 1962

Account	No.	Debit	Credit
Cash	11	1 5 8 6 00	
Automobile	12	2 1 8 0 00	
Office Furniture	13	7 3 0 00	
Office Machines	14	4 9 8 00	
Adams Company	21		1 2 5 00
McIntyre Company	22		2 6 7 00
Triangle Motors	23		6 5 5 00
M. W. Wood, Capital	31		2 2 5 5 00
Commissions Income	41		2 0 1 2 00
Advertising Expense	51	1 2 2 00	
Automobile Expense	52	3 6 00	
Entertainment Expense	53	1 3 00	
Miscellaneous Expense	54	1 4 00	
Rent Expense	55	1 3 5 00	
		5 3 1 4 00	5 3 1 4 00

Step 5

Trial balance

How to prepare a trial balance

Step 1.   Write the trial balance heading at the top of a sheet of paper that has two amount columns.

The heading consists of three lines: (1) the name of the business, (2) the words "Trial Balance," and (3) the date. The date is the month, the day, and the year for which the trial balance is prepared.

Step 2.   Enter on the trial balance each account in the ledger that has a balance. In each case record the account title, the account number, and the balance. If the balance is a debit, enter it in the left-hand or debit amount column; if the balance is a credit, enter it in the right-hand or credit amount column.

Step 3.   Rule a single line across both amount columns under the last amount listed to show that each amount column is to be added.

Step 4.   Add each amount column. Write the totals on the first line below the single ruling.

Step 5.   Rule a double line under the totals across the amount columns· Note how the totals have been entered and the trial balance has been ruled in the illustration.

84

In bookkeeping a double ruling indicates that the work has been completed. The double line should not be drawn until the trial balance is in balance. All lines should be drawn with the aid of a ruler.

Proof provided by the trial balance

If the two totals of the trial balance are equal, the trial balance is said to be in balance. When the trial balance is in balance, the bookkeeper can assume that there is equality of debits and credits in the ledger.

Errors not detected by a trial balance

A trial balance that is in balance does not always prove the complete accuracy of the bookkeeping records. The following kinds of errors in journalizing and posting are not detected by a trial balance:

(1) If an amount is posted to the correct side, but to the wrong account, the trial balance will still be in balance. For example, if the $100.00 debited to the Adams Company account on October 1 had been posted by mistake to the debit side of the Triangle Motors account, the trial balance would still be in balance. An error of this kind should be discovered when monthly statements of account are received from these two creditors and are compared with their accounts.

(2) If the recording of a transaction is omitted entirely, the ledger will still be in balance and the error will not be indicated by the trial balance.

If, however, the omitted transaction affects cash, the error will be shown when the cash balance is proved. The balance of the cash account will not agree with the cash actually on hand.

Finding errors when a trial balance does not balance

In checking a trial balance that does not balance, proceed as follows:

Step 1. Add again each column of the trial balance. (One or both of the columns may have been added incorrectly.)

Step 2. Find the amount of the difference between the debit total and the credit total of the trial balance. Look in the ledger for this amount. The amount of the difference may be the balance of an account that has been omitted from the trial balance. Also look in the journal for this amount. Perhaps this amount was not posted when it should have been.

Step 3. Divide the amount of the difference between the two totals of the trial balance by 2. Look through the accounts to see if this amount has been recorded on the wrong side of an account. Also check to see if this amount has been written as a balance in the wrong column of the trial balance. For example, if the difference between the two columns of the trial balance is $80.00, look for $40.00 on the wrong side of an account or in the wrong column of the trial balance.

85

Step 4. Divide the amount of the difference between the two totals of the trial balance by 9. If this difference is evenly divisible by 9, look through the accounts for an amount that has been transposed. Also look for an amount in the trial balance that has been transposed in copying the balance from the ledger. For example, if the trial balance is out of balance $27.00, this amount is divisible by 9 with a quotient of 3. Look for amounts that have a spread of three, such as $14.00 written as $41.00, or $25.00 written as $52.00, or $36.00 written as $63.00.

Step 5. Compare the balances on the trial balance with the balances in the ledger accounts. An error may have been made in copying the account balance on the trial balance.

Step 6. Verify the pencil footings and the account balances in the ledger. An error may have been made in footing an account or in determining the balance.

Step 7. Verify the posting of each item in the journal. As each posting is verified, place a small check mark ($\sqrt{}$) on the double vertical line at the left of the corresponding amount in both the journal and the ledger. An item may have been (a) posted twice, (b) not posted at all, (c) entered on the wrong side of an account, or (d) copied incorrectly.

Step 8. Examine first the journal and then the ledger to find items not checked or items that have been checked twice.

The error or errors should now be found because all of the work has been retraced.

Correcting errors in the ledger

If an item has been posted to the wrong side of an account, a line should be drawn through the incorrect posting and the item should then be posted correctly, as follows:

Correction of the posting to the wrong side of an account

If an incorrect amount has been posted to the right account, a line should be drawn through the incorrect amount and the correct amount should then be written above it, as follows:

Correction of the posting of an incorrect amount

If an item has been posted to the wrong account, a line should be drawn through the incorrect posting and the item should be posted correctly. If the posting of an item has been omitted, the amount should be posted at once. If an item has been posted twice, a line should be drawn through the second posting in the account.

An error in a pencil footing in the ledger should be erased and the correct pencil footing should be substituted for it.

Correcting errors in the trial balance

If an account balance has been omitted from the trial balance, it should be inserted in its proper position. If an account balance has been placed in the wrong column of the trial balance, the amount should be erased or canceled with a line and the same amount should be written in the correct column. A similar correction should be made for a balance copied incorrectly. The trial balance totals should also be corrected.

Increasing your business vocabulary

What is the meaning of each of the following:

(a) account balance   (b) trial balance

Chapter questions

1. What steps are used in finding the balance of the cash account?
2. Where is the pencil footing of each side of an account written?
3. Why should the pencil footings of an account be written very small?
4. Where is the amount of the pencil balance of any account written?
5. What is the purpose of the trial balance?
6. What are the three parts of the heading of a trial balance?
7. What are the steps used in preparing a trial balance?
8. What kinds of errors in journalizing and posting are not detected by a trial balance even though it is in balance?
9. How is the posting of an amount to the wrong side of an account corrected?
10. How is the posting of an incorrect amount to the right account corrected?

Cases for discussion

1. The balance of R. J. Lane's cash account does not agree with the amount of cash on hand. What steps should he take to find the error?

2. Which of the following errors would not be indicated by the trial balance:
   (a) In posting, a debit of $42.00 was posted to the debit side of the wrong account.
   (b) On October 16 a debit of $4.50 to the miscellaneous expense account was posted to the credit side of that account.
   (c) The automobile account balance was not listed on the trial balance.
   (d) The debit balance of $17.41 in the advertising expense account was written in the credit column of the trial balance.

Drill for understanding

Drill 7-A. Analyzing accounts

Instructions: 1. On a sheet of paper, copy in one column the ledger account titles that are given below.

1. Advertising Expense
2. Atlas Company (creditor)
3. Automobile
4. Automobile Expense
5. Cash
6. Commissions Income
7. Drake Company (creditor)
8. Electricity Expense
9. Kenneth Hackett, Capital
10. Office Furniture
11. Office Machines
12. Rent Expense
13. Rolfe Garage (creditor)
14. Stationery Expense

Instructions: 2. Rule three columns at the right of your list of accounts and write in the headings shown in the form below.

ACCOUNT TITLES	CLASSIFI-CATION	TRIAL BALANCE DEBIT	CREDIT
1. Advertising Expense	E	√	

Instructions: 3. Classify each item on your list as an asset, a liability, proprietorship, an income, or an expense by writing in the Classification column a capital: A for Asset   L for Liability   I for Income   P for Proprietorship   E for Expense

Instructions: 4. Indicate whether the balance of each account will appear in the Debit column or the Credit column of the trial balance by making a check mark in the appropriate column.

The first item, Advertising Expense, is given as an example.

5. Now cover your answers and see how rapidly you can classify these accounts mentally without looking at your answers. Repeat this mental drill several times for increased speed and accuracy.

Application problems

Problem 7-1. Taking a trial balance

If you are not using the workbook correlating with this textbook, complete Exercise 7-A in the Appendix instead of this problem.

The ledger accounts of the Grant Realty Agency are in your workbook.

Instructions: 1. Foot the ledger accounts. Write the footings in very small figures with a sharp pencil and place each footing close to the last item. If an account has entries on both sides, write the balance in small pencil figures in the Items column of the larger side.

2. Prove the cash account. The cash on hand on October 31 of the current year, by actual count, is $740.32. This amount should agree with the balance of the cash account in the ledger.

3. Prepare a trial balance dated October 31 of the current year. If the two totals of the trial balance are equal, rule single and double lines as shown on the model trial balance on page 84.

Self-checking: Compare your ledger with the illustrations on pages 81 to 83 and ask yourself the following questions:

(a) Were the pencil footings written in the ledger in small figures with a sharp, firm pencil?

(b) Was each amount column of an account footed when, and only when, it contained two or more entries?

(c) For each account having one or more entries on both the debit and the credit sides, was the balance of the account written in small pencil figures in the Items column of the larger side?

Problem 7-2. Finding and correcting errors indicated by a trial balance

If you are not using the workbook correlating with this textbook, complete Exercise 7-B in the Appendix instead of this problem.

The journal and the ledger accounts of William Johnson after the posting of the entries for November of the current year are given in the workbook.

Instructions: 1. Foot the ledger accounts. Write the footings in very small figures with a sharp pencil and place each footing close to the last item. If an account has entries on both sides, write the balance in small pencil figures in the Items column of the larger side.

2. Prove the cash account. The cash on hand on November 30 of the current year, by actual count, is $2,002.96.

3. Prepare a trial balance dated November 30 of the current year. Use as a heading the name of the proprietor. If the two totals of the trial balance are not equal, proceed as you were directed in Steps 1-8, pages 85 and 86, to find the error or errors. Correct any errors in the journal or the ledger, using the methods explained and illustrated on pages 53, 86, and 87. Then complete the trial balance.

Project 1

Journal, ledger, and trial balance

Work required in Project 1

This project makes use of all the steps in the bookkeeping process that have been developed in the preceding seven chapters. It requires:

(a) Opening all of the accounts in the ledger that are needed in this project.
(b) Recording the balances in all accounts that have a beginning balance.
(c) Journalizing a series of selected transactions in a columnar cash journal.
(d) Posting from the cash journal to the ledger.
(e) Footing, proving, totaling, and ruling the cash journal.
(f) Footing the accounts in the ledger and preparing a trial balance.

Taylor Realty Agency

Michael Taylor is the owner of the Taylor Realty Agency. In the operation of his bookkeeping system he uses the following chart of accounts:

Taylor Realty Agency Chart of Accounts			
(1) ASSETS	ACCT. No.	(4) INCOME	ACCT. No.
Cash.....................	11	Commissions Income........	41
Automobile...............	12	(5) EXPENSES	
Office Furniture............	13		
Office Machines............	14	Advertising Expense.........	51
		Automobile Expense.........	52
(2) LIABILITIES		Entertainment Expense......	53
Cummings Garage..........	21	Miscellaneous Expense.......	54
Hale Brothers..............	22	Rent Expense..............	55
(3) PROPRIETORSHIP			
Michael Taylor, Capital......	31		

Analysis of expense accounts

Expense transactions are to be charged to the expense accounts as follows:

Advertising Expense is debited for all advertising for the business.

Automobile Expense is debited for the cost of operating the automobile for business purposes.

Entertainment Expense is debited for the cost of entertaining prospective customers.

Miscellaneous Expense is debited for expenses such as postage, stationery, electricity, telephone service, and any expense item not covered by other expense accounts.

Rent Expense is debited for rent.

Opening accounts in the ledger

Instructions: 1. Open accounts in the ledger in the order in which they are listed in the chart of accounts on the preceding page. Allow five lines for each account. Number the accounts with the account numbers given in the chart of accounts.

2. Copy the following balances in your ledger, using as the date November 1 of the current year. As you copy these balances, write the word "Balance" in the Items column of each account.

	DEBIT BALANCE	CREDIT BALANCE
Cash....................................	1,375.00	
Automobile.............................	4,600.00	
Office Furniture.........................	875.00	
Office Machines.........................	600.00	
Cummings Garage.......................		1,700.00
Hale Brothers..........................		750.00
Michael Taylor, Capital.................		5,000.00

Recording transactions in the journal

Instructions: 3. Record the following transactions on page 11 of a cash journal similar to the one illustrated on page 68.

Nov. 1. Received $800.00 as commission on the sale of a house. (Receipt No. 101)
1. Paid $150.00 for rent for November. (Check No. 171)
2. Paid $10.00 for postage stamps. (Check No. 172)
4. Paid $10.00 for dinner for prospective customers. (Check No. 173)
5. Paid $30.00 for additional office furniture. (Check No. 174)
5. Received $120.00 as commission for the rental of a house. (Receipt No. 102)
6. Paid $250.00 for a new typewriter. (Check No. 175)
6. Paid $34.00 for advertising handbills. (Check No. 176)
9. Received $22.00 as commission for renting a garage. (Receipt No. 103)
11. Paid $10.80 for gas and oil for the automobile. (Check No. 177)
11. Received $200.00 as commission on the sale of a house. (Receipt No. 104)
12. Paid $69.18 for advertisements in last week's paper. (Check No. 178)
15. Received $800.00 as commission on the sale of a house. (Receipt No. 105)
20. Received $60.00 as commission on the rental of an apartment. (Receipt No. 106)
20. Paid $45.00 for a new chair for the office. (Check No. 179)
22. Paid $26.50 for advertisements. (Check No. 180)

Nov. 22. Paid $13.00 for dinner for prospective customers. (Check No. 181)
22. Paid $9.60 for gas and oil for the automobile. (Check No. 182)
23. Received $22.00 from sale of old office furniture. (Receipt No. 107)
23. Received $74.00 as commission for rental of a house. (Receipt No. 108)
25. Paid $60.00 to Hale Brothers on account. (Check No. 183)
26. Received $70.00 as commission for rental of a house. (Receipt No. 109)
29. Paid $10.00 for gas and oil for the automobile. (Check No. 184)
30. Received $160.00 as commission for the rental of a store building. (Receipt No. 110)
30. Paid $24.60 for the electric light bill for the month of November. (Check No. 185)
30. Paid $14.00 for telephone service for the month. (Check No. 186)
30. Paid $500.00 to Cummings Garage on account. (Check No. 187)

Footing, proving, totaling, and ruling the cash journal

Instructions: 4. Foot all columns of the cash journal.

5. Prove cash. The cash on hand is $2,436.32.

6. Prove the equality of debits and credits in the cash journal. The sum of the totals of the two debit columns should equal the sum of the totals of the three credit columns.

7. Total and rule the cash journal. (See model on page 68.)

Posting the cash journal entries and totals to the ledger accounts

Instructions: 8. Post each amount in the General Debit column and in the General Credit column. Make a check mark under the totals of the General Debit column and the General Credit column to show that these totals are not to be posted. (See model on page 68.)

9. Post the total of each of the three special columns of the cash journal: Cash Debit, Cash Credit, and Commissions Income Credit. Write the proper account number under each total after the posting is completed. (See model on page 68.)

Footing the accounts in the ledger

Instructions: 10. Foot the accounts in the ledger that have more than one entry on either side of the account. If an account has entries on both sides of the account, write the balance in small pencil figures in the Items column. (Use as your guide the models on pages 81 to 83.)

Preparing a trial balance

Instructions: 11. Prepare a trial balance. (See model on page 84.)

Chapter 8

The six-column work sheet

Need for interpreting the trial balance

At regular intervals, the owner of any business should calculate whether his transactions have resulted in a profit or a loss. All of the information needed to find the profit or the loss of the Wood Realty Agency is in the ledger. Since the ledger is summarized in the trial balance, it is possible to calculate the amount of the profit or the amount of the loss directly from the trial balance.

Analyzing the trial balance

The trial balance lists accounts in the order in which they appear in the ledger. The accounts in the trial balance of the Wood Realty Agency are arranged as follows:

Wood Realty Agency
Trial Balance
October 31, 1962

Balance Sheet Items					
(1) Assets........	Cash.................	11	1,586 00		
	Automobile...........	12	2,180 00		
	Office Furniture.....	13	730 00		
	Office Machines......	14	498 00		
(2) Liabilities.....	Adams Company........	21	....	125 00	
	McIntyre Company.....	22	....	267 00	
	Triangle Motors......	23	....	655 00	
(3) Proprietorship.	M. W. Wood, Capital..	31	....	2,255 00	
Income and Expense Items					
(4) Income.......	Commissions Income...	41	....	2,012 00	
(5) Expenses......	Advertising Expense..	51	122 00		
	Automobile Expense...	52	36 00		
	Entertainment Expense	53	13 00		
	Miscellaneous Expense	54	14 00		
	Rent Expense........	55	135 00		
			5,314 00	5,314 00	

Analysis paper

The modern method of analyzing the trial balance is to use a single sheet of paper with six or more amount columns and to distribute the balances among these amount columns. The number of columns used depends on the kind and the size of the enterprise. Accounting paper with a number of amount columns that are used for analysis purposes is known as *analysis paper*.

The work sheet

Analysis paper that provides for the sorting and the interpreting of the trial balance on a single sheet of paper is called a *work sheet*. The work sheet of the Wood Realty Agency for the month ended October 31, 1962, is shown on the next page.

Analyzing the work sheet

The work sheet is a bookkeeper's working paper and is not a part of the permanent bookkeeping records. It may therefore be prepared with a pencil. The chief purpose of the work sheet is to provide a sorting process that makes it possible to calculate the net income (or the net loss) with the minimum amount of work. The work sheet also provides a convenient method of summarizing the bookkeeping records and proving the accuracy of all calculations.

Step 1. *Write the heading.* Use three lines for the heading. The first line is the name of the business, "Wood Realty Agency"; the second line is the name of the form, "Work Sheet"; and the third line shows the length and the date of the period for which the analysis is made, "For Month Ended October 31, 1962." The period for which an analysis of the operations of the business is made is called a *fiscal period.* It may be any length of time desired, such as four weeks, one month, three months, six months, or one year.

Step 2. *Write the column headings if they are not printed on the work sheet.* The column headings shown on the work sheet on page 95 are Account Titles, Account Number, Trial Balance Debit and Credit, Income Statement Debit and Credit, Balance Sheet Debit and Credit.

> The modern trend in business is to use the term *income statement* in preference to the older term *profit and loss statement.* Therefore, this textbook uses the term *income statement.*

Step 3. *Record the trial balance.* When a work sheet is prepared at the same time that a trial balance is taken, the trial balance is recorded directly on the work sheet. The steps used in writing the trial balance on the work sheet are the same as Steps 2 to 5 on page 84.

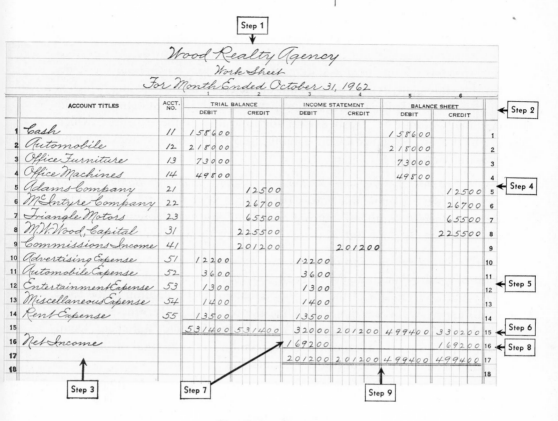

Six column work sheet

Step 4. *Extend the balance sheet items to the Balance Sheet columns.* At the end of each fiscal period a report is prepared to show the assets (what is owned), the liabilities (what is owed), and the proprietorship (what the business is worth). The report showing the assets, the liabilities, and the proprietorship on a specified date is known as the *balance sheet*.

To sort out the items for the balance sheet, extend the amount of each asset from the Trial Balance Debit column to the Balance Sheet Debit column (Column 5). Then extend the amount of each liability and the amount of the proprietorship from the Trial Balance Credit column to the Balance Sheet Credit column (Column 6).

Step 5. *Extend the income and expense items to the Income Statement columns.* At the end of each fiscal period a report is also prepared to show the income earned during the period, the expenses incurred during the period, and the amount of the net income or the net loss. If the income is larger than the expenses, the amount of the difference is called *net income*. If the expenses are larger than the income, the amount of the

95

difference is called *net loss*. The report showing the income, the expenses, and the net income or the net loss is known as the *income statement*.

The Income Statement columns of the work sheet provide the information from which the income statement is prepared. To sort out the items for this statement, extend the amount of the commissions income, which is in the Trial Balance Credit column, into the Income Statement Credit column (Column 4). Also extend the amounts of the expenses, which are in the Trial Balance Debit column, into the Income Statement Debit column (Column 3).

Step 6. *Total the Income Statement columns and the Balance Sheet columns.* Rule a single line across the Income Statement columns and the Balance Sheet columns to indicate addition. Add each column and write the totals on the same line as the Trial Balance totals. (See page 95.)

Step 7. *Find the net income from the Income Statement columns.* The total of the Income Statement Credit column is the total of all income for the month. The total of the Income Statement Debit column is the total of all expenses for the month. When the total of the Income Statement Credit column is larger than the total of the Income Statement Debit column, subtract the total of the debit column from the total of the credit column to find the amount of the net income.

Total of Income Statement Credit column (income). . . . $2,012.00
Total of Income Statement Debit column (expenses). . . 320.00
Net Income (income minus expenses). $1,692.00

When the total of the Income Statement Debit column is larger than the total of the Income Statement Credit column, subtract the total of the credit column from the total of the debit column to find the amount of the net loss.

Write the amount of the net income, $1,692.00, immediately below the smaller of the two totals in the Income Statement columns. Write the words *Net Income* in the Account Titles column on the same line as the amount. Rule a single line across the Income Statement columns and add these columns.

When these two proving totals of the Income Statement columns are equal, the amount of the net income (or the net loss) from these two columns is assumed to be correct.

Step 8. *Extend the net income to the Balance Sheet Credit column.* The net income for the month increases proprietorship. The balance of the proprietorship account without this increase is shown in the Balance Sheet Credit column. Therefore the increase in proprietorship from net income, $1,692.00, is extended to the Balance Sheet Credit column because that is the column in which the entire proprietorship must be shown. A single line is ruled across the Balance Sheet columns, and these columns are added. When these two proving totals are equal, the amount of the net income (or the net loss) as extended from the Income Statement columns is assumed to be correct.

If there is a net loss for the month, the proprietorship is decreased. The amount of a net loss is therefore extended to the Balance Sheet Debit column because that is the column in which deductions in proprietorship must be shown.

Step 9.   *Rule the Income Statement section and the Balance Sheet section.* Rule double lines below the final totals of these four amount columns to show that all work has been completed.

Increasing your business vocabulary

What is the meaning of each of the following:

(a) analysis paper   (d) balance sheet   (f) net loss
(b) work sheet   (e) net income   (g) income statement
(c) fiscal period

Chapter questions

1. What is the chief purpose of the work sheet?
2. What are the three parts of the heading of the work sheet?
3. What is the columnar heading of each of the six amount columns of the six-column work sheet?
4. To what two debit columns in the six-column work sheet illustrated on page 95 are the debit amounts in the trial balance extended?
5. To what two credit columns in the six-column work sheet illustrated on page 95 are the credit amounts in the trial balance extended?
6. When the total of the Income Statement Credit column is larger than the total of the Income Statement Debit column, how do you find the amount of the net income?
7. When the total of the Income Statement Debit column is larger than the total of the Income Statement Credit column, how do you find the amount of the net loss?
8. Why is the amount of the net income obtained from the Income Statement columns of the work sheet extended to the Balance Sheet Credit column?
9. Why is the amount of the net loss that is obtained from the two Income Statement columns of the work sheet extended to the Balance Sheet Debit column?

1. The accounts in the ledger of the Wood Realty Agency are arranged in the following order: (1) assets, (2) liabilities, (3) proprietorship, (4) income, (5) expenses.

   (a) What is the purpose of this arrangement?

   (b) Why would it not be desirable to arrange all accounts in the ledger in alphabetic order?

2. The balance of the automobile expense account was transferred by error to the Balance Sheet Debit column of the work sheet.

   (a) Will this error be discovered by the calculation of the net income on the work sheet?

   (b) What is the effect of this error on the net income as calculated on the work sheet?

   (c) When is an error of this type likely to be discovered?

3. The amount of the net income is placed at the bottom of the *debit* column of the Income Statement section of the work sheet. Why is this same amount placed at the bottom of the *credit* column of the Balance Sheet section of the work sheet?

Drill for understanding

Drill 8-A. Classification of accounts

Instructions: 1. On the left side of a sheet of paper write *Account Titles* and copy the ledger account titles that are given below. At the top of the right side of the paper write the heading *Classification*.

1. Adams Company	8. Louis Larsen, Capital
2. Advertising Expense	9. McIntyre Company
3. Automobile	10. Miscellaneous Expense
4. Automobile Expense	11. Office Furniture
5. Cash	12. Office Machines
6. Commissions Income	13. Rent Expense
7. Entertainment Expense	14. Triangle Motors

Instructions: 2. You are to show to which section of the work sheet the amounts in the trial balance will be extended. If the account balance is shown in the income statement section of the work sheet, write *Income Statement* after the account name. If the account balance is shown in the balance sheet section of the work sheet, write *Balance Sheet* after the account name. The first item, Adams Co., is given as an example.

ACCOUNT TITLES	CLASSIFICATION
1. Adams Co....	Balance Sheet

98

Application problem

Problem 8-1. Work sheet for an insurance agency

On October 31 of the current year, the end of a fiscal period of one month, the account balances in the ledger of the Upham Insurance Agency were:

Cash	Baxter Company	Advertising Expense
1,469.32	495.00	100.00

Automobile	Hale Company	Automobile Expense
2,500.00	798.30	75.00

Office Furniture	State Garage	Entertainment Expense
650.00	1,200.34	50.00

Office Machines	Ethel Upham, Capital	Miscellaneous Expense
595.00	2,000.00	150.32

Premiums Income	Rent Expense
1,216.00	120.00

Instructions: Prepare a six-column work sheet for the Upham Insurance Agency dated October 31 of the current year. Use the account titles and the account balances shown above. Use as your model the work sheet illustrated on page 95.

Self-checking: Compare your completed work sheet with the model work sheet on page 95 and check the accuracy of your work by asking yourself the following questions:

(a) Did you rule a single line across all six amount columns on the line immediately above the trial balance totals?

(b) Do the two totals of your trial balance agree?

(c) Did you rule a double line under both trial balance totals across two amount columns only?

(d) Did you write a total for each of the two Income Statement columns and for each of the two Balance Sheet columns? Did you place all four of these totals on the same line?

(e) Did you write the amount of the net income in the Income Statement Debit column and also in the Balance Sheet Credit column?

(f) Did you rule a single line across the last four amount columns immediately under the amount of the net income?

(g) Do the two proving totals of the Income Statement columns of your work sheet agree?

(h) Do the two proving totals of the Balance Sheet columns of your work sheet agree?

(i) Are the proving totals of the last four amount columns of your work sheet all written on the same line?

(j) Did you rule a double line across the last four amount columns immediately under the proving totals to show that all of your work sheet has been completed?

This problem will be continued in the next chapter. If it is collected by your teacher at this time, it will be returned to you before it is needed in Problem 9-1.

★Supplementary Problem 8-S. Work sheet for a theater

The account balances in the ledger of Frank Peck, proprietor of the Strand Theater, on October 31 of the current year, the end of a fiscal period of one month, were as follows:

Cash, $2,031.12

Air Conditioning Equipment, $3,750.00

Projection Equipment, $9,000.00

Sound Equipment, $542.00

Film Producers, Inc. (creditor), $62.50

International Studios (creditor), $145.00

Majestic Films (creditor), $96.00

Midwest Sound Service (creditor), $34.90

National Supply Co. (creditor), $53.72

Frank Peck, Capital, $14,290.18

Admissions Income, $1,932.75

Advertising Expense, $108.50

Electricity Expense, $57.50

Film Rental Expense, $837.00

Maintenance Expense, $35.00

Projection Expense, $26.50

Rent Expense, $200.00

Water Expense, $27.43

Instructions: Prepare a six-column work sheet for the Strand Theater, using the account balances given above.

Self-checking: Except for the omission of account numbers, is your work sheet similar in all respects to the model on page 95?

★Bonus Problem 8-B. Work sheet for a theater showing net loss

The account balances in the ledger of Frank Peck, proprietor of the Strand Theater, on November 30 of the current year, the end of a fiscal period of one month, were as follows:

Cash, $1,922.50

Air Conditioning Equipment, $3,750.00

Projection Equipment, $9,000.00

Sound Equipment, $542.00

Film Producers, Inc. (creditor), $178.00

International Studios (creditor), $121.00

Majestic Films (creditor), $137.50

Midwest Sound Service (creditor), $24.00

National Supply Company (creditor), $15.75

Frank Peck, Capital, $14,931.00

Admissions Income, $1,129.00

Advertising Expense, $195.00

Electricity Expense, $63.25

Film Rental Expense, $775.00

Maintenance Expense, $35.00

Projection Expense, $29.00

Rent Expense, $200.00

Water Expense, $24.50

Instructions: Prepare a six-column work sheet for the Strand Theater, using the account balances given above.

Self-checking: (a) Did you write the amount of the net loss in the Income Statement Credit column and in the Balance Sheet Debit column?

(b) Did you write the words *Net Loss* in the Account Titles column on the same line with the amount of the net loss?

Chapter 9

The income statement and the balance sheet

Need for financial statements

If the enterprise is small, the work sheet may be a sufficient analysis for the proprietor. There may, however, be individuals or institutions outside the business that are entitled to some of the information included in the work sheet but not to all of the information. For this reason, two financial reports are prepared from the information on the work sheet: (1) the income statement and (2) the balance sheet. The income statement shows the progress of the business for the period of time stated in the heading of the statement. The balance sheet shows the condition of the business for the day that it is prepared.

Income statement

The income statement of the Wood Realty Agency is prepared from the Income Statement columns of the work sheet. The part of the work sheet that is needed in the preparation of the income statement is shown below.

	ACCOUNT TITLES	ACCT. NO.	TRIAL BALANCE		INCOME STATEMENT	
			DEBIT	CREDIT	DEBIT	CREDIT
9	Commissions Income	41		2 0 1 2 0 0		2 0 1 2 0 0
10	Advertising Expense	51	1 2 2 0 0		1 2 2 0 0	
11	Automobile Expense	52	3 6 0 0		3 6 0 0	
12	Entertainment Expense	53	1 3 0 0		1 3 0 0	
13	Miscellaneous Expense	54	1 4 0 0		1 4 0 0	
14	Rent Expense	55	1 3 5 0 0		1 3 5 0 0	
15			5 3 1 4 0 0	5 3 1 4 0 0	3 2 0 0 0	2 0 1 2 0 0
16	Net Income				1 6 9 2 0 0	
17					2 0 1 2 0 0	2 0 1 2 0 0
18						

The income statement of the Wood Realty Agency for the month of October prepared from the Income Statement columns of the work sheet is shown on the next page.

Heading of the income statement

Each income statement covers a definite fiscal period. The fiscal period may be a month, three months, six months, or a year. It is the same as the fiscal period shown on the work sheet from which the statement is prepared. The length of the fiscal period should always be shown clearly in the heading of the income statement.

The heading of the income statement for the Wood Realty Agency includes:

Line 1 — Name of the business: *Wood Realty Agency*

Line 2 — Name of the form: *Income Statement*

Line 3 — {Length of the accounting period: *For Month*
{Date: *Ended October 31, 1962*

Wood Realty Agency				
Income Statement				
For Month Ended October 31, 1962				
Income:				
Commissions Income				2 0 1 2 00
Expenses:				
Advertising Expense		1 2 2 00		
Automobile Expense		3 6 00		
Entertainment Expense		1 3 00		
Miscellaneous Expense		1 4 00		
Rent Expense		1 3 5 00		
Total Expenses				3 2 0 00
Net Income				1 6 9 2 00

Income statement

Income section of the income statement

The information for preparing the income section of the income statement is obtained directly from the Income Statement Credit column of the work sheet (Column 4).

The heading of the income section of the income statement is the single word "Income." This heading is written on the first line, beginning at the vertical line at the left. Then the title of the income account, Commissions Income, is written on the second line, indented about one-half inch. Since the Wood Realty Agency receives income from commissions only, the amount of the commissions income is also the total income. The amount of commissions income is therefore written in the *second* amount column, which is used for totals.

Expense section of the income statement

The information for preparing the expense section of the income statement is obtained directly from the Income Statement Debit column of the work sheet (Column 3).

The heading of the second section of the income statement is "Expenses." This heading is written at the left margin. The titles of the individual expense accounts are listed in the same order in which they are given on the work sheet. Each account title is indented one-half inch from the vertical red line. The amount of each expense account is written in the first amount column of the income statement. The total of the expenses is written in the totals column, the second amount column. The total expenses, $320.00, can then be subtracted easily from the total income, $2,012.00, because both totals are in the same column.

Net income

The amount of the net income has already been calculated on the work sheet. The net income is calculated also on the income statement by subtracting the total expenses from the total income. The amount of the net income shown on the income statement should, of course, agree with the amount of the net income shown on the work sheet.

Ruling the income statement

The illustration of the income statement on page 102 shows where single lines and double lines should be ruled.

In all bookkeeping forms, a single line is ruled across an amount column to indicate either addition or subtraction. In the illustration of the income statement on page 102, a single line is ruled across the first amount column to indicate addition of all the expense amounts. A single line is ruled across the second amount column to indicate subtraction of the total expenses from the total income to find the net income.

Double lines are ruled across the amount columns of a bookkeeping form after all work has been completed.

Two forms of balance sheet

The balance sheet may be prepared in either of two forms: (1) account form or (2) report form. A balance sheet with the assets at the left and the liabilities and the proprietorship at the right is called the *account form* of balance sheet. A balance sheet with the assets, the liabilities, and the proprietorship in a vertical arrangement is called the *report form* of balance sheet. The account form of balance sheet is illustrated in Chapter 1. The report form of balance sheet is illustrated in this chapter.

Report form of balance sheet

The balance sheet of the Wood Realty Agency is prepared from the Balance Sheet columns of the work sheet. The Balance Sheet section and a part of the Trial Balance section of the work sheet are shown below.

	ACCOUNT TITLES	ACCT. NO.	TRIAL BALANCE DEBIT	TRIAL BALANCE CREDIT	BALANCE SHEET DEBIT	BALANCE SHEET CREDIT	
1	Cash	11	1586 00		1586 00		1
2	Automobile	12	2180 00		2180 00		2
3	Office Furniture	13	730 00		730 00		3
4	Office Machines	14	498 00		498 00		4
5	Adams Company	21		125 00		125 00	5
6	McIntyre Company	22		267 00		267 00	6
7	Triangle Motors	23		655 00		655 00	7
8	M. W. Wood, Capital	31		2255 00		2255 00	8
14	Rent Expense	55	135 00				14
15			5314 00	5314 00	4994 00	3302 00	15
16	Net Income					1692 00	16
17					4994 00	4994 00	17
18							18

The balance sheet of the Wood Realty Agency for the month of October prepared from the Balance Sheet columns of the work sheet is shown below.

Wood Realty Agency
Balance Sheet
October 31, 1962

Assets		
Cash	1586 00	
Automobile	2180 00	
Office Furniture	730 00	
Office Machines	498 00	
Total Assets		4994 00
Liabilities		
Adams Company	125 00	
McIntyre Company	267 00	
Triangle Motors	655 00	
Total Liabilities		1047 00
Proprietorship		
M. W. Wood, Capital		3947 00
Total Liabilities and Proprietorship		4994 00

Balance sheet in report form

104

Heading of the balance sheet

The heading of the balance sheet in report form requires three lines to show: (1) the name of the business, (2) the name of the form, and (3) the date for which the balance sheet was prepared. The heading of the balance sheet does not show the length of the fiscal period.

Assets section of the balance sheet

The information for the assets section of the balance sheet is obtained from the Balance Sheet Debit column of the work sheet (Column 5). All of the account balances of the asset accounts are written in the first amount column of the balance sheet in report form. The total of the assets is placed in the second amount column.

Liabilities section of the balance sheet

The information for the liabilities section of the balance sheet is obtained from the Balance Sheet Credit column of the work sheet (Column 6). The account balances are written in the first amount column of the balance sheet. The total of the liabilities is placed in the second amount column.

Proprietorship section of the balance sheet

The information for the proprietorship section of the balance sheet is obtained from the Balance Sheet Credit column of the work sheet (Column 6). The present capital as shown on the work sheet consists of:

(1) The balance of the proprietor's capital account......... $2,255.00
(2) The increase in proprietorship caused by the net income.. 1,692.00
Present capital to be shown on the balance sheet........ $3,947.00

The amount of the present capital is written in the second amount column of the balance sheet. The present capital is then added to the total liabilities to obtain the Total Liabilities and Proprietorship, $4,994.00.

To prove the accuracy of these calculations, the Total Liabilities and Proprietorship is compared with the Total Assets on the balance sheet. If these two amounts agree, all calculations on the balance sheet are assumed to be correct.

Ruling the balance sheet

A single line is ruled across an amount column of the balance sheet to indicate addition. Double lines are ruled to indicate that the balance sheet has been completed and found to be in balance. Double lines are ruled under each of the totals of the two main divisions of the balance sheet: (1) the assets division and (2) the liabilities and proprietorship division.

In the balance sheet of the Wood Realty Agency the two proving totals are $4,994.00. Double lines are ruled under the two proving totals across both amount columns.

What is the meaning of each of the following:

(a) account form of balance sheet
(b) report form of balance sheet

Chapter questions

1. What is the purpose of the income statement?
2. What is the purpose of the balance sheet?
3. From which columns of the work sheet is all of the information for construction of the income statement obtained?
4. What are the three parts of the heading of the income statement?
5. What are the two main sections of the body of the income statement?
6. How is the net income calculated from the information on the income statement?
7. How do you prove the accuracy of the amount of the net income that is shown on the income statement?
8. From which columns of the work sheet is all of the information for construction of the balance sheet obtained?
9. How does the report form of the balance sheet differ from the account form?
10. How does the heading of the balance sheet differ from the heading of the income statement?
11. What are the three main sections of the body of the balance sheet?
12. How does a bookkeeper prove the accuracy of the present capital figure shown on the balance sheet?

Cases for discussion

1. The heading of the income statement of the Wood Realty Agency includes the phrase "For Month Ended October 31, 1962." The heading of the balance sheet does not include the words "For Month Ended."
   (a) Which financial statement is a report for a given date only?
   (b) Which financial statement is a report covering a period of time?
   (c) Why are the words "For Month Ended" omitted in the heading of the balance sheet on page 104?

2. In the income statement of the Wood Realty Agency the total income is $1,692.00 larger than the total expenses. In the balance sheet of the Wood Realty Agency the total of the assets is $1,692.00 larger than the total of the liabilities plus the beginning proprietorship. Why are these two amounts the same?

Drill for understanding

Drill 9-A. Classification of accounts

This drill is planned to give you additional skill in determining which ledger account balances are found on the balance sheet and which ledger account balances are found on the income statement.

Instructions: 1. On a sheet of paper, rule a form similar to the form illustrated below. Fill in the headings as shown in the illustration. Then in the Account Titles column (Column 1), copy the list of account titles given below.

1	2	3
ACCOUNT TITLES	INCOME STATEMENT	BALANCE SHEET
1. Adams Company (Creditor)		√

LIST OF ACCOUNT TITLES

1. Adams Company (creditor)
2. Admissions Income
3. Advertising Expense
4. Tom Alby, Capital
5. Automobile
6. Automobile Expense
7. Cash
8. Commissions Income
9. Electricity Expense
10. Entertainment Expense
11. William Johnson, Capital
12. Kitchen Equipment
13. McIntyre Company (creditor)
14. Miscellaneous Expense
15. Office Equipment
16. Office Furniture
17. Office Machines
18. Premiums Income
19. Professional Library
20. Rent Expense
21. Shop Equipment
22. Stationery Expense
23. Supplies Expense
24. Telephone Expense
25. Triangle Motors (creditor)
26. M. W. Wood, Capital

Instructions: 2. If the account title appears on the income statement, place a check mark in Column 2, Income Statement column. If the account title appears on the balance sheet, place a check mark in Column 3, Balance Sheet column.

The first item, Adams Company (creditor), is given as an example. Since this is a liability account, it appears on the balance sheet. A check mark is placed in Column 3.

Problem 9-1. *Financial reports for an insurance agency*

The work sheet prepared in Problem 8-1 of Chapter 8 is required for this problem. If it has not been returned to you, complete Exercise 9-A in the Appendix.

Instructions: 1. Prepare an income statement from the Income Statement columns of the work sheet that you completed in Problem 8-1. Use as your model the income statement on page 102.

2. Prepare a balance sheet in report form from the Balance Sheet columns of the work sheet that you completed in Problem 8-1. Use as your model the balance sheet in report form on page 104.

Self-checking: Ask yourself the following questions:

(a) Did you center each line of the heading of your income statement?

(b) Did you place the headings of the two sections of the income statement, Income and Expenses, close to the vertical red line?

(c) Did you keep an even indention for all of the account titles listed on your income statement?

(d) Did you rule a double line under the amount of the net income to show completion of all work?

(e) Did you center each of the three lines of the heading of your balance sheet?

(f) Did you center the heading of each of the three main divisions of the balance sheet: Assets, Liabilities, and Proprietorship?

(g) Did you place only totals in the second amount column of your balance sheet?

(h) Did you rule the double lines neatly under the two proving totals of your balance sheet?

Problem 9-2. *Work sheet and financial reports for a doctor*

The account balances in the ledger of Dr. Melvin Sanger on May 31 of the current year, the end of a fiscal period of one month, were as follows:

Cash, $1,708.15

Automobile, $3,600.00

Equipment, $3,621.75

Office Furniture, $1,462.50

Medical Supply Co. (creditor), $163.00

Parker Company (creditor), $225.00

Swift Equipment Co. (creditor), $450.00

Melvin Sanger, Capital, $8,835.45

Fees Income, $1,345.00

Automobile Expense, $65.80

Miscellaneous Expense, $23.45

Rent Expense, $150.00

Salary Expense, $350.00

Utilities Expense, $36.80

Instructions: 1. Prepare a six-column work sheet for Dr. Melvin Sanger, using the account balances given above. Use as your model the work sheet on page 95.

2. Prepare an income statement from the Income Statement columns of the work sheet. Use as your model the income statement on page 102.

3. Prepare a balance sheet in report form from the Balance Sheet columns of the work sheet. Use as your model the balance sheet on page 104.

Self-checking: 1. Except for the omission of account numbers, is your work sheet similar in all respects to the model on page 95?

2. Check the accuracy of your financial reports by using the questions that are listed under Problem 9-1.

Optional problems

★*Supplementary Problem 9-S. Financial reports for a theater*

The work sheet for the Strand Theater for the month of December of the current year is given below.

Strand Theater
Work Sheet
For Month Ended December 31, 19--

Account Titles	Trial Balance Debit	Trial Balance Credit	Income Statement Debit	Income Statement Credit	Balance Sheet Debit	Balance Sheet Credit
Cash...................	2,873 50				2,873 50	
Air Conditioning Equip...	3,375 00				3,375 00	
Projection Equip.........	8,900 00				8,900 00	
Sound Equip.............	878 50				878 50	
Film Producers, Inc......		50 00				50 00
International Studios....		114 00				114 00
Majestic Films..........		28 00				28 00
Midwest Sound Service....		60 00				60 00
National Supply Company..		34 25				34 25
Frank Peck, Capital......		14,931 00				14,931 00
Admissions Income........		2,304 00		2,304 00		
Advertising Expense......	130 00		130 00			
Electricity Expense......	105 75		105 75			
Film Rental Expense......	925 00		925 00			
Maintenance Expense......	64 00		64 00			
Projection Expense.......	33 00		33 00			
Rent Expense............	200 00		200 00			
Water Expense...........	36 50		36 50			
	17,521 25	17,521 25	1,494 25	2,304 00	16,027 00	15,217 25
Net Income..............			809 75			809 75
			2,304 00	2,304 00	16,027 00	16,027 00

Instructions: 1. Prepare an income statement.

2. Prepare a balance sheet in report form.

Self-checking: 1. Is your income statement similar to the model on page 102? Check your work by asking yourself the questions that are listed for the income statement in Problem 9-1.

2. Is your balance sheet similar to the model on page 104? Check your work by asking yourself the questions that are listed for the balance sheet in Problem 9-1.

★Bonus Problem 9-B. Financial reports for a laundry

The work sheet for the Crown Laundry on December 31 of the current year is given below.

Crown Laundry
Work Sheet
For Month Ended December 31, 19--

Account Titles	Trial Balance Debit	Trial Balance Credit	Income Statement Debit	Income Statement Credit	Balance Sheet Debit	Balance Sheet Credit
Cash....................	1,655 15				1,655 15	
Delivery Equipment.......	3,000 00				3,000 00	
Machinery...............	17,478 50				17,478 50	
Office Equipment.........	892 10				892 10	
Faber Equipment Company..		3,450 00				3,450 00
Zenith Supply Company....		532 90				532 90
Paul Calvert, Capital....		19,608 65				19,608 65
Sales....................		468 25		468 25		
Delivery Expense.........	248 85		248 85			
Labor Expense...........	450 00		450 00			
Miscellaneous Expense....	41 10		41 10			
Power Expense...........	83 90		83 90			
Rent Expense............	140 00		140 00			
Supplies Expense.........	70 20		70 20			
	24,059 80	24,059 80	1,034 05	468 25	23,025 75	23,591 55
Net Loss...............				565 80	565 80	
			1,034 05	1,034 05	23,591 55	23,591 55

Instructions: 1. Prepare an income statement.

2. Prepare a balance sheet in report form.

Self-checking: (1) Compare your income statement with the model on page 102. You should use the words "Net Loss" on the last line of your income statement for this problem.

(2) Compare your balance sheet with the model on page 104. In calculating the present capital, did you subtract the net loss from the balance of the proprietor's capital account?

Chapter 10

Closing the ledger

Getting the ledger ready for a new fiscal period

Every income transaction increases Mr. Wood's proprietorship. Every expense transaction decreases his proprietorship. The increases in proprietorship are recorded in the commissions income account. The decreases in proprietorship are recorded in the various expense accounts. Separate accounts are used to record income and expenses so that detailed information will be available for preparing the income statement. But as a result of using separate income and expense accounts, Mr. Wood's capital account does not show these increases or decreases during the fiscal period.

After the income statement is completed, it is therefore desirable to:
1. Show in Mr. Wood's capital account the net income (or the net loss) for the fiscal period just ended.
2. Clear the income account and the expense accounts of their balances so as to make these accounts ready for the next fiscal period.

Need for an income and expense summary account

In order to complete the two steps indicated above, the balances of the various income and expense accounts are first transferred to a temporary account. The account to which the balances of all income and expense accounts are transferred at the end of each fiscal period is called *Income and Expense Summary.*

The transfer of the balances from the income and the expense accounts to Income and Expense Summary must be authorized by journal entries. An entry that transfers the balance from one account to another is called a *closing entry.* An account that has had its balance transferred to another account is called a *closed account.*

After the balances are transferred, the income and expense summary account shows the total expenses on the debit side and the total income on the credit side. The difference between the two sides of the account shows the net increase or the net decrease in proprietorship. The balance of the income and expense summary account is transferred to the proprietor's capital account.

The income and expense summary account is placed in the proprietorship section of the ledger because it shows the net increase or the net decrease in proprietorship. The entire process of transferring the balances in the income and the expense accounts through the income and expense summary account to the proprietor's capital account is called *closing the ledger*.

Procedure for closing the ledger

In closing Mr. Wood's ledger, three steps are taken. The chart below diagrams these steps.

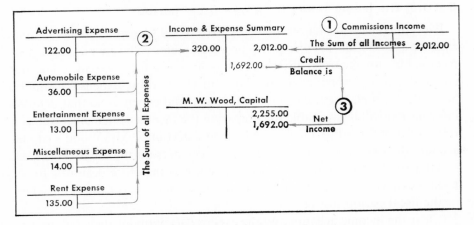

**Diagram showing the transfer of account balances
at the time the ledger is closed**

Step 1. The credit balance of the commissions income account is transferred to the credit side of the income and expense summary account.

Step 2. The sum of the debit balances of the expense accounts is transferred as a single amount to the debit side of the income and expense summary account.

Step 3. The credit balance of the income and expense summary account is transferred to the credit side of the proprietor's capital account.

When these transfers of account balances have been completed Mr. Wood's capital account shows the net increase in proprietorship for the period. As a result, his proprietorship account in the ledger now agrees with the amount shown in the proprietorship section of the end-of-period balance sheet.

Closing the income account

The information necessary for closing the income and the expense accounts is found in the Income Statement columns of the work sheet. The balances of the income and the expense accounts are transferred to the income and expense summary account in the same order in which they appear on the work sheet. According to the work sheet, the first account balance in the ledger to be transferred to the income and expense summary account is Commissions Income. The balance of the commissions income account, $2,012.00, is shown in the Income Statement Credit column of the work sheet as follows:

	ACCOUNT TITLES	ACCT. NO.	TRIAL BALANCE		INCOME STATEMENT	
			DEBIT	CREDIT	DEBIT	CREDIT
9	Commissions Income	41		2012 00		2012 00

Before any closing entry is made, the commissions income account and the income and expense summary account appear as shown below.

Income and Expense Summary ACCOUNT NO. 32

DATE	ITEMS	POST. REF.	DEBIT	DATE	ITEMS	POST. REF.	CREDIT

Commissions Income ACCOUNT NO. 41

DATE	ITEMS	POST. REF.	DEBIT	DATE	ITEMS	POST. REF.	CREDIT
				1962 Oct. 31		C1	2012 00

Since the balance of the commissions income account is a *credit* before the transfer, it will be a *credit* item in the income and expense summary account after the transfer. The amount to be *credited* to Income and Expense Summary is $2,012.00.

The general journal entry to transfer the credit balance of the commissions income account to the credit side of the income and expense summary account is shown below.

		GENERAL JOURNAL				PAGE 1	
	DATE	NAME OF ACCOUNT	POST. REF.	DEBIT		CREDIT	
12		Closing Entries					12
13	31	Commissions Income	41	2012 00			13
14		Income and Expense Summary	32			2012 00	14

The form of general journal used was illustrated in Chapter 2 when the opening entry was discussed. Mr. Wood also uses his general journal for recording his closing entries.

The words "Closing Entries" are written in the Name of Account column before the first closing entry is made. This heading explains the nature of the three closing entries, and therefore a separate explanation for each closing entry is unnecessary.

The procedure of using a journal entry to transfer an account balance in the ledger is desirable because (1) it helps the bookkeeper avoid errors and (2) it is easier to audit the work of the bookkeeper if all transfers of account balances are first recorded together in the journal.

After the general journal entry illustrated on page 113 has been posted, the two accounts affected by it appear as follows:

Income and Expense Summary — Account No. 32

DATE	ITEMS	POST. REF.	DEBIT	DATE	ITEMS	POST. REF.	CREDIT
				1962 Oct. 31		J 1	2 0 1 2 00

Commissions Income — Account No. 41

DATE	ITEMS	POST. REF.	DEBIT	DATE	ITEMS	POST. REF.	CREDIT
1962 Oct. 31		J 1	2 0 1 2 00	1962 Oct. 31		C 1	2 0 1 2 00

Note that the commissions income account illustrated above is now closed. Note also that the original balance of the commissions income account, which had a *credit* balance of $2,012.00, has now been transferred to the *credit* side of the income and expense summary account.

If there were other income accounts, their balances would be transferred to Income and Expense Summary in the same manner.

Closing the expense accounts

The balances of the expense accounts as shown in the Income Statement Debit column of the work sheet are:

	ACCOUNT TITLES	ACCT. NO.	TRIAL BALANCE DEBIT	TRIAL BALANCE CREDIT	INCOME STATEMENT DEBIT	INCOME STATEMENT CREDIT
10	Advertising Expense	51	1 2 2 0 0		1 2 2 0 0	
11	Automobile Expense	52	3 6 0 0		3 6 0 0	
12	Entertainment Expense	53	1 3 0 0		1 3 0 0	
13	Miscellaneous Expense	54	1 4 0 0		1 4 0 0	
14	Rent Expense	55	1 3 5 0 0		1 3 5 0 0	
15			5 3 1 4 0 0	5 3 1 4 0 0	3 2 0 0 0	2 0 1 2 0 0

The expense accounts are closed in the order in which they appear on the work sheet. All of the expense account balances are transferred to the income and expense summary account in one entry. Since all of the expense account balances are *debits* before the transfer is made, the total of all the expense account balances will be a *debit* item in the income and expense summary account after the transfer is completed. The sum of the expense account balances is $320.00. The amount to be *debited* to Income and Expense Summary is therefore $320.00.

The general journal entry to transfer the debit balances of the expense accounts to the debit side of the income and expense summary account is:

	DATE	NAME OF ACCOUNT	POST. REF.	DEBIT	CREDIT	
15	31	Income and Expense Summary	32	.320 00		15
16		Advertising Expense	51		1 22 00	16
17		Automobile Expense	52		36 00	17
18		Entertainment Expense	53		1 3 00	18
19		Miscellaneous Expense	54		1 4 00	19
20		Rent Expense	55		1 35 00	20
21						21

GENERAL JOURNAL — PAGE /

When an entry contains two or more debits or two or more credits, it is known as a *combined entry*.

After this entry has been posted, the income and expense summary account and the first of the expense accounts are as follows:

Income and Expense Summary ACCOUNT NO. 32

DATE	ITEMS	POST. REF.	DEBIT	DATE	ITEMS	POST. REF.	CREDIT
1962 Oct. 31		J 1	3 20 00	1962 Oct. 31		J 1	2 0 1 2 00

Advertising Expense ACCOUNT NO. 51

DATE	ITEMS	POST. REF.	DEBIT	DATE	ITEMS	POST. REF.	CREDIT
1962 Oct. 9		C 1	5 0 00	1962 Oct. 31		J 1	1 2 2 00
19		C 1	7 2 00				

The credits to the other expense accounts are posted in the same manner as the credit to Advertising Expense. All expense accounts are shown in the complete ledger on pages 120 to 122.

Closing the income and expense summary account

The net income as shown on Mr. Wood's work sheet is $1,692.00 (see page 95). This amount is the same as the balance in the income and expense summary account after all income and expense accounts were closed into this summary account. (A credit of $2,012.00 minus a debit of $320.00 equals $1,692.00.) The next step in closing the ledger is to transfer the credit balance of the income and expense summary account to the credit of the proprietor's capital account.

The general journal entry to transfer the credit balance of the income and expense summary account to the credit side of the proprietor's capital account is as follows:

	DATE	NAME OF ACCOUNT	POST. REF.	DEBIT	CREDIT	
GENERAL JOURNAL					PAGE	
21	31	Income and Expense Summary	32	1 6 9 2 00		21
22		M. W. Wood, Capital	31		1 6 9 2 00	22
23						23

After this entry has been posted, the income and expense summary account and the proprietor's capital account are as follows:

M. W. Wood, Capital — ACCOUNT NO. 31

DATE	ITEMS	POST. REF.	DEBIT	DATE	ITEMS	POST. REF.	CREDIT
				1962 Oct. 1	Balance	J 1	2 2 5 5 00
				31		J 1	1 6 9 2 00

Income and Expense Summary — ACCOUNT NO. 32

DATE	ITEMS	POST. REF.	DEBIT	DATE	ITEMS	POST. REF.	CREDIT
1962 Oct. 31		J 1	3 2 0 00	1962 Oct. 31		J 1	2 0 1 2 00
31		J 1	1 6 9 2 00				

The income and expense summary account now has a zero balance. As a result, it is said to be in balance and therefore closed. Mr. Wood's capital account now shows (1) the amount of capital at the start of this fiscal period, $2,255.00, and (2) the net increase in proprietorship during this fiscal period, $1,692.00. The sum of these two amounts now equals his present capital, $3,947.00. Since the present capital shown on the end-of-period balance sheet is also $3,947.00, Mr. Wood's capital account now agrees with the proprietorship section of the new balance sheet.

Summary of closing the ledger

This chapter has explained step by step the three journal entries that are needed to complete the bookkeeping process known as *closing the ledger*. These three journal entries as they appear in the general journal of the Wood Realty Agency after being posted are:

	DATE	NAME OF ACCOUNT	POST. REF.	DEBIT	CREDIT	
12		*Closing Entries*				12
13	31	*Commissions Income*	41	2 0 1 2 00		13
14		*Income and Expense Summary*	32		2 0 1 2 00	14
15	31	*Income and Expense Summary*	32	3 2 0 00		15
16		*Advertising Expense*	51		1 2 2 00	16
17		*Automobile Expense*	52		3 6 00	17
18		*Entertainment Expense*	53		1 3 00	18
19		*Miscellaneous Expense*	54		1 4 00	19
20		*Rent Expense*	55		1 3 5 00	20
21	31	*Income and Expense Summary*	32	1 6 9 2 00		21
22		*M. W. Wood, Capital*	31		1 6 9 2 00	22
23						23

GENERAL JOURNAL — PAGE 1

Closing entries for Wood Realty Agency after posting

These three entries are made from the work sheet illustrated on page 95 in the following order:

Step 1. Income and Expense Summary is credited for the total of the Income Statement Credit column. Each income account is debited for its balance.

Step 2. Income and Expense Summary is debited for the total of the Income Statement Debit column. Each expense account is credited for its balance.

Step 3. Income and Expense Summary is debited for the amount of the net income. The proprietor's capital account is credited for the same amount.

After the three closing entries in the journal are posted, the accounts in the income and expense divisions of the ledger appear as follows:
1. Each income account is now in balance because its credit balance has been transferred to the credit side of Income and Expense Summary.
2. Each expense account is now in balance because its debit balance has been transferred to the debit side of Income and Expense Summary.

117

3. The account Income and Expense Summary is in balance because its credit balance has been transferred to the credit side of the proprietor's capital account.

> In case of a net loss, the balance of the income and expense summary account is a debit balance and is transferred to the debit side of the proprietor's capital account.

4. The proprietor's capital account now shows on its credit side the increase in proprietorship because of the net income.

> In case of a net loss, the proprietor's capital account will show the decrease in proprietorship on its debit side.

Ruling accounts that are closed

As a result of the posting of the closing entries, each income account, each expense account, and the income and expense summary account are in balance and are said to be closed. In order to show that these accounts are closed, the accounts are ruled. This ruling will prevent the amounts now recorded in these accounts from being confused with the amounts that are entered during the following fiscal period. The advertising expense account after ruling is shown below.

The following steps are usually taken in ruling an income or an expense account:

Step 1. The totals of the debit and the credit sides of the account are written on the same line.

Step 2. A single line is ruled across the amount columns on the line above each total. This single line indicates addition.

Step 3. Double lines are ruled on the line under the totals across all columns except the Items column to show that the account is closed.

When an account that is closed has only one debit and one credit, it is clear that the debit equals the credit. It is therefore unnecessary to total the amount columns. The account is ruled with double lines across all columns except the Items columns as shown on page 119.

118

DATE	ITEMS	POST. REF.	DEBIT	DATE	ITEMS	POST. REF.	CREDIT
1962 Oct. 3		C 1	1 3 5 00	1962 Oct. 31		Q 1	1 3 5 00

Rent Expense   ACCOUNT NO. 55

Balancing asset, liability, and proprietorship accounts

When an asset, a liability, or a proprietorship account has one or more entries on each side, it may be balanced as follows:

Step 1. Enter the balance of the account on the side having the smaller total. Write the word "Balance" in the Items column, and place a check mark in the Post. Ref. column to show that this item was not posted from a journal. (See the cash account on page 120.)

Step 2. Total and rule the account in the manner in which an income or an expense account is totaled and ruled when it is closed.

Step 3. Enter the balance again, this time below the double ruling on the side originally having the larger footing. Enter the complete date (day, month, and year) of the new balance, using the first day of the new fiscal period. Write the word "Balance" in the Items column, and place a check mark in the Post. Ref. column.

The process of determining the balance of an account, writing it on the smaller side, totaling and ruling the account, and bringing the balance into the new section of the account below the double lines is known as *balancing an account.*

On the following pages the asset and the liability accounts that are balanced are Cash, Office Furniture, Office Machines, Adams Company, McIntyre Company, and Triangle Motors.

The asset account Automobile and the proprietorship account M. W. Wood, Capital are not balanced because they have entries on one side of the account only. Some bookkeepers prefer to balance such accounts, especially if numerous entries are made in them.

Ledger that has been closed, balanced, and ruled

The ledger of the Wood Realty Agency after the closing entries have been posted and the accounts have been balanced and ruled is shown on pages 120 to 122.

Cash
ACCOUNT NO. 11

DATE	ITEMS	POST. REF.	DEBIT		DATE	ITEMS	POST. REF.	CREDIT	
1962 Oct. 1	Balance	J1	491	00	1962 Oct. 31		C1	1075	00
31		C1	2170	00	31	Balance	✓	1586	00
	1586.00		2661	00				2661	00
			2661	00					
1962 Nov. 1	Balance	✓	1586	00					

Automobile
ACCOUNT NO. 12

DATE	ITEMS	POST. REF.	DEBIT		DATE	ITEMS	POST. REF.	CREDIT
1962 Oct. 1	Balance	J1	2180	00				

Office Furniture
ACCOUNT NO. 13

DATE	ITEMS	POST. REF.	DEBIT		DATE	ITEMS	POST. REF.	CREDIT	
1962 Oct. 1	Balance	J1	745	00	1962 Oct. 1		C1	45	00
3		C1	30	00	31	Balance	✓	730	00
	730.00		775	00				775	00
			775	00					
1962 Nov. 1	Balance	✓	730	00					

Office Machines
ACCOUNT NO. 14

DATE	ITEMS	POST. REF.	DEBIT		DATE	ITEMS	POST. REF.	CREDIT	
1962 Oct. 1	Balance	J1	236	00	1962 Oct. 24		C1	113	00
15		C1	375	00	31	Balance	✓	498	00
	498.00		611	00				611	00
			611	00					
1962 Nov. 1	Balance	✓	498	00					

Adams Company
ACCOUNT NO. 21

DATE	ITEMS	POST. REF.	DEBIT		DATE	ITEMS	POST. REF.	CREDIT	
1962 Oct. 1		C1	100	00	1962 Oct. 1	Balance	J1	275	00
23		C1	50	00		125.00				
			150	00					
31	Balance	✓	125	00					
			275	00				275	00
					1962 Nov. 1	Balance	✓	125	00

Ledger of Wood Realty Agency closed, balanced, and ruled

McIntyre Company — ACCOUNT NO. 22

DATE	ITEMS	POST. REF.	DEBIT	DATE	ITEMS	POST. REF.	CREDIT
1962 Oct. 12		C1	75 00	1962 Oct. 1	Balance	J1	342 00
31	Balance	✓	267 00		267.00		
			342 00				342 00
				1962 Nov. 1	Balance	✓	267 00

Triangle Motors — ACCOUNT NO. 23

DATE	ITEMS	POST. REF.	DEBIT	DATE	ITEMS	POST. REF.	CREDIT
1962 Oct. 9		C1	125 00	1962 Oct. 1	Balance	J1	780 00
31	Balance	✓	655 00		655.00		
			780 00				780 00
				1962 Nov. 1	Balance	✓	655 00

M. W. Wood, Capital — ACCOUNT NO. 31

DATE	ITEMS	POST. REF.	DEBIT	DATE	ITEMS	POST. REF.	CREDIT
				1962 Oct. 1	Balance	J1	2255 00
				31		J1	1692 00
							3947 00

Income and Expense Summary — ACCOUNT NO. 32

DATE	ITEMS	POST. REF.	DEBIT	DATE	ITEMS	POST. REF.	CREDIT
1962 Oct. 31		J1	320 00	1962 Oct. 31		J1	2012 00
31		J1	1692 00				
			2012 00				2012 00

Commissions Income — ACCOUNT NO. 41

DATE	ITEMS	POST. REF.	DEBIT	DATE	ITEMS	POST. REF.	CREDIT
1962 Oct. 31		J1	2012 00	1962 Oct. 31		C1	2012 00

Advertising Expense — ACCOUNT NO. 51

DATE	ITEMS	POST. REF.	DEBIT	DATE	ITEMS	POST. REF.	CREDIT
1962 Oct. 9		C1	50 00	1962 Oct. 31		J1	122 00
19		C1	72 00				
			122 00				122 00

Ledger of Wood Realty Agency closed, balanced, and ruled (continued)

Automobile Expense ACCOUNT NO. 52

DATE	ITEMS	POST. REF.	DEBIT	DATE	ITEMS	POST. REF.	CREDIT
1962 Oct. 5		C1	23 00	1962 Oct. 31		J1	36 00
30		C1	13 00				
			36 00				36 00

Entertainment Expense ACCOUNT NO. 53

DATE	ITEMS	POST. REF.	DEBIT	DATE	ITEMS	POST. REF.	CREDIT
1962 Oct. 17		C1	6 00	1962 Oct. 31		J1	13 00
26		C1	7 00				
			13 00				

Miscellaneous Expense ACCOUNT NO. 54

DATE	ITEMS	POST. REF.	DEBIT	DATE	ITEMS	POST. REF.	CREDIT
1962 Oct. 25		C1	9 00	1962 Oct. 31		J1	14 00
31		C1	5 00				
			14 00				14 00

Rent Expense ACCOUNT NO. 55

DATE	ITEMS	POST. REF.	DEBIT	DATE	ITEMS	POST. REF.	CREDIT
1962 Oct. 3		C1	135 00	1962 Oct. 31		J1	135 00

Ledger of Wood Realty Agency closed, balanced, and ruled (concluded)

Post-closing trial balance

After the closing entries have been posted and the accounts have been
ruled, it is customary to take a trial balance to test the equality of debits
and credits in the ledger. The trial balance taken after the closing entries
have been posted and the accounts have been ruled is called a *post-closing
trial balance.*

The post-closing trial balance of the Wood Realty Agency appears on
page 123. No income or expense account appears on this post-closing
trial balance because each has been closed. The open asset, liability, and
proprietorship accounts (those containing balances) are the only accounts
appearing on a post-closing trial balance. The post-closing trial balance
is used as a final means of checking to see that the ledger is in balance and
ready for use in the new fiscal period.

Wood Realty Agency
Post-Closing Trial Balance
October 31, 1962

Cash	11	1 5 8 6 00	
Automobile	12	2 1 8 0 00	
Office Furniture	13	7 3 0 00	
Office Machines	14	4 9 8 00	
Adams Company	21		1 2 5 00
McIntyre Company	22		2 6 7 00
Triangle Motors	23		6 5 5 00
M. W. Wood, Capital	31		3 9 4 7 00
		4 9 9 4 00	4 9 9 4 00

Post-closing trial balance of the Wood Realty Agency

Summary of the bookkeeping cycle

The post-closing trial balance is the final step in the complete book-keeping cycle. All the steps in the bookkeeping cycle are summarized below in order to give a clear picture of the steps in the cycle.

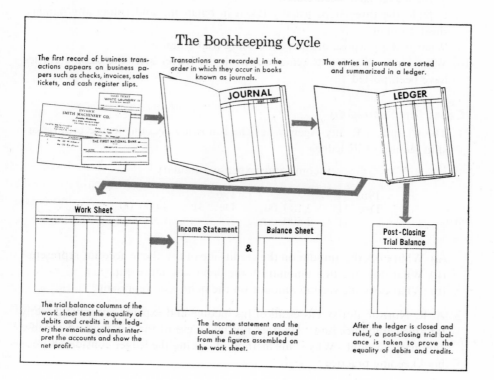

The Bookkeeping Cycle

The first record of business transactions appears on business papers such as checks, invoices, sales tickets, and cash register slips.

Transactions are recorded in the order in which they occur in books known as journals.

The entries in journals are sorted and summarized in a ledger.

JOURNAL

LEDGER

Work Sheet

Income Statement & Balance Sheet

Post-Closing Trial Balance

The trial balance columns of the work sheet test the equality of debits and credits in the ledger; the remaining columns interpret the accounts and show the net profit.

The income statement and the balance sheet are prepared from the figures assembled on the work sheet.

After the ledger is closed and ruled, a post-closing trial balance is taken to prove the equality of debits and credits.

Increasing your business vocabulary

What is the meaning of each of the following:

(a) income and expense summary account
(b) closing entry
(c) closed account
(d) closing the ledger
(e) combined entry
(f) balancing an account
(g) post-closing trial balance

Chapter questions

1. How do income transactions and expense transactions affect proprietorship?
2. Why doesn't the proprietorship account during a fiscal period show increases and decreases as a result of income and expense transactions?
3. What account is used for the purpose of summarizing the income and the expense accounts?
4. Explain the three steps in transferring the income and the expenses of a business to the proprietor's capital account.
5. What two columns of the work sheet are used as a guide for the closing entries in the general journal?
6. Give two reasons why it is desirable to use general journal entries to transfer account balances in the ledger.
7. After the first two closing entries have been posted, what kinds of accounts in the ledger have been closed?
8. Explain the three steps usually taken in balancing and ruling any balance sheet account.
9. What is the purpose of the post-closing trial balance?
10. What kinds of accounts remain open in the ledger after the closing entries have been posted?

Cases for discussion

1. The Chapman Realty Agency has the following account in the proprietorship section of its ledger:

Income and Expense Summary				
1962			1962	
Dec. 31	2,100.00		Dec. 31	4,600.00
31	2,500.00			

(a) What does the amount on the credit side of the above account represent?
(b) What does the first amount on the debit side represent?
(c) What does the second amount on the debit side represent?

2. A. R. Norton, florist, closes all of his income and expense accounts directly into his capital account. He does not make use of the income and expense summary account. Why is his method of closing the ledger considered poor bookkeeping practice?

Drill for understanding

Drill 10-A. *Identification of accounts as open or closed*

Instructions: 1. On the left side of a sheet of paper, write the heading *Account Titles;* then copy the ledger account titles that are given below. Rule a one-inch wide column at the right of the list. Head this column *Answers.*

1. Admissions Income
2. Advertising Expense
3. Air Conditioning Equipment
4. Cash
5. Electricity Expense
6. Film Producers, Inc. (creditor)
7. Film Rental Expense
8. International Studios (creditor)
9. Maintenance Expense
10. Midwest Sound Service (creditor)
11. Projection Equipment
12. Projection Expense
13. Rent Expense
14. Frank Rimer, Capital
15. Sound Equipment
16. Water Expense

2. If the account is closed after the closing entries are posted, write capital *C* (for "Closed") in the Answers column. If the account remains open after all closing entries are posted, write capital *O* (for "Open"). The first item is given as an example.

3. Now cover your answers and see

ACCOUNT TITLES	ANSWERS
1. Admissions Income	C

how rapidly you can do this drill mentally without looking at your answers. Repeat this mental drill several times for increased speed and accuracy.

Application problems

Problem 10-1. *Recording closing entries in a general journal*

A partial work sheet for Sommers' Appliance Store on August 31 of the current year is shown below.

ACCOUNT TITLES	ACCT. NO.	TRIAL BALANCE DEBIT	TRIAL BALANCE CREDIT	INCOME STATEMENT DEBIT	INCOME STATEMENT CREDIT
James Sommers, Capital	31		3,100 00		
Sales	41		1,456 90		1,456 90
Advertising Expense	51	16 53		16 53	
Delivery Expense	52	23 45		23 45	
Electricity Expense	53	8 90		8 90	
Rent Expense	54	130 00		130 00	
Salary Expense	55	375 00		375 00	
Water Expense	56	3 95		3 95	
		6,299 90	6,299 90	557 83	1,456 90
Net Income				899 07	
				1,456 90	1,456 90

Instructions: Record in a two-column general journal the three closing entries that are required at the end of the fiscal period.

Self-checking: Compare your work with the model closing entries on page 117.

Problem 10-2. Closing the ledger

If you are not using the workbook correlating with this textbook, complete Exercise 10-A in the Appendix instead of this problem.

Instructions: 1. Foot the ledger accounts of John Norris provided for this problem in the workbook. If an account has entries on both sides, write the balance in small pencil figures in the proper Items column.

2. Prove cash. The cash on hand on November 30, 19--, by actual count is $1,581.62. This amount should agree with the balance in the cash account in the ledger.

3. Prepare a work sheet on six-column work sheet paper.

4. Prepare an income statement.

5. Prepare a balance sheet in report form.

6. Record the closing entries in a general journal.

7. Post the closing entries.

8. Rule the income and expense summary account, the income account, and the expense accounts.

9. Balance all asset, liability, and proprietorship accounts that need to be balanced.

10. Prepare a post-closing trial balance.

Self-checking: (1) Were the pencil footings written in your ledger in small figures with a sharp, firm pencil?

(2) Was each amount column of an account footed when, and only when, it contained two or more entries?

(3) Is your work sheet similar to the model on page 95?

(4) Is your income statement similar to the model on page 102?

(5) Is your balance sheet similar to the model on page 104?

(6) Are your closing entries similar to the model on page 117?

(7) After you have closed, ruled, and balanced your ledger, is it similar to the model ledger on pages 120 to 122?

(8) Is your post-closing trial balance similar to the model on page 123?

Project 2

The complete bookkeeping cycle

Work required in Project 2

In this project you will record the transactions for a fiscal period and you will do the work required at the end of the fiscal period.

Strand Theater

The Strand Theater is a motion picture theater owned and operated by James Anderson. In the operation of his bookkeeping system he uses the following chart of accounts:

Chart of Accounts			
(1) ASSETS	ACCT. No.	(4) INCOME	ACCT. No.
Cash......................	11	Admissions Income...........	41
Projection Equipment..........	12	(5) EXPENSES	
Sound Equipment.............	13	Advertising Expense..........	51
(2) LIABILITIES		Film Rental Expense.........	52
Dempsey Sound Service........	21	Fuel Expense................	53
Price Optical Company........	22	Maintenance Expense.........	54
(3) PROPRIETORSHIP		Projection Expense...........	55
James Anderson, Capital.......	31	Rent Expense................	56
Income and Expense Summary.	32	Utilities Expense.............	57

Opening accounts in the ledger

Instructions: 1. Open accounts in the ledger in the order in which they are listed in the chart of accounts. Allow five lines for each account. Number the accounts with the account numbers given in the chart of accounts.

2. Copy the following balances in your ledger, using as the date November 1 of the current year. As you copy these balances, write the word "Balance" in the Items column of each account.

	DEBIT BALANCE	CREDIT BALANCE
Cash........................	2,135.00	
Projection Equipment........................	9,250.00	
Sound Equipment........................	1,500.00	
Dempsey Sound Service........................		219.00
Price Optical Company........................		166.00
James Anderson, Capital........................		12,500.00

Recording transactions in a seven-column cash journal

A businessman may have as many amount columns in his journal as he desires. Amount columns should be added in the journal only when they will bring about a saving in time and effort in posting. The best test as to whether or not a special amount column should be provided in a journal is the number of times that the column will be used.

The Strand Theater uses a cash journal with seven amount columns as illustrated below.

CASH JOURNAL

PAGE 10

	CASH DEBIT	ADVERTISING EXPENSE DEBIT	FILM RENTAL EXPENSE DEBIT	GENERAL DEBIT	DATE	NAME OF ACCOUNT	CHK. NO.	P. R.	GENERAL CREDIT	ADMISSIONS INCOME CREDIT	CASH CREDIT	
	1	2	3	4			5		6	7		
					1962 Oct.							
1		21 50			1	Advertising Exp....	222	√			21 50	1
2				300 00	2	Rent Expense......	223	56			300 00	2
3			95 00		4	Film Rental Exp....	224	√			95 00	3
4	243 25				5	Admissions Inc.....		√		243 25		4
25			110 00		31	Film Rental Exp....	240	√			110 00	25
26	1368 25	86 90	440 00	312 50	31	Totals...........			6 75	1361 50	839 40	26
27	11)	(51)	(52)	(√)					√)	(41)	(11)	27

Analysis of the seven-column cash journal of the Strand Theater

The cash journal of the Strand Theater differs from the one used in Project 1 in the following respects:

Advertising Expense Debit. Advertising expenses occur often. Each payment for an advertising expense is recorded in the Advertising Expense Debit column and in the Cash Credit column.

Film Rental Expense Debit. As payments for film rentals are made each week, a special column is provided for film rental expense. Each payment for film rental is recorded as a debit in the Film Rental Expense column and as a credit in the Cash Credit column.

Check No. column. The Check No. column replaces the No. column used in Project 1. The Strand Theater receives its income from admissions and does not issue receipts. The Check No. column is used only to record the number of each check written.

Admissions Income Credit. The Strand Theater receives its income from the sale of tickets. Each day's total receipts are recorded in the Cash Debit column and in the Admissions Income Credit column.

128

Recording transactions in the seven-column cash journal

Instructions: 3. Record the following transactions on page 11 of a seven-column cash journal similar to the one illustrated on page 128.

Nov. 1. Paid $120.00 for film rental. (Check No. 241)

2. Received $280.50 from admissions.

3. Received $210.25 from admissions.

5. Paid $80.00 to Price Optical Company on account. (Check No. 242)

5. Paid $25.00 for advertising. (Check No. 243)

6. Paid $100.00 to Dempsey Sound Service on account. (Check No. 244)

6. Paid $300.00 for rent for November. (Check No. 245)

8. Paid $135.00 for film rental. (Check No. 246)

9. Received $175.75 from admissions.

10. Paid $6.75 for new fuses for the projector. This is Projection Expense. (Check No. 247.)

10. Received $125.75 from admissions.

12. Paid $20.00 for advertising. (Check No. 248)

13. Paid $58.60 for repair of seats. This is Maintenance Expense. (Check No. 249)

15. Paid $45.00 for some new sound equipment. (Check No. 250)

15. Paid $75.00 for film rental. (Check No. 251)

16. Received $175.00 from admissions.

16. Received $15.00 from sale of old sound equipment.

17. Received $193.00 from admissions.

19. Paid $18.00 for advertising. (Check No. 252)

20. Paid $13.00 for repair of carpet. This is Maintenance Expense. (Check No. 253)

23. Received $165.50 from admissions.

24. Received $143.00 from admissions.

24. Paid $85.00 for film rental. (Check No. 254)

26. Received $25.00 from sale of some old projection equipment.

27. Paid $25.00 for advertising. (Check No. 255)

29. Paid $115.00 for film rental. (Check No. 256)

30. Paid $53.00 for fuel for November. (Check No. 257)

30. Paid $62.70 for electricity for November. This is Utilities Expense. (Check No. 258)

30. Paid $12.35 for water service for November. This is Utilities Expense. (Check No. 259)

30. Received $102.00 from admissions.

Work at the end of the month

Instructions: 4. Foot all columns of the cash journal.

5. Prove cash. The cash on hand is $2,396.35.

6. Prove the equality of debits and credits in the cash journal.

7. Total and rule the cash journal. (See model on page 68.)

8. Post each amount in the General Debit column and in the General Credit column. Place a check mark in the posting reference column opposite each amount entered in a special column. Place check marks in parentheses under the total of each General column to show that these two totals are not posted.

9. Post the total of each of the five special columns in the cash journal. Write the proper account number in parentheses under each total after the posting is completed.

10. Foot the accounts in the ledger that have more than one entry on either side of the account. If an account has entries on both sides of the account, write the balance in small pencil figures in the Items column.

Work at the end of the fiscal period

Instructions: 11. Prepare a trial balance on six-column work sheet paper, using the first two amount columns of the work sheet for the trial balance. Note that the name of the business is Strand Theater and that the work sheet is prepared for the month ended November 30 of the current year. The entire work sheet should be prepared with pencil.

12. Complete the work sheet. (See model on page 95.)

13. Prepare the income statement. (See model on page 102.)

14. Prepare the balance sheet in report form. (See model on page 104.)

15. Record the closing entries in your cash journal. (Use as your guide the illustration of closing entries on page 117, but note that the General Debit amount column in your cash journal is at the left of the Name of Account column.)

16. Post the closing entries.

17. Rule the income and expense summary account, the income account, and the expense accounts. (Use as your guide the model accounts on pages 121 and 122.)

18. Balance and rule all asset accounts, all liability accounts, and all proprietorship accounts that need to be balanced. (Use as your guide the model accounts on pages 120 and 121.)

19. Prepare a post-closing trial balance. (See model on page 123.)

Chapter 11

Recording the buying of merchandise on account

Merchandise

Mr. Fred Morton owns and operates an office supplies and equipment store. It is known as Morton Supplies. The business carries in stock for sale such items as typewriters, adding machines, filing cabinets, and office supplies. Goods carried in stock for sale are known as *merchandise*.

Buying procedures

Morton Supplies buys merchandise from different manufacturers and wholesalers. Merchandise may be ordered by letter, on an order blank supplied by the manufacturer or the wholesaler, or on a printed form. A business form prepared by the buyer that describes merchandise to be purchased is called a *purchase order*. The buyer keeps a carbon copy of each purchase order so he can later check quantities received and prices.

The immediate record — the invoice

A business form listing goods sold, the method of shipment, and the cost of the items is called an *invoice*. Morton Supplies receives an invoice from the seller for each order it places. The invoice is the immediate record from which the bookkeeping entry for each purchase is made.

An invoice for a purchase made by Morton Supplies from the Richmond Metal Company is shown below.

Invoice

RICHMOND METAL COMPANY ✓   #120

296 River Road
GARY 6, INDIANA   NOV 5 RECD

Sold to Morton Supplies
         460 Main Street   Date Nov. 1, 1962
         Portland 2, Oregon

                                  No. 4120
Terms 30 days
                                  How Shipped Van Truck Co.
         Purchase Order No. 2060

QUANTITY	DESCRIPTION	UNIT PRICE	TOTAL
4 ✓	3-drawer visible card files #82	18.00	72.00 ✓
6 ✓	Letter-size personal files #76M	2.50	15.00 ✓
10 ✓	Square metal wastebaskets #24D	2.80	28.00 ✓
1 doz. ✓	Letter-size metal desk trays #21T	16.00	16.00 ✓
6 ✓	3-drawer letter-size files #2266	50.00	300.00 ✓
			431.00 ✓

Invoices differ from business to business. Most invoices, however, include the following:
1. The name and the address of the one who sells the merchandise.
2. The name and the address of the purchaser.
3. The date of the invoice.
4. The seller's invoice number.
5. The method of shipment.
6. The terms.
7. The buyer's purchase order number.
8. The quantity, description, and unit price of items purchased.
9. The total cost of each item and the total of the invoice.

Checking an invoice

It is important for the buyer to know that he has received the items he ordered and that they are priced correctly. The following steps are taken to prove the correctness of the invoice:

Step 1.   The invoice is compared with the purchase order to see that the quantity, the description, and the price of each item on the invoice agree with those on the purchase order. A check mark is placed at the right of each amount in the Quantity column of the invoice for each item that is approved. (See invoice on page 131.)

Step 2.   The accuracy of the multiplication on each line and the addition of the Total column are checked. A check mark is placed at the right of each item in the Total column of the invoice as each amount is found to be correct. (See invoice on page 131.)

Journals for a merchandising business

A business that buys and sells merchandise often finds that it can save time in recording and posting transactions by using several journals. When such a plan is used, it is common to have the following journals: (1) purchases journal; (2) sales journal; (3) cash receipts journal; (4) cash payments journal; and (5) general journal.

The purchases journal

A transaction in which merchandise is bought with an agreement that it is to be paid for at a later date is called a *purchase on account*. When a business makes many purchases on account, time can be saved by recording all purchases of merchandise on account in a separate journal. A special journal for recording purchases of merchandise on account is called a *purchases journal*. Other terms used instead of purchases journal are *purchases book* and *purchases register*.

Purchases journal entry No. 1

November 5, 1962. Purchased merchandise from the Richmond Metal Company on account, $431.00.

As each invoice is received, it is stamped with the current date. The Richmond Metal Company invoice on page 131 is stamped Nov. 5. Invoices are also numbered by the buyer when they are received in the order in which they are received. The invoice shown on page 131 is numbered 120 in the upper right-hand corner.

All of the information on an invoice is recorded on a single line of the purchases journal. The invoice for the purchase from the Richmond Metal Company is recorded on Line 1 of the purchases journal as shown below.

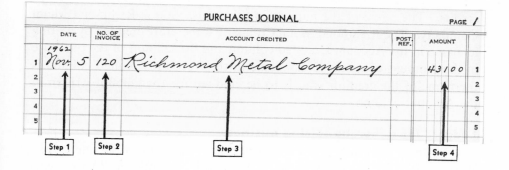

The steps to record the invoice received from the Richmond Metal Company are:

Step 1. The date the invoice was received, Nov. 5, 1962, is recorded in the Date column on the first line of the purchases journal. Since this is the first entry on the page, the year, month, and day are recorded. The year and the month are not repeated on the same page for additional entries.

Step 2. The number written on the invoice, 120, is recorded in the No. of Invoice column. This number is shown in the upper right-hand corner of the invoice on page 131.

Step 3. The name of the business from which the purchase was made, Richmond Metal Company, is written in the Account Credited column.

Step 4. The total of the invoice, $431.00, is recorded in the Amount column.

Step 5. A check mark is placed on the invoice at the right of the name to show that the invoice has been recorded. (See the invoice on page 131.) The invoice is then filed so that it can be referred to when necessary.

The debit part of the entry. In the purchases journal, as in previous journals, every entry has a debit part and a credit part. The account used to record all purchases of merchandise in a merchandising business has the title *Purchases*. The cost of merchandise sold is a deduction from the income of the business. For this reason the debit part of this entry is a debit to Purchases.

It is not necessary to write the word "Purchases" on each line of the purchases journal because each amount in the Amount column is a debit to Purchases. These debits to Purchases are not posted individually. At the end of the month the total of the Amount column will be posted.

The credit part of the entry. The purchase of merchandise on account also increased a liability. Increases in liabilities are always recorded as credits. The name of the liability in this transaction is Richmond Metal Company. The Richmond Metal Company is therefore credited by writing its name in the Account Credited column and the amount of the purchase in the Amount column. Every name in the Account Credited column is the name of the creditor who is to be credited for the amount written in the Amount column.

Ledgers for a merchandising business

A business with only a few ledger accounts often uses only one ledger. When a business has many accounts both with customers and with creditors, it is a common practice to have the following ledgers:

1. A ledger for creditors' accounts. A ledger that contains accounts with creditors only is called an *accounts payable ledger*.

2. A ledger for customers' accounts. A ledger that contains accounts with customers only is called an *accounts receivable ledger*.

3. A ledger for accounts needed to make the financial reports. A ledger that contains all of the accounts needed to make the income statement and the balance sheet is called a *general ledger*.

When a separate ledger is used for all accounts with creditors, this accounts payable ledger must be summarized in a single account in the general ledger. The title of this summarizing account in the general ledger is *Accounts Payable*. When a separate ledger is used for the accounts with customers, this accounts receivable ledger must also be summarized in a single account in the general ledger. The title of this summarizing account in the general ledger is *Accounts Receivable*.

A ledger that is summarized in a single account in the general ledger is called a *subsidiary ledger*. The accounts payable ledger and the accounts receivable ledger are subsidiary ledgers.

134

An account in the general ledger that summarizes all of the accounts in a subsidiary ledger is called a *controlling account*. The accounts payable account in the general ledger is a controlling account for the accounts payable ledger. The accounts receivable account in the general ledger is a controlling account for the accounts receivable ledger.

The accounts payable ledger

Morton Supplies keeps all accounts with creditors in a separate ledger called the accounts payable ledger. The accounts payable ledger has balance-column rulings as shown below.

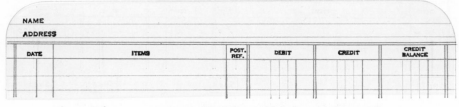

NAME

ADDRESS

DATE	ITEMS	POST. REF.	DEBIT	CREDIT	CREDIT BALANCE

Account in an accounts payable ledger with balance-column ruling

Each account in the accounts payable ledger of Morton Supplies has three amount columns. One column is for debit amounts, one is for credit amounts, and one is for credit balance amounts. The Credit Balance column makes it possible to record the balance of the account after each posting. This is desirable because it shows at any time how much is owed to a creditor.

Posting individual items from the purchases journal

Each individual amount in the purchases journal is posted to the credit of the account of the creditor named in the Account Credited column. All of the accounts with these creditors are placed in the accounts payable ledger.

The purchases journal entry and the creditor's account in the accounts payable ledger after Entry No. 1 is posted are shown at the top of page 136.

The account for the Richmond Metal Company is opened in the accounts payable ledger by writing the name and the address on the first two lines of the ledger page. The address of this new account is obtained from the invoice.

The steps in posting the entry on Line 1 of the purchases journal are as follows:

Step 1. The amount owed for this purchase on account, $431.00, is recorded in the Credit column of the Richmond Metal Company account because this transaction increases this liability.

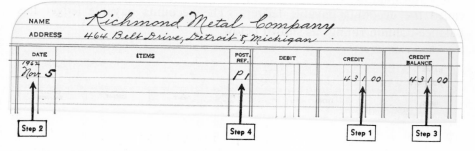

Step 2. The year, 1962, is written at the top of the Date column. The month and the day, Nov. 5, are written on the first line of the Date column.

Step 3. The amount of the credit, $431.00, is extended to the Credit Balance column. As there is no previous balance in this account, this credit is also the balance.

The Credit Balance column in each creditor's account makes it possible to record the balance immediately after each posting. This is desirable because it shows at any time how much is owed to each creditor.

Step 4. *P1* is written in the Post. Ref. column of the account to show that the entry came from page 1 of the purchases journal.

Step 5. A check mark is placed in the Post. Ref. column of the purchases journal to show completion of the posting of this transaction.

Accounts with creditors are placed in alphabetic order in the accounts payable ledger. Since these accounts keep changing, they are not numbered. A check mark, therefore, must be used on each line of the purchases journal to indicate the posting of the entry to the creditor's account.

Recording an opening balance in a creditor's account

Morton Supplies opened accounts with creditors on November 1, 1962, in a new accounts payable ledger. At that time the account of the Union Paper Company had a balance of $80.40. This balance is properly recorded as a credit balance in the account of the Union Paper Company shown at the top of the next page.

NAME	*Union Paper Company*							
ADDRESS	*2964 State Street, Chicago 10, Illinois*							

DATE	ITEMS	POST. REF.	DEBIT	CREDIT	CREDIT BALANCE
1962 *Nov. 1*	*Balance*	✓			*80 40*

The name and the address of the creditor are written at the top of the account. The date, Nov. 1, 1962, is recorded in the Date column. The word *Balance* is written in the Items column, and the credit balance of $80.40 is recorded in the Credit Balance column. To show that this entry did not come from a journal, a check mark is placed in the Post. Ref. column.

Purchases journal entry No. 2

November 5, 1962. Purchased merchandise from Union Paper Company on account, $125.00.

The journal entry to record this purchase is shown on Line 2 of the purchases journal below.

	DATE	NO. OF INVOICE	ACCOUNT CREDITED	POST. REF.	AMOUNT	
1	*1962* *Nov. 5*	*120*	*Richmond Metal Company*	✓	*431 00*	1
2	*5*	*121*	*Union Paper Company*		*125 00*	2
3						3

PURCHASES JOURNAL — PAGE *1*

Posting to an accounts payable account with a previous balance

The account of the Union Paper Company in the accounts payable ledger after posting Line 2 of the purchases journal is shown below.

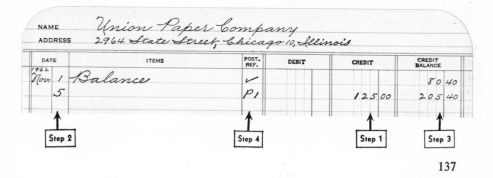

NAME	*Union Paper Company*							
ADDRESS	*2964 State Street, Chicago 10, Illinois*							

DATE	ITEMS	POST. REF.	DEBIT	CREDIT	CREDIT BALANCE
1962 *Nov. 1*	*Balance*	✓			*80 40*
5		*P1*		*125 00*	*205 40*

Step 2   Step 4   Step 1   Step 3

137

The steps in posting the entry on Line 2 of the purchases journal are:

Step 1.　The amount owed for this purchase, $125.00, is recorded on the second line in the Credit column of the Union Paper Company account.

Step 2.　The day, 5, is written on the second line in the Date column. The year and the month are not repeated.

Step 3.　The new credit, $125.00, is added to the credit balance of $80.40. The new credit balance of $205.40 is recorded in the Credit Balance column.

Step 4.　*P1* is written in the Post Ref. column of the account.

Step 5.　A check mark is placed in the Post. Ref. column of the purchases journal to show completion of the posting.

| | | PURCHASES JOURNAL | | | PAGE / |
	DATE	NO. OF INVOICE	ACCOUNT CREDITED	POST. REF.	AMOUNT
1	1962 Nov. 5	120	Richmond Metal Company	✓	431 00
2	5	121	Union Paper Company	✓	125 00

Step 5

The purchases journal of Morton Supplies

The complete purchases journal of Morton Supplies for the month of November, showing all entries to creditors' accounts posted to the accounts payable ledger, is given below.

| | | PURCHASES JOURNAL | | | PAGE / |
	DATE	NO. OF INVOICE	ACCOUNT CREDITED	POST. REF.	AMOUNT
1	1962 Nov. 5	120	Richmond Metal Company	✓	431 00
2	5	121	Union Paper Company	✓	125 00
3	7	122	Arco Typewriter Company	✓	480 60
4	9	123	Metal Desk Company	✓	540 35
5	13	124	Union Paper Company	✓	96 45
6	16	125	Wills Office Machines	✓	646 20
7	19	126	Metal Desk Company	✓	480 15
8	26	127	Bell Business Machines	✓	397 60
9	29	128	Acme Carbon Company	✓	72 80
10	30		Purchases Dr./Accounts Payable Cr.	51	3270 15
11					
12					
13					
14					
15					
16					

Purchases journal after posting to all creditors' accounts

Posting the individual amounts in the purchases journal

In order to keep all accounts with creditors up to date, individual entries in the purchases journal are posted frequently, often daily. The separate posting of each line of the purchases journal affects only the accounts in the accounts payable ledger. Only the total of the purchases journal is posted to the general ledger.

Ruling the purchases journal

The purchases journal is totaled and ruled with single and double lines as shown above. A single line is ruled across the Amount column only. The amount column is totaled and the total, $3,270.15, is written immediately below the single line. Double lines are ruled under the total across all of the columns except the Account Credited column.

The debit part of the total line of the purchases journal

The total of the Amount column of the purchases journal is the amount of merchandise purchased on account during the month. Purchases are a part of the cost of merchandise sold. All costs of merchandise sold are recorded as debits because they are a deduction from the income of the business. The total of the Amount column of the purchases journal is therefore posted to the debit of the purchases account in the general ledger.

To show that the total is to be posted to the debit of the purchases account, *Purchases Dr.* is written in the Account Credited column of the purchases journal on the line with the total. The date, 30, is written in the Date column on the total line. (See the illustration on page 140.)

The credit part of the total line of the purchases journal

The total of the Amount column of the purchases journal is also the sum of the amounts posted as credits to the individual accounts in the accounts payable ledger. A summary of all of these postings must be posted to the general ledger in order to complete the liabilities section of the general ledger. Therefore, the total of the Amount column of the purchases journal is posted as a credit to an account in the general ledger that has the title *Accounts Payable.*

In order to show that the total in the Amount column of the purchases journal is to be posted to the credit of the accounts payable account in the general ledger, *Accounts Payable Cr.* is written on the total line immediately following *Purchases Dr.* The names of these two accounts are separated by writing a diagonal line between them. A diagonal line is also placed in the Post. Ref. column of the total line to show that the total is to be posted to two accounts. (See the illustration on page 140.)

Posting the total of the purchases journal

The total line of the purchases journal and the two accounts to which the total is posted are shown below.

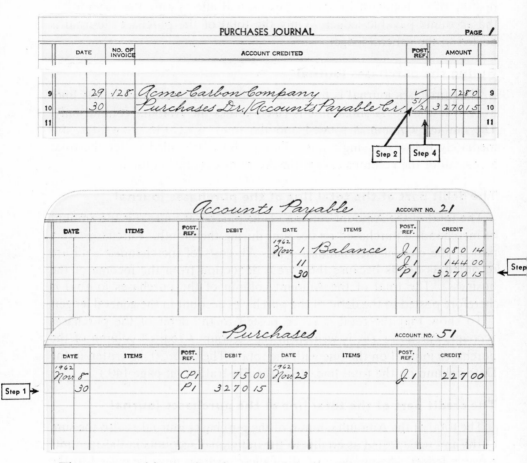

The steps used in posting the total of the purchases journal are:

Step 1. The total of the purchases journal, $3,270.15, is posted to the debit of the purchases account in the general ledger. The date, 30, is written in the Date column. *P1* is written in the Post. Ref. column of the purchases account to show that this debit came from page 1 of the purchases journal.

Step 2. The account number of the purchases account, 51, is written in the left half of the Post. Ref. column of the purchases journal to show completion of the posting of the debit part of the total.

An explanation of the account numbers used by Morton Supplies is given on page 262.

Step 3.   The total of the purchases journal is also posted to the credit of the controlling account, Accounts Payable, in the general ledger. The date, 30, is written in the Date column. *P1* is written in the Post. Ref. column of the accounts payable account to show that this credit came from page 1 of the purchases journal.

Step 4.   The account number of the accounts payable account, 21, is written in the right half of the Post. Ref. column of the purchases journal to show the completion of the posting of the credit part of the total.

Relationship of the purchases journal, the accounts payable ledger, and the general ledger

The total of the purchases journal is posted as a debit to the purchases account in the general ledger. It is also posted as a credit to the accounts payable account in the general ledger. The equality of debits and credits in the general ledger is therefore maintained, because the purchases account is debited and the accounts payable account is credited for the same amount.

Each entry in the purchases journal is posted as a credit to a creditor's account in the accounts payable ledger. The one credit posted to Accounts Payable in the general ledger is therefore equal to the sum of all the credits posted to the individual accounts in the accounts payable ledger. The balance of the accounts payable account is used in the trial balance. The balances of the individual accounts in the subsidiary ledger are not used in the trial balance, but they are useful in showing the amount owed to each individual creditor.

Advantages of a separate ledger for all creditors' accounts

The use of an accounts payable ledger for the accounts of all creditors has the following advantages:

1. It reduces the size of the general ledger and thereby keeps it from becoming bulky in some businesses.

2. It makes it unnecessary to list the names of each creditor on the trial balance. These many credit balances are shown in one amount on the trial balance with the account title Accounts Payable.

3. The balance of the accounts payable account in the general ledger is used to prove the accuracy of all of the postings to the accounts payable ledger after posting to it from both the purchases journal and the cash payments journal. This type of proof will be explained in detail in Chapter 12.

141

A second method — using purchases invoices as a purchases journal

Some businesses file or bind the purchases invoices together and use them as a purchases journal. When this method is used, the posting is done from the original invoices and the purchases journal is not used.

The method of using the purchases invoices for the purchases journal is not the same in all businesses, but a satisfactory method is as follows:

Step 1.　The invoices are numbered consecutively as they are received and are filed together.

Step 2.　The amount of each purchases invoice is posted directly to the creditor's account in the accounts payable ledger. The number of the invoice is placed in the posting reference column of the creditor's account to show the source of the entry. A check mark is placed at the right of the name of the creditor printed at the top of the purchases invoice to show that the invoice has been posted.

Step 3.　At the end of the month the amounts of all purchases invoices for the month are added. Ordinarily an adding machine is used for this purpose. The invoices for a month, with the adding machine list showing the totals, are illustrated below.

```
            230.50 *
            313.75
            115.80
            492.25
             78.60
            274.50
            396.20
            135.30
            206.25
            219.65
            154.15
             29.90
            148.00
            112.40
            154.65
           3061.90 *
```

Roland and Sons ✓

2476 Cedar Road, New York

Sold to McGregor Luggage Shop　　　Date Oct.
229 Main Street
Manchester, Connecticut

Shipped via New England Trucking Co.

QUANTITY	DESCRIPTION	AMOUNT
12 ✓	#410–B Handbags	25.80 ✓
6 ✓	#070–A Overnight Bag	77.70 ✓
24 ✓	#306–B Billfolds	36.00 ✓
10 ✓	#163–C Jewel Case	91.00 ✓
		230.50 ✓

Invoices with an adding machine list showing the total

Step 4. The total of the invoices for the month is recorded in a general journal as a debit to Purchases and a credit to Accounts Payable. Such an entry is illustrated below.

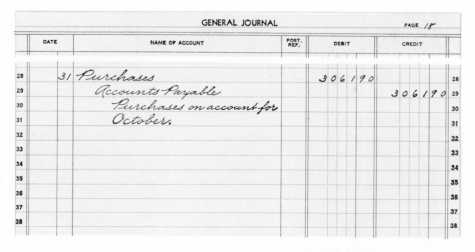

Step 5. The general journal entry is posted to the debit of Purchases and to the credit of Accounts Payable in the general ledger.

Using automated equipment to record and post purchases on account

A business that has a great volume of purchases on account each month often finds that it can get the bookkeeping work done more rapidly and with fewer errors by eliminating hand recording and posting. Equipment that does recording and posting automatically from an original record is called *automated equipment*. The use of automated equipment to replace some hand operations in business or industry is called *automation*.

When automated equipment is used to record and post purchases on account, a clerk makes a punched card or tape from the information on the purchases invoice. This punched card or tape is fed into a machine that automatically makes a purchases journal record of all transactions for the day. These same cards or tapes can then be fed into a machine that will post the amounts of the invoices to the creditors' accounts.

The cards or tapes can also be used to record automatically on stock records the number of items of each type of merchandise purchased.

Automated equipment does much of the routine work of recording purchases and posting the entries to the proper accounts after the invoice and the punched card or tape have been prepared by hand. All of these operations must be planned and directed by a person who has learned the principles of bookkeeping that are involved.

Increasing your business vocabulary

What is the meaning of each of the following:

(a) merchandise

(b) purchase order

(c) invoice

(d) purchase on account

(e) purchases journal

(f) accounts payable ledger

(g) accounts receivable ledger

(h) general ledger

(i) subsidiary ledger

(j) controlling account

(k) automated equipment

(l) automation

Chapter questions

1. Why should one who orders merchandise keep a copy of the purchase order?
2. What business paper is the basis for each entry in the purchases journal?
3. What steps are taken after an invoice is received and before it is recorded?
4. What journals are commonly used when a business buys and sells merchandise on account?
5. In what special journal are all purchases of merchandise on account recorded?
6. How do you determine what number to record in the No. of Invoice column of the purchases journal?
7. How do you indicate on the invoice that the invoice has been recorded?
8. What ledgers are commonly used in a merchandising business?
9. What is the name of the ledger in which Morton Supplies keeps its accounts with creditors?
10. What is the advantage of using balance-column ruling for creditors' accounts?
11. Why is a check mark used in the Post. Ref. column of the purchases journal instead of a number to indicate that the item has been posted?
12. What is the meaning of "P1" in the Post. Ref. column of the creditor's account illustrated on page 136?
13. When the November 1 balance was recorded, why was a check mark used in the Post. Ref. column of the Union Paper Company account illustrated on page 137 instead of a page number?
14. What account in the general ledger is debited for the total of the purchases journal?
15. What account in the general ledger is credited for the total of the purchases journal?

Cases for discussion

1. The Valley Furniture Company purchased eight desks from the Holt Manufacturing Company. One of these desks was for use in the office. The remaining seven were for resale to customers. The amount of the invoice was $800.00. The bookkeeper debited Purchases for the full amount of the invoice. Did the bookkeeper make the correct entry? If not, what should he have done?
2. The total of the purchases journal of Alden's Record Shop was $1,876.00. At the end of the month the accounts payable account in the general ledger

did not agree with the sum of the balances of all creditors' accounts in the accounts payable ledger. There was a difference of $1,876.00. What was the probable cause of the difference?

3. Instead of recording purchases on account in a purchases journal, Danny's Record Shop posts each invoice directly to the creditor's account. What entry does the bookkeeper make at the end of the month to record such purchases? In what journal is the entry made?

Drill for understanding
Drill 11-A. Using accounts payable accounts

This drill is planned to give you practice in opening accounts with creditors and in determining account balances.

Instructions: 1. Open an account for each creditor listed below, using a ledger with balance-column ruling. Allow four lines for each account.

2. Record the amounts given for each account and find the account balance after each amount is recorded. Use the current year for each transaction.

1. T. R. Adams, 2164 8th Street, San Francisco 7, California:
    Feb. 1, beginning balance $70.00; Feb. 10, credit $100.00;
    Feb. 15, credit $120.00.

2. Harry Baker, 4268 Bay View Avenue, San Francisco 37, California:
    Feb. 9, credit $264.00; Feb. 14, credit $200.00;
    Feb. 16, credit $180.00.

3. M. J. Corey, 1922 Morris Street, San Jose 14, California:
    Feb. 1, beginning balance $890.75; Feb. 14, credit $228.60;
    Feb. 20, credit $338.60.

4. J. R. Durgen, 1347 Alameda Drive, Burlingame, California:
    Feb. 1, credit $16.95; Feb. 8, credit $41.40;
    Feb. 15, credit $103.18; Feb. 22, credit $36.67.

5. James Egan, 168 Circle Drive, Los Angeles 13, California:
    Feb. 1, beginning balance $110.00; Feb. 23, credit $103.25;
    Feb. 26, credit $63.83.

6. W. L. Fox, 2649 Vine Street, Tucson, Arizona:
    Feb. 16, credit $445.24; Feb. 20, credit $234.26;
    Feb. 21, credit $336.20; Feb. 27, credit $415.65.

7. H. R. Grant, 329 Stanley Street, Berkeley 14, California:
    Feb. 1, beginning balance $350.00; Feb. 14, credit $175.00;
    Feb. 20, credit $264.40.

8. I. J. Warren, 340 Wells Street, Oakland 32, California:
    Feb. 10, credit $286.90; Feb. 23, credit $239.20;
    Feb. 28, credit $321.16.

9. C. L. White, 5314 Oxnard Avenue, San Jose 12, California:
    Feb. 1, beginning balance $25.00; Feb. 4, credit $15.28;
    Feb. 8, credit $21.95; Feb. 11, credit $5.45.

Application problems

Problem 11-1. *Recording purchases on account of a retail dress shop*

The following purchases of merchandise on account were made by the Bell Dress Shop during March of the current year:

Mar.	2. Barton and Lane	$ 272.80
	5. Lansing Dress Co.	980.20
	8. Walker Apparel Co.	600.00
	12. Home Clothing Co.	424.80
	15. Allen & Co.	601.25
	18. Lansing Dress Co.	409.60
	21. Street Brothers	380.40
	23. Home Clothing Co.	729.20
	26. Barton and Lane	641.30
	29. Lansing Dress Co.	460.90

Instructions: 1. Record each purchase on page 3 of a purchases journal like the one on page 138. Number the invoices beginning with No. 431.

2. Total and rule the purchases journal.

The purchases journal prepared in this problem will also be used in Problem 11-2.

Problem 11-2. *Opening two ledgers and posting a purchases journal*

The creditors of the Bell Dress Shop and the amounts owed to each as of March 1 of the current year are:

Allen & Co., 4660 Fourth Street, City	$ 780.00
Barton and Lane, 1216 Main Street, City	245.60
Home Clothing Co. 2679 Clark Street, Chicago 17, Ill.	235.00
Lansing Dress Co. 1860 7th Avenue, New York 8, N. Y.	580.40
Street Brothers, 2146 Broad Street, St. Louis 23, Mo.	360.20
Walker Apparel Co., 1890 7th Avenue, New York 8, N. Y.	497.30

Instructions: 1. Open accounts for the creditors in an accounts payable ledger with balance-column ruling. Allow five lines for each account. Record the balance in each account. Use the account shown on page 137 as a model.

General ledger accounts of the Bell Dress Shop and the balances of the accounts as of March 1 of the current year are:

ACCT. NO.	ACCOUNT TITLE	BALANCE	ACCT. NO.	ACCOUNT TITLE
11	Cash	$7,910.50 (Dr.)	63	Miscellaneous Expense
21	Accounts Payable	2,698.50 (Cr.)	64	Rent Expense
32	Mary Bell, Drawing		65	Salary Expense
51	Purchases			

Note that this is not a complete general ledger but only the accounts that will be used in this series of problems. The drawing account will be discussed and used in Chapter 12.

Instructions: 2. Open accounts in a general ledger for the accounts listed and record the balances. Allow four lines for each account.

3. Post the entries in the purchases journal prepared in Problem 11-1 to the proper accounts in the accounts payable ledger.

4. Post the total of the purchases journal to the proper accounts in the general ledger.

The ledgers prepared in this problem will be used in Problem 12-2.

Optional problems

★*Supplementary Problem 11-S. Recording and posting purchases on account*

Martha Walker is the owner and manager of The Book Nook. During the month of October of the current year the following purchases on account were made:

Oct. 1.	Wildman School Supplies	$ 147.50
4.	Brant Book Company	49.80
10.	Swift Publishing Company	346.90
16.	Wildman School Supplies	63.80
20.	Clayton Card Company	67.90
27.	Brant Book Company	264.50

Instructions: 1. Record each of the purchases on page 5 of a purchases journal similar to the one illustrated on page 138. Number the invoices in order beginning with No. 81.

The creditors of The Book Nook and the amounts owed to each as of October 1 of the current year are:

Brant Book Company, 795 Sixth Street, City	$ 165.50
Clayton Card Company 45 S. LaSalle Street, Chicago 9	43.75
Swift Publishing Company, 423 Madison Avenue, New York 14	292.80
Wildman School Supplies, 719 Central Parkway, City	91.70

Instructions: 2. Open accounts for the creditors in an accounts payable ledger with balance-column ruling. Allow four lines for each account. Record the balance in each account.

The general ledger accounts that are used in this problem and the balance of the accounts payable account as of October 1 of the current year are:

Acct. No.	Account Title	Balance
21	Accounts Payable	$ 593.75 (Cr.)
51	Purchases	——

Instructions: 3. Open the two accounts in the general ledger. Record the balance of the accounts payable account. Allow four lines for each account.

4. Post the entries from the purchases journal to the proper accounts in the accounts payable ledger.

5. Total and rule the purchases journal; post the total to the proper accounts in the general ledger.

★*Bonus Problem 11-B. Journalizing and posting purchases on account*

The Melvin Store uses several books of original entry. One of these books is a purchases journal similar to the one illustrated on page 138. In this journal, only purchases of merchandise on account are recorded. All other transactions are recorded in other journals.

During the month of October, the Melvin Store completed the transactions given below.

Oct. 1. Paid cash, $300.00, for rent for October.
3. Purchased merchandise on account from Robinson Brothers, $275.00.
6. Sold merchandise on account to J. F. Stocker, $350.00.
8. Received $100.00 from A. D. Hall an account.
9. Purchased merchandise on account from Robinson Brothers, $750.00.
9. Purchased a typewriter on account for use in the office from the Burton Supply Company, $275.00.
10. Purchased merchandise on account from Meyer and Company, $635.00.
13. Paid cash, $11.80, for the telephone bill for September.
16. Sold merchandise on account to C. A. King, $79.50.
20. Purchased merchandise on account from J. Frederick Thompson, $125.00.
20. Purchased a display case for the salesroom on account from Burton Supply Company, $325.00.
20. Received $350.00 from J. F. Stocker on account.
22. Paid $275.00 to Robinson Brothers on account.
23. Purchased merchandise on account from J. Frederick Thompson, $395.00.
27. Sold merchandise on account to L. R. Robbins, $265.50.
29. Purchased supplies for use in the office on account from the Burton Supply Company, $25.40.
31. Received $2,650.00 from cash sales for the month.
31. Purchased merchandise on account from Robinson Brothers, $135.00.

Instructions: 1. From the above transactions select only those that are purchases of merchandise on account and record them on page 7 of the purchases journal. Number the invoices in order beginning with No. 75.

2. Open accounts in an accounts payable ledger for the following creditors. Allow four lines for each account. Record the balances.

Burton Supply Company, 397 Main Street, Muncie.................$ 93.75
Meyer and Company, 819 Westfield Boulevard, Indianapolis........ ——
Robinson Brothers, 27 East Fifth Street, Peoria................... 425.50
J. Frederick Thompson, 2901 Mound Street, St. Louis............. ——

3. Open accounts in the general ledger for Account No. 21, Accounts Payable, and Account No. 51, Purchases. Allow four lines for each account. Record the credit balance of the accounts payable account, $519.25.

4. Post the entries from the purchases journal to the proper accounts in the accounts payable ledger.

5. Total and rule the purchases journal; post the total to the proper accounts in the general ledger.

Chapter 12

Recording cash payments

Importance of accurate cash records

Cash payments and cash receipts are among the most frequent of business transactions. Those who own or operate a business should know at all times the amount of cash paid out, the amount of cash received, and the amount of cash on hand. A plan for recording these facts in detail is therefore very important.

Making cash payments

A transaction in which cash is paid is known as a *cash payments transaction*. Most businesses issue a check for each cash payment transaction. Checks are used not only because it is unsafe to send coins or bills through the mails, but also because a check is good evidence that payment has been made. Morton Supplies makes all cash payments by check.

The immediate record of a cash payment — the check stub

When a cash payment is made by check, the check stub is the immediate record of the transaction. The check stub and the check issued by Morton Supplies in payment for rent for November are illustrated below.

Check and check stub

Writing the check stub

The check stub should be filled out completely so that the bookkeeper will have all the information needed for making the entry. The check stub should always be filled out before the check is written. If this is not done, blank stubs often are found in the checkbook after the checks have been sent out. The information that should be on the stubs may be forgotten.

A record should be kept on the check stubs of all deposits made and all checks written. This record makes it possible to know the amount of cash in the bank at all times. This record also prevents the depositor's writing a check for more than he has on deposit. The method of keeping the record on the check stub is shown in the illustration on page 149.

The amount of each deposit is added to the previous balance. The amount of each check is subtracted from the previous balance plus the deposit, if a deposit has been made. The stub, therefore, shows the new bank balance after each check has been written. The writer of the check also writes on the check stub (1) the check number, (2) the date, (3) the name of the one who is to receive the check, and (4) the purpose for which the check is written.

Writing the check

An order in writing, signed by the depositor, ordering a bank to pay cash from his account is known as a *check*. The one who orders the bank to pay cash from his account is called the *drawer*. The one to whom the bank is ordered to pay the cash is called the *payee*. In the illustration on the preceding page, Morton Supplies is the drawer and Modern Realty Company is the payee.

In writing a check the drawer should fill in (1) the date, (2) the name of the payee, (3) the amount in figures, (4) the amount in words, and (5) his signature.

The three-column cash payments journal

A special journal in which only cash payments are recorded is called a *cash payments journal*. The cash payments journal used by Morton Supplies is shown below.

	DATE	ACCOUNT DEBITED	CHK. NO.	POST. REF.	GENERAL DEBIT	ACCOUNTS PAYABLE DEBIT	CASH CREDIT	
					1	2	3	
1								1
2								2
3								3

CASH PAYMENTS JOURNAL   PAGE

The cash payments journal contains columns in which to record:

1. The date of the transaction.
2. The name of the account to be debited for each transaction.
3. The number of the check that is issued.
4. The posting reference.
5. The debit and credit amounts.

The complete entry for each cash payment transaction is recorded on a single line of the cash payments journal. Each cash payments transaction is a decrease in the asset Cash. For each entry, therefore, Cash is credited. A special Cash Credit amount column is provided for recording the amount of each cash payment. The use of a special column for each cash credit saves time in posting to the cash account in the general ledger because only the total of the Cash Credit column is posted.

Each cash payment to a creditor decreases the amount of the liability Accounts Payable. Each payment to a creditor is therefore debited to Accounts Payable. Because such transactions occur frequently, time can be saved in posting if a special column is provided for Accounts Payable Debit.

Many cash payments transactions affect accounts for which there are no special columns. All payments of cash for which special columns are not provided are recorded in the General Debit amount column.

Cash payments entry No. 1 — paying rent expense

November 2, 1962. Paid cash, $180.00, for November rent. Issued Check No. 172.

Check Stub No. 172 is the immediate record for this cash payments transaction. The entry to record this transaction is made on the first line of the cash payments journal as follows:

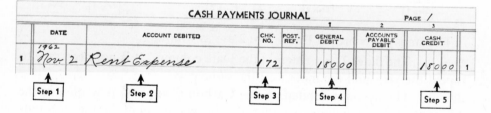

Note that the entire entry for this cash payment is written on one line. The parts of this entry are: (1) the date, (2) the name of the account to be debited, (3) the check number, (4) the amount debited, and (5) the amount credited.

The steps in recording Entry No. 1 are as follows:

Step 1. The year, 1962, is written at the top of the Date column. The month and day, Nov. 2, are written on the first line of the Date column.

Step 2. The name of the account to be debited, Rent Expense, is written in the Account Debited column. Every payment of an expense causes a debit to some expense account.

Step 3. The number of the check, 172, is written in the Check No. column.

Step 4. The amount, $180.00, is recorded in the General Debit column. Rent is paid only once each month; therefore, a special column for Rent Expense Debit would not save time in posting.

Step 5. The amount, $180.00, is also recorded in the Cash Credit column. Every time a cash payment is recorded, the amount will be recorded in the Cash Credit column. The word "Cash" is not written because there is a special column for cash credits.

Step 6. A check mark is placed on the check stub after the check number to show that the check has been recorded. (See the check mark on the check stub on page 149.)

Cash payments entry No. 2 — paying cash on account

November 7, 1962. Paid cash, $196.80, to Acme Carbon Company on account. Issued Check No. 173.

The entry to record this transaction is made on the second line of the cash payments journal as shown below.

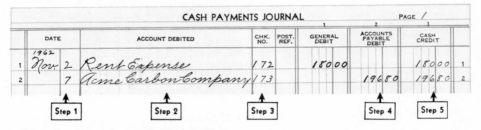

The steps in recording Entry No. 2 are as follows:

Step 1. The date, 7, is written in the Date column. It is not necessary to repeat the year and the month on the same page.

Step 2. The account debited, Acme Carbon Company, is written in the Account Debited column so that the proper account in the accounts payable ledger will be debited.

Step 3. The check number, 173, is written in the Check No. column.

Step 4. The amount, $196.80, is recorded in the special column Accounts Payable Debit. Accounts Payable is debited because this liability account in the general ledger is decreased by the amount of the cash payment. Entries to the debit of Accounts Payable occur often. The use of a special column for Accounts Payable Debit saves time in posting to the accounts payable account in the general ledger because only the total is posted.

Step 5. The amount of the cash payment, $196.80, is recorded in the Cash Credit column.

Step 6. A check mark is placed on the check stub to show that the check has been recorded.

152

Cash payments entry No. 3 — cash withdrawal by the proprietor

November 7, 1962. Paid cash, $100.00, to Fred Morton, proprietor, for personal use. Issued Check No. 174.

Assets taken out of the business by the owner are known as *withdrawals*. Withdrawals result in a decrease in proprietorship and are therefore a debit to a proprietorship account. Withdrawals are not debited to the proprietor's capital account but to a separate account called the proprietor's drawing account. When all withdrawals are debited to a drawing account, the proprietor can readily observe how much the withdrawals have been in a fiscal period.

Mr. Morton's drawing account has the title *Fred Morton, Drawing*. It is assigned the account number 32 because it is in the proprietorship section of the ledger.

The entry to record this transaction is made on Line 3 of the cash payments journal as shown below.

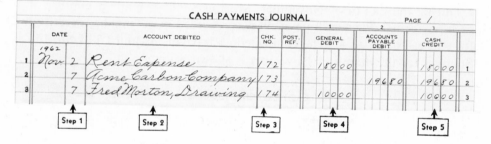

The steps in recording Entry No. 3 are as follows:

Step 1. The date, 7, is written in the Date column.

Step 2. The account debited, Fred Morton, Drawing, is written in the Account Debited column.

Step 3. The check number, 174, is written in the Check No. column.

Step 4. The amount of the withdrawal, $100.00, is recorded in the General Debit column. Withdrawals are not common enough to justify a special column for them. All debits that cannot be recorded in one of the special columns of the cash payments journal are recorded in the General Debit column.

Step 5. The amount of the cash payment, $100.00, is recorded in the Cash Credit column.

Step 6. A check mark is placed on the check stub to show that the check has been recorded.

153

Cash payments entry No. 4 — cash purchase of merchandise

November 8, 1962. Paid cash, $75.00, to Owens Filing Company for purchase of merchandise. Issued Check No. 175.

A cash purchase is recorded in the cash payments journal. Only purchases on account are recorded in the purchases journal.

A special column for Purchases Debit is not provided in the cash payments journal used by Morton Supplies because it makes very few cash purchases. Nearly all of its purchases are made on account.

In recording a purchase of merchandise for cash, the amount of the debit to Purchases is recorded in the General Debit column and the title of the account to be debited, Purchases, is written in the Account Debited column. The amount of the credit to Cash is recorded in the Cash Credit column.

The entry to record the cash purchase from Owens Filing Company is on Line 4 of the cash payments journal shown below.

Completed cash payments journal

During the month of November, Morton Supplies made a number of cash payments. Each cash payment was recorded in the manner described for entries Nos. 1 to 4. The completed cash payments journal of Morton Supplies for the month of November is shown below.

CASH PAYMENTS JOURNAL   PAGE 1

	DATE	ACCOUNT DEBITED	CHK. NO.	POST. REF.	GENERAL DEBIT	ACCOUNTS PAYABLE DEBIT	CASH CREDIT	
1	1962 Nov 2	Rent Expense	172	64	180 00		180 00	1
2	7	Acme Carbon Company	173	✓		196 80	196 80	2
3	7	Fred Morton, Drawing	174	32	100 00		100 00	3
4	8	Purchases	175	51	75 00		75 00	4
5	8	Wills Office Machines	176	✓		714 20	714 20	5
6	8	Miscellaneous Expense	177	63	15 80		15 80	6
7	9	Richmond Metal Company	178	✓		431 00	431 00	7
8	13	Delivery Expense	179	61	27 80		27 80	8
9	15	Salary Expense	180	65	200 00		200 00	9
10	16	Union Paper Company	181	✓		80 40	80 40	10
11	17	Miscellaneous Expense	182	63	10 00		10 00	11
12	26	Arco Typewriter Company	183	✓		280 00	280 00	12
13	28	Delivery Expense	184	61	25 00		25 00	13
14	29	Bell Business Machines	185	✓		88 74	88 74	14
15	30	Fred Morton, Drawing	186	32	100 00		100 00	15
16	30	Salary Expense	187	65	200 00		200 00	16
17	30	Totals			933 60 933 60	1 791 14 1 791 14	2 724 74 2 724 74	17
18					(✓)	(21)	(11)	18

Three-column cash payments journal

The problems of recording withholding taxes and social security taxes when salaries are paid will be dealt with in a later chapter.

Proving the totals of the cash payments journal

When there are a number of cash payments transactions daily, it is customary to pencil foot the columns of the journal at frequent intervals. The pencil footings are used to prove the equality of debits and credits and to prove cash. (The method of proving cash will be explained in a later chapter.) Since Morton Supplies has only a few transactions, daily pencil footings are not shown.

To prove the equality of debits and credits in the cash payments journal illustrated above, the following steps are taken:

Step 1. Each column of the cash payments journal is footed in small pencil figures.

Step 2. The debit totals, $933.60 and $1,791.14, are added on a separate sheet of paper. The sum of the debit totals, $2,724.74, is the same as the total of the Cash Credit column. Therefore, the equality of debits and credits in the cash payments journal is proved.

Ruling and totaling the cash payments journal

After the equality of debits and credits in the cash payments journal is proved, a single line is ruled across all amount columns below the last amount in the Cash Credit column. The totals are recorded below the ruled line. A double line is then ruled under the totals and across all columns except the Account Debited column.

If the cash payments journal has ruled lines at the bottom of the page for totals, the totals are written between these ruled lines. In order to avoid making other entries on this page, it is customary to rule a diagonal line across the page beginning with the date of the last entry and ending with the single ruled line for the total.

Posting the first entry in the cash payments journal

The debit part of the entry. The entry on Line 1 of the cash payments journal shows the amount, $180.00, in the General Debit column. Each amount in the General Debit column must be posted as a debit to the account named in the Account Debited column. The entry on Line 1 is therefore posted as a debit to the account Rent Expense. This account, after the entry has been posted, appears as follows:

The steps in posting Line 1 of the cash payments journal are as follows:

Step 1. The amount, $180.00, is posted to the Debit amount column of the rent expense account in the general ledger.

Step 2. The date is written at the top of the Date column in the account.

Step 3. *CP1* is written in the Post. Ref. column of the account to show that the entry was posted from page 1 of the cash payments journal.

Step 4. The rent expense account number, 64, is written in the Post Ref. column of the cash payments journal to show the completion of the posting of this entry.

An explanation of the account numbers used by Morton Supplies is given on page 262.

The credit part of the entry. The credit to the cash account on Line 1 of the cash payments journal is not posted at this time. Instead of posting each cash payment separately to the cash account in the general ledger, only the total of this column is posted.

Posting additional entries in the General Debit column of the cash payments journal

Each entry in the General Debit column of the cash payments journal is posted separately to the debit side of the account named in the Account Debited column. The amounts in the General Debit column of the cash payments journal are usually posted at frequent intervals during the month. In this way the bookkeeper keeps his work up to date and avoids having to do a large amount of posting at the end of the month.

Note that in the cash payments journal illustrated on page 154 the account number has been entered in the Post Ref. column for each entry in the General Debit column. This shows that all of the amounts in the General Debit column are posted.

Posting each amount in the Accounts Payable Debit column of the cash payments journal

Amounts are posted to creditors' accounts at frequent intervals during the month. It is useful to have the accounts payable ledger show the exact amount owed to each creditor at all times.

The entry on Line 2 of the cash payments journal on page 154 shows a payment to the Acme Carbon Company. This amount is posted to the debit of the creditor's account in the accounts payable ledger. The ledger account of the Acme Carbon Company after the transaction is posted is shown at the top of the following page.

NAME	*Acme Carbon Company*					
ADDRESS	*42 Harbor Ave., Toledo 5, Ohio*					

DATE	ITEMS	POST. REF.	DEBIT	CREDIT	CREDIT BALANCE
1962 Nov 1	Balance	✓			1 9 6 80
7		CP 1	1 9 6 80		—

Step 2 — **Step 4** — **Step 1** — **Step 3**

The steps in posting a cash payment to the Acme Carbon Company account are:

Step 1. The amount, $196.80, which is recorded in the Accounts Payable Debit column of the cash payments journal, is posted as a debit to the Acme Carbon Company account in the accounts payable ledger.

Step 2. The date, 7, is written in the Date column of the account.

Step 3. The debit amount, $196.80, is subtracted from the previous credit balance. If a balance were left, it would be entered in the Credit Balance column. Since there is no balance, a short line is drawn in that column.

Step 4. *CP1* is written in the Post Ref. column of the account to show that the transaction was posted from page 1 of the cash payments journal.

Step 5. A check mark is placed in the Post Ref. column of the cash payments journal to show the completion of the posting. Page numbers are not used when posting to creditors' accounts because the accounts are arranged alphabetically and are not numbered.

Each entry in the Accounts Payable Credit column is posted in the same way. The check mark in the Post. Ref. column opposite each of the amounts in the Accounts Payable Debit column of the cash payments journal on page 154 shows that each amount has been posted.

Posting the totals of the cash payments journal

During the month each of the entries in the General Debit column has been posted individually to the general ledger. Each of the entries in the Accounts Payable Debit column has been posted individually to the accounts payable ledger. At the end of the month the total of the Accounts Payable Debit column is posted to the accounts payable account in the general ledger. Also, at the end of the month the total of the Cash Credit column is posted to the cash account in the general ledger.

The Totals line of the cash payments journal after posting and the two accounts in the general ledger to which the totals are posted are shown on the following page.

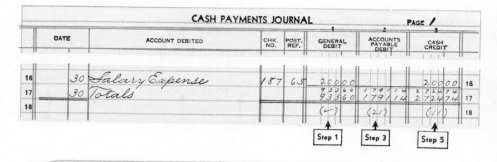

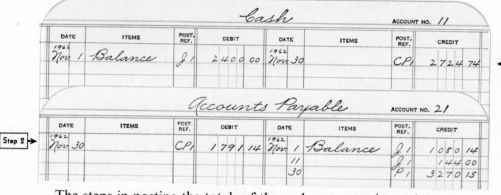

The steps in posting the totals of the cash payments journal are:

Step 1. A check mark is placed in parentheses on the first line below the total of the General Debit column. This check mark shows that the total of the General Debit column is not to be posted. Each amount in this column was posted separately to an account in the general ledger.

Step 2. The total of the Accounts Payable Debit column, $1,791.14, is posted to the debit side of the accounts payable account in the general ledger. The date, 1962, Nov. 30, is written in the Date column of the account. *CP1* is written in the Post. Ref. column of the account to show that this entry came from page 1 of the cash payments journal.

Step 3. The number of the accounts payable account, 21, is written in parentheses on the first line below the total of the Accounts Payable Debit column of the cash payments journal to show completion of the posting of this column.

Step 4. The total of the Cash Credit column, $2,724.74, is posted to the credit of the cash account in the general ledger. The date, 1962, Nov. 30, is written in the Date column of the account. *CP1* is written in the Post. Ref. column of the account.

Step 5. The number of the cash account, 11, is written in parentheses on the first line below the total of the Cash Credit column of the cash payments journal to show the completion of the posting of this column.

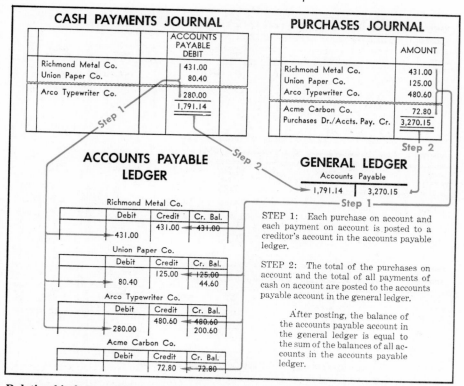

CASH PAYMENTS JOURNAL		
	ACCOUNTS PAYABLE DEBIT	
Richmond Metal Co.	431.00	
Union Paper Co.	80.40	
Arco Typewriter Co.	280.00	
	1,791.14	

Step 1

PURCHASES JOURNAL	
	AMOUNT
Richmond Metal Co.	431.00
Union Paper Co.	125.00
Arco Typewriter Co.	480.60
Acme Carbon Co.	72.80
Purchases Dr./Accts. Pay. Cr.	3,270.15

Step 2

ACCOUNTS PAYABLE LEDGER

GENERAL LEDGER
Accounts Payable

| | 1,791.14 | 3,270.15 |

Step 1

Richmond Metal Co.

	Debit	Credit	Cr. Bal.
		431.00	431.00
	431.00		

Union Paper Co.

	Debit	Credit	Cr. Bal.
		125.00	125.00
	80.40		44.60

Arco Typewriter Co.

	Debit	Credit	Cr. Bal.
		480.60	480.60
	280.00		200.60

Acme Carbon Co.

	Debit	Credit	Cr. Bal.
		72.80	72.80

STEP 1: Each purchase on account and each payment on account is posted to a creditor's account in the accounts payable ledger.

STEP 2: The total of the purchases on account and the total of all payments of cash on account are posted to the accounts payable account in the general ledger.

After posting, the balance of the accounts payable account in the general ledger is equal to the sum of the balances of all accounts in the accounts payable ledger.

Relationship between the accounts payable ledger and the accounts payable account in the general ledger

Accounts payable ledger of Morton Supplies

The accounts payable ledger of Mortons Supplies after all posting for the month of November is completed is shown below and on page 160.

NAME *Acme Carbon Company*
ADDRESS *42 Harbor Ave., Toledo 5, Ohio*

DATE	ITEMS	POST. REF.	DEBIT	CREDIT	CREDIT BALANCE
1962 Nov 1	Balance	✓			196 80
7		CP 1	196 80		
29		P 1		72 80	72 80

NAME *Alfred Supply Company*
ADDRESS *4441 B Street, City*

DATE	ITEMS	POST. REF.	DEBIT	CREDIT	CREDIT BALANCE
1962 Nov 11		P 1		144 00	144 00

Accounts payable ledger — Morton Supplies

NAME	Arco Typewriter Company					
ADDRESS	2424 State Street, City					

DATE	ITEMS	POST. REF.	DEBIT	CREDIT	CREDIT BALANCE
1962 Nov. 7		P1		480 60	480 60
26		CP1	280 00		200 60

NAME	Bell Business Machines					
ADDRESS	424 Broadway, Cleveland 6, Ohio					

DATE	ITEMS	POST. REF.	DEBIT	CREDIT	CREDIT BALANCE
1962 Nov. 1	Balance	✓			88 74
26		P1		397 60	486 34
29		CP1	88 74		397 60

NAME	Metal Desk Company					
ADDRESS	1296 Ash Street, Lansing 3, Michigan					

DATE	ITEMS	POST. REF.	DEBIT	CREDIT	CREDIT BALANCE
1962 Nov. 9		P1		540 35	540 35
19		P1		480 15	1020 50

NAME	Richmond Metal Company					
ADDRESS	464 Belt Drive, Detroit 8, Michigan					

DATE	ITEMS	POST. REF.	DEBIT	CREDIT	CREDIT BALANCE
1962 Nov. 5		P1		431 00	431 00
9		CP1	431 00		—

NAME	Union Paper Company					
ADDRESS	2964 State Street, Chicago 10, Illinois					

DATE	ITEMS	POST. REF.	DEBIT	CREDIT	CREDIT BALANCE
1962 Nov. 1	Balance	✓			80 40
5		P1		125 00	205 40
13		P1		96 45	301 85
16		CP1	80 40		221 45

NAME	Wills Office Machines					
ADDRESS	44 Broadway, Grand Rapids 4, Michigan					

DATE	ITEMS	POST. REF.	DEBIT	CREDIT	CREDIT BALANCE
1962 Nov. 1	Balance	✓			714 20
8		CP1	714 20		
16		P1		646 20	646 20

Accounts payable ledger — Morton Supplies (concluded)

The schedule of accounts payable

In Chapter 11, creditors' accounts in the accounts payable ledger were credited when merchandise was bought from them on account. At the end of the month the controlling account in the general ledger, Accounts Payable, was credited for the total of the purchases journal. The total posted from the purchases journal to the controlling account in the general ledger was equal to the sum of the credits posted to the individual creditors' accounts in the accounts payable ledger.

In this chapter, creditors' accounts in the accounts payable ledger were debited for cash payments to creditors. At the end of the month the controlling account in the general ledger, Accounts Payable, was debited for the total of the Accounts Payable Debit column in the cash payments journal. The total posted from the cash payments journal to the controlling account in the general ledger was equal to the sum of the debits posted to the individual creditors' accounts in the accounts payable ledger.

If all of the posting from the purchases journal and from the cash payments journal was completed accurately, the sum of the balances of the creditors' accounts in the accounts payable ledger should agree with the balance of the controlling account, Accounts Payable, in the general ledger. In making this proof of posting to the accounts payable ledger, all balances of the creditors' accounts are listed and totaled. A list of all creditors that shows the balance owed to each creditor and the total amount owed to all creditors is called a *schedule of accounts payable.*

The following schedule of accounts payable was prepared from the accounts payable ledger shown on pages 159 and 160.

Morton Supplies		
Schedule of Accounts Payable		
November 30, 1962		
Acme Carbon Company	72 80	
Alfred Supply Company	1 44 00	
Arco Typewriter Company	2 00 60	
Bell Business Machines	3 97 60	
Metal Desk Company	1 02 0 50	
Union Paper Company	2 2 1 45	
Wills Office Machines	6 46 20	
Total Accounts Payable		27 03 15

Schedule of accounts payable

The steps used in proving the creditors' accounts in the accounts payable ledger and the controlling account in the general ledger are:

161

Step 1. A list of all creditors who have credit balances at the end of the month is prepared from the accounts payable ledger. The list shows the name of each creditor and the amount owed to each creditor. The amounts are totaled to show the total amount owed to all creditors according to the accounts in the accounts payable ledger. The completed schedule of accounts payable for the month of November is shown on page 161.

Step 2. The controlling account in the general ledger, Accounts Payable, is footed and the balance is determined. The balance is a credit balance and shows the total amount owed to all creditors. The accounts payable account in the general ledger with its footings and balance is shown below.

DATE	ITEMS	POST. REF.	DEBIT	DATE	ITEMS	POST. REF.	CREDIT
1962 Nov. 30		CP1	1 791 14	*1962* Nov. 1	Balance	J1	1 080 14
				11		J1	144 00
				30		P1	3 270 15
					2703.15		4 494 29

Accounts payable account in the general ledger

Step 3. The balance of the accounts payable account in the general ledger is compared with the total of the schedule of accounts payable prepared from the accounts payable ledger. The balance of the accounts payable account of Morton Supplies on November 30 is $2,703.15. The total of the schedule of accounts payable on November 30 is also $2,703.15. When the two amounts agree, it is assumed that all posting affecting creditors' accounts and Accounts Payable is accurate.

The accounts payable account shown above receives posting from three journals: the purchases journal, the cash payments journal, and the general journal. The two credit entries from the general journal will be explained in Chapter 15, but it is desirable to show the complete account at this time.

Using automated equipment to record and post cash payments

When automated equipment is used to record and post cash payments, a clerk makes punched cards or tapes for all cash payments from the immediate record of each cash payment. These cards or tapes are fed into a machine that makes a complete record of all the cash payments. The cards or tapes are then fed into a machine that posts the record of cash payments to accounts in the accounts payable ledger and to accounts in the general ledger. The planning of the automation procedures for cash payments is based on the principles of bookkeeping taught in this chapter.

Increasing your business vocabulary

What is the meaning of each of the following?

(a) cash payments transaction
(b) check
(c) drawer
(d) payee

(e) cash payments journal
(f) withdrawals
(g) schedule of accounts payable

Chapter questions

1. What are two reasons for making cash payments by check?
2. When a cash payment is made by check, what is the immediate record of the transaction?
3. Why should the check stub be written before the check is written?
4. How many lines of the cash payments journal are needed to record a cash payments transaction?
5. Why does the cash payments journal have a special column for Accounts Payable Debit?
6. What payments of cash are recorded in the General Debit amount column?
7. What account is debited and what account is credited for the payment of rent?
8. What accounts are debited and what account is credited when a cash payment is made to a creditor?
9. In what section of the ledger does the proprietor's drawing account appear?
10. In what journal are cash purchases of merchandise recorded?
11. How are the totals of the cash payments journal proved?
12. Why is the amount of each cash payment not posted individually to the credit of the cash account?
13. Why is a check mark placed below the total of the General Debit amount column in the cash payments journal at the time of posting the totals?
14. What is the source of the account balances used in preparing the schedule of accounts payable?

Cases for discussion

1. Mr. R. L. Coleman writes only the name of the payee and the amount on a check stub when he writes checks. What problems does this raise with the bookkeeper when he gets ready to make an entry in the cash payments journal?
2. Fred Atkins, who has never studied bookkeeping, does not understand why, when a cash payment entry is recorded in the cash payments journal, the name of the account debited and the name of the account credited are not both written. How would you explain the reason to him?
3. The Jones Hardware Company has a special column in its cash payments journal for rent expense. In the chapter you have just studied there is no special column for rent expense. Explain why the plan you have studied is a satisfactory plan.

163

Drill for understanding

Drill 12-A. Analyzing cash payments

Instructions: 1. For each cash payment indicate (a) what account will be debited and (b) what account will be credited.

(1) Paid cash to Harmon and Company, a creditor, on account.

(2) Paid cash for advertising.

(3) Paid cash for salaries.

(4) Paid cash for rent.

(5) Paid cash for personal use.

(6) Paid cash for office equipment.

(7) Paid cash for repairs on delivery truck.

(8) Paid cash for cleaning windows.

(9) Paid cash for merchandise.

Application problems

Problem 12-1. Recording cash payments of a retail dress shop

The following checks were issued by the Bell Dress Shop during March of the current year:

Mar. 1. Check No. 210 for $360.20 to Street Brothers on account.
2. Check No. 211 for $200.00 to L. B. Harris for March rent.
9. Check No. 212 for $100.00 to Molly Bell as a withdrawal.
12. Check No. 213 for $1,560.60 to Lansing Dress Company on account.
13. Check No. 214 for $235.00 to Home Clothing Company on account.
14. Check No. 215 for $12.75 to the Bell Telephone Company for March telephone bill. (Miscellaneous Expense)
15. Check No. 216 for $518.40 to Barton and Lane on account.
19. Check No. 217 for $780.00 to Allen & Company on account.
25. Check No. 218 for $1,097.30 to Walker Apparel Company on account.
28. Check No. 219 for $424.80 to Home Clothing Company on account.
29. Check No. 220 for $160.00 for cash purchase of merchandise.
30. Check No. 221 for $250.00 for salaries.
30. Check No. 222 for $150.00 to Molly Bell as a withdrawal.

Instructions: 1. Record each of these cash payments transactions on page 3 of a cash payments journal similar to the one illustrated on page 154.

2. Foot, prove, total, and rule the cash payments journal.

The cash payments journal for this problem will also be used in Problem 12-2.

Problem 12-2. Posting the cash payments journal and making a schedule of accounts payable

This problem requires the accounts payable ledger and the general ledger used in Problem 11-2 and the cash payments journal in Problem 12-1. If these are not available, complete Exercise 12-A in the Appendix.

Instructions: 1. Post the amounts in the Accounts Payable Debit column to the creditors' accounts in the accounts payable ledger.

2. Post the amounts in the General Debit column to the general ledger.

3. Post the totals of the special columns to the general ledger.

4. Prepare a schedule of accounts payable from the accounts payable ledger. If the total of the schedule of accounts payable does not agree with the balance of the accounts payable account, recheck your work until the error is found.

164

Optional problems

If you are not using the workbook correlating with this textbook, complete Exercise 12-B in the Appendix instead of either of these optional problems.

★ Supplementary Problem 12-S. *Recording and posting cash payments*

J. R. Dillon owns a gift shop. During the month of October of the current year he completed the cash payments transactions given below. He made all cash payments by check. The check numbers began with No. 391.

Oct. 2. Paid $125.00 for rent for October.
  4. Paid $100.00 to J. M. Watson Company on account.
  10. Paid $155.60 to T. M. Adams Company on account.
  13. Paid $300.00 to Excel Greeting Card Company on account.
  15. Paid $96.00 for semimonthly payroll. (Salary Expense)
  16. Paid $138.00 to J. M. Watson Company on account.
  16. Paid $75.00 to A. L. Grant Company for a cash purchase of merchandise.
  18. Paid $153.60 to Marlin Company on account.
  20. Paid $14.20 for telephone bill. (Miscellaneous Expense)
  20. Paid $13.90 for electric bill. (Miscellaneous Expense)
  23. Paid Clayton Card Company $79.80 on account.
  30. Withdrew $200.00 for personal use.
  30. Paid $100.00 to A. J. Frank Company on account.
  31. Paid $96.00 for semimonthly payroll.

Instructions; 1. Record the cash payments transactions on page 10 of a cash payments journal similar to the one illustrated on page 154.

2. Foot, prove, total, and rule the cash payments journal.

3. Open the following accounts in the general ledger, using the account numbers shown in parentheses. Record the balance for each account for which a balance is given. Date the balance October 1 of the current year.

Cash (11), $1,760.00   Miscellaneous Expense (61)
Accounts Payable (21), $1,786.25   Rent Expense (62)
J. R. Dillon, Drawing (32)   Salary Expense (63)
Purchases (51)

4. Post the amounts in the Accounts Payable Debit column to the creditors' accounts in the accounts payable ledger.

5. Post the amounts in the General Debit column and the totals of the special columns to the proper accounts in the general ledger.

6. Prepare a schedule of accounts payable.

★ Bonus Problem 12-B. *Recording and posting cash payments transactions*

A. R. Hoskins is the owner of the Hoskins Gift Shop. He finds he can save time in posting if he has a cash payments journal with a special column for Purchases Debit and a special column for Miscellaneous Expense Debit. The form of cash payments journal he uses is shown at the top of the following page.

Date	Account Debited	Chk. No.	Post. Ref.	General Debit	Accounts Payable Debit	Purchases Debit	Misc. Expense Debit	Cash Credit

During the month of October of the current year he had the following cash payments transactions, all of which were paid by check.

Oct. 1. Paid $300.00 for October rent. (Check numbers begin with No. 249)
  2. Paid $14.80 for telephone bill. (Miscellaneous Expense)
  3. Paid $16.20 for electric bill. (Miscellaneous Expense)
  3. Paid $238.00 to J. M. Watson Company on account.
  4. Paid $148.20 to Globe Company for cash purchase of merchandise.
  5. Paid $28.60 to T. M. Adams Company on account.
  8. Paid $14.50 for water bill. (Miscellaneous Expense)
  10. Paid $200.00 to A. J. Frank Company on account.
  12. Paid $250.00 to Excel Greeting Card Company on account.
  16. Paid $39.80 to Bauer & Bruns for cash purchase of merchandise.
  22. Paid $203.60 to Marlin Company on account.
  26. Paid $296.30 to Peerless Company for cash purchase of merchandise.
  26. Paid $17.50 for neon lighting tubes. (Miscellaneous Expense)
  29. Paid $127.00 to T. M. Adams Company on account.
  30. Paid $65.00 for salary of clerk.
  30. Paid $179.80 to Clayton Card Company on account.
  30. Withdrew $300.00 for personal use.

Instructions: 1. Record each of the cash payments in a cash journal with five amount columns as shown above.

2. Foot, prove, total, and rule the cash payments journal.

3. Open the following accounts in the general ledger using the account numbers shown in parentheses. Record the balance for each account for which a balance is given. Date the balance October 1 of the current year.

Cash (11), $3,700.00   Miscellaneous Expense (61)
Accounts Payable (21), $1,786.25   Rent Expense (62)
A. R. Hoskins, Drawing (32)   Salary Expense (63)
Purchases (51)

4. Post the amounts in the Accounts Payable Debit column to the creditors' accounts in the accounts payable ledger.

5. Post the amounts in the General Debit column and the totals of the special columns to the proper accounts in the general ledger.

6. Prepare a schedule of accounts payable.

Chapter 13

Recording the selling of merchandise on account

Selling merchandise

Morton Supplies sells merchandise both for cash and on account. A transaction in which cash is received at the time of sale is known as a *cash sale*. A transaction in which merchandise is sold with an agreement that the amount is to be paid at a later date is known as a *sale on account*. Other terms used to describe a sale on account are *charge sale* or a *sale on credit*. Those to whom a business sells merchandise are known as *customers*. A customer to whom a sale is made on account is known as a *charge customer*.

The immediate record — the sales slip

A business form that shows all the details about a sale is known as a *sales slip* or *sales ticket*. Morton Supplies uses a sales slip as its immediate record of each sale on account. A copy of a sales slip is the basis for the bookkeeping entry required for each sale on account.

In most stores in which sales are made on account, each salesclerk has his own sales slip book in which to record each sale as it is completed. Each sales slip in the book is numbered, and the salesclerk must account for each number. The original copy of the sales slip is usually kept by the store as a basis for its bookkeeping records.

The customer is often required to sign the original sales slip to show that he approves the charge to his account. Usually one of the carbon copies of the sales slip is handed to the customer or is wrapped with the merchandise that is given or delivered to him.

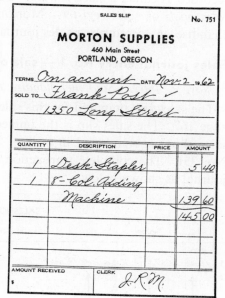

Sales slip

The form and the arrangement of items on sales slips vary with the particular needs of the business. The sales slip on page 167 was prepared by salesclerk JRM for a sale made on account to Frank Post on November 2, 1962. This sales slip shows the following information:

1. The sales slip number.
2. The terms of the sale.
3. The date of the sale.
4. The name and the address of the customer.
5. The quantity and the description of each item.
6. The price of each item.
7. The total amount of the sale.
8. The amount of cash received at the time of the sale.
9. The salesclerk's number or initials.

If a business needs to record other information on its sales slips, additional space is provided. For example, a business with more than one department may provide space for the department name or number.

On many items sold by retailers, the retailer must collect sales taxes for the government. Methods of recording taxes collected from the consumer and the paying of these taxes to tax authorities will be discussed in Chapter 28.

The sales journal

A special journal in which all sales of merchandise on account are recorded is called a *sales journal*. Other terms used for sales journal are *sales book* or *sales register*. Morton Supplies records all sales of merchandise on account in a sales journal.

Sales journal entry No. 1 — sale of merchandise on account

Nov. 2, 1962. Sold merchandise to Frank Post on account, $145.00.

The sales slip prepared for this sale on account transaction is shown on page 167. The sales slip is the immediate record of the transaction. The sales slips are numbered in order. The sales slip for this transaction is No. 751. The complete transaction is recorded on one line in the sales journal as shown below.

The steps in recording Sales Slip No. 751 are as follows:

Step 1.   The year, the month, and the day of the sales slip are recorded in the Date column on the first line of the sales journal.

Step 2.   The number of the sales slip, 751, is recorded in the No. of Sale column.

Step 3.   The name of the customer to whom the sale was made, Frank Post, is written in the Account Debited column.

Step 4.   The amount of the sale on account, $145.00, is recorded in the Amount column.

Step 5.   A check mark is placed on the sales slip at the right of Frank Post's name to show that the sales slip has been recorded.   (See illustration of sales slip on page 167.)

The debit part of the entry in the sales journal.   The sale to Frank Post on account increases the amount to be collected from customers. Amounts to be collected from customers are known as *accounts receivable*. All accounts receivable are assets.   Therefore the asset account Accounts Receivable in the general ledger must be debited for each sale on account recorded in the sales journal.

It is not necessary to write the words *Accounts Receivable Debit* on each line of the sales journal. It is understood that each amount in the Amount column is a debit to the asset account Accounts Receivable in the general ledger.

The credit part of the entry in the sales journal.   Each sale of merchandise results in an income to the business.   The account in the general ledger in which all income from sales is shown has the title *Sales*. All incomes are recorded as credits because they increase proprietorship.   Therefore the income account Sales in the general ledger must be credited for each sale on account recorded in the sales journal.

It is not necessary to write the words *Sales Credit* on each line of the sales journal. It is understood that all amounts in the Amount column are credits to the income account Sales in the general ledger.

All of the credits to the sales account in the general ledger will be posted as a single amount when the total of the column is posted at the end of the month.

The accounts receivable ledger

Morton Supplies keeps all accounts with charge customers in an accounts receivable ledger. The accounts receivable ledger used by Morton Supplies has balance-column ruling similar to the ruling used in the accounts payable ledger. The only difference is that for customers' accounts the balance column is headed Debit Balance instead of Credit Balance.

Posting individual items from the sales journal

Amounts to be collected from others are assets. Each sale on account increases the amount to be collected from a customer. Each amount in the sales journal, therefore, must be posted as a debit to a customer's account in the accounts receivable ledger. Each customer's account is on a separate page in the accounts receivable ledger. The customers' accounts in the accounts receivable ledger are arranged in alphabetic order and do not have account numbers.

The entry in the sales journal for the sale to Frank Post and his account in the accounts receivable ledger after this entry has been posted are shown below.

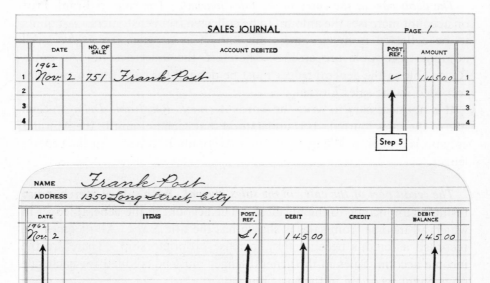

The name and the address of the customer are written on the first two lines of the customer's account. As Frank Post is a new charge customer, his address is obtained from the sales slip.

The steps in posting the sale to Frank Post are as follows:

Step 1. The amount of the sale on account, $145.00, is recorded in the Debit column of the Frank Post account.

Step 2. The year, month, and day are written in the Date column.

Step 3. The amount of the debit, $145.00, is extended to the Debit Balance column of his account. As there is no previous balance in this account, this debit is also the balance.

Step 4. *S1* is written in the Post. Ref. column of the account to show that the entry came from page 1 of the sales journal.

Step 5. A check mark is placed in the Post. Ref. column of the sales journal to show completion of the posting.

Recording additional sales slips in the sales journal

Each sales slip for merchandise sold on account is recorded in the same manner as the Frank Post sales slip. All the essential information on each sales slip is summarized on one line of the sales journal. Entries in the sales journal are posted daily to the accounts receivable ledger in order to keep the individual accounts with customers up to date.

Posting additional amounts to a customer's account

The effect of posting additional entries to a customer's account is shown in the following illustration:

DATE	ITEMS	POST. REF.	DEBIT	CREDIT	DEBIT BALANCE
NAME *Walter Love*					
ADDRESS *360 Elm Street, City*					
1962 Nov. 1	*Balance*	✓			69 00
9		S1	295 40		364 40

The entry of November 9 in the sales journal is posted to Walter Love's account as shown above. The amount, $295.40, is recorded in the Debit column of the customer's account. It is then added to the previous balance, and the new balance, $364.40, is recorded in the Debit Balance column. The page of the sales journal from which this entry came, S1, is written in the Post. Ref. column of the customer's account. The completion of the posting is indicated by placing a check mark in the Post. Ref. column of the sales journal.

The sales journal of Morton Supplies

The complete sales journal of Morton Supplies for the month of November, showing all entries to customers' accounts posted to the accounts receivable ledger, is shown on the following page.

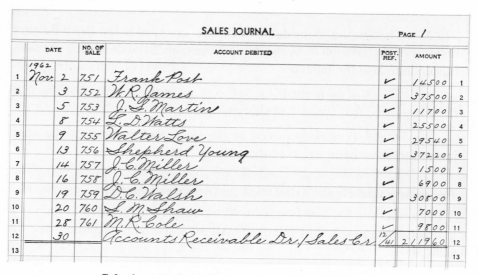

	DATE	NO. OF SALE	ACCOUNT DEBITED	POST. REF.	AMOUNT	
1	1962 Nov. 2	751	Frank Post	✓	145 00	1
2	3	752	W. R. James	✓	375 00	2
3	5	753	J. L. Martin	✓	117 00	3
4	8	754	L. D. Watts	✓	255 00	4
5	9	755	Walter Love	✓	295 40	5
6	13	756	Shepherd Young	✓	372 20	6
7	14	757	J. C. Miller	✓	15 00	7
8	16	758	J. C. Miller	✓	69 00	8
9	19	759	D. C. Walsh	✓	308 00	9
10	20	760	L. M. Shaw	✓	70 00	10
11	28	761	M. R. Cole	✓	98 00	11
12	30		Accounts Receivable Dr./Sales Cr.	12/41	2119 60	12
13						13

Sales journal after posting to all customers' accounts

Ruling the sales journal

The sales journal is totaled and ruled with single and double lines as shown above. A single line is ruled across the Amount column only. The amount column is totaled and the total, $2,119.60, is written immediately below the single line. Double lines are then ruled across all of the columns except the Account Debited column.

The debit part of the total line of the sales journal

The total of the Amount column of the sales journal is the sum of the amounts posted as debits to the individual accounts in the accounts receivable ledger. A summary of all of these postings must be posted to the general ledger in order to complete the assets section of the general ledger. Therefore, the total of the Amount column of the sales journal is posted as a debit to the accounts receivable account in the general ledger.

In order for the sales journal to show that the total is to be posted to the accounts receivable account in the general ledger, *Accounts Receivable Dr.* is written in the sales journal on the line with the total. The date, 30, is written in the Date column. (See the illustration above.)

The credit part of the total line of the sales journal

The total of the Amount column of the sales journal is the amount of merchandise sold on account during the month. Sales are an income to the business. In bookkeeping, all incomes are recorded as credits. The account in the general ledger in which all sales of merchandise are recorded has the title *Sales*. The total of the Amount column of the sales journal is therefore posted as a credit to the sales account in the general ledger.

172

In order for the sales journal to show that the total is to be posted as a credit to the sales account, *Sales Cr.* is written on the total line of the sales journal immediately after *Accounts Receivable Dr.* The names of the two accounts are separated by a diagonal line. A diagonal line is also placed in the Post. Ref. column of the sales journal to show that the total is to be posted to two accounts. (See the illustration on page 172.)

Posting the total of the sales journal

The Total line of the sales journal and the two accounts to which the totals are posted are shown below.

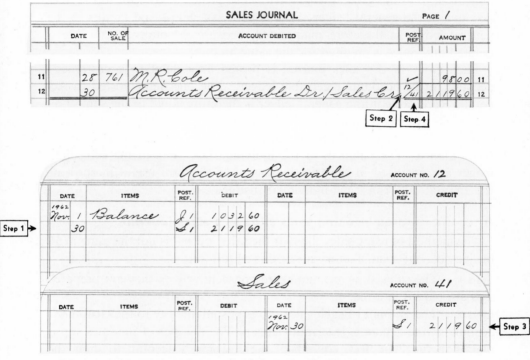

The steps in posting the total of the sales journal are:

Step 1. The total of the sales journal, $2,119.60, is posted to the debit of the controlling account Accounts Receivable in the general ledger. The date, 30, is written in the Date column. *S1* is written in the Post. Ref. column of the accounts receivable account to show that the posting came from page 1 of the sales journal.

Step 2. The number of the accounts receivable account, 12, is written in the left half of the Post. Ref. column of the sales journal to show completion of the posting of the debit part of the total.

Step 3.   The total of the sales journal is also posted to the credit of the sales account in the general ledger. The date, 1962, Nov. 30, is written in the Date column. *S1* is written in the Post. Ref. column of the sales account to show the source of the entry.

Step 4.   The sales account number, 41, is written in the right half of the Post. Ref. column of the sales journal to show the completion of the posting of the credit part of the total.

Relationship of the sales journal, the accounts receivable ledger, and the general ledger

The total of the sales journal is posted as a debit to the accounts receivable account in the general ledger. It is also posted as a credit to the sales account in the general ledger. The equality of debits and credits in the general ledger is therefore maintained, because Accounts Receivable is debited and Sales is credited for the same amount.

Each entry in the sales journal is posted as a debit to a customer's account in the accounts receivable ledger. The one debit posted to Accounts Receivable in the general ledger is therefore equal to the sum of all the debits posted to the individual accounts in the accounts receivable ledger.   The balance of the accounts receivable account is used in the trial balance. The balances of the individual accounts in the subsidiary ledger are not used in the trial balance, but they are useful in showing the amount due from each individual customer.

A second method — using sales slips as a sales journal

The method of using sales slips for the sales journal is not the same in all businesses, but a satisfactory method is as follows:

Step 1.   The sales slips are numbered consecutively as they are prepared and are placed in a file.

Step 2.   The amount of each sales slip is posted directly to the customer's account in the accounts receivable ledger. The number of the sales slip is placed in the Post. Ref. column of the customer's account to show the source of the entry. A check mark is placed at the right of the customer's name on the sales slip to show that the slip has been posted.

Step 3.   The amounts of all sales slips are totaled at the end of the month. Ordinarily an adding machine is used for this purpose.

Step 4.   The total of the sales slips for the period is recorded in a general journal as a debit to Accounts Receivable and a credit to Sales. Such an entry is illustrated at the top of the opposite page.

Step 5.   The journal entry is posted to the debit of Accounts Receivable and to the credit of Sales in the general ledger.

174

	DATE	NAME OF ACCOUNT	POST. REF.	DEBIT	CREDIT	
32	31	*Accounts Receivable*		2 1 9 6 1 0		32
33		*Sales*			2 1 9 6 1 0	33
34		*Sales on account for*				34
35		*October.*				35
36						36

GENERAL JOURNAL — PAGE *15*

Using automation to record and post sales on account

When the volume of business is large enough to justify the investment in automated equipment, it is possible to record and post sales on account in the same manner that was described for the recording and the posting of purchases on account. The procedure is as follows:

A clerk makes a record of each sales slip on a punched card or tape. This punched card or tape is then fed into machines that are set up to do the following:

1. Record all sales slips in a sales journal record.
2. Post the sales slips to the proper customers' accounts.
3. Record on stock cards the number of units of each item that was sold and automatically subtract this number to get a new balance for each item of merchandise on hand.

Increasing your business vocabulary

What is the meaning of each of the following:

(a) cash sale
(b) sale on account
(c) charge customer
(d) sales slip
(e) sales journal
(f) accounts receivable

Chapter questions

1. What are some other terms that are used to describe a sale on account?
2. What is the immediate record for entries of sales on account?
3. What kinds of sales are recorded in a sales journal?
4. What are some other terms that are used for sales journal?
5. What important facts are recorded on one line of the sales journal for a sale on account?
6. What is the name of the ledger in which Morton Supplies keeps its accounts with charge customers?
7. What is the difference between the headings of the amount columns of the accounts receivable ledger accounts and those of the accounts payable ledger accounts?

8. Why are sales on account posted to the debit of customers' accounts?

9. What is the meaning of "S1" in the Post. Ref. column of the customer's account illustrated on page 171?

10. What is written on the total line of the sales journal to show that the amount is to be posted to two accounts in the general ledger?

11. Why is a diagonal line placed in the Post. Ref. column on the total line of the sales journal?

Cases for discussion

1. A grocer sold a typewriter that he had used in the store. He recorded this transaction in the sales journal. Was this procedure correct? Why?

2. Ronald Eastman makes 450 sales on account in an average month. He records each sale in the sales journal, from which he posts to the subsidiary and the general ledgers.

   (a) How much work might be saved by posting directly from the sales slips to the customers' accounts in the subsidiary ledger?

   (b) If this method were followed, how should he record the total sales for the month?

Drill for understanding

Drill 13-A. Accounts receivable

Warren's Hardware keeps its customers' accounts in its general ledger. A portion of the debit column of the trial balance for the year ended December 31 of the current year is shown at the left.

Cash..................	$3,000.00
Merchandise Inventory..	5,000.00
Frederick Adams.......	130.00
M. R. Cole...........	150.00
W. R. James.........	90.00
J. M. Smith..........	70.00
K. R. Jones..........	250.00
Joseph Peart..........	80.00
J. W. Owens..........	75.00
M. W. Morrison.......	150.00
B. J. Cutler...........	95.00
M. R. Abbott.........	175.00
Supplies..............	110.00
Prepaid Insurance......	90.00

Instructions: Answer the following questions:

(1) What was the total amount due from customers?

(2) If Warren's Hardware had used an accounts receivable ledger:

   (a) What is the name of the controlling account that he would have used?

   (b) What would be the balance of this controlling account on the trial balance of December 31?

   (c) How many lines would be saved on the trial balance?

Application problems

Problem 13-1. *Recording sales on account for a wholesale grocer*

The following sales of merchandise on account were made by Hoffman Wholesale Groceries during November of the current year:

DATE	SALE NO.	CUSTOMER	AMOUNT OF SALE
Nov. 1	201	M. E. Creager	$180.00
3	202	Hull Grocery	260.40
5	203	J. B. Johnston	70.80
8	204	R. K. Wise	210.00
10	205	Stambaugh Bros.	390.00
14	206	Bard and Co.	240.60
17	207	T. D. Shirk	160.20
17	208	R. K. Wise	210.30
19	209	M. E. Creager	190.40
20	210	Stambaugh Bros.	110.10
22	211	Hull Grocery	210.70
25	212	J. B. Johnston	150.80
26	213	Bard and Co.	80.00
26	214	T. D. Shirk	250.50
29	215	R. K. Wise	110.80

Instructions: 1. Record each of these transactions on page 11 of a sales journal similar to the one illustrated on page 172.

2. Total and rule the sales journal.

The sales journal prepared in this problem will also be used in Problem 13-2.

Problem 13-2. *Opening two ledgers and posting a sales journal*

Instructions: 1. Open accounts for the customers of Hoffman Wholesale Groceries listed below in an accounts receivable ledger that has balance-column ruling. Use the customer's account on page 171 as a model. Allow five lines for each account. Record the balances as of November 1 of the current year.

Bard and Co., 20 Broadway, Hilton.	$ 500.30
M. E. Creager, 698 Railroad Street, City.	305.20
Hull Grocery, 2932 Daly Avenue, City.	220.40
J. B. Johnston, 598 June Street, City.	165.00
T. D. Shirk, 3625 Morton Street, City.	340.80
Stambaugh Bros., 336 Main Street, City.	360.40
R. K. Wise, Kingston.	130.00

2. Post the entries in the sales journal that you prepared in Problem 13-1 to the appropriate customers' accounts in the accounts receivable ledger.

3. Open the five accounts in the general ledger that are needed in this problem and at the end of the next chapter. These accounts, their account numbers, and their balances are shown below. Allow four lines for each account. Record their balances as of November 1 of the current year.

ACCOUNT TITLE	ACCT. NO.	BALANCE
Cash	11	$3,460.20 (Dr.)
Accounts Receivable	12	2,022.10 (Dr.)
Office Supplies	13	300.00 (Dr.)
R. J. Hoffman, Capital	31	5,782.30 (Cr.)
Sales	41	————

4. Post the total of the sales journal to the appropriate accounts in the general ledger.

The accounts receivable ledger and the general ledger prepared in this problem will also be used in Problem 14-2.

Optional problems

★Supplementary Problem 13-S. Recording and posting sales on account

Max Walton is the owner and manager of the Walton Hi-Fi Store. During the month of July of the current year the following sales on account were made:

July 2. D. E. Wilkes		$ 274.80
5. L. A. Gaines		461.50
9. Henry Newton		105.32
13. Stephen Corey		152.60
18. L. A. Gaines		75.00
24. Stephen Corey		53.96
28. Roger Stimson		109.60
30. L. A. Gaines		113.50

Instructions: 1. Record each of the sales listed above. Use page 7 of a sales journal similar to the one illustrated on page 173. Number the sales in order beginning with No. 315.

2. Total and rule the sales journal.

3. Open accounts for the customers in an accounts receivable ledger that has balance-column ruling and record their balances. Allow four lines for each customer's account. The customers' accounts and their balances are as follows:

Stephen Corey, 4318 Kings Road, City	$ 103.85
L. A. Gaines, 1515 Madison Avenue, City	————
Henry Newton, 4010 Broadway, City	155.50
Roger Stimson, 723 Suffolk Street, City	87.50
D. E. Wilkes, 2133 Mellon Street, City	321.15

4. Post the entries in the sales journal to the proper customers' accounts in the accounts receivable ledger.

5. Open the two accounts in the general ledger that are needed in this problem: Accounts Receivable, 12, and Sales, 41. Record the debit balance of the accounts receivable account, $668.00, as of July 1 of the current year.

6. Post the total of the sales journal to the appropriate accounts in the general ledger.

★ *Bonus Problem 13-B. Journalizing and posting sales on account in a columnar sales journal*

The Corey Manufacturing Company makes kitchen utensils and appliances. It sells merchandise to customers on account and it charges the customers for delivery costs. The Corey Manufacturing Company wants its sales journal to show both the amount of each sale and the delivery costs. It therefore uses a sales journal with the following headings:

SALES JOURNAL   Page 3

Date	No. of Sale	Account Debited	Post. Ref.	Accounts Receivable Debit	Sales Credit	Delivery Expense Credit

The sales on account transactions and the delivery costs for the month of March of the current year are:

Date	Customer	Amount of Sale	Delivery Costs
Mar. 1	R. E. Wilson Company	$ 244.60	$14.90
5	J. R. Watkins Company	348.90	Called for by Watkins truck
8	Olsen Company	348.60	17.80
12	Iowa Sales Company	1,257.00	42.65
15	R. E. Wilson Company	2,240.80	37.40
18	Olsen Company	1,676.87	46.20
21	Iowa Sales Company	2,233.60	62.80
26	J. R. Watkins Company	560.40	Called for by Watkins truck
30	Cornell Company	1,340.65	42.20

Instructions: 1. Record the sales transactions in a three-column sales journal like the one illustrated above. Number the sales in consecutive order beginning with number 238. Note that the amount to be recorded in the Accounts Receivable column for each entry is the sum of the amounts entered in the two credit columns.

2. Total and rule the sales journal.

3. Open accounts for the customers in an accounts receivable ledger that has balance-column ruling and record their balances. Allow four lines for each customer's account. The customers' accounts and their balances are as follows:

Cornell Company, 2318 Harvey Road, Omaha 5, Nebraska....... $1,061.25
Iowa Sales Company, 192 Main Street, Des Moines 3, Iowa....... 1,899.66
Olsen Company, 472 Ninth Street, Madison 2, Wisconsin......... 2,354.70
J. R. Watkins Company, 1417 Vine Street, Detroit 8, Michigan.... 1,392.48
R. E. Wilson Company, 246 A Street, Ann Arbor, Michigan...... 531.80

4. Post each amount in the Accounts Receivable column of the sales journal to the proper customer's account in the accounts receivable ledger.

5. Open the three accounts in the general ledger that are needed in this problem: Accounts Receivable, 12; Sales, 41; and Delivery Expense, 61. The accounts receivable debit balance is $7,239.89 as of March 1 of the current year.

6. Post the totals in the sales journal to the proper accounts in the general ledger.

Chapter 14

Recording cash receipts

The immediate record of cash receipts

Morton Supplies receives cash from (1) collections from customers on account, (2) cash sales, and (3) miscellaneous sources.

When Morton Supplies receives a check from a customer on account, the check is the immediate record of the transaction. When it receives cash in the form of currency or coins, the cash register tape is the immediate record of these cash transactions. All cash received transactions at Morton Supplies are recorded in a cash receipts journal.

The four-column cash receipts journal

A special journal in which all cash receipts and only cash receipts are recorded is called a *cash receipts journal*. The cash receipts journal used by Morton Supplies is shown below.

	DATE	ACCOUNT CREDITED	POST. REF.	GENERAL CREDIT	SALES CREDIT	ACCOUNTS RECEIVABLE CREDIT	CASH DEBIT	
1								1
2								2
3								3

CASH RECEIPTS JOURNAL — PAGE 1

Cash receipts journal

The cash receipts journal used by Morton Supplies contains columns in which to record:

1. The date of the transaction.
2. The name of the account to be credited for each transaction.
3. The posting reference.
4. The debit and the credit amounts.

Each cash receipts transaction is recorded on a single line of the cash receipts journal. Each cash receipts transaction increases the asset Cash. For each cash receipts entry, therefore, Cash is debited. A special column with the heading *Cash Debit* is provided in the cash receipts journal for recording the amount of each cash receipt. The use of this special column saves time in posting because only the total of the column is posted.

Each cash receipt from a charge customer decreases the balances of two accounts: (1) a customer's account in the accounts receivable ledger and (2) the controlling account Accounts Receivable in the general ledger. Each cash receipt from a customer is therefore credited to a customer's account in the accounts receivable ledger and to the accounts receivable account in the general ledger.

A special column in the cash receipts journal with the heading *Accounts Receivable Credit* saves time in posting to the controlling account in the general ledger. Only the total of the column is posted to the credit of the controlling account in the general ledger.

Cash is received often for cash sales. In order to save time in posting the cash sales to the credit of the sales account in the general ledger, a special column with the heading *Sales Credit* is provided in the cash receipts journal. Only the total of the column is posted.

A few cash receipts transactions each month affect accounts for which there are no special columns in the cash receipts journal. All credits in the cash receipts journal for which there are no special columns are recorded as follows: (1) the name of the account credited is written in the Account Credited column and (2) the amount to be credited to this account is written in the General Credit column.

Cash receipts journal entry No. 1 — recording the beginning balance

November 1, 1962. Cash on hand, $2,400.00.

To avoid having to refer to the general ledger to get the amount of cash on hand at the beginning of each month, the cash balance is written in the Account Credited column of the cash receipts journal. This entry is not posted. An entry that records information that is not to be posted is called a *memorandum entry*.

The cash account in the general ledger shows the cash balance on November 1 to be $2,400.00. The memorandum entry to record this information in the cash receipts journal is shown below.

	DATE	ACCOUNT CREDITED	POST. REF.	GENERAL CREDIT	SALES CREDIT	ACCOUNTS RECEIVABLE CREDIT	CASH DEBIT	
1	1962 Nov. 1	Balance on hand $2,400.00	✓					1
2								2
3								3
4								4

CASH RECEIPTS JOURNAL PAGE 1

Memorandum entry for the cash balance

The memorandum entry of the cash balance is written on the first line of the cash receipts journal at the beginning of each month. The year, the month, and the day are written in the Date column. The entire entry, *Balance on hand, $2,400.00,* is written in the Account Credited column. Nothing is written in the amount columns. A check mark is placed in the Post. Ref. column to show that nothing is to be posted from this line.

The reason for not posting the memorandum entry is that the cash balance on November 1, 1962, $2,400.00, is already accounted for in the cash account in the general ledger. To prevent adding the cash balance to the current month's cash receipts, the amount of the cash balance does not appear in any amount column in the cash receipts journal.

Cash receipts journal entry No. 2 — receipt of cash on account

November 1, 1962. Received a check for $29.70 from J. S. Martin to apply on account.

The check received from J. S. Martin is the basis for the entry in the cash receipts journal. This cash receipts transaction is recorded on Line 2 of the cash receipts journal as shown below.

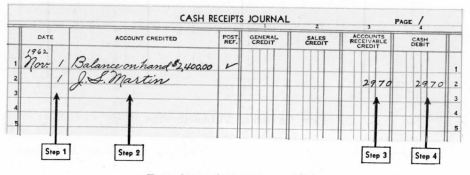

Entry for cash received on account

The steps used in recording the receipt of cash from a customer on account are:

Step 1.   The date, 1, is written in the Date column.

Step 2.   The name of the customer's account to be credited, J. S. Martin, is written in the Account Credited column.

Step 3.   The amount of the credit, $29.70, is written in the special column that has the heading Accounts Receivable Credit. The reason for this special column is that the same amount that is credited to J. S. Martin in the accounts receivable ledger must be credited to the controlling account, Accounts Receivable, in the general ledger.

Step 4.   The amount of cash received, $29.70, is recorded as a debit to Cash by writing this amount in the Cash Debit column.

Cash receipts journal entry No. 3 — cash sales of merchandise

November 2, 1962. Cash sales as shown by the cash register are $442.50.

Sales on account are recorded in the sales journal only. Cash sales are recorded in the cash receipts journal only. The entry in the cash receipts journal for the cash sales recorded on the cash register is shown on Line 3 below.

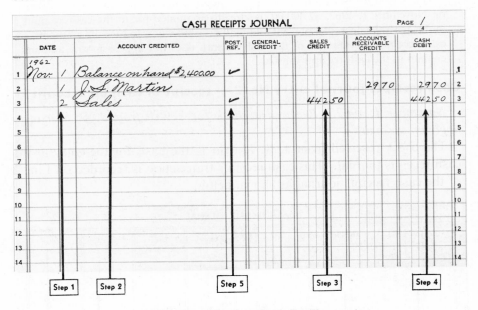

Entry for cash sales of merchandise

The steps in recording the cash sales shown on Line 3 are as follows:

Step 1. The date, 2, is written in the Date column.

Step 2. The account to be credited, Sales, is written in the Account Credited column to show the source of the cash receipt.

Step 3. The credit amount, $442.50, is recorded in the Sales Credit column. Sales is credited because the amount represents an income to the business. All incomes are recorded as credits.

Step 4. The debit amount, $442.50, is recorded in the Cash Debit column.

Step 5. A check mark is placed in the Post. Ref. column on Line 3 of the cash receipts journal to show that nothing on this line is to be posted separately. The debit to Cash is posted as a part of the total of the Cash Debit amount column. The credit to Sales is posted as a part of the total of the Sales Credit column.

184

Cash receipts journal entry No. 4 — additional investment of cash

November 6, 1962. Received from the proprietor, Mr. Morton, a personal check for $1,000.00 as an additional investment in Morton Supplies.

It is customary for one who owns and operates his own business to have a personal bank account separate from his business bank account. A check received by the business from the owner is recorded like any other cash receipt transaction.

The entry to record the additional investment is shown on Line 4 of the cash receipts journal below.

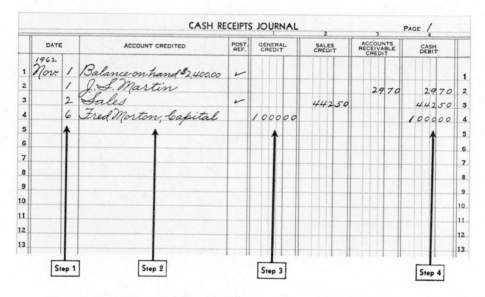

Entry for additional investment by the proprietor

The steps in recording the additional investment of Mr. Morton are:

Step 1. The date, 6, is written in the Date column.

Step 2. The account to be credited, Fred Morton, Capital, is written in the Account Credited column. Fred Morton, Capital is credited because all increases in proprietorship are recorded as credits.

Step 3. The credit amount, $1,000.00, is recorded in the General Credit column. The amount is recorded in the General Credit column because all credits that cannot be recorded in one of the special columns are recorded in the General Credit column.

Step 4. The debit amount, $1,000.00, is recorded in the Cash Debit column.

Completed cash receipts journal for Morton Supplies

During the month of November, Morton Supplies had a number of cash receipts transactions similar to those described. Each cash receipt was recorded in the manner illustrated on Lines 2 to 4. The completed cash receipts journal is shown below.

	DATE	ACCOUNT CREDITED	POST. REF.	GENERAL CREDIT 1	SALES CREDIT 2	ACCOUNTS RECEIVABLE CREDIT 3	CASH DEBIT 4	
1	1962 Nov 1	Balance on hand $2,400.00	✓					1
2	1	J. S. Martin	✓			2970	2970	2
3	2	Sales	✓		44250		44250	3
4	6	Fred Morton, Capital	31	100000			100000	4
5	8	J. C. Miller	✓			8000	8000	5
6	9	Sales	✓		37480		37480	6
7	14	J. C. Miller	✓			37500	37500	7
8	15	L. D. Watts	✓			17440	17440	8
9	16	Sales	✓		66974		66974	9
10	20	Shepherd Young	✓			15000	15000	10
11	20	W. R. Moore	✓			11700	11700	11
12	23	Walter Love	✓			29540	29540	12
13	23	Sales	✓		47336		47336	13
14	25	W. R. Moore	✓			1500	1500	14
15	28	Walter Love	✓			6900	6900	15
16	29	S. M. Shaw	✓			7000	7000	16
17	29	J. C. Miller	✓			2030	2030	17
18	30	Frank Post	✓			14500	14500	18
19	30	S. M. Shaw	✓			15220	15220	19
20	30	Sales	✓		43560		43560	20
21	30	Totals		100000	239600	169300	508900	21
22			(✓)	(41)	(12)	(11)		22
23								23
24								24

Cash receipts journal for November after footing and ruling

Footing, proving, and ruling the cash receipts journal

To prove the equality of debit and credits of the cash receipts journal illustrated above, the following steps are taken:

Step 1. Foot each column of the cash receipts journal in small pencil figures.

Step 2. Add the credit totals, $1,000.00, $2,396.00, and $1,693.00, on a separate sheet of paper. The sum of the credit totals, $5,089.00, is the same as the total of the Cash Debit column; therefore, the equality of debits and credits in the cash receipts journal is proved.

Step 3. After the equality of debits and credits is proved, the page is ruled with single and double lines as shown in the illustration on page 186.

If the cash receipts page has ruled lines at the bottom of the page for totals, the totals may be written between these ruled lines. In order to avoid making other entries on this page, it is customary to rule a diagonal line across the page beginning with the date of the last entry and ending with the single ruled line for the total.

Proving cash on hand

Determining that the amount of cash on hand agrees with the book-keeping records is called *proving cash*. Cash should be proved before the totals in the cash receipts journal and the cash payments journal are posted. The formula for proving cash is as follows:

Beginning balance + cash receipts − cash payments = cash on hand

Using this formula, cash is proved by the following calculations:

Beginning balance (Line 1 of the cash receipts journal, page 186)......................................	$2,400.00
Plus cash receipts (total of Cash Debit column of cash receipts journal, page 186).........................	5,089.00
Total..	$7,489.00
Minus cash payments (total of Cash Credit column of cash payments journal, page 154)........................	2,724.74
Balance of cash on hand November 30 according to journals.	$4,764.26
Balance of cash on hand according to check stub...........	$4,764.26

If the business has some cash on hand that has not been deposited, this amount is added to the check-stub balance to get the amount of cash on hand.

The cash on hand according to the two cash journals agrees with the cash on hand according to the check-stub balance. This is proof that the amounts of the entries in the two cash journals and the records on the check stubs are correct.

Cash is usually proved each day. When this is done, the amount columns in both cash journals are footed in small pencil figures. The calculations are then made as shown above.

Cash short and over

Errors are sometimes made in making change at the time cash is received. If the cash on hand is less than it should be as shown by the records, the cash is said to be *short*. If the cash on hand is more than it should be as shown by the records, the cash is said to be *over* or *long*. If the error cannot be found, an entry is made in a cash journal to record the amount by which the cash is short or over. The account in the expense section of the general ledger in which the amount of cash short or over is recorded is given the title *Cash Short and Over*.

If the cash is short, it is assumed that more cash was paid out than was recorded. Therefore an entry is made in the cash payments journal for the amount by which cash is short. The account Cash Short and Over is debited for the amount and the account Cash is credited.

If the cash is over, it is assumed that more cash was received than was recorded. Therefore an entry is made in the cash receipts journal for the amount by which cash is over. Cash is debited for the amount cash is over and Cash Short and Over is credited for the same amount.

The entries made to record cash short or over may be made each time an error occurs. Another method is to make an entry at the end of the month for the net amount that cash on hand is short or over at that time.

Posting each amount in the Accounts Receivable Credit column of the cash receipts journal

The owner of a business frequently wishes to know how much each customer owes the business so that he will know whether to permit further sales on account to a particular customer. For this reason, the amounts in the Accounts Receivable Credit column of the cash receipts journal are posted frequently to the credit of customers' accounts in the accounts receivable ledger.

The entry in the cash receipts journal and the account of J. S. Martin in the accounts receivable ledger after posting Line 2 are shown below.

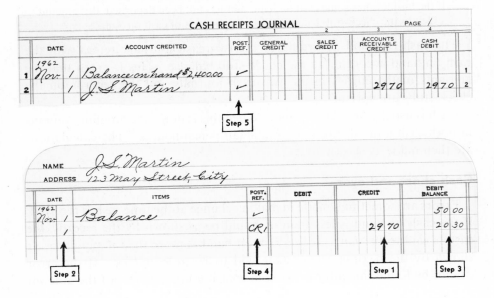

The steps in posting the entry on Line 2 to J. S. Martin's account are:

Step 1. The amount, $29.70, that is recorded in the Accounts Receivable Credit column on Line 2 of the cash receipts journal is posted as a credit to J. S. Martin's account in the accounts receivable ledger.

Step 2. The date, 1, is written in the date column.

Step 3. The credit amount, $29.70, is subtracted from the previous debit balance, leaving a balance of $20.30. This balance, $20.30, is written in the Debit Balance column.

Step 4. *CR1* is written in the Post. Ref. column of the account to show that this entry is posted from page 1 of the cash receipts journal.

Step 5. A check mark is placed in the Post. Ref. column of the cash receipts journal to show the completion of the posting. Numbers are not used when amounts are posted to customers' accounts because the accounts are arranged alphabetically and are not numbered.

Each entry in the Accounts Receivable Credit column is posted in the same way.

The debit to the cash account on this line of the cash receipts journal is not posted as a separate amount. Only the total of this column is posted.

Posting each amount in the General Credit column

The cash receipts journal after the posting of Line 4 and the capital account in the general ledger with this entry posted are shown below.

CASH RECEIPTS JOURNAL   PAGE *1*

	DATE		ACCOUNT CREDITED	POST. REF.	GENERAL CREDIT	SALES CREDIT	ACCOUNTS RECEIVABLE CREDIT	CASH DEBIT	
1	1962 Nov.	1	Balance on hand $2,400.00	✓					1
2		1	J. S. Martin	✓			29 70	29 70	2
3		2	Sales	✓		442 50		442 50	3
4		6	Fred Morton, Capital	31	1 000 00			1 000 00	4

Fred Morton, Capital   ACCOUNT NO. *31*

DATE	ITEMS	POST. REF.	DEBIT	DATE	ITEMS	POST. REF.	CREDIT
				1962 Nov. 1	Balance	J1	8 083 56
				6		CR1	1 000 00

Each item in the General Credit column must be posted separately. The account Fred Morton, Capital is credited for the amount shown in the General Credit column. The date of the transaction, 6, is written in the Date column. *CR1* is written in the Post. Ref. column of the account.

The completion of the posting is shown by writing the account number, 31, in the Post. Ref. column of the cash receipts journal.

If there were other entries in the General Credit column, they would be posted in the same way.

Posting the totals of the cash receipts journal

As the entries in the General Credit column have been posted during the month, the total of this column need not be posted. The entries in the Accounts Receivable Credit column have been posted individually to the customers' accounts in the accounts receivable ledger, but nothing from this column has been posted to the general ledger. The column total must therefore be posted. Also the totals of the Sales Credit and the Cash Debit columns must be posted.

The Totals line of the cash receipts journal and the three accounts in the general ledger to which the totals are posted are shown below.

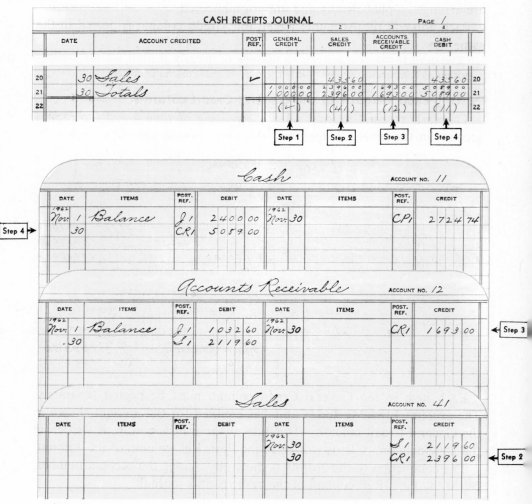

190

The steps in posting the totals of the cash receipts journal are:

Step 1. A check mark is placed in parentheses on the first line below the General Credit column to show that the items in this column have been posted individually to accounts in the general ledger and that the total is not to be posted.

Step 2. The total of the Sales Credit column, $2,396.00, is posted to the credit of Sales in the general ledger. The completion of posting is shown by placing the sales account number, 41, in parentheses below the total.

Step 3. The total of the Accounts Receivable Credit column, $1,693.00, is posted to the credit of Accounts Receivable in the general ledger. The completion of posting is shown by placing the accounts receivable account number, 12, in parentheses below the total.

Step 4. The total of the Cash Debit column, $5,089.00, is posted to the debit of Cash in the general ledger. The completion of posting is shown by placing the cash account number, 11, in parentheses below the total.

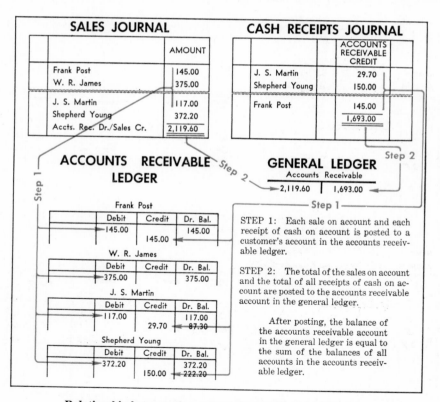

Relationship between the accounts receivable ledger and the accounts receivable account in the general ledger

Accounts receivable ledger of Morton Supplies

The customers' accounts in the accounts receivable ledger of Morton Supplies are shown on this and the following pages.

NAME *M. R. Cole*
ADDRESS *121 West Third Street, City*

DATE	ITEMS	POST. REF.	DEBIT	CREDIT	DEBIT BALANCE
1962 Nov. 28		S1	98 00		98 00

NAME *W. R. James*
ADDRESS *134 North Franklin Street, City*

DATE	ITEMS	POST. REF.	DEBIT	CREDIT	DEBIT BALANCE
1962 Nov. 3		S1	375 00		375 00

NAME *Walter Love*
ADDRESS *360 Elm Street, City*

DATE	ITEMS	POST. REF.	DEBIT	CREDIT	DEBIT BALANCE
1962 Nov. 1	Balance	✓			69 00
9		S1	295 40		364 40
23		CR1		295 40	69 00
28		CR1		69 00	

NAME *J. S. Martin*
ADDRESS *123 May Street, City*

DATE	ITEMS	POST. REF.	DEBIT	CREDIT	DEBIT BALANCE
1962 Nov. 1	Balance	✓			50 00
1		CR1		29 70	20 30
5		S1	117 00		137 30
27		J1		20 30	117 00

Accounts receivable ledger — Morton Supplies

NAME J. C. Miller
ADDRESS 400 Laurel Street, City

DATE		ITEMS	POST. REF.	DEBIT	CREDIT	DEBIT BALANCE
1962						
Nov.	1	Balance	✓			455 00
	8		CR1		80 00	375 00
	14		S1	15 00		390 00
	14		CR1		375 00	15 00
	16		S1	69 00		84 00
	27		S1	20 30		104 30
	29		CR1		20 30	84 00

NAME W. R. Moore
ADDRESS 4827 Cumberland Road, City

DATE		ITEMS	POST. REF.	DEBIT	CREDIT	DEBIT BALANCE
1962						
Nov.	1	Balance	✓			132 00
	20		CR1		117 00	15 00
	25		CR1		15 00	

NAME Frank Post
ADDRESS 1350 Long Street, City

DATE		ITEMS	POST. REF.	DEBIT	CREDIT	DEBIT BALANCE
1962						
Nov.	2		S1	145 00		145 00
	30		CR1		145 00	

NAME S. M. Shaw
ADDRESS 635 Lee Street, Marion

DATE		ITEMS	POST. REF.	DEBIT	CREDIT	DEBIT BALANCE
1962						
Nov.	1	Balance	✓			152 20
	20		S1	70 00		222 20
	29		CR1		70 00	152 20
	30		CR1		152 20	

Accounts receivable ledger — Morton Supplies (continued)

NAME D.C. Walsh
ADDRESS 516 Jones Road, City

DATE	ITEMS	POST. REF.	DEBIT	CREDIT	DEBIT BALANCE
1962 Nov. 19		S1	308 00		308 00

NAME L. D. Watts
ADDRESS 310 Main Street, Brantford

DATE	ITEMS	POST. REF.	DEBIT	CREDIT	DEBIT BALANCE
1962 Nov. 1	Balance	✓			174 40
8		S1	255 00		429 40
15		CR1		174 40	255 00

NAME Shepherd Young
ADDRESS 503 Mill Road, Warren

DATE	ITEMS	POST. REF.	DEBIT	CREDIT	DEBIT BALANCE
1962 Nov. 13		S1	372 20		372 20
20		CR1		150 00	222 20

Accounts receivable ledger — Morton Supplies (concluded)

The schedule of accounts receivable

In Chapter 13, customers' accounts in the accounts receivable ledger were debited when merchandise was sold to them on account. The accounts receivable account was debited for the total amount of sales on account.

In this chapter, customers' accounts in the accounts receivable ledger were credited when cash was received on account from customers. At the end of the month, the accounts receivable account in the general ledger was credited for the total amount received from customers.

If the work was done correctly, the sum of all balances of customers' accounts in the accounts receivable ledger should agree with the balance of the accounts receivable account in the general ledger. In order to prove the accuracy of the posting, a list is prepared showing the balances of all accounts in the accounts receivable ledger. A list showing the account titles and the balances in the accounts receivable ledger is known as a *schedule of accounts receivable*.

Schedule of accounts receivable for Morton Supplies

The following schedule of accounts receivable is prepared from the accounts in the accounts receivable ledger that is shown on pages 192–194.

Morton Supplies Schedule of Accounts Receivable November 30, 1962		
M. R. Cole	98 00	
W. R. James	375 00	
J. F. Martin	117 00	
J. C. Miller	84 00	
D. C. Walsh	308 00	
L. D. Watts	255 00	
Shepherd Young	222 20	
Total Accounts Receivable		1459 20

Schedule of accounts receivable

Proving the accuracy of posting the sales journal and the cash receipts journal

The steps used in proving the accuracy of posting the sales journal and the cash receipts journal are as follows:

Step 1. A schedule of accounts receivable is prepared from the accounts receivable ledger.

Step 2. The controlling account in the general ledger, Accounts Receivable, is footed with small pencil figures. The balance is determined and written with pencil.

Step 3. The total of the schedule of accounts receivable taken from the accounts receivable ledger is compared with the pencil balance of the accounts receivable account in the general ledger. If the two amounts agree, it is assumed that all posting affecting customers' accounts in the accounts receivable ledger and the accounts receivable account in the general ledger is correct.

Statement of account

A business form that shows the charges to a customer's account, the amounts credited to his account, and the balance of his account is known as a *statement of account*. It is customary for a business to send each charge customer a statement of account at regular intervals, usually monthly. When a customer receives his statement of account, he should compare it with his own records. If his records do not agree with the statement he has received, he should notify the creditor from whom he received the statement.

One of the statements of account sent out by Morton Supplies is illustrated below.

<table>
<tr><td colspan="4" align="center">*Statement*</td></tr>
<tr><td colspan="4" align="center">**MORTON SUPPLIES**</td></tr>
<tr><td colspan="4" align="center">460 Main Street
PORTLAND, OREGON</td></tr>
<tr><td colspan="4">Date Dec. 1, 1962</td></tr>
<tr><td colspan="4">To J. C. Miller
400 Laurel Street
City</td></tr>
<tr><td>Date</td><td>Debits</td><td>Credits</td><td>Balance</td></tr>
<tr><td>1962
Nov. 1</td><td></td><td></td><td>455.00</td></tr>
<tr><td>8</td><td></td><td>80.00</td><td>375.00</td></tr>
<tr><td>14</td><td>15.00</td><td></td><td>390.00</td></tr>
<tr><td>14</td><td></td><td>375.00</td><td>15.00</td></tr>
<tr><td>16</td><td>69.00</td><td></td><td>84.00</td></tr>
<tr><td>27</td><td>20.30</td><td></td><td>104.30</td></tr>
<tr><td>29</td><td></td><td>20.30</td><td>84.00</td></tr>
</table>

Statement of account

Using automation to record cash receipts

Automation can be applied to the handling of cash receipts in much the same manner as that used for cash payments. A clerk punches cards or tapes from records furnished to him of cash receipts. The cards or tapes are fed into a machine that is set to prepare a complete record of all cash receipts and to post the cash receipts to the proper accounts in the accounts receivable and general ledgers.

Increasing your business vocabulary

What is the meaning of each of the following:

(a) cash receipts journal
(b) memorandum entry
(c) proving cash
(d) cash short

(e) cash over
(f) schedule of accounts receivable
(g) statement of account

196

Chapter questions

1. What is the immediate record for cash received from a customer on account?
2. If there is no special column in a cash receipts journal for a credit entry, in what amount column is the amount recorded?
3. Why is it desirable to make a memorandum entry of the cash balance in the cash receipts journal at the beginning of each month?
4. Why is a check mark placed in the Post. Ref. column of the cash receipts journal each time a cash sale is recorded?
5. If there are 25 entries to Sales Credit in the cash receipts journal, how many separate postings are saved through the use of a special column with the heading Sales Credit?
6. If some of the cash received has not been deposited, what is done with this amount in proving cash?
7. Why is it desirable to post the amounts in the Accounts Receivable Credit column frequently?
8. Why are the individual amounts in the Cash Debit column not posted?
9. With what account in the general ledger should the total of the schedule of accounts receivable agree?

Cases for discussion

1. R. A. Allison operates a retail radio and television shop. He uses a cash receipts journal with columns similar to those used by Morton Supplies as shown on page 186. J. O. Jacks, who operates the same kind of store, uses a cash receipts journal without a special column for Sales Credit. What are the advantages of Mr. Allison's plan?
2. Hugh Hilts operates a retail shoe store and sells for cash only. What changes in the cash receipts journal used by Morton Supplies as shown on page 186 would you recommend for Mr. Hilts and why?
3. The Crown Retail Store proves cash only once a week. What are the disadvantages of this plan as compared with the plan of a store that proves cash every day?

Drill for understanding

Drill 14-A. *Cash receipts transactions*

The following are the cash receipts for the week of December 1–6:

1. Balance on hand.....	$3,300.00	5. Cash Sales..........	$	720.00
2. Cash Sales..........	270.00	Accounts Receivable.		70.00
3. Accounts Receivable.	450.00	6. Cash Sales..........		640.00
Cash Sales..........	500.00	Accounts Receivable.		120.00
4. Accounts Receivable.	60.00	Office Furniture.....		40.00
Accounts Receivable.	130.00			

197

Instructions: Answer each of the following questions:

(1) In what journal should these transactions be recorded?
(2) What is the total of cash sales for the week?
(3) What is the total of cash received from charge customers?
(4) Will Cash be debited or credited for each cash receipt?
(5) What was the total amount of cash received during the week?
(6) Will Accounts Receivable be debited or credited? Why?

Application problems

Problem 14-1. *Recording cash receipts of a wholesale grocer*

On November 1 of the current year R. J. Hoffman, proprietor of Hoffman Wholesale Grocers, had a cash balance of $3,460.20. During the month of November he completed the following cash receipts transactions:

Nov. 1. Recorded the cash balance with a memorandum entry.
1. Received $2,400.00 from cash sales of merchandise.
4. Received $220.40 from Hull Grocery on account.
7. Received $485.20 from M. E. Creager on account.
8. Received $9,110.50 from cash sales of merchandise.
14. Received $360.40 from Stambaugh Bros. on account.
15. Received $7,120.80 from cash sales of merchandise.
18. Received $260.40 from Hull Grocery on account.
21. Received $235.80 from J. B. Johnston on account.
22. Received $8,110.10 from cash sales of merchandise.
27. Received $820.90 from Bard and Co. on account.
28. Received $550.30 from R. K. Wise on account.
29. Received $6,560.80 from cash sales of merchandise.

Instructions: 1. Record each of these cash receipts transactions on page 14 of a cash receipts journal similar to the one illustrated on page 186 of this chapter.

2. Foot, prove, total, and rule the cash receipts journal.

The cash receipts journal prepared in this problem will also be used in Problem 14-2.

Problem 14-2. *Posting the cash receipts journal and preparing a schedule of accounts receivable*

This problem requires the accounts receivable ledger and the general ledger used in Problem 13-2 and the cash receipts journal used in Problem 14-1. If these are not available, complete Exercise 14-A in the Appendix.

Instructions: 1. Post the entries from the Accounts Receivable Credit column of the cash receipts journal prepared in Problem 14-1 to customers' accounts in the accounts receivable ledger used in Problem 13-2.

2. Post the totals of the special columns in the cash receipts journal to the general ledger used in Problem 13-2.

3. Prepare a schedule of accounts receivable from the accounts in the accounts receivable ledger in a form similar to the one illustrated on page 195.

4. Compare the total of the schedule of accounts receivable with the balance of the accounts receivable account in the general ledger. If there is a difference, recheck your work until the error is found.

Optional problems

★Supplementary Problem 14-S. *Recording and posting cash receipts*

Theodore Winston, a retail jeweler, completed cash received transactions during December of the current year as shown below. The cash balance as of December 1 was $1,300.00.

Dec. 1. Recorded the cash balance with a memorandum entry.
  1. Received $85.00 from M. E. Hedges on account.
  4. Received $301.60 from cash sales of merchandise.
  8. Received $62.25 from A. R. Kelley on account.
  11. Received $910.20 from cash sales of merchandise.
  11. Received $15.00 from the sale of office supplies to a neighboring merchant.

> Office supplies are not a part of the merchandise kept in stock for sale. For this reason, the sales account was not credited for this transaction; instead Office Supplies was credited.

  15. Received $142.80 from Daniel Cabot on account.
  18. Received $200.00 from Michael Murphy on account.
  18. Received $412.60 from cash sales of merchandise.
  23. Received $60.00 from Susan Crane on account.
  25. Received $529.25 from cash sales of merchandise.
  28. Received $100.00 from George Graham on account.
  31. Received $476.20 from cash sales of merchandise.

Instructions: 1. Record the cash received transactions on page 12 of a cash receipts journal similar to the one illustrated on page 186.

2. Foot, prove, total, and rule the cash receipts journal.

3. In a general ledger open the following accounts, using the account numbers shown in parentheses. Allow four lines for each account. Record the balance for each account for which a balance is given. Date the balance December 1 of the current year.

Cash (11), $1,300.00   T. R. Winston, Capital (31), $2,310.75
Accounts Receivable (12), $658.85   Sales (41)
Office Supplies (13), $177.60

4. Post the individual items in the General Credit amount column and the totals of the special columns to the accounts in the general ledger.

★Bonus Problem 14-B. *Recording and posting cash receipts*

The Chase Furniture Company calls its cash receipts journal a cash received record. The form of the cash received record is shown below.

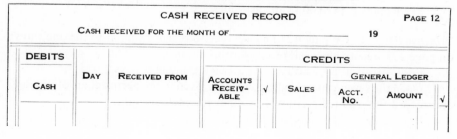

Note that immediately after the Accounts Receivable column and after the General Ledger Amount column there are columns headed with a check mark. These check mark columns are used in place of Post. Ref. columns. When items from these columns are posted, a check mark is placed after the amount to show completion of the posting.

Also note that there is an Account Number column immediately before the General Ledger Amount column. The account number is recorded at the time of the entry instead of the account title. When you record an amount in the General Ledger Amount column, refer to the following partial chart of accounts for the account number.

The numbers, titles, and balances of the accounts used in this problem are:

ACCT. NO.	ACCOUNT TITLE	BALANCES
11	Cash	4,896.00
12	Accounts Receivable	1,630.00
13	Store Equipment	270.00
14	Office Equipment	1,306.00
15	Delivery Equipment	3,560.00
31	L. C. Chase, Capital	10,500.00
41	Sales	———

The following cash received transactions were completed by the Chase Furniture Company during the month of December of the current year:

Dec. 1. Cash balance, $4,896.00. (Record this balance as a memorandum entry on the first line.)
  3. Received $450.00 from cash sales.
  6. Received $75.00 from J. R. Hall on account.
  8. Received $80.00 from the sale of an old display counter to A. L. Marks. (Store Equipment)
  10. Received $375.00 from cash sales.
  15. Received $460.00 from H. R. Milton on account.
  17. Received $390.00 from cash sales.
  20. Received $45.00 from the sale of an old typewriter to J. C. Warren· (Office Equipment)
  21. Received $2,000.00 from L. C. Chase as an additional investment.
  24. Received $640.00 from cash sales.
  27. Received $86.00 from L. K. Cook on account.
  28. Received $960 from the sale of an old delivery truck to J. R. Bodie. (Delivery Equipment)
  31. Received $820.00 from cash sales.

Instructions: 1. On page 12 of a cash received record similar to the one shown on page 199, record the cash received transactions.

2. Foot, prove, total, and rule the amount columns.

3. Open the seven general ledger accounts given in the partial chart of accounts and record the balances. Allow four lines for each account.

4. Post to the general ledger accounts.

Chapter 15

The general journal

Need for a general journal

During the operation of any business, there are various transactions that are not purchases of merchandise on account, sales of merchandise on account, cash receipts, or cash payments. These transactions cannot be recorded in the purchases journal, the sales journal, the cash receipts journal, or the cash payments journal. Entries that cannot be recorded in a special journal are called *miscellaneous entries*. A journal that is used to record miscellaneous entries is usually called a *general journal*.

Examples of miscellaneous entries that are recorded in a general journal are:

1. An opening entry to record the beginning balance sheet of a business when a new bookkeeping system is installed.
2. Entries to record the purchase on account of items other than merchandise.
3. Entries to record withdrawals of merchandise by the proprietor.
4. Entries to record the sale on account of items other than merchandise.
5. Entries to correct errors.
6. Entries to adjust accounts at the end of a fiscal period.
7. Entries to close accounts at the end of a fiscal period.

Beginning balance sheet of Morton Supplies

When Morton Supplies installed a new bookkeeping system on November 1, 1962, the following balance sheet was prepared.

Morton Supplies Balance Sheet November 1, 1962					
Assets			**Liabilities**		
Cash	2400	00	Accounts Payable	1080	14
Accounts Receivable	1032	60			
Merchandise Inventory	5500	50	**Proprietorship**		
Supplies	124	60	Fred Morton, Capital	8083	56
Prepaid Insurance	106	00			
Total Assets	9163	70	Total Liabilities + Prop.	9163	70

Balance sheet of Morton Supplies

General journal entry No. 1 — recording an opening entry

The balance sheet dated November 1, 1962, is the immediate record for the opening entry. It is recorded in the general journal as follows:

		GENERAL JOURNAL			PAGE 1
	DATE	NAME OF ACCOUNT	POST. REF.	DEBIT	CREDIT
Step 1 → 1	1962 Nov. 1	Cash		2 400 00	
2		Accounts Receivable		1 032 60	
Step 2 → 3		Merchandise Inventory		5 500 50	
4		Supplies		124 60	
5		Prepaid Insurance		106 00	
Step 3 → 6		Accounts Payable			1 080 14
7		Fred Morton, Capital			8 083 56
8		To record the October 31			
Step 4 → 9		balance sheet.			
10					
11					

Opening entry in the general journal

The steps in recording the balance sheet in the general journal are:

Step 1. The year, the month, and the day are written in the Date column.

Step 2. The assets are listed in the Name of Account column of the general journal in the same order in which they appear on the balance sheet. The name of each asset account is written at the extreme left margin of the Name of Account column. The amount of each asset is recorded in the Debit amount column.

Step 3. The liabilities and the proprietorship are listed in the Name of Account column of the general journal. Each line is indented about one-half inch to show that each of these items is to be posted as a credit. The amounts for these items are written in the Credit amount column.

Step 4. A brief explanation is written in the Name of Account column to describe the entry. Each line is indented about one inch to distinguish between the explanation and the accounts credited.

Opening accounts in the general ledger

The posting of the opening entry in the general journal produces a new general ledger that is in balance. Through the process of posting, accounts are opened for all of the assets, the liabilities, and the proprietorship listed on the balance sheet. The sum of all of the debit balances in this new ledger equals the sum of all of the credit balances in it.

Opening accounts in the accounts receivable ledger

After the opening entry is posted to the general ledger, the accounts receivable account shows a debit balance of $1,032.60. This debit balance in the controlling account in the general ledger shows the total amount to be collected from all customers, but it does not show the amount to be collected from each individual customer. It is therefore necessary to open an account in the accounts receivable ledger for each customer and to record the proper debit balance in each account.

A schedule of accounts receivable is prepared at the time the balance sheet is prepared. The new accounts receivable ledger is prepared from the information given on this schedule. The schedule of accounts receivable that is used is shown below.

Morton Supplies		
Schedule of Accounts Receivable		
November 1, 1962		
Walter Love	69 00	
J. S. Martin	50 00	
J. C. Miller	4 55 00	
W. R. Moore	1 32 00	
S. M. Shaw	1 52 20	
L. D. Watts	1 74 40	
Total Accounts Receivable		1 03 2 60

Schedule of accounts receivable

It is not necessary to record the schedule of accounts receivable in the general journal. The reason is that the total of all balances in the accounts receivable ledger is accounted for in the opening entry already in the general journal. The accuracy of the work in opening a new accounts receivable ledger is proved by comparing the total of all of its balances with the balance in the controlling account, Account Receivable, in the general ledger. The two amounts must agree.

Opening accounts in the accounts payable ledger

The method of opening accounts for all creditors in a new accounts payable ledger is similar to the method used in opening accounts for all customers in a new accounts receivable ledger.

After the opening entry is posted to the general ledger, the accounts payable account shows a credit balance of $1,080.14. This credit balance in the accounts payable account shows the total amount owed to all creditors but it does not show the amount owed to each individual creditor.

It is therefore necessary to open an account in the accounts payable ledger for each creditor and to record the proper credit balance in each account.

A schedule of accounts payable is prepared at the same time that the balance sheet and the schedule of accounts receivable is prepared. The new accounts payable ledger is prepared from the information given on the schedule of accounts payable. The schedule of accounts payable that is used is shown below.

Morton Supplies Schedule of Accounts Payable November 1, 1962		
Acme Carbon Company	196 80	
Bell Business Machines	88 74	
Union Paper Company	80 40	
Mills Office Machines	714 20	
Total Accounts Payable		1080 14

Schedule of accounts payable

It is not necessary to record the schedule of accounts payable in the general journal. The reason is that the total of all balances in the accounts payable ledger is accounted for in the opening entry already in the general journal. The accuracy of the work in opening a new accounts payable ledger is proved by comparing the sum of all balances in the accounts payable ledger with the balance in the controlling account, Accounts Payable, in the general ledger. The two amounts must agree.

General journal entry No. 2 — purchase of supplies on account

November 12, 1962. Purchased store supplies from Alfred Supply Company on account, $144.00.

Morton Supplies purchases supplies such as wrapping paper, twine, bags, and cleaning supplies for use in the store. Supplies are not purchased for resale to customers; therefore they are not merchandise. Since Morton Supplies records only purchases of merchandise on account in the purchases journal, this transaction must be recorded in the general journal.

The invoice received from Alfred Supply Company is the immediate record of the transaction. The general journal entry to record this transaction is shown on the following page.

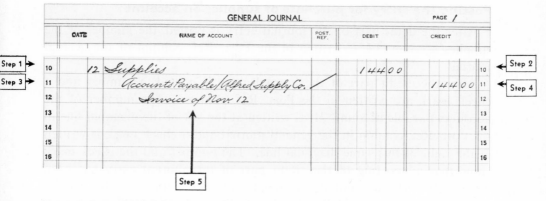

Recording the purchase of supplies on account

The steps in recording the purchase of store supplies on account are:

Step 1.   The date, 12, is written in the Date column. The month is not repeated on the page unless the month changes.

Step 2.   Supplies is debited for $144.00 by writing *Supplies* in the Name of Account column and the amount, $144.00, in the Debit amount column. Supplies is debited because supplies at the time of purchase are an asset of the business.

Step 3.   *Accounts Payable* and *Alfred Supply Company* are credited by writing the names of these two accounts in the Name of Account column. This line is indented to show that both accounts are to be credited. A diagonal line is placed between these two account titles to separate them clearly.

These two accounts are credited in this transaction because (1) the balance of the creditor's account in the accounts payable ledger, Alfred Supply Company, is increased $144.00 and (2) the balance of the account in the general ledger, Accounts Payable, is increased the same amount.

Step 4.   The amount of the credit to each of these two accounts is written in the Credit amount column of the general journal.   The amount, $144.00, need be written only once because each of these two accounts is credited for the same amount. A diagonal line is placed in the Post. Ref. column to show that the amount is to be posted to two accounts.

Step 5.   *Invoice of Nov. 12* is written in the Name of Account column as the journal explanation.   This explanation is indented twice as much as the credit line above it. This journal explanation describes the immediate record that is used as the basis of this journal entry and indicates where the immediate record may be found in the files.

205

Posting the entry for purchase of supplies on account

After the debit part of the journal entry is posted, the number of the supplies account, 14, is written in the Post. Ref. column of the general journal.

After the credit part of the journal entry is posted, a number and a check mark are written in the Post. Ref. column. The number of the accounts payable account, 21, is written at the left of the diagonal line in the Post. Ref. column in the general journal and a check mark is written at the right of this same diagonal line. The number and the check mark show that all posting of the credit part of this journal entry has been completed. The amount in the Credit amount column of the general journal has been posted: (a) to the credit of the controlling account, Accounts Payable, in the general ledger, and (b) to the credit of the creditor's account, Alfred Supply Company, in the subsidiary ledger.

> Transactions with creditors are not recorded frequently in the general journal of Morton Supplies. For this reason a special column for Accounts Payable is not provided in the general journal. It is therefore necessary to post the credit amount to both the accounts payable account in the general ledger and to the creditor's account in the accounts payable ledger. When a balance in the accounts payable ledger is increased, the balance of the controlling account must also be increased the same amount.

General journal entry No. 3 — withdrawal of merchandise by the proprietor

November 23, 1962. Fred Morton, the proprietor, withdrew merchandise for personal use, one typewriter and one desk at cost, $227.00.

Withdrawals of merchandise by the proprietor for personal use reduce the amount of merchandise available for sale. Such amounts are therefore recorded as a reduction in the cost of purchases. The entry is made in the general journal as follows:

	DATE	NAME OF ACCOUNT	POST. REF.	DEBIT	CREDIT	
13	23	Fred Morton, Drawing		2 2 7 00		13
14		Purchases			2 2 7 00	14
15		Typewriter and desk for				15
16		personal use				16

Entry for withdrawal of merchandise by proprietor

In the general journal entry, Fred Morton, Drawing is debited for $227.00 and Purchases is credited for the same amount. A brief explanation is written to describe the entry.

General journal entry No. 4 — correcting entry

November 27, 1962. J. S. Martin, a customer, reported that he had been charged $20.30 in the month of October for merchandise that he had not ordered or received.

In investigating this complaint from J. S. Martin, the bookkeeper finds that one sales slip in October was recorded incorrectly. He finds that J. S. Martin's account was debited for a sale when the debit should have gone to J. C. Miller's account.

An error in two or more accounts in the ledger may be corrected by an entry in the general journal. Entries made in the general journal to correct errors in two or more ledger accounts are known as *correcting entries*. The correcting entry in the general journal to correct the errors in the two accounts in the accounts receivable ledger is as follows:

	DATE	NAME OF ACCOUNT	POST. REF.	DEBIT	CREDIT	
17	27	J. C. Miller		20 30		17
18		J. S. Martin			20 30	18
19		To correct error in				19
20		posting sale of Oct. 29.				20
21						21
22						22
23						23
24						24
25						25

GENERAL JOURNAL — PAGE 1

Correcting entry

J. C. Miller is debited for $20.30 in this correcting entry in the general journal because he received the merchandise and was not charged for it. When the debit part of this journal entry is posted, the omission in his account will be corrected.

J. S. Martin is credited for $20.30 in this correcting entry in order to cancel the debit that was made to his account in error. When the credit part of this journal entry is posted, the error in Martin's account will be corrected.

The balance of the controlling account in the general ledger, Accounts Receivable, shows the total amount to be collected from all customers. The total amount to be collected from all customers has not been changed by corrections in the accounts in the subsidiary ledger. Therefore, no posting needs to be made to the accounts receivable account in the general ledger.

Adjusting and closing entries in the general journal

Entries that are made at the end of a fiscal period to bring various accounts up to date are known as *adjusting entries*. Entries that are made at the end of a fiscal period to transfer the balance of one account to another are called *closing entries*.

The method of making adjusting and closing entries in the general journal will be discussed and illustrated in Chapter 19.

General journal of Morton Supplies

The general journal of Morton Supplies for the month of November after posting is shown below.

	DATE	NAME OF ACCOUNT	POST. REF.	DEBIT	CREDIT	
1	1962 Nov. 1	Cash	11	2 4 0 0 0		1
2		Accounts Receivable	12	1 0 3 2 6 0		2
3		Merchandise Inventory	13	5 5 0 0 5 0		3
4		Supplies	14	1 2 4 6 0		4
5		Prepaid Insurance	15	1 0 6 0 0		5
6		Accounts Payable	21		1 0 8 0 1 4	6
7		Fred Morton, Capital	31		8 0 8 3 5 6	7
8		To record the October 31				8
9		balance sheet.				9
10	12	Supplies	14	1 4 4 0 0		10
11		Accounts Payable/Alfred Supply Co.	21/✓		1 4 4 0 0	11
12		Invoice of Nov. 12.				12
13	23	Fred Morton, Drawing	32	2 2 7 0 0		13
14		Purchases	51		2 2 7 0 0	14
15		Typewriter and desk for				15
16		personal use.				16
17	27	J. C. Miller	✓	2 0 3 0		17
18		J. S. Martin	✓		2 0 3 0	18
19		To correct error in				19
20		posting sale of Oct. 29.				20
21						21
22						22

GENERAL JOURNAL   PAGE 1

General journal of Morton Supplies after miscellaneous entries for November have been recorded and posted

Order of posting when several journals are used

As a general rule, all items affecting customers' accounts and creditors' accounts are posted frequently so that the balances of these accounts in the customers' ledger and in the creditors' ledger will always be up-to-date. Items affecting accounts in the general ledger are posted less frequently during the month. But all items, including the totals of special columns, must be posted before a trial balance is taken.

It is usually found satisfactory to post the special journals in the following order: (1) purchases journal; (2) cash payments journal; (3) sales journal; (4) cash receipts journal; and (5) general journal. This order of posting will help to bring the debits and the credits to the accounts in the ledger in the order in which the transactions happened.

General ledger of Morton Supplies

The general ledger of Morton Supplies on November 30 after the completion of the posting of the five journals presented in Chapters 11–15, and after the accounts have been footed, is shown on pages 210 and 211.

Proving the posting

To prove the equality of debits and credits in the general ledger, a trial balance is prepared. The steps in preparing the trial balance are given on page 84. The completed trial balance is shown below.

Morton Supplies
Trial Balance
November 30, 1962

Account	No.	Debit	Credit
Cash	11	4 7 6 4 2 6	
Accounts Receivable	12	1 4 5 9 2 0	
Merchandise Inventory	13	5 5 0 0 5 0	
Supplies	14	2 6 8 6 0	
Prepaid Insurance	15	1 0 6 0 0	
Accounts Payable	21		2 7 0 3 1 5
Fred Morton, Capital	31		9 0 8 3 5 6
Fred Morton, Drawing	32	4 2 7 0 0	
Sales	41		4 5 1 5 6 0
Purchases	51	3 1 1 8 1 5	
Delivery Expense	61	5 2 8 0	
Miscellaneous Expense	63	2 5 8 0	
Rent Expense	64	1 8 0 0 0	
Salary Expense	65	4 0 0 0 0	
		1 6 3 0 2 3 1	1 6 3 0 2 3 1

Trial balance of Morton Supplies

Cash   ACCOUNT NO. 11

DATE	ITEMS	POST. REF.	DEBIT	DATE	ITEMS	POST. REF.	CREDIT
1962 Nov 1	Balance	J1	2400 00	1962 Nov 30		CP1	2724 74
30	4764.26	CR1	5089 00				
			7489 00				

Accounts Receivable   ACCOUNT NO. 12

DATE	ITEMS	POST. REF.	DEBIT	DATE	ITEMS	POST. REF.	CREDIT
1962 Nov 1	Balance	J1	1032 60	1962 Nov 30		CR1	1693 00
30	1459.20	J1	2119 60				
			3152 20				

Merchandise Inventory   ACCOUNT NO. 13

DATE	ITEMS	POST. REF.	DEBIT	DATE	ITEMS	POST. REF.	CREDIT
1962 Nov 1	Balance	J1	5500 50				

Supplies   ACCOUNT NO. 14

DATE	ITEMS	POST. REF.	DEBIT	DATE	ITEMS	POST. REF.	CREDIT
1962 Nov 1	Balance	J1	124 60				
11		J1	144 00				
			268 60				

Prepaid Insurance   ACCOUNT NO. 15

DATE	ITEMS	POST. REF.	DEBIT	DATE	ITEMS	POST. REF.	CREDIT
1962 Nov 1	Balance	J1	106 00				

Accounts Payable   ACCOUNT NO. 21

DATE	ITEMS	POST. REF.	DEBIT	DATE	ITEMS	POST. REF.	CREDIT
1962 Nov 30		CP1	1791 14	1962 Nov 1	Balance	J1	1080 14
				11		J1	144 00
				30	2703.15	P1	3270 15
							4494 29

Fred Morton, Capital   ACCOUNT NO. 31

DATE	ITEMS	POST. REF.	DEBIT	DATE	ITEMS	POST. REF.	CREDIT
				1962 Nov 1	Balance	J1	8083 56
				6		CR1	1000 00
							9083 56

**General ledger after all journals have been posted
and the accounts have been footed**

Fred Morton, Drawing
ACCOUNT NO. 32

DATE	ITEMS	POST. REF.	DEBIT	DATE	ITEMS	POST. REF.	CREDIT
1962 Nov 7		CP1	100 00				
23		J1	227 00				
30		CP1	100 00				
			427 00				

Sales
ACCOUNT NO. 41

DATE	ITEMS	POST. REF.	DEBIT	DATE	ITEMS	POST. REF.	CREDIT
				1962 Nov 30		J1	2119 60
				30		CR1	2396 00
							4515 60

Purchases
ACCOUNT NO. 51

DATE	ITEMS	POST. REF.	DEBIT	DATE	ITEMS	POST. REF.	CREDIT
1962 Nov 8		CP1	75 00	1962 Nov 23		J1	227 00
30	3118.15	P1	3270 15				
			3343 15				

Delivery Expense
ACCOUNT NO. 61

DATE	ITEMS	POST. REF.	DEBIT	DATE	ITEMS	POST. REF.	CREDIT
1962 Nov 13		CP1	27 80				
28		CP1	25 00				
			52 80				

Miscellaneous Expense
ACCOUNT NO. 63

DATE	ITEMS	POST. REF.	DEBIT	DATE	ITEMS	POST. REF.	CREDIT
1962 Nov 8		CP1	15 80				
17		CP1	10 00				
			25 80				

Rent Expense
ACCOUNT NO. 64

DATE	ITEMS	POST. REF.	DEBIT	DATE	ITEMS	POST. REF.	CREDIT
1962 Nov 2		CP1	180 00				

Salary Expense
ACCOUNT NO. 65

DATE	ITEMS	POST. REF.	DEBIT	DATE	ITEMS	POST. REF.	CREDIT
1962 Nov 15		CP1	200 00				
30		CP1	200 00				
			400 00				

**General ledger after all journals have been posted
and the accounts have been footed (concluded)**

What is the meaning of each of the following:

(a) miscellaneous entries   (b) general journal   (c) correcting entries

Chapter questions

1. What kinds of transactions are recorded in the general journal?
2. Give examples of entries that would be recorded in the general journal.
3. What is the immediate record for an opening entry in the general journal?
4. What business paper was the source for recording balances in the accounts receivable ledger? in the accounts payable ledger?
5. Why are supplies purchased on account for use in a business not recorded in the purchases journal?
6. Why is it advisable to draw a diagonal line in the Post. Ref. column of the journal at the time of making the entry when one amount is to be posted to two accounts?
7. Why is it important to post items to customers' and creditors' accounts frequently?
8. What does a trial balance prove?

Cases for discussion

1. When the bookkeeper for M. R. Hunt started to record the beginning balance sheet in the general journal, he found that the total assets did not equal the total liabilities plus proprietorship. The difference was $100.00. What steps must the bookkeeper take before he makes the opening entry?
2. Mr. Ballard operates a garage. He repairs and services cars; sells gasoline, oil, tires, etc.; and also operates a tow service. Whenever the driver of the towing truck needs gasoline for the truck, he fills the tank from the garage service pump. No record is made of the amounts of gasoline taken. (a) If you were Mr. Ballard's bookkeeper, what kinds of records would you want kept? (b) What journal entry would you make?

Drill for understanding

Drill 15-A. *Journalizing transactions*

The following are selected business transactions of the Fenton Grocery Company. The business uses a purchases journal, a sales journal, a cash receipts journal, a cash payments journal, and a general journal.

Instructions: For each transaction, state:

(a) The journal in which the transaction would be recorded.
(b) The account or accounts that would be debited.
(c) The account or accounts that would be credited.

1. Purchased merchandise on account from Wholesalers Incorporated, $400.00.
2. Received cash, $300.00, from cash sales of merchandise.
3. Purchased office furniture on account from Ideal Furniture Company, $900.00.
4. Sold merchandise on account to J. R. Tomkins, $45.60.
5. Paid cash, $218.30, to Wholesalers Incorporated on account.
6. Received cash, $146.80, from W. L. Cody on account.
7. A. L. Fenton, the proprietor, withdrew merchandise from the business for personal use, $72.40.
8. Paid cash, $312.50, for cash purchase of merchandise.
9. Paid cash, $85.00, for store supplies.
10. Purchased supplies on account from Mason Supply Company, $116.90·
11. Paid cash, $410.00, for salaries.
12. Paid cash, $240.00, for rent.
13. Paid cash, $65.00, to City Delivery Company for delivery service.
14. Paid cash, $15.00, for window cleaning service.

Application problems

Problem 15-1. *Recording an opening entry*

F. H. Olsen, an auto supply dealer, decided to open a new set of books on April 1 of the current year. His balance sheet on March 31 was as follows:

F. H. Olsen					
Balance Sheet					
March 31, 19——					
Assets			Liabilities		
Cash..................	3,600	00	Accounts Payable......	1,100	00
Accounts Receivable....	1,200	00			
Merchandise Inventory..	4,300	00	Proprietorship		
Supplies..............	80	00	F. H. Olsen, Capital.....	8,200	00
Prepaid Insurance......	120	00			
Total Assets..........	9,300	00	Total Liab. & Prop......	9,300	00

Instructions; Record the opening entry on page 1 of a general journal.

Problem 15-2. *Recording miscellaneous entries*

The transactions given below are some of the transactions completed during the month of April by F. H. Olsen. Mr. Olsen records transactions in a purchases journal, a sales journal, a cash receipts journal, a cash payments journal, and a general journal.

Apr. 1. Paid $225.00 for the April rent (Check No. 45).
   3. Purchased office furniture on account from T. F. Rice Company, $700.00; invoice of April 2 (Invoice No. 33).
   5. Received $138.40 from F. W. Arden in full of April 1 balance.
   8. Sold merchandise on account to B. M. Bell, $116.80 (Sale No. 65).
   12. Paid $269.70 to the Kelton Manufacturing Co. in full of April 1 balance (Check No. 46).
   13. Sold merchandise on account to R. D. Thomas, $234.76 (Sale No. 66).
   15. Received $1,646.80 from cash sales for April 1 to 15.

Apr. 17. Took from stock for personal use a car radio costing $110.00.
  20. Paid $197.80 to the Gregory Manufacturing Co. in full of April 1 balance (Check No. 47).
  22. Purchased office supplies on account from the Acme Supply Co., $70.00; invoice of April 20 (Invoice No. 34).
  24. Discovered that a March 22 sale of merchandise on account for $160.00 to F. W. Arden had been posted incorrectly to the account of F. V. Warden.
  28. Took $300.00 for personal use (Check No. 48).
  30. Paid $350.00 for clerks' salaries for the month (Check No. 49).
  30. Purchased merchandise on account from the Kelton Manufacturing Co., $569.74; invoice of April 29 (Invoice No. 35).
  30. Sold office supplies on account as an accommodation to L. D. Toll, $15.00.
  30. Received $1,872.55 from cash sales for April 16 to 30.

Instructions: Select only those entries that should be made in a general journal and record them on two-column journal paper.

Optional problems

★*Supplementary Problem 15-S. Recording miscellaneous transactions*

R. L. Woods owned and operated a paint shop. During the month of July of the current year he had the following transactions that could not be recorded in any of his special journals:

July 6. R. D. Wilkey reported that he was charged $54.80 for merchandise that he had not purchased. The sales journal shows that this charge should have been made to R. D. Wilkes.
  12. Purchased supplies on account from Mills Supply Company, for use in the business, $46.90; invoice dated July 10.
  18. Took merchandise that cost $92.60 for use in painting home.
  26. Donald Wilson reported that he was charged $64.20 for merchandise he had not purchased. The sales journal shows that this debit should have been made to Donald Wilton.

Instructions: Record the above transactions in a general journal.

★*Bonus Problem 15-B. Recording miscellaneous transactions*

J. T. Harvard owned and operated a retail clothing store. During the month of January of the current year he had the following transactions that could not be recorded in any of his special journals:

Jan. 10. Purchased new display counters on account from the Store Supply Company, $675.80. The invoice was dated January 9.
  13. Agreed with a show card artist to exchange a suit of clothes that cost $40.00 for advertising display cards.
  16. Donated clothing that cost $45.00 to the Salvation Army. (The store has an account titled Contributions.)
  22. Withdrew from stock for personal use merchandise that was priced to sell for $60, which was one third more than it cost.
  27. Sold an old display counter for $130 to Joe's Secondhand Store on account.

Instructions: Record the above transactions in a general journal.

Chapter 16

Bank deposits and reconciliation of bank statements

Protecting cash receipts

It is not safe to keep large amounts of cash at a store or an office, on one's person, or at home. It is therefore desirable to deposit all receipts of cash in a bank. Cash is safe in a bank, not only because it is protected by the bank, but also because in most banks each depositor's account is insured up to $10,000 by the Federal Deposit Insurance Corporation. This corporation is an agency of the federal government.

Banking services

Among the many services that banks render to their depositors are: (1) receive cash for safekeeping; (2) pay out cash on the order of depositors; (3) report to each depositor at regular times his deposits, his withdrawals, and his bank account balance.

A business receives cash from customers in the form of coins, bills, checks, money orders, and bank drafts. Businesses and individuals usually place all cash received in a bank for safekeeping and withdraw it as needed by writing checks. Placing cash with a bank is called *making a deposit*. The one in whose name the cash is deposited is called a *depositor*. The report the bank makes to a depositor showing his deposits, his withdrawals, and his bank account balance is called a *bank statement*.

Two types of bank accounts

Most banks provide at least two kinds of accounts with depositors: (1) accounts that permit depositors to withdraw cash at will by check; and (2) accounts on which the bank pays interest to the depositor for cash left with it. An account with a bank that permits the depositor to withdraw cash by check is called a *checking account*. An account with a bank on which a bank pays interest to the depositor is called a *savings account*.

Opening a bank account — the signature card

Each new depositor is required to sign his name on a card so that the bank may verify his signature on all business papers that come to the bank. The card a depositor signs to provide the bank with a copy of his authorized signature is called a *signature card*.

Two signature cards are illustrated below. The one at the left is the card for Morton Supplies. It shows that only Fred Morton, the proprietor, is authorized to sign checks for the business. The one at the right is the signature card of the Palmer Paint Shop. It shows that either R. A. Palmer or B. L. Moore is authorized to sign checks for the business.

SIGNATURE CARD	SIGNATURE CARD
Date *March 27, 1962* ___ THE PACIFIC NATIONAL BANK WILL PLEASE RECOGNIZE IN PAYMENT OF FUNDS, OR THE TRANSACTION OF OTHER BUSINESS ON THIS ACCOUNT, THE AUTHORIZED SIGNATURES BELOW.	Date *June 19, 1962* ___ THE MERCHANTS NATIONAL BANK WILL PLEASE RECOGNIZE IN PAYMENT OF FUNDS, OR THE TRANSACTION OF OTHER BUSINESS ON THIS ACCOUNT, THE AUTHORIZED SIGNATURES BELOW.
Name of Firm *Morton Supplies*	Name of Firm *Palmer Paint Shop*
By *Fred Morton* Signature	By *R. A. Palmer* Signature
By Signature	By *B. L. Moore* Signature
By Signature	By Signature
Phone *Main 1-8871* *460 Main St.* Address	Phone *871-3934* *1142 Erie Ave.* Address
Name to be filled in by Bank. ADDRESS AS— Morton Supplies 460 Main St., City	Name to be filled in by Bank. ADDRESS AS— Palmer Paint Shop 1142 Erie Ave., City

Signature cards

The signature card is a safeguard established by the bank to protect against forgeries. The depositor must make certain that he always signs his checks exactly as his signature appears on the signature card on file with the bank. If the signature on the check is not the same as that shown on the signature card, the bank will refuse to pay the check.

The deposit ticket

The business form provided by the bank on which the depositor lists all cash and cash items that he wishes to deposit is called a *deposit ticket*. The term *deposit slip* is also used. Two commonly used forms of deposit tickets are shown at the top of the following page.

Analyzing the two deposit tickets

Each deposit ticket provides space for: (1) the account number; (2) the date; (3) the name of the depositor and his address; (4) the total amount in currency and coins; (5) the individual amount of each check; (6) the identification of each check; and (7) the total of the deposit.

If such items as postal money orders, express money orders, and bank drafts are deposited, they are listed with the checks.

In the deposit ticket at the left, Morton Supplies uses the identification column to record the name of the person from whom the check was received. This information is useful if questions arise about a check.

In the deposit ticket at the right, Kane's Hobby Shop uses the identification column to record the banks' identification numbers. Some banks prefer this method. A depositor should use the method preferred by his bank.

216

PACIFIC NATIONAL BANK

ACCOUNT NUMBER

`1 2 1 - 6 4 9 7`

MORTON SUPPLIES
PLEASE PRINT EXACT TITLE OF ACCOUNT

460 Main Street

DATE December 12 1962

Checks and other items are received for deposit subject to the terms and conditions of this bank's collection agreement.

CURRENCY	84	00
SILVER	7	35
CHECKS J. C. Miller	69	00
2 D. C. Walsh	308	00
3		
4		
5		
6		
7		
TOTAL ⟶	468	35

Deposit ticket
Checks identified by person
from whom received

LINCOLN BANK OF DETROIT

ACCOUNT NUMBER

`2 5 0 - 1 9 7 7 3`

KANE'S HOBBY SHOP
PLEASE PRINT EXACT TITLE OF ACCOUNT

1416 RIVER STREET

DATE DECEMBER 14, 1962

Checks and other items are received for deposit subject to the terms and conditions of this bank's collection agreement.

CURRENCY	213	00
SILVER	18	26
CHECKS 9-42	68	40
2 74-457	16	45
3 74-419	19	20
4 15-119	21	80
5		
6		
7		
TOTAL ⟶	357	11

Deposit ticket
Checks identified by A.B.A. number

A.B.A. numbers

Identification numbers assigned to banks by the American Bankers Association are called *A.B.A. numbers*. The first check listed on the deposit ticket of Kane's Hobby Shop is shown below.

JOHN R. WILSON
415 2nd Avenue
Detroit 6, Michigan

No. 421

DETROIT, MICHIGAN Dec. 16 1962

9-42
720

PAY TO THE
ORDER OF Kane's Hobby Shop $68 40/100

Sixty-eight and 40/100 _____ DOLLARS

**LINCOLN BANK
OF DETROIT**

DETROIT, MICHIGAN

John R. Wilson

⑆0720⑈0042⑆ 890 123 4⑈

Check with magnetic ink numbers for sorting purposes

The numbers listed on the deposit ticket, 9-42, are the A.B.A. identification numbers of the Lincoln Bank of Detroit. The first part of the number, 9, is the number assigned to all banks in Detroit. The second part, 42, is the number assigned to the Lincoln Bank of Detroit.

The number below the line is called the Federal Reserve number. The first digit, 7, is the number of the Federal Reserve District in which the bank is located. The second digit indicates whether the bank is served by the head office or a branch of the Federal Reserve Bank. If the digit is 1, the bank is served by a head office; if the digit is larger than 1, the bank is served by a branch. The third digit, in this case 0, is used for additional sorting of checks.

In the illustration, bank numbers are printed in magnetic ink on the lower edge of the check. These magnetic ink numbers make it possible for the bank to use automated equipment in sorting checks.

Depositor's record of deposits

When cash is deposited in a bank, the teller provides the depositor with one of the following: (1) a copy of the deposit ticket with the date and the name of the bank stamped on it; or (2) a receipt issued by the bank that shows the name of the depositor, the date, and the amount of the deposit; or (3) a record of the deposit in a small book that the bank issues to the depositor in which all deposits are recorded. The small book issued to the depositor in which the receiving teller records the date and the amount of the deposit is called a *bank passbook*.

Endorsing checks

Before a bank will accept a check for deposit, the depositor must sign or stamp his name on the back of the check. The signature or stamp of the depositor on the back of a check is called an *endorsement*. An endorsement is written or stamped on the back of a check at a right angle to the writing on the front as shown in the illustration at the right.

The purpose of the endorsement is to transfer the title of the check to the bank. In addition, the depositor guarantees payment of the check by his endorsement.

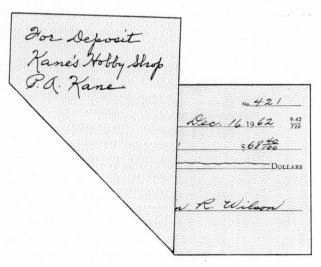

Endorsed check

218

Kinds of endorsements

Different kinds of endorsements serve different purposes. The principal forms of endorsements are discussed and illustrated below.

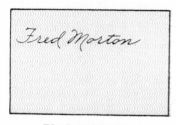

Blank endorsement

Blank endorsement. An endorsement that consists only of the name of the endorser is called a *blank endorsement*. Since a lost or stolen check with a blank endorsement can be cashed by a finder or a thief, a blank endorsement should be used only at the time the check is being cashed or deposited in a bank.

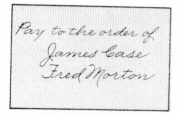

Endorsement in full

Endorsement in full. An endorsement that states on whose order the check is to be paid, together with the name of the endorser, is called an *endorsement in full*. This kind of endorsement states that the check can be cashed or transferred only on the order of the person named in the endorsement.

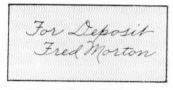

Restrictive endorsement

Restrictive endorsement. An endorsement that limits the receiver of the check as to the use he may make of the funds collected is called a *restrictive endorsement*. Restrictive endorsements are commonly used when checks are prepared for deposit.

Writing a check

A check may be written in ink or by a machine. First, the check stub should be filled out completely. It should contain all the information about the transaction, for the check stub is the immediate record for every entry in the cash payments journal. Second, the check should be written. In writing a check, the steps given below should be followed.

Step 1. *Date.* The current date should be used as the date of the check. Banks will not cash a check that is dated later than the date it is presented for payment. For example, if a check dated February 14 is presented for payment on February 10, the bank will refuse to cash it.

Step 2. *Name of payee.* A check made out to a business as the payee should be made payable to the business — not the proprietor. A check made payable to a married woman should be made out in her given name and her husband's last name.

Step 3. *The amount*. The amount should be written both in figures and in words. For example, a check for $25.10 is written in figures as follows: $25\frac{10}{}$. The figures are written very close to the printed dollar sign on the check so that it is impossible to write another number in front of them. The amount is also written in words as follows: Twenty-five $\frac{10}{100}$. These words are written at the extreme left of the line so that nothing else can be written before the words.

Some businesses use check-writing machines for writing amounts on their checks. A check-writing machine usually perforates the amount of the check. This makes it almost impossible for anyone to alter the amount of the check.

Step 4. *Signature*. The signature of the drawer of the check must be exactly as it appears on the signature card.

Voiding a check

When the books of a business are audited by tax authorities or accountants, they expect to find every check number accounted for. Therefore it is important to keep all checks returned by the bank and all checks that may have to be rewritten because of errors.

Banks usually refuse to cash a check that has been altered in any way. If an error is made in writing a check, a new check should be written. The check on which the error is made should be filed. Before filing it, the word "Void" is written across the face of the check and the stub of the check. Writing the word "void" across the face of the check and the stub to indicate that the check and stub are not to be used is called *voiding a check*.

When a check is voided, a memorandum entry is usually made in the cash payments journal so that the cash payments journal will show that each check number is accounted for. This is done by writing: (1) the date in the Date column; (2) the words "Voided check" in the Account Debited column; (3) the number of the check in the Check No. column; and (4) a check mark in the Post. Ref. column. Nothing is written in an amount column.

Recording a dishonored check

A check that a bank refuses to pay is called a *dishonored check*. The bank may refuse to pay the check for a number of reasons. For example, the check may have been altered, the signature of the drawer of the check may not be the same as the signature on the signature card, or the drawer may not have enough funds in his account to cover the check.

When a depositor is notified by his bank that a check he has deposited has been dishonored, he must pay the bank the amount of the check. The depositor writes his own check payable to the bank for the amount of the dishonored check. This cash payment by the depositor is recorded in his cash payments journal. The account debited is the customer from whom the dishonored check was received. This entry, when posted to the customer's account, will show that the customer still owes the depositor the amount of the dishonored check.

The bank's record of each depositor's account

The bank keeps a ledger account for each of its depositors. The deposit slips and the checks are posted to the depositor's account each business day.

The amount in a depositor's account after adding all deposits to the previous balance and subtracting the checks drawn by the depositor is known as the *bank balance*. At regular intervals, usually once each month, banks send each depositor a statement that shows all deposits, all withdrawals, and the balance of his account. This bank statement is used by the depositor to check the accuracy of his own records as well as the accuracy of the statement received from the bank.

The depositor's record of his bank account

A depositor who has a complete and accurate system of bookkeeping knows his bank balance at all times. The check stubs, if kept properly, can be referred to at any time and the last stub will show the bank balance.

The bank records of a depositor, when all cash has been deposited, are proved as follows:

Beginning cash balance as shown in the cash receipts journal
> *plus*

the total of the Cash Debit column of the cash receipts journal
> *minus*

the total of the Cash Credit column of the cash payments journal
> *equals*

the check-stub balance.

Checking the accuracy of bank records

Although it is uncommon for banks to make errors in their records, there are instances when unavoidable errors do occur. For example, the bank may have accounts with several John Smiths. Unless great care is used by the bank to compare the different signatures of these Smith accounts, a check may be charged to the wrong account or a deposit may be credited to the wrong account.

Another instance in which a bank may make a mistake is that of paying a check that has been forged. If a bank pays a forged check, the bank must stand the loss. When a depositor discovers the bank has made an error, he should notify the bank at once.

The depositor may also make errors in addition and subtraction on his own check stubs. He may locate the error when he proves cash or he may not locate it until he gets his bank statement at the end of the month.

In any of the above cases, the records of the bank and the records of the depositor would not agree. Good business practice, therefore, requires that the depositor compare his records with those of the bank immediately upon receipt of the bank statement.

Bank service charges

Banks obtain income by using part of the funds deposited with them to purchase interest-bearing securities, such as government bonds. They also lend part of the funds deposited and charge interest on the loans. If a depositor has a rather large balance so that a considerable sum is available for investment, a bank will receive more than enough in interest to pay for all of the clerical work and supplies used in handling the customer's account.

If the balance of an account is small, the expense of handling the depositor's account may exceed the possible income to the bank. Banks usually make a monthly charge whenever the depositor's balance is small compared to the number of checks written. A charge made by a bank for servicing an account is called a *bank service charge*. Service charges vary in different communities.

The bank statement

A bank statement shows in detail (1) the balance the depositor had at the beginning of the month, (2) the checks paid by the bank, (3) bank service charges, if any, (4) the amounts deposited, and (5) the depositor's balance at the end of the month.

When a bank sends a bank statement to a depositor, it also returns each check paid by the bank during the month. The checks paid by the bank during the month are stamped or punched on a machine that shows the date they were paid by the bank. Checks that the bank has paid and returned to the depositor are known as *canceled checks*. It is good business practice to keep all canceled checks because they are evidence of the payment of bills.

The bank statement for Morton Supplies

On February 1, Morton Supplies received its bank statement for the month of January. The bank returned with the statement the checks that it had paid for the business during January and a form showing that a service charge of $2.00 has been made. The bank statement is illustrated on the opposite page.

STATEMENT OF YOUR ACCOUNT					
		121-6497			
PACIFIC NATIONAL BANK		Morton Supplies 460 Main Street Portland, Oregon			

CHECKS	CHECKS	DEPOSITS	NO. OF CHECKS	DATE	BALANCE
116.25				Jan 1'63	1,863.90
		429.87	1	Jan 2'63	1,747.65
9.80	223.15			Jan 6'63	2,177.52
15.80	58.63	280.00	3	Jan 7'63	1,944.57
322.50	63.25		5	Jan 8'63	2,150.14
		174.61	7	Jan 9'63	1,764.39
27.80				Jan10'63	1,939.00
100.00	150.00	549.40	8	Jan13'63	1,911.20
15.00			10	Jan15'63	2,210.60
		369.18	11	Jan16'63	2,195.60
410.33		750.76		Jan17'63	2,564.78
326.85	100.00		12	Jan24'63	2,905.21
150.00	17.50		14	Jan28'63	2,478.36
2.00SC	12.00	571.80	16	Jan30'63	2,310.86
			17	Jan31'63	2,868.66

CC—Certified Check CM—Credit Memo DM—Debit Memo	EC—Error Corrected LS—List of Checks NC—Check Not Counted	OD—Overdrawn RT—Returned Item SC—Service Charge

Bank statement

Analysis of the bank statement

The bank statement of Morton Supplies illustrated above shows:

1. The balance as of January 1, $1,863.90.
2. The checks paid by the bank during January.
3. The charge made by the bank for services.

> Some banks make the service charge at the beginning of the month for services of the previous month.

4. The deposits made during January.
5. The balance of the account for each date during the month.

Proving records with the bank statement

The bank statement at the end of the month is valuable proof of the accuracy of the bookkeeping records. When all cash receipts are deposited in the bank, the cash receipts as shown by the cash receipts journal must be the same as the deposits shown on the bank statement. When all cash payments are made by check, the bank statement must agree with the cash payments journal except for outstanding checks, for which the bookkeeper must account. A check that has been issued but not presented to a bank for payment is known as an *outstanding check*.

223

The process of bringing into agreement the bank balance as shown on the bank statement and the balance as shown on the check stub is called *reconciling the bank statement*.

Reconciling the bank statement

When Morton Supplies receives the bank statement, the balance shown on the last check stub is compared with the bank balance shown on the bank statement. The check stub shows the balance to be $2,234.16. The balance on the bank statement is $2,868.66. As the two balances are not equal, it is necessary to reconcile the bank statement. The following steps are taken:

Step 1. The canceled checks received from the bank are arranged in order by check number.

Step 2. A check mark is placed on the stub of each check that has been returned.

Step 3. A reconciliation of the bank statement is prepared in the following form:

Reconciliation of bank statement

Analyzing the reconciliation of the bank statement

The following steps are taken to reconcile the bank statement:

Step 1. The last check stub in the checkbook shows a balance on January 31 of $2,234.16. This amount is recorded as shown above.

Step 2. The bank service charge, $2.00, as shown on the bank statement is deducted from the check-stub balance, giving a corrected check-stub balance of $2,232.16.

Step 3. The balance as shown on the bank statement for January 31, $2,868.66, is recorded as shown above.

224

Step 4. Each check stub that does not have a check mark on it is listed, together with the check number and the amount. The column is totaled and labeled "Total Outstanding Checks." The total is written under the bank statement balance to make subtraction easy.

Step 5. The total of the outstanding checks is deducted from the balance shown on the bank statement. This gives the corrected bank balance of $2,232.16.

The corrected check-stub balance and the corrected bank balance are the same. The bank statement is therefore said to be reconciled.

Recording service charges in the cash payments journal

When a service charge is made by a bank, the amount is deducted from the balance on the check stub. It is also necessary to record the service charge in the cash payments journal. This is done by a debit to Miscellaneous Expense in the General Debit column and a credit to Cash in the Cash Credit column. The entry in the cash payments journal is as follows:

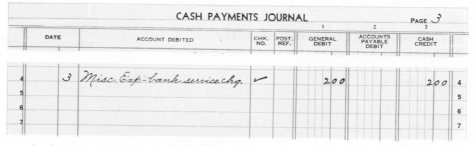

		CASH PAYMENTS JOURNAL			1	2	PAGE 3 3	
	DATE	ACCOUNT DEBITED	CHK. NO.	POST. REF.	GENERAL DEBIT	ACCOUNTS PAYABLE DEBIT	CASH CREDIT	
4		3 *Misc. Exp.-bank service chg.* ✓			2 00		2 00	4
5								5
6								6
7								7

A check is not written for this entry; therefore a check mark is placed in the Check No. column. Since there is no check stub to provide an explanation of this entry, the words "bank service charge" are written after the name of the account debited.

Use of automation in banking

Banks in increasing numbers are making use of automation. The automatic equipment will post the deposit slips and the checks to the proper depositors' accounts. It will also sort checks for distribution to banks on which they are drawn.

The illustration on page 226 shows a check on which is printed in the lower left-hand corner the bank's identification number. This is followed by the customer's account number. The numbers printed in the lower right-hand corner show the amount of the check. This amount was printed by the bank after the check was received by the bank.

```
JOHN R. MURPHY
2275 Sunset Pike
                                                                    No. 47
                              PORTLAND, OREGON   Oct. 6  1962   24-75
                                                                1230
PAY TO THE
ORDER OF   The National Dept. Store        $ 31 23
   Thirty-one  23/100                                        DOLLARS
PACIFIC NATIONAL BANK
   PORTLAND, OREGON
                                          John R Murphy

⑆1230⑈0075⑇   390⑈17685⑈        ⑈0000003123⑈
```

All numbers on the lower margin of the check are in magnetic ink. This makes it possible to feed these checks into machines for one or all of the following purposes:

1. To sort checks by bank identification numbers.
2. To sort checks by customers' account numbers.
3. To add the amount of all checks received.
4. To post the amounts of all checks to customers' accounts.

These operations can be performed at very high speeds and without error.

Increasing your business vocabulary

What is the meaning of each of the following:

(a) depositor
(b) bank statement
(c) checking account
(d) savings account
(e) signature card
(f) deposit ticket
(g) A.B.A. numbers
(h) bank passbook
(i) endorsement

(j) blank endorsement
(k) endorsement in full
(l) restrictive endorsement
(m) dishonored check
(n) bank balance
(o) bank service charge
(p) canceled checks
(q) outstanding check
(r) reconciling the bank statement

Chapter questions

1. Why should all cash received by a business be deposited in a bank?
2. What are three common services that banks render to their depositors?
3. What are the different forms in which a business usually receives cash from a customer?
4. What two kinds of accounts do most banks provide for their depositors?
5. Why does the bank require a depositor to fill out a signature card when he opens his account?
6. What are two ways of identifying checks listed on a deposit slip?
7. What is the purpose of the endorsement on the back of a check?

8. When writing a check, why is it important to place the amount written in figures very close to the printed dollar sign?

9. If a business learns that a check that it has deposited has been dishonored, what entry should it make in its books of account?

10. What use does the depositor make of the bank statement?

11. What information does a bank statement contain?

12. Why is it advisable to keep all canceled checks in a file?

13. What entry is made on a check stub to record a bank service charge?

14. What account is debited and what account is credited in the cash payments journal to record a bank service charge?

Cases for discussion

1. J. T. Zolla prefers to keep large sums of money in the store safe and to pay most of his bills by cash instead of by check. What are the disadvantages of this plan over depositing all cash and paying bills by check?

2. J. M. Ford receives his bank statement each month but does not reconcile his bank statement. What are some of the problems that might arise from this practice?

Drills for understanding

Drill 16-A. Reconciling a bank statement

Robert Wise has a checkbook balance of $223.00 at the end of January. His bank statement shows the balance to be $230.50. When he compared the stubs with the canceled checks, Mr. Wise discovered that he did not receive Check No. 4 for $7.50 presented to the Wilson Co. the day before. Reconcile Mr. Wise's bank statement.

Drill 16-B. Reconciling a bank statement

Janet Emory received her bank statement, which showed a balance of $553.80. Janet's check stub showed a balance of $554.70. When Janet compared the canceled checks with her check stubs, she discovered that all checks written had been returned. She also noticed on the bank statement a service charge of 90 cents, which was not recorded on her check stubs. Reconcile Janet's bank statement.

Drill 16-C. Reconciling a bank statement

Barbara Green has a check-stub balance of $345.10. The bank statement indicates Barbara's balance to be only $231.55. While Barbara was comparing the bank statement with her checkbook, she found that all checks written had been returned. She also noticed that a deposit of $113.00, made the day before, had not been recorded on the bank statement and that there was a service charge of 55 cents. Reconcile Barbara's bank statement.

Application problems

Problem 16-1. Preparing a deposit ticket

On November 15 of the current year, B. L. Stewart, 917 Walnut Street, made a deposit consisting of the following items:

9 ten-dollar bills	6 half dollars	15 dimes
6 one-dollar bills	16 quarters	10 nickels

A check from Herman Dietz on the First National Bank, Chicago, Illinois, A.B.A. number 2-1 .... $150.00

A check from Arthur Merton on the Citizens Bank, Troy, New York, A.B.A. number 50-65 .... 60.00

A check from J. D. Hancock on the Union Trust Bank, City, A.B.A. number 51-66 .... 115.00

A check from Duane Philips on the First State Bank, City, A.B.A. number 51-68 .... 80.00

A postal money order from Charles Benson 20.00

Instructions: Prepare a deposit ticket for the deposit, identifying checks by the A.B.A. numbers.

Problem 16-2. Reconciliation of the bank statement of A. B. Norris

On July 1 of the current year, A. B. Norris received from the Citizens State Bank his bank statement for June, his canceled checks, and charge slips as follows: a service charge of 75 cents and a charge of $2.00 for collecting a note.

Instructions: 1. Record the two charge slips in the cash payments journal. In each case debit Miscellaneous Expense. After the first write the explanation "bank service charge"; after the second, "collection of note."

2. Prepare a reconciliation of Mr. Norris' bank statement in the same form as that on page 224. Additional data needed are:

(a) Mr. Norris' checkbook balance on June 30 was $700.00.

(b) The June 30 balance on the bank statement was $657.25. A deposit of $180.00 made on the evening of June 30 was not shown on the statement.

> Banks often provide a means whereby customers can make a deposit at the end of a business day or night. When a deposit is made after banking hours on the last day of the month, the amount of the deposit should be added to the balance shown on the bank statement before the outstanding checks are subtracted.

(c) When the canceled checks were compared with the check stubs, the following checks were found to be outstanding: No. 105, $20.00; No. 109, $50.00; and No. 120, $70.00.

Practice Set 1

Bradford wholesale grocery

Part 1 - Recording, posting, and trial balance

Purpose of this practice set

This practice set illustrates the entire accounting process. It includes all the work of a fiscal period of one month for the Bradford Wholesale Grocery, owned and operated by William Bradford.

Although the records are those of a small wholesale grocery business, they illustrate the application of general principles of accounting that apply to all businesses.

Only Part 1 will be completed at this time. Part 2, the work at the end of the fiscal period, will be completed after the class has studied Chapters 17, 18, and 19.

Required materials

The transactions of this practice set may be recorded from the narrative of transactions given on pages 232 to 236 inclusive. The work may be completed in bound blank books that may be obtained from the publishers or on unbound sheets of ruled paper. If the use of business papers and more realism are desired, a practice set using incoming and outgoing business papers and bound blank books may be obtained from the publishers.

Model illustrations

The journals, ledgers, and forms used in this practice set are listed below. Also listed are the pages of this textbook on which similar books and forms are illustrated.

Chart of accounts

The accounts needed in the general ledger of the Bradford Wholesale Gorcery are listed on the inside front cover of the bound ledger that is provided by the publishers for this practice set. They are also given in the following chart of accounts.

Bradford Wholesale Grocery

Chart of Accounts

(1) ASSETS	ACCOUNT NUMBER	(4) INCOME	ACCOUNT NUMBER
Cash.....................	11	Sales.....................	41
Accounts Receivable........	12		
Merchandise Inventory......	13	(5) COST OF MERCHANDISE	
Supplies..................	14	Purchases................	51
Prepaid Insurance.........	15		
		(6) EXPENSES	
(2) LIABILITIES		Delivery Expense...........	61
Accounts Payable..........	21	Insurance Expense..........	62
		Miscellaneous Expense......	63
(3) PROPRIETORSHIP		Rent Expense..............	64
William Bradford, Capital...	31	Salary Expense.............	65
William Bradford, Drawing..	32	Supplies Expense...........	66
Income and Expense Summary	33		

Opening a set of books for the Bradford Wholesale Grocery

Instructions: 1. Open the accounts needed in the general ledger by writing the account titles in the order in which they are given in the chart of accounts illustrated above. Use the account numbers shown on the chart.

If loose sheets (8 ½″ x 11″) are used, place four accounts on each sheet but number each account with the account number shown on the chart of accounts.

Instructions: 2. Open all of the customers' accounts in the accounts receivable ledger. These accounts are arranged in alphabetic order for quick finding. The names and the addresses of the customers of the Bradford Wholesale Grocery are listed at the top of the following page.

If the blank books obtainable from the publisher are used, each customer's account in the accounts receivable ledger is placed on a separate page. If loose sheets of ruled ledger paper are used, three customers' accounts may be placed on each ledger sheet.

LIST OF CUSTOMERS AND THEIR ADDRESSES

Benner's Market, 501 South Janesville Street, City

Culver Brothers, 875 Prince Street, Elkhorn

East Side Grocery, 208 South Highland Street, City

Engsbergs, 133 West Center Street, Jefferson

Five Points Grocery, 804 West Walworth Avenue, City

Grocery Basket, 14 Second Street, Cambridge

Handy Food Shop, 207 Main Street, City

Johnson's Market, 212 South Second Street, Milton

Platner & Son, 27 Eighth Avenue, Palmyra

Red Hen Inn, 841 East Milwaukee Street, City

Ridge Grocery, 192 Main Street, City

Instructions: 3. Open all of the creditors' accounts in the accounts payable ledger. These accounts are listed alphabetically below.

If the blank books obtainable from the publisher are used, each creditor's account is placed on a separate page. If loose sheets of ruled paper are used, three creditors' accounts may be placed on each ledger sheet.

LIST OF CREDITORS AND THEIR ADDRESSES

Baker Supply Company, 210 North Park Street, City

George Baskin, 716 West Harper Avenue, Madison

Mason Company, 148 East Main Street, Janesville

Nelson & Smith, 9136 Homan Avenue, Chicago

Reese Corporation, 75 Highland Street, Springfield

Rogers & Rogers, 417 South Prince Street, Rockford

Steck, Inc., 7580 North Fremont Street, Evansville

Instructions: 4. Record in the general ledger the balance of each account that is listed below, using the balances that are given. Date each balance October 1 of the current year.

LIST OF BALANCE SHEET ACCOUNTS AND THEIR BALANCES

	DEBIT	CREDIT
Cash............................	3,195.50	
Accounts Receivable...............	4,824.00	
Merchandise Inventory.............	59,284.00	
Supplies.........................	743.00	
Prepaid Insurance.................	880.00	
Accounts Payable.................		4,504.50
William Bradford, Capital..........		64,422.00

Instructions: 5. Record the cash balance in the cash receipts journal as a memorandum entry in the manner shown in the illustration on page 182.

Instructions: 6. Record each customer's balance in his account in the accounts receivable ledger, dating each balance October 1. The amount of each customer's balance is shown in the schedule of accounts receivable on the next page.

| Bradford Wholesale Grocery |
| Schedule of Accounts Receivable |
| September 30, 19-- |

Benner's Market...............................	$1,233.25
East Side Grocery..............................	987.00
Engsbergs.....................................	860.75
Grocery Basket................................	909.00
Ridge Grocery.................................	834.00
Total Accounts Receivable.....................	$4,824.00

Instructions: 7. Record each creditor's balance in his account in the accounts payable ledger, dating each balance October 1. The amount of each creditor's balance is shown in the following schedule of accounts payable.

| Bradford Wholesale Grocery |
| Schedule of Accounts Payable |
| September 30, 19-- |

George Baskin.................................	$1,230.25
Nelson & Smith................................	912.00
Rogers & Rogers...............................	1,083.00
Steck, Inc....................................	1,279.25
Total Accounts Payable........................	$4,504.50

Narrative of transactions for October

October 1
No. 1. Paid $475.00 for rent for October (Check No. 201).

October 2
No. 2. Purchased merchandise on account from Mason Company, $12,101.50 (Invoice No. 91).

No. 3. Sold merchandise on account to East Side Grocery, $805.00 (Sale No. 181).

No. 4. Received $1,233.25 from Benner's Market on account.

October 3
No. 5. Sold merchandise on account to Engsbergs, $1,740.50 (Sale No. 182).

No. 6. Paid $912.00 to Nelson & Smith on account (Check No. 202).

No. 7. Sold merchandise on account to Red Hen Inn, $956.80 (Sale No. 183).

October 4
No. 8. Sold merchandise on account to Culver Brothers, $1,691.00 (Sale No. 184).

No. 9. The cash sales for October 1 to 4 were $8,820.30.

Cash proof. Foot and prove the two cash journals and determine the cash balance. Use small pencil figures for the footings. See the discussion on pages 186 and 187. The cash balance, ascertained by counting the cash on hand and by adding to this amount the bank balance on the check stub, is $11,862.05.

Posting. Post from each of the five journals the items that are to be posted individually. Column totals are not to be posted at this time but at the end of the month only.

October 6

No. 10. Paid $1,083.00 to Rogers & Rogers on account (Check No. 203).

No. 11. Sold merchandise on account to Platner & Son, $324.76 (Sale No. 185).

No. 12. Received $600.00 from Ridge Grocery on account.

No. 13. Purchased merchandise on account from Nelson & Smith, $8,519.00 (Invoice No. 92).

October 7

No. 14. Paid $1,279.25 to Steck, Inc. on account (Check No. 204).

No. 15. Sold merchandise on account to Handy Food Shop, $1,827.00 (Sale No. 186).

No. 16. Sold merchandise on account to Grocery Basket, $951.33 (Sale No. 187).

October 8

No. 17. Paid $35.40 for telephone bill for September (Check No. 205).

No. 18. Sold merchandise on account to Five Points Grocery, $1,246.45 (Sale No. 188).

October 9

No. 19. Purchased wrapping paper and cartons on account from the Baker Supply Company, $205.00.

See page 204 for a discussion of purchases of supplies on account and an illustration of a general journal entry of this type.

No. 20. Sold merchandise on account to Benner's Market, $165.37 (Sale No. 189).

No. 21. Purchased merchandise on account from Nelson & Smith, $6,835.75 (Invoice No. 93).

October 10

No. 22. Received $867.30 from East Side Grocery on account.

No. 23. The East Side Grocery reported that they had been charged $119.70 on September 25 for merchandise that they had not received. This sale should have been charged to Five Points Grocery.

See page 207 for a discussion and an illustration of a correcting entry of this type in the general journal.

October 11

No. 24. Cash sales for October 6 to 11 were $12,798.75.

Cash proof. Foot and prove the two cash journals and determine the cash balance. The cash balance is $23,730.45.

Posting. Post the items that are to be posted individually from each of the five journals.

October 13

No. 25. Received $909.00 from Grocery Basket on account.

No. 26. Paid $8,519.00 to Nelson & Smith on account (Check No. 206).

No. 27. Received $119.70 from Five Points Grocery on account.

No. 28. Purchased merchandise on account from George Baskin, $9,870.50 (Invoice No. 94).

October 14

No. 29. Received $234.00 from Ridge Grocery on account.

No. 30. Sold merchandise on account to Engsbergs, $36.46 (Sale No. 190).

No. 31. Paid $175.50 for miscellaneous supplies (Check No. 207).

October 15

No. 32. The proprietor, William Bradford, withdrew $350.00 for personal use (Check No. 208).

No. 33. Paid $1,450.00 for salaries for first half of month (Check No. 209).

October 16

No. 34. Sold merchandise on account to Johnson's Market, $2,039.40 (Sale No. 191).

No. 35. Sold merchandise on account to Handy Food Shop, $2,350.00 (Sale No. 192).

October 17

No. 36. Sold merchandise on account to Ridge Grocery, $746.45 (Sale No. 193).

No. 37. Sold merchandise on account to Culver Brothers, $2,329.60 (Sale No. 194).

No. 38. Received $805.00 from East Side Grocery on account.

No. 39. Paid $265.00 to Rolf Trucking Company for delivery service for the first half of the month. (Check No. 210). Debit Delivery Expense.

October 18

No. 40. Paid $6,835.75 to Nelson & Smith on account (Check No. 211).

No. 41. Received a check for $956.80 from Red Hen Inn on account.

No. 42. Received a check for $1,691.00 from Culver Brothers on account.

No. 43. Cash sales for October 13 to 18 were $10,717.25.

Cash proof. Foot and prove the two cash journals and determine the cash balance. The cash balance is $21,567.95.

Posting. Post the items that are to be posted individually from each of the five journals.

October 20

No. 44. Paid $11,100.75 to George Baskin on account (Check No. 212).

No. 45. Purchased supplies on account from the Baker Supply Company, $124.75.

No. 46. Purchased merchandise on account from Nelson & Smith, $9,452.20 (Invoice No. 95).

No. 47. Sold merchandise on account to East Side Grocery, $203.00 (Sale No. 195).

October 21

No. 48. Sold merchandise on account to the Grocery Basket, $1,376.10 (Sale No. 196).

No. 49. Received $20.00 from the Rolf Trucking Company. The trucking company sent a letter with the check, explaining that in figuring the bill paid on October 17 there was an error of $20.00 and that a refund was therefore being made.

> Record this transaction in the cash receipts journal as a credit to Delivery Expense. Enter the amount in the General Credit column.

October 22

No. 50. Received a check for $951.33 from Grocery Basket on account.

No. 51. Purchased merchandise on account from Rogers & Rogers, $7,898.00 (Invoice No. 96).

No. 52. Sold merchandise on account to Platner & Son, $2,325.45 (Sale No. 197).

October 23

No. 53. The proprietor, William Bradford, took canned goods for personal use; cost price was $75.00.

> See the discussion of withdrawals by the proprietor on page 206. Since this transaction is not a sale to a customer, credit the purchases account. Record this transaction in the general journal.

No. 54. Purchased merchandise on account from the Reese Corporation, $8,775.00 (Invoice No. 97).

October 24

No. 55. Sold merchandise on account to Engsbergs, $1,610.15 (Sale No. 198).

No. 56. Received $1,000.00 from Platner & Son on account.

October 25

No. 57. Purchased merchandise on account from Steck, Inc., $9,487.67 (Invoice No. 98).

No. 58. Sold merchandise on account to Five Points Grocery, $2,865.34 (Sale No. 199).

No. 59. Paid $12,101.50 to Mason Company on account (Check No. 213).

No. 60. Received $860.75 from Engsbergs on account.

No. 61. Cash sales for October 20 to 25 were $12,536.00.

Cash proof. Foot and prove the two cash journals and determine the cash balance. The cash balance is $13,733.78.

Posting. Post the items that are to be posted individually from each of the five journals.

October 27

No. 62. Sold merchandise on account to Johnson's Market, $497.85 (Sale No. 200).

No. 63. Paid $45.00 for miscellaneous supplies (Check No. 214).

October 28

No. 64. Received $165.37 from Benner's Market on account.

No. 65. Received $1,246.45 from Five Points Grocery on account.

October 29

No. 66. Received $2,039.40 from Johnson's Market on account.

No. 67. Paid $9,452.20 to Nelson & Smith on account (Check No. 215).

No. 68. Paid $45.20 for electricity bill for October (Check No. 216).

No. 69. Paid $24.70 for water bill for October (Check No. 217).

October 30

No. 70. Received $1,827.00 from the Handy Food Shop on account.

No. 71. The proprietor, William Bradford, withdrew $350.00 for personal use (Check No. 218).

No. 72. Paid $7,898.00 to Rogers & Rogers on account (Check No. 219).

October 31

No. 73. Received $1,776.96 from Engsbergs on account.

No. 74. Purchased merchandise for cash from A. H. Crosby Company, $910.65 (Check No. 220).

No. 75. Paid $1,450.00 for salaries for last half of month (Check No. 221).

No. 76. Paid $315.00 to Rolf Trucking Co. for delivery service (Check No. 222).

No. 77. The cash sales for October 27 to 31 were $9,863.50.

Cash proof. Foot and prove the two cash journals and determine the cash balance. The cash balance is $10,161.71.

Posting. Post the items that are to be posted individually from each of the five journals.

Completing and posting the journals

Instructions: 1. Total and rule the purchases journal. Post the total. Compare your work with the purchases journal shown on page 138.

2. Total and rule the sales journal. Post the total. Compare your work with the sales journal shown on page 172.

3. Total and rule the cash receipts journal. Post the totals of the special columns. Compare your work with the cash receipts journal on page 186.

4. Total and rule the cash payments journal. Post the totals of the special columns. Compare your work with the cash payments journal on page 154.

Schedules and trial balance

Instructions; 5. Prepare a schedule of accounts receivable and a schedule of accounts payable. Compare your work with the schedules on pages 195 and 161. Prove the accuracy of the subsidiary ledgers by comparing the schedule totals with the balances of the controlling accounts in the general ledger.

6. Prepare a trial balance. Use as your guide the model trial balance on page 209.

Chapter 17

Work sheet with adjustments

Need for adjusting some ledger accounts at the end of a fiscal period

At the end of a fiscal period, some of the accounts of a business need to be brought up to date. In the ledger of Morton Supplies, Merchandise Inventory is an example of such an account.

As shown in the T account at the right, the merchandise inventory account shows the value of the goods on hand at the beginning of the fiscal period. This merchandise inventory account does not show that the inventory has been changed during the fiscal period as a result of purchases and sales.

Merchandise Inventory	
Nov. 1 5,500.50	

Each purchase increased the amount of merchandise on hand, but all purchases were recorded in the purchases account. Each sale decreased the amount of merchandise on hand, but all sales were recorded in the sales account. This plan of recording purchases and sales in separate accounts was used in order to make it easier to determine quickly the total purchases and the total sales at the end of the fiscal period. However, it does leave the merchandise inventory account in need of adjustment at the time the financial reports are to be prepared.

Other accounts in the ledger of Morton Supplies that need to be adjusted are Supplies and Prepaid Insurance. These accounts are developed later in this chapter.

Changes that are recorded in accounts at the end of a fiscal period so that these accounts will be brought up to date are called *adjustments*. All changes in ledger accounts must result from the posting of journal entries. No adjustments should be made directly in ledger accounts. Journal entries to record adjustments are called *adjusting entries*.

Work sheet with columns for adjustments

When a business records adjustments, two columns for adjustments are provided on the work sheet immediately after the Trial Balance columns. This form of work sheet has the following column headings:

		1	2	3	4	5	6	7	8
ACCOUNT TITLES	ACCT. NO.	TRIAL BALANCE		ADJUSTMENTS		INCOME STATEMENT		BALANCE SHEET	
		DEBIT	CREDIT	DEBIT	CREDIT	DEBIT	CREDIT	DEBIT	CREDIT

Eight-column work sheet with Adjustments columns

The Adjustments columns of the work sheet are used by the bookkeeper to plan all of the adjusting entries *before* the adjusting entries are made in the journal. The planning of the adjusting entries on the work sheet provides proof of the accuracy of the work and helps to assure that no adjusting entry is overlooked.

Entering the trial balance on the work sheet

The trial balance of the general ledger of Morton Supplies is entered in the Trial Balance columns of the work sheet as follows:

Morton Supplies
Work Sheet
For Month Ended November 30, 19

| | ACCOUNT TITLES | ACCT. NO. | TRIAL BALANCE | | ADJUSTMENTS | | INCOME |
			DEBIT	CREDIT	DEBIT	CREDIT	DEBIT
1	Cash	11	4 764 26				
2	Accounts Receivable	12	1 459 20				
3	Merchandise Inventory	13	5 500 50				
4	Supplies	14	268 60				
5	Prepaid Insurance	15	106 00				
6	Accounts Payable	21		2 703 15			
7	Fred Morton, Capital	31		9 083 56			
8	Fred Morton, Drawing	32	427 00				
9	Income and Expense Summary	33					
10	Sales	41		4 515 60			
11	Purchases	51	3 118 15				
12	Delivery Expense	61	52 80				
13	Insurance Expense	62					
14	Miscellaneous Expense	63	25 80				
15	Rent Expense	64	180 00				
16	Salary Expense	65	400 00				
17	Supplies Expense	66					
18			16 302 31	16 302 31			
19							

Work sheet showing Trial Balance columns completed

Every account in the ledger of Morton Supplies is listed on the work sheet regardless of whether it has a balance. All accounts are arranged in the Trial Balance section of the work sheet in the same order in which they appear in the ledger.

238

Planning the adjustments in the Adjustments column of the work sheet

The work sheet is a working paper in bookkeeping. It is therefore customary to prepare the work sheet in pencil so that if errors are made they can be corrected easily.

The Adjustments Debit and Credit amount columns of the work sheet are used in planning all adjustments. Before any amounts are written in the Adjustments columns, it is necessary to determine which accounts in the Trial Balance section of the work sheet are not up to date. These are the accounts that must be adjusted.

Mr. Morton finds that there are three accounts in his trial balance that are not up to date: (1) Merchandise Inventory, (2) Supplies, and (3) Prepaid Insurance. For these three accounts he must find:

1. The value of merchandise on hand at the end of this fiscal period.
2. The value of supplies used during this fiscal period.
3. The amount of insurance that has expired during this fiscal period.

Every adjustment has a debit part and a credit part. Two accounts must therefore be used in each adjustment. The adjustment transfers part or all of the balance of one account to another account. This transfer is planned by writing the debit part of the adjustment in the Adjustments Debit column of the work sheet and the credit part of the adjustment in the Adjustments Credit column.

Adjusting the merchandise inventory account

The two accounts used in the adjustment of the merchandise inventory account are: *Income and Expense Summary* and *Merchandise Inventory*. Two separate adjustments are made in adjusting the merchandise inventory account as follows:

1. In the first adjustment of the merchandise inventory account, the inventory of merchandise on hand at the beginning of the fiscal period is transferred to the income and expense summary account.
2. In the second adjustment of the merchandise inventory account, the new inventory of merchandise on hand at the end of the fiscal period is recorded in the merchandise inventory account. At the same time the amount of this ending inventory is credited to the income and expense summary account.

Work sheet adjustment for the beginning merchandise inventory

The entry on the work sheet to adjust the beginning merchandise inventory is shown in the Adjustments columns of the partial work sheet at the top of the next page.

	ACCOUNT TITLES	ACCT. NO.	TRIAL BALANCE		ADJUSTMENTS	
			DEBIT	CREDIT	DEBIT	CREDIT
1	Cash	11	4 7 6 4 2 6			
2	Accounts Receivable	12	1 4 5 9 2 0			
3	Merchandise Inventory	13	5 5 0 0 5 0			(a) 5 5 0 0 5 0
9	Income and Expense Summary	33			(a) 5 5 0 0 5 0	

Work sheet adjustment for beginning merchandise inventory

The adjustment for the beginning merchandise inventory is made as follows:

Step 1. *The debit part of the adjustment.* The amount of the beginning merchandise inventory is transferred to the debit of the income and expense summary account because it is a part of the cost of merchandise sold. This transfer is planned on the work sheet by writing the amount of the beginning inventory, $5,500.50, in the Adjustments Debit column on the line with Income and Expense Summary.

Step 2. *The credit part of the adjustment.* The amount of the beginning inventory, $5,500.50, is credited to Merchandise Inventory in the Adjustments Credit column. This credit of $5,500.50 cancels the debit of the same amount that appears in the Trial Balance Debit column.

Step 3. *Labeling the two parts of the adjustment.* The small letter "a" is written in parentheses before the amounts in the Adjustments columns to aid in locating the two parts of the adjustment when the adjusting entry is made in the journal.

Effect of the adjustment for beginning merchandise inventory on ledger accounts

The following illustration in T-account form shows the accounts Merchandise Inventory and Income and Expense Summary before and after the adjustment labeled (a) was journalized and posted. (The journal entries prepared from the work sheet will be presented in the next chapter.)

Before first adjustment	*After first adjustment*
Merchandise Inventory	Merchandise Inventory
Nov. 1 Bal. 5,500.50	Nov. 1 Bal. 5,500.50 Nov. 30 (a) 5,500.50
Income and Expense Summary	Income and Expense Summary
	Nov. 30 (a) 5,500.50

Before the adjustment was journalized and posted, the merchandise inventory account had a debit balance of $5,500.50, the value of the beginning inventory. The income and expense summary account had no entries recorded in it.

The beginning inventory is the first of the amounts in the income and expense summary account needed to find the cost of merchandise sold. After the adjustment is journalized and posted, the merchandise inventory account is in balance because the beginning merchandise inventory debit of $5,500.50 has been transferred to the debit side of the income and expense summary account.

Work sheet adjustment for the ending merchandise inventory

The entry on the work sheet to adjust the ending merchandise inventory is shown in the Adjustments columns of the partial work sheet below.

	ACCOUNT TITLES	ACCT. NO.	TRIAL BALANCE		ADJUSTMENTS	
			DEBIT	CREDIT	DEBIT	CREDIT
1	Cash	11	4 7 6 4 2 6			
2	Accounts Receivable	12	1 4 5 9 2 0			
3	Merchandise Inventory	13	5 5 0 0 50		(b) 5 7 1 9 55	(a) 5 5 0 0 50
9	Income and Expense Summary	33			(a) 5 5 0 0 50	(b) 5 7 1 9 55
10						
11						

Work sheet adjustment for ending merchandise inventory

The adjustment for the ending merchandise inventory is made as follows:

Step 1. *The debit part of the adjustment.* The amount of the ending merchandise inventory, $5,719.55, is debited to Merchandise Inventory in the Adjustments Debit column. Merchandise Inventory is debited because this account should show the amount of the ending inventory at the end of the fiscal period.

Step 2. *The credit part of the adjustment.* The amount of the ending inventory is credited to Income and Expense Summary in the Adjustments Credit column. This is a credit because the ending inventory is a deduction from the cost of merchandise available for sale.

Step 3. *Labeling the two parts of the adjustment.* The small letter "b" is written in parentheses before each amount to show the corresponding debit and credit.

Effect of the adjustment for ending merchandise inventory on ledger accounts

The following illustration in T-account form shows how the merchandise inventory account and the income and expense summary account appear before and after the adjustment for the ending merchandise inventory is journalized and posted.

Before second adjustment			*After second adjustment*		
Merchandise Inventory			Merchandise Inventory		
Nov. 1 Bal. 5,500.50	Nov. 30	5,500.50	Nov. 1 Bal. 5,500.50	Nov. 30	5,500.50
			30 (b) 5,719.55		
Income and Expense Summary			Income and Expense Summary		
Nov. 30 5,500.50			Nov. 30 5,500.50	Nov. 30 (b) 5,719.55	

After the two adjustments of the merchandise inventory account are journalized and posted, the income and expense summary account shows two of the amounts needed in calculating the cost of merchandise sold. The beginning inventory is a part of the cost of merchandise available for sale and is therefore shown on the debit side of the summary account. The ending inventory is a deduction from the cost of merchandise available for sale and is therefore shown on the credit side of the summary account. The merchandise inventory account is brought up to date and shows the asset value, $5,719.55, of merchandise inventory at the end of the fiscal period.

Adjusting the supplies account and the supplies expense account

By referring to the ledger account Supplies on page 210, it will be seen that this account had a beginning balance of $124.60, that the supplies bought during the fiscal period amounted to $144.00, and that the total debit at the end of the fiscal period was $268.60. However, when the inventory of supplies on hand was taken at the end of the fiscal period, November 30, the value of supplies on hand was found to be $160.00. The supplies account must there-

Supplies	
Nov. 1 Bal. 124.60	
11 144.00	
268.60	

fore be adjusted to show the asset value of the supplies on hand at the end of the fiscal period. The supplies expense account must be adjusted to show the cost of the supplies used during the fiscal period. In the adjustment columns of the work sheet, Supplies Expense is debited for the cost of the supplies used, $108.60, and Supplies is credited for $108.60, the amount to be deducted in this asset account.

Calculating the amount of supplies expense

The following calculation shows how the cost of supplies used is determined:

Supplies account balance at the beginning of this fiscal period as shown on the debit side of the supplies account in the ledger.... $124.60

Plus

Supplies purchased during this fiscal period as also shown on the debit side of the supplies account in the ledger.............. 144.00

Equals

Total cost of all supplies available for use during this fiscal period. This amount is the total of the debit side of the supplies account and is shown on the trial balance as the balance in this account .. $268.60

Deduct

Inventory of supplies on hand at the end of the fiscal period as reported by the proprietor after taking inventory.............. 160.00

Equals

Supplies expense for this fiscal period........................ $108.60

This is the amount, $108.60, to be debited to Supplies Expense on the work sheet in the Adjustments Debit column and credited to Supplies in the Adjustments Credit column.

Recording the adjustment of Supplies and Supplies Expense on the work sheet

The adjustment in the work sheet Adjustments columns to record Supplies Expense for this fiscal period and the deduction from Supplies is shown on the partial work sheet illustrated below.

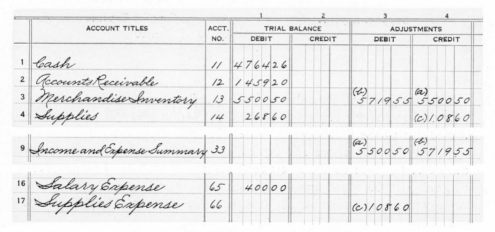

Work sheet adjustment for supplies used

The steps used in making the adjustment for supplies used on the work sheet are given on the following page.

Step 1. *The debit part of the adjustment.* Supplies Expense is debited for $108.60 in the Adjustments Debit column. Supplies Expense is debited for this amount because this is the cost of the supplies used during the fiscal period.

Step 2. *The credit part of the adjustment.* Supplies is credited for the amount of the supplies used, $108.60, in the Adjustments Credit column. Supplies is credited to show the deduction from this asset account for the supplies used. The new debit balance is the value of supplies on hand at the end of the fiscal period.

Step 3. *Labeling the two parts of the adjustment.* The small letter "c" is written in parentheses before the amount of each part of this adjustment to show the location of the corresponding debit and credit.

Effect of the adjustment of the supplies account and the supplies expense account

The supplies account and the supplies expense account before and after the adjustment is journalized and posted are shown in T-account form below.

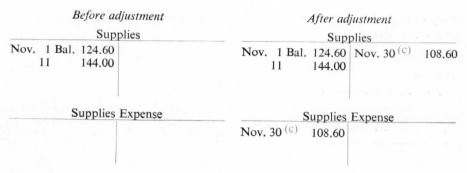

Before adjustment, the balance of the supplies account includes the balance on hand at the beginning of the fiscal period plus the supplies purchased during the fiscal period. After the adjustment labeled (c) on the work sheet is journalized and posted, the supplies account in the ledger has a credit of $108.60 and a new debit balance of $160.00. This new debit balance, $160.00, is the amount of supplies on hand according to the inventory taken on November 30. It is the value of the asset Supplies at the end of the fiscal period.

Before adjustment, the supplies expense account has no balance. After adjustment (c) is journalized and posted, the supplies expense account in the ledger has a debit balance of $108.60. The debit balance of the supplies expense account is the cost of supplies used during the fiscal period.

244

Adjusting the prepaid insurance account and the insurance expense account

By referring to the ledger account Prepaid Insurance on page 210, it will be seen that this account has a debit balance of $106.00 as of the beginning of this fiscal period.

Prepaid Insurance	
Nov. 1 Bal. 106.00	

When the insurance policies were examined, it was found that $20.00 of this prepaid insurance had expired and that the value of the prepaid insurance at the end of the fiscal period was $86.00. The prepaid insurance account must therefore be adjusted so that it will show its present asset value at the end of this fiscal period. At the same time the insurance expense account must be adjusted to show the cost of expired insurance for this fiscal period.

Recording the adjustment of Prepaid Insurance and Insurance Expense on the work sheet

The adjustment in the work sheet Adjustments columns to record Insurance Expense for this fiscal period and the deduction from Prepaid Insurance is shown on the partial work sheet illustrated below.

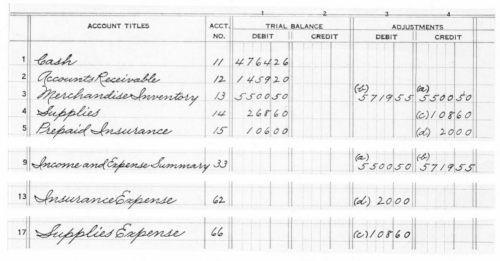

Work sheet adjustment for expired insurance

The adjustment on the work sheet to record the insurance expense for this fiscal period and to adjust the two accounts affected is made as follows:

Step 1. *The debit part of the adjustment.* Insurance Expense is debited for $20.00 in the Adjustments Debit column to record the cost of the expired insurance for this fiscal period. All expenses are recorded as debits.

245

Step 2. *The credit part of the adjustment.* Prepaid Insurance is credited for $20.00 in the Adjustments Credit column to record the decrease in the value of the asset Prepaid Insurance. This decrease is due to expired insurance.

Step 3. *Labeling the two parts of the adjustment.* The small letter "d" is written in parentheses before the amount of each part of this adjustment to show the location of the corresponding debit and credit.

Effect of the adjustment of the prepaid insurance account and the insurance expense account

The prepaid insurance account and the insurance expense account before and after adjustment (d) on the work sheet is journalized and posted are shown in T-account form below.

Before adjustment	*After adjustment*
Prepaid Insurance	Prepaid Insurance
Nov. 1 Bal. 106.00	Nov. 1 Bal. 106.00 Nov. 30 (d) 20.00
Insurance Expense	Insurance Expense
	Nov. 30 (d) 20.00

Before the adjustment, the prepaid insurance account has a debit balance of $106.00 dated November 1. This balance is the value of the asset Prepaid Insurance at the beginning of the fiscal period. After adjustment (d) is journalized and posted, the prepaid insurance account has a credit of $20.00, representing the deduction for expired insurance for this fiscal period. The new balance is $86.00, the value of the asset Prepaid Insurance at the end of the fiscal period.

Before adjustment, the insurance expense account has no balance. After adjustment (d) is journalized and posted, the insurance expense account in the ledger has a debit balance of $20.00. This new debit balance of $20.00 is the insurance expense for this fiscal period.

Proving the accuracy of the adjustments on the work sheet

To prove the equality of debits and credits in the two Adjustments columns of the work sheet, the two Adjustments columns are totaled. The total of the debit column, $11,348.65, equals the total of the credit column, $11,348.65. The two totals are written on the same line as the totals of the trial balance. Single and double lines are ruled as shown in the illustration of the partial work sheet on the opposite page.

Morton Supplies
Work Sheet
For Month Ended November 30, 1962

ACCOUNT TITLES	ACCT. NO.	TRIAL BALANCE DEBIT	TRIAL BALANCE CREDIT	ADJUSTMENTS DEBIT	ADJUSTMENTS CREDIT	INCOME STATEMENT DEBIT	INCOME STATEMENT CREDIT
Cash	11	4764 26					
Accounts Receivable	12	1459 20					
Merchandise Inventory	13	5500 50		(b) 5719 55	(a) 5500 50		
Supplies	14	268 60			(c) 108 60		
Prepaid Insurance	15	106 00			(d) 20 00		
Accounts Payable	21		2 703 15				
Fred Morton, Capital	31		9 083 56				
Fred Morton, Drawing	32	427 00					
Income and Expense Summary	33			(a) 5500 50	(b) 5719 55		
Sales	41		4515 60				
Purchases	51	3118 15					
Delivery Expense	61	52 80					
Insurance Expense	62			(d) 20 00			
Miscellaneous Expense	63	25 80					
Rent Expense	64	180 00					
Salary Expense	65	400 00					
Supplies Expense	66			(c) 108 60			
		16 302 31	16 302 31	11 348 65	11 348 65		

Section of work sheet showing **Trial Balance** and **Adjustments** columns

Extending the balance sheet items to the Balance Sheet columns of the work sheet

The work sheet on page 249 shows the extension of the balance sheet items to the Balance Sheet Debit and Credit columns. The steps in extending these items are:

Step 1.   The cash account and the accounts receivable account are not adjusted. The balances of these asset accounts as shown in the Trial Balance Debit column are therefore extended into the Balance Sheet Debit column.

Step 2.   The merchandise inventory account is debited for $5,500.50 in the Trial Balance Debit column and is credited for the same amount in the Adjustments Credit column. This debit and this credit cancel each other. Therefore, only the debit amount, $5,719.55, in the Adjustments Debit column is extended to the Balance Sheet Debit column. The amount extended is the value of the inventory at the end of the fiscal period.

Step 3. The supplies account has a debit balance of $268.60 in the Trial Balance Debit column and a credit of $108.60 in the Adjustments Credit column. The credit is subtracted from the debit to get the present value of this asset, $160.00. This new debit balance, $160.00, is then extended to the Balance Sheet Debit column.

Step 4. The prepaid insurance account has a debit balance of $106.00 in the Trial Balance Debit column and a credit of $20.00 in the Adjustments Credit column. The credit is subtracted from the debit to get the present value of this asset, $86.00. This new debit balance, $86.00, is then extended to the Balance Sheet Debit column.

Step 5. The accounts payable account and the Fred Morton, Capital account are not adjusted. The credit balance of the liability account, Accounts Payable, and the credit balance of the proprietorship account, Fred Morton, Capital, are therefore extended from the Trial Balance Credit column to the Balance Sheet Credit column.

Step 6. The drawing account is not adjusted. The debit balance of Fred Morton, Drawing, $427.00, is therefore extended from the Trial Balance Debit column to the Balance Sheet Debit column. This amount represents a deduction from proprietorship.

Extending the income, cost, and expense items to the Income Statement columns of the work sheet

The work sheet on page 249 shows the extension of income, cost, and expense items to the Income Statement Debit and Credit columns. The steps in extending these items are:

Step 1. The income and expense summary account has both a debit amount and a credit amount in the Adjustments columns. Both of these amounts are extended to the Income Statement columns.

The beginning inventory and the ending inventory will be needed in the preparation of the income statement. Both of these inventories, therefore, should be available in the Income Statement columns of the work sheet.

The debit amount, $5,500.50, represents the beginning inventory and is a part of the cost of merchandise sold. This amount is extended to the Income Statement Debit column. The credit amount, $5,719.55, represents the ending inventory and decreases the cost of merchandise sold. This amount is extended to the Income Statement Credit column.

Step 2. The credit balance of the sales account, $4,515.60, is extended to the Income Statement Credit column. If there were other income accounts, they also would be extended to this column.

248

Morton Supplies
Work Sheet
For Month Ended November 30, 1962

ACCOUNT TITLES	ACCT. NO.	TRIAL BALANCE Debit	TRIAL BALANCE Credit	ADJUSTMENTS Debit	ADJUSTMENTS Credit	INCOME STATEMENT Debit	INCOME STATEMENT Credit	BALANCE SHEET Debit	BALANCE SHEET Credit
1 Cash	11	4764.26						4764.26	
2 Accounts Receivable	12	1459.20						1459.20	
3 Merchandise Inventory	13	5500.50		(b) 5719.55	(a) 5500.50			5719.55	
4 Supplies	14	268.60			(c) 108.60			160.00	
5 Prepaid Insurance	15	106.00			(d) 20.00			86.00	
6 Accounts Payable	21		2703.15						2703.15
7 Fred Morton, Capital	31		9083.56						9083.56
8 Fred Morton, Drawing	32	427.00						427.00	
9 Income and Expense Summary	33			(a) 5500.50	(b) 5719.55	5500.50	5719.55		
10 Sales	41		4515.60				4515.60		
11 Purchases	51	3118.15				3118.15			
12 Delivery Expense	61	52.80				52.80			
13 Insurance Expense	62			(d) 20.00		20.00			
14 Miscellaneous Expense	63	25.80				25.80			
15 Rent Expense	64	180.00				180.00			
16 Salary Expense	65	400.00				400.00			
17 Supplies Expense	66			(c) 108.60		108.60			
18		16302.31	16302.31	11348.65	11348.65	9405.85	10235.15	12616.01	11786.71
19 Net Income						829.30			829.30
20						10235.15	10235.15	12616.01	12616.01

Work sheet with Adjustment columns

Step 3. The debit balance of the purchases account, $3,118.15, is extended to the Income Statement Debit column because purchases make up a part of the cost of merchandise sold.

Step 4. All expense account balances in the Trial Balance Debit column are extended to the Income Statement Debit column. The adjustments of the supplies expense account and the insurance expense account in the Adjustments Debit column are also extended to the Income Statement Debit column.

Step 5. A single line is ruled across the Income Statement and Balance Sheet columns to indicate addition. Each of these columns is added, and the totals are written on the same line as the Trial Balance totals.

Calculating the net income

The net income is found from the Income Statement columns. The two columns are totaled as shown in the illustration on page 249. The total of the Income Statement Credit column, $10,235.15, is the sum of the income and the deduction from cost amounts. The total of the Income Statement Debit column, $9,405.85, is the sum of the cost and expense amounts. Since the total of the Credit column is larger than the total of the Debit column, the difference is the net income.

Total of the Income Statement Credit column.............. $10,235.15
Total of the Income Statement Debit column..............   9,405.85
Net income... $ 829.30

Ruling and balancing the Income Statement columns

To complete the Income Statement columns, the amount of the net income, $829.30, is written in the Income Statement Debit column on the line immediately under the Debit column total. The words *Net Income* are written in the Account Titles column on the line with the amount. The columns are then totaled and ruled. The proof of the work is shown by the fact that the debit total is the same as the credit total.

Ruling and balancing the Balance Sheet columns

The net income for the period, $829.30, represents the increase in proprietorship. The amount of the net income, $829.30, is therefore extended to the Balance Sheet Credit column so that it can be added to the total liabilities and proprietorship. The columns are then totaled and ruled. Since the Balance Sheet Debit total equals the Balance Sheet Credit total, the calculations on the work sheet are considered correct.

Work sheet showing net loss

If the total of the Income Statement Debit column exceeds the total of the Income Statement Credit column, the difference is called *net loss*. For example, the footings of the Income Statement columns and the Balance Sheet columns of the work sheet for J. L. Garrett are:

ACCOUNT TITLES	INCOME STATEMENT		BALANCE SHEET	
	DEBIT	CREDIT	DEBIT	CREDIT
Net Loss.............	2,340 30	2,201 30	4,598 40	4,737 40
		139 00	139 00	
	2,340 30	2,340 30	4,737 40	4,737 40

The total of the Income Statement Debit column, $2,340.30, is larger than the total of the Income Statement Credit column, $2,201.30. This means that the cost of merchandise sold plus the expenses exceeds the total income. The difference between the two columns is always written under the smaller amount. The amount of the net loss, $139.00, is therefore written in the Income Statement Credit column.

The amount of the net loss, $139.00, is extended to the Balance Sheet Debit column because it represents a decrease in proprietorship. If the amount of the net loss is correct, it represents the difference between the totals of the Balance Sheet columns of the work sheet. Therefore, as proof of the accuracy of the work sheet, the net loss is added to the Balance Sheet Debit column.

Taking an inventory

In order to take an inventory, it is necessary to count each item of merchandise and each item of supplies on hand. A part of the form used by Morton Supplies in taking the merchandise inventory on November 30 is shown below.

Items	Stock Number	Unit of Count	No. of Units on Hand	Unit Cost Price	Value
Paper, typing	T1196	Reams	30	3.50	105.00
Paper, typing	T1190	Reams	40	2.00	80.00
Folders, file	F379	100	6	3.20	19.20
Typewriter ribbons	TR3345	Doz.	8	3.00	24.00
Total					5,719.55

MERCHANDISE INVENTORY
FOR THE MONTH ENDED NOVEMBER 30, 1962

Inventory record sheet

Each column of the inventory form is filled out in the following manner:

Items. The name of each item on hand is listed in the Items column.

Stock number. When merchandise is ordered from a supplier, the items are usually ordered by stock number. The stock number usually appears on the package or other container in which the goods are placed in stock. As each item is listed, the stock number is recorded in the Stock Number column.

Unit of count. The Unit of Count column is used to record the way the goods are priced on the invoice received from the supplier. For example, paper is priced by the ream; file folders, by the hundred; and typewriter ribbons, by the dozen.

Number of units on hand. The No. of Units on Hand column is used to record the actual count made at the time the inventory is taken.

Unit cost price. The amounts in the Unit Cost Price column are taken from the invoices received from the supplier. Sometimes goods are marked at the time of placing them on the shelves with a letter or number code that gives the cost. When this plan is used, the cost is recorded at the time the goods are counted.

Value. The Value column is used to record the extensions. The number of units times the unit cost gives the value of the item on hand.

When all of the items have been counted and the extensions made, the Value column is totaled. The total of the inventory of Morton Supplies at the end of November is $5,719.55. This is the amount that appears as the ending inventory on the work sheet.

Perpetual inventories

An inventory record that shows changes in amounts on hand as the changes occur is called a *perpetual inventory*. Other terms used are *running inventory* and *book inventory*. When an actual count of items is made, it is called a *physical inventory*. Perpetual inventory records supply the necessary information for most purposes. It is important, however, when a perpetual inventory is kept to take a physical inventory at least once each year to make certain that items do not disappear from stock without a record being made of them.

Increasing your business vocabulary

What is the meaning of each of the following:

(a) adjustments
(b) adjusting entries
(c) perpetual inventory
(d) physical inventory

Chapter questions

1. Why is it necessary to adjust the merchandise inventory account at the end of each fiscal period?

2. What is the purpose of the two Adjustments columns of the work sheet?

3. If the merchandise inventory account shows a beginning inventory at the end of the fiscal period, what account is debited and what account is credited in the first adjustment?

4. What account is debited and what account is credited in order to record the ending inventory?

5. Why is each adjustment in the Adjustments columns of the work sheet labeled with an identifying letter?

6. Why must the supplies account be adjusted at the end of each fiscal period?

7. In adjusting the supplies account, what account is debited and what account is credited?

8. Why must the prepaid insurance account be adjusted at the end of each fiscal period?

9. In adjusting the prepaid insurance account, what account is debited and what account is credited?

10. In extending the two adjustments for merchandise inventory on the Income and Expense Summary line of the work sheet, why are both amounts recorded in the Income Statement columns?

Cases for discussion

1. The Trial Balance columns of the work sheet of Hugh Moore on June 30 show that Merchandise Inventory has a balance of $6,000.00. Mr. Moore has sold all of the beginning inventory and the merchandise purchased during the month. What adjustment will be made for the merchandise inventory account?

2. When J. R. Oakley footed the Income Statement columns of his work sheet, he obtained a debit footing of $7,000.00 and a credit footing of $6,000.00. Did the operation of the business result in a net income or a net loss?

Drills for understanding

Drill 17-A. Adjusting the merchandise inventory account

Beginning and ending inventories for four different businesses are given below and on the following page.

Business 1		*Business 2*	
1. Beginning Inventory......	$6,000	2. Beginning Inventory......	$ none
Ending Inventory.........	4,000	Ending Inventory.........	5,000

Business 3			Business 4	
3. Beginning Inventory.......	$ 3,000	4. Beginning Inventory.......	$ 7,000
Ending Inventory..........	none	Ending Inventory..........	10,000

Instructions: For each business state the adjustments needed for Merchandise Inventory.

Drill 17-B. *Adjustment columns of the work sheet*

The income and expense summary account adjustments for merchandise inventory for a number of different fiscal periods are shown below as they appear on work sheets.

Merchandise Inventory Adjustments

	Debit	Credit
Work Sheet 1. Income and Expense Summary	4,000	1,000
Work Sheet 2. Income and Expense Summary	3,000	5,000
Work Sheet 3. Income and Expense Summary	———	6,000
Work Sheet 4. Income and Expense Summary	2,000	———

Instructions: Answer the following questions:

(a) What amounts represent the beginning inventories?
(b) What amounts represent the ending inventories?
(c) What does the blank in the Debit column for Work Sheet 3 indicate?
(d) What does the blank in the Credit column for Work Sheet 4 indicate?

Drill 17-C. *Extensions on the work sheet*

Instructions: From the information given below, state (a) the amount of the adjustment needed to have the account show the actual value of the asset at the end of the period, (b) which adjustment column the amount would be recorded in, and (c) the amount that would be extended to the Balance Sheet Debit column:

Trial Balance Debit		End-of-Period Information	
1. Supplies................	$300.00	Supplies on hand...........	$200.00
2. Supplies................	600.00	Supplies on hand...........	none
3. Prepaid Insurance........	120.00	To be charged to each month.	20.00
4. Prepaid Insurance........	10.00	Policy expires at end of this period	

Application problem

Problem 17-1. *Work sheet for an auto parts retailer*

On December 31 of the current year, the end of a fiscal period of one year, the accounts and their balances in the general ledger of Bard Auto Supply Company and the list of inventories were as shown on the following page.

Account Titles	Acct. No.	Balance	Account Titles	Acct. No.	Balance
Cash...............	11	$ 8,495.63	Sales...............	41	$95,896.25
Accounts Receivable..	12	13,109.85	Purchases...........	51	72,185.50
Merohandise Inventory	13	26,268.77	Delivery Expense.....	61	2,467.29
Supplies............	14	986.42	Insurance Expense....	62	——
Prepaid Insurance.....	15	1,190.00	Miscellaneous Expense	63	1,469.53
Accounts Payable.....	21	12,843.56	Rent Expense........	64	5,400.00
R. H. Bard, Capital...	31	43,208.18	Salary Expense.......	65	13,800.00
R. H. Bard, Drawing..	32	6,575.00	Supplies Expense.....	66	——
Income and Expense Summary..........	33	——			

Inventories, December 31

Merchandise inventory......................	$31,000.00
Supplies inventory.........................	$ 400.00
Value of insurance policies...................	$ 900.00

Instructions: Prepare an eight-column work sheet for the Bard Auto Supply Company. Use as your guide the eight-column work sheet illustrated on page 249.

This problem will be continued in the next chapter. If it is collected by your teacher at this time, it will be returned to you before it is needed in Problem 18-1.

Optional problems

★ *Supplementary Problem 17-S. Work sheet for a women's wear shop*

On May 31 of the current year, the end of a fiscal period of one month, the accounts and their balances in the general ledger of Carson's, a women's wear shop owned by Janet Carson, and the list of inventories were as follows:

Account Titles	Acct. No.	Balance	Account Titles	Acct. No.	Balance
Cash...............	11	$ 2,987.64	Sales...............	41	$ 7,846.19
Accounts Receivable..	12	5,138.50	Purchases...........	51	3,996.81
Merchandise Inventory	13	21,659.76	Delivery Expense.....	61	119.45
Supplies............	14	187.65	Insurance Expense....	62	——
Prepaid Insurance.....	15	395.00	Miscellaneous Expense	63	173.29
Accounts Payable.....	21	4,091.18	Rent Expense........	64	300.00
Janet Carson, Capital..	31	23,958.73	Salary Expense.......	65	425.00
Janet Carson, Drawing	32	513.00	Supplies Expense.....	66	——
Income and Expense Summary..........	33	——			

Inventories, May 31

Merchandise inventory......................	$19,497.61
Supplies inventory..........................	$ 117.45
Value of insurance policies....................	$ 305.00

Instructions: Prepare an eight-column work sheet for Carson's Women's Wear. Use as your guide the eight-column work sheet illustrated on page 249.

★ *Bonus Problem 17-B.* **Preparing a work sheet with no beginning merchandise inventory and showing a net loss**

Mr. J. R. Paulson owns the Star Grocery Store. He started this business on October 1 of the current year without any merchandise inventory. On December 31 of the current year, the end of a quarterly fiscal period, the accounts and their balances in the general ledger and the list of inventories were as shown below.

Account Titles	Acct. No.	Balance	Account Titles	Acct. No.	Balance
Cash...............	11	$ 3,820.96	Sales...............	41	$17,468.38
Accounts Receivable..	12	894.56	Purchases............	51	16,219.56
Merchandise Inventory	13	——	Advertising Expense...	61	488.48
Supplies............	14	114.90	Delivery Expense.....	62	746.19
Prepaid Insurance.....	15	65.00	Insurance Expense....	63	——
J. R. Paulson, Capital..	31	7,169.59	Miscellaneous Expense	64	63.32
J. R. Paulson, Drawing	32	835.00	Rent Expense........	65	600.00
Income and Expense			Salary Expense.......	66	790.00
Summary..........	33	——	Supplies Expense.....	67	——

Inventories, December 31

Merchandise inventory......................	$ 1,400.00
Supplies inventory..........................	$ 40.00
Expired insurance for three months...........	$ 20.00

Instructions: Prepare an eight-column work sheet for the Star Grocery Store. Use as your guide the eight-column work sheet illustrated on page 249.

Chapter 18

Financial reports

Preparing financial reports from the work sheet

The work sheet summarizes all facts about the operations of a business for a fiscal period, but it does not provide this information in a convenient form. Statements that can be used conveniently are therefore prepared from the work sheet. The most commonly prepared statements are (1) the income statement and (2) the balance sheet.

Use of the income statement

At the end of a fiscal period, the proprietor may compare his income statement for that period with those prepared for other periods. From a comparison of the income statements for different periods, he can learn whether his income is increasing or decreasing. He can also learn whether the costs and the expenses are reasonable when compared with the income or whether some costs and expenses have been increasing more rapidly than they should. He can note any changes in his net income and the reasons for these changes. These comparisons assist him in making decisions about such items as: (1) how to increase income; (2) how to decrease costs; and (3) how to decrease expenses without reducing services.

Use of the balance sheet

By studying the balance sheet, the proprietor can obtain additional information that is useful to him in the management of his business. He can observe whether he has sufficient cash on hand to enable him to pay his liabilities when they are due. By comparing the balance sheet with earlier balance sheets, he can observe whether his accounts receivable and his inventory are increasing more than they should; whether his liabilities are decreasing or increasing; and whether his proprietorship is decreasing or increasing. He can then decide if these changes are desirable and if there should be changes in business methods.

The income statement section of the work sheet

The income statement of Morton Supplies is prepared from the Income Statement columns of the work sheet. The part of the work sheet that is needed for the preparation of the income statement for the fiscal period ended November 30, 1962, is shown on the following page.

257

ACCOUNT TITLES	ACCT. NO.	INCOME STATEMENT DEBIT	INCOME STATEMENT CREDIT
9 Income and Expense Summary	33	5500 50	5719 55
10 Sales	41		4515 60
11 Purchases	51	3118 15	
12 Delivery Expense	61	52 80	
13 Insurance Expense	62	20 00	
14 Miscellaneous Expense	63	25 80	
15 Rent Expense	64	180 00	
16 Salary Expense	65	400 00	
17 Supplies Expense	66	108 60	
18		9405 85	10235 15
19 Net Income		829 30	
20		10235 15	10235 15

Section of work sheet showing income statement columns

The income statement

The three main sections of the income statement for a merchandising business are: (1) income, (2) cost of merchandise sold, and (3) expenses. The income statement of Morton Supplies prepared from the information shown in the Income Statement columns of the work sheet is shown below.

Morton Supplies
Income Statement
For Month Ended November 30, 1962

Income:		
Sales		4515 60
Cost of Merchandise Sold:		
Merchandise Inventory, Nov. 1, 1962	5500 50	
Purchases	3118 15	
Total Cost of Mdse. Available for Sale	8618 65	
Less Merchandise Inventory, Nov. 30, 1962	5719 55	
Cost of Merchandise Sold		2899 10
Gross Profit on Sales		1616 50
Expenses:		
Delivery Expense	52 80	
Insurance Expense	20 00	
Miscellaneous Expense	25 80	
Rent Expense	180 00	
Salary Expense	400 00	
Supplies Expense	108 60	
Total Expenses		787 20
Net Income		829 30

Income statement

Steps used in preparing the income statement

Step 1. *The heading.* The heading is written on three lines to include: (1) the name of the business: *Morton Supplies*; (2) the name of the report: *Income Statement*; and (3) the fiscal period that the income statement covers: *For Month Ended November 30, 1962.*

Step 2. *The income section.* The name of this section of the report, "Income," is written at the extreme left of the wide column. The only income item shown on the work sheet is Sales. "Sales" is written on the next line, indented about a half inch, and the amount, $4,515.60, is written in the second amount column so that the cost of merchandise sold can be subtracted from it.

Step 3. *The cost of merchandise sold section.* The name of this section of the report, "Cost of Merchandise Sold," is written at the extreme left of the wide column.

To arrive at the cost of merchandise sold, the following calculations are made from the information shown in the Income Statement columns of the work sheet:

Beginning merchandise inventory, November 1.............. $5,500.50
   (This amount is shown as a debit to Income and Expense
   Summary in the Income Statement Debit column of the
   work sheet.)

Plus purchases during November........................ 3,118.15
   (This amount is shown as a debit to Purchases in the Income
   Statement Debit column of the work sheet.)

Total cost of merchandise available for sale................ $8,618.65

Less ending merchandise inventory, November 30.......... 5,719.55
   (This amount is shown as a credit to Income and Expense
   Summary in the Income Statement Credit column of the
   work sheet.)

Cost of merchandise sold............................. $2,899.10

When these calculations are completed, the information is recorded on the income statement in the manner shown on page 258. The amounts are written in the first amount column so that the amounts do not interfere with the calculations that must be made in the second amount column. Single ruled lines are drawn under amounts to be added or subtracted.

The cost section is completed by recording the cost of merchandise sold, $2,899.10, in the second amount column and subtracting it from sales. The resulting amount, $1,616.50, is written in the second amount column. The difference between the sales and the cost of merchandise sold is called the *gross profit on sales*. The words "Gross Profit on Sales" are written at the extreme left on the line with the amount.

Step 4. *The expenses section.* The name of this section of the report, "Expenses," is written at the extreme left of the wide column. The expense accounts are listed in the order in which they appear on the work sheet. The amount of each expense is written in the first amount column. The expenses are totaled and the total amount, $787.20, is written in the second amount column. The words "Total Expenses" are written on the line with this amount.

The income statement is completed by subtracting the total expenses from the gross profit on sales. The difference, $829.30, is written in the second amount column. When the expenses are less than the gross profit, the difference is called *net income*. The words "Net Income" are therefore written at the extreme left on the line with the amount.

The income statement is considered correct because the net income on the income statement, $829.30, is the same as the net income on the work sheet.

Net loss on the income statement

If the expenses are greater than the gross profit, the difference between the gross profit and the expenses is called *net loss*. For example, J. L. Garrett, a part of whose work sheet is illustrated on page 251, suffered a loss in one fiscal period. The final part of his income statement appears as follows:

Gross Profit on Sales......................		464 50
Expenses:		
Delivery Expense........................	32 50	
Insurance Expense.......................	15 00	
Miscellaneous Expense...................	57 60	
Rent Expense...........................	200 00	
Salary Expense..........................	275 00	
Supplies Expense........................	23 40	
Total Expenses.........................		603 50
Net Loss................................		139 00

Section of income statement showing net loss

The balance sheet

The balance sheet of Morton Supplies is prepared from the Balance Sheet columns of the work sheet. The part of the work sheet that is needed for the preparation of the balance sheet for the fiscal period ended November 30, 1962, is shown at the top of the following page.

The three main sections of the balance sheet are: (1) assets, (2) liabilities and (3) proprietorship. The balance sheet of Morton Supplies prepared from the information shown in the balance sheet columns of the work sheet is shown at the bottom of the following page.

	ACCOUNT TITLES	ACCT. NO.	BALANCE SHEET DEBIT	BALANCE SHEET CREDIT	
1	Cash	11	476426		1
2	Accounts Receivable	12	145920		2
3	Merchandise Inventory	13	571955		3
4	Supplies	14	16000		4
5	Prepaid Insurance	15	8600		5
6	Accounts Payable	21		270315	6
7	Fred Morton, Capital	31		908356	7
8	Fred Morton, Drawing	32	42700		8
18			1261601	1178671	18
19	Net Income			82930	19
20			1261601	1261601	20

Section of work sheet showing balance sheet columns

Morton Supplies
Balance Sheet
November 30, 1962

	Assets		
	Cash	476426	
	Accounts Receivable	145920	
	Merchandise Inventory	571955	
	Supplies	16000	
	Prepaid Insurance	8600	
	Total Assets		1218901
	Liabilities		
	Accounts Payable		270315
	Proprietorship		
	Fred Morton, Capital		948586
	Total Liabilities and Proprietorship		1218901

Balance sheet in report form

Preparing the balance sheet

In the first section of the balance sheet, the assets section, the amount of each asset is written in the first amount column. The total is placed in the second amount column and the words "Total Assets" are written on the same line.

In the second section of the balance sheet, the liabilities section, there is only one item, Accounts Payable. The amount of accounts payable is therefore written in the second amount column because this amount is also the total of this section of the balance sheet.

In the third section of the balance sheet, the proprietorship section, there is only one item, Fred Morton, Capital. The amount of the proprietorship, $9,485.86, is obtained from the Balance Sheet columns of the work sheet by the following computations:

Fred Morton, Capital, credit balance.....................	$9,083.56
Plus net income...	829.30
	$9,912.86
Less Fred Morton, Drawing, debit balance................	427.00
Present capital to be shown on balance sheet..............	$9,485.86

The amount of the present capital is written in the second amount column of the balance sheet because this amount represents the total of this section. The present capital is then added to the total liabilities to obtain the Total Liabilities and Proprietorship, $12,189.01.

To prove the accuracy of these calculations, the Total Liabilities and Proprietorship is compared with the Total Assets on the balance sheet. If these two amounts agree, all calculations on the balance sheet are assumed to be correct.

Classification of accounts in the general ledger

The accounts in a ledger are arranged according to their location on the balance sheet and on the income statement. The chart of accounts used by Morton Supplies shows the account titles and the account numbers for all accounts. This chart of accounts is shown on the following page.

Analyzing the chart of accounts

The first group of accounts is the *assets* group. The cash account is placed first and is followed by the other assets arranged in the order in which they can be most quickly converted into cash. The assets group is assigned account numbers 11 to 19.

The second group of accounts is the *liabilities* group, to which account numbers 21 to 29 are assigned.

The third group of accounts is the *proprietorship* group, to which account numbers 31 to 39 are assigned.

```
                     CHART OF ACCOUNTS FOR MORTON SUPPLIES

            BALANCE SHEET ACCOUNTS          INCOME STATEMENT ACCOUNTS

                 (1) Assets                        (4) Income
       Acct.                              Acct.
        No.                                No.
        11   Cash                          41    Sales
        12   Accounts Receivable
        13   Merchandise Inventory
        14   Supplies                          (5) Cost of Merchandise
        15   Prepaid Insurance
                                           51    Purchases
                (2) Liabilities
                                               (6) Expenses
        21   Accounts Payable
                                           61    Delivery Expense
               (3) Proprietorship          62    Insurance Expense
                                           63    Miscellaneous Expense
        31   Fred Morton, Capital          64    Rent Expense
        32   Fred Morton, Drawing          65    Salary Expense
        33   Income and Expense Summary    66    Supplies Expense
```

Classified chart of accounts

The fourth group of accounts is the *income* group, to which account numbers 41 to 49 are assigned.

The fifth group of accounts is the *cost of merchandise* group. This group is assigned account numbers 51 to 59. As Morton Supplies buys and sells merchandise, the chart of accounts provides a section entitled "Cost of Merchandise." In this respect the Morton Supplies chart of accounts with six groups of accounts differs from that of the Wood Realty Agency illustrated on page 62, which has only five groups.

The sixth group of accounts is the *expenses* group. This group is assigned account numbers 61 to 69. If Morton Supplies later finds that it needs expense account numbers beyond 69, the next numbers would be 610, 611, etc.

Supplementary reports

The balance sheet lists the total amount of the accounts receivable and the total amount of the accounts payable. It does not, however, list the individual balances of accounts with customers and creditors. When these details are desired, it is customary to attach the schedule of accounts receivable and the schedule of accounts payable to the balance sheet. Schedules of accounts receivable and accounts payable used with the balance sheet as supplementary reports are commonly referred to as *supporting schedules*. The supporting schedules for Morton Supplies for November 30 are shown on pages 161 and 195.

Reporting business income or loss on federal income tax returns

Income tax laws require each individual who operates a single proprietorship, such as Morton Supplies, to report the details of the business operations as a part of his annual income tax return. A special income tax form known as Schedule C, Form 1040, must be used for this purpose.

In order to have the necessary information for filling out Schedule C, Form 1040, an income statement is prepared by Morton Supplies for the year ended December 31, 1962. This income statement is shown below.

```
                          MORTON SUPPLIES
                         Income Statement
                 For Year Ended December 31, 1962

Income:
  Sales . . . . . . . . . . . . . . . . . . . . .       $57,600.00

Cost of Merchandise Sold:
  Merchandise Inventory, January 1, 1962. . . .    $ 6,500.00
  Purchases . . . . . . . . . . . . . . . . . .     40,150.00
  Total Cost of Merchandise Available for Sale.    $46,650.00
  Less Merchandise Inventory, December 31, 1962     6,200.00
  Cost of Merchandise Sold. . . . . . . . . . .                    40,450.00

Gross Profit on Sales. . . . . . . . . . . . . .       $17,150.00

Expenses:
  Delivery Expense. . . . . . . . . . . . . . .    $    640.00
  Insurance Expense . . . . . . . . . . . . . .        240.00
  Miscellaneous Expense . . . . . . . . . . . .        390.00
  Rent Expense. . . . . . . . . . . . . . . . .      2,160.00
  Salary Expense. . . . . . . . . . . . . . . .      4,800.00
  Supplies Expense. . . . . . . . . . . . . . .      1,260.00
  Total Expenses. . . . . . . . . . . . . . . .                    9,490.00

Net Income . . . . . . . . . . . . . . . . . . .                 $ 7,660.00
```

Income statement

A part of Schedule C, Form 1040, with the information filled in from the income statement is shown on the opposite page. The income statement contains most of the information needed to fill out this form. The procedure in filling out the form is as follows:

The name and the residence address of the owner of Morton Supplies is written at the top of Schedule C. Since Morton Supplies is a single proprietorship business, this schedule when completed must be attached to Fred Morton's personal income tax return.

Line A. Since Morton Supplies is a retail business, the words "Retail trade" are written on this line.

Lines B and C. The name of the business, "Morton Supplies," and the employer's identification number, "93-0764295," are written on this line.

Every employer subject to social security taxes is assigned an identification number by the federal government. In the offices of the internal revenue service all records with Fred Morton are filed under this identification number.

SCHEDULE C	**PROFIT (OR LOSS) FROM BUSINESS OR PROFESSION**
(Form 1040) U.S. Treasury Department Internal Revenue Service	(Compute social security self-employment tax on Schedule C–3 (Form 1040))

Attach this Schedule to your Income Tax Return, Form 1040 — Partnerships, Joint Ventures, Etc., Must File On Form 1065

Name and address as shown on page 1, Form 1040

Fred Morton, 4145 Riverside Drive, Portland, Oregon

A. Principal business activity ... Retail trade
(See separate instructions)   (Retail trade, wholesale trade, lawyer, etc.)   (Principal product or service)

B. Business name ... Morton Supplies

C. Employer Identification Number 93-0764295

D. Business location ... 460 Main Street   Portland   Oregon
(Number and street or rural route)   (City or post office)   (State)

1.	Total receipts $ 57,600.00 , less allowances, rebates, and returns $	none	57,600 | 00
2.	Inventory at beginning of year (If different than last year's closing inventory attach explanation)	6,500.00	
3.	Merchandise purchased $ 40,800.00 , less any items withdrawn from business for personal use $ 650.00	40,150.00	
4.	Cost of labor (do not include salary paid to yourself)		
5.	Material and supplies		
6.	Other costs (explain in Schedule C–2)		
7.	Total of lines 2 through 6	46,650.00	
8.	Inventory at end of this year	6,200.00	
9.	**Cost of goods sold** (line 7 less line 8)		40,450 | 00
10.	**Gross profit** (subtract line 9 from line 1)		17,150 | 00

OTHER BUSINESS DEDUCTIONS

11.	Salaries and wages not included on line 4 (exclude any paid to yourself)	4,800.00	
12.	Rent on business property	2,160.00	
13.	Interest on business indebtedness		
14.	Taxes on business and business property		
15.	Losses of business property (attach statement)		
16.	Bad debts arising from sales or services		
17.	Depreciation (explain in Schedule C–1)		
18.	Repairs (explain in Schedule C–2)		
19.	Depletion of mines, oil and gas wells, timber, etc. (attach schedule)		
20.	Amortization (attach statement)		
21.	Insurance	240.00	
22.	Legal and professional fees		
23.	Commissions		
24.	Other business expenses (explain in Schedule C–2)	2,290.00	
25.	Total of lines 11 through 24		9,490 | 00
26.	**Net profit (or loss)** (subtract line 25 from line 10). Enter here; on line 1, Schedule C–3; and on line 6, page 1, Form 1040		7,660 | 00

SCHEDULE C–2. EXPLANATION OF LINES 6, 18, AND 24					Page 2
Line No.	Explanation	Amount	Line No.	Explanation	Amount
24	Delivery Expense	$ 640.00			$
24	Misc. Expense	390.00			
24	Supplies Expense	1,260.00			
24	Total	2,290.00			

Portion of Schedule C, Form 1040, from Internal Revenue Service

Line D. The business address of Morton Supplies is written on this line.

Line 1. These amounts are copied directly from the income statement. (See income statement on page 264.)

Line 2. The amount of the beginning inventory is obtained from the income statement.

Line 3. These two amounts must be obtained directly from the purchases account in the general ledger because these amounts are not shown on the income statement. The merchandise purchased, $40,800.00, is the total of the debit column of the purchases account in the general ledger. The withdrawal of merchandise by the proprietor, $650.00, is the total of the credit column of the purchases account. When the subtraction of the withdrawal is completed, the remainder, $40,150.00, should agree with the amount of purchases shown on the income statement.

Lines 4, 5, 6, and 7. In Morton Supplies there are no amounts for Lines 4, 5, and 6. The calculation for Line 7 is completed according to the instructions on the government form.

Line 8. The amount of the ending merchandise inventory is obtained from the income statement.

Lines 9 and 10. The calculations are completed as instructed on the form, the amounts are written in the proper spaces, and the gross profit on sales on the form is compared with the gross profit on sales shown on the income statement. The two amounts should agree.

Lines 11 through 23. All of these amounts are taken directly from the income statement.

Line 24. "Other business expenses" are the business expenses that are not listed on Lines 11 through 23. They are obtained from the income statement. These expenses are listed in Schedule C-2, which is page 2 of the government form. (See partial illustration of Schedule C-2 at bottom of page 265.) The total of all expenses listed in Schedule C-2 is written on Line 24 of page 1 of the government form.

Line 25. All of the amounts on Lines 11 through 24 are added and the total, $9,490.00, is written on Line 25. This total should agree with the total expenses on the income statement.

Line 26. The net profit is obtained by subtracting the amount on Line 25 from the amount on Line 10. The amount of the net profit on Schedule C, $7,660.00, should agree with the amount of the net income shown on the income statement.

The terms "net profit" and "net income" are often used interchangeably. The term "net profit" is used on the government form. The term "net income" is generally preferred among accountants. Since Schedule C is a part of an income tax report, it is quite probable that the federal government forms of the near future will use the term "net income from business" instead of "net profit."

Increasing your business vocabulary

What is the meaning of each of the following:

(a) gross profit on sales
(b) net income

(c) net loss
(d) supporting schedules

Chapter questions

1. What are the two most common financial reports of any business?
2. What information can the proprietor of a business obtain from a comparison of his income statements for two or more fiscal periods?
3. What information can the proprietor of a business obtain from a comparison of two or more of his balance sheets?
4. From what source is the information obtained that is needed in preparing the income statement?
5. What are the three main sections of the income statement of a merchandising business such as Morton Supplies?
6. How is the cost of merchandise sold determined?
7. From what source is the information obtained that is needed in preparing a balance sheet?
8. What are the three main sections of a balance sheet?
9. What determines the order in which asset accounts are listed on the chart of accounts?
10. Why does the Morton Supplies chart of accounts on page 263 have six groups of accounts when the Wood Realty Agency chart of accounts on page 62 has only five groups?

Cases for discussion

1. By analyzing his income statement for April and comparing it with the income statements for previous fiscal periods, J. A. Meyers notes that his total sales have been increasing. His net income, however, has remained approximately the same. What would cause this situation?

2. The balance sheet of Mark Loftus on June 30 showed his proprietorship to be $10,450.00. His balance sheet on July 31 showed the proprietorship to be $11,200.00. Discuss two probable causes of this change in proprietorship.

3. James Sommers' income statement for the month of April shows a net income of $600.00. During the same period he withdrew $700.00 in cash from the business for personal use. Why would it not be correct to say that he incurred a net loss of $100.00 in April?

Drill 18-A. *Classification of accounts*

The following are the accounts that appear in the ledger of the Trenton Radio Shop. Mr. Trenton has never classified his accounts.

Instructions: For each account tell whether it is an asset, a liability, a proprietorship, an income, a cost of merchandise, or an expense account.

T. R. Trenton, Capital	Accounts Payable	Salary Expense
Cash	Merchandise Inventory	Store Furniture
T. R. Trenton, Drawing	Insurance Expense	Income and Expense Summary
Supplies Expense	Purchases	Sales
Supplies	Prepaid Insurance	Miscellaneous Expense
Accounts Receivable	Office Furniture	Rent Expense

Drill 18-B. *Cost of merchandise*

The following items are found in the Income Statement columns of the work sheets of several different businesses:

	Income Statement Debit	Credit
Business No. 1:		
Purchases..............................	3,000	
Income and Expense Summary..............	4,000	2,000
Business No. 2:		
Purchases..............................	6,000	
Income and Expense Summary..............	.....	5,000
Business No. 3:		
Purchases..............................	7,000	
Income and Expense Summary..............	8,000	.....

Instructions: Compute the cost of merchandise sold for each business.

Drill 18-C. *Present capital*

Instructions: From the following information find the present capital of each of the four businesses.

	Business No. 1	Business No. 2	Business No. 3	Business No. 4
Beginning Capital.........	$9,000.00	$10,000.00	$8,000.00	$5,000.00
Net Income..............	1,000.00	1,500.00		
Net Loss................			500.00	500.00
Withdrawals.............	500.00	none	700.00	none

268

Application problem

Problem 18-1. *Financial reports for a furniture dealer*

The work sheet completed in Problem 17-1 of the preceding chapter is required for this problem. If Problem 17-1 has not been returned to you, complete Exercise 18-A in the Appendix.

Instructions: 1. Prepare an income statement similar to the model given in the illustration on page 258.

2. Prepare a balance sheet in report form similar to the model given in the illustration on page 261.

Optional problems

★Supplementary Problem 18-S. *Eight-column work sheet and financial statements*

The account balances and the inventories on June 30 of the current year, the end of a quarterly fiscal period, for Peter Lowe, a clothing merchant, are:

Account Titles	Acct. No.	Debit	Credit
Cash	11	3,723.58	
Accounts Receivable	12	4,094.10	
Merchandise Inventory	13	9,605.33	
Supplies	14	352.24	
Prepaid Insurance	15	234.08	
Accounts Payable	21		5,255.38
Peter Lowe, Capital	31		11,990.80
Peter Lowe, Drawing	32	1,260.00	
Income and Expense Summary	33		——
Sales	41		17,008.25
Purchases	51	11,751.73	
Delivery Expense	61	258.72	
Insurance Expense	62	——	
Miscellaneous Expense	63	379.75	
Rent Expense	64	840.00	
Salary Expense	65	1,754.90	
Supplies Expense	66	——	

Inventories, June 30

Merchandise inventory	$9,982.84
Supplies inventory	$ 231.70
Prepaid insurance	$ 130.76

Instructions: 1. Prepare an eight-column work sheet similar to the model given in the illustration on page 249.

2. From the Income Statement columns of the work sheet, prepare an income statement similar to the model given in the illustration on page 258.

3. From the Balance Sheet columns of the work sheet, prepare a balance sheet in report form similar to the model given in the illustration on page 261.

The account balances and the inventories on May 31 of the current year, the end of a fiscal period of one month, for H. C. Leffingwell, the owner of Leffingwell's Clothing Store, are shown below.

Account Titles	Acct. No.	Balances Debit	Credit
Cash..	11	4,348.10	
Accounts Receivable..........................	12	2,294.00	
Merchandise Inventory........................	13	20,236.76	
Supplies.......................................	14	208.00	
Prepaid Insurance............................	15	335.00	
Accounts Payable............................	21		3,710.00
H. C. Leffingwell, Capital....................	31		21,926.86
H. C. Leffingwell, Drawing...................	32	500.00	
Income and Expense Summary.................	33		——
Sales...	41		6,993.45
Purchases....................................	51	3,793.47	
Delivery Expense............................	61	117.38	
Insurance Expense...........................	62	——	
Miscellaneous Expense.......................	63	160.10	
Rent Expense................................	64	250.00	
Salary Expense..............................	65	387.50	
Supplies Expense............................	66	——	

Inventories, May 31

Merchandise inventory........................	$17,360.30
Supplies inventory...........................	$ 170.00
Value of insurance policies...................	$ 295.00

Instructions: 1. Prepare an eight-column work sheet similar to the model given in the illustration on page 249.

2. From the Income Statement columns of the work sheet, prepare an income statement similar to the model given in the illustration on page 258.

3. From the Balance Sheet columns of the work sheet, prepare a balance sheet in report form similar to the model given in the illustration on page 261.

Chapter 19

Adjusting and closing entries

Reason for recording all adjustments in the general journal

The Adjustments columns of the work sheet show the changes that must be made in the general ledger accounts at the end of the fiscal period. It is necessary to record an adjustment in the general journal for each adjustment on the work sheet because changes in the ledger should be made only as a result of posting journal entries.

An entry that is made in the general journal at the end of a fiscal period to bring an account up to date is called an *adjusting entry*. All adjusting entries are first planned on a work sheet. Adjusting entries are then made in the general journal from the information on the work sheet.

After the adjusting entries are recorded in the general journal, they are posted to the proper accounts in the general ledger. These postings bring up to date those accounts that need to be adjusted.

The adjusting entry for the beginning merchandise inventory

A section of the work sheet of Morton Supplies showing the adjustment for the beginning inventory at the end of the fiscal period is as follows:

			1	2	3	4
	ACCOUNT TITLES	ACCT. NO.	TRIAL BALANCE DEBIT	CREDIT	ADJUSTMENTS DEBIT	CREDIT
3	Merchandise Inventory	13	5 5 0 0 50			(a) 5 5 0 0 50
9	Income and Expense Summary	33			(a) 5 5 0 0 50	

The adjusting entry in the general journal for the above adjustment is shown below:

	GENERAL JOURNAL			PAGE 2	
	DATE	NAME OF ACCOUNT	POST. REF.	DEBIT	CREDIT
1		*Adjusting Entries*			
2	1962 Nov. 30	Income and Expense Summary	33	5 5 0 0 50	
3		Merchandise Inventory	13		5 5 0 0 50

Journal entry for the adjustment of beginning merchandise inventory

Analyzing the adjusting entry for the beginning inventory

The adjusting entries in the general journal are made in the usual general journal form with one exception. Instead of writing an explanation after each adjusting entry, the words "Adjusting Entries" are written above the first entry and are not repeated for the remaining adjusting entries.

In the Trial Balance columns of the work sheet, the merchandise inventory account shows a debit balance of $5,500.50. The Adjustments columns of the work sheet show that this debit balance in the merchandise inventory account is to be transferred to the debit side of the income and expense summary account. The adjusting entry in the general journal makes the transfer by debiting Income and Expense Summary and crediting Merchandise Inventory.

The income and expense summary account is debited because the beginning merchandise inventory is a part of the cost of merchandise sold. The merchandise inventory account is credited in order to cancel the debit and thereby show that the amount of the beginning inventory has been transferred to another account.

The accounts Merchandise Inventory and Income and Expense Summary after the first adjusting entry has been posted are shown below.

Note in the accounts illustrated above that (a) the merchandise inventory account is in balance and (b) the income and expense summary account now shows the beginning inventory, which is the first amount to be used in determining the cost of the merchandise sold.

The adjusting entry for the ending merchandise inventory

The ending merchandise inventory is an asset of the business. It must be recorded in the merchandise inventory account so that this asset account will be brought up to date.

A section of the work sheet of Morton Supplies showing the adjustment for the ending merchandise inventory at the end of the fiscal period is shown at the top of the opposite page.

	ACCOUNT TITLES	ACCT. NO.	TRIAL BALANCE DEBIT	CREDIT	ADJUSTMENTS DEBIT	CREDIT
3	Merchandise Inventory	13	5 5 0 0 50		(b) 5 7 1 9 55	(a) 5 5 0 0 50
9	Income and Expense Summary	33			(a) 5 5 0 0 50	(b) 5 7 1 9 55

The adjusting entry in the general journal for the above adjustment is shown below.

		GENERAL JOURNAL				PAGE 2
	DATE	NAME OF ACCOUNT	POST. REF.	DEBIT	CREDIT	
4	30	Merchandise Inventory	13	5 7 1 9 55		4
5		Income and Expense Summary	33		5 7 1 9 55	5

Journal entry for the adjustment of ending merchandise inventory

Analyzing the adjusting entry for the ending inventory

Merchandise Inventory is debited for $5,719.55, the merchandise inventory at the end of the fiscal period. Income and Expense Summary is credited for the same amount because this amount is a deduction from the cost of merchandise sold.

The accounts Merchandise Inventory and Income and Expense Summary after the second adjusting entry is posted are shown below.

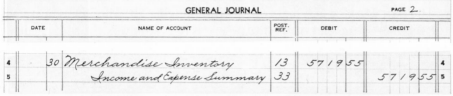

Merchandise Inventory — ACCOUNT NO. 13

DATE	ITEMS	POST. REF.	DEBIT	DATE	ITEMS	POST. REF.	CREDIT
1962 Nov. 1	Balance	J1	5 5 0 0 50	1962 Nov. 30		J2	5 5 0 0 50
30		J2	5 7 1 9 55				

Income and Expense Summary — ACCOUNT NO. 33

DATE	ITEMS	POST. REF.	DEBIT	DATE	ITEMS	POST. REF.	CREDIT
1962 Nov. 30		J2	5 5 0 0 50	1962 Nov. 30		J2	5 7 1 9 55

The merchandise inventory account now has a debit balance of $5,719.55, the amount of the ending inventory.

The income and expense summary account now has a debit of $5,500.50, the amount of the beginning merchandise inventory. It has a credit of $5,719.55, the amount of the ending inventory.

The adjusting entry for supplies

The supplies account needs to be adjusted at the end of each fiscal period because the supplies used have not been recorded. The supplies used have not been recorded because it is not convenient to record a debit to Supplies Expense and a credit to Supplies each time some of the supplies are used.

The part of the work sheet of Morton Supplies showing the adjustment for supplies at the end of the fiscal period is as follows:

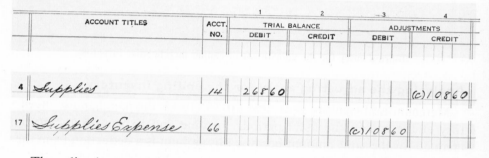

The adjusting entry in the general journal for the above adjustment is shown below.

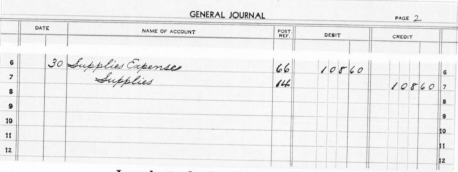

Journal entry for the adjustment of supplies

Supplies Expense is debited to record the expense resulting from the use of supplies during the fiscal period. Supplies is credited to show the decrease in the balance of this asset account.

After the entry is posted, the two accounts Supplies and Supplies Expense appear as shown at the top of the opposite page.

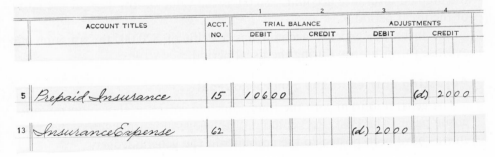

			Supplies				ACCOUNT NO. 14	
DATE	ITEMS	POST. REF.	DEBIT	DATE	ITEMS	POST. REF.	CREDIT	
1962 Nov 1	Balance	J1	1 24 60	1962 Nov 30		J2	1 0 8 60	
11		J1	1 44 00					
			2 6 8 60					

			Supplies Expense				ACCOUNT NO. 66	
DATE	ITEMS	POST. REF.	DEBIT	DATE	ITEMS	POST. REF.	CREDIT	
1962 Nov 30		J2	1 0 8 60					

Analyzing the supplies account and the supplies expense account

The asset account Supplies has two debits. The debit of November 1 is the amount of supplies on hand at the beginning of the fiscal period. The debit of November 11 represents the purchase of supplies during the fiscal period. The credit to the supplies account on November 30, $108.60, is the amount of supplies used during the fiscal period. The balance, $160.00, is the amount of supplies on hand as of November 30, the end of this fiscal period.

The account Supplies Expense has a debit of $108.60. This debit is the amount of supplies used during the fiscal period. Supplies used are an expense of the business.

The adjusting entry for prepaid insurance

Part of the value of the insurance premiums has expired during the fiscal period. The part that has expired is an expense. To record this expense for insurance, Insurance Expense is debited. Prepaid Insurance is credited to show the decrease in this asset account because of the expired insurance.

The part of the work sheet of Morton Supplies showing the adjustment for prepaid insurance at the end of the fiscal period is as follows:

			1	2	3	4
	ACCOUNT TITLES	ACCT. NO.	TRIAL BALANCE		ADJUSTMENTS	
			DEBIT	CREDIT	DEBIT	CREDIT
5	Prepaid Insurance	15	1 06 00			(d) 20 00
13	Insurance Expense	62			(d) 20 00	

The adjusting entry in the general journal for the above adjustment is shown below.

	DATE	NAME OF ACCOUNT	POST. REF.	DEBIT		CREDIT	
8	30	Insurance Expense	62	20 00			8
9		Prepaid Insurance	15			20 00	9
10							10

GENERAL JOURNAL — PAGE 2

Journal entry for the adjustment of prepaid insurance

The prepaid insurance account and the insurance expense account after this entry is posted are shown below.

Prepaid Insurance ACCOUNT NO. 15

DATE	ITEMS	POST. REF.	DEBIT	DATE	ITEMS	POST. REF.	CREDIT
1962 Nov. 1	Balance	J1	106 00	1962 Nov. 30		J2	20 00

Insurance Expense ACCOUNT NO. 62

DATE	ITEMS	POST. REF.	DEBIT	DATE	ITEMS	POST. REF.	CREDIT
1962 Nov. 30		J2	20 00				

Analyzing the prepaid insurance account and the insurance expense account

The prepaid insurance account has a debit of $106.00, the value of this asset at the beginning of the fiscal period. It has a credit of $20.00, the decrease in the value of this asset during the fiscal period. The balance of the prepaid insurance account, $86.00, is the value of this asset at the end of the fiscal period.

The insurance expense account has a debit of $20.00, the amount of expense for insurance during the fiscal period.

Adjusting entries in the general journal

The general journal with the four adjusting entries is shown on the opposite page. The Post. Ref. column of the general journal shows that the entries have been posted to the accounts in the general ledger.

	DATE		NAME OF ACCOUNT	POST. REF.	DEBIT	CREDIT	
			GENERAL JOURNAL			PAGE 2	
1	*1962*		*Adjusting Entries*				1
2	*Nov.*	30	*Income and Expense Summary*	33	5 5 0 0 50		2
3			*Merchandise Inventory*	13		5 5 0 0 50	3
4		30	*Merchandise Inventory*	13	5 7 1 9 55		4
5			*Income and Expense Summary*	33		5 7 1 9 55	5
6		30	*Supplies Expense*	66	1 0 8 60		6
7			*Supplies*	14		1 0 8 60	7
8		30	*Insurance Expense*	62	2 0 00		8
9			*Prepaid Insurance*	15		2 0 00	9
10							10
11							11
12							12

Adjusting entries at the end of the fiscal period

Reason for recording closing entries

Closing entries are needed at the end of each fiscal period for the following reasons:

(1) To clear the balances of all income accounts, all cost accounts, and all expense accounts by transferring their balances to the income and expense summary account.

The clearing of these accounts causes the postings of the next fiscal period to be clearly separated from the entries of the past fiscal period. As a result of closing entries, each income account, each cost account, and each expense account begins a new fiscal period with a zero balance.

(2) To bring the proprietor's capital account in the general ledger up to date.

For this purpose two journal entries are required: (a) a journal entry to transfer the balance of the income and expense summary account to the proprietor's capital account, and (b) a journal entry to transfer the balance of the proprietor's drawing account to the proprietor's capital account.

No amount may be transferred from one account in the general ledger to another account unless the transfer results from the posting of a journal entry. Therefore, all closing entries are made in the general journal and are posted to the accounts.

Recording entries to close income, cost, and expense accounts

All entries to close income, cost, and expense accounts are made from the information given in the Income Statement columns of the work sheet. The part of the work sheet that is needed in making the closing entries for the fiscal period ended November 30, 1962, is shown on the next page.

ACCOUNT TITLES	ACCT. NO.	INCOME STATEMENT DEBIT	CREDIT
10 Sales	41		451560
11 Purchases	51	311815	
12 Delivery Expense	61	5280	
13 Insurance Expense	62	2000	
14 Miscellaneous Expense	63	2580	
15 Rent Expense	64	18000	
16 Salary Expense	65	40000	
17 Supplies Expense	66	10860	
18			
19			
20			

The closing entries for income, cost, and expense accounts in the general journal for the fiscal period ended November 30, 1962, are shown below.

GENERAL JOURNAL — PAGE 2

DATE	NAME OF ACCOUNT	POST. REF.	DEBIT	CREDIT
	Closing Entries			
30	Sales	41	451560	
	Income and Expense Summary	33		451560
30	Income and Expense Summary	33	390535	
	Purchases	51		311815
	Delivery Expense	61		5280
	Insurance Expense	62		2000
	Miscellaneous Expense	63		2580
	Rent Expense	64		18000
	Salary Expense	65		40000
	Supplies Expense	66		10860

Closing entries for income, cost, and expense accounts

The balances of all income accounts are transferred to the *credit* of the income and expense summary account. The balances of all cost accounts and all expense accounts are transferred to the *debit* of the income and expense summary account.

The income and expense summary account

After all of the adjusting entries and all of the closing entries have been journalized and posted, the income and expense summary account in the general ledger appears as follows:

DATE	ITEMS	POST. REF.	DEBIT	DATE	ITEMS	POST. REF.	CREDIT
1962 Nov. 30		J2	5 5 0 0 50	*1962* Nov. 30		J2	5 7 1 9 55
30		J2	3 9 0 5 35	30		J2	4 5 1 5 60
30		J2	8 2 9 30				

Income and Expense Summary ACCOUNT NO. 33

The income and expense summary account in the general ledger brings together in one account all of the amounts that have been used on the income statement in calculating the net income or the net loss. The income and expense summary account contains the following information:

Income and Expense Summary

(a) Beginning merchandise inventory	(b) Ending merchandise inventory
(d) Total of purchases account balance plus all expense account balances	(c) Total of all income account balances
(e) Net income	

Sometimes in the process of closing the ledger the sum of entries (a) and (d) on the debit side of the income and expense summary account is larger than the sum of entries (b) and (c) on the credit side. When this occurs, the income and expense summary account contains the following information:

Income and Expense Summary

(a) Beginning merchandise inventory	(b) Ending merchandise inventory
(d) Total of purchases account balance plus all expense account balances	(c) Total of all income account balances
	(e) Net loss

If the total of the credit side of the income and expense summary account is larger than the total of the debit side, the credit balance is the amount of the *net income* for the fiscal period. If the total of the debit side of the income and expense summary account is larger than the credit side, the debit balance is the amount of the *net loss* for the fiscal period.

Closing the income and expense summary account into the proprietor's capital account

The part of the work sheet needed in making the journal entry to close Income and Expense Summary into the proprietor's capital account is:

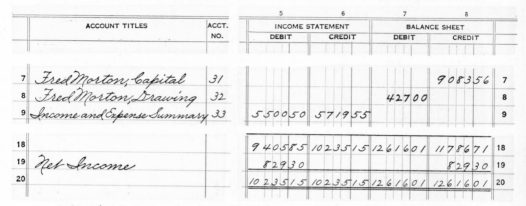

	ACCOUNT TITLES	ACCT. NO.	INCOME STATEMENT		BALANCE SHEET		
			5 DEBIT	**6** CREDIT	**7** DEBIT	**8** CREDIT	
7	Fred Morton, Capital	31				9 083 56	7
8	Fred Morton, Drawing	32			4 2 7 00		8
9	Income and Expense Summary	33	5 500 50	5 719 55			9
18			9 405 85	10 235 15	12 6 1 6 0 1	11 786 7 1	18
19	Net Income		829 30			829 30	19
20			10 235 15	10 235 15	12 6 1 6 0 1	12 6 1 6 0 1	20

The balance of the income and expense summary account is closed into the proprietor's capital account. The information for this closing entry is obtained from the Net Income line of the work sheet. The closing entry in the general journal is as follows:

GENERAL JOURNAL

PAGE 2

	DATE	NAME OF ACCOUNT	POST. REF.	DEBIT	CREDIT	
21	30	Income and Expense Summary	33	829 30		21
22		Fred Morton, Capital	31		829 30	22

Closing entry for income and expense summary account

Closing the proprietor's drawing account into the proprietor's capital account

The balance of the proprietor's drawing account is closed into the proprietor's capital account. The information for this closing entry is obtained from the drawing account line on the work sheet in the Balance Sheet columns. The journal entry to close the drawing account is as follows:

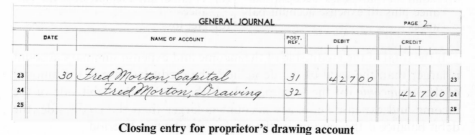

GENERAL JOURNAL

PAGE 2

	DATE	NAME OF ACCOUNT	POST. REF.	DEBIT	CREDIT	
23	30	Fred Morton, Capital	31	4 2 7 00		23
24		Fred Morton, Drawing	32		4 2 7 00	24
25						25

Closing entry for proprietor's drawing account

After this journal entry is posted, Fred Morton's drawing account in the general ledger appears as follows:

DATE	ITEMS	POST. REF.	DEBIT		DATE	ITEMS	POST. REF.	CREDIT	
Fred Morton, Drawing							ACCOUNT NO. 32		
1962 Nov 7		CP1	1 00	00	1962 Nov 30		J2	4 27	00
23		J1	2 27	00					
30		CP1	1 00	00					
			4 27	00					

Proprietor's drawing account after all closing entries have been posted

After all of the closing entries have been journalized and posted, the proprietor's capital account appears as follows:

DATE	ITEMS	POST. REF.	DEBIT		DATE	ITEMS	POST. REF.	CREDIT	
Fred Morton, Capital							ACCOUNT NO. 31		
1962 Nov 30		J2	4 27	00	1962 Nov 1	Balance	J1	8 0 83	56
					6		CR1	1 0 00	00
					30		J2	8 29	30
								9 0 4 3 56	

Proprietor's capital account after all closing entries have been posted

The debit side of Fred Morton's capital account has only one entry. This debit of $427.00 shows the decrease in his proprietorship because of his total withdrawals of cash and merchandise for personal use during this fiscal period.

These withdrawals are accumulated in the proprietor's drawing account during each fiscal period and are then closed into the proprietor's capital account at the end of each fiscal period.

The credit side of Fred Morton's capital account has three entries: (a) the balance of his capital account at the beginning of this fiscal period, $8,083.56; (b) the increase in his proprietorship on November 6 because of his adding to his investment in Morton Supplies, $1,000.00; and (c) the increase in his proprietorship from the operations of this business for this fiscal period because of a net income of $829.30.

The balance of Fred Morton's capital account on November 30 is his new net worth at the end of this fiscal period, $9,485.86.

Closing entries in the general journal

All of the closing entries of Morton Supplies for the fiscal period ended November 30, 1962, are shown on the following page.

	DATE	NAME OF ACCOUNT	POST. REF.	DEBIT	CREDIT	
10		*Closing Entries*				10
11	30	Sales	41	4 5 1 5 6 0		11
12		Income and Expense Summary	33		4 5 1 5 6 0	12
13	30	Income and Expense Summary	33	3 9 0 5 3 5		13
14		Purchases	51		3 1 1 8 1 5	14
15		Delivery Expense	61		5 2 8 0	15
16		Insurance Expense	62		2 0 0 0	16
17		Miscellaneous Expense	63		2 5 8 0	17
18		Rent Expense	64		1 8 0 0 0	18
19		Salary Expense	65		4 0 0 0 0	19
20		Supplies Expense	66		1 0 8 6 0	20
21	30	Income and Expense Summary	33	8 2 9 3 0		21
22		Fred Morton, Capital	31		8 2 9 3 0	22
23	30	Fred Morton, Capital	31	4 2 7 0 0		23
24		Fred Morton, Drawing	32		4 2 7 0 0	24

Closing entries at the end of the fiscal period

The words "Closing Entries" are written in the Name of Account column of the general journal immediately above the first closing entry. A separate explanation for each closing entry in the journal is not necessary.

The first closing entry in the journal transfers the credit balance in the sales account to the credit side of the income and expense summary account. After this entry is posted, the sales account is closed and the credit side of the income and expense summary account shows the income from sales for the fiscal period.

The second closing entry in the journal transfers the debit balance of the purchases account and the debit balances of all expense accounts to the debit side of the income and expense summary account. After this entry is posted, the purchases account and all of the expense accounts are closed and the debit side of the income and expense summary account shows the purchases and the total expenses for the fiscal period.

The third closing entry in the journal transfers the credit balance of the income and expense summary account to the credit side of the proprietor's capital account, Fred Morton, Capital.

If there had been a net loss, the income and expense summary account would have had a debit balance. Then the closing entry would have transferred this debit balance to the debit side of the proprietor's capital account.

The fourth closing entry in the journal transfers the debit balance of the proprietor's drawing account, Fred Morton, Drawing, to the debit side of the proprietor's capital account, Fred Morton, Capital.

Cash

ACCOUNT NO. 11

DATE		ITEMS	POST. REF.	DEBIT	DATE		ITEMS	POST. REF.	CREDIT
1962 Nov.	1	Balance	J1	2400 00	1962 Nov.	30		CP1	2724 74
	30		CR1	5089 00		30	Balance	✓	4764 26
		4764.26		7489 00					7489 00
1962 Dec.	1	Balance	✓	4764 26					

Accounts Receivable

ACCOUNT NO. 12

DATE		ITEMS	POST. REF.	DEBIT	DATE		ITEMS	POST. REF.	CREDIT
1962 Nov.	1	Balance	J1	1032 60	1962 Nov.	30		CR1	1693 00
	30		S1	2119 60		30	Balance	✓	1459 20
		1459.20		3152 20					3152 20
1962 Dec.	1	Balance	✓	1459 20					

Merchandise Inventory

ACCOUNT NO. 13

DATE		ITEMS	POST. REF.	DEBIT	DATE		ITEMS	POST. REF.	CREDIT
1962 Nov.	1	Balance	J1	5500 50	1962 Nov.	30		J2	5500 50
	30		J2	5719 55					

Supplies

ACCOUNT NO. 14

DATE		ITEMS	POST. REF.	DEBIT	DATE		ITEMS	POST. REF.	CREDIT
1962 Nov.	1	Balance	J1	124 60	1962 Nov.	30		J2	108 60
	11		J1	144 00		30	Balance	✓	160 00
				268 60					268 60
1962 Dec.	1	Balance	✓	160 00					

Prepaid Insurance

ACCOUNT NO. 15

DATE		ITEMS	POST. REF.	DEBIT	DATE		ITEMS	POST. REF.	CREDIT
1962 Nov.	1	Balance	J1	106 00	1962 Nov.	30		J2	20 00
						30	Balance	✓	86 00
				106 00					106 00
1962 Dec.	1	Balance	✓	86 00					

General ledger closed, balanced, and ruled

Accounts Payable — ACCOUNT NO. 21

DATE	ITEMS	POST. REF.	DEBIT	DATE	ITEMS	POST. REF.	CREDIT
1962 Nov 30		CP1	1791 14	1962 Nov 1	Balance	J1	1080 14
30	Balance	✓	2703 15	11		J1	144 00
				30	2703.15	P1	3270 15
			4494 29				4494 29
				1962 Dec 1	Balance	✓	2703 15

Fred Morton, Capital — ACCOUNT NO. 31

DATE	ITEMS	POST. REF.	DEBIT	DATE	ITEMS	POST. REF.	CREDIT
1962 Nov 30		J2	427 00	1962 Nov 1	Balance	J1	8083 56
30	Balance	✓	9485 86	6		CR1	1000 00
				30		J2	829 30
			9912 86				9912 86
				1962 Dec 1	Balance	✓	9485 86

Fred Morton, Drawing — ACCOUNT NO. 32

DATE	ITEMS	POST. REF.	DEBIT	DATE	ITEMS	POST. REF.	CREDIT
1962 Nov 7		CP1	100 00	1962 Nov 30		J2	427 00
23		J1	227 00				
30		CP1	100 00				
			427 00				
			427 00				427 00

Income and Expense Summary — ACCOUNT NO. 33

DATE	ITEMS	POST. REF.	DEBIT	DATE	ITEMS	POST. REF.	CREDIT
1962 Nov 30		J2	5500 50	1962 Nov 30		J2	5719 55
30		J2	3905 35	30		J2	4515 60
30		J2	829 30				
			10235 15				10235 15

Sales — ACCOUNT NO. 41

DATE	ITEMS	POST. REF.	DEBIT	DATE	ITEMS	POST. REF.	CREDIT
1962 Nov 30		J2	4515 60	1962 Nov 30		S1	2119 60
				30		CR1	2396 00
			4515 60				4515 60

General ledger closed, balanced, and ruled (continued)

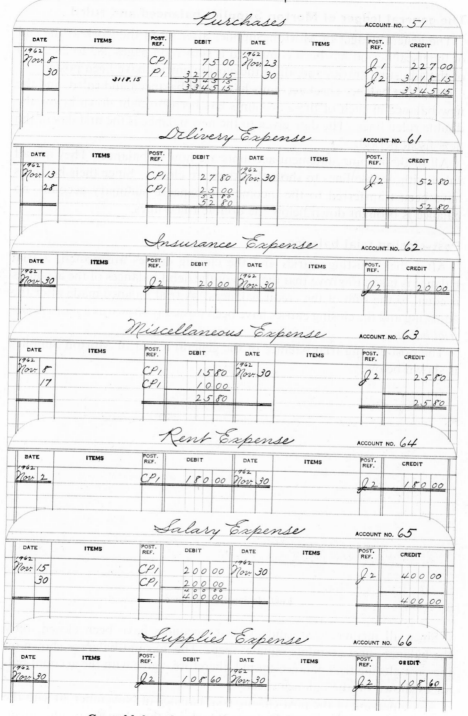

Purchases ACCOUNT NO. 51

DATE	ITEMS	POST. REF.	DEBIT	DATE	ITEMS	POST. REF.	CREDIT
1962 Nov. 8		CP1	75 00	1962 Nov. 23		J1	227 00
30	3118.15	P1	3270 15	30		J2	3118 15
			3345 15				3345 15
			3345 15				

Delivery Expense ACCOUNT NO. 61

DATE	ITEMS	POST. REF.	DEBIT	DATE	ITEMS	POST. REF.	CREDIT
1962 Nov. 13		CP1	27 80	1962 Nov. 30		J2	52 80
28		CP1	25 00				
			52 80				52 80
			52 80				

Insurance Expense ACCOUNT NO. 62

DATE	ITEMS	POST. REF.	DEBIT	DATE	ITEMS	POST. REF.	CREDIT
1962 Nov. 30		J2	20 00	1962 Nov. 30		J2	20 00

Miscellaneous Expense ACCOUNT NO. 63

DATE	ITEMS	POST. REF.	DEBIT	DATE	ITEMS	POST. REF.	CREDIT
1962 Nov. 8		CP1	15 80	1962 Nov. 30		J2	25 80
17		CP1	10 00				
			25 80				25 80

Rent Expense ACCOUNT NO. 64

DATE	ITEMS	POST. REF.	DEBIT	DATE	ITEMS	POST. REF.	CREDIT
1962 Nov. 2		CP1	180 00	1962 Nov. 30		J2	180 00

Salary Expense ACCOUNT NO. 65

DATE	ITEMS	POST. REF.	DEBIT	DATE	ITEMS	POST. REF.	CREDIT
1962 Nov. 15		CP1	200 00	1962 Nov. 30		J2	400 00
30		CP1	200 00				
			400 00				400 00
			400 00				

Supplies Expense ACCOUNT NO. 66

DATE	ITEMS	POST. REF.	DEBIT	DATE	ITEMS	POST. REF.	CREDIT
1962 Nov. 30		J2	108 60	1962 Nov. 30		J2	108 60

General ledger closed, balanced, and ruled (concluded)

285

The general ledger of Morton Supplies balanced and ruled

The general ledger of Morton Supplies after all of the work at the end of the fiscal period has been completed is shown on pages 283 to 285. All of the adjusting entries and all of the closing entries have been posted.

All of the balance sheet accounts have been balanced and ruled, and the new balance in each of these accounts has been brought down below the double ruled lines. The date given to the new balance is the first day of the next fiscal period.

All of the income statement accounts are now in balance. They are all ruled with double lines to show that they are closed. Since their balances have been transferred to the income and expense summary account, no balance is brought down below the double ruled lines.

Post-closing trial balance

After the adjusting entries and the closing entries are posted, a trial balance is taken to prove that the sum of the debit balances of the accounts is equal to the sum of the credit balances. A trial balance made after the adjusting and the closing entries have been posted is known as a *post-closing trial balance*.

The post-closing trial balance of the general ledger of Morton Supplies is shown below.

	Morton Supplies Post-Closing Trial Balance November 30, 1962			
Cash	11	4 7 6 4 26		
Accounts Receivable	12	1 4 59 20		
Merchandise Inventory	13	5 7 1 9 55		
Supplies	14	1 6 0 00		
Prepaid Insurance	15	8 6 00		
Accounts Payable	21		2 7 03 15	
Fred Morton, Capital	31		9 4 8 5 86	
		1 2 1 89 01	1 2 1 89 01	

Post-closing trial balance

Since all income, cost, and expense accounts have been closed, only the balance sheet accounts remain open. The account balances shown on the post-closing trial balance should, therefore, agree with the account balances shown on the balance sheet.

A comparison of the post-closing trial balance of November 30 with the balance sheet on November 30, page 261, shows that they are in agreement.

This is proof that the ledger has been brought up to date. The entire general ledger of Morton Supplies is represented by the following bookkeeping equation:

$$\begin{array}{ccccc} \text{ASSETS} & = & \text{LIABILITIES} & + & \text{PROPRIETORSHIP} \\ \$12,189.01 & = & \$2,703.15 & + & \$9,485.86 \end{array}$$

Increasing your business vocabulary

What is the meaning of each of the following:

(a) adjusting entry   (b) post-closing trial balance

Chapter questions

1. Why is it necessary to record entries in the general journal for each adjustment on the work sheet?
2. Why is it necessary to adjust the supplies account at the end of each fiscal period?
3. After the adjusting entry for expired insurance is posted, what does the debit balance of the prepaid insurance account in the general ledger represent?
4. What are the two reasons for making closing entries?
5. From what columns of the work sheet is the information obtained for making entries to close the income accounts, the cost accounts, and the expense accounts?
6. To what account are the balances of all income accounts, cost accounts, and expense accounts transferred?
7. To what account is the balance of the income and expense summary account transferred?
8. Why should a trial balance be taken after the adjusting and the closing entries have been posted?

Cases for discussion

1. At the end of a fiscal period, Dale Dodge, an auto supply merchant, prepares a trial balance and the two financial reports, but he does not adjust and close the ledger. What effect will this omission of the adjusting and the closing entries have on the records at the end of the next fiscal period?
2. At the end of his fiscal period on October 31, G. L. Smith, a florist, had sold his complete stock of merchandise. He therefore had no ending inventory of merchandise. How would his adjusting entry for merchandise inventory differ from that of Morton Supplies presented in this chapter?
3. O. H. Helstrom, a druggist, says that the accuracy of all of his work has been proved definitely by his post-closing trial balance. To what extent does the post-closing trial balance prove that the work at the end of the fiscal period was correctly completed?

Drills for understanding

Drill 19-A. *Adjusting entries*

A part of the Trial Balance columns and a part of the Adjustments columns of the work sheet of Ronald Schmidt are shown below.

Account Titles	Trial Balance		Adjustments	
	Debit	Credit	Debit	Credit
Merchandise Inventory........	10,000 00	....	(b) 6,000 00	(a) 10,000 00
Supplies....................	120 00	....	....	(c) 60 00
Prepaid Insurance...........	80 00	....	....	(d) 40 00
Income and Expense Summary .	....	....	(a) 10,000 00	(b) 6,000 00
Insurance Expense...........	....	....	(d) 40 00	....
Supplies Expense............	....	....	(c) 60 00	....

Instructions: 1. What account is debited and what account is credited in the adjusting entry for the beginning merchandise inventory?

2. What account is debited and what account is credited in the adjusting entry for the ending merchandise inventory?

3. What account is debited and what account is credited in the adjusting entry for supplies?

4. What account is debited and what account is credited in the adjusting entry for prepaid insurance?

Drill 19-B. *Closing entries*

A part of the Income Statement columns and a part of the Balance Sheet columns of the work sheet of Ronald Schmidt are shown below.

Account Titles	Income Statement		Balance Sheet	
	Debit	Credit	Debit	Credit
Ronald Schmidt, Capital.........	....	....	....	18,000 00
Ronald Schmidt, Drawing........	....	....	400 00	....
Income and Expense Summary....	10,000 00	6,000 00	....	....
Sales...........................	....	9,800 00	....	....
Purchases......................	3,000 00	....	....	....
Insurance Expense..............	40 00	....	....	....
Miscellaneous Expense...........	80 00	....	....	....
Rent Expense...................	300 00	....	....	....
Salary Expense.................	800 00	....	....	....
Supplies Expense...............	60 00	....	....	....
Totals.......................	14,280 00	15,800 00	24,520 00	23,000 00
Net Income...................	1,520 00	....	....	1,520 00
	15,800 00	15,800 00	24,520 00	24,520 00

Instructions; 1. What accounts will be debited and credited to close Sales?

2. What accounts will be debited and credited to close the purchases account and all of the expense accounts?

3. What accounts will be debited and credited to close the income and expense summary account into the proprietor's capital account?

4. What accounts will be debited and credited to close the proprietor's drawing account into the proprietor's capital account?

Application problems

Problem 19-1. Work at the end of the fiscal period

If you are not using the workbook correlating with this textbook, complete Exercise 19-A in the Appendix instead of this problem.

The ledger accounts of the Bowman Electric Shop as of May 31 of the current year are given in the workbook.

Instructions: 1. Foot the ledger accounts. Write the footings in very small figures with a sharp pencil and place each footing close to the last item.

2. Prove cash. The cash on hand and in the bank on May 31, 19--, is $3,879.60, which should agree with the balance in the cash account.

3. Prepare a trial balance. You may prepare this trial balance in the Trial Balance columns of the work sheet, but in a trial balance recorded on the work sheet you should record each account regardless of whether it has a balance.

4. Complete the work sheet, using the following additional data as of May 31:

Merchandise inventory......................	$11,480.40
Supplies on hand...........................	225.00
Prepaid insurance..........................	240.00

Compare your work with the work sheet illustrated on page 249.

5. Prepare an income statement from the information given on the work sheet. Compare your work with the income statement illustrated on page 258.

6. Prepare a balance sheet from the information given on the work sheet. Compare your work with the balance sheet illustrated on page 261.

7. Record on page 2 of a general journal the adjusting entries shown in the Adjustments columns of the work sheet. Compare your work with the adjusting entries illustrated on page 277.

8. Record in the general journal the closing entries from the information shown in the Income Statement columns and the Balance Sheet columns of the work sheet. Compare your work with the closing entries illustrated on page 282.

9. Post the adjusting entries and the closing entries.

10. Rule the accounts that balance. Balance each remaining account in the general ledger that has both debits and credits. Compare your work with the general ledger accounts illustrated on pages 283 to 285.

11. Prepare a post-closing trial balance. Compare your work with the post-closing trial balance illustrated on page 286.

Bradford wholesale grocery

Part 2 - Work at the end of the fiscal period

At this time you are to complete the work at the end of a fiscal period for the Bradford Wholesale Grocery. For this work you will need all of the records that you completed for the month of October in Part 1 of this practice set.

Instructions: 1. Prepare an eight-column work sheet as follows:

(a) Write the heading for the monthly fiscal period ended October 31 of the current year.

(b) Enter in the Account Titles column all the account titles given in the chart of accounts. Then enter in the Trial Balance columns the account balances shown in the trial balance prepared at the end of Part 1.

(c) Record adjustments in the Adjustments columns of the work sheet from the following data as of October 31 of the current year:

Merchandise inventory, $57,856.00
Supplies on hand, $912.00
Prepaid insurance, $750.00

(d) Complete the work sheet. Compare your work with the work sheet on page 249.

2. Prepare an income statement from the information given on the work sheet. Compare your work with the income statement illustrated on page 258.

3. Prepare a balance sheet from the information given on the work sheet. Compare your work with the balance sheet illustrated on page 261.

4. Record in the general journal the adjusting entries for the adjustments shown in the Adjustments columns of the work sheet. Compare your work with the adjusting entries illustrated on page 277.

5. Record in the general journal the closing entries from the information shown in the Income Statement columns of the work sheet. Compare your work with the closing entries illustrated on page 282.

6. Post the adjusting entries and the closing entries and rule the accounts in the general ledger that balance. Compare your work with the general ledger accounts illustrated on pages 283 to 285.

7. Balance each remaining account in the general ledger that has both debits and credits. Compare your work with the general ledger accounts illustrated on pages 283 to 285.

8. Prepare a post-closing trial balance. Compare your work with the post-closing trial balance illustrated on page 286.

Chapter 20

The combination journal and the petty cash fund

Why don't all businesses use the same kind of journals?

The number and kinds of business transactions vary from business to business. It is not practical, therefore, for all businesses to use the same kind and the same number of journals. The books of original entry should be adapted to the needs of the business.

The combination journal

In earlier chapters we saw how a columnar journal may be used as the only book of original entry of a small service business. Later we used special journals as well as a general journal to record the transactions of a business buying and selling merchandise on account. Now we shall see how some small merchandising businesses can retain the benefits of special journals by combining several or all of their journals into one. A multi-column journal that combines several journals or all journals into one book of original entry is called a *combination journal*.

In a combination journal similar types of transactions are sorted and summarized by columns as shown in the illustration on pages 292 and 293. Note that this journal is much the same as the columnar journal used in the first ten chapters, but columns have been added for accounts payable, accounts receivable, purchases, and sales.

Analyzing the combination journal

The use of the combination journal may be readily understood from a study of the recording of a few typical transactions. The transactions recorded on the first nine lines of the combination journal illustrated on pages 292 and 293 are therefore discussed in the following paragraphs.

Line 1 — May 1, sold merchandise on account to J. B. Wall, $29.65. The amount of the debit to Accounts Receivable, $29.65, is written in the Accounts Receivable Debit column. As this amount must also be posted to the account of the customer in the accounts receivable ledger, the name of the customer, J. B. Wall, is written in the Name of Account column. The credit to Sales, $29.65, is recorded by writing the amount in the Sales Credit column.

Line 2 — May 1, purchased merchandise on account from Western Hardware Company, $329.62. Purchases is debited by an entry in the

Purchases Debit column, and Accounts Payable is credited by an entry in the Accounts Payable Credit column. In order that the credit may also be posted to the account of the creditor in the accounts payable ledger, the name of the creditor, Western Hardware Company, is written in the Name of Account column.

Line 3 — May 1, issued Check No. 127 for $269.75 to Franklin Mfg. Co. on account. The amount of the debit, $269.75, is recorded in the Accounts Payable Debit column. To indicate that this amount is also to be debited to the creditor's account in the accounts payable ledger, the name of the creditor, Franklin Mfg. Co., is written in the Name of Account column. The amount of the credit to Cash, $269.75, is written in the Cash Credit column. The check number, 127, is written in the Check No. column.

Line 4 — May 1, issued Check No. 128 for $150 for the May rent. A special column is provided only when it will be used frequently. As Rent Expense is debited only once a month, a special column is not provided; instead the debit is recorded in the General Debit column. The title of the account debited, Rent Expense, is written in the Name of Account column. The amount credited to Cash is recorded in the Cash Credit column. The number of the check, 128, is written in the Check No. column.

Line 5 — May 2, received cash, $79.65, from Robert Norton on account. The amount of the cash received, $79.65, is recorded in the Cash Debit column. The same amount is written in the Accounts Receivable Credit column. To show that Robert Norton's account in the accounts receivable ledger is to be credited, his name is written in the Name of Account column.

	CASH		CHK. NO.	DATE	NAME OF ACCOUNT	POST. REF.	
	DEBIT	CREDIT					
1				1962 May 1	J. B. Wall	✓	1
2				1	Western Hardware Co.	✓	2
3		269 75	127	1	Franklin Mfg. Co.	✓	3
4		150 00	128	1	Rent Expense	65	4
5	79 65			2	Robert Norton	✓	5
6				3	Equipment	16	6
7					A. M. Allen	✓	7
8	90 00		129	3	Purchases	✓	8
9	289 77			4	Sales	✓	9
35	35 39			25	Sales	✓	35
36	1884 83	1635 17		25	Carried Forward	✓	36

PAGE 10   COMBINATION JOURNAL

Combination journal (left page)

Lines 6 and 7 — *May 3, purchased equipment on account from A. M. Allen, $125.* Since there is no special column for the equipment account, the debit amount must be recorded in the General Debit column. The title of the account to be debited, Equipment, is written in the Name of Account column.

The accounts payable account in the general ledger must be credited for $125, and the creditor's account, A. M. Allen, in the accounts payable ledger must also be credited for $125. The amount, $125, is therefore written in the Accounts Payable Credit column and the name of the creditor is written in the Name of Account column.

When the account titles for both the debit and the credit of a single transaction must be written, two lines are used. The account title for the debit is written on the first line. The account title for the credit is written on the next line and is indented about one-half inch.

Line 8 — *May 3, issued Check No. 129 for $90 for cash purchase of merchandise.* The amount of the debit to Purchases is entered in the Purchases Debit column, and the amount of the credit to Cash is entered in the Cash Credit column. The account title, Purchases, is written in the Name of Account column to show the nature of this transaction.

Line 9 — *May 4, total cash receipts for cash sales for May 1–4 were $289.77.* The amount of the debit to Cash is entered in the Cash Receipts Debit column, and the amount of the credit to Sales is entered in the Sales Credit column. The account title, Sales, is written in the Name of Account column to show the nature of this transaction.

FOR MONTH OF *May* 19 62   PAGE 10

| | GENERAL | | ACCOUNTS PAYABLE | | ACCOUNTS RECEIVABLE | | PURCHASES | SALES | |
	3 DEBIT	4 CREDIT	5 DEBIT	6 CREDIT	7 DEBIT	8 CREDIT	9 DEBIT	10 CREDIT	
1					29 65			29 65	1
2				329 62			329 62		2
3			269 75						3
4	150 00								4
5						79 65			5
6	125 00								6
7				125 00					7
8							90 00		8
9								289 77	9
35	521 38	169 10	1583 50	1624 80	460 33	226 80	1594 93	351 30	35
36	521 38	169 10	1583 50	1624 80	460 33	226 80	1594 93	2389 10	36

Combination journal (right page)

293

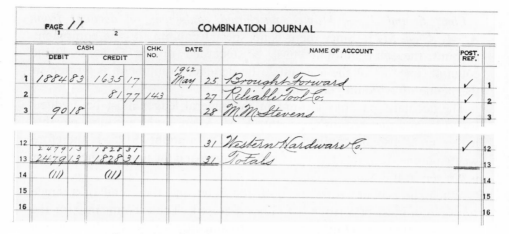

COMBINATION JOURNAL

| CASH | | CHK. | DATE | NAME OF ACCOUNT | POST. | |
DEBIT	CREDIT	NO.			REF.	
1884 83	1635 17		1962 May 25	Brought Forward	✓	1
	81 77	143	27	Reliable Tool Co.	✓	2
90 18			28	M. M. Stevens	✓	3
2479 13	1828 31		31	Western Hardware Co.	✓	12
2479 13	1828 31		31	Totals		13
(11)	(11)					14
						15
						16

Combination journal footed, ruled, and posted (left page)

Forwarding the combination journal totals

When a page of the combination journal is filled before the end of a month, the totals of the first page are forwarded to the second page. The bottom line in the illustration on page 292 shows how the "Totals" line is prepared for forwarding. The illustration above shows how the first line on a new page indicates the totals brought forward. The procedure in forwarding totals is:

Step 1.   Each of the amount columns is totaled. The totals are entered in small pencil footings immediately below the line of the last entry.

Step 2.   The equality of debits and credits is proved. This is done by adding on a separate sheet of paper the totals of all debit columns and the totals of all credit columns. The total debits should equal the total credits.

Step 3.   When the total debits are found to equal the total credits, the column totals are entered in ink. A single line is drawn above the column totals to indicate addition. A double line is drawn below the totals in the manner shown in the illustration on pages 292 and 293.

Many printed forms provide single- and double-ruled lines at the bottom of each page. In such cases it is not necessary to rule lines.

Step 4.   The date is entered in the Date column, "Carried Forward" is written in the Name of Account column, and a check mark is placed in the Post. Ref. column. None of these totals is to be posted, as these totals are to be included with the figures on the next page.

Step 5.   The column totals are written on the first line of the next page.

Step 6.   The date is written in the Date column and the words "Brought Forward" are written in the Name of Account column. A check mark is placed in the Post. Ref. column.

FOR MONTH OF *May*, 1962   PAGE 11

| | GENERAL | | ACCOUNTS PAYABLE | | ACCOUNTS RECEIVABLE | | PURCHASES | SALES | |
	DEBIT	CREDIT	DEBIT	CREDIT	DEBIT	CREDIT	DEBIT	CREDIT	
1	521 38	169 10	1583 50	1624 80	460 33	226 80	1594 93	2389 10	1
2				81 77					2
3						90 18			3
12	727 88	169 10	1665 27	1850 30	540 18	458 60	1725 30	2831 45	12
13	727 88	169 10	1665 27	1850 30	540 18	458 60	1725 30	2831 45	13
14	(✓)	(✓)	(21)	(21)	(12)	(12)	(51)	(41)	14
15									15
16									16

Combination journal footed, ruled, and posted (right page)

Any columnar or special journal might require more than one page for recording all the transactions for a month. The forwarding procedure described and illustrated for the combination journal is the same procedure used for forwarding in any of these other journals.

Posting the individual items in the combination journal

Each amount in the General Debit column is posted to the debit of the account shown in the Name of Account column. Each amount in the General Credit column is posted to the credit of the account shown in the Name of Account column. The completion of the posting of each amount in the General columns is indicated by writing in the Post. Ref. column the number of the account to which the amount was posted.

Each amount in the Accounts Receivable columns must be posted to a customer's account in the accounts receivable ledger. Each amount in the Accounts Payable columns must be posted to a creditor's account in the accounts payable ledger. The titles of the customers' and the creditors' accounts are given in the Name of Account column. The completion of the posting of each item is indicated by a check mark in the Post. Ref. column.

A check mark is also placed in the Post. Ref. column for each cash sales entry and for each cash purchases entry (see Lines 8, 9 and 35 on page 292). This check mark indicates that neither the debit nor the credit is to be posted separately.

When a business makes a combination journal its only book of original entry, only the page number from which the posting is made is shown in the Post. Ref. column of the ledger accounts. When a business uses two or more journals, letters are placed before the page number to show from which journal the posting was made. For example, S1 is used for page 1 of the sales journal, CP4 for page 4 of the cash payments journal, and J6 for page 6 of the general journal.

Posting the column totals of the combination journal

At the end of the month all columns of the combination journal are footed, proved, totaled, and ruled. The total of each special column is posted to the account indicated by the column heading. The completion of the posting of each column total is indicated by writing the number of the account in parentheses below the column total.

The totals of the General columns are not posted, since each amount in these columns is posted individually. To indicate that these totals are not to be posted, a check mark is placed in parentheses under each total.

Variations in the use of the combination journal

Some small businesses make a combination journal their only book of original entry. More frequently, however, businesses that use a combination journal retain the general journal for recording special entries such as adjusting, closing, and correcting entries. Some businesses will also retain one or more of their special journals for recording sales, or purchases, or cash and then record only the summary totals from the special journal in the combination journal. For example, when invoices are filed or bound together and are used as the special sales journal, one entry would be made in the combination journal at the end of the month debiting Accounts Receivable and crediting Sales. Such a practice enables assistant bookkeepers to keep the subsidiary records, while the head bookkeeper controls the posting to the accounts in the general ledger.

Why do many businesses keep a petty cash fund?

Most businesses have small expenses that are best paid in cash. For example, the postman presents a letter or a package on which a few cents are due; the expressman delivers a collect package; or the office boy is sent to the post office to send a registered letter. An amount of cash kept on hand and used for making small payments is called a *petty cash fund*.

The use of a petty cash fund enables a business to follow the common practice of depositing *all* cash receipts in the bank and of making *all* withdrawals of such cash by writing checks. When this is done, the monthly bank statements may be used to prove the cash records of the business. This gives the bookkeeper a double check on the accuracy of the cash account.

Using the petty cash fund

The petty cash fund is established by drawing a check in favor of Petty Cash and by cashing this check. The amount of the check is often $50 or less. The money is kept separate from cash receipts. One person is usually responsible for making petty cash payments.

When cash is paid from the petty cash fund, a form is filled out to show to whom the cash was paid, what it was paid for, the amount spent, and the expense account to be debited. It may also show the signature of the person receiving the payment and the signature of the person making or approving the payment. A form that provides written authority for a bookkeeping transaction is known as a *voucher*. One form of a petty cash voucher is shown in the illustration at the right.

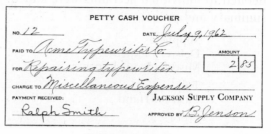

PETTY CASH VOUCHER

NO. *12*   DATE *July 9, 1962*

PAID TO *Acme Typewriter Co.*   AMOUNT

FOR *Repairing typewriter*   *2 85*

CHARGE TO *Miscellaneous Expense*

PAYMENT RECEIVED: JACKSON SUPPLY COMPANY

Ralph Smith   APPROVED BY *B. Jenson*

Petty cash voucher

Whenever a payment is made from the petty cash fund, the voucher for the payment is filled out and is placed in the petty cash drawer. The sum of the petty cash vouchers and the money in the drawer should equal the original amount of the petty cash fund.

At the end of each fiscal period and at any other time when the petty cash fund is low, a check made out to Petty Cash for an amount equal to the sum of the vouchers is written and cashed. At that time the vouchers are sorted according to the accounts to be debited. All amounts to be debited to one account are added together. An entry is then made in the combination journal debiting the various accounts for the proper amounts and crediting Cash for the total amount of the check.

Recording petty cash in a combination journal

At the time the petty cash fund is established, Petty Cash is debited and Cash is credited. This entry is shown on Line 1 of the combination journal illustrated below. The effect of the transaction is to reduce the cash amount and to set up a new asset account, Petty Cash.

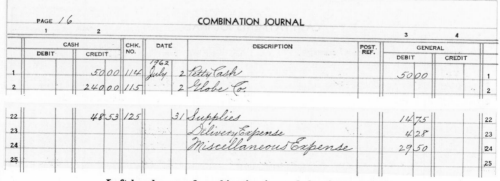

PAGE *16*   COMBINATION JOURNAL

	CASH		CHK. NO.	DATE	DESCRIPTION	POST. REF.	GENERAL		
	DEBIT	CREDIT					DEBIT	CREDIT	
1		50 00	114	1962 July 2	Petty Cash		50 00		1
2		240 00	115	2	Globe Co.				2
22		48 53	125	31	Supplies		14 75		22
23					Delivery Expense		4 28		23
24					Miscellaneous Expense		29 50		24
25									25

Left-hand page of combination journal showing entries to establish and to replenish petty cash fund

On July 31 the petty cash fund was replenished. The following steps were made to bring the cash in the fund back up to $50:

Step 1. The petty cash vouchers were sorted and the amounts to be debited to individual accounts were added. This resulted in the following summary and proof:

Supplies....................................	.$14.75
Delivery Expense...........................	4.28
Miscellaneous Expense......................	29.50
Total......................................	$48.53
Cash on Hand..............................	1.47
Proof.....................................	$50.00

Step 2. A check for $48.53 was then drawn to bring the petty cash fund up to its original amount. The check was made out to Petty Cash. The check stub from which the entry was made indicated that Supplies was to be debited for $14.75, Delivery Expense for $4.28, and Miscellaneous Expense for $29.50.

Step 3. The check for $48.53 was cashed and the cash was put into the petty cash drawer along with the remaining $1.47.

The entry to record the check that replenished the petty cash fund is shown on Lines 22, 23, and 24 in the combination journal illustrated on the preceding page. The titles of the accounts, Supplies, Delivery Expense, and Miscellaneous Expense, were written in the Name of Account column. The number of the check, 125, was written in the Check No. column on Line 22.

If this business used a cash payments journal instead of a combination journal, the entries to record petty cash transactions would be the same. The following illustration shows how the entries for establishing and replenishing the petty cash fund would appear in a cash payments journal.

	DATE	ACCOUNT DEBITED	CHK. NO.	POST. REF.	GENERAL DEBIT	ACCOUNTS PAYABLE DEBIT	CASH CREDIT	
					1	2	3	
1	1962 July 2	Petty Cash	114		50 00		50 00	1
2	2	Globe Co.	115			240 00	240 00	2
12	31	Supplies			14 75			12
13		Delivery Expense			4 28			13
14		Miscellaneous Expense	125		29 50		48 53	14

CASH PAYMENTS JOURNAL   PAGE 7

Cash payments journal with entries for petty cash

Increasing your business vocabulary

What is the meaning of each of the following:

  (a) combination journal   (b) petty cash fund   (c) voucher

Chapter questions

1. Why do not all businesses use the same kind and the same number of journals?
2. When is it necessary to use two lines, instead of one, in the Name of Account column of a combination journal for recording a business transaction?
3. When are the columns in the combination journal totaled?
4. How is the combination journal proved?
5. What amounts in the combination journal illustrated on pages 292 and 293 are posted individually?
6. In the combination journal illustrated on pages 294 and 295, how is the posting of the column totals indicated?
7. When a business uses a general journal as well as a combination journal, what kind of entries are usually recorded in the general journal?
8. Why do some businesses retain their special journals and record only the summary totals of these special journals in their combination journal once a month?
9. Why is it a good business practice to bank *all* cash receipts and to make *all* withdrawals of such cash by check?
10. Why do many businesses keep a petty cash fund?
11. In the combination journal illustrated on page 297, what entry is made to establish the petty cash fund?
12. When is the petty cash fund replenished?
13. When a check is drawn to replenish the petty cash fund, what entry is made?

Cases for discussion

1. Assume that you are the only bookkeeper for A. J. Smith, the owner of a small toy shop. You have been using a cash journal similar to that illustrated on page 51. Mr. Smith has asked you to suggest improvements in his bookkeeping system. Under what circumstances would you recommend shifting from this cash journal to a combination journal with additional amount columns?
2. One high school bookkeeping student, when he first learned about forwarding, said that he did not see the need for it. He claimed that it would be satisfactory to show the final total only for each column. Why is his suggestion a poor one?
3. Michael Rocco, a florist, deposited all cash receipts in the bank. All large payments were made by check. Small payments were made from a petty cash fund. Why was this method better than that of making small cash payments from cash receipts?

Application problem

Problem 20-1. Recording transactions in a combination journal

Instructions: 1. Record on page 6 of a combination journal like the one illustrated on pages 294 and 295 the following transactions completed by Charles W. North during the month of June of the current year:

June 1. Issued Check No. 48 for $35.00 to establish a petty cash fund.
     1. Issued Check No. 49 for $200.00 for the June rent.
     2. Received $126.10 from Peter Potter on account.
     3. Purchased merchandise on account from Starrett Bros., $409.33.
     4. Sold merchandise on account to V. M. Moore, $88.20.
     5. Received $220.48 from Henry Jackson on account.
     5. Cash sales for June 1–5 were $293.85.
     8. Issued Check No. 50 for $269.75 to Bailey Company on account.
     9. Issued Check No. 51 for $73.88 for a cash purchase of merchandise.
    10. Purchased merchandise on account from Moss & Menke, $612.21.
    11. Received $15.00 for an old display case. (Store Equipment)
    12. Cash sales for June 7–12 were $375.57.
    14. Issued Check No. 52 for $168.90 to Starrett Bros. on account.
    17. Sold merchandise on account to J. M. Handy, $28.50.
    19. Cash sales for June 14–19 were $413.25.
    21. Received $41.80 from T. B. Dent on account.
    22. Issued Check No. 53 for $25.00 for advertising. (Advertising Expense)
    24. Issued Check No. 54 for $303.67 for cash purchase of merchandise.
    25. Issued Check No. 55 for $231.90 to the Hammitt Company on account.
    26. Issued Check No. 56 for $250.00 to Mr. North for a withdrawal for personal use.

Instructions: 2. Assume at this point of the problem that you have reached the bottom of the page. Total all columns and forward to the next page of the combination journal. Then continue to journalize the following transactions:

June 26. Cash sales for June 21–26 were $408.17.
    28. Sold merchandise on account to T. W. Baxter, $43.88.
    29. Issued Check No. 57 for $66.19 for utility bills for the month. (Miscellaneous Expense)
    30. Issued Check No. 58 for $31.85 to replenish the petty cash fund. The petty cash payments were as follows: Supplies, $9.80; Advertising Expense, $2.50; Delivery Expense, $2.25; and Miscellaneous Expense, $17.30.
    30. Issued Check No. 59 for $440 for the monthly payroll. (Salary Expense)
    30. Cash sales for June 28–30 were $227.13.

Instructions: 3. Foot all columns of the combination journal and prove the equality of debits and credits.

4. Total and rule the combination journal.

Problem 20-2. Establishing, proving, and replenishing the petty cash fund

Instructions: 1. On November 1 of the current year, John O'Brien drew and cashed Check No. 61 for $40.00 to establish a petty cash fund. Record this check on page 11 of a combination journal like the model on page 297.

Mr. O'Brien paid cash from the petty cash fund as given below. The accounts to be charged are:

Supplies — for all supplies, such as ink, tape, wrapping supplies, and stamps.
Advertising Expense — for all advertising, such as newspaper advertisements.
Delivery Expense — for the delivery of goods sold.
Miscellaneous Expense — for all other expenses.

Nov. 2. Paid $1.65 for a telegram.
    4. Paid $1.25 for special delivery of a sale.
    7. Paid 85 cents for ink and cellophane tape.
    9. Paid $7.00 for having the office cleaned.
    12. Paid $2.50 for a newspaper advertisement.
    16. Paid $3.95 for wrapping supplies.
    19. Paid $1.65 for two telegrams.
    21. Paid $1.50 to himself for a luncheon purchased for a customer.
    23. Paid $5.00 for having the office cleaned.
    25. Paid $8.00 for postage stamps.
    28. Paid $1.00 for immediate delivery of a sale.
    29. Paid $3.25 for repairs to the typewriter.
    29. At the close of this day, $2.40 remained in the petty cash fund.

Instructions: 2. On a separate sheet of paper, sort and summarize these transactions by accounts.

3. Prove the petty cash fund.

4. Check No. 88 was drawn to replenish the petty cash fund. Record in the combination journal the entry for replenishing the petty cash fund.

Optional problems

★Supplementary Problem 20-S. Recording transactions in a combination journal

Instructions: 1. Record on page 7 of a combination journal like the one illustrated on pages 294 and 295 the following transactions completed by Kenneth Parker during the month of July of the current year:

July 1. Purchased merchandise on account from Atkins Bros., $320.00.
    1. Issued Check No. 231 for $200.00 for July rent.
    2. Sold merchandise on account to J. B. Dane, $25.50.
    3. Received $60.00 from Michael Grey on account.
    5. Issued Check No. 232 for $310.00 for cash purchase of merchandise.
    6. Cash sales for July 1–6 were $620.70.
    8. Issued Check No. 233 for $320.00 to Atkins Bros. on account.
    9. Issued Check No. 234 for $33.50 for cash purchase of supplies.
    9. Received $20.00 for sale of old typewriter. (Office Equipment)

July 10. Issued Check No. 235 for $63.80 to Office Supply Company on account.
12. Purchased merchandise on account from Lawton Wholesalers, $431.40.
13. Cash sales for July 8–13 were $770.14.
16. Purchased merchandise on account from Atkins Bros., $280.80.
18. Issued Check No. 236 for $50.00 to Office Supply Company on account.
19. Issued Check No. 237 for $23.50 for newspaper advertising. (Advertising Expense)
20. Received $83.75 from J. B. Dane on account.
20. Sold merchandise on account to M. M. Milton, $183.20.
20. Cash sales for July 15–20 were $610.40.
23. Sold merchandise on account to Ronald Carr, $23.90.
23. Issued Check No. 238 for $200.00 to Lawton Wholesalers on account.
27. Cash sales for July 22–27 were $590.63.
31. Issued Check No. 239 to replenish the petty cash fund. The summary of petty cash payments was as follows: Delivery Expense, $16.00; Advertising Expense, $14.80; Miscellaneous Expense, $7.60; and Supplies, $6.20.
31. Issued Check No. 240 for $310.25 for the monthly payroll. (Salary Expense)
31. Issued Check No. 241 for $150.00 to Mr. Parker for a withdrawal for personal use.
31. Cash sales for July 29–31 were $280.10.

Instructions: 2. Foot all columns of the combination journal and prove the equality of debits and credits.

3. Total and rule the combination journal.

★Bonus Problem 20-B. A combination journal with different rulings

Introductory remarks. The rulings of combination journals follow two common patterns. The one illustrated on pages 292 and 293 is called a divided-column form. Its amount columns are divided by the Name of Account column, some placed on the left and others on the right of this wide column. The other common pattern is for *all* of the amount columns to be *on the right* of the wide column.

Instructions: 1. Use a 10-column combination journal with rulings and column headings as follows:

DATE	NAME OF ACCOUNT	CHK. NO.	POST. REF.	GENERAL		CASH		ACCOUNTS PAYABLE		ACCOUNTS RECEIVABLE		PURCHASES DR.	SALES CR.
				DR.	CR.	DR.	CR.	DR.	CR.	DR.	CR.		

Instructions: 2. Record the transactions given in Supplementary Problem 20-S.

3. Foot all columns of the combination journal and prove the equality of debits and credits.

4. Total and rule the combination journal.

Chapter 21

Problems relating to sales and purchases

Sales returns and allowances

A *sales return* is the return of goods previously sold to a customer for which the merchant grants credit or refunds cash. Sales returns are usually the result of a customer's changing his mind about a purchase, receiving the wrong item, or receiving damaged goods. A *sales allowance* is the credit given to a customer for part of the sales price of goods that are not returned. Sales allowances are generally the result of damaged or imperfect goods or a shortage in the shipment.

Sales returns and sales allowances represent a decrease in sales. As a result, some businesses debit the amount of the sales returns and allowances to the sales account. It is recommended, however, that these debits be recorded in a separate account with the title *Sales Returns and Allowances*. A business can then readily see how large these sales returns and allowances are and whether they are increasing or decreasing from year to year. If the amounts are very large, one account may be kept for sales allowances and another account for sales returns. Usually it is satisfactory to combine the two into the same account.

The credit memorandum

A special business form that contains a record of the credit that the seller has granted for returns, overcharges, allowances, and similar items is known as a *credit memorandum*. A typical credit memorandum is shown at the right.

Recording sales returns and allowances

This credit memorandum shows that R. J. Wallace has given W. B. Hanley a credit of $10.50 for merchandise that Hanley has returned. The entry for this credit transaction is the first one shown in the combination journal on pages 304 and 305.

CREDIT MEMORANDUM	No. 16
R. J. WALLACE	July 2, 1962
Book and Writing Papers	W. B. Hanley
	2016 State Street
HAMILTON	Gary, Indiana
WE CREDIT YOUR ACCOUNT AS FOLLOWS:	
1 M Sheets 21 x 32-100# Posting Ledger	10.50

Credit memorandum

To record the debit to Sales Returns and Allowances, the account title was written in the Name of Account column and the amount of the debit, $10.50, was entered in the General Debit column.

To record the credit to the customer's account, the customer's name was written in the Name of Account column on the next line of the journal and was indented. The amount of the credit, $10.50, was entered in the Accounts Receivable Credit column.

The effect of this credit-granting transaction on accounts in the general and accounts receivable ledgers is shown in T account form below.

GENERAL LEDGER

Sales Returns and Allowances

July 2	10.50	

ACCOUNTS RECEIVABLE LEDGER

W. B. Hanley

July 1 Bal. 186.60	July 2	10.50

Accounts Receivable

July 1 Bal. 4,310.14	July 2	10.50

The sales returns and allowances account, a minus sales account, has been debited for $10.50. The accounts receivable account has been credited for the same amount. Also, Mr. Hanley's account in the accounts receivable ledger has been credited for $10.50.

Receiving credit for purchases returns and allowances

The buyer of merchandise may be allowed credit by the seller for the return of part or all of the merchandise purchased. He may also be allowed

	CASH		CHK. NO.	DATE	NAME OF ACOUNT	POST. REF.	GENERAL		
	DEBIT	CREDIT					DEBIT	CREDIT	
				1962					
1				July 2	Sales Returns and Allow.		10 50		1
2					W. B. Hanley				2
3				2	Atlas Manufacturing Co.				3
4				2	Joseph Reed				4
5				5	Johnson Manufacturing Co.				5
6					Purchases Returns + Allow.			16 50	6
15		456 29	191	12	Atlas Manufacturing Co.				15
16	294 00			12	Joseph Reed				16
17									17

PAGE 17   COMBINATION JOURNAL

Combination journal with entries for returns and allowances (left page)

credit by the seller if the merchandise received was inferior in quality or was damaged in transit. In the latter case the merchandise is usually retained by the buyer. Merchandise returned by a purchaser for which he receives credit is called a *purchases return*. Credit that is given for merchandise that is not completely satisfactory but that is not returned is called a *purchases allowance*.

The buyer usually receives a credit memorandum from the seller showing the amount of the purchases return or the purchases allowance. As purchases returns and purchases allowances are ordinarily few in number, they are usually recorded in the same account with the title *Purchases Returns and Allowances*.

Recording purchases returns and allowances

A credit memorandum was received on July 5 from the Johnson Manufacturing Company for $16.50 worth of merchandise that had been returned. The entry on Lines 5 and 6 in the combination journal below shows this transaction recorded.

To record the debit to the creditor's account, the creditor's name was written in the Name of Account column and the amount of the debit, $16.50, was entered in the Accounts Payable Debit column.

To record the credit to Purchases Returns and Allowances, the account title was written in the Name of Account column on the next line of the journal and was indented. The amount of the credit was entered in the General Credit column.

	ACCOUNTS PAYABLE		DISCOUNT ON PURCHASES CREDIT	ACCOUNTS RECEIVABLE		DISCOUNT ON SALES DEBIT	PURCHASES DEBIT	SALES CREDIT		
	DEBIT	CREDIT		DEBIT	CREDIT					
1										1
2					10 50					2
3		465 60					465 60			3
4				300 00				300 00		4
5	16 50									5
6										6
15	465 60			9 31						15
16					300 00	6 00				16
17										17

FOR MONTH OF *July* 1962 PAGE *17*

Combination journal with entries for returns and allowances (right page)

The effect of this credit-receiving transaction on accounts in the general and accounts payable ledgers is shown in T account form below.

GENERAL LEDGER

Accounts Payable

| July 5 | 16.50 | July 1 Bal. 1,614.20 |

Purchases Returns and
Allowances

| | July 5 | 16.50 |

ACCOUNTS PAYABLE LEDGER

Johnson Manufacturing Co.

| July 5 | 16.50 | July 1 Bal. 136.50 |

The accounts payable account has been debited for the amount of the credit received, $16.50. At the same time, the individual account in the accounts payable ledger has been debited for $16.50. The purchases returns and allowances account, a minus purchases account, has been credited for the amount of the purchases return.

Trade discount

In many lines of business, manufacturers and wholesalers print price lists and catalogs showing prices greater than those that the retailer will actually pay. These prices are known as *list prices*. The deduction from the list price allowed to retailers is called a *trade discount*.

When a trade discount is granted, the invoice shows the actual amount charged after the trade discount has been deducted. The invoice is recorded by both the seller and the buyer at this amount. For this reason, the fact that a trade discount has been granted has no effect on the bookkeeping records.

Why are cash discounts granted?

When merchandise is bought on credit, the buyer is expected to pay the seller within the time agreed upon. To encourage the buyer to make payment before the end of the credit period, the seller may allow a deduction from the amount owed. A deduction that the seller allows on the amount of an invoice to encourage the purchaser to make prompt payment is known as a *cash discount*.

The cash discount on purchases taken by the buyer is called a *discount on purchases*. When the buyer takes advantage of this cash discount, he pays less than the purchase price recorded on his books. This cash discount is a deduction from purchases and is credited on the books of the buyer to an account with the title *Discount on Purchases*.

The cash discount on sales granted a customer is known as a *discount on sales*. When the customer takes advantage of a cash discount, the seller receives a sum less than the sales price recorded on his books. This cash discount is a deduction from sales and is debited on the books of the seller to an account with the title *Discount on Sales*.

Terms of sale

The understanding arrived at between the buyer and the seller as to payment for merchandise is called the *terms of sale*. If payment is to be made immediately, the terms are said to be "cash" or "net cash." When the buyer is allowed a period of time before payment, the sale is called a credit sale.

The period for a credit sale usually begins with the date of the invoice. It may extend to the end of the month in which the sale was made. It may extend for 30 or 60 days, or for any stipulated time agreed upon.

Invoices usually contain the terms of a credit sale. When a cash discount is included in the terms of a credit sale, it is usually expressed as a percentage of the amount of the invoice. The terms of a sale showing the rate of discount, the period in which the discount may be taken, and the time when full payment is due are shown on the invoice below.

ATLAS MANUFACTURING COMPANY

Wholesale Papers and Twines

917 Front Street

Sold to	R. J. Wallace 506 Fourth Street Hamilton	Date	July 2, 1962
		Our No.	**956**
Terms	2/10, n/60	Shipped Via	Arrow Express Co.

40 M sheets 36 x 48--120/M
Atlas Publishers Text E.F.   4800#   9.70cwt   465.60

Invoice showing terms of payment

The terms of the invoice are written 2/10, n/60. These cash discount terms, which are commonly read "two ten, net sixty," mean that the buyer may deduct 2% of the amount of the invoice if payment is made within 10 days from the date of the invoice. If he does not pay the invoice within 10 days, he is expected to pay the total amount of the invoice in 60 days.

Other businesses may offer different terms. For example, the terms of one business may be 1/10, n/30 EOM. "EOM" means "end of month." If the terms are 1/10, n/30 EOM, a 1% discount may be taken if the invoice is paid within 10 days after the end of the month in which the invoice was dated. The full amount of the invoice must be paid on or before 30 days after the end of the month.

Discount on purchases

On July 2, Mr. Wallace purchased merchandise amounting to $465.60 from the Atlas Manufacturing Company, terms 2/10, n/60. This invoice was paid on July 12. As payment was made within the discount period indicated in the terms, Mr. Wallace was entitled to take a discount of 2%. The calculations for the payment were: $465.60, total of invoice — $9.31, discount (2% of $465.60 = $9.31) = $456.29, the amount to be paid in cash.

The one debit and the two credits that result from this transaction are as follows:

	DR.	CR.
Accounts Payable — Atlas Mfg. Co....	465.60	
Cash............................		456.29
Discount on Purchases.............		9.31

Recording discount on purchases

The entry on Line 3 in the combination journal illustrated on pages 304 and 305 shows the July 2 purchase transaction with the Atlas Manufacturing Company. The entry on Line 15 records the payment on July 12 for this purchase, with purchases discount taken. Observe in this payment transaction that the total of the invoice, $465.60, is recorded in the Accounts Payable Debit column; the amount of the cash paid, $456.29, is recorded in the Cash Credit column; and the amount of the discount on purchases, $9.31, is recorded in a special Discount on Purchases Credit column.

The debit and the two credits are all entered in special columns, but the debit to Accounts Payable must also be posted as a debit to the creditor's account in the accounts payable ledger. The title of the creditor's account, Atlas Manufacturing Co., is therefore entered in the Name of Account column.

When discounts on purchases or sales are recorded frequently, special columns in the combination journal are usually provided for them.

The effect of this discount-taking transaction on accounts in the general and subsidiary ledgers is shown in T account form below.

GENERAL LEDGER			ACCOUNTS PAYABLE LEDGER

Accounts Payable

| July 5 | 16.50 | July 1 | 1,614.20 |
| 12 | 465.60 | | |

Cash

| July 1 | 3,161.40 | July 12 | 456.29 |

Atlas Manufacturing Co.

| July 12 | 465.60 | July 2 | 465.60 |

Discount on Purchases

| | | July 12 | 9.31 |

The accounts payable account in the general ledger has been debited for $465.60, the total amount of the July 2 invoice. Also, the individual account in the accounts payable ledger has been debited to show this account paid in full. Cash was credited for $456.29, the amount of cash actually paid. Discount on Purchases, a minus purchases account, was credited for $9.31, the amount of discount because of early payment within the discount period. The two credits in the general ledger, therefore, equal the one debit.

Discount on sales

On July 2, Mr. Wallace sold merchandise for $300 to Joseph Reed, a charge customer. The terms of the invoice were 2/10, n/30. On July 12, Mr. Wallace received cash, $294, from Joseph Reed in full payment of this invoice of July 2. The invoice was paid within the discount period; Mr. Reed was therefore entitled to a discount of 2% on the amount that he owed. The check that Mr. Wallace received was for $294 (the face of the invoice, $300, less the cash discount, $6.) The two debits and the one credit that result from this transaction are as follows:

	Dr.	Cr.
Cash...............................	$294.00	
Discount on Sales....................	6.00	
Accounts Receivable — Joseph Reed.		$300.00

Recording discount on sales

The entry on Line 4 in the combination journal shows the July 2 sale of $300 to Joseph Reed. The entry on Line 16 records the receipt of $294 in payment of the invoice of $300 less a cash discount of $6.

Cash was debited in the Cash Debit column for the amount actually received, $294. Discount on Sales was debited in the Discount on Sales Debit column for $6. Accounts Receivable was credited in the Accounts Receivable Credit column for the full amount of the invoice, $300. The name of the customer was written in the Name of Account column so that the amount could be posted to the proper account in the accounts receivable ledger.

The effect of this discount-granting transaction on accounts in the general and subsidiary ledgers is shown in T account form below.

GENERAL LEDGER		ACCOUNTS RECEIVABLE LEDGER

Cash		Accounts Receivable		Joseph Reed	
July 1 3,161.40		July 1 4,310.14	July 1 10.50	July 2 300.00	July 12 300.00
12 294.00			12 300.00		

Discount on Sales	
July 12 6.00	

R. J. Wallace
Work Sheet
For Month Ended July 31, 1962

ACCOUNT TITLES	ACCT. NO.	TRIAL BALANCE DEBIT	TRIAL BALANCE CREDIT	ADJUSTMENTS DEBIT	ADJUSTMENTS CREDIT	INCOME STATEMENT DEBIT	INCOME STATEMENT CREDIT	BALANCE SHEET DEBIT	BALANCE SHEET CREDIT
Cash	11	215690						215690	
Petty Cash	12	5000						5000	
Accounts Receivable	13	250333						250333	
Merchandise Inventory	14	634695		(a) 767132	(a) 634695			767132	
Supplies	15	48731			(c) 12297			36434	
Prepaid Insurance	16	100800			(b) 4200			96600	
Accounts Payable	21		528606						528606
R. J. Wallace, Capital	31		746040						746040
R. J. Wallace, Drawing	32	50000						50000	
Income and Expense Summary	33			(a) 634695	(a) 767132	634695	767132		
Sales	41		1541926				1541926		
Sales Returns and Allowances	41.1	232775				232775			
Discount on Sales	41.2	7852				7852			
Purchases	51	1343224				1343224			
Purchases Returns and Allowances	51.1		23541				23541		
Discount on Purchases	51.2		27300				27300		
Delivery Expense	61	64230				64230			
Insurance Expense	62			(b) 4200		4200			
Miscellaneous Expense	63	7858				7858			
Rent Expense	64	32000				32000			
Salary Expense	65	837225				837225			
Supplies Expense	66			(c) 12297		12297			
		2867413	2867413	1418324	1418324	2213356	2359899	1421189	1274646
Net Income						1465343			1465343
						2359899	2359899	1421189	1421189

Work sheet of R. J. Wallace

310

The cash account was debited for $294, the total amount of cash received. Discount on Sales, a minus sales account, was debited for $6, the amount of sales discount granted for early payment. The accounts receivable account was credited for $300, the total amount of the July 2 invoice. Also, Mr. Reed's individual account in the accounts receivable ledger was credited for $300 to show that his July 2 purchase was paid in full.

The work sheet

The work sheet of R. J. Wallace for the month ended July 31 is shown on page 310. This work sheet includes the four new accounts discussed in this chapter: Sales Returns and Allowances, Purchases Returns and Allowances, Discount on Purchases, and Discount on Sales. Of these new accounts, those having debit balances in the trial balance are extended into the Income Statement Debit column. Those having credit balances in the trial balance are extended into the Income Statement Credit column.

Accounts numbered with decimals

The account numbers 41.1 and 41.2 on Lines 11 and 12 of the work sheet indicate that these accounts are reported as deductions from the account numbered 41. Similarly, in this book any account that has a decimal in its number is a deduction from the account having the same number without the decimal. Many variations in the system of numbering accounts are used in business.

The income statement

The income statement prepared from the work sheet on page 310 is shown at the top of the following page.

This income statement includes the two new accounts related to sales: Sales Returns and Allowances and Discount on Sales. Since both of these accounts are minus sales accounts, their amounts were totaled and then deducted from the total sales. The total sales less Sales Returns and Allowances and Discount on Sales is known as *Net Sales.*

This income statement also includes the two new accounts related to purchases: Purchases Returns and Allowances and Discount on Purchases. Purchases Returns and Allowances and Discount on Purchases are both minus purchases accounts. The amounts in these two accounts were totaled and then deducted from the total purchases. The total purchases less Purchases Returns and Allowances and Discount on Purchases is known as *Net Purchases.*

Some businesses treat Discount on Sales as an expense account instead of a minus sales account and Discount on Purchases as an income account instead

R. J. Wallace
Income Statement
For Month Ended July 31, 1962

Income:				
Sales				1541926
Less: Sales Returns and Allowances			23275	
Discount on Sales			7852	31127
Net Sales				1510799
Cost of Merchandise Sold:				
Merchandise Inventory, July 1, 1962			634695	
Purchases		1343224		
Less: Purchases Returns and Allow. 235.41				
Discount on Purchases 273.00		50841		
Net Purchases			1292383	
Total Cost of Mdse. Available for Sale			1927078	
Less Merchandise Inventory, July 31, 1962			767132	
Cost of Merchandise Sold				1159946
Gross Profit on Sales				350853
Operating Expenses:				
Delivery Expense			64230	
Insurance Expense			4200	
Miscellaneous Expense			7858	
Rent Expense			32000	
Salary Expense			83725	
Supplies Expense			12297	
Total Operating Expenses				204310
Net Income				146543

Income statement

of a minus purchases account. When this is done, Discount on Sales is not considered to be a regular operating expense of the business. Neither is Discount on Purchases considered to be a part of the regular operating income of the business. These items are reported at the bottom of their income statements under the separate headings "Other Income" and "Other Expense." This procedure is becoming less common.

Closing entries

The closing entries made from the work sheet illustrated on page 310 are similar to those presented in earlier chapters. The four new accounts introduced in this chapter must, however, also be closed. The closing entries shown on the opposite page include these new accounts.

		CHK.			POST.	GENERAL		
DEBIT	CREDIT	NO.	DATE	NAME OF ACOUNT	REF.	DEBIT	CREDIT	

PAGE 18

COMBINATION JOURNAL

10					*Closing Entries*				10
11				31	*Sales*		15419 26		11
12					*Pur. Returns and Allow.*		235 41		12
13					*Discount on Purchases*		273 00		13
14					*Income and Expense Summary*			15927 67	14
15				31	*Income and Expense Summary*		15786 61		15
16					*Sales Returns and Allow.*			232 75	16
17					*Discount on Sales*			78 52	17
18					*Purchases*			13432 24	18
19					*Delivery Expense*			642 30	19
20					*Insurance Expense*			42 00	20
21					*Miscellaneous Expense*			78 58	21
22					*Rent Expense*			320 00	22
23					*Salary Expense*			837 25	23
24					*Supplies Expense*			122 97	24
25				31	*Income and Expense Summary*		1465 43		25
26					*R. J. Wallace, Capital*			1465 43	26
27				31	*R. J. Wallace, Capital*		500 00		27
28					*R. J. Wallace, Drawing*			500 00	28

Closing entries in the combination journal

Increasing your business vocabulary

What is the meaning of each of the following:

(a) sales return
(b) sales allowance
(c) credit memorandum
(d) purchases return
(e) purchases allowance
(f) trade discount
(g) cash discount
(h) discount on purchases
(i) discount on sales
(j) terms of sale
(k) net sales
(l) net purchases

Chapter questions

1. What is the difference between a sales return and a sales allowance?
2. What common business form supplies the information for recording a transaction granting credit for allowances and returns?

3. In the combination journal on pages 304 and 305, what entry is required to record a transaction in which:

(a) Merchandise is returned by a charge customer?

(b) An allowance for returned merchandise is received from a creditor?

4. Why does a trade discount have no effect on the bookkeeping records?

5. Why does the seller of merchandise often allow a cash discount if payment is made within a short time after the sale is made?

6. In the combination journal on pages 304 and 305, what four accounts are affected when a purchase on account is paid with a cash discount being taken? Which of these are general ledger accounts?

7. In this book, what does a decimal in an account number indicate?

8. How does a business that has granted credit for sales returns and allowances and discount on sales determine its net sales for a fiscal period?

9. Under what divisional heading or section in the income statement is each of the following accounts reported:

(a) Sales Returns and Allowances   (c) Discount on Sales

(b) Purchases Returns and Allowances   (d) Discount on Purchases

Cases for discussion

1. Company X never recorded a purchases return transaction until it received a credit memorandum. Company Y recorded such a transaction on the same day that the merchandise was shipped back. Which company followed the better plan?

2. On December 13 the bookkeeper for Charles Madison received a check for $196 dated December 11. This was in payment of a $200 invoice dated December 1 with the terms 2/10, n/60. Thus the payment was received two days after the discount-taking period. The envelope in which the check was mailed showed a December 11 postmark. If you were the bookkeeper for Mr. Madison, how would you handle this situation?

Drill for understanding

Drill 21-A. Calculating the terms of sale

Instructions: 1. Find the selling price for each of the following sales on account:

INVOICE DATE	LIST PRICE	TRADE DISCOUNT	CREDIT TERMS	DATE PAID
(1) January 10	$100	20%	n/30	February 8
(2) January 10	250	none	2/10, n/30	February 9
(3) January 21	300	40%	2/10, n/30	January 31
(4) January 21	200	25%	1/10, n/30EOM	February 10
(5) January 31	600	33⅓%	2/10, n/60	April 1

Instructions: 2. Find the amount to be paid by the purchaser in each case.

314

Application problems

Problem 21-1. Recording transactions in a combination journal

Instructions: 1. Record the following selected transactions, which were completed by Richard Smart during the month of December of the current year, in a combination journal like the one on pages 304 and 305. All sales are made on account.

Dec. 1. Issued Check No. 315 for $60.00 for cash purchase of merchandise.

1. Purchased merchandise amounting to $440.90 from Norton and Co.

1. Received a check for $617.10 from D. T. Hamilton for our invoice of November 22 for $623.33 less a 1% discount of $6.23.

4. Issued Check No. 316 for $123.16 to Brandon and Company in payment of their invoice of November 26 for $125.67 less a 2% discount of $2.51.

5. Norton and Co. allowed us credit for $20.00 for defective merchandise.

9. Sold merchandise amounting to $830.60 to B. F. Woolman.

9. Issued Check No. 320 for $412.48 to Norton and Co. in payment of the balance of $420.90 on their invoice of December 1 less a 2% discount of $8.42.

> The amount of the invoice of December 1 was $440.90, but a credit of $20.00 was received on December 5. The balance of the invoice to which the discount applied was therefore $420.90, and the discount was 2% of this amount.

13. Purchased merchandise amounting to $1,122.80 from Varden Bros.

15. Issued a credit memorandum for $30.00 to B. F. Woolman for merchandise returned.

19. Received a check for $792.59 from B. F. Woolman and gave him credit for that amount plus $8.01, a 1% discount.

> The amount of the invoice of December 9 was $830.60. A credit of $30.00 was given on December 15. The balance of the invoice to which the discount applied was therefore $800.60.

20. Sold merchandise amounting to $527.70 to A. O. Prince.

23. Issued Check No. 324 for $1,100.34 to Varden Bros. in payment of their invoice of December 13 for $1,122.80 less a 2% discount of $22.46.

25. Received a credit memorandum for $13.00 from Mason Bros. for merchandise returned by us.

26. Sold merchandise amounting to $450.00 to D. T. Hamilton.

29. Received a check for $522.42 from A. O. Prince for our invoice of December 20 for $527.70 less a 1% discount of $5.28.

30. Issued Check No. 326 for $37.60 to replenish the petty cash fund. The expenses were: Supplies, $6.10; Miscellaneous Expense, $25.00; and Delivery Expense, $6.50.

Instructions: 2. Total the amounts in each column, prove the equality of debits and credits, and rule the journal.

Problem 21-2. Work at the end of a fiscal period

The accounts and the account balances in the general ledger of Ben Adamson, a retail merchant, on June 30 of the current year, the end of a quarterly fiscal period, were as follows:

ACCOUNT TITLE	ACCT. No.	DEBIT BALANCE	CREDIT BALANCE
Cash..	11	2,917.23	
Petty Cash..	12	45.00	
Accounts Receivable..............................	13	1,963.75	
Merchandise Inventory...........................	14	6,385.50	
Supplies..	15	478.63	
Prepaid Insurance................................	16	250.00	
Accounts Payable.................................	21		2,036.45
Ben Adamson, Capital............................	31		7,100.00
Ben Adamson, Drawing...........................	32	900.00	
Income and Expense Summary.....................	33	——	——
Sales...	41		16,340.40
Sales Returns and Allowances.....................	41.1	244.40	
Discount on Sales.................................	41.2	163.89	
Purchases..	51	10,680.30	
Purchases Returns and Allowances.................	51.1		167.50
Discount on Purchases............................	51.2		138.10
Insurance Expense................................	61	——	
Miscellaneous Expense............................	62	303.75	
Rent Expense.....................................	63	400.00	
Salary Expense...................................	64	1,050.00	
Supplies Expense.................................	65	——	

Instructions: 1. Prepare an eight-column work sheet for the quarterly fiscal period ended June 30 of the current year. The additional data needed at the end of the period are:

> Merchandise inventory, June 30, $5,160.80
> Supplies inventory, June 30, $208.03
> Prepaid insurance, June 30, $165.00

2. Prepare an income statement and a balance sheet.

3. Record the adjusting entries and the closing entries.

Project 3

Bookkeeping cycle using the combination journal

Turner Wholesale Toys

Turner Wholesale Toys, of which R. S. Turner is proprietor, uses as its book of original entry a combination journal with the same column headings as the one illustrated on pages 304 and 305. A general ledger, an accounts receivable ledger, and an accounts payable ledger are maintained.

Opening accounts in the ledgers

Instructions: 1. Open the following accounts in the general ledger, using the account numbers given. If a workbook is not used, allow five lines in each account in the general ledger. Number the accounts with the account numbers given in the chart of accounts.

<table>
<tr><td colspan="4" align="center">Turner Wholesale Toys
Chart of Accounts</td></tr>
<tr><td></td><td align="center">ACCT.
NO.</td><td></td><td align="center">ACCT.
NO.</td></tr>
<tr><td align="center">(1) ASSETS</td><td></td><td align="center">(4) INCOME</td><td></td></tr>
<tr><td>Cash.....................</td><td>11</td><td>Sales.....................</td><td>41</td></tr>
<tr><td>Petty Cash...............</td><td>12</td><td>Sales Returns and Allowances</td><td>41.1</td></tr>
<tr><td>Accounts Receivable........</td><td>13</td><td>Discount on Sales..........</td><td>41.2</td></tr>
<tr><td>Merchandise Inventory......</td><td>14</td><td colspan="2" align="center">(5) COST OF MERCHANDISE</td></tr>
<tr><td>Supplies..................</td><td>15</td><td>Purchases..................</td><td>51</td></tr>
<tr><td>Prepaid Insurance..........</td><td>16</td><td>Purchases Returns and</td><td></td></tr>
<tr><td align="center">(2) LIABILITIES</td><td></td><td> Allowances..............</td><td>51.1</td></tr>
<tr><td>Accounts Payable..........</td><td>21</td><td>Discount on Purchases......</td><td>51.2</td></tr>
<tr><td align="center">(3) PROPRIETORSHIP</td><td></td><td align="center">(6) EXPENSES</td><td></td></tr>
<tr><td>R. S. Turner, Capital.......</td><td>31</td><td>Insurance Expense..........</td><td>61</td></tr>
<tr><td>R. S. Turner, Drawing......</td><td>32</td><td>Miscellaneous Expense......</td><td>62</td></tr>
<tr><td>Income and Expense Summary</td><td>33</td><td>Rent Expense..............</td><td>63</td></tr>
<tr><td></td><td></td><td>Salary Expense.............</td><td>64</td></tr>
<tr><td></td><td></td><td>Supplies Expense...........</td><td>65</td></tr>
</table>

Instructions: 2. Copy the following balances in your general ledger, using as the date December 1 of the current year. As you copy these balances, write the word "Balance" in the Items column of each account.

	DEBIT BALANCE	CREDIT BALANCE
Cash...................................	3,170.00	
Petty Cash..............................	50.00	
Accounts Receivable......................	1,872.40	
Merchandise Inventory....................	18,282.85	
Supplies.................................	1,725.60	
Prepaid Insurance........................	342.00	
Accounts Payable........................		1,527.90
R. S. Turner, Capital.....................		20,500.00
R. S. Turner, Drawing....................	6,000.00	
Sales....................................		59,149.30
Sales Returns and Allowances..............	741.95	
Discount on Sales........................	145.60	
Purchases...............................	39,564.20	
Purchases Returns and Allowances..........		690.20
Discount on Purchases....................		740.45
Miscellaneous Expense....................	2,752.25	
Rent Expense............................	1,938.00	
Salary Expense..........................	6,023.00	

Instructions: 3. Open the following accounts in the accounts receivable ledger and record the balance to be collected from each customer. As you copy these balances in your accounts receivable ledger, write the word "Balance" in the Items column of each account, using as the date December 1 of the current year. If the workbook is not used, allow three lines for each customer's account.

	DEBIT BALANCE
Paul Baker, 950 W. Charles Street, City............	$575.15
J. F. Dunn, 301 Main Street, City.................	402.60
N. L. Gage, 633 Starin Road, City.................	———
Edward A. Ritter, 426 North Street, City...........	389.25
J. R. Thayer, 180 Esterly Avenue, City.............	505.40

Instructions: 4. Open the following accounts in the accounts payable ledger and record the balance owed to each creditor. As you copy these balances in your accounts payable ledger, write the word "Balance" in the Items column of each account, using as the date December 1 of the current year. If the workbook is not used, allow four lines for each creditor's account.

	CREDIT BALANCE
Clark Brothers, 434 Fremont Street, Toledo...............	$321.00
Harris Toy Company, 2611 Vine Street, Cincinnati	344.40
Larkin Plastic Toy Company, 839 Walworth Ave., St. Paul...	———
Service Toy Company, 106 High Street, Lima..............	862.50

Recording transactions for December

Instructions: 5. Record in the combination journal the following transactions completed by Turner Wholesale Toys during the month of December of the current year:

Dec. 1. Issued Check No. 301 for $190.00 for the December rent.

3. Issued a credit memorandum for $12.00 to Edward A. Ritter for merchandise returned by him.

4. Received a check for $394.55 from J. F. Dunn in payment of our invoice of November 26 for $402.60 less a 2% discount of $8.05.

4. Issued Check No. 302 for $853.87 to Service Toy Company in payment of their invoice of November 25 for $862.50 less a 1% discount of $8.63.

7. Received a check for $369.70 from Edward A. Ritter and gave him credit for that amount plus a 2% discount of $7.55.

8. Harris Toy Co. allowed us credit for $18.00 for defective merchandise.

9. Purchased merchandise on account from Larkin Plastic Toy Co., $891.25.

11. Sold merchandise on account to J. R. Thayer, $181.35.

12. Purchased merchandise on account from Clark Brothers, $1,283.00.

14. Issued Check No. 303 for $23.65 for the telephone bill.

14. Sold merchandise on account to N. L. Gage, $388.75.

15. The cash sales for December 1 to 15 were $2,029.00.

   Post from the combination journal to the accounts receivable ledger and the accounts payable ledger.

17. Issued Check No. 304 for $27.00 for the electricity bill.

17. Received a check for $505.40 from J. R. Thayer in payment of our invoice of November 18 for that amount.

19. Issued Check No. 305 for $873.42 to Larkin Plastic Toy Co. in payment of their invoice of December 9 for $891.25 less a 2% discount of $17.83.

21. Received a check for $177.72 from J. R. Thayer in payment of our invoice of December 11 for $181.35 less a 2% discount of $3.63.

21. Issued Check No. 306 for $1,257.34 to Clark Brothers in payment of their invoice of December 12 for $1,283.00 less a 2% discount of $25.66.

22. Sold merchandise on account to N. L. Gage, $464.15.

22. Issued Check No. 307 for $326.40 to Harris Toy Company on account.

22. Sold merchandise on account to J. F. Dunn, $290.35.

24. Received a check for $380.97 from N. L. Gage in payment of our invoice of December 14 for $388.75 less a 2% discount of $7.78.

26. Purchased merchandise on account from Larkin Plastic Toy Co., $535.75.

Dec. 28. Purchased merchandise on account from Clark Brothers, $718.00.

    30. Larkin Plastic Toy Co. allowed us credit for $33.00 for shipment of wrong merchandise to us.

    31. Issued Check No. 308 for $850.00 for the monthly payroll.

    31. Issued Check No. 309 for $475.00 to the proprietor, R. S. Turner, for a personal withdrawal.

    31. The petty cash vouchers were sorted and the petty cash payments for the month were found to be as follows: supplies, $18.55; miscellaneous expense, $22.35. Issued Check No. 310 for $40.90 to replenish the petty cash fund.

    31. The cash sales for December 16 to 31 were $1,265.00.

Post from the combination journal to the accounts receivable ledger and the accounts payable ledger.

Work at end of the fiscal year

Instructions: 6. Foot all columns of the combination journal and prove the equality of the debits and the credits. Prove cash; the cash on hand and in the bank is $3,374.76. Total and rule the journal.

7. Post each amount in the two General columns. Post the totals of the special columns.

8. Prepare a schedule of accounts receivable and a schedule of accounts payable.

9. Prepare an eight-column work sheet. Additional data for the adjustments are:

        Merchandise inventory, December 31, $22,731.00
        Supplies inventory, December 31, $175.00
        Prepaid insurance, December 31, $110.00

10. Prepare an income statement and a balance sheet for the year.

11. Record the adjusting entries and the closing entries in the combination journal. Post these entries to the general ledger and rule the accounts that balance. Balance each remaining account that has both debits and credits.

12. Prepare a post-closing trial balance.

Chapter 22

Payroll records

The payroll

Employees are often paid once a week. In some businesses, however, they are paid biweekly (once every two weeks), or semimonthly (twice a month), or monthly. Before these payments are made, a list of all employees entitled to pay, with the amounts due each, is prepared. A special business form showing the wage or salary payable to each employee for a certain period is called a *payroll*. In large businesses, one or more payroll clerks may spend all or most of their time keeping payroll records. In smaller businesses the bookkeeper usually keeps the payroll records.

Payroll taxes

The trend of legislation, both federal and state, has been to place several kinds of taxes on a pay-as-you-go basis and to require employers to withhold these taxes from the wages of their employees. Not only must an employer withhold the amount of the taxes from the pay of each employee, but also he must keep a detailed record of the amounts, give reports to each employee, and send reports and payments to the government. For these taxes the employer serves as the government's collection agent and bookkeeper.

Income taxes withheld from employees by employer

A business is required to help the government in collecting the federal income taxes levied upon the employees of that business. The employer does this by withholding for income tax purposes a part of his employees' wages. The amounts withheld by the employer represent a liability for him until he makes payment to a district director of internal revenue or to a bank that is authorized to receive such funds.

Social security taxes

The social security laws of our federal government provide:

(a) Old-age, survivors, and disability insurance benefits for covered employees and their wives or husbands, widows or widowers, dependent children, and parents.

(b) Grants to states that provide pay for persons temporarily unemployed and for certain relief and welfare purposes, such as aid to the blind.

A general term that is used to refer to taxes imposed under the terms of the social security laws is *social security taxes.*

A social security tax paid to the federal government by both employees and employers for use in paying old-age, survivors, and disability insurance benefits is called *FICA tax.* FICA tax is the abbreviated name for Federal Insurance Contributions Act tax. This tax is also known as OAB or old-age benefits tax. It is based on the wages paid to employees. The employee's tax is withheld from his wages by the employer. The amount deducted from the employee's wages, together with a similar amount that must be contributed by the employer, is paid to the government by the employer.

A social security tax paid only by the employer and used by the federal government to assist the states in paying persons who are temporarily unemployed is called *federal unemployment tax.*

A tax paid to the state, usually by employers only, for use in paying persons temporarily unemployed is called *state unemployment tax.*

FICA taxes at the time this book was published were based on the first $4,800 paid to an employee during a calendar year. Federal and state unemployment taxes were based on the first $3,000 paid to an employee during a calendar year. These amounts may be changed by Congress, but the same principles of bookkeeping will apply regardless of changes in amounts.

Obtaining a social security card

Every employee in an occupation covered by the social security laws is required to have a social security card. This card is issued to anyone upon request without charge by the Social Security Administration. The application form may be obtained from any local post office. The appli-

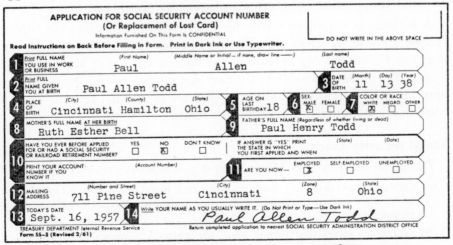

Application for social security account number

SOCIAL SECURITY
ACCOUNT NUMBER

194-08-0862

HAS BEEN ESTABLISHED FOR

Paul Allen Todd

SIGNATURE *Paul A. Todd*

FOR SOCIAL SECURITY PURPOSES • NOT FOR IDENTIFICATION

Social security card

cation should be sent to the nearest field office of the Social Security Administration.

Any person may make application for a social security card even though he is not employed at the time. In fact, every person seeking a job should obtain a social security card in advance of employment because having a card simplifies making application for employment. If a person is not employed at the time of making application for a social security card, he places an "x" under the word "Unemployed" in Item 11 on the application.

After filing an application, the employee will receive from the Social Security Administration a card showing the social security account number that has been assigned to him. If a person loses his social security card, he may apply for a new card. In this case he should write at the top of the application "Request for duplicate."

If an employee changes her name by marriage, she should notify the Social Security Administration of the change. A form for reporting the change may be obtained from the Social Security field office.

Payroll time cards

The first requirement of an adequate payroll record system is an accurate record of the time each employee has worked. Time cards and a time clock are often used to obtain this information.

The Barry Machine Shop uses a time clock to record the time of arrival and departure of each employee each day. Each employee has a card with his name on it in a rack beside the time clock. He "rings in" each morning and after lunch, and he "rings out"

PAYROLL NO.	37						
NAME	Paul A. Todd						
WEEK ENDING	September 22, 1962						

MORNING		AFTERNOON		OVERTIME		HOURS
IN	OUT	IN	OUT	IN	OUT	
Σ 7:56	Σ 12:00	Σ 12:55	Σ 5:02			8
⊐ 7:58	⊐ 12:01	⊐ 12:57	⊐ 5:01			8
≥ 8:00	≥ 12:03	≥ 1:00	≥ 5:03			8
⊤ 7:57	⊤ 12:02	⊤ 1:01	⊤ 5:00	⊤ 6:00	⊤ 9:00	8⅜
⌐ 7:59	⌐ 12:02	⌐ 12:59	⌐ 5:08			8

	HOURS	RATE	EARNINGS	
REGULAR	40	2.42	96	00
OVERTIME	3	3.60	10	80
TOTAL	43		106	80

Payroll time card

at noon and when he leaves at night. Each time an employee "rings in" or "rings out," the clock records the time on the card. The payroll clerk uses the time cards in making the weekly payroll record for each employee.

Mr. Paul A. Todd, a grinder in the finishing department, began work for the Barry Machine Shop on September 17, 1962. His payroll time card for the week ended September 22, 1962, is shown on page 323.

Analyzing the time card

At the top of the card is a number, which is Mr. Todd's payroll number. The use of the number makes it easier to place each time card in the rack in its proper place than it would be if the cards were filed alphabetically. On the next lines are Mr. Todd's name and the payroll period.

For recording the time there are three sections — Morning, Afternoon, and Overtime — with an "In" and an "Out" under each section. When Mr. Todd reported for work on Monday, he inserted the card in the slot in the time clock and recorded his time of arrival as M7:56. The other entries on this line indicate that he checked out at lunch time at 12:00 and in at 12:55 and that he left for the day at 5:02. The entries following are for the remaining days of the week. On Thursday he worked three hours overtime. This is recorded as shown on the line for Thursday.

At the end of the week the payroll clerk entered the number of hours for each day in the right-hand column. Each firm has its own rules regarding deductions for tardiness. The payroll clerk must know these rules in order to make the proper deductions if employees are late.

Determining the employee's earnings

Each employee's hours of work and earnings are found as follows:

Step 1. The time card is examined for records of tardiness and early leaving, and notations are made.

Mr. Todd reported to work one minute late on Thursday afternoon. Deductions are not made by the Barry Machine Shop for such short periods of time.

Step 2. The regular hours are extended into the Hours column.

The regular hours for Mr. Todd are 8 for Monday through Friday.

Step 3. The amount of overtime for each day is calculated and is entered above the regular hours for the day.

Mr. Todd worked from 6:00 p.m. to 9:00 p.m. on Thursday; hence the figure 3 is written above the figure 8 for that day.

Step 4. The regular hours and the overtime hours are added separately and are entered in the spaces provided at the bottom of the card.

Step 5. The rates for regular time and overtime are entered, and the earnings are computed.

324

Step 6.   The Hours and the Earnings columns are then added to show the total hours and the total earnings.

After the payroll for the week is completed, the time cards are filed.

Payroll register

Each week information about the entire payroll is entered in the pay-roll register. A part of the payroll register prepared for the week ended September 22 is shown below.

PAYROLL REGISTER

WEEK ENDED   September 22, 1962   DATE OF PAYMENT   September 24, 1962

No.	EMPLOYEE'S NAME	No. OF EXEMP-TIONS	TOTAL EARNINGS	FICA TAX	INCOME TAX	OTHER		TOTAL	NET PAY AMOUNT	CHK. No.
11	Thomas Aylward	1	84 00	2 63	13 00	CC	1 00	16 63	67 37	691
3	Richard Bradley	4	108 50	3 39	10 10			13 49	95 01	692
12	Alex M. Caldwell	2	99 70	3 12	13 20	CC	1 00	17 32	82 38	693
6	Philip Dalton	1	75 00	2 34	11 20	B	2 00	15 54	59 46	694
9	William Parker	2	92 80	2 90	12 10	B	1 50	16 50	76 30	725
18	Howard Price	3	89 00	2 78	9 10			11 88	77 12	726
20	James Randolph	4	108 50	3 39	10 10			13 49	95 01	727
31	Allen J. Ross	2	92 50	2 89	12 10	CC	1 50	16 49	76 01	728
16	Henry Stahl	4	75 00	2 34	4 30			6 64	68 36	729
37	Paul A. Todd	3	106 80	3 34	12 40	B	2 00	17 74	89 06	730
42	Walter Williams	2	106 50	3 33	14 70			18 03	88 47	731
	Totals		4000 00	125 00	382 50	CC B	36 00 54 50	598 00	3402 00	

OTHER DEDUCTIONS: CC—COMMUNITY CHEST;   GI—GROUP INSURANCE;   HC—HOSPITAL CARE;   B—U.S. SAVINGS BONDS;   UD—UNION DUES

Payroll register

Analyzing the payroll register

At the top of the payroll register the last day of the payroll week, September 22, and the date of payment, September 24, are entered.

A few days before the end of the payroll period, the time card numbers, the names of the employees, and the number of their exemptions for income tax purposes are listed in the register.

> An *exemption* is an amount of money on which a person does not have to pay income tax. Each person is allowed one exemption for himself, one exemption for his wife (or husband), and one exemption for each additional person who is dependent on him. The number of exemptions a worker declares affects the amount that is deducted each period for his income tax.

When the time cards for the week are computed, the total earnings figure from each card is written in the Total Earnings column of the payroll register opposite the employee's name.

The section headed "Deductions" is used to record the various amounts that are deducted from the employees' earnings. The column headed "FICA Tax" is used to record the amount that is deducted for old-age, survivors, and disability benefit taxes. The FICA tax on the earnings of Paul A. Todd is $3.34. The amount of the FICA tax may be found by multiplying the total earnings by the tax rate. It may also be found from a social security wage tax table. A section of such a table is illustrated below.

The tax rates used in this chapter were taken from the laws in effect at the time this book was published. At that time, the FICA tax rate for each calendar year was as follows: 1962, 3⅛%; 1963 through 1965, 3⅝%; 1966 through 1967, 4⅛%; 1968 and after, 4⅝%. These rates may be changed by Congress, but the same principles will apply regardless of any changes in rates.

SOCIAL SECURITY WAGE TAX TABLE FOR 1962

This table applies to all payroll periods. The rate is 3⅛% for employers and 3⅛% for employees, so that the amounts shown below are the taxes for which each is liable. (Example: Tax on wages of $55.20 to and including $55.51 is $1.73.)

Wages including	Tax	Wages including	Tax	Wages including	Tax	Wages including	Tax	Wages including	Tax	Wages including	Tax
$55.19	$1.72	$64.79	$2.02	$75.03	$2.34	$85.59	$2.67	$94.87	$2.96	$106.71	$3.33
55.51	1.73	65.11	2.03	75.35	2.35	85.91	2.68	95.19	2.97	107.03	3.34
55.83	1.74	65.43	2.04	75.67	2.36	86.23	2.69	95.51	2.98	107.35	3.35
56.15	1.75	65.75	2.05	75.99	2.37	86.55	2.70	95.83	2.99	107.67	3.36
56.47	1.76	66.07	2.06	76.31	2.38	86.87	2.71	96.15	3.00	107.99	3.37
56.79	1.77	66.39	2.07	76.63	2.39	87.19	2.72	96.47	3.01	108.31	3.38
57.11	1.78	66.71	2.08	76.95	2.40	87.51	2.73	96.79	3.02	108.63	3.39
57.43	1.79	67.03	2.09	77.27	2.41	87.83	2.74	97.11	3.03	108.95	3.40
57.75	1.80	67.35	2.10	77.59	2.42	88.15	2.75	97.43	3.04	109.27	3.41
58.07	1.81	67.67	2.11	77.91	2.43	88.47	2.76	97.75	3.05	109.59	3.42

Section of Social Security Wage Tax Table

The column headed "Income Tax" is used to record the amount of income tax withheld from each employee's earnings. This amount is determined from a table furnished by the government that takes into account the amount of wages earned and the number of income tax exemptions claimed. Part of such a table showing the withholdings based on weekly wages is illustrated on page 327. To determine Paul A. Todd's tax on the $106.80 he earned during the week ended September 22, the proper wage bracket in the first two columns was found. This was the $105–$110 bracket. The income tax to be withheld was the amount shown on this line under the column for 3 withholding exemptions — $12.40.

In addition to withholding tax tables for weekly payroll periods, the government provides separate tables for daily, biweekly, semimonthly, and monthly payroll periods.

If the payroll period with respect to an employee is WEEKLY—Concluded

And the wages are—		And the number of withholding exemptions claimed is—										
At least	But less than	0	1	2	3	4	5	6	7	8	9	10 or more
		The amount of tax to be withheld shall be—										
$55	$56	$10.00	$7.70	$5.40	$3.10	$ .80	$0	$0	$0	$0	$0	$0
56	57	10.20	7.90	5.60	3.20	.90	0	0	0	0	0	0
57	58	10.40	8.00	5.70	3.40	1.10	0	0	0	0	0	0
58	59	10.50	8.20	5.90	3.60	1.30	0	0	0	0	0	0
59	60	10.70	8.40	6.10	3.80	1.50	0	0	0	0	0	0
60	62	11.00	8.70	6.40	4.10	1.70	0	0	0	0	0	0
62	64	11.30	9.00	6.70	4.40	2.10	0	0	0	0	0	0
64	66	11.70	9.40	7.10	4.80	2.50	.20	0	0	0	0	0
66	68	12.10	9.80	7.40	5.10	2.80	.50	0	0	0	0	0
68	70	12.40	10.10	7.80	5.50	3.20	.90	0	0	0	0	0
70	72	12.80	10.50	8.20	5.90	3.50	1.20	0	0	0	0	0
72	74	13.10	10.80	8.50	6.20	3.90	1.60	0	0	0	0	0
74	76	13.50	11.20	8.90	6.60	4.30	2.00	0	0	0	0	0
76	78	13.90	11.60	9.20	6.90	4.60	2.30	0	0	0	0	0
78	80	14.20	11.90	9.60	7.30	5.00	2.70	.40	0	0	0	0
80	82	14.60	12.30	10.00	7.70	5.30	3.00	.70	0	0	0	0
82	84	14.90	12.60	10.30	8.00	5.70	3.40	1.10	0	0	0	0
84	86	15.30	13.00	10.70	8.40	6.10	3.80	1.50	0	0	0	0
86	88	15.70	13.40	11.00	8.70	6.40	4.10	1.80	0	0	0	0
88	90	16.00	13.70	11.40	9.10	6.80	4.50	2.20	0	0	0	0
90	92	16.40	14.10	11.80	9.50	7.10	4.80	2.50	.20	0	0	0
92	94	16.70	14.40	12.10	9.80	7.50	5.20	2.90	.60	0	0	0
94	96	17.10	14.80	12.50	10.20	7.90	5.60	3.30	.90	0	0	0
96	98	17.50	15.20	12.80	10.50	8.20	5.90	3.60	1.30	0	0	0
98	100	17.80	15.50	13.20	10.90	8.60	6.30	4.00	1.70	0	0	0
100	105	18.50	16.10	13.80	11.50	9.20	6.90	4.60	2.30	0	0	0
105	110	19.40	17.00	14.70	12.40	10.10	7.80	5.50	3.20	.90	0	0

Section of Weekly Wage Bracket Withholding Table

The column headed "Other" is used to list withholdings for which no special column is provided. The various deductions that are entered in this column are identified by initials, which are keyed at the bottom of the payroll register. For example, withholdings for Community Chest are marked "CC." The different items in this column are sorted and classified and a separate total is shown for each class. Paul A. Todd had $2.00 withheld to be applied toward the purchase of United States Savings Bonds.

The section headed "Net Pay" is used to record the amount due each employee and the number of the payroll check issued to him. The net pay is secured by subtracting each employee's total deductions from his total earnings.

After all the deductions have been computed and the net pay has been recorded for each employee, each of the amount columns is totaled. The accuracy of these additions is verified by comparing the total of the Total Earnings column with the sum of the totals of the Net Pay column and the Total Deductions columns.

Before checks are written for the net pay amounts, the manager or some person designated by him examines the payroll computations and approves the payroll.

Record of employee's earnings

A detailed account is kept of all items affecting the payments made to each employee. This record, known as the employee's earnings record, is kept on cards or sheets. A separate card or sheet is kept for each employee. The employee's earnings record for Mr. Todd is shown below.

EARNINGS RECORD FOR QUARTER ENDING					Sept. 29, 1962				
Todd	Paul	A.	37	194--08--0862			Sal. Exp.		
LAST NAME	FIRST	MIDDLE	TIME CLOCK NO.	SOC. SEC. NO.			ACCOUNT CHARGED		

PAY PERIOD		TOTAL EARNINGS	DEDUCTIONS				NET PAY	
WEEK NO.	WEEK ENDED		FICA TAX	INCOME TAX	OTHER	TOTAL	AMOUNT	CHECK NO.
1								
2								
11								
12	9/22	106 80	3 34	12 40	B 2 00	17 74	89 06	730
13	9/29	103 20	3 23	11 50	B 2 00	16 73	86 47	793
QUARTERLY TOTALS		210 00	6 57	23 90	B 4 00	34 47	175 53	

Employee's earnings record

Analyzing the employee's earnings record

The illustration of the employee's earnings record provides information for thirteen weeks, a quarter of a year. The record is made with quarterly divisions because the government requires the employer to make reports on special forms for each quarter.

Mr. Todd's name is entered at the top of the card, together with his payroll number and his social security number.

Mr. Todd began work for the Barry Machine Shop on Monday, September 17. The first entry in his earnings record is therefore made at the end of that week, September 22; hence there is no record before this date. The week ended September 22 is the twelfth week in the quarter; therefore the payroll clerk enters the information on the twelfth line. The date September 22 is entered on the twelfth line as 9/22.

The amount columns of the employee's earnings record are the same as the amount columns of the payroll register. The amounts opposite each employee's name in the payroll register are transferred to the corre-

328

sponding columns of the employee's earnings record. The Barry Machine Shop also records the number of the payroll check in the employee's earnings record.

The Quarterly Totals line provides space for the totals for the quarter. The form for the final quarter in the year also provides space for entering the totals for the year. These totals are needed in making reports to the government on both a quarterly and an annual basis.

The law requires that the employee's earnings record shall be kept on file for a period of at least four years. This requirement is made in order to give the government time to check back on records of payments to employees and to audit the reports of employers.

Paying the payroll by check

The Barry Machine Shop pays its employees weekly by check. It uses a special payroll check form that has a space in the upper left-hand corner to record amounts deducted from weekly earnings.

The payroll checks are drawn against a special payroll bank account. Each pay period a check for the total amount of the net pay is drawn on the regular checking account in favor of the payroll account and is deposited in the separate account against which the payroll checks are drawn. On September 24, the Barry Machine Shop drew a check for $3,402.00 and deposited it in its payroll account, and then it drew payroll checks for each employee.

The check for Mr. Todd for the week ended September 22 appears below. The information for the check is taken directly from the payroll register.

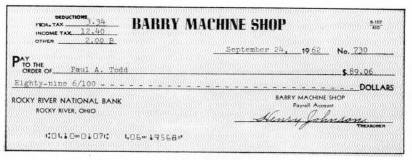

Payroll check

Some firms make a carbon copy of the check containing all the information that is on the check with the exception of the signature of the employer and the name of the bank. The employee detaches the carbon copy and keeps it as his record of deductions and cash received.

Paying the payroll in cash

Some firms prefer to pay their employees in cash. This practice is usually followed when the employees find it difficult to get to a bank to have their checks cashed or when the employer is required by law to allow time off from work for the employees to deposit or cash their checks.

When the payroll is to be paid in cash, the payroll clerk must obtain the cash from the bank in the proper denominations so that he will have the necessary change when he distributes the money into the individual envelopes. In order to have the necessary change, he prepares a payroll change form similar to the one at the right.

From the employee's earnings record, each employee's number and the amount due him are entered in the first two columns of the payroll

PAYROLL CHANGE SHEET										
DATE Oct 22, 1962										
EMPLOYEE NO.	AMOUNT DUE	$20	$10	$5	$1	50¢	25¢	10¢	5¢	1¢
1	77 50	3	1	1	2	1				
2	84 26	4			4		1			1
3	84 88	4			4	1	1	1		3
4	61 21	3			1			2		1
75	67 06	3			1	2			1	1
76	78 61	3	1		1	3	1		1	1
77	57 33	2	1		1	2		1		3
78	84 12	4			4			1		2
TOTAL	4696 12	2/2	2/2	1/88	72	32	47	65	117	

Payroll change sheet

change sheet. Then the bills and the coins required for the employee's pay envelope are listed in the columns at the right. For example, Employee No. 1 has $77.50 due him. To pay this amount, the payroll clerk needs three $20 bills, one $10 bill, one $5 bill, two $1 bills, and one 50-cent piece.

After the payroll change sheet is completed, all the columns are totaled and a payroll requisition form is prepared. This form shows the number of each denomination desired and the amount of each denomination. The total of the amounts must equal the total of the payroll shown on the payroll change sheet. A typical payroll requisition form is shown in the illustration at the left.

A check for the total amount of the payroll is then drawn. This check and the payroll requisition form are given to the bank clerk, who gives the payroll clerk the

PAYROLL REQUISITION		
DENOMINATION	NUMBER OF EACH DENOMINATION	AMOUNT
$20.00	2/2	4240 00
10.00	2/	210 00
5.00	2/	105 00
1.00	88	88 00
.50	72	36 00
.25	32	8 00
.10	47	4 70
.05	65	3 25
.01	117	1 17
TOTAL PAYROLL		4696 12

Payroll requisition form

number of each denomination needed. The payroll clerk places the money in the envelopes for the employees.

Payroll receipt

A payroll receipt is prepared in duplicate for each employee. The receipt contains a summary of the earnings record showing the employee's name, his gross earnings, an itemized list of the deductions, and the net amount he receives. When the employee receives his pay envelope, he signs one copy of the payroll receipt, which the business keeps, and he retains the other copy as his record of earnings and deductions. An illustration of a payroll receipt is shown below.

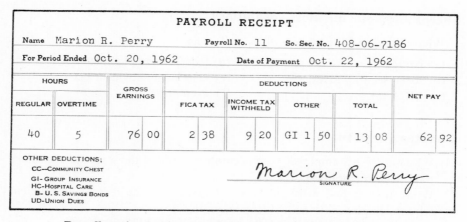

Payroll receipt showing the earnings, deductions, and net pay of an employee who is paid in cash

This payroll receipt shows that, for the week ended October 20, Marion R. Perry had gross earnings of $76. The total deductions of $13.08 were: $2.38 for FICA taxes, $9.20 for income taxes withheld, and $1.50 for group insurance.

Where a time clock is not used

Firms employing a small number of persons usually do not find it economical to use a time clock. Employees are assumed to be present unless the payroll clerk is notified of absence. Also, many executives and junior executives do not use a time clock because they are paid at a certain rate a month and their pay is not affected by brief absences.

Even though a time clock is not used, an employee's earnings record must be kept for each employee. The method of paying the employee by check or by cash is similar to one of the methods discussed in this chapter.

Automation for payroll work

Organizations with many employees often use automated equipment for payroll work. They have found that the use of automated equipment makes it possible to prepare all payroll records, including the preparation and the signing of payroll checks, in a small fraction of the time formerly required.

A clerk records all of the information shown on the time cards on punched cards or tapes. These cards or tapes are then fed into machines, which make the calculations and prepare the payroll register, the individual payroll record, and the individual payroll checks. Payroll work that formerly required days to do by hand can now be done in a few hours by machine.

Increasing your business vocabulary

What is the meaning of each of the following:

(a) payroll

(b) social security taxes

(c) FICA tax

(d) federal unemployment tax

(e) state unemployment tax

(f) exemption

Chapter questions

1. Why must every employer keep accurate records of the wages or the salary paid to each employee?
2. What are the two principal types of taxes that the federal government requires employers to deduct from payrolls?
3. How is a social security card obtained?
4. What are the principal types of information recorded on the time card illustrated on page 323?
5. On what day did Paul A. Todd work overtime according to his time card on page 323?
6. What are the six steps commonly followed in determining each individual employee's earnings and the amount to be paid to each employee?
7. What are the principal types of information recorded in the payroll register illustrated on page 325?
8. What are the chief differences between the payroll register on page 325 and the employee's earnings record on page 328?
9. (a) What were Paul A. Todd's earnings for the week ended September 22?
   (b) How much did he actually receive?
10. How is the amount of income tax withheld from employees' wages determined?
11. On the employee's earnings record illustrated on page 328, what is the column headed "Other" used to record?
12. How is the payroll change sheet illustrated on page 330 prepared and used?

Cases for discussion

1. Lang's Music Shop pays its employees by check. Elmer Bantry pays his employees in cash. What are the advantages and the disadvantages of each method?

2. The Oakdale Manufacturing Company uses a time clock and time cards in recording employees' working time. Swain & Storey do not use a time clock, but the payroll clerk assumes that employees are present unless he is notified otherwise. What are the advantages and the disadvantages of each system?

3. The Meade Company requires each employee to sign a payroll receipt, similar to the one illustrated on page 331, each time wages are paid. The Standish Company, on the other hand, does not require employees to sign payroll receipts. What difference in payroll procedures might make payroll receipts desirable for one company but not for the other?

Application problems

Problem 22-1. *Applying for a social security account number*
If the workbook correlating with this textbook is not available, this problem may be omitted.

Instructions: Fill in the application for a social security account number given in the workbook. Use your own personal data. Compare your application with the illustration on page 322.

Problem 22-2. *Using payroll time cards*
If the workbook correlating with this textbook is not available, complete Exercise 22-A in the Appendix instead of this problem.

Instructions: 1. Complete the time cards given in the workbook.

2. Record the time cards in a payroll register similar to the one on page 325 of the textbook. The date of payment is May 18.

3. Prepare a payroll change sheet similar to the one on page 330.

4. Prepare a payroll requisition form similar to the one on page 330.

Problem 22-3. *Preparing an employee's earnings record*
The total earnings of Janet Carter for the thirteen weeks in the quarterly period April through June of the current year are given below, together with the deductions for hospital care.

Week Ended	Total Earnings	Deductions	Week Ended	Total Earnings	Deductions
4/5	$65.00		5/24	65.00	
4/12	66.00		5/31	67.00	
4/19	67.00		6/7	66.00	
4/26	65.00		6/14	65.00	6.00
5/3	67.00	$4.50	6/21	66.00	
5/10	66.00		6/28	67.00	
5/17	67.00				

Instructions: Prepare an employee's earnings record, similar to the one on page 328, for Janet Carter for the second quarter of the current year. Additional data needed to complete the record are as follows:

(a) Miss Carter's time card number is 57.

(b) Miss Carter's social security number is 268–05–9847.

(c) Miss Carter's earnings should be charged to Salary Expense.

(d) In addition to her deductions for hospital care, the following deductions for taxes should be made:

(1) A deduction of $3\frac{1}{8}\%$ of her total earnings for each week is to be made for FICA taxes. Use the social security wage tax table on page 326 for calculating the FICA tax on each week's total earnings.

(2) A deduction is to be made from her total earnings for each week for her income tax withheld. Miss Carter claims only one withholding exemption for herself. Use the weekly wage bracket withholding table on page 327 for figuring each of her weekly income tax deductions.

Problem 22-4. *Preparing a payroll*

The Hoffman Company pays its employees in cash. For each pay period the payroll clerk prepares a payroll register showing the earnings, the deductions, and the net pay of each employee.

A part of the payroll register for the week ended June 23 of the current year, showing the number, the name, the number of exemptions, the total earnings, and other deductions of each employee, is given below.

PAYROLL REGISTER

WEEK ENDED   June 23, 19––   DATE

No.	Employee's Name	No. of Exemptions	Total Earnings	FICA Tax	Income Tax	Other	
1	Wm. S. Baxter........	5	$107 00			B	2 00
2	John Bennett.........	1	96 00				
3	Steven Cary..........	1	88 00				
4	Ida M. Cook.........	2	76 00			CC	50
5	Jean Denham.........	1	56 00			B	1 00
6	R. S. Foster..........	2	95 00			CC	1 50
7	Ruth Horn...........	1	65 00				
8	Sandra Klein.........	1	56 00				
9	Mary Mitchell........	1	88 00				
10	C. F. Parks..........	4	108 00			B	2 00

Other Deductions: CC—Community Chest, B—Bonds

An additional deduction of 3⅛% of each employee's total earnings is to be made for FICA taxes. (Use the wage tax table on page 326.) An income tax deduction, based on the wage bracket withholding table on page 327, is also to be made for each employee.

Instructions: 1. Prepare a payroll register similar to the one illustrated on page 325. The date of payment is June 25.

2. Prepare a payroll change sheet similar to the one illustrated on page 330.

3. Prepare a payroll requisition form similar to the one illustrated on page 330.

Optional problems

★ *Supplementary Problem 22-S. Preparing a payroll*

A part of a payroll register for the week ended April 7 of the current year, showing the number, the name, the number of exemptions, the total earnings, and other deductions of each employee, is given below.

An additional deduction of 3⅛% of each employee's total earnings is to be made for FICA taxes. (Use the wage tax table on page 326.) An income tax deduction, based on the withholding tax table on page 327, is also to be made for each employee.

PAYROLL REGISTER
WEEK ENDED APRIL 7, 19--

No.	Employee's Name	No. of Exemptions	Total Earnings	Deductions		
				FICA Tax	Income Tax	Other
1	Laura Cox.............	1	55 50			B 1 00
2	Jean Dabney...........	1	65 00			
3	Clement Earle.........	4	107 00			HC 1 90
4	J. G. Fisher............	3	95 00			
5	Esther Harris..........	2	57 50			
6	Walter Kern...........	3	109 50			HC 1 60
7	Mary Z. Long.........	2	86 25			
8	Harriet Nyer...........	1	58 00			B 1 00
9	Betty Pringle...........	1	57 00			
10	Ethel L. Stone.........	2	86 50			B 2 50
11	George Swift..........	3	95 60			HC 1 90
12	Paul Thorne	4	106 /5			HC 1 90
13	Ruth Vetter...........	1	75 50			
14	Betty Lee Wagner.....	1	67 25			B 1 00
15	C. L. Young..........	2	88 33			

Other Deductions: HC—Hospital Care, B—Bonds

Instructions: 1. Prepare a payroll register similar to the one illustrated on page 325. The date of payment is April 10.

2. Prepare a payroll change sheet similar to the one illustrated on page 330.

3. Prepare a payroll requisition form similar to the one illustrated on page 330.

Introductory remarks. Production workers in factories are frequently paid on the basis of the number of units they produce. This is called the piecework incentive wage plan. Most piecework wage plans include a guaranteed hourly rate to employees regardless of the number of units they produce. This guaranteed hourly rate is called the base rate.

Time and motion study engineers usually determine the standard time required for producing a single unit. For example, if the time studies determined that 6 minutes is the standard time required to produce a unit, then the standard rate for one hour would be 10 units (60 minutes ÷ 6 minutes = 10 units per hour). If the worker's base pay is $1.80 per hour, the piece rate is 18¢ ($1.80 ÷ 10 units = 18¢ per unit). Therefore, if the worker produces 10 or less units per hour, he is paid only $1.80 per hour, his base pay. But for every unit in excess of 10 that he produces each hour, he is paid 18¢ in addition to his base pay.

The Billings Manufacturing Company has a crew of three men working in the welding department and a crew of three men working in the assembly department. Standard production for the welding department is 12 units per hour per man. Standard production for the assembly department is 8 units per hour per man. Each of the men in both departments worked 8 hours a day during the first week in July. Payroll records for the week ended July 6 show:

No.	Worker	No. of Exemptions	Guaranteed Hourly Rate	Units Produced					Weekly Total
				M	Tu	W	Th	F	
	Welding Dept.:								
W6	Charles Archer..	1	$2.40	96	98	96	100	96	486
W14	James Cobb	2	2.40	90	93	95	96	90	464
W12	William West...	4	2.40	106	105	115	106	103	535
	Assembly Dept.:								
A3	John Bently.....	3	1.80	68	66	66	71	73	344
A12	Lewis Dalton...	1	1.80	70	70	68	68	70	346
A16	Edward Price...	2	1.80	65	67	65	68	70	335

A piecework incentive of 20¢ per unit is in operation for the welding department and 22.5¢ per unit is in operation for the assembly department.

Instructions: 1. Prepare a payroll register similar to the one illustrated on page 325. The date of payment is July 8. None of the employees had "Other" deductions. Use the wage tax table on page 326 to find the deduction of 3⅛% of each employee's total earnings for FICA tax. Use the wage bracket withholding table on page 327 to find the income tax deduction for each employee.

2. Prepare a payroll change sheet similar to the one illustrated on page 330.

3. Prepare a payroll requisition form similar to the one illustrated on page 330.

Chapter 23

Payroll taxes and reports

Debits and credits required in recording the payroll

The payroll register illustrated in the previous chapter summarizes the payroll information for each pay period. This information must also be recorded in a journal and posted to the accounts.

A part of the payroll register of the Barry Machine Shop for the week ended September 22 is illustrated below.

PAYROLL REGISTER

WEEK ENDED   September 22, 1962   DATE OF PAYMENT   September 24, 1962

No.	EMPLOYEE'S NAME	No. OF EXEMP- TIONS	TOTAL EARNINGS	DEDUCTIONS				NET PAY	
				FICA TAX	INCOME TAX	OTHER	TOTAL	AMOUNT	CHK. No.
11	Thomas Aylward	1	84 00	2 63	13 00	CC 1 00	16 63	67 37	691
3	Richard Bradley	4	108 50	3 39	10 10		13 49	95 01	692
12	Alex M. Caldwell	2	99 70	3 12	13 20	CC 1 00	17 32	82 38	693
6	Philip Dalton	1	75 00	2 34	11 20	B 2 00	15 54	59 46	694
9	William Parker	2	92 80	2 90	12 10	B 1 50	16 50	76 30	725
18	Howard Price	3	89 00	2 78	9 10		11 88	77 12	726
20	James Randolph	4	108 50	3 39	10 10		13 49	95 01	727
31	Allen J. Ross	2	92 50	2 89	12 10	CC 1 50	16 49	76 01	728
16	Henry Stahl	4	75 00	2 34	4 30		6 64	68 36	729
37	Paul A. Todd	3	106 80	3 34	12 40	B 2 00	17 74	89 06	730
42	Walter Williams	2	106 50	3 33	14 70		18 03	88 47	731
	Totals		4000 00	125 00	382 50	CC 36 00 B 54 50	598 00	3402 00	

OTHER DEDUCTIONS: CC—COMMUNITY CHEST;   GI—GROUP INSURANCE;   HC—HOSPITAL CARE;   B—U.S. SAVINGS BONDS;   UD—UNION DUES

Payroll register

The total of the Total Earnings column, $4,000, is the salary expense for the period. Salary Expense must therefore be debited for this amount.

The total of the FICA Tax column, $125, is the amount withheld from the salaries of employees for FICA taxes. Until this amount is paid to the government, it is a liability of the business. In order to record this liability, FICA Taxes Payable must be credited for $125.

The total of the Income Tax column, $382.50, is the amount withheld from salaries of employees for income taxes. Until this amount is paid to

337

the government, it is a liability of the business. To record this liability, Employees Income Taxes Payable must be credited for $382.50.

The $36 total in the "Other" column is the amount withheld from salaries to apply on the pledges that employees have made to the annual Community Chest drive. The other total of $54.50 in this column is the amount withheld from the salaries of employees who wish to have U. S. Savings Bonds purchased for them. Until these respective amounts have been paid by the employer, they are liabilities of the business. To record these liabilities, Community Chest Donations Payable is credited for $36 and U. S. Savings Bonds Payable is credited for $54.50.

The total of the Net Pay Amount column, $3,402, is the amount of cash actually paid to employees. To record the decrease in the asset Cash, the cash account is credited for this amount.

The debits and the credits based on the column totals of the payroll register are equal, as shown below:

Salary Expense Debit		FICA Taxes Payable Credit		Employees' Income Taxes Payable Credit		Community Chest Donations Pay. Credit		U. S. Savings Bonds Pay. Credit		Cash Credit
$4,000.00	=	$125.00	+	$382.50	+	$36.00	+	$54.50	+	$3,402.00

Recording the payroll in the journal

When the payroll check was drawn on September 24, the following entry was made in the combination journal to record the totals of the September 22 payroll register of the Barry Machine Shop:

PAGE 19

COMBINATION JOURNAL

	CASH DEBIT	CASH CREDIT	CHK. NO.	DATE	NAME OF ACOUNT	POST REF.	GENERAL DEBIT	GENERAL CREDIT	
11		3402 00	451	24	Salary Expense		4000 00		11
12					FICA Taxes Payable			125 00	12
13					Employees Income Taxes Pay.			382 50	13
14					Community Chest Donations Pay.			36 00	14
15					U S Savings Bonds Pay.			54 50	15
16									16

The amount of the Salary Expense, $4,000, is entered in the General Debit column. The credit to Cash, $3,402, is entered in the Cash Credit column. The amounts of the two tax liabilities and the two "Other" liabilities are entered in the General Credit column.

Tax liability accounts

After this payroll entry was posted, the two tax liability accounts, Employees Income Taxes Payable and FICA Taxes Payable, appeared as follows:

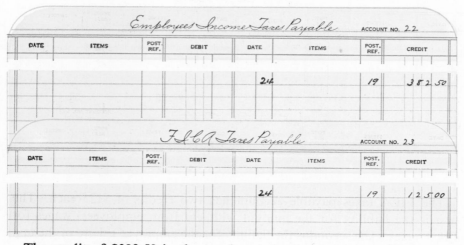

The credit of $382.50 in the employees income taxes payable account represents a liability of the business to pay the amount of income taxes withheld from the employees' salaries. The credit of $125 in the FICA taxes payable account represents a liability of the business to pay the amount of the FICA taxes withheld from the employees' salaries.

Recording the employer's share of FICA taxes

The FICA taxes of the employer are the same as those of the employees. For the pay period ended September 22, 1962, the FICA taxes of the Barry Machine Shop were therefore $125. To record this liability, the following entry was made in the combination journal of the Barry Machine Shop:

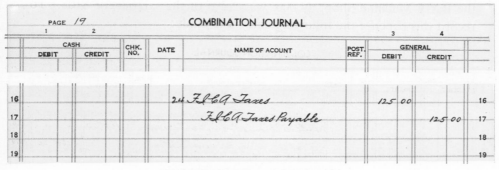

Entry for employer's FICA taxes

FICA Taxes is debited to record the expense for the taxes. FICA Taxes Payable is credited to record the liability. After the entry was posted, these two accounts appeared as follows:

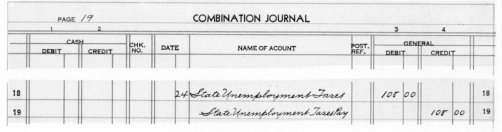

DATE	ITEMS	POST. REF.	DEBIT	DATE	ITEMS	POST. REF.	CREDIT
				24		19	125 00
				24		19	125 00

FICA Taxes Payable   ACCOUNT NO. 23

FICA Taxes   ACCOUNT NO. 63

DATE	ITEMS	POST. REF.	DEBIT	DATE	ITEMS	POST. REF.	CREDIT
24		19	125 00				

The FICA taxes payable account has two credits of $125 each. The first is the liability for the amount withheld from employees' wages for FICA taxes. The second is the liability for the employer's share of the tax.

The expense account FICA Taxes has a debit of $125, which is the employer's tax expense.

Recording the employer's state unemployment taxes

Under the provisions of the federal and the state unemployment insurance laws, employers are required to pay taxes that are used for the payment of unemployment compensation. Compensation is available under certain circumstances for those who are unemployed and who are unable to obtain employment. The taxes for unemployment purposes are based on the amount of the salaries and are, in most states, levied on the employers only.

The state unemployment tax on the salaries paid on September 24 by the Barry Machine Shop, $4,000, was 2.7% of the salaries, or $108. To record this expense the following entry was made:

	CASH		CHK. NO.	DATE	NAME OF ACOUNT	POST. REF.	GENERAL		
	DEBIT	CREDIT					DEBIT	CREDIT	
18				24	State Unemployment Taxes		108 00		18
19					State Unemployment Taxes Pay			108 00	19

PAGE 19   COMBINATION JOURNAL

Entry for state unemployment taxes

In a few states an unemployment tax is levied against the employee as well as against the employer. In these states the amount of the unemployment taxes withheld from employees is credited to the liability account State Unemployment Taxes Payable.

The expense account State Unemployment Taxes is debited for the amount of the tax expense, which is 2.7% of the total earnings, or $108. The amount of this tax is a liability until it is paid; therefore State Unemployment Taxes Payable is credited for $108.

After this entry was posted, the two accounts appeared as follows:

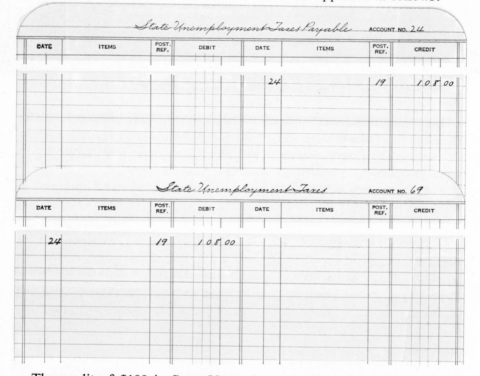

The credit of $108 in State Unemployment Taxes Payable is the employer's liability for the state unemployment tax for the week ended September 22. The debit of $108 in State Unemployment Taxes is the employer's expense for the state unemployment tax for the week ended September 22.

Recording the employer's federal unemployment taxes

The federal unemployment tax on the salaries paid on September 24 by the Barry Machine Shop, $4,000, was .8% of the wages, or $32. The entry to record this expense is shown at the top of the next page.

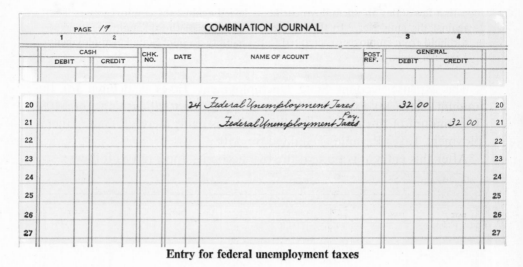

Entry for federal unemployment taxes

The expense account Federal Unemployment Taxes was debited for the amount of taxes owed, .8% of the total earnings, or $32. The amount of this tax was a liability until it was paid; therefore, Federal Unemployment Taxes Payable was credited for $32.

After this entry was posted, the two accounts involved appeared as follows:

The credit of $32 in the account Federal Unemployment Taxes Payable is the employer's liability for the federal unemployment tax for the week ended September 22. The debit of $32 in the account Federal Unemployment Taxes is the employer's expense for the federal unemployment tax for the week ended September 22.

Paying the liability for employees income taxes and for FICA taxes

At the end of September the liability account Employees Income Taxes Payable had a credit balance of $1,530.50 and the liability account FICA Taxes Payable had a credit balance of $960. On October 15 the Barry Machine Shop drew Check No. 489 for $2,490.50 in payment of these two liabilities. The entry to record this payment was as follows:

| | CASH | | CHK. | DATE | NAME OF ACOUNT | POST. | GENERAL | | |
	DEBIT	CREDIT	NO.			REF.	DEBIT	CREDIT	
10		2490 50	489	15 Employees Income Taxes Payable			1530 50		10
11				F.I.C.A Taxes Payable			960 00		11
12									12
13									13
14									14
15									15
16									16
17									17
18									18

PAGE 21   COMBINATION JOURNAL

Entry for payment of liability for employees income taxes and for FICA taxes

The liability accounts Employees Income Taxes Payable and FICA Taxes Payable were debited to record the decreases in these liabilities, and Cash was credited to record the decrease in the asset Cash.

After each quarter of the year, every employer must pay to the government the amount of the income tax withheld and the FICA taxes for which he is liable. If the total of these taxes for any month (except the third month of the quarter) exceeds $100, the employer is required to deposit these amounts in the Federal Reserve Bank that serves his district. Special rules apply for handling such taxes if the employees are household or agricultural workers.

Since the taxes for the Barry Machine Shop exceeded $100 for both July and August, these taxes were deposited within 15 days after the close of each month. Then when the September payment was made, receipts for the deposits of the July and August taxes were attached to the quarterly report that accompanied the payment for September. The bookkeeping entries at the time the July and August taxes were deposited were similar to the one shown for the payment of the September taxes.

Paying the liability for state unemployment taxes

On October 29, the Barry Machine Shop paid its liability for the state unemployment taxes for the three-month period ended September 30. The amount of this liability, $1,404, was obtained by adding the weekly credits in the account State Unemployment Taxes Payable. The entry to record this payment was as follows:

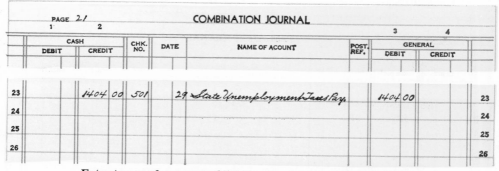

Entry to record payment of liability for state unemployment taxes

This payment covered the state unemployment taxes based on the payrolls of July, August, and September.

Paying the liability for federal unemployment taxes

The federal unemployment taxes payable are paid by the Barry Machine Shop at the end of the year. On December 31 the balance of the account Federal Unemployment Taxes Payable in the ledger of the Barry Machine Shop was $1,624. On January 21 of the following year a check for this amount was sent to the District Director of Internal Revenue. To record the payment of the liability the following entry was made:

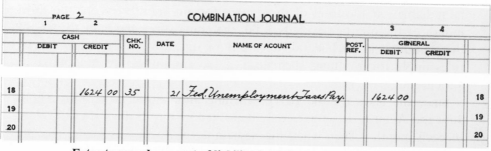

Entry to record payment of liability for federal unemployment taxes

This payment covered the federal unemployment taxes based on the payrolls for 1962.

Reports to employees of taxes withheld

Every employer who is required to withhold taxes from employees' wages must furnish each of his employees with a statement showing the total earnings of the employee and the amounts withheld for taxes. This statement is made on a Form W-2 that is furnished by the District Director of Internal Revenue.

The Form W-2 prepared for Paul A. Todd by the Barry Machine Shop for 1962 wages is illustrated below.

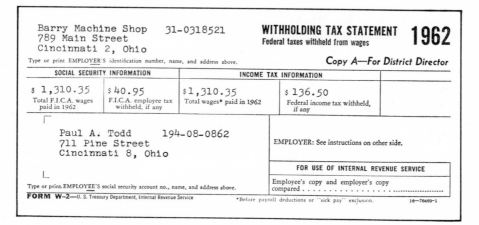

Statement given to the employee for taxes withheld

When the employee files his income tax return, he must attach the original of this form to his income tax return. An employee should have a withholding statement from each employer for whom he worked during the taxable year.

Chapter questions

1. The total earnings of the employees for the week ended September 22, 1962, as shown in the payroll register on page 337, amount to $4,000 and the total cash paid amounts to $3,402. What causes this difference?

2. What entry was made in the combination journal on page 338 to record the payment of the payroll and the amounts withheld from the employees' salaries?

3. What entry was made in the combination journal on page 339 to record the employer's share of the FICA taxes?

4. The FICA taxes payable account on page 340 has two credits. What do these amounts represent?

5. In most states who pays the unemployment tax?

6. What entry was made in the combination journal on page 340 to record the liability of the employer for state unemployment taxes?

7. What entry was made in the combination journal on page 342 to record the liability of the employer for federal unemployment taxes?

8. What entry was made in the combination journal on page 343 to record the payment of the liability for employees income taxes and for FICA taxes?

9. What entry was made in the combination journal on page 344 to record the payment of the liability for state unemployment taxes?

10. What entry was made in the combination journal on page 344 to record the payment of the liability for federal unemployment taxes?

11. What statement is the employer required to submit to each employee at the end of the year? What does it show?

Cases for discussion

1. R. L. King, the owner of a food-canning company, had a weekly payroll of $5,000, with the following deductions: employees income taxes, $400; FICA taxes, 3⅛%. Mr. King's liabilities for payroll taxes were as follows: FICA taxes, 3⅛%; state unemployment taxes, 2.7%; and federal unemployment taxes, .8%. What entry should Mr. King make in his combination journal each payday to record (a) the payment of wages and the amounts withheld and (b) the liability for his payroll taxes?

2. On January 8 of the current year, A. B. Kohn sent checks to the proper government authorities in payment of the following taxes previously recorded in his books: employees income taxes withheld, $264; FICA taxes, $156; federal unemployment taxes, $240; and state unemployment taxes, $202. What accounts should be debited and credited to record these payments?

Application problems

Problem 23-1. Recording payrolls and payroll taxes

The payroll register totals of Excel Television Service for the week ended May 24 are given below:

No.	EMPLOYEE'S NAME	No. OF EXEMP- TIONS	TOTAL EARNINGS	FICA TAX	INCOME TAX	OTHER	TOTAL	AMOUNT	CHECK No.
				DEDUCTIONS				NET PAY	
	Totals.........		840 00	26 25	78 00		104 25	735 75	

346

The employer's liabilities for payroll taxes included the following:

FICA taxes   3⅛%
State unemployment taxes   2.7%
Federal unemployment taxes   .8%

Instructions: 1. Make the entry in the combination journal to record the payroll and the withholdings.   The payroll was paid by Check No. 482 on May 27 of the current year.

2. Make the entries in the combination journal to record the employer's share of the payroll taxes.

Problem 23-2. *Recording payroll transactions*

F. O. Butler, owner of a stationery store, completed the payroll transactions given below.

Feb. 28. Issued Check No. 34 for $1,205.65 in payment of the monthly payroll of $1,400 less a deduction of $150.60 for income taxes and a deduction of $43.75 for FICA taxes.

      28. Recorded the employer's payroll taxes at the following rates: FICA taxes, 3⅛%; state unemployment taxes, 2.7%; federal unemployment taxes, .8%.

Mar. 10. Issued Check No. 43 for $238.10 in payment of the liabilities for payroll taxes and taxes withheld as follows: income taxes, $150.60; FICA taxes, $87.50.

      31. Issued Check No. 56 for $1,162.81 in payment of the monthly payroll of $1,350 less a deduction of $145 for income taxes and a deduction of $42.19 for FICA taxes.

      31. Recorded the employer's payroll taxes at the same rates as in February.

Apr. 10. Issued Check No. 69 for $229.38 in payment of the liabilities for payroll taxes and taxes withheld as follows: income taxes, $145; FICA taxes, $84.38.

      10. Issued Check No. 70 for $111.35 in payment of the liability for state unemployment taxes.

Instructions: Record the transactions in a combination journal. Use the current year in the date.

Problem 23-3. *Recording and posting payroll transactions*

The Arrow Electrical Shop completed the payroll transactions given below during the period January 1 to April 10. The Arrow Electrical Shop is liable for payroll taxes at the following rates: FICA taxes, 3⅛%; state unemployment taxes, 2.7%; and federal unemployment taxes, .8%. It is also liable for the purchase of U. S. Savings Bonds as the accumulated withholdings for each particular employee reaches the necessary amount.

Instructions: 1. Open the accounts that are given at the top of the next page and record the balances as of January 1 of the current year.

Acct No.	Account Title	Credit Balance
22	Employees Income Taxes Payable....................	$280.00
23	FICA Taxes Payable...............................	156.25
24	State Unemployment Taxes Payable..................	195.75
25	Federal Unemployment Taxes Payable...............	230.40
26	U. S. Savings Bonds Payable.......................	146.50
63	Federal Unemployment Taxes.......................	_____
66	FICA Taxes.......................................	_____
68	Salary Expense...................................	_____
69	State Unemployment Taxes.........................	_____

Instructions: 2. Record the following selected transactions in a combination journal.

3. After each entry is journalized, post the items recorded in the General Debit and General Credit columns.

Jan. 10. Issued Check No. 15 for $436.25 in payment of the liabilities for employees income taxes and FICA taxes.
   10. Issued Check No. 16 for $195.75 in payment of the liability for state unemployment taxes.
   10. Issued Check No. 17 for $230.40 in payment of the liability for federal unemployment taxes.
   31. Issued Check No. 29 for $2,027 in payment of the monthly payroll of $2,400 less deductions of $250 for income taxes, $75 for FICA taxes, and $48 for U. S. Savings Bonds deductions.
   31. Recorded the employer's payroll tax liabilities.
Feb. 2. Issued Check No. 31 for $75 to purchase U. S. Savings Bonds (4 at $18.75) for employees.
   10. Issued Check No. 38 for $400 in payment of the liabilities for employees income taxes and FICA taxes.
   28. Issued Check No. 61 for $1,940.12 in payment of the monthly payroll of $2,300 less deductions of $240 for income taxes, $71.88 for FICA taxes, and $48 for U. S. Savings Bonds deductions.
   28. Recorded the employer's payroll tax liabilities.
Mar. 1. Issued Check No. 66 for $37.50 to purchase U. S. Savings Bonds (2 at $18.75) for employees.
   10. Issued Check No. 74 for $383.76 in payment of the liabilities for employees income taxes and FICA taxes.
   31. Issued Check No. 88 for $2,200.75 in payment of the monthly payroll of $2,600 less deductions of $270 for income taxes, $81.25 for FICA taxes, and $48 for U. S. Savings Bonds deductions.
   31. Recorded the employer's payroll tax liabilities.
Apr. 2. Issued Check No. 92 for $56.25 to purchase U. S. Savings Bonds (3 at $18.75) for employees.
   10. Issued Check No. 97 for $432.50 in payment of the liabilities for employees income taxes and FICA taxes.
   10. Issued Check No. 98 for $197.10 in payment of the liability for state unemployment taxes.

Optional problems

★ *Supplementary Problem 23-S. Recording and posting payroll transactions*

The Congreve Company completed the payroll transactions given below during the period October 1 to January 10. The Congreve Company is liable for payroll taxes at the following rates: FICA taxes, $3\frac{1}{8}\%$; state unemployment taxes, 2.7%; and federal unemployment taxes, $.8\%$. It is also liable for Hospital Care premiums and Community Chest donations withheld from employees' wages.

Instructions: 1. Open the following accounts in the general ledger and record the balances as of October 1 of the current year:

Acct No.	Account Title	Credit Balance
22	Employees Income Taxes Payable..........................	$710.00
23	FICA Taxes Payable......................................	375.00
24	State Unemployment Taxes Payable.......................	405.00
25	Federal Unemployment Taxes Payable....................	360.00
26	Hospital Care Premiums Payable..........................	33.50
27	Community Chest Donations Payable.....................	108.00
63	Federal Unemployment Taxes.............................	———
66	FICA Taxes...	———
68	Salary Expense..	———
69	State Unemployment Taxes...............................	———

Instructions: 2. Record the following selected transactions in a combination journal. After each entry is journalized, post the items recorded in the General Debit and General Credit columns.

Oct. 10. Issued Check No. 862 for $1,085 in payment of the liabilities for employees income taxes and FICA taxes for September.

10. Issued Check No. 863 for $405 in payment of the liability for state unemployment taxes for the third quarter.

10. Issued Check No. 864 for $33.50 in payment of the liability for Hospital Care premiums for September.

10. Issued Check No. 865 for $108 in payment of the liability for Community Chest donations for the third quarter.

31. Issued Check No. 884 for $4,194.25 in payment of the monthly payroll of $5,000 less deductions of $580 for income taxes, $156.25 for FICA taxes, $33.50 for Hospital Care premiums, and $36 for Community Chest donations.

31. Recorded the employer's payroll tax liabilities.

Nov. 10. Issued Check No. 893 for $33.50 in payment of the liability for Hospital Care premiums for October.

10. Issued Check No. 894 for $892.50 in payment of the liabilities for employees income taxes and FICA taxes for October.

30. Issued Check No. 916 for $4,070.50 in payment of the monthly payroll of $4,800 less deductions of $510 for income taxes, $150 for FICA taxes, $33.50 for Hospital Care premiums, and $36 for Community Chest donations.

30. Recorded the employer's payroll tax liabilities.

Dec. 10. Issued Check No. 927 for $810 in payment of the liability for employees income taxes and FICA taxes for November.

10. Issued Check No. 928 for $33.50 in payment of the liability for Hospital Care premiums for November.

31. Issued Check No. 966 for $4,352.80 in payment of the monthly payroll of $5,200 less deductions of $615.20 for income taxes, $162.50 for FICA taxes, $33.50 for Hospital Care premiums, and $36 for Community Chest donations.

31. Recorded the employer's payroll tax liabilities.

Jan. 10. Issued Check No. 23 for $940.20 in payment of the liability for employees income taxes and FICA taxes for December.

10. Issued Check No. 24 for $405 in payment of the liability for state unemployment taxes for the fourth quarter.

10. Issued Check No. 25 for $480 in payment of the liability for federal unemployment taxes for the year.

10. Issued Check No. 26 for $33.50 in payment of the liability for Hospital Care premiums for December.

10. Issued Check No. 27 for $108 in payment of the liability for Community Chest donations for the fourth quarter.

*Bonus Problem 23-B. Computing and recording payroll taxes

Royal Plastics employs twenty factory workers. Ten are paid at the rate of $1.80 per hour and ten at the rate of $2.10 per hour. They work a total of 40 hours per week and are paid weekly. Royal Plastics also employs five salaried persons and pays them monthly as follows: 2 office clerks at $280 each; 2 factory foremen at $430 each; and 1 factory manager at $800. All employees worked the entire year.

The following social security tax rates apply:

(a) FICA, $3\frac{1}{8}\%$ on a maximum of $4,800.

(b) State unemployment, 1.6% on a maximum of $3,000. (Note: Because Royal Plastics had an excellent employment record, the state in which they conducted their business granted them the benefit of a tax rate lower than the basic rate.)

(c) Federal unemployment, .8% on a maximum of $3,000.

Royal Plastics uses only one tax expense account for recording all of its share of the payroll taxes. This account has the title *Payroll Tax Expense*. At the time that this single account is debited for the *total* of the employer's payroll taxes, the individual tax liability accounts — FICA Taxes Payable, State Unemployment Taxes Payable, and Federal Unemployment Taxes Payable — are credited for the specific amounts owed.

Instructions: Record in a combination journal the entries for the employer's payroll taxes for the current year for:

(1) The first weekly payroll of the year.

(2) The last (the 52nd) weekly payroll of the year.

(3) The first monthly payroll of the year.

(4) The last (the 12th) monthly payroll of the year.

Chapter 24

Depreciation of fixed assets

What is depreciation?

Everyone knows that a bicycle worth $50 one Christmas is not worth that much the following Christmas. Similarly, in a business a delivery truck bought in January for $3,000 may not be worth more than $2,100 at the end of the year. This decrease in the value of the truck is the result of (a) wear and tear from use and from weather, and (b) the tendency of new models to replace old ones. This constant decrease in the value of an asset because of wear and of the passage of time is referred to as *depreciation.*

Why is depreciation recorded?

The amount by which an asset depreciates is an expense to the business. Depreciation expense is a constant expense occurring during the life of the asset. Like any other expense, depreciation expense must be subtracted from gross income each fiscal period in order for a business to arrive at its true net income. If depreciation expense is ignored, the business is understating its expenses and overstating its income.

Fixed assets

Assets that can be used for a number of fiscal periods in the operation of a business are known as *fixed assets.* Examples of fixed assets are equipment, machinery, buildings, and land.

Fixed assets such as typewriters, desks, display cases, tables, and delivery trucks are known as *equipment.* In smaller businesses where only a few items of equipment are owned, these fixed assets are frequently recorded in a single account with the title Equipment. Other and larger businesses prefer to record them in separate accounts with such descriptive titles as Office Equipment, Store Equipment, and Delivery Equipment.

Recording the purchase of fixed assets

Fixed assets may be bought either for cash or on credit. When a fixed asset is purchased, it is recorded at the cost price.

For example, on July 2, 1962, C. W. Lane, the proprietor of a feed and grain store, bought a typewriter for $180 in cash. Mr. Lane recorded the purchase of the typewriter as a debit to Equipment and a credit to Cash. After the entry was posted, the equipment account in the assets section of the general ledger appeared as shown on the next page.

Equipment

DATE	ITEMS	POST. REF.	DEBIT	DATE	ITEMS	POST. REF.	CREDIT
1962 Jan 1	Balance	1	2751 00				
Mar 1		4	1800 00				
July 2		9	180 00				
			4731 00				

The total of the debit side of the equipment account, $4,731, showed the *cost price* of all equipment.

Calculating depreciation

Before a bookkeeper can record the depreciation expense of a fixed asset, he must know how to calculate that expense. The simplest way to calculate depreciation expense requires a knowledge of two things. These are: (1) the cost of the fixed asset and (2) its probable life. The typewriter that Mr. Lane purchased on July 2, 1962, for $180 was estimated to have a life of 5 years. This meant that the estimated depreciation expense on this item of equipment for *each year* was $36 ($180 ÷ 5 years = $36).

The annual depreciation is frequently referred to as a percentage of the cost price. For example, a typewriter that depreciates $\frac{1}{5}$ each year is said to depreciate at the rate of 20%.

The value at which a fixed asset is shown on the books is known as *book value*. The book value is, then, the original cost minus the total recorded depreciation.

The following table shows Mr. Lane's estimate of depreciation expense and the book value of the typewriter for the years he plans to use it:

Typewriter	Recorded Depreciation for Each Year	Total Recorded Depreciation	Book Value
Cost at time of purchase, July 2, 1962.............			$180
Last half of fiscal year ending 12/31/62..............	$18	$18	162
Fiscal year ending 12/31/63.	36	54	126
Fiscal year ending 12/31/64.	36	90	90
Fiscal year ending 12/31/65.	36	126	54
Fiscal year ending 12/31/66.	36	162	18
First half of fiscal year ending 12/31/67.............	18	180	0

Sometimes it is difficult for the businessman or the bookkeeper to estimate with reasonable accuracy how fast certain fixed assets will depreciate. Tables that list the probable useful life of hundreds of common fixed assets are available in Bulletin "F" of the Internal Revenue Service. These tables are based on the experience of business and industry. They serve as excellent guides for estimating the life of fixed assets and the rates of depreciation.

Card record of fixed assets

When Mr. Lane purchased the typewriter on July 2, 1962, he made out the card record shown below.

FIXED ASSET RECORD

ITEM __Typewriter__ GENERAL LEDGER ACCOUNT __Equipment__

SERIAL NO. __3979666__ DESCRIPTION __Majestic Typewriter__

FROM WHOM PURCHASED __Bell Equipment Co., City__

ESTIMATED LIFE __5 years__ DEPRECIATION PER YEAR __20%__

| DATE | | | EXPLANATION | ASSET | | | DEPRECIATION ALLOWANCE | | | BOOK VALUE | |
MO.	DAY	YR.		DR.	CR.	BAL.	DR.	CR.	BAL.		
7	2	62		180 00		180 00				180	00
12	31	62						18 00	18 00	162	00
12	31	63						36 00	54 00	126	00
12	31	64						36 00	90 00	90	00

Card record of a fixed asset

At the time the typewriter was purchased, Mr. Lane recorded a complete description of the machine, including its serial number. He also recorded the date of purchase, the cost price, the estimated life, and the annual rate of depreciation. At the close of each fiscal period he brought the card up to date by recording the depreciation for that period. The card record shown above indicates how the record would appear at the close of the 1964 fiscal period.

Determining depreciation for the fiscal period

On December 31, 1962, the end of the annual fiscal year, Mr. Lane referred to each of his card records of fixed assets and calculated the total amount of the depreciation. According to these card records, the total depreciation of equipment for this fiscal year was $312.60. This meant that during the fiscal year ended December 31 the equipment had decreased in value an amount estimated to be $312.60.

Valuation of fixed assets

The equipment account, like all fixed asset accounts, is debited for the cost price at the time of purchase. When equipment is discarded or sold, the fixed asset account is credited for the cost price. The balance of the fixed asset account Equipment, therefore, should always represent the cost price of the equipment on hand.

To determine the book value of equipment on hand, Mr. Lane must subtract the total estimated depreciation of the equipment from the balance of the equipment account. The calculation is as follows:

Equipment, cost		$4,731.00
Less total depreciation:		
For previous years.............................	$1,491.35	
For current year..............................	312.60	1,803.95
Book value of equipment on hand..................		$2,927.05

C. W.

Work

For Year Ended

	ACCOUNT TITLES	ACCT. NO.	TRIAL BALANCE DEBIT	TRIAL BALANCE CREDIT	
6	Equipment	121	4731 00		6
7	Allowance for Depr. of Equip.	121.1		1491 35	7
21	Depreciation Expense	612			21
28	State Unemployment Taxes	619	93 83		28
29	Supplies Expense	620			29
30			23816 65	23816 65	30
31	Net Income				31
32					32
33					33

Work sheet with

Since the book value of equipment on December 31, 1962, was $2,927.05, that amount was the value which should be shown on the December 31 balance sheet.

Allowance for depreciation of equipment account

Depreciation cannot be credited to the equipment account, as that would indicate that some of the equipment had been sold or discarded. Whenever depreciation expense for equipment is recorded, the estimated amount of depreciation is credited to an account called *Allowance for Depreciation of Equipment.* The equipment account debit balance then continues to show the original cost of all equipment on hand. The credit balance in this new account, Allowance for Depreciation of Equipment, shows the estimated decrease in the value of the equipment because of depreciation. The difference between the balances of the two accounts is the book value.

Adjustment for depreciation on the work sheet

At the end of the fiscal year on December 31, Mr. Lane made an adjustment for depreciation of equipment in the Adjustments columns of his work sheet. A partial work sheet is illustrated below.

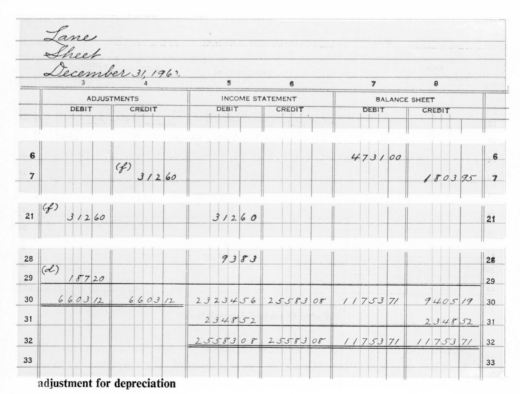

adjustment for depreciation

In the Trial Balance columns of the work sheet, Allowance for Depreciation of Equipment had a credit balance of $1,491.35, the sum of amounts credited to this account in previous fiscal periods. In the Adjustments columns, Allowance for Depreciation of Equipment was credited for $312.60 to record the decrease in the value of equipment as a result of the depreciation during the period. The credit of $312.60 to Allowance for Depreciation of Equipment was added to the credit balance of $1,491.35, and the total, $1,803.95, was extended to the Balance Sheet Credit column of the work sheet. This credit balance in the allowance for depreciation of equipment account will be deducted from the equipment account debit balance when the balance sheet is prepared.

The amount of the depreciation for the year, $312.60, was an expense and was debited to an expense account with the title *Depreciation Expense*. This amount, like the other expenses, was extended into the Income Statement Debit column.

Adjusting entry in the journal to record depreciation

Mr. Lane made the following adjusting entry in the combination journal from the Adjustments columns of his work sheet to record the depreciation:

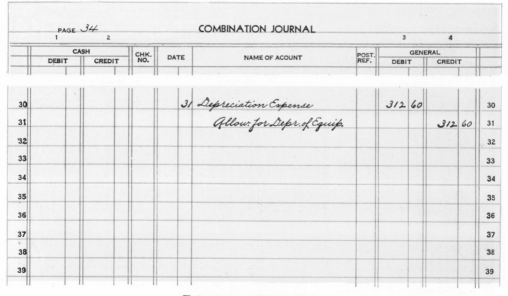

Entry to record depreciation

When the entry to record the depreciation of equipment was posted, the asset account, the allowance account, and the expense account appeared as shown on the opposite page.

356

Equipment   ACCOUNT NO. *121*

DATE	ITEMS	POST. REF.	DEBIT	DATE	ITEMS	POST. REF.	CREDIT
1962 Jan. 1	Balance	1	2 7 5 1 00				
Mar. 1		4	1 8 0 0 00				
July 2		9	1 8 0 00				
			4 7 3 1 00				

Allowance for Depreciation of Equipment   ACCOUNT NO. *121.1*

DATE	ITEMS	POST. REF.	DEBIT	DATE	ITEMS	POST. REF.	CREDIT
				1962 Jan. 1	Balance	1	1 4 9 1 35
				Dec. 31		34	3 1 2 60
							1 8 0 3 95

Depreciation Expense   ACCOUNT NO. *612*

DATE	ITEMS	POST. REF.	DEBIT	DATE	ITEMS	POST. REF.	CREDIT
1962 Dec. 31		34	3 1 2 60				

The debit balance of the equipment account, $4,731, showed the original cost of the equipment. The credit balance of the allowance account, $1,803.95, showed the total amount of the depreciation of all the equipment to date. The difference between these two balances, $2,927.05, was the book value. The debit balance of the depreciation expense account, $312.60, was the depreciation expense for the fiscal period.

Depreciation expense is a deductible expense in computing the state and federal income taxes of the business. Failure to record this $312.60 depreciation expense properly would result in an overstatement of the net income of the business for the period. It could also cause the business to pay higher taxes than it should.

Depreciation expense on the income statement

When Mr. Lane prepared his income statement from the work sheet on December 31, he indicated the depreciation expense as an operating expense as shown below.

C. W. Lane			
Income Statement			
For Year Ended December 31, 1962			
Gross Profit on Sales			8 4 6 5 50
Operating Expenses:			
Delivery Expense	2 6 6 45		
Depreciation Expense	3 1 2 60		
FICA Taxes	7 8 1 5		
Federal Unemployment Taxes	1 0 43		
Insurance Expense	6 3 1 5		
Miscellaneous Expense	4 3 0 1 4		
Rent Expense	1 2 0 0 00		
Salary Expense	3 4 7 5 00		
State Unemployment Taxes	9 3 83		
Supplies Expense	1 8 7 20		
Total Operating Expenses		6 1 1 6 95	
Net Income		2 3 4 8 52	

Income statement showing depreciation expense

Equipment and allowance accounts on the balance sheet

When Mr. Lane prepared his balance sheet from the work sheet on December 31, he indicated (a) the original cost of the equipment, (b) the decrease in value because of depreciation, and (c) the book value of the equipment. (See the balance sheet on the opposite page.)

The total cost of all equipment, $4,731, was shown in the first amount column on the line with Equipment. The depreciation of these fixed assets, $1,803.95, was placed immediately under the cost of the equipment and was subtracted from it. The difference between the two amounts, $2,927.05, was the book value of the equipment.

Valuation accounts

An allowance account used in calculating the book value of an asset account to which it is related is known as a *valuation account*. The balance of an allowance account is always a credit. Since an allowance account is reported as a deduction from an asset on the balance sheet, it is referred to as a *minus asset*.

Classification of assets on the balance sheet

Assets that are in the form of cash or that will be turned into cash or consumed relatively soon in the regular operation of the business are called

C. W. Lane		
Balance Sheet		
December 31, 1962		
Assets		
Current Assets:		
Cash	1920 75	
Accounts Receivable	185 68	
Merchandise Inventory	2757 86	
Supplies	77 30	
Prepaid Insurance	65 60	
Total Current Assets		5007 19
Fixed Assets:		
Equipment	4731 00	
Less Allow. for Depr. of Equip.	1803 95	
Total Fixed Assets		2927 05
Total Assets		7934 24
Liabilities		
Current Liabilities:		
Accounts Payable	486 68	
Employees Income Taxes Payable	52 20	
F.I.C.A. Taxes Payable	26 06	
State Unemployment Taxes Payable	23 46	
Federal Unemployment Taxes Payable	10 43	
Total Current Liabilities		598 83
Proprietorship		
C. W. Lane, Capital		7335 41
Total Liabilities and Proprietorship		7934 24

Balance sheet showing allowance for depreciation

current assets. Examples of current assets are Cash, Accounts Receivable, Merchandise Inventory, Supplies, and Prepaid Insurance.

Fixed assets, as explained earlier, include such items as equipment, buildings, and other assets that will be used in the operation of the business for a number of fiscal periods.

When a business owns both current and fixed assets, it is customary to list them on the balance sheet under the headings "Current Assets" and "Fixed Assets." Anyone examining the balance sheet can then more easily determine whether the current assets will provide sufficient cash to pay the liabilities of the business and whether too much or too little has been invested in fixed assets for the successful operation of the business.

The correct order for listing current assets is to start with Cash and to have this account followed by the other current asset accounts in the order in which they could most readily be converted into cash. The order of listing fixed assets is not so uniform in practice. One common order is to list those with the shortest life first.

When Mr. Lane prepared the balance sheet shown on page 359, he classified the assets under the headings "Current Assets" and "Fixed Assets." The only item to be listed under the heading "Fixed Assets" was Equipment. For Equipment he listed:

(1) The original cost of the equipment on hand.
(2) The decrease in the value of the equipment because of depreciation.
(3) The book value, that is, the difference between the cost and the recorded depreciation.

A business having several fixed assets might list them in the following manner:

Total Current Assets............................			16,660 50
Fixed Assets:			
Equipment........................ 4,230.00			
Less Allow. for Depr. of Equip... 1,200.00	3,030 00		
Building.........................11,000.00			
Less Allow. for Depr. of Bldg.... 1,500.00	9,500 00		
Land..	3,500 00		
Total Fixed Assets............................			16,030 00
Total Assets..................................			32,690 50

Section of a balance sheet showing three fixed assets

Allowances for depreciation were recorded for Equipment and Buildings, but no such allowance was recorded for Land. There is ordinarily no depreciation of land as a result of its use for business purposes.

Classification of liabilities on the balance sheet

Liabilities that will be due within a relatively short time, usually within a year, are called *current liabilities.* Examples of current liabilities are Accounts Payable, Employees Income Taxes Payable, FICA Taxes Payable, State Unemployment Taxes Payable, and Federal Unemployment Taxes Payable.

Liabilities that do not have to be paid for a number of years in the normal operation of the business are known as *long-term liabilities* or *fixed liabilities.* An example of a long-term liability is Mortgage Payable.

A common order of arrangement for listing liability accounts on the balance sheet is the order in which they should be paid.

All of the liabilities of Mr. Lane are current liabilities. He included on his balance sheet, shown on page 359, the heading "Current Liabilities" to show that all of these liabilities should be paid within a year.

Increasing your business vocabulary

What is the meaning of each of the following:

(a) depreciation
(b) fixed assets
(c) equipment
(d) book value
(e) valuation account
(f) current assets
(g) current liabilities
(h) fixed liabilities

Chapter questions

1. Why are most fixed assets worth less than their purchase price after they have been used for a fiscal period?
2. If the expense of using a fixed asset is not recorded, how will this affect the total expenses of the business? How will this omission affect the net income for the period?
3. What two things must a bookkeeper know about a fixed asset before he can calculate its depreciation expense?
4. Why is the amount of depreciation credited to the allowance for depreciation of equipment account rather than to the equipment account?
5. When is the depreciation of fixed assets recorded?
6. On the work sheet on pages 354 and 355, what accounts are debited and credited in making the adjustment for estimated depreciation?
7. Why is the allowance for depreciation of equipment called a valuation or minus asset account?
8. What is the difference between a current asset and a fixed asset? Between a current liability and a long-term liability?
9. What is a correct order for listing assets on the balance sheet? For listing liabilities on the balance sheet?

Cases for discussion

1. Suppose that Mr. Stone, the proprietor of a small business, maintains that since he makes no actual cash payments for depreciation he is not entitled to record depreciation as an expense. What is wrong with Mr. Stone's point of view?

2. When R. G. O'Grady purchased a new delivery truck, he told his book-keeper to determine what the annual depreciation expense should be. What steps should be taken to determine what the annual depreciation expense should be?

3. C. W. Potter rents a typewriter for $6 a month. He can buy a new typewriter for $190. He estimates the life of a new typewriter to be 5 years. If interest and repair costs are ignored, how much would he save by buying the machine?

Drills for understanding

Drill 24-A. Calculating depreciation

Instructions: For each of the following fixed assets find the amount of annual depreciation.

Fixed Asset	Initial Cost	Estimated Life
1	$ 400	4 years
2	600	5 years
3	300	3 years
4	720	20 years
5	6,400	8 years
6	12,800	16 years

Drill 24-B. Finding book value

Instructions: For each of the following items of equipment find as of December 31, 1962, (a) the total amount of estimated depreciation and (b) the book value.

Fixed Asset	Date of Purchase	Initial Cost	Annual Rate of Depreciation
1	Jan. 3, 1960	$412.00	25%
2	July 1, 1960	360.00	20%
3	Jan. 3, 1961	972.40	5%
4	Nov. 1, 1961	150.00	8%
5	Jan. 2, 1962	738.50	10%
6	Dec. 1, 1962	200.00	12%

Problem 24-1. *Calculating and recording depreciation*

G. W. Ranger purchased the following items of office equipment during the first two years that he was in business:

Office Equipment	Date of Purchase	Initial Cost	Annual Rate of Depreciation
1	January 3, 1961	$ 440	10%
2	July 1, 1961	80	25%
3	March 1, 1962	72	20%
4	July 2, 1962	470	8%
5	November 1, 1962	960	12%
6	December 1, 1962	1,600	5%

Instructions: 1. Record the adjusting journal entry for the total depreciation expense for the year ended December 31, 1961.

2. Record the adjusting journal entry for the total depreciation expense for the year ended December 31, 1962.

Problem 24-2. *Work at the end of the fiscal period*

The account numbers, titles, and balances in the general ledger of A. P. May, a dealer in building materials, on June 30 of the current year were as follows:

111 Cash, $1,300.20	411 Sales, $13,156.80
112 Accounts Receivable, $319.97	411.1 Sales Returns and Allowances, $160.30
113 Merchandise Inventory, $2,326.98	
114 Supplies, $170.00	511 Purchases, $10,067.40
115 Prepaid Insurance, $223.65	511.1 Purchases Returns and Allowances, $170.50
121 Equipment, $2,750.00	
121.1 Allowance for Depreciation of Equipment, $420.00	611 Delivery Expense, $622.25
	612 Depreciation Expense, —
211 Accounts Payable, $1,267.20	613 Insurance Expense, —
311 A. P. May, Capital, $5,724.50	614 Miscellaneous Expense, $278.25
312 A. P. May, Drawing, $1,320 (Dr.)	615 Salary Expense, $1,200.00
313 Income and Expense Summary, —	616 Supplies Expense, —

The additional data needed at the end of the annual fiscal period are: merchandise inventory, $5,238.65; supplies inventory, $58.45; prepaid insurance, $128.25; annual rate of estimated depreciation of equipment, 10%.

Instructions: 1. Prepare an eight-column work sheet for the annual fiscal period ended June 30 of the current year.

2. Prepare an income statement and a balance sheet from the work sheet.

3. Record the adjusting and closing entries in a combination journal.

★*Supplementary Problem 24-S. Calculating depreciation, recording depreciation, and finding book value*

L. B. Blair purchased the following items of store equipment during the first two years that he was in business:

Store Equipment	Date of Purchase	Initial Cost	Annual Rate of Depreciation
1	January 3, 1961	$240	10%
2	July 1, 1961	300	15%
3	April 2, 1962	640	25%
4	September 1, 1962	840	5%
5	November 1, 1962	72	12%
6	December 1, 1962	480	8%

Instructions: 1. Record the adjusting entry for the total depreciation expense for the year ended December 31, 1961.

2. Record the adjusting entry for the total depreciation expense for the year ended December 31, 1962.

3. Find the book value as of December 31, 1962, of each item of equipment.

★*Bonus Problem 24-B. Calculating and recording depreciation of fixed assets with a trade-in or scrap value*

Introductory remarks. When it is expected that a fixed asset will have a trade-in or scrap value after it is no longer serviceable, this value should be subtracted from the cost in determining depreciation. For example, if a machine costs $1,200 and it is expected that the trade-in value will be $300, depreciation would be calculated on $900.

R. S. Richards purchased the following items of equipment during the first two years that he was in business:

Equipment	Date of Purchase	Initial Cost	Estimated Trade-in or Scrap Value	Estimated Life
1	Jan. 3, 1961	$1,000	$100	10 years
2	Jan. 3, 1961	300	50	5 years
3	Jan. 3, 1961	180	none	12 years
4	July 3, 1961	3,600	900	3 years
5	Jan. 2, 1962	108	none	6 years
6	July 1, 1962	650	50	15 years

Instructions: 1. Record the adjusting entry for the total depreciation expense for the year ended December 31, 1961.

2. Record the adjusting entry for the total depreciation expense for the year ended December 31, 1962.

3. Find the book value as of December 31, 1962, of each item of equipment.

Chapter 25

Disposing of fixed assets

Ways of disposing of fixed assets

A fixed asset, such as a machine, a typewriter, or a desk, cannot be used forever. It may wear out, or the business may replace it with a newer model.

When a fixed asset is no longer useful to a business, it may be disposed of in any one of three ways: (1) it may be discarded; (2) it may be sold; or (3) it may be traded in as part of the purchasing price of a new asset.

Calculating loss or gain on the disposal of a fixed asset

A business will frequently experience a loss or a gain when one of its fixed assets is disposed of. This is so because depreciation is an estimate and the value of the fixed asset at the time it is discarded or sold will probably not equal its book value. For example, a fixed asset that cost $50 was estimated to have a useful life of 5 years. Thus it was estimated to depreciate 20% or $10 a year. The following outline shows the loss or the gain that would be experienced under different circumstances:

Situation	Description of Transaction	Cost Price	Allow. for Depr.	Book Value	Cash for Sale	Loss	Gain
1	Asset was discarded as worthless at the end of 4 years.	$50	$40	$10	..	$10	..
2	Asset was discarded as worthless at the end of 5 years.	50	50	..	..	..	..
3	Asset was sold for $15 at the end of 4 years.	50	40	10	$15	..	$5
4	Asset was sold for $10 at the end of 4 years.	50	40	10	10	..	..
5	Asset was sold for $10 at the end of 3½ years.	50	35	15	10	5	..
6	Asset was sold for $10 after 5 years.	50	50	..	10	..	10

As can be seen from the above illustrations, the book value of the fixed asset *at the time of its disposal* is necessary in determining loss or gain. It is important, therefore, that the depreciation expense be recorded at the time of disposal for that part of the final fiscal period during which the asset was used. Usually, the depreciation expense for this final period is considered sufficiently accurate if it is calculated to the nearest month.

Thus an asset disposed of during the first half of a month need not have any depreciation expense charged to it for that month. Similarly, a fixed asset sold or discarded during the last half of a month would have a full month's depreciation expense recorded.

Discarding a fixed asset

On January 7, 1963, Earl Hill, a grocer, discarded a refrigerator. It had no trade-in or sale value. An analysis of the card record for this asset showed the following summary information:

Purchase price on January 5, 1954.........	$400
Total depreciation (9 yrs. @ 10%)........	360
Book value, January 7, 1963..............	$ 40

At the time Mr. Hill purchased this refrigerator, he made a reasonable estimate that it would be used for 10 years and that it would depreciate 10% a year. But the refrigerator lasted only 9 years and his books showed that it still had a value of $40. It would not have been practical to distribute this $40 expense back over the 9 years that the refrigerator was in use. Therefore, to record the discarding of the refrigerator and the loss from discarding an asset with a book value, Mr. Hill made the following entry in the combination journal:

	CASH		CHK. NO.	DATE	NAME OF ACCOUNT	POST. REF.	GENERAL		
	DEBIT	CREDIT					DEBIT	CREDIT	
				1963					
1				Jan. 7	Allow. for Depr. of Equip.		360 00		1
2					Loss on Fixed Assets		40 00		2
3					Equipment			400 00	3

PAGE 3 — COMBINATION JOURNAL

Entry to record the discarding of a fixed asset

The effect of this transaction is shown in the following T accounts:

EQUIPMENT (Refrigerator)

1/5/54	400	1/7/63	400

LOSS ON FIXED ASSETS

1/7/63	40

ALLOWANCE FOR DEPRECIATION OF EQUIPMENT (Refrigerator)

1/7/63	360	12/31/54	40
		12/31/55	40
		12/31/56	40
		12/31/57	40
		12/31/58	40
		12/31/59	40
		12/31/60	40
		12/31/61	40
		12/31/62	40
			360

Analysis of journal entry showing discarding of a fixed asset

The debit of $360 to Allowance for Depreciation of Equipment canceled the amount of the allowance previously recorded for the refrigerator.

The debit to the expense account Loss on Fixed Assets recorded the loss when a fixed asset with a book value of $40 was discarded. A loss that a business incurs when it discards a fixed asset with a book value or sells a fixed asset for less than its book value is known as a *loss on fixed assets*.

The credit of $400 to Equipment canceled the debit to that account that was recorded when the refrigerator was purchased.

Selling a fixed asset

On January 11, 1963, Mr. Hill sold one of his display cases for $150 in cash. The card record for the display case showed the following summary information:

Purchase price on July 2, 1959............ $200
Total depreciation (3½ years @ 10%)...... 70
Book value, January 11, 1963............. $130

Mr. Hill, in receiving $150 for this used display case, sold it for $20 more than its book value ($150 − $130 = $20). To record this transaction he made the following entry:

CASH DEBIT	CASH CREDIT	CHK. NO.	DATE	NAME OF ACOUNT	POST. REF.	GENERAL DEBIT	GENERAL CREDIT	
23	150 00			11	Allow. for Depr. of Equip.		70 00		23
24					Equipment			200 00	24
25					Gain on Fixed Assets			20 00	25
26									26

PAGE 3 — COMBINATION JOURNAL

Entry to record the sale of a fixed asset

The effect of this transaction is shown in the following T accounts:

CASH		ALLOWANCE FOR DEPRECIATION OF EQUIPMENT (Display Case)	
1/11/63 150		1/11/63 70	12/31/59 10
			12/31/60 20
EQUIPMENT (Display Case)			12/31/61 20
7/2/59 200	1/11/63 200		12/31/62 20
			70
GAIN ON FIXED ASSETS			
	1/11/63 20		

Analysis of journal entry showing sale of a fixed asset

The debit to Cash, $150, was the amount actually received for the display case.

The debit to Allowance for Depreciation of Equipment, $70, canceled the amount of the allowance recorded for the used display case.

The credit to Equipment, $200, canceled the debit recorded in the equipment account when the display case was purchased.

The credit to the income account Gain on Fixed Assets for $20 recorded the gain when a fixed asset with a book value of $130 was sold for $150. The profit that a business makes when it sells a fixed asset for an amount that is more than its book value is known as *gain on fixed assets*.

If a fixed asset is sold for a price less than its book value, the journal entry to record the transaction would be similar to the illustration on page 367. Instead of crediting Gain on Fixed Assets, however, the expense account *Loss on Fixed Assets* is debited for the difference between the selling price and the book value.

Trading in a fixed asset

According to income tax regulations, a loss or a gain is not recognized when one fixed asset of a business is traded in for another similar fixed asset. The new asset is recorded at a value equal to the sum of the cash actually paid plus the book value of the old asset.

On March 4, 1963, Mr. Hill purchased a new delivery truck and gave for it his old truck and $2,500 in cash. The fixed asset account for the truck, Delivery Equipment, and its valuation account, Allowance for Depreciation of Delivery Equipment, in T form, appeared as follows on March 4, 1963, immediately before the trade-in transaction was completed:

DELIVERY EQUIPMENT		ALLOWANCE FOR DEPRECIATION OF DELIVERY EQUIPMENT	
1/2/60	3,000	12/31/60	600
		12/31/61	600
		12/31/62	600

When the truck was purchased on January 2, 1960, it was estimated that it would have a useful life of 5 years and that it would therefore depreciate 20% or $600 each year. Since this old truck was used during the first 2 months of the 1962 fiscal period, it was necessary to record the depreciation expense for this time in order to bring the book value of the truck up to date. This was done in the journal entry shown at the top of the following page.

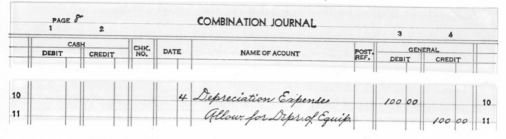

CASH		CHK. NO.	DATE	NAME OF ACOUNT	POST. REF.	GENERAL		
DEBIT	CREDIT					DEBIT	CREDIT	
			4	*Depreciation Expense*		100 00		10
				Allow. for Depr. of Equip.			100 00	11

Entry to record estimated depreciation for part of a fiscal period

After this entry was posted, the two balance sheet accounts showing the book value of the old truck appeared as follows:

DELIVERY EQUIPMENT		ALLOWANCE FOR DEPRECIATION OF DELIVERY EQUIPMENT	
1/2/60	3,000	12/31/60	600
		12/31/61	600
		12/31/62	600
		3/ 4/63	**100**
			1,900

Since the old truck was purchased for $3,000 and the total allowance for depreciation was $1,900, the old truck had a book value of $1,100 ($3,000 − $1,900 = $1,100) on March 4, 1963, the day it was traded in. As Mr. Hill paid an additional $2,500 cash for the new truck, the value of this new truck to be recorded on the books in the delivery equipment account was $3,600. This amount was found as follows:

Original cost of old truck...............	$3,000
Less allowance for depreciation..........	1,900
Book value of old truck.................	$1,100
Add cash paid for new truck............	2,500
Initial book value of new truck.........	$3,600

The account Delivery Equipment should show the initial book value of the new truck, and the allowance account should be balanced. Mr. Hill made the following entry in his combination journal:

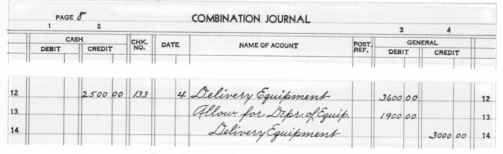

CASH		CHK. NO.	DATE	NAME OF ACOUNT	POST. REF.	GENERAL		
DEBIT	CREDIT					DEBIT	CREDIT	
	2 500 00	133	4	*Delivery Equipment*		3600 00		12
				Allow. for Depr. of Equip.		1900 00		13
				Delivery Equipment			3000 00	14

Entry to record trading in a fixed asset

Analysis of journal entry showing trading in of a fixed asset

The debit to Delivery Equipment, $3,600, for the new truck was considered the actual cost of the new truck and thus the new truck's initial book value. The debit to Allowance for Depreciation of Delivery Equipment, $1,900, canceled the amount of the allowance recorded for the old truck. The credit to Cash, $2,500, was the amount of cash actually paid. The credit to Delivery Equipment, $3,000, canceled the debit made in the delivery equipment account when the old truck was purchased.

The delivery equipment account and its valuation account, in T form, appeared as follows after posting, balancing, and ruling:

DELIVERY EQUIPMENT				ALLOWANCE FOR DEPRECIATION OF DELIVERY EQUIPMENT			
1/2/60	3,000	3/4/63	3,000	3/4/63	1,900	12/31/60	600
						12/31/61	600
3/4/63	3,600					12/31/62	600
						3/ 4/63	100
					1,900		1,900

The delivery equipment account now shows the initial book value of the new truck. The allowance account has been balanced and ruled so that future entries in this account will apply to the depreciation of the new truck only.

It should be observed that no record was made of the amount the dealer said the new truck was worth or the amount he said he was giving as an allowance for the old truck. These amounts were ignored, and the new truck was recorded at a value equal to the amount of cash paid plus the book value of the truck traded in.

Other income and other expenses on the income statement

When a business has income and expenses that are not considered to be a part of the regular operation of the business, such nonoperating income and expense items are classified separately on the income statement. The income statement of Universal Furniture on the next page includes the nonoperating income account Gain on Fixed Assets and the nonoperating expense account Loss on Fixed Assets. How this income statement differs from previously illustrated statements is discussed in the following paragraphs.

Line 1. The first heading is *Income from Sales* rather than *Income* as used previously. The more complete title is used to distinguish between income from sales reported at the beginning of the statement and other income reported near the end of the statement.

Universal Furniture
Income Statement
For Year Ended December 31, 1962

Income from Sales:					
Sales					9833585
Less: Sales Returns and Allowances			103450		
Discount on Sales			84128	187578	
Net Sales				9646007	
Cost of Merchandise Sold:					
Merchandise Inventory, January 1, 1962			930763		
Purchases	7408039				
Less: Purchases Ret. and Allow. 560.85					
Discount on Purchases 1429.03	198988				
Net Purchases			7209051		
Total Cost of Mdse. Available for Sale			8139814		
Less Mdse. Inventory, Dec. 31, 1962			815966		
Cost of Merchandise Sold				7323848	
Gross Profit on Sales				2322159	
Operating Expenses:					
Delivery Expense			363056		
Depreciation Expense			62450		
FICA Taxes			22969		
Federal Unemployment Taxes			19845		
Insurance Expense			24000		
Miscellaneous Expense			65311		
Rent Expense			240000		
Salary Expense			735015		
State Unemployment Taxes			5880		
Supplies Expense			83198		
Total Operating Expenses				1621724	
Net Income from Operations				700435	
Other Income:					
Gain on Fixed Assets			22040		
Other Expense:					
Loss on Fixed Assets			16020		
Net Addition				6020	
Net Income				706455	

Income statement showing Other Income and Other Expense sections

Line 25. *Net Income from Operations* is the excess of operating income, which in a mercantile business is gross profit on sales, over operating expenses. The term *net income from operations* is used to distinguish between net income that came entirely from the regular operation of the business and net income that did not.

Lines 26 and 27 — Other Income. Universal Furniture is not in business for the major purpose of making a profit on the sale of its fixed assets. A gain on the sale of a fixed asset is not, therefore, considered to be a part of the regular operating income of a business. As a result, Gain on Fixed Assets is listed separately on the income statement under the heading *Other Income*.

Lines 28 and 29 — Other Expense. A business will sometimes have an expense that is not a regular operating expense of the business. The expense account Loss on Fixed Assets is an example of a nonoperating expense. It is listed separately on the income statement under the heading *Other Expense*.

Lines 30 and 31. The amount by which the Other Income exceeds the Other Expense is labeled *Net Addition* and is added to the Net Income from Operations. The sum is the *Net Income* of the business for the period.

When the Other Income during a fiscal period is less than the Other Expense, the difference is entitled *Net Subtraction*. This amount is then subtracted from the Net Income from Operations. The final lines of an income statement showing Other Income less than Other Expense is illustrated below.

Net Income from Operations.................		1,728 33
Other Income:		
Gain on Fixed Assets......................	116 50	
Other Expense:		
Loss on Fixed Assets......................	245 00	
Net Subtraction...........................		128 50
Net Income..............................		1,599 83

Closing other income and other expense accounts

Other Income and Other Expense accounts are closed into Income and Expense Summary in the same manner and at the same time that the operating income and expense accounts are closed.

increasing your business vocabulary

What is the meaning of each of the following:

(a) loss on fixed assets

(b) gain on fixed assets

(c) net income from operations

Chapter questions

1. What are the three ways of disposing of a fixed asset?

2. Why, at the time a fixed asset becomes worn out and worthless, do the bookkeeping records sometimes show that it has a book value?

3. Why, when a fixed asset is discarded, sold, or traded in, must the depreciation expense of that asset be recorded for the part of the final fiscal period that it was used?

4. What is meant by calculating depreciation expense "to the nearest month"?

5. When is it necessary in the disposal of a worthless fixed asset to debit the account Loss on Fixed Assets?

6. How does a bookkeeper determine whether a gain or a loss has been made on the sale of a fixed asset?

7. How does a bookkeeper determine the value to be recorded for a new fixed asset that is acquired by trading in a similar item?

8. How is Gain on Fixed Assets shown on the income statement?

9. How is Loss on Fixed Assets shown on the income statement?

Cases for discussion

1. When A. J. Peters reported to his bookkeeper the discarding of a worthless file cabinet, its card record showed that it no longer had any book value. Mr. Peters then told his bookkeeper that since all possible depreciation expense had been recorded and no loss on the fixed asset had been incurred, no further bookkeeping entry was necessary. What was wrong with Mr. Peters' advice?

2. Suppose that one of your friends in the bookkeeping class made the mistake of assuming that an allowance account shows an amount of money set aside for use in the replacement of a fixed asset. How would you explain to him that this is not true?

3. When a new adding machine that cost $160 was purchased by Jones and Smith, partners in a lumber business, one thought they should estimate its useful life at 10 years and the other thought that 12 years would be a better estimate. Finally Mr. Jones stated, "Whether we decide on 10 years or 12 years will make little difference in the long run. The total expense to the business will be $160 in either case." Is there anything wrong with Mr. Jones's statement? Explain your answer.

4. Under what circumstances could a worthless fixed asset be discarded without requiring an entry debiting the account Loss on Fixed Assets?

Application problems

Problem 25-1. Discarding fixed assets

R. G. Conover, an insurance agent, discarded as worthless the following items of office equipment:

Items	Date of Purchase	Initial Cost	Annual Rate of Depreciation	Date of Disposal
#1	January 2, 1959	$360	25%	January 7, 1963
#2	June 2, 1954	160	10%	March 7, 1963
#3	July 5, 1957	500	20%	January 7, 1963
#4	April 28, 1945	180	5%	March 18, 1963

Instructions: 1. Calculate the book value and the amount of loss, if any, for each fixed asset.

2. Make the journal entries necessary to record depreciation for 1963 to the date of disposal of the assets. Calculate depreciation to the nearest month.

3. Make the journal entries necessary to record the discard of each item of office equipment.

Problem 25-2. Selling fixed assets

Fred Carr, a grocer, sold the following items of store equipment on December 1, 1962:

Item	Purchase Price	Book Value Dec. 1, 1962	Cash Received for Sale of Fixed Asset
Cash register	$600	$100	$130
Refrigerator	540	90	50

Instructions: Make the journal entries necessary to record the sale of these used fixed assets.

Problem 25-3. Trading in fixed assets

Assume that, instead of selling the items in Problem 25-2 for cash, Mr. Carr traded them in on December 1, 1962, for new and similar items of store equipment as follows:

(a) A new cash register for his old cash register plus $500 in cash.

(b) A new refrigerator for his old refrigerator plus $400 in cash.

Instructions: Make the journal entries necessary to record the trade-in of these fixed assets.

Optional problems

★Supplementary Problem 25-S. Purchase and disposition of fixed assets

Instructions: 1. Open the following accounts in the ledger of Harvey Lewis and record the balances as of January 1 of the current year.

No.	ACCOUNT TITLE	BALANCE
121	Delivery Equipment	$4,000
121.1	Allowance for Depreciation of Delivery Equipment	2,650
122	Office Equipment	1,080
122.1	Allowance for Depreciation of Office Equipment	670
614	Depreciation of Delivery Equipment	_____
615	Depreciation of Office Equipment	_____
712	Gain on Fixed Assets	_____
812	Loss on Fixed Assets	_____

Instructions: 2. Record in a combination journal the following transactions selected from those completed during the current year.

Jan. 2. Issued Check No. 9 for $300 for cash purchase of office equipment.

Jan. 3. Discarded office equipment for which there was no further use and which could not be sold. The office equipment cost $200 and had a book value of $15 at the time it was discarded.

Jan. 10. Bought a new delivery truck for $2,300 cash (Check No. 413) and the old truck. The old truck cost $2,000 and had a book value of $350 at the time of the trade-in.

Jan. 12. Sold old office equipment for cash, $25. The equipment cost $80 and had a book value of $35 when it was sold.

June 30. Sold a truck for $900. The truck had been purchased two years ago on January 2 for $2,000. The depreciation rate was $500 a year. Allowance for depreciation for that amount was recorded at the end of the two previous years.
(a) Record the depreciation for the current year to June 30.
(b) Record the sale of the truck.

June 30. Office equipment costing $800, with depreciation at the rate of 10% a year, has a total allowance for depreciation of $440 on January 1 of the current year. On June 30 it is traded in on a new office machine. The cost of the new machine was the book value of the old machine plus $500 that was paid in cash (Check No. 554).
(a) Record the depreciation for the current year to June 30.
(b) Record the purchase of the new machine and the trade-in of the old.

Instructions: 3. Post all amounts in the General columns.

4. Make the necessary adjusting entries to record depreciation for the year ended December 31 and based on the following annual rates: delivery equipment, 25%; office equipment, 10%.

5. Post the adjusting entries.

★*Bonus Problem 25-B. Purchase and disposition of fixed assets*

Instructions: 1. Open the following accounts in the ledger of R. Swan, using the account numbers indicated: Delivery Equipment, 121; Allowance for Depreciation of Delivery Equipment, 121.1; Office Machines, 122; Allowance for Depreciation of Office Machines, 122.1; Depreciation of Delivery Equipment, 614; Depreciation of Office Machines, 615; Gain on Fixed Assets, 712; Loss on Fixed Assets, 812.

2. Record in a combination journal the following selected transactions:

Jan.   3, 1961. Purchased a used delivery truck for cash, $1,600. (Check No. 6.)

Jan.   6, 1961. Purchased a used adding machine for cash, $15. (Check No. 21.)

Dec. 31, 1961. Made adjusting entries to record depreciation for the year. The estimated life of the used truck is 2 years. The annual rate of depreciation for the used adding machine is $33\frac{1}{3}\%$.

Dec. 31, 1961. Made an entry to close the depreciation expense accounts.

Instructions: 3. Post the foregoing entries to the accounts that you opened in the ledger. As you do not have a complete ledger, you need not at this time post to the account Income and Expense Summary.

4. Rule the accounts that have been closed.

5. Record in a combination journal the following selected transactions:

Jan. 10, 1962. Discarded adding machine which was broken and could not be sold.

Jan. 11, 1962. Purchased new adding machine for cash, $250. (Check No. 33.)

July   2, 1962. Sold truck for cash, $600.
(a) Record the depreciation for the current year to July 2.
(b) Record the sale of the truck.

July   3, 1962. Bought a new delivery truck for cash, $3,000. (Check No. 413.)

Dec. 28, 1962. Traded in truck bought on July 3 for a 1963 model. The cost of the new truck was the book value of the old truck plus $500 in cash. (Check No. 860.)
(a) Record the depreciation from July 3 to December 28 of the current year at an annual rate of 20%.
(b) Record the purchase of the new truck and the trade-in of the old.

Dec. 31, 1962. Made adjusting entry to record for the year the depreciation expense that had not previously been recorded. The new adding machine bought on January 11 has an estimated life of 10 years.

Dec. 31, 1962. Made an entry to close the income account.

Dec. 31, 1962. Made an entry to close the expense accounts.

Instructions: 6. Post the foregoing entries to the accounts that you opened in the ledger. As you do not have a complete ledger, you need not at this time post to the account Income and Expense Summary.

7. Rule the accounts that have been closed.

8. Prepare the Fixed Assets section of R. Swan's balance sheet for December 31, 1962.

Chapter 26

Bad debts and accounts receivable

Why do businesses grant credit?

Many businesses find that they can increase their volume of sales and thus their income by selling on account. This practice of granting credit and allowing customers time in which to pay for their purchases is an added service that accommodates and thus draws more customers.

Most of the sales made by wholesale houses and manufacturers to retailers are credit sales. Many retail stores make sales to charge customers who pay at stated intervals, usually once a month. Federal statistics show that hundreds of the larger department stores throughout the United States report that less than 50% of their sales are cash sales.

Investigating customer credit

Before a business extends credit, it usually obtains information about the credit standing of the prospective charge customer. Retailers usually obtain the credit rating of a prospective charge customer from a local credit bureau. Wholesalers and manufacturers may obtain this information from the financial reports submitted by the prospective customer and from national credit agencies such as Dun & Bradstreet.

Dun & Bradstreet, Inc. publishes a credit-rating book containing information about the financial condition of business houses throughout the United States. This reference book is available to businesses subscribing for it.

Uncollectible accounts

Even though a business is careful in extending credit to charge customers, there are usually some accounts that cannot be collected. Accounts receivable that cannot be collected are called *bad debts*. The expense caused by the uncollectible accounts is called *bad debts expense*. This bad debts expense, like any other expense of the business, must be subtracted from gross income in order to arrive at a true net income. If this is not done, the business will be understating its expenses and overstating its net income.

An account receivable does not become a bad debt until it is known to be uncollectible. Sometimes this is several months or even a year or more after the date when the sale was made. During the time that this account receivable which proved to be uncollectible was carried on the books, the value of the asset Accounts Receivable was overstated. Furthermore, the expense resulting from selling goods to a customer who did not pay was not recorded. It is desirable, therefore, for a business to make entries that will keep the accounts receivable account from being overstated and that will charge the bad debts expense to the period in which the sale is made.

Valuation of accounts receivable

The books of M. F. Conway, a wholesale hardware merchant, showed a balance of $5,515.77 in Accounts Receivable at the end of the quarterly fiscal period ended December 31, 1962. Mr. Conway knew from past experience that some of the individual accounts included in the balance of Accounts Receivable would eventually prove to be uncollectible. As a result, the $5,515.77 debit balance in Accounts Receivable was an overstatement of the value of this asset.

Mr. Conway has found from past records and experience that his uncollectible accounts usually amounted to about ½% (.005) of his net sales for a fiscal period. Mr. Conway's net sales for the quarterly fiscal period ended December 31, 1962, were $22,064. He was therefore justified in *estimating* that $110.32 ($22,064 × .005 = $110.32) of his Accounts Receivable would be bad debts expense for this period.

In order for Mr. Conway to determine the estimated value of his accounts receivable on December 31, it was necessary to subtract the estimated amount of uncollectible accounts from the balance of the accounts receivable account. The following calculation shows this:

Accounts receivable..................	$5,515.77
Less estimated loss from bad debts....	110.32
Estimated value of accounts receivable.	$5,405.45

Some businesses find that they can secure their best estimate of bad debts expense by taking a percentage of their total *charge* sales for the period instead of a percentage of their total net sales. Others will take a percentage of the balance in the accounts receivable account at the end of a fiscal period. In any case, a business should use the method that results in the most accurate estimate. A change in policy concerning sales on account or a change in economic conditions may cause a business to raise or lower its percentage figure so as to keep its estimate of bad debts as accurate as possible.

Establishing the allowance for bad debts account

Mr. Conway desired to have his ledger as well as his balance sheet show the estimated value of the accounts receivable. It was therefore necessary to record the estimated decrease in value of the accounts receivable because of uncollectible accounts.

378

Even though Mr. Conway estimated that accounts receivable to the amount of $110.32 would not be collected, he was not certain which of his customers would fail to pay. He could record the estimated loss by debiting an expense account; but without knowing which customers would not pay, he could not credit certain customers' accounts. Likewise, he could not credit the accounts receivable account in the general ledger because the balance of that account had to equal the sum of the balances of the customers' accounts. He therefore, by an adjusting entry, credited the estimated amount of the bad debts to an account with the title *Allowance for Bad Debts*. Since the loss from bad debts, $110.32, was one of the expenses of operating his business, he debited this amount to an expense account with the title *Bad Debts Expense*.

The entry in the combination journal to adjust the ledger record of accounts receivable and to show the estimated bad debts expense was as follows:

	CASH		CHK. NO.	DATE	NAME OF ACCOUNT	POST. REF.	GENERAL		
	DEBIT	CREDIT					DEBIT	CREDIT	
29				31	Bad Debts Expense		110 32		29
30					Allowance for Bad Debts			110 32	30

PAGE 24 — COMBINATION JOURNAL

Adjusting entry to establish allowance for bad debts

When the adjusting entry was posted, the accounts receivable account, the allowance for bad debts account, and the bad debts expense account in the general ledger appeared as follows:

Accounts Receivable — ACCOUNT NO. 12

DATE	ITEMS	POST. REF.	DEBIT	DATE	ITEMS	POST. REF.	CREDIT
1962 Oct. 1	Balance	✓	3 6 9 9 68	1962 Oct. 31		17	2 8 5 5 55
31		17	3 1 2 6 83	Nov. 30		22	3 2 1 4 27
Nov. 30		22	3 8 7 2 90	Dec. 31		24	3 4 9 4 70
Dec. 31		24	4 3 8 0 83				9 5 6 4 47
		5515.77	1 5 0 8 0 24				

Allowance for Bad Debts — ACCOUNT NO. 12.1

DATE	ITEMS	POST. REF.	DEBIT	DATE	ITEMS	POST. REF.	CREDIT
				1962 Dec. 31		24	1 1 0 32

DATE	ITEMS	POST. REF.	DEBIT	DATE	ITEMS	POST. REF.	CREDIT
1962 Dec 31		24	1 1 0 32				

The accounts receivable account has a debit balance of $5,515.77 and is classified as an *asset*. The Allowance for Bad Debts has a credit balance of $110.32 and is classified as a *minus asset*. Because Allowance for Bad Debts is used on the balance sheet in calculating the real value of Accounts Receivable, it is often called a *valuation account*. The bad debts expense account has a debit balance of $110.32 and is classified as an *operating expense*.

The debit balance of the accounts receivable account, $5,515.77, showed the total amount due from charge customers. The credit balance of the allowance for bad debts account, $110.32, showed the amount to be subtracted from the accounts receivable account because of estimated uncollectible accounts. The difference between these two balances, $5,405.45, was the estimated real value of the accounts receivable on December 31, 1962.

M. F.
Work
For Quarter Ended

	ACCOUNT TITLES	ACCT. NO.	TRIAL BALANCE DEBIT	TRIAL BALANCE CREDIT	
1	Cash	11	2 1 3 0 63		1
2	Accounts Receivable	12	5 8 7 2 15		2
3	Allowance for Bad Debts	12.1		1 1 0 32	3
19	Bad Debts Expense	61			19
20	Delivery Expense	62	4 1 5 90		20
29	Supplies Expense	71			29
30			4 6 4 3 2 37	4 6 4 3 2 37	30
31	Net Income				31
32					32

Work sheet with

Until recent years valuation accounts were titled "Reserve for Bad Debts" and "Reserve for Depreciation." Today, however, the American Institute of Certified Public Accountants recommends the term *allowance* be used in preference to the term *reserve* in these account titles.

Adjustment of the allowance for bad debts account

Because new charge sales are made constantly, the amount of uncollectible accounts changes constantly. At the end of each fiscal period, Mr. Conway estimates his bad debts expense by taking ½% of the total net sales.

On March 31, 1963, the end of the quarterly fiscal period, Mr. Conway determined the total amount of net sales for January, February, and March. This total was $21,480. The estimated bad debts expense for the period was therefore ½% of this amount, or $107.40.

Bad debts on the work sheet

On March 31, 1963, Mr. Conway made an adjustment for bad debts expense in the Adjustments columns of his work sheet. In the illustration below, the break indicates the omission of account titles and amounts not needed in this discussion.

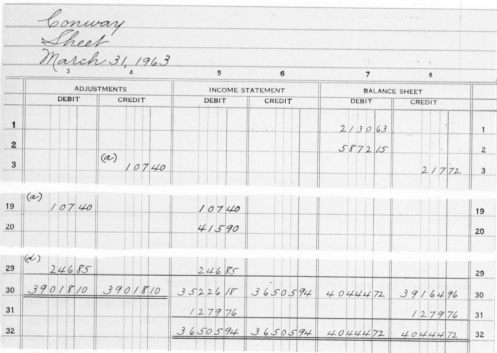

adjustment for bad debts

The estimated bad debts expense, $107.40, was entered as a credit to Allowance for Bad Debts to record the additional allowance for bad debts for this fiscal period. The same amount was entered as a debit to Bad Debts Expense to record the estimated bad debts expense for the period.

Bad debts expense on the income statement

When Mr. Conway prepared his income statement from the work sheet on March 31, he indicated the bad debts expense as shown below. As Bad Debts Expense is one of the expenses of operating the business, it is listed with the operating expenses.

M. F. Conway Income Statement For Quarter Ended March 31, 1963		
Gross Profit on Sales		5 2 3 2 10
Operating Expenses :		
Bad Debts Expense	1 0 7 40	
Delivery Expense	4 1 5 90	
Depreciation Expense	1 3 9 35	
FICA Taxes	1 2 6 88	
Federal Unemployment Taxes	1 4 00	
Insurance Expense	4 9 75	
Miscellaneous Expense	1 3 1 36	
Rent Expense	9 0 0 00	
Salary Expense	1 7 5 0 00	
State Unemployment Taxes	4 7 25	
Supplies Expense	2 4 6 85	
Total Operating Expenses		3 9 2 8 74
Net Income from Operations		1 3 0 3 36
Other Income :		
Gain on Fixed Assets	1 1 9 20	
Other Expense :		
Loss on Fixed Assets	1 4 2 80	
Net Subtraction		2 3 60
Net Income		1 2 7 9 76

Bad Debts Expense on the income statement

Allowance for bad debts on the balance sheet

When Mr. Conway prepared his balance sheet from the work sheet on March 31, he indicated (1) the total amount due from charge customers, (2) the decrease in value because of estimated uncollectible accounts, and (3) the estimated real value of account receivable as follows:

M. F. Conway
Balance Sheet
March 31, 1963

Assets			
Current Assets:			
Cash		2 1 3 0 63	
Accounts Receivable	5872.15		
Less Allowance for Bad Debts	217.72	5 6 54 43	
Merchandise Inventory		2 8 80 3 41	
Supplies		1 78 66	
Prepaid Insurance		1 2 5 00	
Total Current Assets			3 6 8 92 13
Fixed Assets:			
Equipment		3 7 54 00	
Less Allowance for Depr. of Equip.		1 1 42 50	
Total Fixed Assets			2 6 1 1 50
Total Assets			3 9 5 0 3 63

Allowance for Bad Debts on the balance sheet

The total amount due from charge customers, $5,872.15, was written on the line with Accounts Receivable. The estimated allowance for bad debts, $217.72, was placed immediately under the accounts receivable balance and was subtracted from it. The difference between these two amounts, $5,654.43, was the estimated real value of the accounts receivable. This amount was written in the first amount column so that it could be added with the other assets.

Adjusting entry for bad debts

Mr. Conway made the following adjusting entry in the combination journal from the Adjustments columns of his work sheet to record the estimated bad debts.

	CASH		CHK. NO.	DATE	NAME OF ACOUNT	POST. REF.	GENERAL		
	DEBIT	CREDIT					DEBIT	CREDIT	
26				31	Bad Debts Expense		107 40		26
27					Allowance for Bad Debts			107 40	27

PAGE 37   COMBINATION JOURNAL

Adjusting entry for estimated bad debts

When this entry was posted, the accounts receivable account, the allowance for bad debts account, and the bad debts expense account in the general ledger appeared as follows:

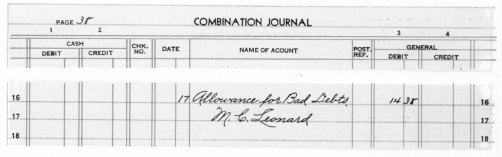

Accounts Receivable — ACCOUNT NO. 12

DATE	ITEMS	POST. REF.	DEBIT	DATE	ITEMS	POST. REF.	CREDIT
1963 Jan. 1	Balance	✓	5 5 1 5 77	1963 Jan. 31		29	6 2 2 8 18
31		29	3 2 6 0 66	Feb. 28		33	3 2 5 6 09
Feb. 28		33	4 9 2 7 26	Mar. 31		36	4 5 2 4 19
Mar. 31		36 5872.15	6 1 7 6 92 / 9 8 8 0 61				1 4 0 0 8 46

Allowance for Bad Debts — ACCOUNT NO. 12.1

DATE	ITEMS	POST. REF.	DEBIT	DATE	ITEMS	POST. REF.	CREDIT
				1962 Dec. 31		24	1 1 0 32
				1963 Mar. 31		37	1 0 7 40 2 1 7 72

Bad Debts Expense — ACCOUNT NO. 61

DATE	ITEMS	POST. REF.	DEBIT	DATE	ITEMS	POST. REF.	CREDIT
1963 Mar. 31		37	1 0 7 40				

The debit balance of the accounts receivable account, $5,872.15, showed the total amount of the accounts due from charge customers. The credit balance of the allowance for bad debts account, $217.72, showed the amount to be subtracted from the accounts receivable account because of estimated uncollectible accounts. The difference between these two balances, $5,654.43, was the estimated real value of the accounts receivable on March 31.

PAGE 35

COMBINATION JOURNAL

	CASH		CHK. NO.	DATE	NAME OF ACOUNT	POST. REF.	GENERAL		
	DEBIT	CREDIT					DEBIT	CREDIT	
	1	2					3	4	
16					17 Allowance for Bad Debts		14 35		16
17					M. C. Leonard				17
18									18

Entry to write off an uncollectible

384

Writing off uncollectible accounts

When it has been decided that a customer's account is uncollectible, the customer's account should be written off the books. To write off a customer's account, one account is debited and two accounts are credited. The allowance for bad debts account in the general ledger is debited. The customer's account in the accounts receivable ledger and the accounts receivable account in the general ledger are credited.

On April 17, Mr. Conway decided that the past-due account of M. C. Leonard, with debit balance of $14.38, was uncollectible. Mr. Conway therefore made the entry shown in the combination journal below to write off the account.

The allowance for bad debts account in the general ledger was debited for $14.38 by writing the title of the account, Allowance for Bad Debts, in the Name of Account column and the amount, $14.38, in the General Debit column. This debit was made because an uncollectible account amounting to $14.38 covered by the allowance account was being eliminated from the accounts receivable ledger. The allowance for bad debts account must therefore be reduced by the amount of the customer's account written off. The debit entry to the allowance for bad debts account indicated this subtraction.

The M. C. Leonard account in the accounts receivable ledger was credited by writing his name in the Name of Account column and the amount of the credit, $14.38, in the Accounts Receivable Credit column. When this entry is posted, the credit to his account will close the account. His account will then be written off.

The accounts receivable account in the general ledger will be credited for $14.38 when this amount is posted as a part of the total of the Accounts Receivable Credit column at the end of the month. Whenever a customer's account is written off, the accounts receivable summary account in the general ledger must be reduced by the amount of the customer's account written off.

			FOR MONTH OF *April* 1963					PAGE *35*	
5	6	7	8	9	10	11	12		
ACCOUNTS PAYABLE		DISCOUNT ON PURCHASES CREDIT	ACCOUNTS RECEIVABLE		DISCOUNT ON SALES DEBIT	PURCHASES DEBIT	SALES CREDIT		
DEBIT	CREDIT		DEBIT	CREDIT					
									16
				14 38					17
									18

account when an allowance account is used

385

Posting the journal entry

After the debit to Allowance for Bad Debts was posted, the allowance for bad debts account appeared as follows:

DATE	ITEMS	POST. REF.	DEBIT	DATE	ITEMS	POST. REF.	CREDIT
1963 Apr. 17		38	14 38	1962 Dec. 31		24	1 10 32
				1963 Mar. 31		37	1 07 40
							2 17 72

Allowance for Bad Debts ACCOUNT NO. 12.1

The corresponding credit to Accounts Receivable in the general ledger will be posted as a part of the column total at the end of the month.

When the credit to the customer's account in the accounts receivable ledger was posted, the account appeared as follows:

NAME M. C. Leonard
ADDRESS 504 Fifth Street, City

DATE	ITEMS	POST. REF.	DEBIT	CREDIT	DEBIT BALANCE
1962 Oct. 18		15	14 38		14 38
1963 Apr. 17	Written off	38		14 38	— —

As a result of posting this amount to the customer's account, that account has been reduced $14.38, the same amount that the accounts receivable account in the general ledger will be reduced when the total of the Accounts Receivable Credit column is posted.

Recording bad debts expense at the time a debt becomes worthless

Most businesses and accountants prefer to follow the previously described method of estimating and recording bad debts expense. Some small businesses with relatively few uncollectible accounts do, however, record this expense at the time a debt is known to be worthless. This is done by debiting the account Bad Debts Expense and crediting Accounts Receivable and the customer's account for the amount of the debt.

This is a simple and acceptable method. It is not generally preferred because (a) it fails to charge the expense to the period in which the debt was incurred and (b) it can cause the accounts receivable account to have its value overstated on the balance sheet.

Increasing your business vocabulary

What is the meaning of each of the following:

(a) bad debts   (b) bad debts expense   (c) allowance for bad debts

Chapter questions

1. What is the major reason why some businesses sell on credit?
2. Why are accounts receivable evaluated at the end of a fiscal period?
3. What three methods are used in estimating in advance what the bad debts expense of a business will be?
4. Why is the amount of estimated uncollectible accounts receivable credited to Allowance for Bad Debts rather than to Accounts Receivable?
5. Why is the allowance for bad debts account called a valuation account?
6. When are allowances for bad debts recorded?
7. In what section of the income statement on page 382 is the bad debts expense listed?
8. What entry was made in the combination journal on page 383 to record the estimated bad debts expense?
9. When is a customer's account written off the books?
10. In the combination journal on pages 384 and 385, what entry was made to write the customer's account off the books?
11. Why is the allowance for bad debts account debited when a customer's account is written off as uncollectible?
12. What simple method of recording bad debts expense is used principally by some small businesses with relatively few accounts receivable?

Cases for discussion

1. W. R. McBride and Son operate a garage. When their financial statements were compiled, no bad debts expense was included. How would this omission affect (a) the total value of the assets on the balance sheet and (b) the net income or the net loss on the income statement?
2. B. M. Morton, a retail merchant, credits Accounts Receivable for the amount of the estimated bad debts for each fiscal period. R. J. Pegolo, another retail merchant, credits Allowance for Bad Debts for the amount of the estimated bad debts. What are the advantages of Mr. Pegolo's method?

Drill for understanding

Drill 26-A. *Computing bad debts expense*

The bookkeeping records of three different furniture stores showed the following summary information for the fiscal period ending December 31:

Furniture Store	Total Net Sales	Total Charge Sales	Balance in Accounts Receivable Account
#1	$27,980.90	$ 9,811.90	$ 945.00
#2	36,777.43	12,530.50	7,864.50
#3	27,890.10	14,211.21	2,160.00

387

Instructions: Compute the bad debts expense on December 31 for each of these stores under the following conditions:

(a) Store #1 estimated its bad debts would amount to ¼% (.0025) of its total *net sales*.

(b) Store #2 used 2% of its total *charge sales* as its estimate of bad debts.

(c) Store #3 used 3% of the *balance* in its accounts receivable account as its estimate of bad debts.

Application problems

Problem 26-1. *Recording transactions with bad debts expense*

Fred Spooner, proprietor of Spooner's Store, records his transactions in a combination journal. In his general ledger he maintains accounts with Bad Debts Expense and Allowance for Bad Debts. At the beginning of the current year the credit balance of the allowance for bad debts account was $126.36.

In this exercise you are given transactions taken from those completed by Spooner's Store during the year. The selected transactions cover only uncollectible accounts, bad debts expense, and allowance for bad debts.

Instructions: Record in a combination journal all of the necessary entries for the following transactions:

Feb. 3. Decided that the past-due account of Carl Smith, $39.80, was uncollectible. Wrote off his account as a bad debt.

Mar. 31. (End of first quarterly fiscal period.) Increased the allowance for bad debts by making the necessary adjusting entry. The estimated bad debts expense for each quarterly fiscal period was 1½% of the total charge sales. The charge sales for the quarterly fiscal period ended March 31 were $8,880.40.

May 15. Henry Johnson, a charge customer, became insolvent. Wrote off his account of $35.00 as a bad debt.

June 30. The charge sales for the second quarterly fiscal period ended June 30 were $5,326.18. Increased the allowance for bad debts 1½% of that amount.

Aug. 11. Decided that the past-due account of R. H. Graham, $104.25, was uncollectible. Wrote off his account as a bad debt.

Sept. 30. The charge sales for the third quarterly fiscal period ended September 30 were $7,196.66. Increased the allowance for bad debts 1½% of that amount.

Dec. 31. Decided that the past-due accounts of the following charge customers were uncollectible:

> L. D. Smith, $50.66
>
> Estelle Edwards, $34.50
>
> E. H. Hoffman, $45.00

Wrote them off as bad debts in one combined entry, debiting Allowance for Bad Debts for the total.

Dec. 31. The charge sales for the fourth quarterly fiscal period ended December 31 were $6,422.30. Increased the allowance for bad debts 1½% of that amount.

Problem 26-2. Work at the end of the fiscal period

If you are not using the workbook correlating with this textbook, complete Exercise 26-B in the Appendix instead of this problem.

The ledger accounts of Decker Lumber Co., B. C. Decker proprietor, are given in the workbook.

Instructions: 1. Foot the ledger accounts. Prove cash. The cash on hand and in the bank on December 31 is $7,087.22.

2. Prepare an eight-column work sheet for the annual fiscal period ended December 31 of the current year, using the following additional data as of December 31:

Additional allowance for bad debts, ½% of net sales
Merchandise inventory, $15,478.90
Supplies inventory, $195.88
Prepaid insurance, $240.00
Annual rate of estimated depreciation, 5%

3. Prepare an income statement and a balance sheet.
4. Record the adjusting entries and the closing entries.
5. Post the adjusting entries and the closing entries.
6. Rule the accounts that balance. Balance each remaining account in the general ledger that has both debits and credits.
7. Prepare a post-closing trial balance.

Optional problems

★Supplementary Problem 26-S. Recording transactions with bad debts expense

R. L. Fuller, a candy manufacturer, records his transactions in a combination journal. In his general ledger he maintains accounts with Bad Debts Expense and Allowance for Bad Debts. At the beginning of the current year the balance of the allowance for bad debts account was $138.65.

In this exercise you are given transactions taken from those completed by Mr. Fuller during the year. The selected transactions in this exercise cover only uncollectible accounts, bad debts expense, and allowance for bad debts.

Instructions: 1. Record in a combination journal all of the necessary entries for the following transactions:

Feb. 18. Decided that the past-due account of Henry Jefferson, $45.25, was uncollectible. Wrote off his account as a bad debt.

Mar. 31. (End of first quarterly fiscal period.) Increased the allowance for bad debts by making the necessary adjusting entry. The estimated bad debts expense for each quarterly fiscal period was ½% (.005) of the total net sales. The net sales for the quarterly fiscal period ended March 31 were $17,472.10.

Apr. 9. C. B. Smith, a charge customer, became insolvent. Wrote off his account of $91.60 as a bad debt.

June 30. The net sales for the second quarterly fiscal period ended June 30 were $15,094.15. Increased the allowance for bad debts ½% (.005) of that amount.

July 23. Decided that the past-due account of B. F. Jackson, $77.50, was uncollectible. Wrote off his account as a bad debt.

Sept. 30. The net sales for the third quarterly fiscal period ended September 30 were $17,908.05. Increased the allowance for bad debts ½% (.005) of that amount.

Dec. 31. Decided that the past-due accounts of the following charge customers were uncollectible:

> C. D. Lambert, $37.50
>
> Elmer Madden, $50.00
>
> S. T. Ruark, $49.85

Wrote them off as bad debts in one combined entry, debiting Allowance for Bad Debts for the total.

Dec. 31. The net sales for the fourth quarterly fiscal period ended December 31 were $16,620.30. Increased the allowance for bad debts ½% (.005) of that amount.

Instructions: 2. Foot, prove, and record the totals in the combination journal.

Bonus Problem 26-B. *Recording the collection of accounts previously written off*

Introductory remarks. Occasionally a customer's account that has been written off as a bad debt is later collected. When this occurs, the customer's account is first reinstated by an entry debiting Accounts Receivable and the customer's account and crediting Allowance for Bad Debts. Then a second entry debiting Cash and crediting Accounts Receivable and the customer's account is made. These two entries provide a complete record of the transaction.

When the old debt is not being paid in full and there is no indication that it will be paid in full, only the actual amount being paid should be used in each of the above transactions.

Instructions: 1. During 1962 Henry Wheeling completed the following transactions in connection with bad debts. Record these transactions in a combination journal.

Mar. 7. Wrote off account of Paul Kinney, $80, as uncollectible.

May 23. Received 30% of the $220 balance owed by Henry Bunker, bankrupt, and wrote off the remainder as uncollectible.

June 6. Received $50 from Arthur King in full payment of his account which was written off on February 8, 1961, as uncollectible.

June 20. Wrote off account of Stephen Frost, $105, as uncollectible.

Sept. 26. Received $35 from the receiver in bankruptcy for Will Larson in final payment of his account which had totaled $70 when it was written off on March 29, 1961.

Dec. 12. Received $40 from Paul Kinney along with a written promise to pay the balance of his account written off on March 7, 1962.

Instructions: 2. Foot, prove, and record the totals in the combination journal.

Chapter 27

The use of the cash register

Need for recording transactions quickly

A retail store often makes hundreds of sales in a single day. The records of these sales must be accurate and complete in order to provide the manager with the information that he needs. A popular business machine that is used to record sales transactions is the *cash register*. Some form of cash register is commonly used wherever the customer deals directly with the cashier.

Use of the cash register

The cash register provides a convenient place for sorting and keeping the money used in the daily transactions. It also makes an immediate record of each transaction. A cash register of the type that is commonly used in retail stores is shown below.

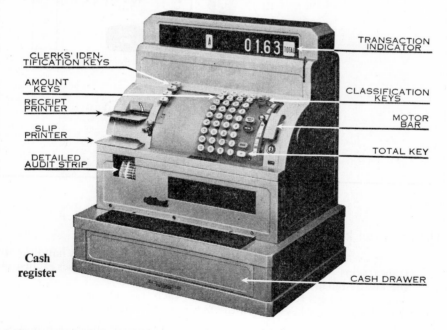

There are many different types of cash registers. The one shown above records each transaction on a paper tape, supplies a receipt for the customer, and provides a convenient, organized money drawer.

Operating the cash register

The clerk operates the machine by pressing several of the keys and the motor bar. At the time the motor bar is pressed, the transaction is recorded on a paper tape in the machine. The transaction indicator in the illustration on page 391 shows that $1.63 was received for a cash sale. As this amount is recorded in full view of the customer, there is little likelihood that the clerk would intentionally record the wrong amount.

A diagram of the key arrangement of the register is shown below.

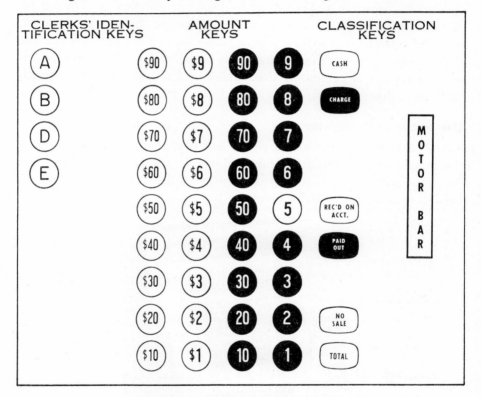

Key arrangement on a cash register

The groups of keys are as follows:

(1) The keys A, B, D, and E are used to identify the salesclerks handling the transactions. Each clerk is assigned one of these letters and uses exclusively the key assigned to him.
(2) The amount keys record the amount of each transaction.
(3) The classification keys record the nature of each transaction.

Cash registers are available with various kinds of classification keys. For example, if a retail store collects sales taxes, its register will also have a Sales Tax key to record the sales tax on each sale.

Recording a cash sale

On July 2, Clerk A of the Style Shop sold merchandise for $1.63 in cash. To record this transaction on the cash register, Clerk A pressed the A key, the $1 key, the 60¢ key, the 3¢ key, the Cash key, and finally the motor bar. When the motor bar was operated, the complete transaction was shown in the transaction indicator at the top of the register and it was printed on a paper tape in the machine. At the same time the cash drawer came open so that the amount received could be placed in it.

$\mathcal{S}tyle\ \mathcal{S}hop$

THANK YOU

JUL 2

–001 $ 01.63CaA

Receipt for a cash sale

When several items are sold to a customer, the amount of each item is recorded and the register operates like an adding machine to total the various items of the sale. Some types of cash registers will also compute the amount of change due.

When the motor bar was operated, the receipt shown at the left was automatically printed and was pushed out of the machine at the point marked "Receipt Printer." This receipt was given to the customer and was further proof that the transaction was properly recorded.

Recording a charge sale

On July 2, Clerk B of the Style Shop sold merchandise for $9.17 to Mrs. J. B. Arthur on account. He prepared the sales slip illustrated at the right. By using carbon paper, two copies were made. Each copy showed: the date; the name and the address of the customer; the clerk's initial or number; a description of the items sold, including the price of each item; and the total amount of the sale. He then inserted both copies of the sales slip in the slip printer of the cash register and recorded the charge sale on the machine.

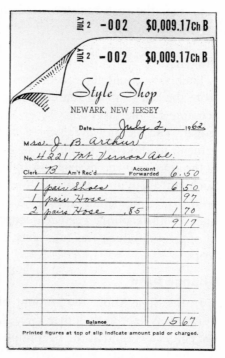

Sales slip in duplicate for a charge sale

393

To record the transaction on the cash register, Clerk B pressed the B key, the $9 key, the 10¢ key, the 7¢ key, the Charge key, and finally the motor bar. The cash register made a permanent record of the charge sale. It also printed the transaction number, the amount, and the clerk's letter, B, on both copies of the sales slip.

Analyzing the sales slip for a charge sale

The cash register did not record the name of the customer or a description of the items sold. The original copy of the sales slip was kept to show this information. The duplicate copy of the sales slip was given to Mrs. Arthur.

In order that the amount owed by the customer, Mrs. Arthur, might be readily observed, the balance owed was carried forward to each new sales slip and was added to the amount of the sale. Mrs. Arthur's balance was $6.50; the amount of the sale was $9.17; the new balance to be carried forward to the next sales slip was, therefore, $15.67.

Using sales slips as the accounts receivable ledger

In the Style Shop sales slips were filed alphabetically in a small file kept near the cash register. This file served the purpose of an accounts receivable ledger. The Style Shop file for sales slips is illustrated at the right.

Each sale could have been posted from the sales slip to the customer's account in the accounts receivable ledger. The file, however, was a convenient method of keeping a record of the amount owed by each customer. Such an accounts receivable file is used by some small businesses in place of an accounts receivable ledger in order to reduce the bookkeeping work.

Accounts receivable file

Change fund

In the Style Shop, the amount of the petty cash fund was $100. This money was kept in the office safe. A definite amount, $20, was taken from the petty cash fund at the beginning of each day and was placed in the cash register for use in making change. At the end of the day this amount, $20, was taken out of the cash register and returned to the petty cash fund in the office safe.

Recording cash payments

On July 2, Clerk B gave Mrs. A. L. James 50 cents, a cash refund for merchandise returned. He prepared a receipt that Mrs. James signed. The receipt was placed in the slip printer of the cash register. Clerk B then pressed the B key, the 50¢ key, the Paid Out key, and finally the motor bar. The receipt for this "paid out" transaction is illustrated at the right. Mrs. James's signature on the receipt was evidence that she received payment. This receipt was placed in the cash drawer.

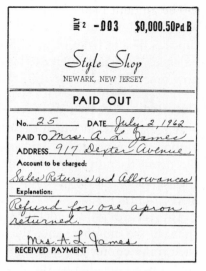

Receipt for cash paid out

Recording "no sale" transactions

A customer gave Clerk B a dollar bill and asked for change to make a pay telephone call. To open the cash drawer, Clerk B pressed the B key, the No Sale key, and the motor bar.

Recording cash received on account

When cash is received from a customer on account, the amount received must be entered in the cash register. A record must also be made on the customer's sales slip in the file cabinet to show the amount received and the remaining balance.

On July 2, Clerk D received $5 from Mrs. A. M. Thorne to apply on her account. Clerk D recorded this cash receipt on a sales slip. He also recorded this transaction in the cash register in the same way as a charge sale, except that the Received on Account key was pressed instead of the Charge key. This sales slip after it was imprinted on the cash register is shown at the left.

To indicate that cash was received, the clerk wrote "Received on Account" in the explanation column of the sales slip. The amount received, $5, was deducted from the old balance, $17.65, and the remaining balance, $12.65, was recorded.

Sales slip for cash received on account

395

The amount of the cash received was recorded in the cash register and was printed on both copies of the sales slip. The original copy of the sales slip was filed in front of the other sales slips of Mrs. Thorne. The present balance, $12.65, written at the bottom of this slip indicated at a glance how much Mrs. Thorne still owed the Style Shop.

Detailed audit strip

A paper tape on which each transaction entered in the cash register is automatically printed is known as the *detailed audit strip*. A section of the detailed audit strip showing the first five transactions completed by the clerks in the Style Shop is illustrated at the right.

The record on the detailed audit strip showed the number and the amount of each transaction. The nature of each transaction was indicated by the symbols *Ca* for a cash sale, *Ch* for a charge sale, *Pd* for an amount paid out, *NS* for no sale, and *Rc* for an amount received on account. The letters A, B, and D indicated the clerk who completed each transaction.

-005	$0,005.00Rc D
-004	$0,000.00NS B
-003	$0,000.50Pd B
-002	$0,009.17Ch B
-001	$0,001.63Ca A

Section of detailed audit
strip showing individual
transactions

Obtaining cash register totals

The cash register accumulated the total for each of the following types of transactions: (1) cash sales, (2) charge sales, (3) received on accounts, and (4) paid outs. At the end of each day the Total key was pressed and the totals for these groups of transactions were printed on the detailed audit strip. When these totals were printed, the cash register was automatically cleared so that none of the figures would be added to the transactions for the following day.

The section of the detailed audit strip of the Style Shop showing the totals at the end of the day, July 2, is shown at the left. The first column of numbers is the operation number, which is imprinted on the strip for each operation of the cash register. The second column shows the totals and the symbols. These symbols have the following meanings:

-086	$0,194.35GT
-085	$0,005.35Pd
-084	$0,030.00Rc
-083	$0,030.70Ch
-082	$0,164.35Ca

Section of the detailed audit
strip showing totals

GT, grand total, $194.35
Pd, paid out, $5.35
Rc, received on account, $30
Ch, charge sales, $30.70
Ca, cash sales, $164.35

Proving cash with the cash register totals

After the cash register was cleared and the total of each type of transaction was printed on the detailed audit strip, the strip was removed from the machine. The change fund of $20 was taken out of the cash register and was returned to the petty cash fund in the office safe. The money remaining in the cash drawer was then counted and entered on a daily balance slip similar to the one shown at the right. The total of each denomination of coin, the total paper money, and the total checks were listed in the spaces provided. The sum of all these items, $189, was the total cash in the drawer. To this amount was added the cash paid out, $5.35. The total, $194.35, was then the total cash received. The

DAILY BALANCE SLIP		
Denominations	Dollars	Cts.
Pennies		05
Nickels	1	55
Dimes	4	40
Quarters	2	50
Halves·	1	50
Silver Dollars		—
Paper Money	164	00
Checks	15	00
Total Cash in Drawer	189	00
Add Cash Paid Out	5	35
Total Cash Received	194	35
Total Cash Received on Detailed Audit Strip	194	35
Cash Short		
Cash Over		
No. of Paid-Out Slips	7	
No. of Charge Sales Slips	3	
No. of Rc. on A/c Slips	4	
Name *L. H. Moore* Date 7/2/62		

Cash proof on daily balance slip

total cash received as shown by the detailed audit strip was then entered on the daily balance slip. As the two amounts were the same, $194.35, the record of all the transactions in the cash register was considered to be correct.

DAILY BALANCE SLIP		
Denominations	Dollars	Cts.
Pennies		35
Nickels	1	15
Dimes	6	80
Quarters	4	50
Halves	12	00
Silver Dollars		—
Paper Money	126	00
Checks	45	00
Total Cash in Drawer	195	80
Add Cash Paid Out	3	55
Total Cash Received	199	35
Total Cash Received on Detailed Audit Strip	198	85
Cash Short		
Cash Over		50
No. of Paid-Out Slips	4	
No. of Charge Sales Slips	7	
No. of Rc. on A/c Slips	3	
Name *L. H. Moore* Date 7/3/62		

Cash proof with cash over

Cash short and over

If the sum of the cash on hand at the end of the day plus the cash paid out during the day is less than the grand total recorded by the cash register, the cash is said to be *short*. If the sum of the cash on hand at the end of the day plus the cash paid out during the day is greater than the grand total recorded by the cash register, the cash is said to be *over*.

Whether the cash is short or over, the error is caused by mistakes in recording transactions on the cash register or by mistakes in making change. If the error is large, the clerks should examine the detailed audit strip and try to recall the transaction that was recorded improperly or the transaction where a mistake was made in making change. If the error is small, usually no attempt is made to find the reason for it.

A record should be made of any error in the cash proof. If the cash is short, the amount of the shortage is entered on the daily balance slip on the line "Cash Short." If the cash is over, the amount of the overage is entered on the daily balance slip on the line "Cash Over" in the manner illustrated on page 397.

Cash short and over voucher

If the cash is short, the amount of the "cash short" is made up from the petty cash fund. A cash short and over voucher is filled out and is placed with the petty cash fund as a receipt for the amount taken out.

If there is too much cash on hand, the "cash over" is taken from the register and is placed with the petty cash. A cash short and over voucher is filled out and is placed with the petty cash as a receipt for the amount placed in the fund.

Cash short and over voucher for an overage

Paid-out slips and the petty cash fund

In the Style Shop, all cash receipts were deposited in the bank. All large payments were made by check. Small cash payments, however, were made from the cash register. A paid-out slip was prepared for each of these transactions, and the amount was recorded by pressing the "Paid Out" key of the cash register. The paid-out slips were kept in the cash register.

At the end of the day, these paid-out slips were placed with the petty cash fund in the office safe, and an amount of cash equal to the total of the paid-out slips was taken from the fund. The cash taken from the petty cash fund was combined with the cash in the cash register, and the sum of these two amounts was proved with the grand total figure on the detailed audit strip (GT). This procedure made it possible to deposit in the bank an amount equal to the total cash receipts for the day.

The petty cash fund, then, was used for three purposes:

(1) To supply the cash register with an adequate amount of change at the beginning of the day.

(2) To adjust the amount of cash short or over each day.

(3) To replace the paid-out slips in the cash register with money.

Replenishing the petty cash fund

When the petty cash fund was running low, the paid-out receipts and the cash short or over vouchers kept with the fund were grouped together according to their nature. The amount of each group of payments was determined.

On July 31, the manager of the Style Shop grouped together the paid-out receipts and found that the various groups of payments were:

Sales Returns and Allowances....................		$12.80
Salary Expense................................		11.50
Miscellaneous Expense........................		17.84
Cash Short...........................	$2.76	
Less Cash Over......................	2.30	
Net Cash Short...............................		.46
Total..		$42.60

As the total of all of the paid-out receipts plus the net cash shortage for the month was $42.60, a check was drawn for that amount. The check was cashed and the money was placed in the petty cash fund. The fund then had $100, the amount for which it was charged on the books. The entry to record this transaction is shown below. All the debits are recorded in the General Debit column, as special columns are not provided for any of these accounts.

	CASH DEBIT	CASH CREDIT	CHK. NO.	DATE	NAME OF ACCOUNT	POST. REF.	GENERAL DEBIT	GENERAL CREDIT	
30		42 60	121	31	Sales Returns and Allowances		12 80		30
31					Salary Expense		11 50		31
32					Cash Short & Over		46		32
33					Miscellaneous Expense		17 84		33
34									34
35									35
36									36
37									37

PAGE 16   COMBINATION JOURNAL

Left-hand page of combination journal showing entry to replenish petty cash

Each time the petty cash fund is replenished, the account Cash Short and Over is debited if cash short exceeds cash over. If cash over exceeds cash short, Cash Short and Over is credited. In the entry recorded on Line 32 of the combination journal on page 399, the total cash short for the period was larger than the total cash over.

If at the end of the fiscal period the cash short and over account in the ledger has a debit balance, it is listed on the income statement in the section with the heading "Other Expenses." If the cash short and over account in the ledger has a credit balance, it is listed on the income statement in the section with the heading "Other Income."

Sales returns and allowances for charge sales

When credit is given to a customer because merchandise is defective or is returned, a sales slip similar to the one at the left is made out in duplicate. The carbon copy is given to the customer. The original copy is used as the basis for an entry in the combination journal debiting Sales Returns and Allowances and crediting Accounts Receivable. This entry is illustrated on Lines 4 and 5 of the combination journal on pages 402 and 403.

The amount owed by the customer before the credit was given and the balance owed after the credit was given are entered on the sales slip. The slip is filed in the accounts

Sales slip for a sales return or allowance

receivable file, illustrated on page 394. It is placed in front of Mr. Wade's other sales slips and shows the new balance due from L. M. Wade.

Recording purchases on account

When the merchandise represented by a purchase invoice was received, the merchandise was examined as to quality and was checked against the purchase invoice as to quantity. All calculations on the invoice were verified. If the purchase invoice was in agreement with the purchase order and the goods received, the purchase invoice was entered in the combination journal. The entry on Line 6 on pages 402 and 403 was an entry of this kind.

Purchases returns and allowances

If goods received were not satisfactory, omissions and errors were noted and reported to the seller. When a credit memorandum was received for merchandise returned or for an allowance granted, the transaction was recorded in the combination journal. An entry of this kind is illustrated on Lines 12 and 13 of the combination journal on pages 402 and 403.

After the credit memorandum was used as the basis for the entry in the combination journal, it was filed with the invoice to which it applied so that only the balance due the creditor would be paid.

Payment of purchases invoices

The Style Shop did not use an accounts payable ledger. After each invoice was verified, it was placed in a file maintained for all unpaid purchases invoices. The purchases invoices were placed in the file in the order in which they were to be paid. In determining the date of payment, it was assumed that each invoice would be paid within the discount period. The file of unpaid invoices was examined each day to see if any invoices should be paid on that day.

All payments were made by check. An entry for each check stub was made in the combination journal. The entry of July 4 on Line 11 of the combination journal on pages 402 and 403 was an entry of this kind.

Paid invoices file

A folder for each creditor was maintained in the *paid invoices file*. As each purchase invoice was paid, it was filed in the folder labeled with the name of the firm from whom the purchase had been made. The folders were arranged in the file in alphabetic order.

The use of an unpaid invoices file and a paid invoices file made it unnecessary to maintain an accounts payable ledger. The unpaid invoices file showed at all times the total accounts payable. The paid invoices file was a record of completed purchases transactions.

The paid invoices file was consulted whenever the management desired information concerning past purchases. It was a convenient source of information on quantities and types of merchandise bought in the past from each creditor. From the contents of each folder it was possible to determine quickly any information desired with reference to the transactions completed with any creditor.

Recording transactions from the detailed audit strip

The Style Shop used a combination journal as its book of original entry. The transactions of July 2 to 5 as they are recorded in this combination journal are illustrated on the two following pages.

	CASH		CHK. NO.	DATE	NAME OF ACCOUNT	POST. REF.	GENERAL		
	DEBIT	CREDIT					DEBIT	CREDIT	
1	164 35			1962 July 2	Sales for cash				1
2				2	Sales on account				2
3	30 00			2	Received on account				3
4				3	Sales Returns & Allow.		1 69		4
5					L M Wade				5
6				3	Lincoln Mfg. Co.				6
7	152 30			3	Sales for cash				7
8				3	Sales on account				8
9	27 80			3	Received on account				9
10		150 00	108	3	Rent Expense		150		10
11		246 57	109	5	Jameson Bros.				11
12				5	Lincoln Mfg. Co.				12
13					Purchases Ret. & Allow.			10 00	13
14									14
15									15
16									16
17									17
18									18
19									19

Combination journal

Analyzing the combination journal of the Style Shop

Lines 1, 2, and 3. These three entries recorded the totals section of the detailed audit strip illustrated on page 396.

Line 1. Cash was debited and Sales was credited for the total of the cash sales (Ca), $164.35. The words "Sales for cash" were written in the Name of Account column to distinguish between this entry and the entry for sales on account given on the following line.

Line 2. Accounts Receivable was debited and Sales was credited for the total of the charge sales (Ch), $30.70. Since the sales slip file was used as the accounts receivable ledger, the amounts entered in the Accounts Receivable Debit column were not posted to customers' accounts. For this reason the customers' names were not given in the Name of Account column. The words "Sales on account" were written to indicate the nature of the transaction.

FOR MONTH OF *July* 19 62   PAGE 16

| | ACCOUNTS PAYABLE | | DISCOUNT ON PURCHASES CREDIT | ACCOUNTS RECEIVABLE | | PURCHASES DEBIT | SALES CREDIT | |
	DEBIT	CREDIT		DEBIT	CREDIT			
1							164 35	1
2				30 70			30 70	2
3					30 00			3
4								4
5					1 69			5
6		295 65				295 65		6
7							152 30	7
8				35 40			35 40	8
9					27 80			9
10								10
11	251 60		5 03					11
12	10 00							12
13								13
14								14
15								15
16								16
17								17
18								18
19								19

of the Style Shop

Line 3. Cash was debited and Accounts Receivable was credited for the total of the cash received on account (Rc), $30. Since the sales slip file was used as the accounts receivable ledger, the customers' names were not given in the Name of Account column. The words "Received on account" were written to indicate the nature of the transaction.

Similar entries were made from the totals section of the detailed audit strip at the end of each day. Note the entries on Lines 7-9.

Lines 4 and 5. To record the debit resulting from the return by L. M. Wade, the account title, Sales Returns and Allowances, was written in the Name of Account column and the amount, $1.69, was entered in the General Debit column. To record the credit, the name of the customer, L. M. Wade, was written in the Name of Account column in the indented position. The amount of the credit was entered in the Accounts Receivable Credit column.

403

The name of the customer was not required for posting because the file of sales slips was used instead of the accounts receivable ledger. The customer's name was written in the Name of Account column, however, so that reference could be made to the proper sales slip if information about the transaction was desired.

Line 6. The purchase on account was recorded in the Purchases Debit column and the Accounts Payable Credit column. The file of unpaid invoices was used instead of the accounts payable ledger; nevertheless the name of the creditor was written in the Name of Account column so that further information could be obtained from the invoice if it was desired.

Lines 12 and 13. To record the debit resulting from the allowance for defective merchandise, the name of the creditor, Lincoln Manufacturing Co., was written in the Name of Account column and the amount, $10, was written in the Accounts Payable Debit column. To record the credit, the account title, Purchases Returns and Allowances, was written in the Name of Account column in the indented position. The amount of the credit was entered in the General Credit column.

The name of the creditor was not required for posting because the file of unpaid invoices was used instead of the accounts payable ledger; nevertheless the name of the creditor was written in the Name of Account column so that further information, if desired, could be obtained from the credit memorandum attached to the invoice.

Chapter questions

1. What is the purpose of a cash register?
2. Why is a file for sales slips sometimes used in place of an accounts receivable ledger?
3. What is the meaning of each of the following symbols on the detailed audit strip on page 396: Ca, Ch, NS, Pd, and Rc?
4. How are the totals obtained for all the transactions entered on the cash register during the day?
5. How is the cash on hand proved each day?
6. In the Style Shop, what records were made to record (a) a cash shortage and (b) a cash overage?
7. How is a sales return for a charge sale recorded?
8. What three entries were made in the combination journal on pages 402 and 403 at the end of each business day from the totals on the detailed audit strip?
9. How is an allowance on a charge purchase recorded?
10. What system did the Style Shop use instead of an accounts payable ledger?

Cases for discussion

1. R. A. Hannon, a retail clothier, employs four salesclerks, who use a cash register that has the key arrangement shown on page 392. Describe how each of the following transactions would be recorded:

    (a) Clerk A sold merchandise for $4.50 in cash.
    (b) Clerk E received $12.75 to apply on account.
    (c) Clerk D paid out $2.50 for merchandise that was returned.
    (d) Clerk B gave a customer change for a dollar.
    (e) Clerk E sold merchandise for $13.98 on account.

2. A. R. Barber, a retail druggist, makes purchases on account in small quantities from a number of wholesalers. He maintains an account for each of his creditors in an accounts payable ledger. Joseph Pine, another druggist, has the same type of transactions as Mr. Barber. Mr. Pine does not maintain an accounts payable ledger; instead he keeps a file of all unpaid invoices. What are the advantages of each of these methods?

Application problems

Problem 27-1. Proving cash

If you are not using the workbook correlating with this textbook, complete Exercise 27-A in the Appendix instead of this problem.

Instructions: 1. Fill in the daily balance slip given in the workbook and prove cash. The count of cash in the cash register, the detailed audit strip totals, and the cash register papers for February 20 are also given in the workbook.

2. Fill in the cash short and over voucher in the workbook for the cash shortage for the day.

Problem 27-2. Replenishing petty cash

If you are not using the workbook correlating with this textbook, complete Exercise 27-B in the Appendix instead of this problem.

On September 30 of the current year, the end of a monthly fiscal period, the petty cash fund of the Johnson Grocery Store contained the petty cash paid-out receipts and the cash short and over vouchers given in the workbook.

Instructions: 1. Detach the cash short and over vouchers and the petty cash paid-out receipts and separate them along the perforated lines.

2. Sort the cash short and over vouchers and the petty cash paid-out receipts into the following groups:

    (a) Cash short.   (d) Miscellaneous expense.
    (b) Cash over.   (e) Sales returns and allowances.
    (c) Delivery expense.   (f) Supplies.

3. Find the net amount by which the cash is short or over.
4. Find the total amount in each group of petty cash paid-out receipts.
5. Record the entry to replenish the petty cash fund (Check No. 328).

Problem 27-3. Recording transactions from business papers

If you are not using the workbook correlating with this textbook, complete Exercise 27-C in the Appendix instead of this problem.

A. J. Booth, who operates an electrical appliance store, records his transactions in a combination journal like the one on pages 402 and 403. On June 27 of the current year, he finds that the page is filled.

Instructions: 1. Forward the following column totals on June 27 to a new page of Mr. Booth's combination journal:

Cash Debit, $3,138.72

Cash Credit, $2,364.53

General Debit, $826.00

General Credit, $24.85

Accounts Payable Debit, $5,059.12

Accounts Payable Credit, $4,317.28

Discount on Purchases Credit, $53.27

Accounts Receivable Debit, $260.75

Accounts Receivable Credit, $253.10

Purchases Debit, $4,553.85

Sales Credit, $6,825.41

Instructions: 2. Record in the combination journal the following transactions completed by Mr. Booth on June 27 to 30. The business papers referred to are numbered and given in consecutive order in the workbook.

June 27. (Business Paper 1.) Issued Check No. 406 in payment of the telephone bill.

27. (Business Paper 2.) Received a credit memorandum from King Bros. for returned merchandise.

27. (Business Paper 3.) Recorded the cash register totals for the day as shown on the detailed audit strip.

28. (Business Paper 4.) Recorded the cash register totals for the day as shown on the detailed audit strip.

30. (Business Paper 5.) Purchased merchandise on account from Osgood Mfg. Co.

30. Issued Check No. 407 for $334.18 in payment of the semimonthly payroll of $375.00 less a deduction of $29.10 for employees income taxes payable and a deduction of $11.72 for FICA taxes payable.

30. Recorded the employer's liability of $11.72 for FICA taxes, $10.13 for state unemployment taxes, and $3.00 for federal unemployment taxes.

30. (Business Paper 6.) Issued Check No. 408 in payment of Emery & Sons' invoice of June 21 less discount. This invoice was previously recorded as a debit to Purchases and a credit to Accounts Payable.

30. (Business Paper 7.) Issued Check No. 409 for $48.13 to replenish the petty cash fund.

30. (Business Paper 8.) Recorded the cash register totals for the day as shown on the detailed audit strip.

Instructions: 3. Foot, prove, and rule the combination journal.

Chapter 28

Sales taxes and other sales and purchases transactions

Collection of sales taxes

A tax levied on sales by a state or a city government is called a *sales tax*. Most sales taxes are on retail sales. In those states and cities that have a sales tax, the law usually provides that the seller shall collect from the retail customer a certain percentage of the total sale as a tax. At regular intervals, the seller must then pay to the state or the city the amount of the sales taxes collected. The percentage of the tax, the kinds of goods taxed, and the procedure of payment to the government vary considerably from state to state and from city to city.

The effect of sales tax transactions on accounts

A merchant who conducts his business in a state or a city where a 2% sales tax is in effect must collect an additional 2% on each sale made. For example, if on October 1 he sells merchandise worth $100 for cash, he must add a 2% sales tax to the sales price and charge his customer a total of $102. The effect of this cash transaction is shown in the following T accounts:

GENERAL LEDGER

Cash	Sales	Sales Taxes Payable
Oct. 1 102	Oct. 1 100	Oct. 1 2

If a sale similar to the above cash sale was made on account to A. L. Dwyer, the following accounts would have been affected as shown:

GENERAL LEDGER

Accounts Receivable	Sales	Sales Taxes Payable
Oct. 1 102	Oct. 1 100	Oct. 1 2

ACCOUNTS RECEIVABLE LEDGER

A. L. Dwyer
Oct. 1 102

407

Note that the sales price plus the sales tax is debited in one amount, $102, to both the accounts receivable account in the general ledger and the customer's account in the subsidiary ledger. Sales is credited for the selling price of the merchandise, $100, and the liability account Sales Taxes Payable is credited for the amount of the sales tax, $2.

When a customer pays his account in full, Cash is debited and both Accounts Receivable in the general ledger and the customer's account in the subsidiary ledger are credited for the total amount.

The seller makes payments of the sales taxes collected from customers to the proper tax agency at stated times. He records the payment as a debit to Sales Taxes Payable and as a credit to Cash.

Handling sales taxes on sales returns and allowances

When a customer is granted credit for a sales return or a sales allowance, he is also entitled to a credit for the sales tax originally charged to his account. For example, on October 5 A. L. Dwyer returns $50 worth of the merchandise he purchased on October 1. The effect of this transaction is shown in the following T accounts:

GENERAL LEDGER

Accounts Receivable		Sales Ret. and Allow.		Sales Taxes Payable	
Oct. 1 102	Oct. 5 51	Oct. 5 50		Oct. 5 1	Oct. 1 2

ACCOUNTS RECEIVABLE LEDGER

A. L. Dwyer	
Oct. 1 102	Oct. 5 51

Since Mr. Dwyer was charged a 2% sales tax on the $50 worth of merchandise he is now returning, he is entitled to a total credit of $51: $50 for the merchandise and $1 for the sales tax. Sales Returns and Allowances is a minus sales account. The seller, therefore, reduces his total sales for the period by debiting Sales Returns and Allowances for $50. He also reduces his liability Sales Taxes Payable by debiting this account for $1.

Recording sales taxes in the columnar sales journal

Many businesses provide a special column in the sales journal headed Sales Taxes Payable Credit in which to record sales taxes. A special column headed Transportation on Sales Credit in which to record delivery charges or mailing charges that the seller prepays may also be included.

408

A portion of the columnar sales journal used during the month of October by Wayside Furniture is shown below.

SALES JOURNAL   PAGE *10*

	DATE	SALE NO.	ACCOUNT DEBITED	POST. REF.	ACCOUNTS RECEIVABLE DEBIT	SALES CREDIT	SALES TAXES PAYABLE CREDIT	
	1962							
1	Oct. 1	321	G. L. Dwyer	✓	102 00	100 00	2 00	1
2	1	322	Arthur R. Jones	✓	331 50	325 00	6 50	2
3	2	323	Harbor View Motel	✓	496 54	486 80	9 74	3
4	2	324	D. L. Logan	✓	89 25	87 50	1 75	4
5	2	325	E. E. Carson	✓	67 93	66 60	1 33	5
27	29	371	Betsy Morton	✓	693 60	680 00	13 60	27
28	30	372	Alvin Lowe	✓	16 83	16 50	33	28
29	31	373	W. R. McConnell	✓	215 22	211 00	4 22	29
30	31		Totals		7819 22	7665 90	153 32	30
31					(13)	(41)	(27)	31

Columnar sales journal

Each of the invoices entered in the sales journal above illustrates the method of recording a sale and a sales tax. Note that the total amount of the sale, including the sales tax, is recorded in the Accounts Receivable Debit column as a debit to Accounts Receivable and to the customer. Sales is credited for the selling price of the goods, and Sales Taxes Payable is credited for the sales tax.

In states or cities where a merchant is required to pay the sales taxes in advance, he debits *Prepaid Sales Taxes* when the payment is made. Then when a sale is made, he credits Prepaid Sales Taxes for the sales tax on that sale.

Posting the columnar sales journal

The individual amounts in the Accounts Receivable Debit column are posted daily to the accounts receivable ledger so that each customer's account is always up to date. Check marks in the Post. Ref. column are used to indicate posting to the accounts receivable ledger accounts.

After the equality of debits and credits has been verified, the totals of the special columns are posted to the general ledger accounts named in the headings of the columns. As each total is posted, the account number is placed in parentheses below the total.

Recording sales taxes in the columnar cash receipts journal

The columnar cash receipts journal used during the month of October by Wayside Furniture is shown on the following page. This columnar cash receipts journal is similar to the one illustrated in Chapter 14, except that a column has been added for Sales Taxes Payable Credit.

	DATE	ACCOUNT CREDITED	POST. REF.	1 GENERAL CREDIT	2 SALES CREDIT	3 SALES TAXES PAYABLE CREDIT	4 ACCOUNTS RECEIVABLE CREDIT	5 CASH DEBIT
1	1962 Oct. 1	Balance on hand $8,314.52	✓					
2	1	R. D. Neal	✓				153 00	153 00
3	1	Sales	✓		310 00	6 20		316 20
4	2	Store Supplies	15	12 00				12 00
29	29	Sales	✓		460 50	9 21		469 71
30	30	A. L. Durjer	✓				51 00	51 00
31	31	Sales	✓		794 10	15 88		809 98
32	31	Totals		311 40	1224 20	244 80	616 80	1895 20
				311 40	1224 20	244 80	616 80	1895 20
				(✓)	(41)	(27)	(13)	(11)

Columnar cash receipts journal after posting

The amount of cash received in each transaction is recorded in the Cash Debit column. Accounts to be credited for which special columns are not provided are recorded in the General Credit column. Special columns are provided to record credits to sales, to customers' accounts, and to sales taxes.

On October 1 a check for $153 is received from Mr. R. D. Neal. The check is in payment of Invoice No. 218 dated September 6 for $153. The invoice shows the selling price to be $150 and the sales tax to be $3. Cash is debited for $153 in the Cash Debit column. Mr. Neal's account is credited for the same amount. Since the sales tax on all credit sales is recorded in the columnar sales journal at the time of the charge sale, the sales tax account is not affected at the time the customer pays his account.

Wayside Furniture uses a cash register with a special tax key for recording the sales taxes on each sale. The detailed audit strip of the cash register for October 1 shows total cash sales of $310 and total sales taxes of $6.20. The amount of the cash sales, $310, is recorded in the Sales Credit column. The amount received for sales taxes, $6.20, is recorded in the Sales Taxes Payable Credit column. Cash is debited for $316.20, the total amount of cash received.

The use of a special tax key on the cash register is especially helpful in businesses that sell both taxable and nontaxable merchandise. But when the sales tax applies to all merchandise sold by a business, the total of the selling price plus the sales tax may be recorded on the cash register in a single amount. When this practice is followed, the total cash sales figure at the end of the day would also include the sales taxes collected.

Posting the columnar cash receipts journal

Amounts in the Accounts Receivable Credit column are posted to the customers' accounts daily. Amounts in the General Credit column are posted frequently to avoid too much work at the end of the fiscal period.

After cash has been proved and the equality of debits and credits has been verified, the totals of the special columns are posted to the accounts named in the headings of the columns. As each total is posted, the account number is placed in parentheses below the total.

Recording the payment of sales taxes and the payroll in the columnar cash payments journal

The columnar cash payments journal used during the month of October by Wayside Furniture is shown below.

CASH PAYMENTS JOURNAL   PAGE 10

	DATE	CHK. NO.	ACCOUNT DEBITED	POST. REF.	GENERAL DEBIT	ACCOUNTS PAYABLE DEBIT	SALARY EXPENSE DEBIT	EMPLOYEES INC. TAXES PAYABLE CREDIT	FICA TAXES PAYABLE CREDIT	DISCOUNT ON PURCHASES CREDIT	CASH CREDIT	
	1962											
1	Oct. 1	171	Rent Expense	67	275 00						275 00	1
2	2	172	Petty Cash	12	40 00						40 00	2
3	2	173	J. R. Towne	✓		332 00				6 64	325 36	3
29	31	191	Sales Taxes Payable	27	462 10						462 10	29
30	31	192	Salary Expense	✓			360 60	30 60	11 27		318 73	30
31	31	193	Store Supplies	15	8 60							31
32			Office Supplies	16	11 65							32
33			Miscellaneous Expense	65	14 80							33
34			Advertising Expense	61	3 75						38 80	34
35	31		Totals		4852 52	10123 60	1442 40	122 40	45 08	143 20	16107 84	
35					4852 52	10123 60	1442 40	122 40	45 08	143 20	16107 84	35
36					(✓)	(21)	(68)	(22)	(23)	(51.2)	(11)	36
37												37

Columnar cash payments journal after posting

The transaction on Line 29 illustrates the payment of sales taxes that had been collected for the third quarter of the year. Sales Taxes Payable was debited in the General Debit column for $462.10 and a similar amount was recorded in the Cash Credit column.

The transaction on Line 30 illustrates the use of special columns relating to payroll payments. Salary Expense was debited in the Salary Expense Debit column for $360.60, which was the amount of the payroll. The credit of $30.60 in Column 4 recorded the employees' income taxes withheld. The credit of $11.27 in Column 5 recorded the FICA taxes withheld. The cash credit of $318.73 recorded the amount of the check that was cashed in order to pay the employees. The three credits equaled the one debit.

Posting the columnar cash payments journal

Amounts in the Accounts Payable Debit column are posted to the creditors' accounts daily. Amounts in the General Debit column are posted frequently to avoid too much work at the end of the fiscal period.

After cash has been proved and the equality of debits and credits has been verified, the totals of the special columns are posted to the accounts named in the headings of the columns. As each total is posted, the account number is placed in parentheses below the total.

A general journal with special amount columns

To make it easier to record and to post miscellaneous transactions with customers and creditors, Wayside Furniture uses special columns for accounts receivable and accounts payable in its general journal as shown below.

GENERAL JOURNAL   PAGE 10

	ACCOUNTS PAYABLE DEBIT	GENERAL DEBIT	DATE	NAME OF ACOUNT	POST. REF.	GENERAL CREDIT	ACCOUNTS RECEIVABLE CREDIT	
1		50 00	1962 Oct 5	Sales Returns and Allowances	41.1			1
2		1 00		Sales Taxes Payable	27			2
3				F. L. Dwyer	✓		51 00	3
4				Credit Memo. No. 18				4
5	70 00		9	Curran & Curran	✓			5
6				Purchases Returns and Allowances	51.1	70 00		6
7				Allowance for damaged				7
8				merchandise				8
9		37 63	12	Allowance for Bad Debts	12.1			9
10				L. B. Dawson	✓		37 63	10
11				To write off an uncol-				11
12				lectible account				12
13		150 75	15	C. A. Murphy	✓			13
14				C. R. Michael	✓	150 75		14
15				To correct error in				15
16				posting sales invoice No. 303				16
38	685 00	1,224 62	31	Totals		1,449 12	460 50	38
39	(21)	(✓)				(✓)	(13)	39
40								40

Miscellaneous entries in the columnar general journal

The differences between this columnar general journal and the general journal in Chapter 15 are: (1) this journal has two additional columns, one headed Accounts Payable Debit and the other headed Accounts Receivable Credit, and (2) the two debit amount columns are at the left of the Name of

Account column and the two credit columns are at the right. The special columns make it possible to debit Accounts Payable or to credit Accounts Receivable without having to write the account title in the Name of Account column.

The entry on Lines 1–4 records a sales return involving sales taxes. Sales Returns and Allowances is debited for $50, the selling price of the returned merchandise, and Sales Taxes Payable is debited for $1, the amount of the sales tax on the returned merchandise. Both of these amounts are recorded in the General Debit column. Accounts Receivable and the customer's account are credited for the total of $51 by writing the customer's name, A. L. Dwyer, in the Name of Account column and the amount, $51, in the Accounts Receivable Credit column.

The entry on Lines 5–8 records a purchases return. Accounts Payable and the creditor's account are debited for the amount of the purchases return by writing the creditor's name, Curran & Curran, in the Name of Account column and the amount, $70, in the Accounts Payable Debit column. Purchases Returns and Allowances is credited for $70 in the General Credit column.

The entry on Lines 9–12 records the writing off of an uncollectible account. Allowance for Bad Debts is debited for $37.63 in the General Debit column. Accounts Receivable and L. B. Dawson are credited for $37.63 in the Accounts Receivable Credit column.

The entry on Lines 13–16 records the correction of an error in posting a sales invoice. The debit of $150.75 to C. A. Murphy charges his account for the sale. The credit of $150.75 to C. R. Michael corrects the error in his account. This correcting entry is recorded in the General columns only, because the accounts receivable account balance already includes this sale.

Posting the four-column general journal

The individual amounts in the Accounts Payable Debit column and in the Accounts Receivable Credit column are posted daily to the appropriate accounts in the accounts payable ledger and the accounts receivable ledger. A check mark is placed in the Post. Ref. column of the general journal to indicate the completion of the posting.

The individual amounts in the General columns that affect accounts in the general ledger are posted to those accounts in the general ledger. The account number is written in the Post. Ref. column of the general journal to indicate the completion of the posting.

Posting the totals of the four-column general journal

At the end of the month the columns of the four-column general journal are totaled and proved. The sum of the totals of the debit columns,

$1,909.62, is equal to the sum of the totals of the credit columns, $1,909.62. The records in the general journal are therefore assumed to be accurate.

The totals of the General columns are not posted because the items in these columns were posted individually to the general ledger accounts during the month. A check mark is placed below each of these columns to show that the total is not to be posted.

The total of the Accounts Payable Debit column, $685.00, is posted to the debit side of the accounts payable account in the general ledger and the account number, 21, is placed below the total to indicate that this amount has been posted. Similarly, the total of the Accounts Receivable Credit column, $460.50, is posted to the credit side of the accounts receivable account in the general ledger and the account number, 13, is placed below the total to indicate that this amount has been posted.

Using sales invoices as a sales journal

Some businesses use the duplicate copies of their sales invoices as their sales journal. When this is done, each sales invoice is posted directly to the proper customer's account in the accounts receivable ledger. (See page 174.) The number of the sales invoice is placed in the posting reference column of the customer's account to show the source of the entry. A check mark is placed at the right of the customer's name on the sales invoice to show that the invoice was posted. As invoices are posted, they are filed in numerical order.

At the end of the month, the amounts on the invoices are totaled on an adding machine. If the business collects a sales tax, three different totals must be secured: (1) the total amount of all invoices, (2) the total sale price on all invoices, and (3) the total sales tax on all invoices. These totals are the basis for a journal entry debiting Accounts Receivable and crediting Sales and Sales Taxes Payable. For example, if the adding machine lists show the grand total of all invoices to be $865.20, the total sales prices to be $840, and the total sales taxes to be $25.20, the following entry would be recorded in the general journal:

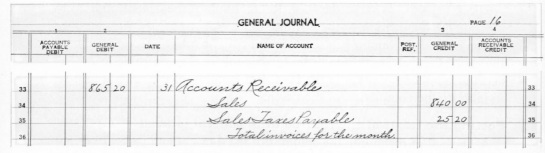

Entry to record total monthly sales on account when sales invoices serve as a sales journal

The cash method of handling purchases on account

Some businesses prefer to handle all purchases on account as though they were cash purchases. This is done by recording each purchase transaction only at the time the invoice is paid. This method makes it unnecessary to maintain a purchases journal, accounts with creditors, or an accounts payable controlling account in the general ledger.

The steps in using the cash method of handling purchases on account are as follows:

Step 1. Each purchase invoice is verified and then is filed under the date it is to be paid.

Step 2. The bookkeeper examines the file each day, and checks are issued to the creditors in payment of the invoices due on that day.

Step 3. The amount of the check is recorded in the cash payments journal as a debit to Purchases and a credit to Cash. If the invoice is subject to a discount, only the amount of the check is recorded as a debit to Purchases.

Step 4. At the end of the month the total of the Purchases Debit column of the cash payments journal is posted to the debit of the purchases account in the general ledger.

Chapter questions

1. Why is the sales taxes payable account a liability of the seller?
2. What two different types of transactions would cause the sales taxes payable account to be debited?
3. What are the differences between the sales journal on page 172 and the one on page 409?
4. What steps need to be taken before the totals of the cash receipts journal are posted?
5. What do the numbers in parentheses below the totals of the cash receipts journal on page 410 show?
6. What was the amount of the invoice that was paid in the transaction on Line 3 of the cash payments journal shown on page 411?
7. What was the amount of cash withdrawn to pay the employees in the transaction on Line 30 of the cash payments journal on page 411?
8. What kinds of entries are recorded in the columnar general journal?
9. Explain the procedure followed when sales invoices are used as the sales journal.
10. Explain the procedure followed when purchases on account are recorded only at the time of payment.

Cases for discussion

1. William Clynes, the proprietor of a small gift shop, had to replace his worn-out cash register with a new one. His old cash register contained no special tax key. A 3% sales tax existed in the state where his shop was located. All

items that he sold were subject to this sales tax. Assuming that a new cash register with a special tax key would cost no more than one without such a key, what advantages can you give for his purchasing a register with a special tax key?

2. The Adkins Novelty Shop uses a columnar cash receipts journal with the following headings: (1) General Credit, (2) Sales Credit, (3) Sales Taxes Payable Credit, (4) Accounts Receivable Credit, and (5) Cash Debit.

(a) From which of these columns are amounts posted individually?
(b) To what accounts are the individual amounts posted?
(c) Which column total of the cash receipts journal is not posted?

Drill for understanding

Drill 28-A. *The effect of sales tax transactions on accounts*

Instructions: 1. Open the following accounts in T-account form:

(a) General Ledger: Cash, Accounts Receivable, Sales Taxes Payable, Sales. (Allow eight lines for each account.)
(b) Accounts Receivable Ledger: B. Jones, A. Smith. (Allow three lines for each account.)

2. In these T accounts record the effect of the following selected transactions. In addition to the sales price listed in each of these transactions, there was a sales tax of 2% on each sale.

(a) Sold merchandise for cash, $25.
(b) Sold merchandise on account to B. Jones, $17.50.
(c) Sold merchandise on account to A. Smith, $8.
(d) Sold merchandise for cash, $43.
(e) Received payment in full for B. Jones's account.
(f) Sold merchandise on account to A. Smith, $23.50.
(g) Sold merchandise for cash, $108.
(h) Received payment in full for A. Smith's account.
(i) Sold merchandise on account to B. Jones, $178.
(j) Drew a check in full payment to the state for all sales taxes payable.

Instructions: 3. Prove the equality of the debits and the credits in the general ledger by taking a trial balance.

Application problem

Problem 28-1. *Recording transactions in columnar sales and cash receipts journals*

Instructions: 1. Record the following transactions completed by the Fields Hardware Store during January of the current year in a sales journal and a cash receipts journal like those illustrated in this chapter.

Jan. 1. Record the cash balance of $1,991.34 in the cash receipts journal (memorandum entry).

Jan. 2. Received a check for $76.80 from Robert Fisher on account.

3. Sold merchandise on account to T. O. Reed, $42.00; sales tax, $1.68; total invoice, $43.68 (Sale No. 1).

5. Sold merchandise on account to P. F. Parker, $68.70; sales tax, $2.75; total invoice, $71.45 (Sale No. 2).

5. Cash sales for January 2 to 5, $589.93; sales taxes, $23.60; total, $613.53.

9. Received a check for $156.33 from E. C. Kemper on account.

12. Cash sales for January 7 to 12, $726.48; sales taxes, $29.06; total, $755.54.

16. Sold some wrapping supplies for $7.50 cash to accommodate a fellow merchant. (In this state there is no sales tax on an accommodation sale of this kind.)

17. Sold merchandise on account to E. C. Kemper, $163.80; sales tax, $6.55; total invoice, $170.35 (Sale No. 3).

18. Received a check for $100 from P. F. Parker on account.

19. Cash sales for January 14 to 19, $684.23; sales taxes, $27.37; total, $711.60.

24. Received a check for $116.62 from T. A. Benjamin on account.

26. Cash sales for January 21 to 26, $796.44; sales taxes, $31.86; total, $828.30.

28. Received a check for $21.84 from T. O. Reed in payment of our invoice of January 3 for $43.68 less the $21.84 credit granted on January 19.

29. Sold merchandise on account to C. A. Hart, $214.20; sales tax, $8.57; total invoice, $222.77 (Sale No. 4).

31. Received a check for $50 from P. F. Parker on account.

31. Sold merchandise on account to P. F. Parker, $78.60; sales tax, $3.14; total invoice, $81.74 (Sale No. 5).

31. Cash sales for January 28 to 31, $240.80; sales taxes, $9.63; total, $250.43.

Instructions: 2. Foot, prove, total, and rule both journals.

Optional problems

★*Supplementary Problem 28-S. Recording transactions in columnar cash payments and general journals*

Instructions: 1. Record the following transactions completed by the Fields Hardware Store during January of the current year in a cash payments journal and a general journal like those illustrated in this chapter.

Jan. 2. Issued Check No. 1 for $50 to establish a petty cash fund.

2. Issued Check No. 2 for $150 for January rent.

4. Issued Check No. 3 for $378.40 to Daniels Company in payment of their invoice of December 26 for $386.12 less $7.72 discount.

8. Issued Check No. 4 for $221.25 in payment of the liability of $140 for employees income taxes payable and the liability of $81.25 for FICA taxes payable for the previous quarterly period.

8. Issued Check No. 5 for $35.10 in payment of the state unemployment taxes payable for the previous quarterly period.

8. Issued Check No. 6 for $41.60 in payment of the federal unemployment taxes payable for the previous year.

10. Wrote off the account of John J. Smith, $27.50, as a bad debt.

Jan. 12. Issued Check No. 7 for $170.75 in payment of the biweekly payroll of $200 less a deduction of $23 for employees income taxes payable and a deduction of $6.25 for FICA taxes payable.

12. Recorded the employer's liability of $6.25 for FICA taxes, $5.40 for state unemployment taxes, and $1.60 for federal unemployment taxes.

15. Issued Check No. 8 for $387.60 in payment of the sales taxes payable for the previous quarterly period.

15. Issued Check No. 9 for $163.79 to Harry Moore in payment of his invoice of December 15.

18. Received a credit memorandum for $12.50 from Tru-Steel Tool Company for merchandise returned to them.

19. Issued Credit Memorandum No. 1 for $21.84 to T. O. Reed for merchandise returned that had been part of the invoice of January 3, $21, and sales tax on the return, 84 cents.

22. Issued Check No. 10 for $16.50 for electricity bill. (Debit Miscellaneous Expense.)

23. Issued Credit Memorandum No. 2 for $6.97 to E. C. Kemper for an allowance granted because of defective merchandise shipped to him as part of the invoice of January 17, $6.70, and sales tax on the allowance, 27 cents.

26. Issued Check No. 11 for $749.99 to Tru-Steel Tool Company in payment of their invoice of January 16 for $777.80 less the $12.50 credit of January 18 and less $15.31 discount.

26. Issued Check No. 12 for $170.75 in payment of the biweekly payroll of $200 less the same deductions as on January 12.

26. Recorded the employer's liability for social security taxes, which were the same as on January 12.

29. Discovered that a December 29 sale of merchandise on account for $150.80, including sales tax, to T. O. Reed had been posted incorrectly to the account of C. R. Read.

30. Issued Check No. 13 for $377.40 to Birch & Company in payment of their invoice of January 20 for $385.10 less $7.70 discount.

31. Issued Check No. 14 for $48 to replenish petty cash. The expenditures were as follows: Supplies, $7.80; Delivery Expense, $10.50; Miscellaneous Expense, $12.66; Sales Returns and Allowances, $16.38; Sales Taxes Payable, 66¢.

Instructions: 2. Foot, prove, total, and rule both journals.

★ Bonus Problem 28-B. *Recording transactions in columnar special journals*

Instructions: 1. Record the following transactions completed by the Slater Company during March of the current year in a sales journal, a cash receipts journal, a cash payments journal, and a general journal like those illustrated in this chapter.

Mar. 1. Recorded the cash balance of $2,361.18 with a memorandum entry.

1. Issued Check No. 302 for $175 for the June rent.

1. Sold merchandise on account to M. A. Tully, $41.50; sales tax, 83¢; total invoice, $42.33. (Sale No. 43).

2. Sold merchandise on account to J. R. Tilton, $142; sales tax, $2.84; total invoice, $144.84 (Sale No. 44).

2. Received a check for $147.90 from John Larkin on account.

2. Issued Check No. 303 for $262.12 in payment of the biweekly payroll

of $300 less a deduction of $28.50 for employees income taxes payable and a deduction of $9.38 for FICA taxes payable.

Mar. 2. Cash sales for March 1 and 2 were $337.50; sales taxes, $6.75; total, $344.25.

4. Wrote off the account of M. A. Stevens, $42.25, as a bad debt.

5. Issued Check No. 304 for $809.72 to Dayton Electrical Co. in payment of their invoice of Feb. 28 for $826.25 less $16.53 discount.

7. Sold merchandise on account to M. A. Tully, $53.50; sales tax, $1.07; total invoice, $54.57 (Sale No. 45).

8. Issued Check No. 305 for $11.75 in payment of the telephone bill. (Debit Miscellaneous Expense.)

9. Cash sales for the week were $890.90; sales taxes, $17.82; total, $908.72.

11. Sold some wrapping supplies for cash to accommodate a customer, $5.50. (There is no sales tax on such a transaction in this city.)

13. Issued Credit Memorandum No. 38 for $21.93 to M. A. Tully for merchandise returned that had been part of the invoice of March 1, $21.50, and sales tax on the return, 43 ¢.

14. Received $75 from H. R. Ward on account.

15. Issued Check No. 306 for $375 for a new display case. (Equipment.)

16. Issued Check No. 307 for $262.12 in payment of the biweekly payroll of $300 less a deduction of $28.50 for employees income taxes payable and a deduction of $9.38 for FICA taxes payable.

16. Cash sales for the week were $810.50; sales taxes, $16.21; total, $826.71.

18. Received a credit memorandum for $12.75 from Dayton Electrical Co. for an allowance on defective merchandise.

19. Sold merchandise on account to J. R. Tilton, $121.50; sales tax, $2.43; total invoice, $123.93 (Sale No. 46).

20. Received a check for $20.40 from M. A. Tully for balance due on our invoice of March 1 less our credit memorandum No. 38 of March 13.

21. Issued Check No. 308 for $231.67 to Randolph Corporation in payment of its invoice of March 12 for $236.40 less $4.73 discount.

23. Cash sales for the week were $912.63; sales taxes, $18.25; total, $930.88.

26. Received a check for $100 from J. R. Tilton on account.

27. Sold merchandise on account to H. R. Ward, $216; sales tax, $4.32; total invoice, $220.32. (Sale No. 47).

28. Received a credit memorandum for $28.30 from Dawson & Co. for merchandise returned.

29. Issued Check No. 309 for $38.05 for delivery service for the month. (Debit Delivery Expense.)

30. Issued Check No. 310 for $262.12 in payment of the biweekly payroll of $300 less a deduction of $28.50 for employees income taxes payable and a deduction of $9.38 for FICA taxes payable.

30. Recorded the employer's liability, for the three payrolls paid this month, of $28.14 for FICA taxes, $24.30 for state unemployment taxes, and $7.20 for federal unemployment taxes.

30. Issued Check No. 311 for $46.47 to replenish petty cash. The expenditures were as follows: Supplies, $24; Delivery Expense, $4.30; Sales Returns and Allowances, $17.81; Sales Taxes Payable, 36¢.

30. Cash sales for the week were $1,010.50; sales taxes, $20.21; total, $1,030.71.

Instructions: 2. Foot, prove, total, and rule all journals.

Chapter 29

Notes and interest

The use of notes

An unconditional written promise to pay a certain amount of money at a definite time signed by a person or the persons agreeing to make payment is known as a *promissory note*, or, more briefly, as a *note*. For example, when a person borrows at a bank, the bank requires the borrower to sign a note. Notes are sometimes given to creditors when the buyer wants credit beyond the usual time for which credit is given.

Notes have an advantage over oral promises or open accounts because, like checks, notes can be endorsed and transferred. Notes can also be useful in a court of law as evidence of a debt.

Notes that a business receives, in which its debtors promise to pay, are known as *notes receivable*. Notes that a business gives creditors, in which it promises to pay, are known as *notes payable*. Notes receivable are assets. Notes payable are liabilities. A form of a note is shown below.

Note

Analyzing a promissory note

In the following table the terms used in connection with promissory notes are defined, and the applications of these terms to the foregoing illustration are shown.

Terms	Definitions	The Illustration
Maker	The one who signs the note and thus promises to make payment.	E. L. Cooper
Payee	The one to whom a note is payable.	Graham & Sons
Date	The day on which the note is issued.	October 24, 1962
Time	The days or months from the date of issue until the note is to be paid.	60 days
Maturity date	The date on which the note is due.	December 23, 1962
Principal	The amount the maker promises to pay—the face of the note.	$700.00
Interest rate	The rate paid for the use of the money.	4%

420

Interest on notes

A note that bears interest is said to be *interest-bearing*. If a note does not bear interest, it is said to be *non-interest-bearing*. Interest is expressed as a percentage of the principal. This percentage is known as the *interest rate*. Interest at 6% means that 6 cents will be paid for the use of each dollar borrowed for a full year. When a note runs for a fraction of a year, the amount of interest is found by multiplying this fraction by the interest for a full year. For example, if the time of a note is 6 months, which is one half of a year, the amount of interest would be one half the amount that would be paid for a full year.

When cash is paid for interest, the amount of the payment is debited to an expense account with the title *Interest Expense*. When cash is received for interest, the amount of the receipt is credited to an income account with the title *Interest Income*.

Computing interest using interest tables

Whenever a business has many calculations of interest, it commonly uses an interest table. Interest tables may be purchased at an office supply store or may be obtained from some banks. The illustration at the right shows an interest table for 6% on a monthly basis. Interest tables are available for almost any interest rate on both a monthly and a daily basis.

Analyzing the interest table

If a business has a note for $500 that is to run for 3 months, compute the interest as follows:

1. Follow down the interest table in the month column to the figure 3. The amount column on this line shows .015, which is the amount of interest for $1 for 3 months.

2. Multiply $500 by .015. The result is $7.50, which is the interest on $500 for 3 months.

INTEREST TABLE 6% for $1.00 on a Monthly Basis	
NUMBER OF MONTHS	AMOUNT OF INTEREST
1	.005
2	.01
3	.015
4	.02
5	.025
6	.03
7	.035
8	.04
9	.045
10	.05
11	.055
12	.06

Computing interest without interest tables

To compute the interest on a given amount for one year, the principal is multiplied by the interest rate. For example, the interest on $300 for 1 year at 5% is $15. The interest is computed as follows:

$$\$300 \times .05 = \$15$$

To calculate the amount of interest for a period of less than one year, the following formula is used:

PRINCIPAL × RATE × FRACTION OF YEAR = AMOUNT OF INTEREST

For example, to find the interest on $600 for 4 months at 5%, the following computation may be made:

PRINCIPAL × RATE × FRACTION OF YEAR = AMOUNT OF INTEREST

$$\$600 \times .05 \times \frac{4}{12} = \frac{\$120}{12} = \$10$$

For convenience in calculating, 360 days are commonly used as the number of days in a year. To find the interest on $400 for 90 days at 4% the following computation may be made:

$$\$400 \times .04 \times \frac{90}{360} = \frac{1440}{360} = \$4$$

Instead of multiplying the numbers and dividing by 360, the cancellation method can be used, as follows:

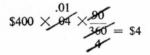

$$\$400 \times \overset{.01}{\cancel{.04}} \times \frac{\cancel{90}}{\underset{4}{\cancel{360}}} = \$4$$

Recording notes receivable

A business may accept a note from a charge customer as a means of granting an extension of time for the payment of an account. The note does not pay the amount the customer owes, but it does change the form of the asset from an account receivable to a note receivable.

On October 29, E. L. Cooper receives from D. C. Walsh a 60-day, 5% note for $400 to apply on Mr. Walsh's account. Mr. Cooper records this transaction in a general journal with special columns for Accounts Payable Debit and Accounts Receivable Credit. The entry is made in a four-column general journal in the following manner:

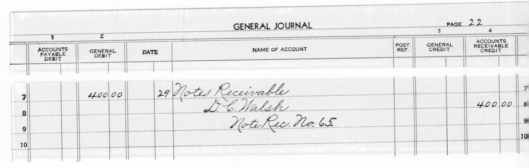

ACCOUNTS PAYABLE DEBIT	GENERAL DEBIT	DATE	NAME OF ACCOUNT	POST. REF.	GENERAL CREDIT	ACCOUNTS RECEIVABLE CREDIT	
	400 00	29	Notes Receivable				7
			D. C. Walsh			400 00	8
			Note Rec. No. 65				9
							10

Entry to record a note received from a customer

Notes Receivable is debited for $400 to record the increase in this asset. The amount of the debit is written in the General Debit column, and the title of the account to be debited, Notes Receivable, is written in the Name of Account column.

Accounts Receivable is credited to record the decrease in the value of this asset. The amount is written in the Accounts Receivable Credit column. The name of the customer, D. C. Walsh, is written in the Name of Account column so that this amount may be posted to the customer's account in the accounts receivable ledger.

Recording the collection of a note with interest

When cash is received in payment of a note and interest, a combined entry with two credits is made in the cash receipts journal. Cash is debited to record the increase in the asset Cash, Notes Receivable is credited to record the decrease in the asset Notes Receivable, and Interest Income is credited to record the increase in this type of income.

On December 28, E. L. Cooper receives a check for $403.33 in payment of the note of October 29 with interest. The following entry is made in the cash receipts journal:

	DATE	ACCOUNT CREDITED	POST. REF.	GENERAL CREDIT	SALES CREDIT	SALES TAXES PAYABLE CREDIT	ACCOUNTS RECEIVABLE CREDIT	CASH DEBIT	
28	28	Notes Receivable		400 00				403 33	28
29		Interest Income		3 33					29
30									30

CASH RECEIPTS JOURNAL   PAGE 41

Entry to record the collection of a note and interest

Dishonored note receivable

A note that the maker refuses or is unable to pay when it is due is said to be a *dishonored note*. The notes receivable account should include only those notes that are not yet due. A dishonored note should therefore be removed from the notes receivable account. Such a note is debited to the customer's account so that the account will show the total amount owed by the customer, including the amount of the dishonored note. This information may be important if the customer requests credit in the future.

Mr. Cooper holds a 60-day note, dated September 20, for $275.80, which the maker, L. C. Spence, is unable to pay when it comes due on November 19. The entry made by Mr. Cooper to record this transaction, after posting, is shown on the following page.

423

ACCOUNTS PAYABLE DEBIT	GENERAL DEBIT	DATE	NAME OF ACCOUNT	POST. REF.	GENERAL CREDIT	ACCOUNTS RECEIVABLE CREDIT	
9		275 80	19 Accounts Receivable / L. C. Spence	15/✓			9
10			Notes Receivable	13	275 80		10
11			To charge the L. C. Spence				11
12			account for Note Rec No. 64				12
13			dishonored today.				13
14							14

Entry to record a dishonored note receivable

The debit to Accounts Receivable, $275.80, is entered in the General Debit column, and the title of the general ledger account, Accounts Receivable, is written in the Name of Account column. As this amount also has to be debited to the account of L. C. Spence, the customer's name is also written in the Name of Account column. When the transaction is posted, the completion of the posting of the debit to the general ledger account is indicated by writing the account number in the Post Ref. column. The completion of the posting to the customer's account is indicated by a check mark. The account number and the check mark are separated by a diagonal line in the manner shown in the illustration.

To record the decrease in the asset Notes Receivable, the account Notes Receivable is credited in the General Credit column and the title of the account is written in the Name of Account column.

If it is later decided that collection cannot be made from Mr. Spence, the balance of the account will be written off as a bad debt. At that time Allowance for Bad Debts will be debited and Accounts Receivable and L. C. Spence will be credited.

Recording notes payable

Not only may a business receive notes, but also it may issue them. It may issue them to those to whom it owes money in order to obtain additional time in which to pay some of its obligations. It may also issue them to a bank for the purpose of borrowing money. In either case a note issued by the business is a liability and is recorded in its books as a note payable.

For example, on October 24, E. L. Cooper gives a creditor, Graham & Sons, a 60-day, 4% note for $700 for the invoice of September 24 that is due on October 24. The entry made to record this transaction is shown at the top of the following page.

| | | | GENERAL JOURNAL | | | PAGE 23 |

| 1 | 2 | | | 3 | 4 |

ACCOUNTS PAYABLE DEBIT	GENERAL DEBIT	DATE	NAME OF ACCOUNT	POST. REF.	GENERAL CREDIT	ACCOUNTS RECEIVABLE CREDIT
4 700 00		24	Graham & Sons			4
5			Notes Payable		700 00	5
6			Note Pay. No. 54.			6
7						7
8						8
9						9

Entry to record a note issued to a creditor

As the liability Accounts Payable is decreased, it is debited for $700 in the Accounts Payable Debit column. The name of the creditor's account is written in the Name of Account column so that this amount can be posted to the creditor's account in the accounts payable ledger.

The liability Notes Payable is increased and therefore the notes payable account is credited in the General Credit column.

Recording the payment of a note with interest

When a business pays a note with interest, a combined entry with two debits is made in the cash payments journal. The debits are to the liability account Notes Payable and to the expense account Interest Expense.

On December 23, E. L. Cooper issues a check for $704.67 to Graham & Sons in payment of the note of October 24 with interest. The following entry is made in the cash payments journal:

| | | | CASH PAYMENTS JOURNAL | | | | | | | PAGE 43 |

| | | | | 1 | 2 | 3 | 4 | 5 | 6 | 7 |

DATE	CHK. NO.	ACCOUNT DEBITED	POST. REF.	GENERAL DEBIT	ACCOUNTS PAYABLE DEBIT	SALARY EXPENSE DEBIT	EMPLOYEES INC. TAXES PAYABLE CREDIT	FICA TAXES PAYABLE CREDIT	DISCOUNT ON PURCHASES CREDIT	CASH CREDIT
32 23	185	Notes Payable		700 00						704 67
33		Interest Expense		4 67						
34										
35										

Entry to record the payment of a note and interest

Both debits are entered in the General Debit column, as special columns are not provided for Notes Payable Debit or Interest Expense Debit. Cash is credited for $704.67 to record the amount of cash paid.

Borrowing money at a bank

If a businessman borrows money from a bank, he may give the bank an interest-bearing note and pay the interest at the maturity of the note. In that case he receives cash or credit for the face of the note, and at the maturity date he pays the face of the note plus the interest. If the note is a 60-day, 6% note for $1,000, he receives $1,000 when he issues the note, and at the maturity date he pays $1,010, the face of the note plus the interest.

The borrower may, however, be required to pay interest in advance. Interest charged in advance by a bank is referred to as *bank discount*. The amount received for a note after the bank has taken this discount is called the *proceeds*. When interest on a note is taken in advance, the note is said to be *discounted*.

E. L. Cooper wishes to borrow from his bank. It is the custom of his bank to charge interest in advance. On October 8, Mr. Cooper draws a 60-day, non-interest-bearing note for $1,000 in favor of his bank. The discount rate charged by the bank is 6%. The interest on $1,000 for 60 days at 6% is $10. The proceeds of the note, the amount received by Mr. Cooper, is therefore $1,000 minus $10, or $990.

When E. L. Cooper issues the note on October 8 and receives credit for $990 from the bank, he records the transaction by the following entries in his cash receipts journal and in his cash payments journal:

CASH RECEIPTS JOURNAL PAGE 33

	DATE	ACCOUNT CREDITED	POST. REF.	GENERAL CREDIT	SALES CREDIT	SALES TAXES PAYABLE CREDIT	ACCOUNTS RECEIVABLE CREDIT	CASH DEBIT	
22	8	Notes Payable		1000 00				1000 00	22

CASH PAYMENTS JOURNAL PAGE 33

	DATE	CHK. NO.	ACCOUNT DEBITED	POST. REF.	GENERAL DEBIT	ACCOUNTS PAYABLE DEBIT	SALARY EXPENSE DEBIT	EMPLOYEES INC. TAXES PAYABLE CREDIT	FICA TAXES PAYABLE CREDIT	DISCOUNT ON PURCHASES CREDIT	CASH CREDIT	
8		8	Interest Expense		10 00						10 00	8
9												9

Entries to record the discounting of a note payable

Two entries are used to record this transaction. In the cash receipts journal, Cash is debited for the face of the note and Notes Payable is credited for the same amount. In the cash payments journal, Interest Expense is debited for the amount of the interest paid in advance and

Cash is credited. The difference between the cash debit of $1,000 and the cash credit of $10 is the amount of cash actually received by Mr. Cooper.

In order for his checkbook balance to agree with his cash record, Mr. Cooper adds $990 to his previous check-stub balance. He then makes the following notation on the check stub: "Discounted $1,000 note; discount $10."

Reporting interest income and interest expense

As interest income is not an income from selling merchandise, it is classified as *other income* and is placed in the Other Income division of the ledger.

As interest expense is not an expense of selling merchandise, it is classified as *other expense* and is placed in the Other Expense division of the ledger.

Interest on the work sheet

When E. L. Cooper prepares his work sheet from the ledger on December 31, the end of his semiannual fiscal period, the accounts with interest appear at the end of the trial balance. Interest Income, which is a credit in the Trial Balance Credit column, is extended into the Income Statement Credit column. Interest Expense, which is a debit in the Trial Balance Debit column, is extended into the Income Statement Debit column.

The method of entering Interest Income and Interest Expense on the work sheet is shown in the following illustration:

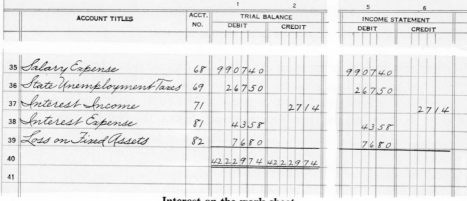

	ACCOUNT TITLES	ACCT. NO.	TRIAL BALANCE DEBIT	TRIAL BALANCE CREDIT	INCOME STATEMENT DEBIT	INCOME STATEMENT CREDIT
35	Salary Expense	68	9 9 0 7 4 0		9 9 0 7 4 0	
36	State Unemployment Taxes	69	2 6 7 5 0		2 6 7 5 0	
37	Interest Income	71		2 7 1 4		2 7 1 4
38	Interest Expense	81	4 3 5 8		4 3 5 8	
39	Loss on Fixed Assets	82	7 6 8 0		7 6 8 0	
40			4 2 2 2 9 7 4	4 2 2 2 9 7 4		
41						

Interest on the work sheet

Interest on the income statement

The illustration on the following page shows how E. L. Cooper reports interest income and interest expense on his income statement on December 31.

E. L. Cooper
Income Statement
For Year Ended December 31, 1962

Income from Sales:				2616843
Sales				
Power Expense	78438			
Rent Expense	180000			
Salary Expense	990740			
State Unemployment Taxes	26750			
Supplies Expense	55957			
Total Operating Expenses		1707275		
Net Income from Operations		90303		
Other Income:				
Interest Income	2714			
Other Expenses:				
Interest Expense	43.58			
Loss on Fixed Assets	76.80			
Total Other Expenses		12038		
Net Subtraction				9324
Net Income				80979

Interest on the income statement

Interest Income is listed in the Other Income section. Interest Expense is listed in the Other Expenses section. Since the Other Expenses exceed the Other Income, the difference is called Net Subtraction and is deducted from the Net Income from Operations to obtain the Net Income.

Increasing your business vocabulary

What is the meaning of each of the following:

(a) promissory note
(b) notes receivable
(c) notes payable
(d) maker of a note
(e) payee of a note
(f) maturity date of a note
(g) principal of a note

(h) interest rate
(i) interest-bearing note
(j) non-interest-bearing note
(k) dishonored note
(l) bank discount
(m) proceeds

Chapter questions

1. What are the advantages of possessing the promissory note of a debtor?
2. When is a promissory note referred to as a note receivable?
3. When is a promissory note referred to as a note payable?
4. What does "6% interest" mean?
5. What are the three steps in computing interest when an interest table is not available?
6. What account is credited when cash is received for interest?
7. What accounts are credited when cash is received in payment for a note and interest?
8. Why is it important to record a dishonored note to the debit of the maker's account?
9. What account is debited when cash is paid for interest on a note?
10. What accounts are debited when cash is paid for the principal of a note and the interest?

Cases for discussion

1. George Lester, a dealer in farm equipment, receives a large number of notes. He has the Farmer's National Bank collect all of his notes for him. What special column would you advise Mr. Lester to add to his cash receipts journal?
2. D. T. Minor, a retail grocer, maintains a cash balance sufficient to pay all of his bills when they become due. J. E. Crane, another retail grocer, finds it necessary to borrow money from his bank at frequent intervals. Both merchants have an equal volume of sales. Which merchant is likely to have the smaller net profit from his business? Why?

Drills for understanding

Drill 29-A. *Computing the due date and the interest*

The Theater Equipment Company held five promissory notes, which contained the following information:

No. of Note	Date of Note	Time	Interest Rate	Principal
1	March 1	1 month	6%	$ 200
2	March 1	60 days	6%	400
3	March 12	6 months	5%	900
4	May 23	75 days	6%	500
5	August 4	30 days	4%	300

Instructions: Find for each of the above notes (a) the due date and (b) the interest.

Drill 29-B. *Computing discount and proceeds*

During the current year the Apex Manufacturing Company discounted five of its own notes as follows:

No. of Note	Date of Note	Date of Maturity	Discount Rate	Face of Note
1	January 1	January 31	6%	$ 300
2	March 4	May 3	6%	600
3	March 15	April 29	4½%	2,000
4	May 28	August 26	6%	470
5	November 5	December 20	6%	300

Instructions: Find for each of the above notes (a) the number of days for which the note was discounted, (b) the amount of the discount, and (c) the proceeds.

Application problem

Problem 29-1. *Recording notes and interest*

The transactions given below were selected from those completed by Frank Norton, a used car dealer, during the months of April, May, and June of the current year.

Instructions: 1. Record the following transactions, using a cash receipts journal, a cash payments journal, and a general journal similar to those illustrated in this chapter.

Apr. 1. Received Note Receivable No. 21 for $300 from Henry Sanders on account.

4. Issued Note Payable No. 15 for $2,500 to Standard Motors Co. for an extension of time on account.

8. Received Note Receivable No. 22 for $595 from Louis Wylie on account.

15. Issued Note Payable No. 16 for $3,600 to the Jet Manufacturing Co. for an extension of time on account.

26. Discounted at the First National Bank our Note Payable No. 17 for $1,000. Received credit for the proceeds, $990.

May 6. Discounted at the First National Bank our Note Payable No. 18 for $5,000. Received credit for the proceeds, $4,979.17.

8. Received a check for $595 from Louis Wylie in payment of non-interest-bearing Note Receivable No. 22 for $595.

13. Received Note Receivable No. 23 for $300 from Ernest Walters on account.

15. Issued Check No. 108 for $3,618 to the Jet Manufacturing Co. in payment of Note Payable No. 16 for $3,600 plus $18 interest.

31. Received notice from the bank that Henry Sanders had refused to pay non-interest-bearing Note Receivable No. 21 for $300 when it became due on May 30. Charged the note to the account of the maker.

430

June 3. Issued Check No. 156 for $2,525 to Standard Motors Co. in payment of Note Payable No. 15 for $2,500 plus $25 interest.
   5. Issued Check No. 161 for $5,000 to the First National Bank in payment of Note Payable No. 18 for $5,000.
   11. Received a check for $301.25 from Ernest Walters in payment of Note Receivable No. 23 for $300 plus $1.25 interest.
   19. Received Note Receivable No. 24 for $1,750 from Joseph Benson on account.
   25. Issued Check No. 188 for $1,000 to the First National Bank in payment of Note Payable No. 17 for $1,000.

Instructions: 2. Foot and prove the columnar special journals.

Optional problems

★*Supplementary Problem 29-S.   Calculating and recording interest and bank discount*

The transactions given below were completed by D. F. Turner, a dealer in farm implements, during October of the current year.

Instructions: 1. Record the following transactions in a cash receipts journal and a cash payments journal similar to those illustrated in this chapter.

Oct. 3. Issued Check No. 172 to Ace Implement Co. in full payment of a 60-day, 5% interest-bearing note due today (Note Payable No. 41). Face of note, $600.
   7. Discounted at the Farmers Bank his 30-day, non-interest-bearing note (Note Payable No. 45). Face of note, $400. Rate of discount, 6%. Received credit for the proceeds.
   8. Received a check from L. D. Lyons in payment of the principal and interest on a 20-day, 5% interest-bearing note due today (Note Receivable No. 78). Face of note, $240.
   10. Issued Check No. 178 to the City National Bank in payment of the principal and interest on a 90-day, 4% interest-bearing note due today (Note Payable No. 36). Face of note, $1,000.
   15. Discounted at the Farmers Bank his 90-day, non-interest-bearing note (Note Payable No. 46). Face of note, $1,500. Rate of discount, 6%. Received credit for the proceeds.
   17. Received a check from James Joyce in full settlement of his 180-day, 6% interest-bearing note due today (Note Receivable No. 61). Face of note, $500.
   18. Issued Check No. 186 to Kent Manufacturing Co. in full payment of the principal and interest on a 60-day, 3% interest-bearing note due today (Note Payable No. 42). Face of note, $648.50.
   24. Discounted at the Farmers Bank his 20-day, non-interest-bearing note (Note Payable No. 47). Face of note, $600. Rate of discount, 6%. Received credit for the proceeds.
   25. Received a check from W. S. Slane in payment of the principal and interest on a 30-day, 5% interest-bearing note due today (Note Receivable No. 79). Face of note, $540.80.
   28. Issued Check No. 195 to Acme Harvester Corporation in full payment of the principal and interest on a 90-day, 4% interest-bearing note due today (Note Payable No. 38). Face of note, $800.

Oct. 28. Received a check from James Berry in full settlement of his 90-day, 6% interest-bearing note due today (Note Receivable No. 72). Face of note, $485.

Instructions: 2. Foot and prove the columnar special journals.

★ Bonus Problem 29-B. Calculating and recording interest and bank discount

Instructions: 1. Record the following selected transactions completed by Robert Vincent during the current fiscal year. Use a cash receipts journal, a cash payments journal, and a general journal similar to those illustrated in this chapter.

Jan. 2. Received from Harry Cobb a 90-day, 6% note (Note Receivable No. 84) for $400, dated December 28, on account.

8. Received from Arthur Doyle a 30-day, 6% note (Note Receivable No. 85) for $300, dated January 7, on account.

24. Issued a 30-day, 6% note (Note Payable No. 1) for $750 to Ralph Crandall for an extension of time on account.

Feb. 6. Received a check from Arthur Doyle in payment of the principal and the interest on Note Receivable No. 85 due today.

23. Issued Check No. 63 to Ralph Crandall in payment of the principal and the interest on Note Payable No. 1 due today.

Mar. 5. Issued a 90-day, 5% note (Note Payable No. 2) for $2,500 to Boyd & Company for an extension of time on account.

11. Purchased office equipment from the Atlas Company for $2,000. Issued Check No. 88 for $500 and a 60-day, 4% note (Note Payable No. 3) for $1,500 to the Atlas Company in payment. (Record the entire transaction in the general journal and the payment in the cash payments journal. Insert check marks where necessary so that duplicate posting will be avoided.)

29. Received notice from the bank that Harry Cobb dishonored Note Receivable No. 84 when it became due on March 28. Charged the principal and the interest to Cobb's account.

May 6. Discounted at the Lincoln National Bank our 30-day, non-interest-bearing note (Note Payable No. 4). Face of note, $900; rate of discount, 6%. Received credit for the proceeds.

10. Issued Check No. 103 to the Atlas Company in payment of the principal and the interest on Note Payable No. 3 due today.

June 3. Issued Check No. 146 to Boyd & Company in payment of the principal and the interest on Note Payable No. 2 due today.

5. Issued Check No. 151 to the Lincoln National Bank in payment of Note Payable No. 4 due today.

Oct. 15. Received a check for 50% of the $406 balance owed by Harry Cobb (see March 29 transaction). Wrote off the remainder of the account as uncollectible. (Record the cash receipt in the cash receipts journal in the usual manner. Record the write-off of the remainder of the account in the general journal.)

Instructions: 2. Foot and prove the columnar special journals.

Chapter 30

Accrued expenses

The need for recording accrued expenses

Some expenses, such as wages and interest, accumulate daily but may not be paid until a later fiscal period. Expenses that are incurred in one fiscal period but not paid during that period are called *accrued expenses*.

The income statement at the close of each fiscal period should show all the expenses for the period even though some have not been paid. Also, since accrued expenses are liabilities, they should appear on the balance sheet. As was learned earlier, accounts may require adjustment in order for the financial statements to show the true facts. This chapter shows the adjustments necessary for accrued expenses.

Accrued salaries

J. M. Miller operates his wholesale grocery on a five-day week. During December, 1962, his expense for salaries is $120 a day or $600 a week, payable on a weekly basis every Friday. The following T account and calendar illustrate Mr. Miller's problem of accrued salaries:

Salary Expense		1962		DECEMBER			1962	
		S	M	T	W	T	F	S
								1
1962		2	3	4	5	6	7	8
Dec. 1 Bal. 28,164.00		9	10	11	12	13	14	15
31 2,400.00		16	17	18	19	20	21	22
		23	24	25	26	27	28	29
		30	31	End of 1962 fiscal period				
	Start of 1963 fiscal period	1963		JANUARY			1963	
			1	2	3	4	5	

The debit balance of the salary expense account on December 1, $28,164, is the total of the salary expense for the first eleven months of the year. The debit of $2,400 on December 31 is the total posted from the Salary Expense Debit column of the cash payments journal. It includes the four $600 payrolls paid on December 7, 14, 21, and 28.

At the close of the business day on Monday, December 31, one day or one fifth of the weekly payroll is owed to employees. The salary expense account needs to be adjusted to show this accrued expense. Since the amount owed to employees is a liability, the liability needs to be recorded.

433

The liability account used to record salaries owed to employees but not yet due is called *Salaries Payable*.

Adjusting entry for accrued salaries

Mr. Miller makes the following adjusting entry for accrued salaries on December 31, 1962:

ACCOUNTS PAYABLE DEBIT	GENERAL DEBIT	DATE	NAME OF ACCOUNT	POST. REF.	GENERAL CREDIT	ACCOUNTS RECEIVABLE CREDIT	
			GENERAL JOURNAL PAGE 42				
	120 00	31	*Salary Expense*				15
			Salaries Payable		120 00		16
							17
							18

Adjusting entry for accrued salaries

The salary expense account is debited for $120 so that it will include the salary expense incurred but not paid during 1962. The liability account Salaries Payable is credited for $120, the amount owed to employees for the last day of December, 1962.

When this adjusting entry is posted, the salaries payable account and the salary expense account in the general ledger appear as follows:

Salaries Payable   ACCOUNT NO. 24

DATE	ITEMS	POST. REF.	DEBIT	DATE	ITEMS	POST. REF.	CREDIT
				1962 Dec. 31		J42	120 00

Salary Expense   ACCOUNT NO. 68

DATE	ITEMS	POST. REF.	DEBIT	DATE	ITEMS	POST. REF.	CREDIT
1962 Dec. 1	Balance	✓	28 164 00				
31		CP12	2 400 00 / 30 564 00				
31		J42	120 00				

The credit balance of the salaries payable account, $120, shows the amount owed by Mr. Miller for salaries on December 31. The debit balance of the salary expense account, $30,684, shows the total amount of the expense for salaries for the fiscal year ended December 31, 1962. This total includes salaries already paid during this period, $30,564, and the accrued salaries for the last day at the end of the fiscal period, $120.

434

Accrued interest

Each day that an interest-bearing note payable is owed, the amount of interest expense that is incurred is increased. Even though the note and the interest will not be paid until a future fiscal period, the amount of the interest that was incurred during the current fiscal period should appear on the financial reports.

On December 31, 1962, Mr. Miller's interest expense account in the general ledger appears as shown below.

DATE	ITEMS	POST. REF.	DEBIT	DATE	ITEMS	POST. REF.	CREDIT
1962 Dec. 6		CP12	9 00				

Interest Expense — ACCOUNT NO. 81

The debit to the interest expense account represents interest expense that was paid on December 6, 1962, on a 3-month note for $600 that became due on that date.

On November 1, Mr. Miller issued another note for $3,500. The note was for 90 days, with interest at the rate of 6%, and was due on January 30. The interest expense on this note, $35, for the months of November and December, which were in the fiscal year ended December 31, 1962, should be debited to the interest expense account on December 31 by means of an adjusting entry. The income statement will then show all the interest expense for the fiscal year ended December 31, 1962, even though some of it has not been paid.

Adjusting entry for accrued interest expense

Mr. Miller makes the following adjusting entry for interest expense on December 31, 1962:

GENERAL JOURNAL — PAGE 42

	ACCOUNTS PAYABLE DEBIT	GENERAL DEBIT	DATE	NAME OF ACCOUNT	POST. REF.	GENERAL CREDIT	ACCOUNTS RECEIVABLE CREDIT	
23		35 00	31	Interest Expense				23
24				Interest Payable		35 00		24
25								25
26								26

Adjusting entry for accrued interest expense

435

The interest expense account is debited for $35 so that it will include the interest expense incurred but not paid during 1962. The liability account Interest Payable is credited for $35, the amount that Mr. Miller owes for interest on notes payable on December 31, 1962.

When this adjusting entry is posted, the interest payable account and the interest expense account in the general ledger appear as follows:

DATE	ITEMS	POST. REF.	DEBIT	DATE	ITEMS	POST. REF.	CREDIT

Interest Payable ACCOUNT NO. 22

DATE	ITEMS	POST. REF.	DEBIT	DATE	ITEMS	POST. REF.	CREDIT
				1962 Dec. 31		J42	35 00

Interest Expense ACCOUNT NO. 81

DATE	ITEMS	POST. REF.	DEBIT	DATE	ITEMS	POST. REF.	CREDIT
1962 Dec. 6		CP12	9 00				
31		J42	35 00				

The credit balance of the interest payable account, $35, shows the amount owed by Mr. Miller for interest on December 31, 1962. The debit balance of the interest expense account, $44, shows the total amount of the interest expense for the fiscal period ended December 31, 1962. This total includes the interest expense already paid during the fiscal period, $9, and the accrued interest expense at the end of the fiscal period, $35.

Other accrued expenses

If there are other expenses (such as taxes and miscellaneous expenses for electricity, telephones, etc.) that have accrued but that have not been paid at the end of a fiscal period, an adjusting entry is made for each one. An appropriate expense account should be debited and a liability account (a "payable" account) should be credited in each adjusting entry.

Accruals on the work sheet

The preceding discussion and illustrations have shown: (a) the need for adjusting entries for accrued expenses, (b) the method of recording these adjusting entries in the columnar general journal, and (c) the effect of these entries on the accounts in the general ledger. Before the adjusting entries for accrued expenses are recorded and posted, the work sheet and the statements are prepared.

436

When Mr. Miller prepares his work sheet on December 31, 1962, he makes the following adjustments for accrued expenses in the Adjustments columns:

	ACCOUNT TITLES	ACCT. NO.	TRIAL BALANCE DEBIT	TRIAL BALANCE CREDIT	ADJUSTMENTS DEBIT	ADJUSTMENTS CREDIT
11	Interest Payable	22				(g) 3500
12	Accounts Payable	23		242633		
13	Salaries Payable	24				(h) 12000
31	Federal Unemployment Taxes	64	16040			
32	Insurance Expense	65			(e) 24000	
33	Miscellaneous Expense	66	76225			
34	Rent Expense	67	480000			
35	Salary Expense	68	306840 0		(h) 12000	
36	State Unemployment Taxes	69	54060			
37	Supplies Expense	610			(d) 43817	
38	Interest Expense	81	900		(g) 3500	
39			1183697 4	1183697 4	1062590 4	1062590 4
40	Net Income					
41						

Work sheet showing adjustments for accrued expenses

Effect of accrued expenses on the income statement

The adjusting entries for accrued expenses increase the balances of the expense accounts concerned. For example, the adjusting entry for accrued salary expense increases the balance of the salary expense account by $120. An accrued expense, therefore, appears on the income statement as a part of the balance of the expense account.

When Mr. Miller prepares his income statement on December 31, 1962, the balance of the salary expense account, which includes the salary expense accrued on that date, is listed in the Operating Expenses section in the manner illustrated on page 358.

The balance of the interest expense account, which includes the accrued interest expense, is listed in the Other Expenses section of the income statement in the manner illustrated on page 428.

Accruals on the balance sheet

When Mr. Miller prepares his balance sheet, the liabilities — Interest Payable and Salaries Payable — are listed in the Current Liabilities section of the balance sheet. This section of Mr. Miller's balance sheet for December 31, 1962, is shown in the illustration at the top of the following page.

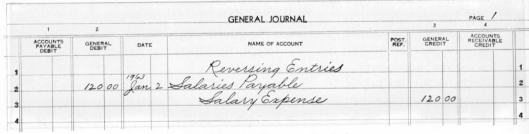

Current liabilities section of the balance sheet

Need for readjusting the salary expense account

When Mr. Miller makes the entry for the next payroll on January 4, 1963, he will debit the entire amount to Salary Expense in the same manner that he recorded the payment of each payroll in 1962. But the salaries for only the first four days of January should be shown as an expense for the fiscal year 1963. This result can be obtained by recording a reversing entry at the beginning of the 1963 fiscal period. A journal entry made at the beginning of a new fiscal period to reverse an adjusting entry that was recorded at the end of the preceding period is called a *reversing entry.*

Reversing entry for accrued salaries

On January 2, 1963, Mr. Miller makes the following entry to readjust the salary expense account:

ACCOUNTS PAYABLE DEBIT	GENERAL DEBIT	DATE	NAME OF ACCOUNT	POST. REF.	GENERAL CREDIT	ACCOUNTS RECEIVABLE CREDIT	
			Reversing Entries				1
	120 00	1963 Jan. 2	Salaries Payable				2
			Salary Expense		120 00		3
							4

GENERAL JOURNAL — PAGE 1

Reversing entry for accrued salaries

Through this entry Salaries Payable is debited for $120, the amount of the accrued salary expense for the preceding fiscal period, the year 1962. Salary Expense is credited for the same amount. This reversing entry is exactly the opposite of the adjusting entry for accrued salary expense recorded on December 31, 1962.

438

The reversing entry is posted to Salaries Payable and to Salary Expense. The salaries payable account is then in balance and is ruled. The accounts after the completion of this work appear as follows:

Salaries Payable — Account No. 24

DATE	ITEMS	POST. REF.	DEBIT	DATE	ITEMS	POST. REF.	CREDIT
1963 Jan. 2		J1	120 00	1962 Dec. 31		J42	120 00

Salary Expense — Account No. 68

DATE	ITEMS	POST. REF.	DEBIT	DATE	ITEMS	POST. REF.	CREDIT
1962 Dec. 1	Balance	✓	28164 00	1962 Dec. 31		J43	30684 00
31		CP12	2400 00				
31		J42	30564 00 / 120 00				
			30684 00				30684 00
				1963 Jan. 2		J1	120 00

The salaries payable account is in balance. The salary expense account has a credit balance of $120, the amount of the salaries incurred but not paid in 1962.

During January, 1963, Mr. Miller pays salaries on January 4, 11, 18, and 25. When the total of the Salary Expense Debit column in the cash payments journal is posted on January 31, the salary expense account in the general ledger appears as follows:

Salary Expense — Account No. 68

DATE	ITEMS	POST. REF.	DEBIT	DATE	ITEMS	POST. REF.	CREDIT
1962 Dec. 1	Balance	✓	28164 00	1962 Dec. 31		J43	30684 00
31		CP12	2400 00				
31		J42	30564 00 / 120 00				
			30684 00				30684 00
1963 Jan. 31		CP1	2400 00	1963 Jan. 2		J1	120 00

The credit of $120 in the salary expense account is the part of the January salary payments that belongs to the preceding year. The balance of the salary expense account, $2,280, is the part of the January salary payments that is actually an expense for 1963.

Need for readjusting the interest expense account

The 90-day, 6% note for $3,500 issued by Mr. Miller on November 1, 1962, is due on January 30, 1963. When Mr. Miller pays this note and the interest on it, he will debit the entire amount of the interest to Interest Expense. But the interest for only one month, January, should be shown as an expense for the fiscal year 1963. This result can be obtained by recording a reversing entry at the beginning of the 1963 fiscal period.

Reversing entry for accrued interest expense

On January 2, 1963, Mr. Miller makes the following reversing entry to readjust the interest expense account:

ACCOUNTS PAYABLE DEBIT	GENERAL DEBIT	DATE	NAME OF ACCOUNT	POST. REF.	GENERAL CREDIT	ACCOUNTS RECEIVABLE CREDIT	
	35 00	2	*Interest Payable*				4
			Interest Expense		35 00		5
							6

GENERAL JOURNAL — PAGE 1

Reversing entry for accrued interest expense

Through this entry Interest Payable is debited for $35, the amount of the accrued interest expense for the preceding fiscal period, the year 1962. Interest Expense is credited for the same amount. This reversing entry is exactly the opposite of the adjusting entry for accrued interest expense recorded on December 31, 1962.

The reversing entry is posted to Interest Payable and to Interest Expense. The interest payable account is then in balance and is ruled. The accounts after the completion of this work appear as follows:

Interest Payable — ACCOUNT NO. 22

DATE	ITEMS	POST. REF.	DEBIT	DATE	ITEMS	POST. REF.	CREDIT
1963 Jan. 2		J1	35 00	1962 Dec. 31		J42	35 00

Interest Expense — ACCOUNT NO. 81

DATE	ITEMS	POST. REF.	DEBIT	DATE	ITEMS	POST. REF.	CREDIT
1962 Dec. 6		CP72	9 00	1962 Dec. 31		J43	44 00
31		J42	35 00				
			44 00				44 00
				1963 Jan. 2		J1	35 00

440

The interest payable account is in balance. The interest expense account has a credit balance of $35, the amount of the interest expense incurred but not paid in 1962.

No additional notes payable are issued prior to January 30, 1963. On January 30, Mr. Miller issues a check for $3,552.50 in payment of his $3,500 note and 90 days' interest, $52.50. This entry is recorded in the columnar cash payments journal as follows:

				1	2	3	4	5	6	7	
DATE	CHK. NO.	ACCOUNT DEBITED	POST. REF.	GENERAL DEBIT	ACCOUNTS PAYABLE DEBIT	SALARY EXPENSE DEBIT	EMPLOYEES INC. TAXES PAYABLE CREDIT	FICA TAXES PAYABLE CREDIT	DISCOUNT ON PURCHASES CREDIT	CASH CREDIT	
30	30 85	Notes Payable		3500 00							30
31		Interest Expense		52 50						3552 50	31

CASH PAYMENTS JOURNAL — PAGE 1

Payment of a note payable and interest

After this entry is posted, the interest expense account appears as follows:

Interest Expense — ACCOUNT NO. 81

DATE	ITEMS	POST. REF.	DEBIT	DATE	ITEMS	POST. REF.	CREDIT
1962 Dec. 6		CP2	9 00	1962 Dec. 31		J43	44 00
31		J42	35 00				
			44 00				44 00
1963 Jan. 31		CP2	52 50	1963 Jan. 2		J1	35 00

The debit entry in the interest expense account shows the interest expense, $52.50, that was paid on January 30. The credit entry in this account, $35, shows the part of this payment that belongs to the preceding fiscal year. The balance of the interest expense account, $17.50, represents the part of the $52.50 interest payment that belongs to the fiscal year 1963.

Accrued income

Income that is earned in one fiscal period but collected in a later fiscal period is called *accrued income*. Examples of accrued income are interest income and rent income. Each accrued income must be recorded before the reports are prepared at the end of the fiscal period so that the income statement will be complete and accurate.

The adjusting entry for any accrued income requires a debit to an asset account (a "receivable" account) and a credit to an income account. For example, an adjusting entry for interest accrued on notes receivable debits Interest Receivable and credits Interest Income.

The reversing entry for any accrued income requires a credit to an asset account (a "receivable" account) and a debit to an income account. For example, a reversing entry for interest accrued on notes receivable debits Interest Income and credits Interest Receivable.

Increasing your business vocabulary

What is the meaning of each of the following:

(a) accrued expenses   (b) reversing entry   (c) accrued income

Chapter questions

1. Why should expenses that have been incurred but not paid be recorded before the financial reports are prepared at the end of the fiscal period?
2. What entry is made in the columnar general journal on page 434 to record the adjusting entry for accrued salaries?
3. What entry is made in the columnar general journal on page 435 to record the adjusting entry for accrued interest expense?
4. Under what heading on the income statement is the balance of the salary expense account listed?
5. Under what heading on the income statement is the balance of the interest expense account listed?
6. Under what heading on the balance sheet are the balances of the interest payable and salaries payable accounts listed?
7. Why is it desirable to record a reversing entry for salaries payable at the beginning of each fiscal period?
8. What reversing entry is made in the columnar general journal on page 438 to readjust the salary expense account?
9. What reversing entry is made in the columnar general journal on page 440 to readjust the interest expense account?

Cases for discussion

1. At the end of the fiscal period the bookkeeper for the Royal Manufacturing Company failed to record a liability of $200 arising from accrued salaries. What effect did this omission have (a) on the income statement and (b) on the balance sheet?
2. After L. C. Russell closed his books on March 31, his ledger included two liability accounts, Salaries Payable and Interest Payable. All of the salaries payable will be paid within three days after the beginning of the next fiscal period. The interest payable has accrued on five notes that will come due on different dates during the next period. For which of these two liabilities will a reversing entry be more beneficial?

Application problems

Problem 30-1. *Adjusting, closing, and reversing entries for accrued expenses*

The following selected accounts from the ledger of Arthur Boyd contained the balances shown below on December 31 of the current year:

ACCT. NO.	ACCOUNT TITLE	ACCOUNT DEBIT	BALANCE CREDIT
212	Interest Payable		——
214	Salaries Payable		——
313	Income and Expense Summary		——
618	Salary Expense	$6,370.00	
811	Interest Expense	87.50	

On December 31, accrued salaries were $121.00 and accrued interest on the two notes payable outstanding amounted to $43.60.

Instructions: 1. Open the five general ledger accounts shown above and record the balances.

2. Record on page 34 of a columnar general journal as of December 31 the adjusting entries for the accrued expenses.

3. Post the adjusting entries for accrued expenses to the ledger accounts.

4. Record in the columnar general journal an entry to close the salary expense and interest expense accounts.

5. Post this closing entry. Rule the two expense accounts.

6. Record the reversing entries on January 2 of the new year.

7. Post the reversing entries to the ledger accounts.

Problem 30-2. *Work at the end of the fiscal period*

The account numbers, titles, and balances in the general ledger of Vanity Fair, a dress shop owned and operated by Norma Curtis, on December 31 of the current year were as follows:

111 Cash, $5,612.48

112 Accounts Receivable, $4,615.40

112.1 Allowance for Bad Debts, $168.15

113 Merchandise Inventory, $10,648.82

114 Supplies, $810.55

115 Prepaid Insurance, $636.00

121 Equipment, $2,137.50

121.1 Allowance for Depreciation of Equipment, $613.49

122 Building, $10,000.00

122.1 Allowance for Depreciation of Building, $1,250.00

211 Notes Payable, $2,000.00

212 Interest Payable, ———

213 Accounts Payable, $3,233.75

214 Sales Taxes Payable, $137.04

215 Salaries Payable, ———

216 Employees Income Taxes Payable, $191.40

217 FICA Taxes Payable, $93.78

218 State Unemployment Taxes Payable, $40.50

219 Federal Unemployment Taxes Payable, $47.36

311	Norma Curtis, Capital, $14,957.00	614	Depreciation of Building, ——
312	Norma Curtis, Drawing, $3,600.00	615	Depreciation of Equipment,——
313	Income and Expense Summary,	616	FICA Taxes, $185.00
	——	617	Federal Unemployment Taxes, $47.36
411	Sales, $71,347.32		
411.1	Sales Returns and Allowances, $2,755.84	618	Heat, Light, and Power, $1,953.27
		619	Insurance Expense, ——
511	Purchases, $41,898.71	620	Miscellaneous Expense, $579.58
511.1	Purchases Returns and Allowances, $566.40	621	Salary Expense, $5,920.00
		622	State Unemployment Taxes, $159.84
511.2	Discount on Purchases, $671.90		
611	Advertising Expense, $1,875.00	623	Supplies Expense, ——
612	Bad Debts Expense, ——	811	Interest Expense, $172.14
613	Delivery Expense, $1,710.60		

The additional data needed at the end of the period are:

Additional allowance for bad debts, 1% of total charge sales of $36,330.20.

Merchandise inventory, December 31, $8,633.75

Supplies on hand, $254.12

Prepaid insurance, $136.00

Annual rate of estimated depreciation of equipment, 8%

Annual rate of estimated depreciation of building, 2½%

Accrued interest expense, $20.00

Accrued salary expense, $21.50

Instructions: 1. Prepare an eight-column work sheet for the annual fiscal period ended December 31 of the current year.

2. Prepare an income statement and a balance sheet from the work sheet.

3. Record the adjusting entries and the closing entries in a columnar general journal.

4. Record the reversing entries for accruals as of January 2 of next year in a columnar general journal.

Optional problems

Supplementary Problems 30-S. *Adjusting, closing, and reversing entries for accrued expenses*

The following selected accounts from the ledger of Albert Whitney contained the balances as shown below on December 31 of the current fiscal year before adjusting entries had been made:

ACCT. NO.	ACCOUNT TITLE	ACCOUNT BALANCE DEBIT	CREDIT
115	Prepaid Insurance	$ 360	
212	Interest Payable		——
214	Salaries Payable		——
612	Insurance Expense	——	
618	Salary Expense	12,635	
811	Interest Expense	110	

Adjustment information at December 31 included the following:

(a) The $360 in the prepaid insurance account was the premium paid on July 1 covering a two-year period.

(b) Accrued salaries payable were $218.

(c) Accrued interest was payable on a 120-day, 6% note for $2,000 dated December 1.

Instructions: 1. Open the six ledger accounts and record the balances.

2. Record on page 12 of a columnar general journal as of December 31 the adjusting entries for the prepaid expenses and the accrued expenses. Post to the ledger accounts.

3. Record the entry to close the expense accounts.

4. Post the credits of the closing entry to the ledger accounts and rule the accounts that should be ruled.

5. Record and post the reversing entries on January 2 of the new year.

Bonus Problem 30-B. *Adjusting, closing, and reversing entries for accrued expenses and accrued income*

The following selected accounts from the ledger of John Tyler contained the balances as shown below on December 31 of the current fiscal year before adjusting entries had been made:

ACCT. No.	ACCOUNT TITLE	ACCOUNT BALANCES DEBIT	CREDIT
114	Interest Receivable	——	
115	Rent Receivable	——	
214	Salaries Payable		——
618	Salary Expense	$ 24,312	
711	Interest Income		——
712	Rent Income		$ 1,000

Adjustment information at December 31 included the following:

(a) Accrued interest receivable was on a 60-day, 6% note for $4,000 dated November 16.

(b) Accrued rent receivable amounted to $200.

(c) Accrued salaries payable were $187.

Instructions: 1. Open the six ledger accounts listed and record the balances.

2. Record on page 19 of a columnar general journal as of December 31 the adjusting entries for the accrued income and for the accrued expenses. Post to the ledger accounts available.

3. Record the entry to close the income accounts and post the debit amounts.

4. Record the entry to close the expense account and post the credit amount.

5. Rule the accounts that should be ruled.

6. Record and post the reversing entries on January 2 of the new year.

Chapter 31

Partnerships

Why are partnerships formed?

Many businesses require more capital than one individual is able to furnish. In such a case two or more persons may combine their assets to provide the necessary capital. Also, the efficiency of a business may be improved when the responsibility for management is divided among two or more owners. The owners may then combine both their assets and their skills with the agreement that they are to share the profits and the losses.

When two or more persons combine their property or their skill or both in one business and agree to share in the profits or the losses, the business is referred to as a *partnership*. Each member of a partnership is known as a *partner*. Partnerships are common in retail stores, in personal services businesses, and among professional men such as lawyers, doctors, and accountants.

A partnership is similar to a single proprietorship, except that in the single proprietorship one person is the owner, while in the partnership two or more persons share in the ownership.

Organization of a partnership

A partnership is formed by an agreement or contract between the partners. This agreement may be oral, but it is desirable to have it in writing to avoid any misunderstandings that might arise from oral agreements. The written agreement by which a partnership is formed is commonly referred to as the *articles of copartnership*.

The articles of copartnership ordinarily show the following:

1. The names of the partners.
2. The kind of business.
3. The length of time the partnership is to run.
4. The name and the location of the business.
5. The amount of the investment of each partner.
6. The investment of each partner.
7. The duties of each partner.
8. The limitations on each partner's activities.
9. How income and losses are to be distributed.

The illustration on the next page contains the information usually included in the articles of copartnership.

ARTICLES OF COPARTNERSHIP

THIS CONTRACT, made and entered into on the first day of November, 1962, by and between Arthur F. Poultney, of Butte, Montana, and David D. Duane, of the same city and state.

WITNESSETH: That the said parties have this day formed a copartnership for the purpose of engaging in and conducting a wholesale drug supply business in the city of Butte under the following stipulations, which are a part of this contract:

FIRST: The said copartnership is to continue for a term of ten years from November 1, 1962.

SECOND: The business is to be conducted under the firm name of Acme Drug Supply Company, at 827 Main Street, Butte, Montana.

THIRD: The investments are as follows: Arthur F. Poultney, cash, $25,000; David D. Duane, cash, $25,000. These invested assets are partnership property in which the equity of each partner is the same.

FOURTH: Each partner is to devote his entire time and attention to the business and to engage in no other business enterprise without the written consent of the other partner.

FIFTH: During the operation of this partnership, neither partner is to become surety or bondsman for anyone without the written consent of the other partner.

SIXTH: Each partner is to receive a salary of $7,200 a year, payable $600 in cash on the last business day of each month. At the end of each annual fiscal period the net income or the net loss shown by the income statement, after the salaries of the two partners have been allowed, is to be shared as follows: Arthur F. Poultney, 60 per cent; David D. Duane, 40 per cent.

SEVENTH: Neither partner is to withdraw assets in excess of his salary, any part of the assets invested, or assets in anticipation of net income to be earned, without the written consent of the other partner.

EIGHTH: In case of the death or the legal disability of either partner, the other partner is to continue the operations of the business until the close of the annual fiscal period on the following December 31. At that time the continuing partner is to be given an option to buy the interest of the deceased or incapacitated partner at not more than 10 per cent above the value of the deceased or incapacitated partner's proprietary interest as shown by the balance of his capital account after the books are closed on December 31. It is agreed that this purchase price is to be paid one half in cash and the balance in four equal installments payable quarterly.

NINTH: At the conclusion of this contract, unless it is mutually agreed to continue the operation of the business under a new contract, the assets of the partnership, after the liabilities are paid, are to be divided in proportion to the net credit to each partner's capital account on that date.

IN WITNESS WHEREOF, the parties aforesaid have hereunto set their hands and affixed their seals on the day and year above written.

Arthur F. Poultney (Seal)

David D. Duane (Seal)

Articles of copartnership

Partnerships accounts

As in a single proprietorship, the number of accounts in the general ledger of a partnership depends upon the kind of business and the information desired. Since two or more persons share in the ownership of a partnership, separate capital accounts should be maintained for each partner. The capital account of each partner should show his share in the business, that is, the value of his ownership.

A separate drawing account may also be maintained for each partner in order to record the partners' withdrawals of cash and merchandise.

Forming a partnership with cash investments

The opening entries of a partnership are similar to the opening entries of a single proprietorship. Ordinarily a separate entry is made to record the investment of each partner.

The illustration on the preceding page shows the articles of copartnership drawn up by A. F. Poultney and D. D. Duane when they formed a partnership to begin a wholesale drug supply business on November 1. Each partner invested $25,000 in cash. To record the investment of each partner, the following entries were made in the columnar cash receipts journal:

	DATE	ACCOUNT CREDITED	POST. REF.	GENERAL CR.	SALES CR.	ACCOUNTS RECEIVABLE CR.	DISCOUNT ON SALES DR.	CASH DR.	
1	1962 Nov. 1	A. F. Poultney, Capital		25000 00				25000 00	1
2	1	D. D. Duane, Capital		25000 00				25000 00	2

CASH RECEIPTS JOURNAL — PAGE 1

Cash investments of a partnership recorded in a cash receipts journal

Converting a single proprietorship business into a partnership

An established business operated by one owner may be converted into a partnership by a merger with another business or by the investment of cash or other assets by another person.

L. K. Holmes operated a supply business. On January 2 he formed a partnership with F. G. Harris. Mr. Holmes invested the assets of his business, and the partnership assumed the liabilities of his business. Mr. Harris invested $10,000 in cash.

The new partnership, Holmes and Harris, decided to open a new set of books. The investment of each partner was recorded with an opening entry in the columnar general journal. The two opening entries as they appeared in the columnar general journal on January 2, 1962, are shown at the top of the following page.

448

GENERAL JOURNAL PAGE 1

ACCOUNTS PAYABLE DR.	GENERAL DR.	DATE	NAME OF ACCOUNT	POST. REF.	GENERAL CR.	ACCOUNTS RECEIVABLE CR.	
	765 50	1962 Jan. 2	Cash				1
	3422 00		Accounts Receivable				2
	20885 00		Merchandise Inventory				3
	450 00		Supplies				4
	5300 00		Equipment				5
			Accounts Payable		822 50		6
			L.K. Holmes, Capital		30000 00		7
			Investment.				8
	10000 00	2	Cash				9
			F.T. Harris, Capital		10000 00		10
			Investment.				11

Opening entries for a partnership recorded in a columnar general journal

The cash investments of the partners are not recorded in the cash receipts journal, as the amount of the cash is posted directly from the general journal. The amount of cash is, however, recorded as a memorandum entry on the first line of the cash receipts journal as a balance for future use in proving cash. The cash receipts journal of Holmes and Harris with the memorandum entry showing the beginning cash balance is illustrated below.

CASH RECEIPTS JOURNAL PAGE 1

DATE	ACCOUNT CREDITED	POST. REF.	GENERAL CR.	SALES CR.	ACCOUNTS RECEIVABLE CR.	DISCOUNT ON SALES DR.	CASH DR.	
1962 Jan. 2	Balance on hand, $10,765.50	✓						1
								2

Beginning cash balance of a partnership recorded in a cash receipts journal

Recording an investment in a going concern

When a going concern of a single proprietorship is converted into a partnership, it may be agreed that the books of the original business are to be continued. It is only necessary then to record the investment of the new partner. This may be done by debiting the asset accounts for the assets invested, crediting the liability accounts for the liabilities assumed, and crediting the new partner's capital account for the net amount of his investment.

449

Partners' salaries

In the partnership of Holmes and Harris, Mr. Holmes had been operating a supply business for several years. Mr. Harris was a young man with no experience in the supply business. The articles of copartnership therefore provided that Mr. Holmes was to receive a monthly salary of $750 and Mr. Harris a monthly salary of $500.

Salaries of partners may be considered as withdrawals and may be debited to the partners' drawing accounts the same as other withdrawals of cash or merchandise. But the federal income tax form used by a partnership provides for reporting payments of partners' salaries as an expense of the business. The partnership of Holmes and Harris therefore debits the payment of salaries to the partners to an account entitled *Partners Salaries.* At the end of the fiscal period this account, together with other expense accounts, is closed to Income and Expense Summary.

Partners are not considered to be employees of the business; therefore the salary payments to partners are not subject to withholding for income taxes or FICA taxes.

Income statement of a partnership

The income statement of a partnership is similar to that of a single proprietorship. The income statement prepared for the Holmes and Harris partnership on December 31, 1962, is illustrated on the next page.

Division of net income or net loss among partners

Partnership net income or net loss may be divided in any way desired by the partners. The method of division is ordinarily stated in the articles of copartnership. If the partnership agreement does not state how the amount of income or loss is to be divided, it is assumed by law that the income or the loss is to be shared equally.

The articles of copartnership of the partnership of Holmes and Harris provided that salaries were to be paid to the partners. These salaries are shown as one of the expenses on the income statement on page 451. The net income or the net loss of the partnership was to be divided as follows:

(a) Each partner was to receive an amount equal to 6% of his capital to provide for the difference in the investments.
(b) The remainder was to be distributed between the partners equally.

Mr. Holmes's capital was $30,000. Mr. Harris' capital was $10,000. The net income as shown on the income statement on page 451 was $4,000. Each partner's share of the net income was determined as shown on page 452.

```
                        Holmes and Harris
                        Income Statement
                 For Year Ended December 31, 1962
```

Income from Sales:
 Sales $99,204.03
 Less: Sales Returns and Allowances . $ 735.46
     Discount on Sales 477.48   1,212.94
 Net Sales. $97,991.09

Cost of Merchandise Sold:
 Merchandise Inventory, Jan. 1, 1962. . $21,432.25
 Purchases. $70,255.80
 Less: Purchases Ret.& Allow.$ 740.82
     Discount on Purchases 1,196.87   1,937.69
 Net Purchases. 68,318.11
 Total Cost of Mdse. Available for Sale $89,750.36
 Less Mdse. Inventory, Dec. 31, 1962. .   23,194.85
 Cost of Merchandise Sold 66,555.51

Gross Profit on Sales $31,435.58

Operating Expenses:
 Bad Debts Expense. . . . . $ 285.68
 Delivery Expense 1,600.82
 Depreciation Expense 975.00
 FICA Taxes 216.45
 Federal Unemployment Taxes 55.41
 Insurance Expense. 248.00
 Miscellaneous Expense. 740.50
 Partners Salaries. 15,000.00
 Property Taxes 535.20
 Salary Expense 7,061.75
 State Unemployment Taxes 187.02
 Supplies Expense 356.29

  Total Operating Expenses 27,262.12

Net Income from Operations. . . . . $ 4,173.46

Other Income:
 Interest Income. . . . . $ 72.16

Other Expense:
 Interest Expense 245.62

Net Deduction 173.46

Net Income. . . . . $ 4,000.00

Income statement of a partnership

451

Net income			$4,000

Less 6% of each partner's capital:

L. K. Holmes (6% of $30,000)		$1,800	
F. G. Harris (6% of $10,000)		600	2,400

Remainder of net income for distribution to partners			$1,600

Division of remaining net income:
L. K. Holmes: ½ of $1,600 = $800
F. G. Harris: ½ of $1,600 = $800

Summary:

L. K. Holmes:	6% of capital	$1,800
	½ of remainder of net income	800
	Total share of net income	$2,600

F. G. Harris:	6% of capital	$ 600
	½ of remainder of net income	800
	Total share of net income	$1,400

Statement showing distribution of net income

After the distribution of net income is calculated, a separate statement that shows the details of the distribution is prepared for the two partners. On December 31, the end of the fiscal year, a distribution of net income statement is prepared as follows:

```
                        Holmes and Harris
                Distribution of Net Income Statement
                  For Year Ended December 31, 1962


L. K. Holmes:
    6% of capital . . . . . . . . . . . . . . . .    $1,800.00
    ½ of remaining net income . . . . . . . . . .       800.00
    Total share of net income                                    $2,600.00

F. G. Harris:
    6% of capital . . . . . . . . . . . . . . . .    $  600.00
    ½ of remaining net income . . . . . . . . . .       800.00
    Total share of net income . . . . . . . . .                  $1,400.00

Net Income . . . . . . . . . . . . . . . . . .                   $4,000.00
```

Distribution of net income statement

Balance sheet of a partnership

The balance sheet of Holmes and Harris on December 31, 1962, is shown on page 453. Note that this balance sheet is similar to that of a single proprietorship except that it shows each partner's present capital as of the date of the balance sheet.

```
                        Holmes and Harris
                         Balance Sheet
                       December 31, 1962
```

Assets

Current Assets:
Cash		$ 4,760.08
Petty Cash		50.00
Notes Receivable		3,100.00
Accounts Receivable	$ 5,582.37	
Less Allowance for Bad Debts . .	267.37	5,315.00
Merchandise Inventory.		21,422.34
Supplies		459.58
Prepaid Insurance		376.00

Total Current Assets $35,483.00

Fixed Assets:
Equipment.	$ 5,300.00	
Less Allow. for Depr. of Equipment	795.00	$ 4,505.00
Building	$ 9,000.00	
Less Allow. for Depr. of Building.	180.00	8,820.00

Total Fixed Assets. 13,325.00

Total Assets. $48,808.00

Liabilities

Current Liabilities:
Notes Payable	$ 2,000.00
Interest Payable	18.00
Accounts Payable	2,562.12
Salaries Payable	135.25
Employees Income Taxes Payable. . .	191.80
FICA Taxes Payable.	101.55
State Unemployment Taxes Payable . .	43.87
Federal Unemployment Taxes Payable .	55.41

Total Current Liabilities . . . . $ 5,108.00

Proprietorship

L. K. Holmes, Capital	$32,400.00
F. G. Harris, Capital	11,300.00

Total Proprietorship. 43,700.00

Total Liabilities and Proprietorship . . $48,808.00

Balance sheet of a partnership

Capital statement of a partnership

The balance sheet of the partnership of Holmes and Harris shows the present capital of each partner at the end of the fiscal period, but it does not show the details of the changes during the fiscal period. Note that each partner may have this detailed information if the following capital statement is prepared.

```
                          Holmes and Harris
                          Capital Statement
                   For Year Ended December 31, 1962


L. K. Holmes:
      Capital, January 1, 1962 . . . . .            $30,000.00
      Share of Net Income  . . . . . . .  $2,600.00
            Less Withdrawals  . . . . . .    200.00
      Net Increase in Capital  . . . . .                2,400.00
      Present Capital, December 31, 1962                           $32,400.00

F. G. Harris:
      Capital, January 1, 1962 . . . . .            $10,000.00
      Share of Net Income  . . . . . . .  $1,400.00
            Less Withdrawals  . . . . . .    100.00
      Net Increase in Capital  . . . . .                1,300.00
      Present Capital, December 31, 1962                           11,300.00

Total Proprietorship, December 31, 1962                           $43,700.00
```

Capital statement of a partnership

Note that the salaries paid the partners are not shown on the capital statement, as they were recorded as expenses of the partnership. The statement does show that L. K. Holmes withdrew $200 and F. G. Harris withdrew $100. These amounts represent withdrawals of cash or merchandise and were recorded as debits in the partners' drawing accounts.

Adjusting entries for a partnership

The adjusting entries for a partnership are similar to those for a single proprietorship type of business. The Adjustments columns of the work sheet are used as the basis for the adjusting entries. The adjusting entries are recorded in the general journal.

Closing entries for a partnership

With the exception of the entries needed to close the income and expense summary account, the closing entries for a partnership are similar to those for a single proprietorship. All closing entries are made from the information given on the work sheet, except that the amount to be credited to each partner's capital account when the income and expense summary account is closed is obtained from the distribution of net income statement. The entries to close the income and expense summary account and the drawing accounts of the partners were as follows:

	ACCOUNTS PAYABLE DEBIT	GENERAL DEBIT	DATE	NAME OF ACCOUNT	POST. REF.	GENERAL CREDIT	ACCOUNTS RECEIVABLE CREDIT	
				GENERAL JOURNAL			PAGE *17*	
24		4000 00	31	Income and Expense Summary				24
25				L. K. Holmes, Capital		2600 00		25
26				F. G. Harris, Capital		1400 00		26
27		200 00	31	L. K. Holmes, Capital				27
28				L. K. Holmes, Drawing		200 00		28
29		100 00	31	F. G. Harris, Capital				29
30				F. G. Harris, Drawing		100 00		30
31								31
32								32

Closing entries for a partnership recorded in a columnar general journal

Increasing your business vocabulary

What is the meaning of each of the following:
(a) partnership   (b) partner   (c) articles of copartnership

Chapter questions

1. Why are partnerships formed?
2. Why should the partnership agreement be in writing?
3. What are the principal provisions of the partnership agreement on page 447?
4. How do the accounts in the general ledger of a partnership differ from those of a single proprietorship?
5. What account is debited to record the payment of partners' salaries?
6. How is the amount of income or loss divided when the partnership agreement does not state the method of division?
7. How is the net income of the partnership of Holmes and Harris divided?
8. What information does the distribution of net income statement show?
9. How does the balance sheet of a partnership differ from the balance sheet of a single proprietorship?
10. What information does the capital statement show?
11. What closing entries are made to close the accounts of a partnership?

Cases for discussion

1. A. R. Brook owns and operates a garage in the center of a large city. The garage is used only for storage. Many of Mr. Brook's customers have asked that their cars be repaired while stored during the day or night. Mr. Brook decides to install a repair department. Alan Cook, an able mechanic, is

available for taking charge of the new repair department. He is willing to consider the position either as a partner or as an employee. Indicate some of the possible advantages and disadvantages to Mr. Brook of admitting Mr. Cook as a partner.

2. For the past thirty-five years Donald Powers has operated a large mercantile store. He has decided to offer a partnership to David Ambler, a young man without capital and without much store experience. How may the partnership profits be divided so as to recognize (a) differences in business experience and (b) differences in investment?

Application problems

Problem 31-1. *Opening entries for cash investment in a partnership*

On May 1 of the current year, Henry Osborn and John Harmon formed a partnership to begin a haberdashery business. Each partner invested $5,000 in cash.

Instructions: Record the opening entry for each partner in a columnar cash receipts journal.

Problem 31-2. *Opening entries for investment of cash and other assets in a partnership*

On August 1 of the current year, Louis Harvey and Daniel Lynn formed a partnership for the purpose of continuing a retail music store that Mr. Harvey had been operating. The partnership, Harvey & Lynn, took over the assets of Mr. Harvey's business and assumed his liabilities. Mr. Lynn invested cash equal to Mr. Harvey's proprietorship. The balance sheet of Louis Harvey appeared as shown below.

	Louis Harvey Balance Sheet July 31, 19--			
Assets			*Liabilities*	
Cash................	3,633 60	Notes Payable........	3,000 00	
Notes Receivable......	560 00	Accounts Payable......	1,763 09	
Accounts Receivable...	2,126 75	Total Liabilities.......	4,763 09	
Merchandise Inventory.	7,930 57			
Supplies.............	388 62			
Equipment..........	2,395 40	*Proprietorship*		
		Louis Harvey, Capital..	12,271 85	
Total Assets.........	17,034 94	Total Liab. and Prop...	17,034 94	

Instructions: 1. Record the opening entry for each partner in a columnar general journal.

2. Record the memorandum entry to show the total cash balance in a columnar cash receipts journal.

Problem 31-3. *Distribution of the net income of a partnership*

J. Roth, L. Sayers, and M. Tyler were partners in the retail clothing business of Roth, Sayers, & Tyler. The partners had invested in the business $16,000, $14,000, and $10,000 respectively. According to the partnership agreement the net income was to be divided as follows:

(1) Each partner was to receive an amount equal to 6% of his capital.
(2) The remainder of the net income or the net loss was to be distributed among the partners equally.

At the end of the annual fiscal period on December 31 of the current year, the income statement showed that the net income for the year, after the payment of partners' salaries, amounted to $6,000.

Instructions: 1. Prepare a distribution of net income statement.

2. Prepare a capital statement. The debit balances of the partners' drawing accounts on December 31 were: Roth, $250; Sayers, $100; Tyler, $120.

Problem 31-4. *Work at the end of the fiscal period*

The account numbers, titles, and balances in the general ledger of Judd & Peck, partners in a household furnishings business, on December 31 of the current year were as follows:

111	Cash, $2,448.18		217	State Unemployment Taxes Payable, $24.30
112	Petty Cash, $50.00			
113	Accounts Receivable, $5,505.66		311	J. A. Judd, Capital, $15,000.00
113.1	Allowance for Bad Debts, $287.50		312	J. A. Judd, Drawing, $361.40 (Dr.)
114	Merchandise Inventory, $17,461.49		313	C. R. Peck, Capital, $10,000.00
115	Supplies, $293.60		314	C. R. Peck, Drawing, $116.15 (Dr.)
116	Prepaid Insurance, $240.00		315	Income and Expense Summary, —
121	Equipment, $2,365.10		411	Sales, $60,618.31
121.1	Allowance for Depreciation of Equipment, $581.80		411.1	Sales Returns and Allowances, $396.14
211	Notes Payable, $1,000.00		511	Purchases, $41,060.63
212	Interest Payable, —		511.1	Purchases Returns and Allowances, $185.00
213	Accounts Payable, $1,630.20			
214	Salaries Payable, —		511.2	Discount on Purchases, $423.82
215	Employees Income Taxes Payable, $120.60		611	Bad Debts Expense, —
			612	Delivery Expense, $1,380.48
216	FICA Taxes Payable, $56.25		613	Depreciation Expense, —

614	FICA Taxes, $112.50	620	State Unemployment Taxes, $97.20
615	Insurance Expense, —		
616	Miscellaneous Expense, $629.75	621	Supplies Expense, —
617	Partners Salaries, $12,000.00	711	Interest Income, $9.00
618	Rent Expense, $1,800.00	811	Interest Expense, $18.50
619	Salary Expense, $3,600.00		

Instructions: 1. Prepare an eight-column work sheet for the annual fiscal period ended December 31 of the current year. The additional data needed at the end of the annual fiscal period are:

Additional allowance for bad debts, 1% of charge sales of $20,731.16
Merchandise inventory, $20,723.40
Supplies inventory, $48.23
Prepaid insurance, $60.00
Annual rate of estimated depreciation of equipment, 5%
Accrued interest expense, $5.00
Accrued salary expense, $75.00

2. Prepare an income statement.

3. Prepare a capital statement. The net income is to be distributed in proportion to the partners' investments as shown by their capital account balances.

4. Prepare a balance sheet.

5. Record the adjusting entries and the closing entries.

6. Record the reversing entries for the accruals as of January 1 of the next year.

Chapter 32

Corporations and cooperatives

Nature of a corporation

Large businesses, such as factories and public utilities, usually require more capital than can be furnished by one individual or by several partners. With the growth of large business units has come a need for amounts of capital that may be obtained only from many individuals. A form of business organization that has the legal right to act as one person but that is owned by many is known as a *corporation*.

Most corporations are authorized by a state government. Some corporations are authorized by the federal government, such as national banks. Each corporation has legal authority to act as an individual. A corporation is an artificial person created by law.

Advantages of corporate organization

The corporate form of organization has many advantages over the single proprietorship and the partnership. Some of these advantages are:

(a) The investors are not responsible for the debts of a corporation.

(b) It permits many investors to combine their capital.

(c) It allows each investor to transfer his interest in the corporation without securing the consent of the other owners and without dissolving the corporation.

(d) It is not terminated by the death of the investors.

Ownership of a corporation

In a corporation there are ordinarily a number of owners, but the ownership of each person is not represented by a separate capital account for each investor as it is in a partnership. The ownership in a corporation is divided into units known as *shares*. All of the shares are referred to as the *capital stock*. The owner of one or more shares of the capital stock is known as a *stockholder*. The evidence of each stockholder's ownership in the corporation is a certificate known as a *stock certificate*. A typical stock certificate is illustrated on page 460.

Organization of a corporation

Corporations are organized through the authority provided by state and federal laws. The laws grant the right to incorporate a business and also prescribe the method of incorporation. Most states require that three or

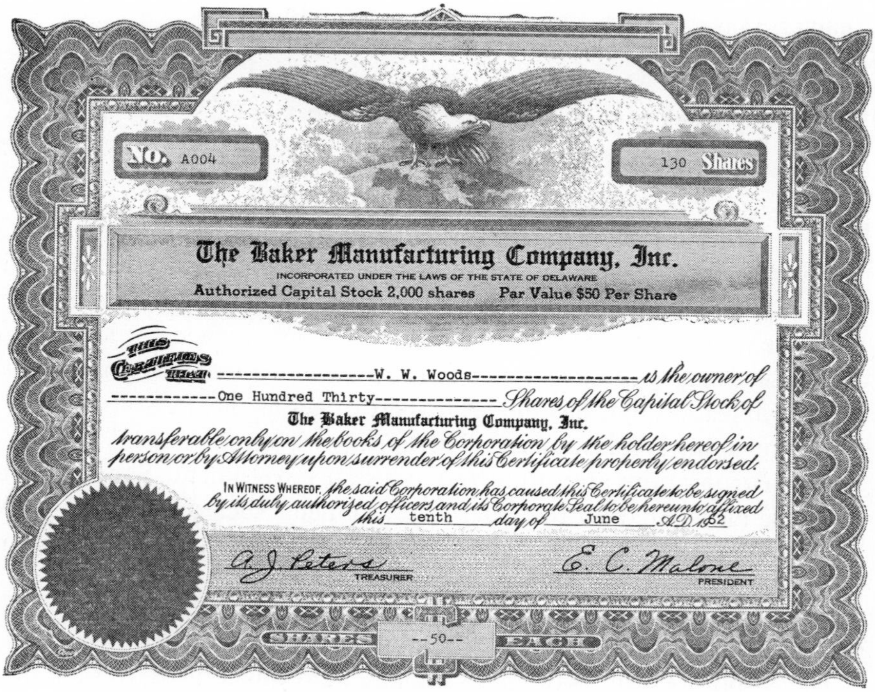

Stock certificate

more individuals provide the assets with which to organize the corporation. The incorporators must make written application to the proper state or federal officials. A written application to the state for permission to incorporate is known as a *certificate of incorporation.*

The certificate of incorporation usually contains: (1) the name under which the business is to be operated; (2) the location of the principal office of the corporation; (3) the object of the proposed corporation; (4) the amount of the capital stock, the kind of stock, and the number of shares; (5) the amount of capital with which the corporation will commence business; (6) the names and the addresses of the incorporators; and (7) the period for which the corporation is formed.

On June 2, 1962, E. C. Malone, F. E. Hill, A. J. Peters, and W. W. Woods decided to organize a corporation to manufacture and sell machinery used by bakers. They drew up the certificate of incorporation and filed it with the secretary of state of the state in which the corporation was to be formed. This certificate of incorporation is shown on page 461. The secretary of state furnished a certified copy of the certificate of incorporation to the organizers. This copy was recorded in the office of the recorder of the county in which the business was located. The certified copy of the certificate of incorporation is referred to as the *charter* of the corporation.

460

CERTIFICATE OF INCORPORATION
of
THE BAKER MANUFACTURING COMPANY, INC.

FIRST: The name of the corporation is The Baker Manufacturing Company, Inc.

SECOND: The principal office of said corporation is located at 105 West Tenth Street, in the City of Wilmington, County of New Castle, Delaware.

THIRD: The nature of the business, or objects or purposes to be transacted, promoted, or carried on are to engage in the business of manufacturing and selling machinery used by bakers and all business incidental to such manufacture and sale.

FOURTH: The total number of shares of stock that the corporation shall have authority to issue is Two Thousand (2,000) and the par value of each of such shares is Fifty Dollars ($50), amounting in the aggregate to One Hundred Thousand Dollars ($100,000).

FIFTH: The amount of capital with which the corporation will commence business is Thirty-three Thousand Dollars ($33,000).

SIXTH: The names and the places of residence of the incorporators are as follows:
E. C. Malone..... 1527 Vineyard Place, Dover, Delaware
F. E. Hill....... 3466 Trimble Avenue, Wilmington, Delaware
A. J. Peters..... 17 Beechcrest Road, Newport, Delaware
W. W. Woods...... 351 Park Avenue, New York, New York

SEVENTH: The corporation is to have perpetual existence.

WE, THE UNDERSIGNED, being each of the incorporators hereinbefore named for the purpose of forming a corporation to do business both within and without the State of Delaware, and in pursuance of the General Corporation Law of the State of Delaware, being Chapter 65 of the Revised Code of Delaware, and the acts amendatory thereof and supplemental thereto, do make this certificate, hereby declaring and certifying that the facts herein stated are true, and accordingly have hereunto set our hands and seals this second day of June, A. D. 1962.

In the presence of:

D. V. Price

R. E. Holt

E. C. Malone (SEAL)
F. E. Hill (SEAL)
A. J. Peters (SEAL)
W. W. Woods (SEAL)

State of Delaware ⎫ ss.:
County of New Castle ⎭

BE IT REMEMBERED, That on this second day of June, A. D. 1962, personally came before me, Matthew J. Moore, a Notary Public for the State of Delaware, all of the parties to the foregoing certificate of incorporation, known to me personally to be such, and severally acknowledged the said certificate to be the act and deed of the signers respectively and that the facts therein stated are truly set forth.

GIVEN under my hand and seal of office the day and year aforesaid.

Matthew J. Moore
Notary Public

Certificate of incorporation

Capital stock

The fourth paragraph of the charter on page 461 indicated that The Baker Manufacturing Company was authorized to issue capital stock in the amount of $100,000. The total amount of stock that a corporation is permitted by its charter to issue is known as the *authorized capital stock*.

According to the fourth paragraph of the charter, the total authorized capital stock of The Baker Manufacturing Company was divided into 2,000 shares, each share having a face value of $50. The face value of each share as stated on the stock certificate is known as the *par value* of the share. Shares of stock that do not have the value stated on the certificate are called *no-par-value stock*. The charter of a corporation that has no-par-value stock states the number of shares of stock that may be issued.

A corporation may issue two kinds of stock. Stock issued by a corporation that gives the holder preference to earnings or other preferences is called *preferred stock*. Stock issued by a corporation that does not give the holder special preferences is called *common stock*.

Stock subscriptions

Before application can be made for a charter, the organizers of a corporation must have definite promises from the incorporators to buy stock. Persons who promise to buy stock to organize a corporation are known as *subscribers*. The total amount of the stock subscribed before organization is listed in the application for the charter.

The Baker Manufacturing Company had 660 shares of stock subscribed before the charter was granted. Mr. Malone subscribed for 200 shares, Mr. Hill for 200 shares, Mr. Peters for 130 shares, and Mr. Woods for 130 shares at $50 for each share. As soon as the subscriptions were paid, they would have $33,000 in cash with which to begin operations.

Management of a corporation

A corporation ordinarily has a number of owners or stockholders. The stockholders hold an annual meeting to elect a group of persons to manage the business. The group of persons elected to manage the business of a corporation is known as the *board of directors*. Each stockholder is ordinarily entitled to one vote for each share of stock that he holds.

The board of directors controls the general policies of the corporation and elects the officers. These officers or their authorized agents carry on the business of the corporation. The officers are responsible to the board of directors, and the board of directors is responsible to the stockholders. All are governed by (a) the charter and (b) the bylaws adopted by the stockholders.

Opening entries for a corporation

The opening entry for a business operated by one person consists of debits to assets, credits to liabilities, and a credit to proprietorship. The opening entry for a partnership consists of debits to assets, credits to liabilities, and credits to the capital account of each partner. The opening entry for a corporation follows the same pattern as that for a single proprietor or for a partnership — assets are debited, liabilities are credited, and an account called Capital Stock is credited for the amount of the proprietorship.

The entry below illustrates the opening entry of a corporation where cash is the only asset and there are no liabilities.

	DATE	ACCOUNT CREDITED	POST. REF.	GENERAL CR.	SALES CR.	ACCOUNTS RECEIVABLE CR.	DISCOUNT ON SALES DR.	CASH DR.	
				1	2	3	4	5	
1	1962 June 11	Capital Stock		3300000				3300000	1
2									2
3									3

CASH RECEIPTS JOURNAL — PAGE

Entry to record the sale of capital stock

Analyzing the opening entry

The certificate of incorporation of The Baker Manufacturing Company provided that the corporation would commence business with a capital of $33,000. On the day the charter was received, the four incorporators purchased for cash 660 shares of stock for $33,000. A stock certificate was issued to each subscriber indicating the number of shares of stock that he owned. To record the receipt of cash by the corporation, the entry shown above was made in the cash receipts journal. The total amount of cash received was credited to one account, Capital Stock. Capital Stock was credited in the General Credit column and Cash was debited in the Cash Debit column.

Purchase of a business by a corporation

The Baker Manufacturing Company decided on June 11 to purchase the business of the partnership of C. J. Nelson and E. H. Tealy. In payment for their business, the partners agreed to accept shares of stock in the corporation. The balance sheet of the partnership showed that the difference between the assets and the liabilities amounted to $15,000. At $50 a share, the corporation would issue the partners 300 shares of stock for their interest in the business. The general journal entry to record this transaction is illustrated at the top of the next page.

	ACCOUNTS PAYABLE DR.	GENERAL DR.	DATE	NAME OF ACCOUNT	POST. REF.	GENERAL CR.	ACCOUNTS RECEIVABLE CR.	
1		584 38	1962 June 11	Cash				1
2		1000 00		Notes Receivable				2
3		575 62		Accounts Receivable				3
4		106.50 00		Merchandise Inventory				4
5		121 50		Supplies				5
6		250 00		Prepaid Insurance				6
7		1000 00		Equipment				7
8				Notes Payable		2500 00		8
9				Accounts Payable		1281 50		9
10				Capital Stock		15000 00		10
11				Purchase of the business				11
12				of Nelson and Tealey.				12

Entry to record the purchase of a going business

Analyzing the entry for purchase of a going business

Each asset purchased was debited in the General Debit column for the amount shown on the balance sheet of the partnership. The two liabilities taken over, Notes Payable and Accounts Payable, were credited in the General Credit column for the amounts shown on the balance sheet. If cash had been paid to the partners, Cash would have been credited; but as the partners had agreed to accept stock for their interest, Capital Stock was credited for the amount of their interest, $15,000.

When this entry and the entry in the cash receipts journal were posted, the capital stock account in the general ledger appeared as follows:

Capital Stock   ACCOUNT NO. 31

DATE	ITEMS	POST. REF.	DEBIT	DATE	ITEMS	POST. REF.	CREDIT
				1962 June 11		CR	3300 00
				11		J1	1500 00

Financial statements of a corporation

At the end of the fiscal period on December 31, The Baker Manufacturing Company prepared its financial statements. During the period it had a net income of $3,913.66. The income statement was prepared in the form illustrated previously for a single proprietorship and a partnership.

The assets and the liabilities of the corporation were shown on the balance sheet in the same manner as the assets and the liabilities of a single proprietorship or a partnership. The only difference in the statements was in the proprietorship section. The proprietorship section of the balance sheet prepared by The Baker Manufacturing Company on December 31 is shown below.

```
                    Proprietorship
  Capital Stock . . . . . . . . . . . . . .   $48,000.00
  Retained Earnings  . . . . . . . . . . .      3,913.66
  Total Proprietorship . . . . . . . . . . .                51,913.66
  Total Liabilities and Proprietorship . . .               $86,982.19
```

Proprietorship section of a corporate balance sheet

The amount earned by a corporation and not yet distributed to stockholders is known as *retained earnings.* Other terms used instead of retained earnings are *earned surplus, earnings retained in the business, retained income,* and *accumulated earnings.* If costs and expenses exceed income, there is a net loss. The amount of net loss is called a *deficit.*

The amount of net income earned by The Baker Manufacturing Company and not yet distributed to the stockholders, $3,913.66, was listed on the balance sheet under the title *Retained Earnings.* This amount was added to the amount of the capital stock to give the total proprietorship of the corporation, $51,913.66.

Closing entries for a corporation

The closing entries for the income, cost, and expense accounts of a corporation are the same as those of a single proprietorship or a partnership. Since there are no separate capital and drawing accounts for each owner in a corporation, the net income of the corporation is credited to a separate account with the title *Retained Earnings.* The retained earnings account summarizes the changes in the proprietorship of the corporation.

When the closing entries were made for The Baker Manufacturing Company on December 31, the following entry was made in the general journal to close the income and expense summary account:

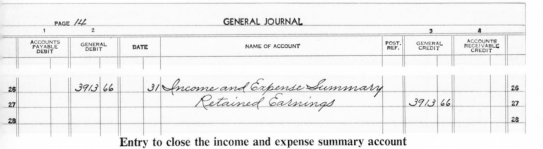

Entry to close the income and expense summary account

Declaring dividends

The balance of the retained earnings account, $3,913.66, represents net income of the corporation that really belongs to the stockholders of the corporation. The stockholders may not claim this income, however, except by order of the board of directors. Corporations ordinarily wish to maintain a credit balance in the retained earnings account to provide funds for the expansion of the business and as a source of dividends in less prosperous years. When the board of directors meets, it decides whether it is advisable to distribute all or part of the earnings to the stockholders.

When the board of directors of The Baker Manufacturing Company met on January 6, it decided that it should distribute $2 for each of the 960 shares of outstanding stock, or a total of $1,920 of the retained earnings, to the stockholders. When the board of directors decides to distribute earnings to stockholders, it is said to have *declared a dividend*. The amount of earnings to be distributed is called the *dividend*. The amount of the dividend is usually expressed in terms of a certain amount per share of outstanding stock. For example, The Baker Manufacturing Company declared a dividend of $2 a share. The dividends are payable in cash by the corporation at the time fixed by the directors.

When the dividend was declared by the board of directors of The Baker Manufacturing Company, the retained earnings account was debited for $1,920, the amount of the earnings to be distributed to the stockholders. The liability account *Dividends Payable* was credited for $1,920 to show the amount owed to the stockholders by the corporation.

The declaration of the board of directors of The Baker Manufacturing Company provided that the dividend was to be paid on January 21. On that date a check was mailed to each of the stockholders for the total amount of the dividend due him.

The entry in the general journal to record the declaration of the dividend on January 7 was as follows:

ACCOUNTS PAYABLE DEBIT	GENERAL DEBIT	DATE	NAME OF ACCOUNT	POST. REF.	GENERAL CREDIT	ACCOUNTS RECEIVABLE CREDIT
	1920 00	7	Retained Earnings			
			Dividends Payable		1920 00	
			To record Dividend No. 1 of			
			$2 a share.			

Entry to record the declaration of a dividend

466

The entry in the cash payments journal to record the payment of the dividend on January 21 was as follows:

	DATE	CHK. NO.	ACCOUNT DEBITED	POST. REF.	GENERAL DR.	ACCOUNTS PAYABLE DR.	SALARY EXPENSE DR.	EMPLOYEES INCOME TAX. PAY. CR.	FICA TAXES PAY. CR.	DISCOUNT ON PURCHASES CR.	CASH CR.	
					1	2	3	4	5	6	7	
12	21 23 28		Dividends Payable		1920 00						1920 00	12
13												13
14												14
15												15
16												16
17												17

CASH PAYMENTS JOURNAL — PAGE 3

Entry to record the payment of a dividend

Cooperatives

A business that is owned by its customers is known as a *cooperative*. A cooperative business is usually organized as a corporation.

One of the chief differences between a cooperative and an ordinary corporation lies in the power that each stockholder has in the stockholders' meetings. In the usual corporation each stockholder has one vote for each share of stock owned. It is possible, therefore, for a few large stockholders to have complete control of such a corporation. In the cooperative, however, each stockholder has one and only one vote, regardless of the number of shares of stock owned.

Earnings are distributed to the members of a cooperative in two ways: (a) participation dividends and (b) dividends on capital stock. The earnings distributed to each member in proportion to the amount of business that he has done with the cooperative during the fiscal period are known as *participation dividends*. The earnings distributed to each member in proportion to the amount of his investment in the cooperative are known as *dividends on capital stock*.

During the yearly fiscal period ended June 30, J. M. Tice, a member of the Lima Consumers Cooperative, bought merchandise totaling $2,500. On June 30 the board of directors of the cooperative declared a participation dividend of 2%. Mr. Tice therefore received a participation dividend of $50.

Mr. Tice owned shares of capital stock in the cooperative, for which he had paid $100. The cooperative declared a dividend on the capital stock of 4%. Mr. Tice's dividend was therefore $4.

Increasing your business vocabulary

What is the meaning of each of the following?

(a) corporation
(b) shares of stock
(c) capital stock
(d) stockholder
(e) stock certificate
(f) certificate of incorporation
(g) charter
(h) authorized capital stock
(i) par value
(j) no-par-value stock

(k) preferred stock
(l) common stock
(m) subscribers
(n) board of directors
(o) retained earnings
(p) deficit
(q) dividend
(r) cooperative
(s) participation dividends

Chapter questions

1. Which of the three types of business organization must secure permission from the state or federal government to organize?
2. What is the evidence of ownership in a corporation?
3. How long does a corporation continue to exist?
4. When does a single proprietorship or a partnership cease to exist?
5. What entry was made in the cash receipts journal on page 463 to record cash received from the sale of stock?
6. What proprietorship account was credited in the general journal entry on page 464 when the partnership of Nelson and Tealy was purchased?
7. What two accounts in the proprietorship section of the balance sheet on page 465 are totaled to arrive at the total proprietorship?
8. Who in a corporation makes the decision to distribute all or part of the earnings to stockholders?
9. What account was debited and what account was credited in the general journal on page 466 to record the declaration of the dividend?
10. What account was debited and what account was credited in the cash payments journal on page 467 to record the payment of the dividend?

Cases for discussion

1. Company A declared a dividend that distributed all of the net earnings to the stockholders. Company B declared a dividend that distributed only half of the net earnings to the stockholders. What is the advantage of the policy of Company B over that of Company A?

2. If you had an opportunity to invest in a partnership or in a corporation with equal opportunities to make a good return on your investment, what factors would you want to consider before making a decision?

468

Application problems

Problem 32-1. *Opening entry to incorporate a going concern*

On January 2 of the current year a charter was granted to Carter-Lane, Inc. that authorized a capital stock of $60,000, consisting of 600 shares (par value $100).

This corporation had agreed to take over the hardware business owned by the partnership of Carter and Lane. On January 2 the corporation took over the assets and assumed the liabilities of the partnership shown in the following balance sheet:

<table>
<tr><td colspan="5" align="center">Carter and Lane
Balance Sheet
December 31, 19--</td></tr>
<tr><td colspan="2" align="center">*Assets*</td><td colspan="3" align="center">*Liabilities*</td></tr>
<tr><td>Cash..................</td><td>864 60</td><td>Notes Payable.........</td><td colspan="2">500 00</td></tr>
<tr><td>Accounts Receivable....</td><td>6,124 85</td><td>Accounts Payable......</td><td colspan="2">3,986 85</td></tr>
<tr><td>Merchandise Inventory..</td><td>24,987 15</td><td></td><td></td><td></td></tr>
<tr><td>Supplies..............</td><td>410 25</td><td>Total Liabilities........</td><td colspan="2">4,486 85</td></tr>
<tr><td>Equipment............</td><td>2,100 00</td><td></td><td></td><td></td></tr>
<tr><td></td><td></td><td colspan="3" align="center">*Proprietorship*</td></tr>
<tr><td></td><td></td><td>J. L. Carter,
    Capital....18,000.00</td><td></td><td></td></tr>
<tr><td></td><td></td><td>M. R. Lane,
    Capital....12,000.00</td><td></td><td></td></tr>
<tr><td></td><td></td><td>Total Proprietorship....</td><td colspan="2">30,000 00</td></tr>
<tr><td>Total Assets...........</td><td>34,486 85</td><td>Total Liab. and Prop...</td><td colspan="2">34,486 85</td></tr>
</table>

On January 2, 180 shares of stock were issued to Mr. Carter and 120 shares of stock were issued to Mr. Lane for the equities in the partnership.

Instructions: Record the opening entry in a general journal.

Problem 32-2. *Declaring and paying a dividend*

Instructions: Record in general journal form the following entries for The Nelson Company.

Dec. 31. The credit balance of the income and expense summary account, $16,420, was transferred to the retained earnings account.

Jan. 6. A dividend of $5 a share was declared on the 1,200 shares of common stock outstanding.

Jan. 30. The dividend declared on January 6 was paid.

Problem 32-3. Balance sheet for a corporation

The Balance Sheet columns of the work sheet of Mercer & Co. for the fiscal year ended December 31 of the current year are shown below.

Account Titles	Balance Sheet	
	Debit	Credit
Cash...	7,520 60	
Accounts Receivable..........................	8,341 25	
Allowance for Bad Debts......................		129 16
Merchandise Inventory........................	43,936 78	
Supplies.....................................	910 54	
Equipment...................................	7,000 00	
Allowance for Depreciation of Equipment.......		612 50
Accounts Payable.............................		6,432 75
Taxes Payable...............................		401 15
Capital Stock................................		50,000 00
Retained Earnings............................		3,913 92
	67,709 17	61,489 48
Net Income.................................		6,219 69
	67,709 17	67,709 17

Instructions: Prepare the balance sheet for Mercer & Co. Add the net income for the current fiscal period to the retained earnings account balance. Use as your model for the proprietorship section the illustration on page 465.

Chapter 33

Bookkeeping and budgeting for the family and the individual

Need for personal and family bookkeeping records

Bookkeeping records aid business in planning for more efficient operations. Bookkeeping records are also important for the individual or the family that wants to plan for more intelligent use of income. If systematic records are not kept, there is no basis upon which to plan for purchases of essentials, to provide adequately for savings, and to make funds available for recreation and some of the luxuries.

The Carl Johnson family

Carl Johnson has a wife and two children. For a number of years the Johnson family has kept a set of books in which to record its income and expenditures. At the beginning of each year the family draws up a budget of its expected income and expenditures. Periodically during the year the expenditures are compared with the budget.

Johnson family balance sheet

At the end of each year Mr. Johnson prepares a balance sheet showing the assets, the liabilities, and the proprietorship of his family. The balance sheet on December 31, 1961, is shown at the top of the following page.

Analyzing the balance sheet

Assets. Several of the assets are similar to those illustrated in other balance sheets. These are Cash, Furniture and Household Equipment, Automobile, and House. Two assets that have not been illustrated before are Life Insurance Cash Value and Social Security Deposits.

Life insurance policies provide for a cash surrender value. The amount the insurance company will pay a policyholder if he wishes to turn his policy in for cash is called the *cash surrender value*. This cash value is an asset. On December 31, 1962, Mr. Johnson examined his policies and found that the cash surrender value totaled $924. This value was therefore listed on the balance sheet as an asset.

An amount is withheld from Mr. Johnson's salary to provide for old-age, survivors, and disability insurance benefits. These amounts are de-

```
                    The Carl Johnson Family
                         Balance Sheet
                       December 31, 1961

                             Assets

Cash . . . . . . . . . . . . . . . . .   $     820.40
Life Insurance Cash Value. . . . . . .         924.00
Furniture and Household Equipment. . .       4,000.00
Automobile . . . . . . . . . . . . . .       1,800.00
House. . . . . . . . . . . . . . . . .      18,900.00
Social Security Deposits . . . . . . .         680.00
Total Assets . . . . . . . . . . . . .                  $27,124.40

                          Liabilities

Eagle Savings and Loan Association . .                  $ 6,800.00

                        Proprietorship

The Carl Johnson Family, Capital . . .                   20,324.40

Total Liabilities and Proprietorship .                  $27,124.40
```

Balance sheet of a family

posited to his credit with the Social Security Administration. The total of Mr. Johnson's social security deposits on December 31, 1962, was $680. Social security deposits are considered to be an asset, because they provide an annuity for old age and benefits for survivors and disability.

Liabilities. Mr. Johnson owed $6,800 to the Eagle Savings and Loan Association. This amount was the balance due on the mortgage the Association held on his home. Each month Mr. Johnson makes a payment to the Association that both pays the interest due on the mortgage for the month and reduces the principal.

Proprietorship. By subtracting the total liabilities from the total assets, Mr. Johnson found that his family proprietorship was $20,324.40.

Income and expense accounts

Family and individual bookkeeping systems need to be as simple as possible and yet show all the important facts needed for making income tax returns and regulating expenditures.

An income account is maintained for Mr. Johnson's salary. Other family income is recorded in the account Other Income. For each of the main types of expenses an account is kept. Income and expense accounts used by the Johnson family are shown at the top of the following page.

Income Accounts:
  Salary
  Other Income

Expense Accounts:
  Automobile Expense — car insurance, repairs, oil, gas, and depreciation.
  Clothing Expense — all wearing apparel, including shoes and hats.
  Donations — church and charities.
  Food Expense — groceries, meat, and milk.
  Gifts — Christmas club installments, birthday and personal gifts.
  Household Expense — depreciation of house, depreciation of furniture and
    equipment, light, heat, water, electricity, telephone, cleaning, laundry.
  Insurance Expense — life insurance and group insurance.
  Interest Expense
  Medical Expense — drugs, hospitalization insurance, dentist and doctor
    bills, hospital bills, etc.
  Personal Expense — all amounts given to the members of the family for
    miscellaneous expenses for which no detailed record was kept.
  Taxes — Federal Income
  Taxes — Real Estate
  Taxes — State Income
  Vacation Expense — Vacation Club installments and additional vacation
    expenses.

Johnson family budget

A family has the problem of distributing its income over all types of expenditures so that the greatest benefits will be received. Plans should be made in advance to show how much income may be received and how the available funds should be spent. A financial statement of estimated income and expenses for a period is called a *budget*. The Carl Johnson family budget for 1962 is shown on the following page.

In preparing their 1962 budget, the family consulted their records for 1961 to determine how much was spent for each type of expense. They talked over changes they anticipated in their spending during the year of 1962 and decided upon an amount that was sufficient for each type of expense. The total of their estimated expense items was $7,320. They subtracted this amount from their estimated income, $7,800, to determine their estimated increase in proprietorship, $480.

Automobile Expense and Household Expense were divided into current expenses and depreciation expenses. This division was made so that Mr. Johnson could estimate how much he had to pay out in cash in each pay period and how much his depreciation expenses would be.

A part of the money collected as life insurance premiums by the life insurance company is used to cover its operating costs and the benefits

473

it must pay under some of its policies. This part of the premiums is an expense to the policyholder. The balance of the premiums accumulates as a cash value that may be withdrawn by the policyholder if he wishes to cancel his policy. This part of the premiums is an investment of the policyholder. The Johnson family expected to pay $280 for insurance premiums during 1962. The expense part, $180, was listed in the expense section of the budget.

Mr. Johnson was paid semimonthly. He had to decide how much of each pay check he should allot on each payday to the various types of expenditures. To determine these amounts he divided the yearly allotment for each expenditure by 24, the number of pay checks that he received.

```
                     The Carl Johnson Family
                             Budget
                            For 1962

                                             Yearly Estimates

Estimated Income:

     Salary . . . . . . . . . . . . . . . .   $7,680.00
     Other Income . . . . . . . . . . . . .      120.00
     Total Estimated Income . . . . . . . .                  $7,800.00

Estimated Expenses:

     Automobile Expense:
          Current . . . . . . . . . . $200.00
          Depreciation. . . . . . . .  300.00   $   500.00
     Clothing Expense . . . . . . . . . . . .        500.00
     Donations. . . . . . . . . . . . . . .          120.00
     Food Expense . . . . . . . . . . . . .         2,100.00
     Gifts. . . . . . . . . . . . . . . . .           150.00
     Household Expense:
          Current . . . . . . . . . . $600.00
          Depreciation of Furniture
            and Household Equip-
            ment . . . . . . . . .     200.00
          Depreciation of House . . .  200.00      1,000.00
     Insurance Expense. . . . . . . . . . . .        180.00
     Interest Expense . . . . . . . . . . . .        400.00
     Medical Expense. . . . . . . . . . . . .        300.00
     Personal Expense . . . . . . . . . . . .        360.00
     Taxes--Federal Income. . . . . . . . . .        910.00
     Taxes--Real Estate . . . . . . . . . . .        260.00
     Taxes--State Income. . . . . . . . . . .        180.00
     Vacation Expense . . . . . . . . . . . .        360.00
     Total Estimated Expenses . . . . . . . .                  7,320.00

Estimated Increase in Proprietorship. . . . .                $   480.00
```

Budget of a family

Recording income and expenses

Mr. Johnson deposits his salary check and other items of income in the bank. He pays all of his monthly and other bills by check. Twice each month he writes a check payable to Cash for the total of the allowances for food, household, and personal expenses.

A combination journal is used to record all income and expenses. The combination journal for the month of January is shown on pages 476 and 477.

Analyzing the combination journal

A few of the transactions recorded in the combination journal that are unusual are explained in the following paragraphs.

Lines 7 and 8. On January 12, Mr. Johnson wrote a check to the Eagle Savings and Loan Association for $90. Of this sum $56 was repayment of part of the principal and $34 was interest on the loan. The Eagle Savings and Loan Association account was debited for $56 and Interest Expense was debited for $34 in the General Debit column. This entry required two lines in the combination journal.

Lines 9 and 15. On January 15 and January 31, Mr. Johnson wrote a check payable to Cash for $103. He cashed the check and recorded the amount he gave to Mrs. Johnson for food, $80, in the Food Expense Debit column. The amount given to Mrs. Johnson for household expenses, $8, was recorded in the Household Expense Debit column. The amount given to various members of the family for personal allowances, $15, was recorded in the Personal Expense Debit column. Cash was credited for $103 in the Cash Credit column.

Line 10. Once each month Mr. Johnson wrote a check and deposited it in a special vacation account at the bank. The amount, $30, was recorded in the Cash Credit column and in the General Debit column. Vacation Expense was debited each month for the amount of the check. This method spread the vacation expense over each month of the year instead of having it all charged in the month when the family takes its vacation.

Lines 11 and 16. Mr. Johnson's semimonthly salary was $320. From his salary the following deductions were made: federal income tax, $39.40; social security, $10. The amount of the net pay received, $270.60, was debited in the Cash Debit column. The amount withheld for federal income tax, $39.40, was debited in the Taxes — Federal Income Debit column. The amount withheld for social security, $10, was debited in the Social Security Deposits Debit column. Salary was credited for the salary earned, $320, in the General Credit column.

COMBINATION JOURNAL

	CASH		CHECK NO.	DATE	NAME OF ACCOUNT	POST. REF.	GENERAL		
	DEBIT	CREDIT					DEBIT	CREDIT	
1				1962 Jan 1	Balance on hand $820.40	✓			1
2		10 40	1	4	Collins Garage - repairs	✓			2
3		32 00	2	5	Furniture and Household Equip.		32 00		3
4		9 20	3	5	City Gas & Electric Co.	✓			4
5		6 80	4	5	General Telephone Co.	✓			5
6		15 00	5	8	Medical Expense - Dr. Grant		15 00		6
7		90 00	6	12	Eagle Savings and Loan Assn.		56 00		7
8					Interest Expense		34 00		8
9		103 00	7	15	Allowances	✓			9
10		30 00	8	15	Vacation Expense		30 00		10
11	270 60			15	Salary			320 00	11
12		20 00	9	20	Insurance Expense		20 00		12
13		12 00	10	26	Moore Department Store	✓			13
14		6 00	11	29	Jack's Clothing Store	✓			14
15		103 00	12	31	Allowances	✓			15
16	270 60			31	Salary			320 00	16
17		8 50	13	31	Donations		8 50		17
18		24 10	14	31	Shore Oil Company	✓			18
19	541 20	470 00		31	Totals		195 50	640 00	19
20									20
21									21
22									22
23									23
24									24
25									25
26									26
27									27
28									28
29									29

Combination journal

Proving cash and the equality of debits and credits

At the end of each month the combination journal is totaled and the equality of debits and credits is proved. Before the amounts are posted to the ledger, cash is proved by making certain that the check-stub balance agrees with the cash balance shown in the combination journal.

FOR MONTH OF *January* 19 62   PAGE *1*

	AUTOMOBILE EXPENSE DEBIT	CLOTHING EXPENSE DEBIT	FOOD EXPENSE DEBIT	HOUSEHOLD EXPENSE DEBIT	PERSONAL EXPENSE DEBIT	TAXES— FEDERAL INCOME DEBIT	SOCIAL SECURITY DEPOSITS DEBIT	
1								1
2	10 40							2
3								3
4				9 20				4
5				6 80				5
6								6
7								7
8								8
9			80 00	8 00	15 00			9
10								10
11						39 40	10 00	11
12								12
13		12 00						13
14		6 00						14
15			80 00	8 00	15 00			15
16						39 40	10 00	16
17								17
18	10 40	18 00	160 00	24 10 / 56 10	30 00	78 80	20 00	18
19	10 40	18 00	160 00	56 10	30 00	78 80	20 00	19
20								20
21								21
22								22
23								23
24								24
25								25
26								26
27								27
28								28
29								29

of a family

Controlling expenditures

Mr. Johnson divided his yearly budget into monthly allotments and entered these amounts on the heading line of the ledger accounts. For example, the yearly allotment for current Automobile Expense was $200. Dividing this amount by 12, he entered the amount of the monthly budget,

$16.67, in the heading of the Automobile Expense account as shown in the illustration below.

DATE	ITEMS	POST. REF.	DEBIT	DATE	ITEMS	POST. REF.	CREDIT
Automobile Expense — Monthly Budget: $16.67 — ACCOUNT NO. 51							
1962							
Jan. 31		1	13 53				
Feb. 28		2	16 46				
Mar. 31		3	20 61 / 50 60				
Apr. 30		4	15 93				
May 31		5	17 88				
June 30		6	18 84 / 1 03 25				

In order to control expenditures each month, Mr. Johnson compared the totals of the accounts with the budget allotments. At the end of June when Mr. Johnson checked the automobile account, he found the total for the first six months of the year was $103.25. The budget allotment for the same period was $100.02 ($16.67 × 6). From these figures Mr. Johnson concluded that he was operating his automobile at about the budget figure.

Analyzing the year-end records

In order to prove the accuracy of the records for the year, a trial balance was taken of all the accounts in the ledger. Mr. Johnson entered the trial balance in the first two columns of an eight-column work sheet so that he could make his adjusting entries and so that his income and expense analysis and his balance sheet for the year would all appear on one work sheet. The work sheet completed for the year ended December 31 is shown on the opposite page.

Adjusting entries

At the end of the year it is necessary that adjusting entries be made so that the asset and the expense accounts will reflect the correct values. Figures for the adjusting entries are taken from the Adjustments columns of the work sheet.

The value of the furniture and household equipment at the beginning of the year and all purchases of furniture and household equipment during the year were entered as debits in the furniture and household equipment account. This furniture and equipment has decreased in value because of depreciation. An entry must therefore be made to record the expense and the decrease in the value of the asset. In order to simplify the records, the

478

The Earl Johnson Family
Work Sheet
For Year Ended December 31, 1962

No.	Account Title	Acct. No.	Trial Balance Debit	Trial Balance Credit	Adjustments Debit	Adjustments Credit	Income Statement Debit	Income Statement Credit	Balance Sheet Debit	Balance Sheet Credit	No.
1	Cash	11	784.32						784.32		1
2	Life Insurance Cash Value	12	924.00		(d)100.00				1024.00		2
3	Furniture & Household Equip.	13	4220.00			(a)200.00			4020.00		3
4	Automobile	14	1800.00			(b)300.00			1500.00		4
5	House	15	18900.00			(c)200.00			18700.00		5
6	Social Security Deposits	16	830.00						830.00		6
7	Eagle Savings & Loan Assn.	21		611.92						611.92	7
8	Cash Johnson Family, Cap.	31		25830.40						25830.40	8
9	Salary	41		7680.00				7680.00			9
10	Other Income	42		120.00				120.00			10
11	Automobile Expense	51	1988.20		(b)300.00		2288.20				11
12	Clothing Expense	52	468.00				468.00				12
13	Donations	53	168.40				168.40				13
14	Food Expense	54	2167.50				2167.50				14
15	Gifts	55	122.80				122.80				15
16	Household Expense	56	672.00		(a)200.00 (c)200.00		1072.00				16
17	Insurance Expense	57	280.00			(d)100.00	180.00				17
18	Interest Expense	58	397.92				397.92				18
19	Medical Expense	59	192.65				192.65				19
20	Personal Expense	60	412.80				412.80				20
21	Taxes - Federal Income	61	893.28				893.28				21
22	Taxes - Real Estate	62	268.30				268.30				22
23	Taxes - State Income	63	192.15				192.15				23
24	Vacation Expense	64	350.00				350.00				24
25			34242.32	34242.32	800.00	800.00	7384.00	7800.00	26858.32	26442.32	25
26	Increase in Proprietorship						416.00			416.00	26
27							7800.00	7800.00	26858.32	26858.32	27

Work sheet of a family

depreciation expense was debited to the account Household Expense; a separate account with depreciation was not set up. The decrease in value was credited directly to the account Furniture and Household Equipment; an allowance for depreciation was not set up.

The value of the automobile at the beginning of the year was shown in the asset account Automobile. The automobile has decreased in value during the year because of depreciation. The depreciation was recorded by debiting Automobile Expense and crediting Automobile.

The value of the house at the beginning of the year was shown in the asset account House. The house has decreased in value during the year because of depreciation. The depreciation was recorded by debiting Household Expense and crediting House.

During the year insurance premiums totaling $280 were debited to Insurance Expense, but this total was not all expense. With the payment of each premium the cash value of some of the life insurance policies was increased, and this increase was an asset.

The balance in the account Life Insurance Cash Value was not correct at the end of the year because, with the payment of premiums, the cash value of the policies had been increased. By checking the cash surrender tables printed on the policies, the ending cash value was determined to be $1,024. This amount was an increase of $100 over the beginning cash value of $924. To record the increase in the cash value, an adjusting entry was made debiting Life Insurance Cash Value and crediting Insurance Expense for the amount of the increase. When this entry was posted, the balance of the life insurance cash value account agreed with the cash surrender value stated on the policy and the balance of the insurance expense account represented the actual expense of insurance.

Closing entries

In order that the income and the expense accounts for one year could be easily compared with the income and the expense accounts for the following year, Mr. Johnson closed each income and each expense account by transferring the balance of each account to an account entitled Income and Expense Summary. He made an entry in the combination journal from the information in the Income and Expense Statement columns of the work sheet. The income and expense summary account was credited for the total of all the items in the Income and Expense Statement Credit column, and each item was debited for its balance. The income and expense summary account was debited for the total of all the items in the Income and Expense Statement Debit column, and each item was credited for its balance.

When these entries were posted, all income and expense accounts were in balance, Each account was ruled. The account Income and Expense Summary had a credit balance of $416. To close this account, an entry was made in the combination journal debiting Income and Expense Summary and crediting Carl Johnson Family, Capital. When this entry was posted, the income and expense summary account was in balance and the capital account had a credit balance of $20,740.40, which was the capital as of December 31, 1962.

Income and expense statement

In order to have a convenient means of comparing the operations of the family with the budget plan, Mr. Johnson prepared an *income and expense statement*. This statement showed the amount and the source of income, the amount and the kind of each expense, and the amount of the increase in proprietorship. The income and expense statement prepared by Mr. Johnson is shown below.

```
                        The Carl Johnson Family
                       Income and Expense Statement
                       For Year Ended December 31, 1962


                                    Budget              Actual

Income:

      Salary . . . . . . .    $7,680.00           $7,680.00
      Other Income . . . .       120.00              120.00
      Total Income . . . .              $7,800.00            $7,800.00

Expenses:

      Automobile Expense . .  $   500.00           $   498.20
      Clothing Expense . . .      500.00               468.00
      Donations. . . . . . .      120.00               168.40
      Food Expense . . . . .    2,100.00             2,167.50
      Gifts. . . . . . . . .      150.00               122.80
      Household Expense. . .    1,000.00             1,072.00
      Insurance Expense. . .      180.00               180.00
      Interest Expense . . .      400.00               397.92
      Medical Expense. . . .      300.00               192.65
      Personal Expense . . .      360.00               412.80
      Taxes--Federal Income.      910.00               893.28
      Taxes--Real Estate . .      260.00               268.30
      Taxes--State Income. .      180.00               192.15
      Vacation Expense . . .      360.00               350.00
      Total Expenses . . . .              7,320.00            7,384.00

Increase in Proprietorship.             $   480.00          $   416.00
```

Income and expense statement of a family

The amounts in the Budget columns of the income and expense statement are based on the amounts in the family budget prepared at the beginning of the year. The amounts in the Actual columns of the income and expense statement are based on the amounts in the Income and Expense Statement columns of the work sheet.

Balance sheet

In order to compare his assets and his proprietorship at the end of the year with those at the beginning of the year, Mr. Johnson prepared the balance sheet shown below from the figures in the balance sheet columns of the work sheet.

```
                    The Carl Johnson Family
                         Balance Sheet
                      December 31, 1962

                            Assets

Cash . . . . . . . . . . . . . . . . . . . .   $    784.32
Life Insurance Cash Value. . . . . . . . .        1,024.00
Furniture and Household Equipment. . . .          4,020.00
Automobile . . . . . . . . . . . . . . .          1,500.00
House. . . . . . . . . . . . . . . . . .         18,700.00
Social Security Deposits . . . . . . . .            830.00
Total Assets . . . . . . . . . . . . . .                     $26,858.32

                          Liabilities

Eagle Savings and Loan Association . . .                     $ 6,117.92

                        Proprietorship

The Carl Johnson Family, Capital . . . .                      20,740.40

Total Liabilities and Proprietorship . .                     $26,858.32
```

Balance sheet of a family

Revising the budget

In preparing the budget for 1963, Mr. Johnson made use of the budget for 1962 and the actual income and expenses for 1962 shown in the statement on the preceding page. He compared the figures for each item of income and each item of expense.

The actual expenses were slightly larger than the amounts budgeted. As a result, the actual increase in proprietorship was less than the budgeted increase.

Mr. Johnson and his family decided that their budget needed only a slight change for the coming year. On the basis of the actual expenses for the year 1962 and in the light of added income and expenses anticipated for the year 1963, the Johnson family prepared a budget. Because the revised budget was based on well-kept records and on anticipated changes in spending, it was a sound one.

Income tax data

Mr. Johnson kept a complete set of records. As a result, he found that he was able to fill out his income tax returns with a minimum of difficulty. Mr. Johnson's records provided all the information he needed to prepare his returns.

From his two income accounts Mr. Johnson obtained his yearly income as follows:

Salary..	$7,680.00
Other Income..	120.00
Total Income..	$7,800.00

The instructions accompanying the income tax form showed that donations to charitable organizations, interest expense, and taxes could be subtracted from the amount on which federal income tax had to be paid. From a study of his accounts and his check stubs, Mr. Johnson found that the following amounts were allowable deductions under the income tax law:

Donations..	$ 168.40
Interest Expense.......................................	397.92
Taxes — Real Estate...................................	268.30
Taxes — State Income.................................	192.15
Taxes — State Gasoline...............................	14.00
Automobile License...................................	13.75
Total Deductions......................................	$1,054.52

Mr. Johnson kept his canceled checks on file and as a result could support the amounts he listed for each of his allowable deductions.

Bookkeeping for the individual

The advantages of keeping a budget are the same for the individual as for the family. The expenses of a family are generally more numerous than those of an individual, but the procedures for recording the expenses of one are essentially the same as for the other. From a periodic study of his records, an individual can determine how nearly his spending agrees with his spending plan.

Increasing your business vocabulary

What is the meaning of each of the following terms:

(a) cash surrender value   (c) income and expense statement

(b) budget

Chapter questions

1. Why is it important for a family to keep accurate records of its expenditures?
2. Why does Mr. Johnson list among his assets the cash value of his life insurance policies?
3. Why does Mr. Johnson list among his assets his social security deposits?
4. What procedure did the Johnson family follow in setting up their budget for 1962?
5. Why were Automobile Expense and Household Expense divided on the budget on page 474 into current expense and depreciation expense?
6. On Lines 7 and 8 of the illustration on pages 476 and 477, what entry was made to record the payment to the Eagle Savings and Loan Association?
7. On Line 11 of the illustration on pages 476 and 477, what entry was made to record Mr. Johnson's semimonthly salary?
8. What arrangement did the Johnson family have for handling household and personal allowances?
9. Why did Mr. Johnson record the amount $16.67 in the heading of the automobile expense account shown on page 478?
10. Which of Mr. Johnson's accounts required adjustment at the end of the year?
11. What use is made of the comparison of budgeted and actual income and expenses in the income and expense statement?

Cases for discussion

1. The family bookkeeping system developed in this chapter illustrated the main books of accounts kept by the Johnson family. In order to maintain control of household and personal allowances, what types of records would you recommend that the Johnson family keep?

2. The Ray Brown family maintained a set of books similar to those illustrated in this chapter. All receipts and all payments were carefully recorded in the combination journal and were posted to the ledger. At the end of the year, however, no statements were made because the Brown family followed the same budget each year. What are the disadvantages of this system?

3. The Harold Attlee family maintains a record of cash income and expenditures but keeps no record of assets, depreciation, liabilities, or capital. What are the advantages of the Johnson family's system in this chapter as compared with the Attlee family's system?

Application problems

Problem 33-1. *Recording the transactions of a family*

The C. D. Green family has been keeping bookkeeping records similar to those of the Johnson family illustrated in this chapter. The chart of accounts and the distribution of expenses for the Green family are the same as those of the Johnson family.

Instructions: 1. Record in a combination journal like the one on pages 476 and 477 the following transactions completed by Mr. Green during the month of April of the current year.

April 1. Balance of cash on hand, $452.80.
2. Issued Check No. 43 for $5.25 for the telephone bill.
3. Issued Check No. 44 for $26.95 for a coffee table for the living room.
4. Issued Check No. 45 for $62.50 for a new suit.
5. Issued Check No. 46 for $87.50 in payment of the semiyearly taxes on the house.
8. Issued Check No. 47 for $24.60 for fuel oil.
10. Issued Check No. 48 for $9.45 for the gas and electric bill.
12. Issued Check No. 49 for $10 to the Community Chest.
15. Received his semimonthly salary of $300 less a deduction of $35.80 for income tax and a deduction of $9.38 for social security tax.
15. Issued Check No. 50 for $106 and cashed it. Gave Mrs. Green her $80 food allowance and her $10 household allowance. Gave the members of the family their personal allowances, $16.
15. Issued Check No. 51 for $25 and deposited it in the Vacation Club account.
15. Issued Check No. 52 for $5 and deposited it in the Christmas Club account.
20. Issued Check No. 53 for $12.50 for the monthly life insurance premium.
25. Issued Check No. 54 for $16.50 for automobile repairs.
27. Issued Check No. 55 for $80 to the Guaranty Savings and Loan Association. Of this amount $50 was repayment of the principal and $30 was interest on the loan.
30. Received his semimonthly salary of $300 less a deduction of $35.80 for income tax and a deduction of $9.38 for social security tax.
30. Issued Check No. 56 for $106 and cashed it. Gave Mrs. Green her $80 food allowance and her $10 household allowance. Gave the members of the family their personal allowances, $16.
30. Issued Check No. 56 for $18.85 for gasoline and oil.
30. Issued Check No. 57 for $10 for monthly church donation.
30. Issued Check No. 58 for $5 for a birthday gift.
30. Issued Check No. 59 for $23.85 for clothing.

Instructions: 2. Total, prove, and rule the columns in the combination journal.

Problem 33-2. *Work at the end of the fiscal period for a family*

At the end of the fiscal year on December 31 of the current year, the account balances in the ledger maintained by the C. D. Green family were as follows:

Cash, $1,331.85

Life Insurance Cash Value, $620.45

Furniture and Household Equipment, $2,784.60

Automobile, $1,050.00

House, $12,800.00

Social Security Deposits, $946.00

Guaranty Savings and Loan Association, $6,742.34

C. D. Green Family, Capital, $11,799.97

Salary, $7,200.00

Other Income, $19.84

Automobile Expense, $243.50

Clothing Expense, $340.25

Donations, $92.00

Food Expense, $2,200.00

Gifts, $122.00

Household Expense, $885.50

Insurance Expense, $243.00

Interest Expense, $352.00

Medical Expense, $122.00

Personal Expense, $432.00

Taxes — Federal Income, $870.00

Taxes — Real Estate, $175.00

Vacation Expense, $152.00

Instructions: 1. Prepare an eight-column work sheet for the year ended December 31 of the current year. Use the following data for adjustments:

(a) Estimated depreciation of furniture and household equipment, $139.

(b) Estimated depreciation of automobile, $250.

(c) Estimated depreciation of house, $250.

(d) Increase in life insurance cash value, $100.

2. Prepare an income and expense statement for the year.

3. Prepare a balance sheet for December 31, 19--.

Chapter 34

Bookkeeping for a professional man

Need of records for a professional man

The keeping of adequate records by the professional man is not only desirable for efficient management of his affairs, but it is also necessary for tax purposes. The state and the federal income tax laws require the professional man to keep accurate records of his income and his expenses in order that he may make accurate tax returns and reports. Since the professional man derives his income primarily from fees for personal services, a few special records are needed.

Daily appointment book of a dentist

Dr. J. L. Carver is a dentist in a moderate-sized city. Virtually all of his work is done by appointment. His dental hygienist and secretary, Ruth Porter, keeps an *appointment book* that also serves as a record of daily charges to patients' accounts and cash collection from patients. A page of the appointment book for a part of one day, April 1, 1962, is shown below.

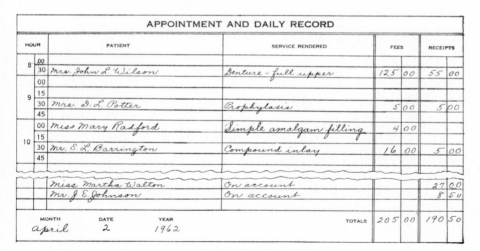

HOUR	PATIENT	SERVICE RENDERED	FEES		RECEIPTS	
8 00 / 30	mrs. John L. Wilson	Denture - full upper	125	00	55	00
9 00 / 15 / 30 / 45	mrs. D. L. Potter	Prophylaxis	5	00	5	00
10 00 / 15 / 30 / 45	miss Mary Radford	Simple amalgam filling	4	00		
	mr. E. L. Barrington	Compound inlay	16	00	5	00
	miss Martha Walton	On account			27	00
	mr. J. E. Johnson	On account			8	50
MONTH april DATE 2 YEAR 1962		TOTALS	205	00	190	50

Dentist's appointment book

Analyzing the appointment book

All appointments for the day were listed in the appointment book at the time the appointments were made. Appointments were often recorded

487

several weeks or months in advance. The name of each patient was re-corded in the appropriate space to indicate the time of his appointment. On the day the work was done, the line was completed to show the type of service rendered, the charge for this service, and the amount collected if money was received.

Several lines at the bottom of the appointment sheet did not have any particular time apportioned to them. These lines were used for recording appointments outside of office hours and collections received from patients on their accounts when not received at the time of a regular appointment.

The appointment book illustrated on page 487 served also as a cash receipts journal. The first amount column, headed "Fees," was used to record the charges for the work. The second column, headed "Receipts," was used to record the amounts actually received. The first entry at the bottom of the page was an immediate record of $27 received on account on April 2 from Miss Martha Walton for work previously completed. The second entry at the bottom of the page was an immediate record of $8.50 received on account from Mr. J. E. Johnson. All of these entries were posted daily to the appropriate patients' record cards.

Patient's record and ledger account card

Dr. Carver used an individual card for each patient. The front of one of these record cards is shown below, and the reverse side is shown at the top of the following page.

NAME Miss Martha Walton			ADDRESS 1423 Center Street							
DATE	OPERATION	TOOTH No.	.DR.	CR.	DATE	OPERATION	TOOTH No.	.DR.	CR.
1962 Feb.14	Prophylaxis		5 00						
14	X-ray		5 00						
21	O. alloy	19	5 00						
21	G. Syn. Porcel	8	7 00						
Mar.5	Extraction	17	5 00						
Apr.2	On account			27 00					
16	M.O. alloy	3	7 00						
16	C. Base		2 00	9 00					

Front of a patient's record card

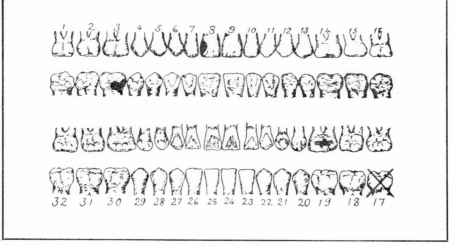

Back of a patient's record card

Analyzing the patient's record card

The patient's record card was an immediate record of the work done and was brought up to date each time the patient was in the dentist's chair. The front of the card was a complete ledger account of the patient. The back of the card had a chart of teeth that was marked by the dentist to supplement many of the entries on the front of the card.

Each entry on the front of the card showed the date the work was done, a description of the work done, the chart number of the tooth involved in the operation, and the amount of the charge for the work. As money was received from the patient, the amount received was credited to the patient in the Cr. amount column of his record card.

On the back of the card, the dentist shaded the diagram of the tooth to show the exact location of the work done. A cross marked through a tooth indicated extraction of that tooth.

Accounts receivable ledger

The patients' record cards were filed in a cabinet quickly accessible to the dentist, near the dentist's chair. This complete file of patients' record cards was Dr. Carver's accounts receivable ledger and also his individual patients' work completed file.

The combination journal of a dentist

All of the transactions completed by Dr. Carver were recorded in a combination journal similar to those developed in preceding chapters. Dr. Carver's combination journal for the month of April is illustrated at the top of the next two pages.

	CASH		CHECK NO.	DATE	NAME OF ACCOUNT	POST. REF.	GENERAL		
	DEBIT	CREDIT					DEBIT	CREDIT	
1		100 00	41	1962 Apr 2	Rent Expense	12	100 00		1
2		15 30	42	2	Burger Laboratories, Inc.				2
3	247 00			6	Professional Fees				3
28		18 20	51	30	To replenish petty cash fund				28
29		123 22	52	30	Salary Expense				29
30				30	FICA Taxes	57	4 78		30
31	1196 50	975 27		30	Totals		227 91	12 25	31
32	(11)	(11)					(✓)	(✓)	32
33									33

Combination journal

Analyzing the combination journal of a dentist

Special columns were provided in the combination journal for accounts that were frequently affected by transactions. The General Debit and Credit columns were used to record the transactions involving accounts for which there were no special columns.

Dr. Carver's secretary recorded in one entry in the combination journal the cash received for fees for an entire week. This entry was made at the close of business at the end of each week and on the last day of each month. The amount to be recorded was found by adding the totals of the Receipts column in the appointment book for the period for which the entry was made. Income from fees was recorded only when the cash had been received. The entry on Line 3 for April 6 illustrates the recording of fees received.

Dr. Carver made all large payments by check. He maintained a petty cash fund of $25 from which minor expenses were paid. Petty cash receipts were made out for each payment and were kept with the petty cash fund. Whenever the fund was running low, a check was drawn to replenish it. The entry for Check No. 51, Line 28, shows the entry to replenish the petty cash fund.

At intervals during the month Dr. Carver's secretary posted the items in the General Debit and Credit columns. On April 30 she totaled and ruled all of the amount columns of the combination journal. The sum of the totals of the debit columns was found to equal the sum of the totals of the credit columns. After this proof was made, the totals of all special columns were posted.

	PROFESSIONAL FEES CREDIT	DENTAL SUPPLIES EXP. DEBIT	LABORATORY EXPENSE DEBIT	MISC. EXPENSE DEBIT	SALARY EXPENSE DEBIT	EMPLOYEES INCOME TAX. PAY CREDIT	FICA TAXES PAY CREDIT	DR. CARVER DRAWING DEBIT	
1									1
2			15 30						2
3	247 00								3
28		8 20	6 20	3 80					28
29					150 00	22 00	4 78		29
30							4 78		30
31	1196 50	46 45	42 10	34 18	300 00	44 00	19 72	400 00	31
31	1196 50	46 45	42 10	34 18	300 00	44 00	19 12	400 00	31
32	(41)	(51)	(54)	(55)	(59)	(21)	(22)	(32)	32
33									33

of a dentist

Work at the end of the fiscal period

At the end of the year, December 31, 1962, Dr. Carver's secretary prepared an eight-column work sheet. From the work sheet, she prepared an income statement as shown below.

```
                          Dr. J. L. Carver
                          Income Statement
                  For Year Ended December 31, 1962


Professional Income:
     Professional Fees . . . . . . .            $17,345.00

Professional Expenses:
     Dental Supplies Expense . . . . $2,128.15
     Depreciation of Equipment . . .    360.88
     FICA Taxes. . . . . . . . . . .    112.50
     Insurance Expense . . . . . . .     72.00
     Laboratory Expense. . . . . . .    850.32
     Miscellaneous Expense . . . . .    228.26
     Office Supplies Expense . . . .    125.75
     Rent Expense. . . . . . . . . .  1,200.00
     Salary Expense. . . . . . . . .  3,600.00
     Total Professional Expenses . .             8,677.86

Net Professional Income. . . . . . .            $ 8,667.14
```

Income statement of a dentist

The information on the income statement was used in the preparation of the income tax return.

A bookkeeping system for an attorney

The customer of a dentist is known as a *patient*; the customer of an attorney is known as a *client*. Unlike the dentist's patient, the attorney's client is seldom present while much of the work for him is being done. The work of an attorney in behalf of a client may be performed over a period of several weeks or months.

The attorney may keep an appointment book; but because of the nature of his work it will be supplemented by records with his clients that are best suited to the attorney's needs.

Collection docket of an attorney

The record kept by an attorney with clients who engage him to make collections for them is known as a *collection docket*. A page of the collection docket of Attorney John Easton is shown below.

Collection docket of an attorney

The collection docket contains space to record all the details relative to the case and to record all money collected and remitted to the client.

Case docket of an attorney

The record kept by an attorney with clients who engage him to represent them in law suits is known as a *case docket*. A page of Attorney Easton's case docket is shown below.

ATTORNEYS' CASE DOCKET

IN THE *Common Pleas* COURT	COURT FILE NO. *A 11063*
COUNTY *Hamilton; State of Ohio*	OFFICE FILE NO. *128*

PARTIES	NATURE OF CASE
Reliable Motor Co., Inc.	ACTION *Lawsuit*
1233 Gilbert Avenue	
City	
	AMOUNT *Minimum fee $100 with costs*
VS. *Howard Orloff* PLAINTIFF	ATTORNEYS FOR PLAINTIFF
	ATTORNEYS FOR DEFENDANT
DEFENDANT	

DATE	PROCEEDINGS IN CAUSE AND DISPOSITION OF CASE
1962 Dec 4	*Suit filed*

DATE OF JUDGMENT   AMOUNT $

DATE	DESCRIPTION	✓	CHARGES	DATE	DESCRIPTION	✓	CREDITS
1962 Nov 28	*Case received*		*100 00*	*1962 Nov 28*	*Retainer*		*50 00*
Dec 4	*Suit fee*		*5 00*	*Dec 18*	*In full*		*55 00*

Case docket of an attorney

The case docket provides space for all the essential information relative to the case and space to record the financial transactions involved.

Combination journal of an attorney

Mr. Easton maintained a combination journal similar to the one kept by Dr. Carver, the dentist. The combination journal kept by Mr. Easton during December is illustrated at the top of the next two pages.

CASH DEBIT	CASH CREDIT	CHECK NO.	DATE	NAME OF ACCOUNT	POST. REF.	GENERAL DEBIT	GENERAL CREDIT	
			1962					
	100 00	271	Dec 1	Rent Expense		100 00		1
326 80			1	Crowell & Co			245 10	2
	245 10	272	3	Crowell & Co		245 10		3
	5 00	273	4	Suit fee – J C Lancer				4
	4 95	274	5	Telephone bill				5
387 50			7	Cash receipts for week				6
25 00			10	Mrs Edna Myer				7
	150 00	275	12	John Easton, Drawing		150 00		8
421 50			14	Cash receipts for week				9

Combination journal

Analyzing the combination journal of an attorney

Mr. Easton's combination journal contained two income columns. The column headed "Legal Fees" was used to record the income from representing clients in law suits. The column headed "Collection Fees" was used to record the income from collecting accounts for clients. Because of the difference in the type of work involved, it was desirable to separate these two most common sources of income.

Two columns headed "Advances for Clients" were used to record the expenses of a case that were paid by the attorney but that would later be collected from the client. It was desirable that a separate record be kept of these accounts receivable in order that the repayments would not be confused with income for services. The advances for clients and the repayment of the advances by clients in no way affected the attorney's income.

Mr. Easton made all large payments by check. He maintained a petty cash fund of $50 from which minor expenses were paid. Petty cash receipts were made out for each payment and were kept with the petty cash fund. Whenever the fund was running low, a check was drawn to replenish it.

At intervals during the month, Mr. Easton posted the items in the General Debit and Credit columns. On December 31 he totaled and ruled all of the amount columns of the combination journal. The sum of the totals of all the debit columns was found to equal the sum of the totals of all the credit columns. After this proof was made, the totals of all special columns were posted.

FOR MONTH OF *December* 1962   PAGE 23

	LEGAL FEES CREDIT	COLLECTION FEES CREDIT	ADVANCES FOR CLIENTS DEBIT	ADVANCES FOR CLIENTS CREDIT	MISC. EXPENSE DEBIT	SALARY EXPENSE DEBIT	EMPLOYEES INCOME TAX. PAY. CREDIT	FICA TAXES PAY. CREDIT		
1										1
2		81 70								2
3										3
4			5 00							4
5					4 95					5
6	300 00			87 50						6
7	25 00									7
8										8
9	250 00	30 00		141 50						9
10										10
11										11

of an attorney

Work at the end of the fiscal period

At the end of the year, December 31, 1962 Mr. Easton prepared an eight-column work sheet. From the work sheet, he prepared the following income statement:

```
                         John Easton
                      Income Statement
               For Year Ended December 31, 1962

Professional Income:
    Legal Fees . . . . . . . . .   $11,970.00
    Collection Fees. . . . . . .     3,625.70
    Total Professional Income. . . .            $15,595.70

Professional Expenses:
    Depreciation of Law Library. . .  $   205.30
    Depreciation of Office Equipment      76.25
    FICA Taxes . . . . . . . . . . .     135.94
    Miscellaneous Expense. . . . . .     317.75
    Rent Expense . . . . . . . . . .   1,440.00
    Salary Expense . . . . . . . . .   4,350.00
    Supplies Expense . . . . . . . .     165.20
    Traveling Expense. . . . . . . .      56.83
    Total Professional Expenses. . .               6,747.27

Net Professional Income . . . . . . .            $ 8,848.43
```

Income statement of an attorney

The information provided by the income statement was used in the preparation of the income tax return.

Increasing your business vocabulary

What is the meaning of each of the following:

(a) appointment book

(b) patient's record card

(c) collection docket

(d) case docket

Chapter questions

1. Why is it desirable for a professional man to maintain complete and accurate bookkeeping records?
2. What is the purpose of the appointment book of a dentist?
3. What information is shown on the patient's record card of a dentist illustrated on page 488?
4. What are the immediate records maintained by a dentist as presented in this chapter?
5. What are the immediate records maintained by an attorney as presented in this chapter?
6. How often were the cash receipts for fees entered in the dentist's combination journal?
7. How were petty cash payments handled by the dentist in this chapter?
8. What financial statement was prepared by the dentist in this chapter to aid him in making government reports and income tax returns?
9. What is the heading of the special column in the attorney's combination journal on pages 494 and 495 that is used to record the expenses of a case paid by the attorney in behalf of his client?
10. What entry was made in the combination journal of the attorney on pages 494 and 495 to record the collection of an account for a client?
11. What entry was made in the combination journal of the attorney on pages 494 and 495 to record the remittance to a client of a collection made in his behalf?

Cases for discussion

1. Dr. C. D. Meade is a dentist in a small town. He does not have a book-keeper. He maintains a columnar cash record book and a summary page without a ledger. His accounts with patients are kept on individual cards. Do you consider this system satisfactory? Why?
2. R. F. Dale is a certified public accountant. Once each year he audits the books of five different manufacturing concerns in the city. During the rest of his time he does miscellaneous auditing work for other businesses. He does considerable consulting with individuals and businesses in filing income tax returns. What type of records is Mr. Dale likely to maintain?

Application problems

Problem 34-1. *Transactions of a dentist*

Dr. Peter Roth, a local dentist, has employed you as a dental hygienist and secretary. He maintains a bookkeeping system like that used by the dentist in this chapter.

Instructions: 1. Record in a combination journal like the one on pages 490 and 491 the following transactions completed by Dr. Roth during the month of May of the current year. All cash payments are made by check.

May 1. Paid the May rent, $125, with Check No. 227.
     2. Paid American Dental Supply Co. $15 for laboratory expenses.
     3. Paid the telephone bill, $7.50.
     4. Paid X-ray Sales Company $135 for equipment. (Debit Dental Equipment.)
     5. The cash receipts for the week were $415.
     5. Withdrew $300 for personal use.
     8. Paid Dental Service Supply Co. $50.30 for dental supplies.
     12. The cash receipts for the week were $478.50.
     15. Paid you your semimonthly salary of $160 less a deduction of $24.20 for income tax withheld and a deduction of $5 for FICA tax.
     15. Recorded the employer's liability of $5 for his share of the FICA tax.
     16. Paid Lanier & Co. $105 for three chairs for the waiting room. (Debit Office Equipment.)
     17. Replenished the petty cash fund with a check for $19.25. The distribution was as follows: Dental Supplies Expense, $8.40; Laboratory Expense, $9.35; Miscellaneous Expense, $1.50.
     18. Paid O. L. Kettwig $17.50 for washing the walls in the office.
     19. The cash receipts for the week were $394.75.
     23. Withdrew $200 for personal use.
     24. Paid American Dental Supply Co. $50 for laboratory expenses.
     26. The cash receipts for the week were $428.50.
     31. Paid you your semimonthly salary of $160 less a deduction of $24.20 for income tax withheld and a deduction of $5 for FICA tax.
     31. Recorded the employer's liability of $5 for his share of the FICA tax.
     31. Withdrew $300 for personal use.
     31. Replenished the petty cash fund with a check for $23.95. The distribution of payments was as follows: Office Supplies Expense, $3.25; Dental Supplies Expense, $5.75; Laboratory Expense, $12.75; Miscellaneous Expense, $2.20.
     31. The cash receipts for May 28 to 31 were $137.

Instructions: 2. Total, prove, and rule the combination journal.

Problem 34-2. Work at the end of the fiscal period for an attorney

At the end of the fiscal year on December 31 of the current year, the account numbers, titles, and balances in the ledger maintained by L. M. Grayson, a local attorney, were as follows:

11   Cash, $2,963.79

12   Petty Cash, $75.00

13   Advances for Clients, $248.40

14   Law Library, $595.00

14.1 Allowance for Depreciation of Law Library, $142.50

15   Office Equipment, $1,250.00

15.1 Allowance for Depreciation of Office Equipment, $125.00

21   Employees Income Taxes Payable, $71.10

22   FICA Taxes Payable, $37.12

31   L. M. Grayson, Capital, $3,838.03

32   L. M. Grayson, Drawing, $7,200.00

33   Income and Expense Summary, —

41   Legal Fees, $12,420.00

42   Collection Fees, $7,587.12

51   Depreciation of Law Library, —

52   Depreciation of Office Equipment, —

53   FICA Taxes, $223.92

54   Miscellaneous Expense, $410.50

55   Rent Expense, $3,600.00

56   Salary Expense, $7,162.30

57   Supplies Expense, $193.75

58   Traveling Expense, $295.21

Instructions: 1. Prepare an eight-column work sheet for the year ended December 31 of the current year, using the following data for adjustments:

Depreciation of law library, $71.25

Depreciation of office equipment, $62.50

2. Prepare an income statement from the data given on the work sheet. Use as your guide the model income statement on page 495.

3. Prepare a balance sheet from the data given on the work sheet.

4. Record the adjusting and closing entries in a combination journal.

Chapter 35

Bookkeeping for a farmer

Need for records of a farmer

Farmers are engaged in the business of raising and selling farm products for a profit. Farming is therefore a business in the same sense that manufacturing and retailing are businesses. A farmer, like any other businessman, should have bookkeeping records that will show him whether or not he is making a fair return on his investment and how he can manage his business so that it will be increasingly profitable.

A farmer must make many decisions regarding what is to be produced on his farm, the amount of labor that is to be employed, the amount of fertilizer that should be used, and similar questions. Complete and accurate records are necessary in guiding a farmer in such decisions. Records are also needed in order that the farmer may make correct income tax reports.

The accrual basis and the cash basis of keeping records

The method of keeping records that shows (1) all income earned during a fiscal period even though the income is not yet received and (2) all expenses incurred during the fiscal period even though the expenses are not yet paid is known as the *accrual basis* of keeping records.

The method of keeping records that shows (1) only income actually received during a fiscal period and (2) only expenses paid during a fiscal period is known as the *cash basis* of keeping records.

Federal and state income tax laws permit the filing of income tax returns either on the accrual basis or the cash basis.

Mr. Thomas Burke, a farmer, keeps his bookkeeping records on the cash basis. He records income only when cash is received. He records expenses, such as purchases of supplies, fertilizers, labor, and other items, only when he pays for them. He therefore makes no adjustments at the end of the fiscal period for any inventories on hand. In order that the fixed assets may show the true value on the books at the end of a fiscal period, he records depreciation on them at that time.

Balance sheet of a farmer

On January 1, 1961, Thomas Burke, a farmer, decided to open a new set of books. As a basis for his records he prepared the balance sheet illustrated at the top of the following page, showing his assets, liabilities, and proprietorship as of December 31, 1960.

```
                           Thomas Burke
                          Balance Sheet
                        December 31, 1960


                              Assets

Cash . . . . . . . . . . . . . . . . . . . . . .  $   789.00
Livestock. . . . . . . . . . . . . . .  $1,450.00
    Less Allowance for Depreciation
    of Livestock. . . . . . . . . . .      280.00    1,170.00
Machinery and Equipment. . . . . . . .  $5,282.50
    Less Allowance for Depreciation
    of Machinery and Equipment. . . .    2,178.00    3,104.50
Buildings. . . . . . . . . . . . . . .  $8,500.00
    Less Allowance for Depreciation
    of Buildings. . . . . . . . . . .    1,250.00    7,250.00
Land . . . . . . . . . . . . . . . . . . . . . .   15,000.00
Total Assets . . . . . . . . . . . . . . . . . .           $27,313.50

                            Liabilities

Notes Payable. . . . . . . . . . . . . . . . . .  $   500.00
Mortgage Payable . . . . . . . . . . . . . . . .    7,500.00
Total Liabilities. . . . . . . . . . . . . . .             $ 8,000.00

                          Proprietorship

Thomas Burke, Capital. . . . . . . . . . . . . .             19,313.50

Total Liabilities and Proprietorship . . . . . .            $27,313.50
```

Beginning balance sheet of a farmer

Analysis of the balance sheet of a farmer

The amounts on the balance sheet were determined from the records maintained by Mr. Burke and by an evaluation of his fixed assets.

As Mr. Burke operated on the cash basis, he did not record income until he had collected cash. Accounts receivable were therefore not listed on the balance sheet. A memorandum record was maintained for accounts receivable until they were collected. Similarly, inventories of things raised on the farm were not included on the balance sheet. When these products were sold, Cash was debited and an income account was credited. There were no supplies or prepaid insurance listed on the balance sheet, as such items were charged to expense accounts when they were paid.

The livestock account shown on Mr. Burke's balance sheet included the value of the dairy cattle and other livestock purchased. At the end of a fiscal period, the depreciation of this livestock was recorded the same as the depreciation of other fixed assets was recorded.

The value of livestock raised on the farm is not shown on the balance sheet because such livestock, like other farm products, is not entered on the books until it is sold and cash is received.

500

Occasionally Mr. Burke purchased livestock for resale that was fed for a few months only and was then sold. This livestock was an asset; but as its value would ordinarily increase during the time that it was kept, it was not subject to depreciation and was therefore not recorded in the fixed asset account Livestock. It was recorded in a special account entitled *Livestock Purchased Cost.* Whenever any of this livestock was on hand at the end of a fiscal period, it was recorded on the balance sheet as an asset at the cost price.

As the notes payable were given in return for cash or fixed assets, it was necessary to record the notes, because the assets should appear on the records. The mortgage payable was recorded for the same reason. No record was made of ordinary accounts payable until the accounts were paid; therefore no accounts payable were listed on the balance sheet.

The combination journal of a farmer

Thomas Burke recorded all of his transactions in a combination journal.

All payments recorded in the combination journal were made by check. Checks written for the purchase of farm assets and to pay farm business expenses were debited to the proper farm asset and expense accounts. Checks written to withdraw cash for personal use and to pay personal expenses were debited to the proprietor's drawing account.

Special columns were provided in the combination journal for accounts that were frequently affected by transactions. The General Debit and Credit columns were used to record the transactions involving accounts for which there were no special columns.

Since he completed relatively few transactions during a month, Mr. Burke did not feel that it was necessary to use two new pages of the combination journal for each month. He therefore recorded transactions until he filled a page. At that time the columns were totaled, the equality of debits and credits was proved, and the columnar totals were posted. The items in the General Debit and Credit columns were posted at intervals during the period. A part of Mr. Burke's combination journal is illustrated on pages 502 and 503. All of the transactions from January 1 through April 30 were recorded on these two pages.

Analyzing the combination journal

Line 21. On March 1, Mr. Burke received cash, $270, for corn that he sold. Cash was debited in the Cash Debit column. *Produce Sales* was credited in the Produce Sales Credit column.

> Whenever both the debit and the credit parts of a transaction are recorded in special columns, a check mark is placed in the Post. Ref. column to indicate that no amount on this line is to be posted separately.

501

	CASH		CHECK NO.	DATE	NAME OF ACCOUNT	POST. REF.	GENERAL		
	DEBIT	CREDIT					DEBIT	CREDIT	
21	270 00			Mar 1	Sold corn	✓			21
22				5	Misc. Received for Produce eggs			3 75	22
23		56 00	7	12	Purchased seed corn	✓			23
24		225 00	8	19	For personal use	✓			24
25	92 00			30	Misc. Income—soil conservation payment			92 00	25
26		135 00	9	31	Hired labor	✓			26
27		43 25	10	Apr. 3	Paris Department Store	✓			27
28		300 00	11	5	Livestock Purchased Cost		300 00		28
29	730 95			17	Sold hogs	✓			29
30		32 50	12	22	Mchry. & Equip.—elec. fm. transformer		32 50		30
31		9 28	13	26	Cox Refining Co.	✓			31
32		135 00	14	30	Hired labor	✓			32
33	2470 21	2967 66		30	Totals		33760 50	33568 50	33

Combination journal

Line 22. On March 5, Mr. Burke exchanged $3.75 worth of eggs for groceries for personal use. The federal income tax law provides that merchandise received in exchange for farm produce shall be reported as an income item separate from produce sales. Mr. Burke therefore maintained a special income account entitled *Merchandise Received for Produce.* This account was credited in the General Credit column. Since the groceries were for personal use, he debited his drawing account in the column headed *T. Burke, Drawing.*

Line 23. On March 12, Mr. Burke issued Check No. 7 for $56 in payment for seed corn. *Seed, Plants, and Trees Purchased* was debited in the special column provided for that account and Cash was credited.

Line 24. On March 19, Mr. Burke wrote Check No. 8 for $225 to withdraw cash from the bank for his personal use. T. Burke, Drawing was debited and Cash was credited.

Line 25. On March 30, Mr. Burke received a check from the government for $92 in payment for conserving soil on part of his farm. Cash was debited for $92 and *Miscellaneous Income* was credited. Since this type of income is infrequent, no special column is provided for it. Miscellaneous Income was therefore credited in the General Credit column. Any income Mr. Burke receives from miscellaneous sources, such as for work away from his farm and for rental of his machinery and equipment to others, would be recorded as a credit to Miscellaneous Income.

FOR MONTH OF *Jan., Feb., March, and April* 1961   PAGE *1*

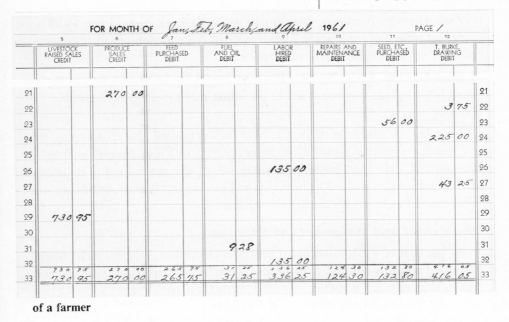

	5 LIVESTOCK RAISED SALES CREDIT	6 PRODUCE SALES CREDIT	7 FEED PURCHASED DEBIT	8 FUEL AND OIL DEBIT	9 LABOR HIRED DEBIT	10 REPAIRS AND MAINTENANCE DEBIT	11 SEED, ETC., PURCHASED DEBIT	12 T. BURKE, DRAWING DEBIT	
21			270 00						21
22								3 75	22
23							56 00		23
24								225 00	24
25									25
26					135 00				26
27								43 25	27
28									28
29	730 95								29
30									30
31				9 28					31
32					135 00				32
32	730 95	270 00	265 75	31 25	,136 25	124 30	132 80	476 05	32
33	730 95	270 00	265 75	31 25	336 25	124 30	132 80	416 05	33

of a farmer

Line 26. On March 31, Mr. Burke issued Check No. 9 for $135 in payment for farm labor. *Labor Hired* was debited in the special column provided for that account and Cash was credited.

Line 27. On April 3, Mr. Burke issued Check No. 10 for $43.25 to the Paris Department Store for purchases made for the family. T. Burke, Drawing was debited and Cash was credited.

Line 28. On April 5, Mr. Burke issued Check No. 11 for $300 for livestock purchased for resale. The schedule of farm income and expenses for farmers' income tax returns, shown on page 507, requires a farmer to report livestock purchased for resale. The cost account *Livestock Purchased Cost* was debited for $300 in the General Debit column. Cash was credited.

When livestock purchased for resale is sold, the income account *Livestock Purchased Sales* is credited for the amount received. The difference between the cost of livestock and the sales price is the profit from livestock that has been purchased for resale.

Line 29. On April 17, Mr. Burke received cash, $730.95, for hogs sold. Cash was debited and *Livestock Raised Sales* was credited in the special column provided.

Line 30. On April 22, Mr. Burke issued Check No. 12 for $32.50 in payment for an electric fence transformer. *Machinery and Equipment* was debited in the General Debit column and Cash was credited.

Line 31. On April 26, Mr. Burke issued Check No. 13 for $9.28 to Cox Refining Co. for tractor fuel. *Fuel and Oil* was debited in the special column provided and Cash was credited.

Line 32. On April 29, Mr. Burke issued Check No. 14 for $135 for farm labor. This was recorded in the same manner as the transaction on Line 26.

Line 33. At the end of April, Mr. Burke totaled the columns of his combination journal, proved the equality of debits and credits, and ruled the journal. He then posted the totals of all the special columns to the proper ledger accounts. The items in the General Debit and Credit columns were posted at intervals during the period.

Work sheet and statements of a farmer

At the end of the annual fiscal year, on December 31, 1961, Mr. Burke prepared an eight-column work sheet. Since he kept his records on the cash basis, the only adjustments required were those for livestock purchased cost and for the depreciation of the fixed assets.

The amount paid for livestock that was sold during the year was no longer an asset. The cost of the livestock sold was therefore credited to

```
                          Thomas Burke
                        Income Statement
                For Year Ended December 31, 1961


Farm Income:
    Livestock Purchased Sales . . . . . . . . . $  1,862.25
    Livestock Raised Sales. . . . . . . . . . .    6,568.50
    Merchandise Received for Produce. . . . . .       94.05
    Miscellaneous Income. . . . . . . . . . . .      192.75
    Produce Sales . . . . . . . . . . . . . . .    2,780.25
    Total Farm Income . . . . . . . . . . . . .               $11,497.80

Farm Expenses:
    Depreciation of Buildings . . . . . . . . . $    170.00
    Depreciation of Livestock . . . . . . . . .      145.00
    Depreciation of Machinery and Equipment . .      552.40
    Feed Purchased. . . . . . . . . . . . . . .      870.37
    Fertilizer and Lime . . . . . . . . . . . .      273.13
    Fuel and Oil (Farm Machinery) . . . . . . .      233.25
    Insurance Expense . . . . . . . . . . . . .       67.00
    Interest Expense. . . . . . . . . . . . . .      375.00
    Labor Hired . . . . . . . . . . . . . . . .    1,020.00
    Machine Hire. . . . . . . . . . . . . . . .      390.00
    Miscellaneous Expense . . . . . . . . . . .      231.30
    Repairs and Maintenance . . . . . . . . . .      156.45
    Seed, Plants, and Trees Purchased . . . . .      277.12
    Taxes . . . . . . . . . . . . . . . . . . .      240.00
    Total Farm Expenses . . . . . . . . . . . .                 5,001.02

Net Farm Income . . . . . . . . . . . . . . . .               $ 6,496.78
```

Income statement of a farmer

```
                        Thomas Burke
                        Balance Sheet
                      December 31, 1961


                           Assets

Cash . . . . . . . . . . . . . . . . . . . . . . $     794.20
Livestock. . . . . . . . . . . . . . . . $1,450.00
    Less Allowance for Depreciation
    of Livestock. . . . . . . . . . . . .    425.00   1,025.00
Machinery and Equipment. . . . . . . . . $5,549.80
    Less Allowance for Depreciation
    of Machinery and Equipment. . . . .    2,730.40   2,819.40
Buildings. . . . . . . . . . . . . . . . $8,500.00
    Less Allowance for Depreciation
    of Buildings. . . . . . . . . . . .    1,420.00   7,080.00
Land . . . . . . . . . . . . . . . . . . . . .   15,000.00
Total Assets . . . . . . . . . . . . . . . .             $26,718.60

                        Liabilities

Notes Payable. . . . . . . . . . . . . . . . . . $     300.00
Mortgage Payable . . . . . . . . . . . . . . . .   6,000.00
Total Liabilities. . . . . . . . . . . . . . .           $ 6,300.00

                      Proprietorship

Thomas Burke, Capital. . . . . . . . . . . . . .         20,418.60

Total Liabilities and Proprietorship . . . . . .         $26,718.60
```

Balance sheet of a farmer

Livestock Purchased Cost and was debited to Livestock Purchased Sales
The balance of the livestock purchased sales account then represented
the gross profit on the livestock that was sold.

The depreciation of the fixed assets of a farmer varies with the type
and the use of each asset. Typical depreciation rates are as follows: frame
buildings, 2%; miscellaneous farm machinery, 10%; horses and cows, 10%;
trucks, tractors, and combines, 10%.

In order to maintain an accurate record of his fixed assets, it was necessary for Mr. Burke to keep information about the date of purchase, the
cost, and the annual depreciation of each fixed asset. He kept a separate
card record for each fixed asset similar to the card shown on page 353.

From the data on the work sheet Mr. Burke prepared the income statement and the balance sheet illustrated.

Adjusting and closing entries for a farmer

From the data in the Adjustments columns of the work sheet that he
prepared for the year ended December 31, 1961, Mr. Burke recorded the
adjusting entries in the combination journal as shown on the following
page.

After the adjusting entries for livestock purchased cost and depreciation were posted, the income and expense accounts were closed into the income and expense summary account. The credit balance of the income and expense summary account was then credited to Mr. Burke's capital ac-

	CASH		CHECK NO.	DATE	NAME OF ACCOUNT	POST. REF.	GENERAL		
	DEBIT	CREDIT					DEBIT	CREDIT	
1				1961	Adjusting Entries				1
2				Dec. 31	Livestock Purchased Sales		1650 00		2
3					Livestock Purchased Cost			1650 00	3
4				31	Depreciation of Livestock		145 00		4
5					Allow. for Depr of Livestock			145 00	5
6				31	Depr. of Machinery & Equip.		552 40		6
7					Allow. for Depr. of Mchry & Equip.			552 40	7
8				31	Depreciation of Buildings		170 00		8
9					Allow. for Depr of Buildings			170 00	9
10					Closing Entries				10
11				31	Livestock Purchased Sales		1862 25		11
12					Livestock Raised Sales		6568 50		12
13					Mdse. Received for Produce		94 05		13
14					Miscellaneous Income		192 75		14
15					Produce Sales		2780 25		15
16					Income and Expense Summary			11497 80	16
17				31	Income and Expense Summary		5001 02		17
18					Feed Purchased			870 37	18
19					Fertilizer and Lime			273 13	19
20					Fuel and Oil (Farm Mchry)			233 25	20
21					Insurance Expense			67 00	21
22					Interest Expense			375 00	22
23					Labor Hired			1020 00	23
24					Machine Hire			390 00	24
25					Miscellaneous Expense			231 30	25
26					Repairs and Maintenance			156 45	26
27					Seed, Etc. Purchased			277 12	27
28					Taxes			240 00	28
29					Depr. of Livestock			145 00	29
30					Depr. of Machinery & Equip.			552 40	30
31					Depr. of Buildings			170 00	31
32				31	Income and Expense Summary		6496 78		32
33					Thomas Burke, Capital			6496 78	33
34				31	Thomas Burke, Capital		5391 68		34
35					Thomas Burke, Drawing			5391 68	35

PAGE 5   COMBINATION JOURNAL

Adjusting and closing entries for a farmer

count. (If the income and expense summary account had had a debit balance, it would have been debited to the capital account.) The debit balance of Mr. Burke's drawing account was also closed into the capital account. The closing entries recorded by Mr. Burke in the General columns of the combination journal are shown on page 506.

Preparing income tax reports

Each farmer who is required to file an income tax return is required by the government to file a special form known as the *schedule of farm income and expenses*. The schedule of farm income and expenses prepared by Mr. Burke is shown below.

SCHEDULE F (Form 1040)
U.S. Treasury Department
Internal Revenue Service

SCHEDULE OF FARM INCOME AND EXPENSES
(Compute social security self-employment tax on Schedule F–1 (Form 1040))
Attach this Schedule to your income tax return, Form 1040

1961

Name and address as shown on Form 1040.
Business name and address Thomas Burke, R. R. #1, Lafayette, Indiana
Location of farm(s) and number of acres in each farm Same, 160 acres
Employer identification number, if any

FARM INCOME FOR TAXABLE YEAR—CASH RECEIPTS AND DISBURSEMENTS METHOD
(Report receipts from sale of livestock held primarily for sale in the applicable column below. Do not include other sales of livestock held for draft, breeding, or dairy purposes; report such sales on Schedule D (Form 1040))

SALES OF MARKET LIVESTOCK AND PRODUCE RAISED AND HELD PRIMARILY FOR SALE						OTHER FARM INCOME	
Kind	Quantity	1. Amount	Kind	Quantity	2. Amount	Items	3. Amount
Cattle	3	$1,125.00	Dairy products		$	Mdse. rec'd for produce	$ 94.05
			Eggs	332 dz	165.75	Machine work	55.00
Horses			Meat products			Breeding fees	
Mules			Poultry, dressed			Wood and lumber	
Sheep			Wool			Other forest products	
Swine	139	4,585.05	Honey			Patronage dividends, rebates or refunds	
Poultry	280	858.45	Sirup and sugar			Agricultural program payments	137.75
Bees			Other (specify):			Other (specify):	
Grain	1330 bu.	2,262.00					
Hay	12 T	322.50					
Cotton							
Tobacco							
Vegetables	11 bu.	30.00					
Fruits and nuts							
Total of columns 1, 2, and 3. Enter here and on line 1 of summary below							$9,635.55

SALES OF PURCHASED LIVESTOCK AND OTHER PURCHASED ITEMS				
a. Description	b. Date acquired	c. Amount received	d. Cost or other basis	e. Profit (or loss)
18 feeder steers	2-6-61	$3,512.25	$1,650.00	$1,862.25
Total (enter on line 2 of summary below)				$1,862.25

F

FARM EXPENSES FOR TAXABLE YEAR (see instructions)
(Do not include personal or living expenses or expenses not attributable to production of farm income, such as taxes, insurance, repairs, etc., on your dwelling)

Items	1. Amount	Items	2. Amount	Items	3. Amount
Labor hired	$ 1,020.00	Veterinary, medicine	$	Freight, trucking	$
Feed purchased	870.37	Gasoline, fuel, oil	233.25	Amortization	
Seed, plants purchased	277.12	Storage, warehousing		Conservation expenses	
Machine hire	390.00	Taxes	240.00	Other farm expenses (specify):	
Supplies purchased		Insurance	67.00	Misc.	231.30
Repairs, maintenance	156.45	Farm interest	375.00		
Breeding fees		Utilities			
Fertilizers, lime	273.13	Rent of farm, pasturage			
Total of columns 1, 2, and 3. Enter here and on line 4 of summary below (cash method) or line 6, page 2 (accrual method)					$4,133.62

SUMMARY OF INCOME AND DEDUCTIONS—CASH RECEIPTS AND DISBURSEMENTS METHOD

1. Sale of livestock and produce raised and other farm income	$ 9,635.55	**4.** Farm expenses (from above)	$ 4,133.62	
2. Profit (or loss) on sale of purchased livestock and other purchased items	1,862.25	**5.** Depreciation (from page 2)	867.40	
		6. Other farm deductions (specify):		
3. Gross profits*	$ 11,497.80	**7.** Total deductions	$ 5,001.02	
8. Net farm profit (or loss) (subtract line 7 from line 3). Enter here and on line 8, page 1, Form 1040. Make your computation of self-employment income and the self-employment tax on Schedule F–1 (Form 1040)			$ 6,496.78	

*Use this amount for optional method of computing net earnings from self-employment. (See line 3, Schedule F–1 (Form 1040))

Schedule of farm income and expenses, page 1

The information reported on the schedule of farm income and expenses was obtained from the income statement prepared by Mr. Burke on December 31. (See illustration on page 504.) Because accurate records were maintained and the income statement was prepared, the preparation of the income tax return was simplified.

Increasing your business vocabulary

What is the meaning of each of the following terms?

(a) accrual basis

(b) cash basis

(c) merchandise received for produce

(d) livestock purchased cost

(e) livestock purchased sales

(f) schedule of farm income and expenses

Chapter questions

1. Why is it desirable for a farmer to maintain complete and accurate book-keeping records of all of his farming operations?
2. When is income earned recorded when books are kept on the accrual basis?
3. When is income earned recorded when books are kept on the cash basis?
4. When are expenses recorded when books are kept on the accrual basis?
5. When are expenses recorded when books are kept on the cash basis?
6. Why do no accounts receivable appear on the balance sheet of a farmer who keeps his books on a cash basis?
7. Why do no accounts payable appear on the balance sheet of a farmer who keeps his books on a cash basis?
8. Why is a special account maintained for merchandise received for produce?
9. What adjusting entries should a farmer make at the end of the fiscal period if he keeps his books on the cash basis?
10. How does a farmer keep an accurate record of his fixed assets?
11. What is the source of the information used in preparing the schedule of farm income and expenses on the income tax return?

Cases for discussion

1. John Moland, a farmer, decided that he should keep his books on the accrual basis. In what respect would Mr. Moland's books differ from those kept by Mr. Burke in this chapter?
2. M. L. Johnson, a dairy farmer, received all of his income from the sale of milk, cream, and butter. He raised some of the grain fed to his cattle and purchased the remainder of it. He delivered his own products. In what ways would his records be likely to differ from those kept by Mr. Burke?

Application problems

Problem 35-1. Recording transactions of a farmer

A. B. Williams, a farmer, maintained a set of books similar to those illustrated in this chapter.

Instructions: 1. Record in a combination journal similar to the one shown on pages 502 and 503 the following transactions completed by Mr. Williams during October, November, and December of the current year. All payments were made by check, the first check for October being No. 63.

Oct. 2. Sold corn for cash, $287.50.
      7. Paid cash for seed for following year, $46.50.
      9. Paid wages for hired labor on the farm, $75.00.
    10. Received cash for use of tractor by neighbor, $20.00.
    14. Paid cash for insurance on house in which he lived, $17.35.
    17. Paid cash for gasoline and oil for farm machines, $14.30.
    20. Withdrew cash for personal use, $150.00.
    23. Paid cash for repairs to tractor and other farm machinery, $23.75.
    25. Received cash from sale of livestock that had been purchased as feeders, $590.25.
    28. Exchanged eggs worth $9.50 for groceries.

Nov. 1. Paid cash for feed for livestock, $83.75.
      7. Received cash from sale of livestock raised on farm, $384.20.
    12. Exchanged eggs and dairy products worth $15.60 for groceries.
    15. Paid $500.00 on the principal of the mortgage and $70.00 interest on the mortgage.
    18. Paid wages for hired labor on the farm, $25.00.
    19. Received $94.20 from sale of turkeys and chickens raised on farm.
    22. Paid for repairs on house in which he lived, $51.30.
    25. Received cash from sale of livestock raised on farm, $331.90.
    28. Paid cash for gasoline and oil for farm machines, $14.65.
    29. Paid note, $200.00, and interest on note, $3.00.

Dec. 5. Received cash from sale of corn and wheat, $351.45.
      6. Paid cash for feed for livestock, $65.75.
    12. Paid cash for seed for following year, $20.55.
    15. Withdrew cash for personal use, $250.00.
    17. Received cash from sale of livestock purchased as feeders, $688.30.
    22. Paid wages for hired labor on the farm, $18.50.
    27. Paid taxes, $107.66. (He estimated that $29.75 of this amount should be debited to his drawing account because it was taxes on the dwelling. Debit Taxes for the remainder.)

Instructions: 2. Total, prove, and rule the combination journal.

Problem 35-2. Work at the end of a fiscal period for a farmer

At the end of the fiscal year on December 31 of the current year, the account numbers, titles, and balances in the ledger maintained by A. B. Williams were as follows:

11	Cash, $853.64	43	Merchandise Received for Produce, $122.40
12	Livestock, $1,225.00		
12.1	Allowance for Depreciation of Livestock, $280.00	44	Miscellaneous Income, $295.25
		45	Produce Sales, $1,198.25
13	Livestock Purchased Cost, $656.00	51	Depreciation of Buildings, —
14	Machinery and Equipment, $2,187.50	52	Depreciation of Livestock, —
		53	Depreciation of Machinery and Equipment, —
14.1	Allowance for Depreciation of Machinery and Equipment, $787.50	54	Feed Purchased, $367.14
		55	Fertilizer and Lime, $93.90
15	Buildings, $4,375.00	56	Fuel and Oil (Farm Machinery), $115.15
15.1	Allowance for Depreciation of Buildings, $655.50	57	Insurance Expense, $37.50
16	Land, $12,000.00	58	Interest Expense, $252.00
21	Notes Payable, $350.00	59	Labor Hired, $281.65
22	Mortgage Payable, $6,000.00	60	Machine Hire, $77.50
31	A. B. Williams, Capital, $11,780.00	61	Miscellaneous Expense, $103.69
32	A. B. Williams, Drawing, $3,618.75	62	Repairs and Maintenance, $78.03
41	Livestock Purchased Sales, $1,333.20	63	Seed, Plants, and Trees Purchased, $188.25
42	Livestock Raised Sales, $3,903.60	64	Taxes, $195.00

Instructions: 1. Prepare an eight-column work sheet for the annual fiscal period ended December 31 of the current year, using the following data for adjustments:

All livestock purchased for resale has been sold
Depreciation of livestock, $122.50
Depreciation of machinery and equipment, $218.75
Depreciation of buildings, $87.50

2. Prepare an income statement from the work sheet. Use as your guide the model on page 504.

3. Prepare a balance sheet from the work sheet. Use as your guide the model on page 505.

Appendix A

Automation in bookkeeping and accounting

The search for improvement in bookkeeping

Business is continually searching for less expensive and more efficient means of keeping necessary records. As a result of this search, businesses have varied their bookkeeping procedures to fit their particular needs. They have used various devices and office machines to do routine and repetitive work. The necessity for high speed in handling many records in today's large and widespread businesses has brought about the development of automatic office machines and the remarkable high-speed electronic equipment we hear so much about.

We have already seen how some businesses organize their bookkeeping procedures and systems to meet their particular needs. In Part 1 of this textbook, the Wood Realty Agency used only a cash journal and a general ledger for recording its daily transactions. In Part 2, Morton Supplies, a merchandising business, used separate journals for purchases, sales, cash receipts, cash payments, and miscellaneous transactions. It used not only a general ledger, but also two subsidiary ledgers. In other parts of the textbook, new accounts and other kinds of records and reports were illustrated for businesses in need of expanded bookkeeping systems.

In this appendix you will be introduced to some of the modern machines used in bookkeeping and the work performed on them. It should be emphasized that the use of machines does not change the basic principles of bookkeeping. Debits and credits have the same meaning regardless of the tools that are used. But the sequence of bookkeeping work may be somewhat different in offices using automatic devices. The division of the work among clerical employees will also differ to some extent because a bookkeeper using machines can process many more routine transactions than would otherwise be possible. A knowledge of current developments in bookkeeping procedures, combined with a knowledge of the bookkeeping and accounting principles presented in this textbook, should help a student to adjust quickly to the bookkeeping practices in any modern office.

Data processing

A term that is often used in business today is data processing. Any handling of figures to provide desired information is *data processing*. Therefore, bookkeeping done either by hand or by the latest automatic devices may be considered a form of data processing. Throughout this textbook we have processed data by hand as we have recorded transactions in journals, posted to ledgers, and prepared financial statements. Now we shall observe how the use of various devices speeds up data processing.

The write-it-once principle — first step toward automation

Each time the Wood Realty Agency in Part 1 of this textbook received cash, Mr. Wood wrote a receipt with a carbon copy. By using carbon paper, Mr. Wood was able to save time by writing two receipts at once. The original was given to the customer, and the copy was retained as the immediate record for use when the transaction was journalized. The procedure of using carbon paper or other means of producing more than one copy with only one writing is called the *write-it-once principle*.

Some businesses use the "write-it-once" principle quite extensively in their bookkeeping systems. For example, the payroll work may require for each employee an entry in the payroll register, an entry in the employee's earnings record, and the writing of a check. Some businesses apply the write-it-once principle to these three operations and perform all of them in one writing. This may be done by hand or by machine.

When the writing is done by hand, a specially designed writing board, such as that shown at the top of page 513, is used. The board has two major purposes: (1) to provide a solid writing base; and (2) to provide a device for holding the bookkeeping forms in proper alignment on the board. The forms are arranged in such a position that, by using carbon paper, entries are made in one writing on the correct line and column of the payroll register and the employee's earnings record as well as on the check. Such standardized systems of manual accounting are often referred to as *writing board*, *accounting board*, or *peg board* systems.

The write-it-once principle applied to bookkeeping machines

Bookkeeping machines also apply the write-it-once principle. A *bookkeeping machine* is a piece of office equipment that will add, subtract, and carry forward balances in the same manner as an adding machine. Unlike an adding machine, however, it has a movable carriage similar to that found on a typewriter, and it may have a typewriter keyboard. This makes it a very good machine for preparing journals and for posting ledgers. The carriage moves the journal and the ledger account from left to

Writing board

Modern bookkeeping machine

right as account names, debits, credits, and balances are entered on the keyboard by the operator.

Most machine bookkeeping systems possess the following major advantages over writing board or other manual bookkeeping systems:

1. The striking power of the keys can usually be adjusted to carry through more carbon copies legibly than when the write-it-once principle is performed by hand on a writing board.
2. Records are uniformly neat and legible because they are printed by machine instead of being handwritten.
3. There is greater accuracy because the machines possess devices that can calculate new balances and retain cumulative balances.

Automation in the office

Large offices today face the problem of handling vast quantities of paper work within a limited time. Weekly payrolls have to be paid to thousands of employees. Inventory records may involve thousands of items, and balances may be desired weekly or even daily. Customers may number in the tens or hundreds of thousands, and both debits and credits may often have to be posted to each account.

A variety of business machines are available to help do this work. These range from simple operator-controlled adding machines to the latest electronically operated equipment. Not all of these machines operate automatically. For example, almost all of the operations performed on an adding machine are manual, and many of the operations performed on a bookkeeping machine are manual. Adding machines and bookkeeping machines are classified, therefore, as manual equipment.

The solution to the problem of handling very large amounts of paper work does not lie in the use of manually operated equipment. It lies in the use of machines that perform operations *with minimum help from an operator*. Such equipment is called *automated equipment*. The use of the equipment to perform bookkeeping and other office work automatically is called *office automation*.

The nature of automated office equipment

Automated office equipment performs much of the bookkeeping work without help from the bookkeeper. Fortunately, the part that is done by the machines is the part that is least interesting to the bookkeeper. For example, automated machines count the number of invoices posted and check the arithmetic involved in posting. Furthermore, they are most commonly used for subsidiary ledger posting. This is a repetitive job in which the same kind of operation is done over and over again many times. If a large enough number of repetitive operations must be performed, it is desirable to have machines do it. The machines must have human supervision, however.

Some new bookkeeping problems are created by the use of automated equipment. A very important problem is the need for presenting information to the machines. Any acceptable means of presenting information to an automated machine is known as *input*. Since the machines are not operated manually for the most part, they must do bookkeeping by *sensing* (reading) information from special kinds of records. These records are called *input media*. The input media are usually prepared from the familiar immediate records or documents described in chapters of this book. Automated bookkeeping, therefore, requires that an additional step be taken between the immediate record of the transaction and the making of an original entry by a machine. This step is the rewriting or *translating* of the information on the immediate record into a language or code that the machine can read — that will cause the automated equipment to respond when the information is put into the machine. Thus it can be seen that in automated systems the manual activities are not completely eliminated. Manual writing is required on the business document, and manual work is also required in writing or coding the information on the input medium.

There is a large variety of automated equipment on the market today. Four kinds of automated equipment are discussed in this appendix. They are called (1) tabulating or punched card equipment, (2) electronic digital computers, (3) magnetic ink character readers, and (4) common language machines. Each of these is explained in the sections that follow. The media used for input to each kind of equipment are also explained.

Punched card bookkeeping

Punched cards are the input media that are used for bookkeeping in systems that use punched card equipment. Punched card equipment consists of a series of machines, each of which performs a different bookkeeping function. Some of the machines, as might be expected, are used to punch holes in cards. Others sense the holes and print business reports from the information that is sensed. There are machines that arrange the cards in sequence before the reports are printed, and there are machines that add, subtract, multiply, and divide the figures represented by the punched holes.

The punched card may be prepared manually on a key punch machine. Data are represented on a punched card by punched holes. The position of the holes on the card and the setup of the machine into which it is fed determine what the machine is to do.

An illustration of a key punch machine is shown on the following page.

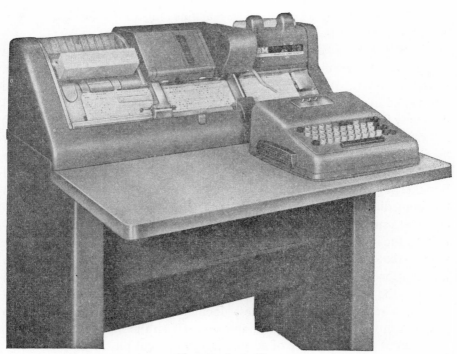

Key punch machine

If the immediate record is typed on an office machine that has a card punching attachment, the immediate record of the transaction and the punched card can be produced at the same time in one operation.

Once a punched card has been prepared, the recorded information on it can be used over and over again when and where needed. The punched cards are fed into a machine that has been planned or *programmed* for a specific purpose, and the punched information is read by electrically conductive brushes or steel pins that sense the position of the holes in the card. The specific purposes may include journalizing, posting, preparing customers' statements, preparing payroll registers, preparing payroll checks, and performing other work of the bookkeeper.

An example of punched cards used for handling accounts receivable

Punched cards may be created from documents. They may themselves be used as documents. In either case, they are used to drive machines that help to perform bookkeeping operations automatically.

Assume that a company wants to automate accounts receivable bookkeeping. Sales invoices are typed for each sale on account. The customer's name or account number, or both, and the amount of the sale are key punched into an *accounts receivable card.* An accounts receivable card is illustrated at the top of the next page.

Accounts receivable card

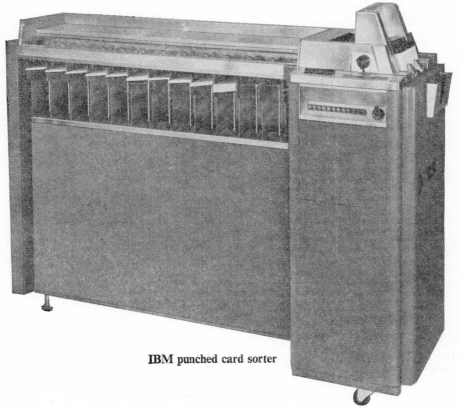

Cards are now brought together in a batch and can be processed automatically. The cards may first be passed through an accounting machine and a total obtained. This total can be checked against an adding machine list of the invoice amounts to make sure no mistakes have been made.

The cards are next sorted. A machine that automatically groups all punched cards of a similar kind and arranges them in numerical or alphabetical order is called a *sorter*. A sorter in common use today is shown below.

IBM punched card sorter

The cards are placed in the hopper of the sorter. The hopper can be seen protruding from the upper right-hand portion of the sorter illustrated above. The sorted cards drop into the pockets that can be seen across the front of the machine. In the case being discussed, the cards are sorted according to customer number.

In a system of this kind there is no ordinary accounts receivable ledger. Instead, there is a file of accounts receivable cards that serves as a ledger. This is called the *customer master file*. For each customer, the master file may contain (1) a name and address card, (2) a card showing the customer's balance at the beginning of the month, and (3) a card for each sales invoice sent to the customer during the month. Each card in the file has the customer's number punched into it.

To post, the sorted cards, representing sales invoices sent to the customer, are merged automatically with the customer master file in a machine called a *collator*. The merging results in an *updated master file*. The result of the automated machine's work is known as *output*. In this instance, the output is the updated master file. What has been done is the same thing that is accomplished in a manual system in posting debits to the accounts receivable subsidiary ledger.

The method described in the preceding paragraphs is only one of the many that may be used. Some offices are more completely automated, and others are less. A method used by one business for processing customer orders is illustrated in the chart on page 519.

The rest of the accounts receivable operations are handled in a similar manner. They include posting cash receipts and preparing monthly statements. When the statements are prepared, the new balance for the next month is calculated and punched into a new card automatically.

An example of punched cards used for handling the payroll

The payroll office is often one of the first offices of a business to be automated. This is so because preparing a payroll each week calls for considerable repetition in computing and recording. For example, the individual employee in most businesses has the same hourly rate of pay, the same FICA tax rate, and the same federal income tax rate each week. He also frequently has the same amount of "other" deductions from week to week.

Information that is repeated each week on the payroll register is therefore punched in machine language into a master card for each employee when he is first hired. This, for many automated payroll systems, includes the employee's (1) name, (2) payroll number, (3) social security number, (4) hourly rate of pay, (5) department number, (6) number of withholding exemptions, and (7) other constant information.

518

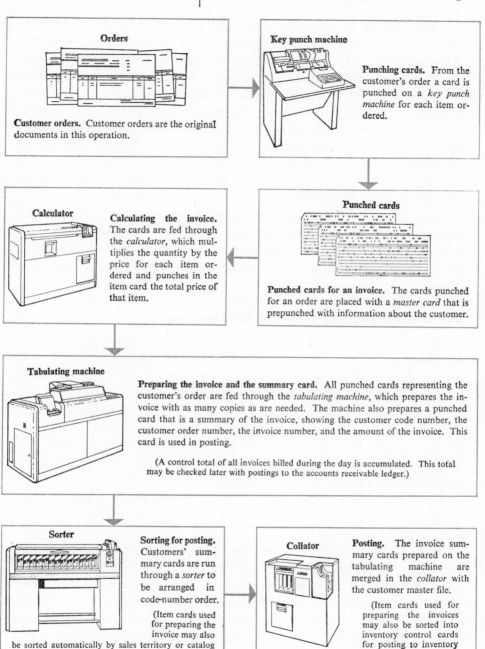

Orders

Customer orders. Customer orders are the original documents in this operation.

Key punch machine

Punching cards. From the customer's order a card is punched on a *key punch machine* for each item ordered.

Calculator

Calculating the invoice. The cards are fed through the *calculator*, which multiplies the quantity by the price for each item ordered and punches in the item card the total price of that item.

Punched cards

Punched cards for an invoice. The cards punched for an order are placed with a *master card* that is prepunched with information about the customer.

Tabulating machine

Preparing the invoice and the summary card. All punched cards representing the customer's order are fed through the *tabulating machine*, which prepares the invoice with as many copies as are needed. The machine also prepares a punched card that is a summary of the invoice, showing the customer code number, the customer order number, the invoice number, and the amount of the invoice. This card is used in posting.

(A control total of all invoices billed during the day is accumulated. This total may be checked later with postings to the accounts receivable ledger.)

Sorter

Sorting for posting. Customers' summary cards are run through a *sorter* to be arranged in code-number order.

(Item cards used for preparing the invoice may also be sorted automatically by sales territory or catalog number for further sales or inventory analysis.)

Collator

Posting. The invoice summary cards prepared on the tabulating machine are merged in the *collator* with the customer master file.

(Item cards used for preparing the invoices may also be sorted into inventory control cards for posting to inventory records.)

One method of processing customer orders

Then, weekly, a current earnings card is punched to record such information as the daily and overtime hours taken from the payroll time card of the employee. After this card is prepared, it is matched and merged with the employee's master card and the two are run through an automated calculating machine for computing the employee's gross pay, his individual as well as his total deductions, and his net or "take-home" pay. As this information is computed, the results are punched into the current earnings card. These cards, along with the master cards, are then run through an automated accounting machine that prints the pay checks, or, if cash is used for payment, pay slips. These same cards are then run through the same machine again, this time for printing the payroll register.

Accounting machines can print more than 50 complete payroll checks each minute, along with accompanying statements of weekly earnings and payroll deductions for each employee. When printing the payroll register, the machines will print as fast as 150 complete lines of the register each minute.

Use of electronic computers in bookkeeping

The most complicated automatic bookkeeping systems are those that use electronic digital computers. Computers are referred to as *electronic* because their components are almost entirely electrical or electronic rather than mechanical. They use vacuum tubes or transistors, as do radios and television sets. *Digital* computers deal with alphabetic letters and with numbers. It would not be necessary to emphasize the word *digital* except for the fact that there is a kind of computer that does not use letters and numbers in the usual way. It is called an *analog computer*. Analog computers are not suitable for bookkeeping.

Electronic *digital* computers are what is usually meant when one uses the simpler term *electronic computers*. In the remainder of this section, the simpler term will be used.

It is not possible to describe electronic computers in detail in this appendix. To understand them fully requires a great deal of study. But some of the things that are unusual about them can be explained here. First of all, they are very fast. One computer now in use will post 80,000 inventory transactions to a file containing 2,000,000 inventory records in about four hours. In doing so, the computer checks each one of the 2,000,000 records to see if any postings to it are required.

Second, electronic computers can be programmed to complete a large number of different tasks. More important, the sequence of these operations is entirely what the computer programmer wants it to be. This means that literally thousands of detailed instructions for the machines must be set up by trained people in exactly the right sequence to get the result desired. The machines cannot perform without people to plan what they should do. Bookkeepers who have the interest and the ability may qualify as programmers for these systems. Their job will be to write the instructions for the computer and to plan the arrangement of transactions information (input files) for the most efficient automatic processing.

Another very important way in which electronic computers differ from other machines used for bookkeeping lies in the completeness of the job that they will do. In punched card machine systems, many machines are needed to sort, summarize, and arrange transactions and to calculate. An electronic computer will do all of these things without physical transportation of data from one machine to the next. This makes it more automatic than any other device used for bookkeeping.

Finally, the input to electronic computers differs from the input to other office equipment systems. In the fastest computers, the transactions are coded onto magnetic tapes. The tapes are similar to the tapes on an ordinary tape recorder. Magnetic tapes are used because the information coded on them can be sensed by the computer at very fast speeds. This helps to make electronic computers much faster in their bookkeeping operations than any other kind of office equipment in use.

Magnetic ink machines

Machines have now been developed that do not require punched cards or tapes in order to perform bookkeeping and sorting operations. A machine that can read and use information that has been properly written in magnetic ink is called a *magnetic ink character reader*. Magnetic ink character readers are used principally by banks for sorting checks and other documents. The illustration below shows a check with magnetic ink numbers printed along the lower margin of the check.

Check with magnetic ink numbers

The Federal Reserve number, the bank's identification number, and the depositor's account number were printed in magnetic ink by the bank before the blank checks were issued to the depositor. The amount of the check, printed in the lower right-hand corner, was placed there by a special machine used by the bank that cashed the check.

Note that the numbers written in magnetic ink on the lower margin of the check follow a style that is not exactly like ordinary numbers. This is because these numbers are read by a device that senses the surface area of each figure and recognizes its shape. Regular numbers, especially 2, 5, 6, and 9, are too much alike to be recognized accurately by an electronic machine. As a result, the American Bankers Association has approved the use of these special numbers. The use of magnetic ink numbers in the processing of bank checks is called *magnetic ink character recognition*. The common abbreviation for this is *MICR*.

The magnetic ink numbers make it possible for the machines that can read such numbers to do any or all of the following operations:

1. Sort the checks by Federal Reserve bank number.
2. Sort the checks by the bank's identification number.
3. Sort the checks by the customer's account number.
4. Feed check amounts and account numbers to an electronic digital computer that processes all checks.
5. Feed check amounts and account numbers to accounting machines that prepare journals and post customers' accounts.

Common language machines

Office machines such as typewriters, adding machines, cash registers, bookkeeping machines, and teletype machines are familiar to most students. Each of these kinds of equipment normally is operated by hand. In recent years, however, the manufacturers of such equipment have learned to create attachments that will partly automate these simpler office devices. The attachments are used to punch holes into reels of paper tape or into cards. The holes are punched as the machines are operated manually. The attachments also have the ability to sense the holes in paper tape or cards. When this is done, the machines will operate automatically. A section of punched paper tape is illustrated below.

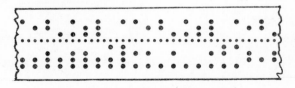

A section of punched paper tape

One of the results of this development is to make it possible for different kinds of machines to communicate with each other. For example, the punched paper tape produced by a special typewriter can be used to drive a teletype machine. The punched tape contains (in the form of punched holes) the same information that was typed. The teletype machine automatically transmits the information by wire from one office of a business to another.

A company may use this method to process orders received from customers. As the orders are typed, a punched tape is created. The orders are then examined for typing errors. If the typed orders are correct, it is evident that the punched tape is also correct. The orders are then teletyped automatically to the company's plants where the orders are filled.

Office machines that can communicate with each other through the medium of punched paper tape or cards are often referred to as *common language machines*.

Principles of bookkeeping apply to all bookkeeping systems

In this chapter we have reviewed the ways in which office equipment is used to automate bookkeeping activities. The *write-it-once* principle was shown to be the first step. It is used both in manual systems and in bookkeeping machine systems. True automation, however, lies in the fields of punched card machines and electronic digital computers. In addition, lesser degrees of automation are found in magnetic ink machine systems and in common language machine systems.

Continuing research and new invention have made office automation a rapidly growing and constantly changing field of work. Automated offices offer many opportunities for employment and careers. These range from the simple work of preparing, handling, and storing materials that the machines use or produce to the more complicated challenges of programming machines for automated systems.

Automated installations differ according to the specific needs of a particular business. As a result, it is generally true that such work will require some special training on the job. However, the basic principles of bookkeeping as presented in this text are the foundation upon which all systems of double-entry bookkeeping are built.

Whether bookkeeping is done by hand or by machine, whether it follows a standardized system or a highly individualized system, whether it is performed wholly or in part by automated equipment, the basic principles of bookkeeping remain the same. A knowledge of these principles is more important to students in school than detailed familiarity with machines. The student should know how and why procedures vary. But the basic principles are the tools that are most important. Students with a knowledge of these principles and an understanding of how and why procedures vary should be well equipped to adjust to the bookkeeping practices in any machine system.

Discussion questions

1. What are some of the reasons why business firms have found it desirable to adopt automated equipment to handle bookkeeping activities?
2. What is meant by the term "data processing"?
3. What is meant by the write-it-once principle?
4. Which of the following applies the write-it-once principle:
   (a) Filling out a check stub and then writing the check.
   (b) Writing a receipt and making a duplicate copy by the use of carbon paper.
5. What are three advantages of a bookkeeping machine over a writing board system in applying the write-it-once principle?
6. Some businesses need office automation more than others. What are some of the reasons that office automation might become necessary in a business?
7. What is the most important feature that distinguishes automated office equipment from nonautomated office equipment?
8. What step that is not required in manual bookkeeping must be taken in automated bookkeeping between the immediate record and the making of an original entry by the machine?
9. Why is a payroll office often one of the first offices of a business to be automated?
10. What are some of the advantages of electronic computing systems over punched card systems?
11. What kind of business makes the greatest use of magnetic ink character readers?
12. In magnetic ink character reader systems, what are some of the functions that the machines can perform?
13. What is a common language machine?
14. Does the use of automated office equipment change the principles of bookkeeping? Explain.

524

Appendix B

Supplementary exercises

Chapter 1

Exercise 1-A. Balance sheet for an individual

Prepare a balance sheet, dated October 31, current year, for C. N. Haney. His assets and his liabilities are listed below.

Assets		Liabilities		
Cash.....................	$ 385.00	Allen Grocery.............	$	88.00
Government Bonds........	2,000.00	Jones Bros................		75.00
Automobile..............	1,925.00	Hanson Dairy.............		12.00
Furniture................	3,748.00			
House...................	17,000.00			

Exercise 1-B. Balance sheet for a small business

Prepare a balance sheet, dated December 31, current year, for the Ideal Laundry. M. T. Weber is the proprietor and manager. The assets and the liabilities are:

Assets		Liabilities		
Cash.....................	$ 973.50	J. M. Greene..............	$	120.00
Office Equipment...........	124.60	Hunt Supply Company......		56.80
Delivery Equipment........	970.00			
Machinery................	5,304.00			

Chapter 2

Exercise 2-A. Opening entry for a professional man

Thomas Bostwick is an attorney with the following business assets and liabilities: Cash, $612.25; Supplies, $37.50; Law Library, $475.00; Office Furniture, $725.50; Office Equipment, $375.00. He owes Avery Book Co. $55.25 and Hagan Equipment Co. $465.00.

Instructions: 1. Prepare a balance sheet dated June 1 of the current year.

2. Record the opening entry in a general journal.

Chapter 3

Exercise 3-A. Recording and posting the opening entry of a small business

The balance sheet of the Bauman Repair Shop, owned by Merlin Bauman, on July 31 of the current year is shown on the following page.

Assets			Liabilities		
Cash.....................	412	00	Jaeger Equipment Co......	197	00
Parts....................	375	00	Davel & Son.............	32	00
Office Equipment........	310	00	Total Liabilities..........	229	00
Shop Equipment........	3,500	00			
			Proprietorship		
			Merlin Bauman, Capital...	4,368	00
Total Assets............	4,597	00	Total Liab. and Prop......	4,597	00

Instructions: 1. Record this opening entry under the date of August 1 of the current year.

2. Post the opening entry to the ledger accounts. Allow one fourth of a page for each account. Number the accounts as follows: asset accounts 11 to 14; liability accounts, 21 and 22; and capital account, 31.

Chapter 4

Exercise 4-A. Analyzing transactions into debit and credit parts using T-accounts

Mr. Ronald Radtke operates a real estate agency. His ledger contains the following accounts:

Cash
Automobile
Office Furniture
Office Machines
Office Supplies
Holmes Equipment Company
Johnson Supply Company

Ronald Radtke, Capital
Commissions Income
Advertising Expense
Automobile Expense
Entertainment Expense
Rent Expense

Instructions: 1. Analyze each of the following transactions, using two accounts arranged in the form shown at the bottom of page 34.

TRANSACTION

1. Received cash, $37.00, for the sale of old office furniture.
2. Paid cash, $50.00, to the Johnson Supply Company in part payment of the amount owed to them.
3. Received cash, $60.00, as commission for renting a house.
4. Paid cash, $150.00, for rent of office for November.
5. Paid cash, $10.50, for entertaining a customer.
6. Received cash, $65.00, as commission for serving as agent in securing a tenant for a house.
7. Paid cash, $9.75, for advertising.
8. Paid cash, $7.50, for gas and oil used in operating the automobile on business.
9. Received cash, $550.00, as commission on the sale of a house.
10. Paid cash, $12.55, for gas and oil used in operating the automobile on business.

11. Paid cash, $25.00, for office supplies.
12. Paid cash, $95.00, to Holmes Equipment Company in part payment of amount owed to them.
13. Paid cash, $8.00, for advertising.
14. Paid cash, $225.00, for new typewriter to be used in the business.
15. Received cash, $490.00, as commission on the sale of a house.
16. Paid cash, $100.00, for a new desk.

Chapter 5

Exercise 5-A. Journalizing cash transactions of a shoe repair shop

Robert Laflin owns and operates the Laflin Shoe Repair Shop. The title he uses for his income account is Sales.

Instructions: 1. Record on page 12 of a five-column cash journal the selected transactions given below. Use as your model the five-column cash journal illustrated on page 51. Use the current year in recording the date. In journalizing these transactions, use the following account titles:

Cash	Advertising Expense
Shop Equipment	Fuel Expense
Shop Supplies	Maintenance Expense
Mason Leather Works	Miscellaneous Expense
Wills Boot Shop	Rent Expense
Robert Laflin, Capital	Wages Expense
Sales	

June 1. Paid cash, $75.00, for June rent. (Check No. 1)
2. Paid cash, $23.75, for a month's supply of nails and leather. (Check No. 2)
3. Paid cash, $10.50, for maintenance of shop equipment. (Check No. 3)
4. Paid cash, $45.00, to Wills Boot Shop in full payment of amount owed to them. (Check No. 4)
6. Paid cash, $25.75, for fuel oil. (Check No. 5)
7. Paid cash, $40.00, for wages of shop employee. (Check No. 6)
9. Paid cash, $5.00, for advertising. (Check No. 7)
11. Paid cash, $3.45, for water bill. (Check No. 8) (Miscellaneous 'Expense)
12. Paid cash, $75.00, for purchase of shop equipment. (Check No. 9)
14. Total cash receipts for cash sales of services for the first half of June amounted to $356.35. (Receipt No. 1)
14. Paid cash, $40.00, for wages of shop employee. (Check No. 10)
16. Received cash, $10.00, for sale of used shop equipment. (Receipt No. 2)
18. Paid cash, $1.50, to extra errand boy. (Check No. 11) (Wages Expense)
21. Paid cash, $40.00, for wages of shop employee. (Check No. 12)
24. Paid cash, $56.80, to Mason Leather Works in part payment of amount owed to them. (Check No. 13)
25. Paid cash, $3.20, for telephone bill. (Check No. 14) (Miscellaneous Expense)
26. Paid cash, $9.00, for advertising. (Check No. 15)
28. Paid cash, $40.00, for wages of shop employee. (Check No. 16)
29. Paid cash, $9.90, for electricity bill. (Check No. 17) (Miscellaneous Expense)
30. Total cash receipts for cash sales of services for the last half of June amounted to $396.85. (Receipt No. 3)

Instructions: 2. Foot, prove, and rule the journal.

Chapter 6

Exercise 6-A. Journalizing and posting the transactions of a doctor

Instructions: 1. Prepare a ledger for L. F. Nelson, a physician, by opening the accounts listed below. Place four accounts on each page of your ledger and use the account numbers shown.

Account Title	Acct. No.	Account Title	Acct. No.
Cash	11	L. F. Nelson, Capital	31
Automobile	12	Fees Income	41
Office Equipment	13	Automobile Expense	51
Office Supplies	14	Miscellaneous Expense	52
Baker Garage	21	Rent Expense	53
Allington Company	22	Stationery Expense	54

Instructions: 2. Copy the balances given below in the proper accounts of your ledger. Date each account balance November 1 of the current year.

Assets (Debit Balances)		Liabilities and Proprietorship (Credit Balances)	
Cash	$1,500.00		
Automobile	3,000.00	Baker Garage	$ 72.50
Office Equipment	6,225.00	Allington Company	550.00
Office Supplies	1,050.00	L. F. Nelson, Capital	11,152.50

Instructions: 3. Record the transactions given below in a five-column cash journal. Use as your model the five-column cash journal illustrated on page 51, but use page 11 as the page number for your journal.

Nov. 1. Paid cash, $250.00, for rent for November. (Check No. 1)
2. Received cash, $90.00, for professional fees. (Receipt No. 1)
3. Paid cash, $19.00, for stationery. (Check No. 2)
5. Paid cash, $83.00, for office equipment. (Check No. 3)
7. Paid cash, $32.50, to Baker Garage. (Check No. 4)
9. Received cash, $45.00, from the sale of old office furniture. (Receipt No. 2)
11. Received cash, $55.00, for professional fees. (Receipt No. 3)
13. Paid cash, $200.00, to Allington Company. (Check No. 5)
15. Paid cash, $8.45, for stamps, a miscellaneous expense. (Check No. 6)
16. Paid cash, $9.50, for gas and oil. (Check No. 7)
17. Received cash, $230.00, for professional fees. (Receipt No. 4)
18. Paid cash, $11.50, for stationery. (Check No. 8)
20. Paid cash, $48.45, for office supplies. (Check No. 9)
23. Received cash, $175.00, for professional fees. (Receipt No. 5)
25. Paid cash, $8.40, for gas and oil. (Check No. 10)
27. Received cash, $150.00, for professional fees. (Receipt No. 6)
30. Paid cash, $16.25, for telephone service for the month, a miscellaneous expense. (Check No. 11)
30. Paid cash, $15.10, for electricity for the month, a miscellaneous expense. (Check No. 12)
30. Received cash, $187.00, for professional fees. (Receipt No. 7)

Instructions: 4. Post the individual amounts in the General Debit and the General Credit columns to the accounts in the ledger.

5. Place a check mark in the Post. Ref. column for each entry that has a credit to Fees Income to show that this entry is not posted individually.

6. Foot each amount column with small pencil figures. Prove the equality of debits and credits in your journal.

7. Prove cash. The balance on hand at the end of the month is $1,729.85.

8. Rule your cash journal.

9. Post the totals of the three special columns. Place a check mark under the columns General Debit and General Credit to indicate that these totals are not posted.

Chapter 7

Exercise 7-A. Trial balance for a personal service business

Mr. Carl Berry is the proprietor and manager of the Berry Parcel Service. The balances in the accounts in Mr. Berry's ledger on June 30 of the current year are as follows:

Cash	Marathon Motors	Labor Expense
1,175.60	182.50	1,327.00

Delivery Equipment	Carl Berry, Capital	Miscellaneous Expense
6,357.00	5,380.81	263.40

Office Equipment	Service Fees	Rent Expense
822.00	4,328.50	307.00

Edgar Gas & Oil Co.	Heating Expense	Truck Expense
1,320.00	273.20	686.61

Instructions: 1. Prepare a trial balance dated June 30 of the current year.

Exercise 7-B. Trial balance for a dentist

The footings in the ledger accounts of Dr. Michael R. Wunsch on October 31 of the current year are as follows:

Account Numbers	Account Titles	Debit Footings	Credit Footings
11	Cash......................................	$1,323.45	$ 735.25
12	Equipment.................................	3,950.00	
13	Office Furniture............................	1,455.00	
21	Athens Equipment Company...................	250.00	675.90
22	Colby Medical Supply Company...............	75.90	75.90
31	Michael R. Wunsch, Capital..................		4,544.75
41	Dental Fees................................		1,504.00
51	Miscellaneous Expense.......................	66.45	
52	Rent Expense...............................	140.00	
53	Salary Expense.............................	275.00	

Instructions: 1. Prove cash. The cash on hand on October 31 of the current year is $588.20.

2. Prepare a trial balance dated October 31 of the current year.

Chapter 8

Exercise 8-A. Work sheet for an optometrist

The account balances in the ledger of A. J. Price, an optometrist, on November 30 of the current year, the end of a fiscal period of one month, were:

Cash, $1,278.45
Automobile, $2,950.00
Equipment, $5,275.00
Office Furniture, $987.10
Baxter Company (creditor), $349.25
Sawyer Optical Supplies (creditor), $95.50

A. J. Price, Capital, $9,304.00
Professional Fees, $1,201.60
Miscellaneous Expense, $34.80
Rent Expense, $150.00
Salary Expense, $275.00

Instructions: Prepare a six-column work sheet for Dr. Price. Use the account titles and the account balances given above.

Chapter 9

Exercise 9-A. Financial reports for an attorney

The work sheet of Alan J. Rogers, an attorney, for the month ended April 30 of the current year is as follows:

Alan J. Rogers
Work Sheet
For Month Ended April 30, 19--

Account Titles	Acct. No.	Trial Balance Debit	Trial Balance Credit	Income Statement Debit	Income Statement Credit	Balance Sheet Debit	Balance Sheet Credit
Cash..............	11	1,078.50	....	......	......	1,078.50	....
Automobile..........	12	3,361.00	....	......	......	3,361.00	....
Office Furniture.......	13	736.00	....	......	......	736.00	....
Professional Library....	14	840.00	....	......	......	840.00	....
Horton Brothers.......	21	....	178.50	......	......	....	178.50
Kennedy Company....	22	....	243.10	......	......	....	243.10
Alan J. Rogers, Capital.	31	....	4,952.65	......	......	....	4,952.65
Fees Income..........	41	....	886.60	......	886.60	....	....
Automobile Expense...	51	45.50	....	45.50	......	....	....
Miscellaneous Expense.	52	31.10	....	31.10	......	....	....
Rent Expense.........	53	150.00	....	150.00	......	....	....
Stationery Expense.....	54	18.75	....	18.75	......	....	....
		6,260.85	6,260.85	245.35	886.60	6,015.50	5,374.25
Net Income..........				641.25	......	....	641.25
				886.60	886.60	6,015.50	6,015.50

Instructions: 1. Prepare an income statement.
2. Prepare a balance sheet in report form.

Chapter 10

Exercise 10-A. Closing entries for an attorney

A work sheet for Alan J. Rogers, an attorney, is given in Exercise 9-A.
Instructions: Record the closing entries in a general journal.

Chapter 11

Exercise 11-A. Recording purchases on account of a book store

The following purchases on account were made by the Avenue Book Store during November of the current year:

Nov. 2. Morrison School Supplies, $246.90
  9. Perkins Paper Company, $125.80
  11. Miller Publishing Company, $320.40
  16. Morrison School Supplies, $180.20
  20. Alton Book Company, $133.40
  24. Miller Publishing Company, $220.60
  24. Welton Greeting Card Company, $98.40
  27. Morrison School Supplies, $220.80
  27. Alton Book Company, $227.60

Instructions: 1. Record each purchase on page 11 of a purchases journal like the one on page 138. Number the invoices beginning with No. 621.

2. Total and rule the purchases journal.

The purchases journal prepared in this problem will also be used in Exercise 11-B.

Exercise 11-B. Opening two ledgers and posting a purchases journal

The creditors of the Avenue Book Store and the amounts owed to each on November 1 of the current year were:

Alton Book Company, 1296 Prairie Avenue, Chicago 46..............	$228.00
Miller Publishing Company, 5101 Madison Road, City...............	———
Morrison School Supplies, 2624 Third Street, City...................	126.00
Perkins Paper Company, 247 Harbor Street, Duluth 24..............	115.20
Welton Greeting Card Company, 1240 Market Street, City...........	68.20

Instructions: 1. Open accounts for the creditors in an accounts payable ledger with balance-column ruling. Record the balance of each account. Allow four lines for each account.

2. In a general ledger open Account No. 21 for Accounts Payable and Account No. 51 for Purchases. Allow four lines for each account. In the accounts payable account record the credit balance of $537.40, dating this balance November 1 of the current year.

3. Post the entries in the purchases journal prepared in Exercise 11-A to the proper accounts in the accounts payable ledger.

4. Post the total of the purchases journal to accounts in the general ledger.

Chapter 12

Exercise 12-A. Recording and posting purchases and cash payments

The creditors of Richard Burton, a wholesale china dealer, and the amounts owed to them on September 30 of the current year are as follows:

	Balances
Lynn China Company, 347 State St., Weston.......................	$230.20
Marshall Potteries, Charleston.....................................	260.00
Monticello China Company, 7863 Marburg Ave., Clinton.............	415.60
Zanesville Pottery Company, Zanesville............................	281.20

Instructions: 1. Open accounts in an accounts payable ledger with balance-column ruling for the creditors listed above. Allow five lines for each account. Record the balance in each account. Date the balance September 30 of the current year.

2. In a general ledger open the following accounts needed in this exercise. Allow four lines for each account. Record the balance for each account for which a balance is given. Date the balance September 30 of the current year.

Acct. No.	Account Title	Balance	Acct. No.	Account Title
11	Cash	$4,124.20 (Dr.)	63	Miscellaneous Expense
21	Accounts Payable	1,187.00 (Cr.)	64	Rent Expense
32	Richard Burton, Drawing		65	Salary Expense
51	Purchases			

The cash payments and purchases transactions completed by Richard Burton during October of the current year are given below.

Instructions: 3. Record the cash payments in a cash payments journal similar to the one illustrated on page 154. All payments are made by check. Number the checks consecutively beginning with No. 110.

Record the purchases in a purchases journal similar to the one illustrated on page 138. Number the purchases consecutively beginning with 81.

Oct. 2. Paid $180.00 for the October rent.
3. Purchased merchandise on account from Monticello China Company, $628.30.
4. Paid $415.60 to Monticello China Company on account.
5. Purchased merchandise on account from Lynn China Company, $764.30.
7. Paid $230.20 to Lynn China Company on account.
14. Paid $325.00 for semimonthly payroll.
15. Purchased merchandise on account from Zanesville Pottery Company, $380.40.
17. Paid $281.20 to Zanesville Pottery Company on account.
21. Paid $16.80 for electricity bill. (Miscellaneous Expense)
22. Purchased merchandise on account from Marshall Potteries, $520.30.
23. Paid $260.00 to Marshall Potteries on account.
26. Paid $16.25 for October telephone bill. (Miscellaneous Expense)
28. Withdrew $350.00 for personal use.
31. Paid $325.00 for the semimonthly payroll.

Instructions: 4. Post the entries from the purchases journal and the cash payments journal to the proper accounts.

5. Total and rule the purchases journal. Post the total to the purchases account and to the accounts payable account in the general ledger.

6. Foot, prove, total, and rule the cash payments journal.

7. Post the totals of the special columns in the cash payments journal.

8. Prepare a schedule of accounts payable from the accounts payable ledger.

Exercise 12-B. Recording and posting cash payments

Frank Webber, a retail paint supplies dealer, completed cash paid transactions during November of the current year as shown on the following page.

Nov. 1. Paid $275.00 for November rent. (Check numbers begin with No. 315)
2. Paid $150.00 to Meyers Supply Company on account.
5. Paid $225.00 to R. L. Davis on account.
8. Paid $310.00 to M. R. Murphy on account.
15. Paid $115.00 for semimonthly payroll. (Salary Expense)
17. Paid $100.00 to Martin Company on account.
18. Paid $65.00 to C. M. Trenton for a cash purchase of merchandise.
20. Paid $13.75 for telephone bill. (Miscellaneous Expense)
20. Paid $15.65 for electric bill. (Miscellaneous Expense)
24. Paid $86.70 to D. J. Barton on account.
30. Withdrew $300.00 for personal use.
30. Paid $115.00 for semimonthly payroll.

Instructions: 1. Record the cash paid transactions on page 15 of a cash payments journal similar to the one illustrated on page 154.

2. Foot, prove, total, and rule the cash payments journal.

3. In a general ledger open the following accounts needed in this exercise. Use the account numbers shown in parentheses. Allow four lines for each account. Record the balance for each account for which a balance is given. Date the balance November 1 of the current year.

Cash (11), $2,100.00
Accounts Payable (21), $1,154.35
Frank Webber, Drawing (32)
Purchases (51)

Miscellaneous Expense (62)
Rent Expense (63)
Salary Expense (64)

4. Post the individual items in the General Debit amount column and the totals of the special columns to the accounts in the general ledger.

Chapter 13

Exercise 13-A. Record sales on account for a furniture store

The following sales of merchandise on account were made by B. R. Turner, a retail furniture dealer, during July of the current year. The sales slips are to be numbered consecutively beginning with No. 76.

July 2. D. E. Wilkes, $276.40
8. L. A. Gaines, $422.95
8. Henry H. Newton, $106.55
17. Stephen Corey, $152.30

July 17. L. A. Gaines, $78.00
25. Stephen Corey, $54.24
29. Roger Stimson, $109.66
29. L. A. Gaines, $112.40

Instructions: 1. Record each of these transactions on page 7 of a sales journal similar to the one illustrated on page 172.

2. Total and rule the sales journal.

The sales journal prepared in this exercise will also be used in Exercise 13-B.

Exercise 13-B. Opening two ledgers and posting a sales journal

Instructions: 1. Open accounts for the customers of B. R. Turner listed below in an accounts receivable ledger that has balance-column ruling. Use the customer's account shown on page 171 as a model. Allow five lines for each account. Record the balances.

Stephen Corey, 2637 Bay Street, Milford.............................. $215.90
L. A. Gaines, 675 Merrit Boulevard, City............................ 321.40
Henry H. Newton, 1640 Hewitt Avenue, City......................... 85.00
Roger Stimson, 241 River Road, City................................ 460.80
D. E. Wilkes, 2730 Maple Park Avenue, City......................... 130.90

2. Post the entries in the sales journal that you prepared in Exercise 13-A to the appropriate customers' accounts in the accounts receivable ledger.

3. In the general ledger open Account No. 12 for Accounts Receivable and Account No. 41 for Sales. Allow four lines for each account. In the accounts receivable account record the debit balance of $1,214.00, dating this balance July 1.

4. Post the total of the sales journal to the appropriate accounts in the general ledger.

Chapter 14

Exercise 14-A. Recording and posting sales and cash receipts of a jewelry store

The names of the customers to whom Thomas Benton, a retail jeweler, sells on account and the amounts due from them on September 30 of the current year are:

	Balances
Daniel Cabot, 1472 Dreman Ave., Erie.............................	$242.40
Susan Crane, 8584 Donegal, City..................................	60.00
George Graham, 4345 Michigan Ave., City........................	110.00
M. E. Hedges, 2311 Lakewood Drive, City........................	85.00
A. R. Kelley, 412 Salem Ave., City..............................	63.45
Michael Murphy, 4340 Trenton St., City..........................	220.00

Instructions: 1. Open accounts in an accounts receivable ledger with balance-column ruling for the customers listed above. Allow five lines for each account. Record the balance in each account.

2. In a general ledger open the following accounts needed in this exercise. Allow four lines for each account. Record the balance for each account.

Acct. No.	Account Title	Balance
11	Cash	$1,468.55 (Dr.)
12	Accounts Receivable	780.85 (Dr.)
13	Office Supplies	177.60 (Dr.)
41	Sales	

The cash receipts and sales transactions completed by Thomas Benton during October of the current year are given below.

Instructions: 3. Record the cash receipts in a cash receipts journal similar to the one illustrated on page 186.

Record the sales in a sales journal similar to the one illustrated on page 172. Number the sales consecutively beginning with 125.

Oct. 1. Recorded the cash balance of $1,468.55 with a memorandum entry.
　　 1. Received $85.00 from M. E. Hedges on account.
　　 3. Sold merchandise on account to A. R. Kelley, $156.20.
　　 4. Received $301.60 from cash sales of merchandise.
　　 8. Received $63.45 from A. R. Kelley on account.
　　 9. Sold merchandise on account to Daniel Cabot, $361.40.
　　 11. Received $910.20 from cash sales of merchandise.

Oct. 11. Received $15.00 from the sale of office supplies to a neighboring merchant. (Office supplies are not a part of the merchandise kept in stock for sale. For this reason, the sales account was not credited for this transaction; instead Office Supplies was credited.)
  14. Sold merchandise on account to Michael Murphy, $85.00.
  15. Received $242.40 from Daniel Cabot on account.
  18. Received $220.00 from Michael Murphy on account.
  18. Received $412.60 from cash sales of merchandise.
  21. Sold merchandise on account to Susan Crane, $63.40.
  23. Received $60.00 from Susan Crane on account.
  25. Received $529.25 from cash sales of merchandise.
  26. Sold merchandise on account to George Graham, $110.50.
  28. Received $110.00 from George Graham on account.
  31. Received $476.20 from cash sales of merchandise.

Instructions: 4. Post the entries from the sales journal and the cash receipts journal to the proper accounts.

5. Total and rule the sales journal. Post the total to the accounts receivable account and to the sales account in the general ledger.

6. Foot, prove, total, and rule the cash receipts journal.

7. Post the totals of the special columns in the cash receipts journal.

8. Prepare a schedule of accounts receivable from the accounts in the accounts receivable ledger.

Chapter 15

Exercise 15-A. Recording miscellaneous entries for a retail clothing store

George Beacom, a retail clothing merchant, decided to open a new set of book on July 1 of the current year. His balance sheet on June 30 was as follows:

George Beacom
Balance Sheet
June 30, 19--

Assets			Liabilities		
Cash......................	2,280	20	Accounts Payable.........	927	80
Accounts Receivable.....	780	60	Proprietorship		
Mdse. Inventory.........	2,420	40			
Supplies................	93	60	George Beacom, Capital...	4,727	00
Prepaid Insurance........	80	00			
Total Assets.............	5,654	80	Total Liab. and Prop......	5,654	80

Instructions: 1. Record the opening entry in a two-column general journal.

2. Record the following selected transactions in the general journal:

July 5. A. L. Benton reported that he was charged $48.30 for merchandise that he had not purchased. The sale was made to A. L. Bender.
  12. Purchased supplies on account from the Wright Supply Co., $41.95; invoice dated July 11.
  18. Took from stock for personal use one suit that cost $62.40.
  25. Donald Marvin reported that he was charged $82.35 for merchandise he had not purchased. The sale was made to D. A. Martin.

Chapter 16

Exercise 16-A. Reconciliation of a bank statement

On August 1 of the current year, the Allen Hardware Store, owned and operated by M. A. Allen, received from the First National Bank the bank statement for July.

Instructions: Prepare a reconciliation of the bank statement using the following data:

(a) The checkbook balance on July 31 was $2,498.20.

(b) The July 31 balance on the bank statement was $2,693.70.

(c) Two charge slips accompanied the bank statement showing that the bank had made the following charges against the account of the Allen Hardware Store:
   (1) A slip showing a service charge of $2.00.
   (2) A slip showing a charge of $1.50 for collecting a note for the Allen Hardware Store.

(d) The following checks were found to be outstanding: No. 91, $36.10; No. 93, $42.90; and No. 96, $120.00.

Chapter 17

Exercise 17-A. Work sheet for an automobile agency

On June 30 of the current year, the end of a fiscal period of one month, the accounts and their balances in the general ledger of the Langer Auto Sales Agency, owned and operated by R. A. Langer, and the list of inventories were as follows:

Account Titles	Acct. No.	Balance	Account Titles	Acct. No.	Balance
Cash	11	$ 3,067.20	Sales	41	$17,960.60
Accounts Receivable	12	7,250.80	Purchases	51	14,241.10
Merchandise Inventory	13	22,000.00	Gas and Oil Expense	61	350.20
Supplies	14	360.20	Insurance Expense	62	——
Prepaid Insurance	15	340.00	Miscellaneous Expense	63	190.60
Accounts Payable	21	7,210.40	Rent Expense	64	300.00
R. A. Langer, Capital	31	25,209.50	Salary Expense	65	1,680.40
R. A. Langer, Drawing	32	600.00	Supplies Expense	66	——
Inc. and Exp. Summary	33	——			

Inventories, June 30, 19--
Merchandise inventory, $22,140.00
Supplies inventory, $265.40
Value of insurance policies, $320.00

Instructions: Prepare an eight-column work sheet, similar to the model given on page 249.

Chapter 18

Exercise 18-A. Financial reports for a pharmacy

A work sheet for the Bliss Pharmacy is given on the following page.
Instructions: 1. Prepare an income statement from this work sheet.
2. Prepare a balance sheet in report form from this work sheet.

Bliss Pharmacy
Work Sheet
For Month Ended March 31, 19--

Account Titles	Acct. No.	Trial Balance Debit	Trial Balance Credit	Adjustments Debit	Adjustments Credit	Income Statement Debit	Income Statement Credit	Balance Sheet Debit	Balance Sheet Credit
Cash...................	11	2460 20						2460 20	
Accounts Receivable......	12	940 85						940 85	
Merchandise Inventory....	13	4985 00		(b) 4145 00	(a) 4985 00			4145 00	
Supplies.................	14	344 90			(c) 74 00			270 90	
Prepaid Insurance.......	15	210 00			(d) 8 00			202 00	
Accounts Payable........	21		1210 65						1210 65
J. L. Bliss, Capital........	31		6627 50						6627 50
J. L. Bliss, Drawing......	32	360 00						360 00	
Income and Expense Sum..	33			(a) 4985 00	(b) 4145 00	4985 00	4145 00		
Sales...	41		4260 35				4260 35		
Purchases.....	51	1974 45				1974 45			
Delivery Expense.........	61	110 30				110 30			
Insurance Expense.......	62			(d) 8 00		8 00			
Miscellaneous Expense....	63	62 80				62 80			
Rent Expense............	64	200 00				200 00			
Salary Expense...........	65	450 00				450 00			
Supplies Expense........	66			(c) 74 00		74 00			
		12098 50	12098 50	9212 00	9212 00	7864 55	8405 35	8378 95	7838 15
Net Income.............						540 80			540 80
						8405 35	8405 35	8378 95	8378 95

Chapter 19

Exercise 19-A. Work at the end of the fiscal period

On January 31 of the current year, the end of a monthly fiscal period, the account balances in the ledger of Burton Electric Supply, owned and operated by W. M. Burton, and the list of inventories were as follows:

Account Titles	Acct. No.	Balance	Account Titles	Acct. No.	Balance
Cash	11	$ 3,460.40	Sales	41	$ 8,545.15
Accounts Receivable	12	2,101.45	Purchases	51	4,870.20
Merchandise Inventory	13	11,310.00	Delivery Expense	61	485.45
Supplies	14	504.00	Insurance Expense	62	———
Prepaid Insurance	15	540.00	Miscellaneous Expense	63	361.25
Accounts Payable	21	1,780.00	Rent Expense	64	300.00
W. M. Burton, Capital	31	15,018.40	Salary Expense	65	960.80
W. M. Burton, Drawing	32	450.00	Supplies Expense	66	———
Inc. and Exp. Summary	33	———			

Inventories, January 31, 19--

Merchandise inventory, $12,210.50
Supplies inventory, $315.00
Prepaid insurance, $520.00

Instructions: 1. Prepare an eight-column work sheet.

2. Prepare the income statement and the balance sheet.

3. Record the adjusting and the closing entries in the general journal.

Chapter 20

Exercise 20-A. Recording transactions in a combination journal

Instructions: 1. Record on page 6 in a combination journal like the one illustrated on pages 292 and 293 the following transactions completed by R. H. Holt during the month of May of the current year:

May 1. Issued Check No. 133 for $50 to establish a petty cash fund.
    1. Received $78.67 from Paul Jones on account.
    2. Issued Check No. 134 for $150 for the May rent.
    3. Sold merchandise on account to Henry Jackson, $33.98.
    3. Cash sales for May 1–3 were $206.80.
    5. Purchased merchandise on account from Lamb & Sons, $361.25.
    6. Issued Check No. 135 for $427.47 to Norton Mfg. Co. on account.
    7. Received $113.50 from Thomas Lucas on account.
    9. Issued Check No. 136 for $75 for a cash purchase of merchandise.
   10. Cash sales for May 5–10 were $488.55.
   12. Received $25 for an old display table. (Store Equipment)
   13. Sold merchandise on account to Fred Piper, $103.75.
   15. Issued Check No. 137 for $141.36 to Baker Bros. on account.
   16. Issued Check No. 138 for $300 to Mr. Holt for a withdrawal for personal use.
   17. Cash sales for May 12–17 were $516.71.
   19. Purchased merchandise on account from Beaver & Bent, $735.15.
   21. Issued Check No. 139 for $33 for advertising. (Advertising Expense)
   23. Sold merchandise on account to Robert Coyne, $45.
   24. Cash sales for May 19–24 were $538.95.
   26. Issued Check No. 140 for $67.89 for a cash purchase of merchandise.

Instructions: 2. Assume at this point of the problem that you have reached the bottom of the page. Total all columns and forward to the next page of the combination journal. Then continue to journalize the following transactions:

May 27. Issued Check No. 141 for $505.40 to Boswell Company on account.
   29. Issued Check No. 142 for $73.15 for utility bills for the month. (Miscellaneous Expense)
   31. Issued Check No. 143 for $38.45 for delivery expense.
   31. Issued Check No. 144 for $330 for the payroll. (Salary Expense)
   31. Issued Check No. 145 for $41.80 to replenish the petty cash fund. The petty cash payments were as follows: Supplies, $18.20; Advertising Expense, $7.50; Delivery Expense, $1.50; and Misc. Expense, $14.60.
   31. Cash sales for May 26–31 were $471.10.

Instructions: 3. Foot all columns of the combination journal and prove the equality of debits and credits.

4. Total and rule the combination journal.

Chapter 21

Exercise 21-A. Recording transactions in a combination journal

Instructions: 1. Record the following selected transactions, which were completed by John Murphy during the month of June, in a combination journal like the one on pages 304 and 305. All purchases and sales are made on account.

June 2. Received a check for $174.54 from B. C. Porter for our invoice of May 23 for $176.30 less a 1% discount of $1.76.

3. Purchased merchandise amounting to $463.81 from McHenry Bros.

4. Sold merchandise amounting to $113.66 to T. B. Baxter.

6. McHenry Bros. allowed us credit for $11.50 for defective merchandise.

6. Issued Check No. 224 for $463.69 to Peyton & Co. in payment of their invoice of May 29 for $473.15 less a 2% discount of $9.46.

9. Issued a credit memorandum for $7.95 to T. B. Baxter for merchandise returned.

11. Issued Check No. 230 for $443.26 to McHenry Bros. in payment of the balance of $452.31 on their invoice of June 3 less a 2% discount of $9.05.

The amount of the invoice of June 3 was $463.81, but a credit of $11.50 was received on June 6. The balance of the invoice to which the discount applied was therefore $452.31, and the discount was 2% of this amount.

12. Sold merchandise amounting to $364.50 to A. D. King.

13. Issued Check No. 235 for $43.60 to Red Arrow Lines for delivery expense on merchandise sold.

14. Received a check for $104.65 from T. B. Baxter and gave him credit for that amount plus $1.06, a 1% discount.

The amount of the invoice of June 4 was $113.66. A credit of $7.95 was given on June 9. The balance of the invoice to which the discount applies was therefore $105.71.

17. Purchased merchandise amounting to $611.44 from the Clyde Co.

22. Received a check for $360.85 from A. D. King for our invoice of June 12 for $364.50 less a 1% discount of $3.65.

24. Sold merchandise amounting to $183.25 to B. F. Vance.

26. Issued Check No. 255 for $599.21 to the Clyde Co. in payment of their invoice of June 17 for $611.44 less a 2% discount of $12.23.

27. Purchased merchandise amounting to $534.65 from Knight & Sons.

30. Issued Check No. 264 for $51.80 to Red Arrow Lines for delivery expense on merchandise sold.

30. Received a credit memorandum for $21.30 from Knight & Sons for merchandise returned by us.

30. Issued Check No. 266 for $46.21 to replenish the petty cash fund. The payments were as follows: Supplies, $12.14; Miscellaneous Expense, $17.32; Delivery Expense, $16.75.

Instructions: 2. Foot, prove and rule the combination journal.

Chapter 22

Exercise 22-A. Determination of earnings

The following table gives the hours worked and the hourly rate for ten employees. Each employee is paid his regular hourly rate for a maximum of 8 hours for Monday through Friday. If he works more than 8 hours on any of these five days, he receives time and a half for the overtime. He also receives time and a half for Saturday.

Name	Hours Worked						Hourly Rate
	M	Tu	W	Th	F	S	
Henry A. Abbott....................	8	8	8	8	8	4	$1.40
Robert C. Barton...................	8	8	8	8	10		1.60
Marvin Easton.....................	8	10	8	8	8		1.70
Laurence Hershey..................	8	8	8	8	8	3	1.30
William Morton....................	8	8	8	0	8		1.95
Richard Parker.....................	8	10	8	8	8		2.20
Raymond R. Ridge.................	8	8	8	8	10		2.00
Frank O. Sutton...................	8	8	8	8	8	4	2.00
Martin Tucker.....................	8	8	8	8	8	2	1.80
David M. Weber...................	8	10	8	8	8		2.10

Instructions: Determine the earnings for the week for each employee and the total earnings for all employees.

Chapter 23

Exercise 23-A. Recording and posting payroll transactions

The Caldwell Print Shop completed the payroll transactions given below during the period January 1 to February 5. The Caldwell Print Shop is liable for payroll taxes at the following rates: FICA taxes, $3\frac{1}{8}\%$; state unemployment taxes, 2.7%; and federal unemployment taxes, .8%. It is also liable for the purchase of U. S. Savings Bonds as the accumulated withholdings for each particular employee reaches the necessary amount.

Instructions: 1. Open the following accounts in the general ledger and record the balances as of January 1 of the current year:

Acct. No.	Account Title	Credit Balance
22	Employees Income Taxes Payable.....................	$253.60
23	FICA Taxes Payable................................	152.48
24	State Unemployment Taxes Payable...................	178.75
25	Federal Unemployment Taxes Payable.................	210.60
26	U. S. Savings Bonds Payable........................	98.00
63	Federal Unemployment Taxes........................	———
66	FICA Taxes..	———
68	Salary Expense....................................	———
69	State Unemployment Taxes..........................	———

Instructions: 2. Record the following selected transactions in a combination journal.

3. After each entry is journalized, post the items recorded in the General Debit and General Credit columns.

Jan. 10. Issued Check No. 18 for $515.54 in payment of the weekly payroll of $610 less deductions of $63.40 for income taxes, $19.06 for FICA taxes, and $12 for U. S. Savings Bonds deductions.

10. Recorded the employer's payroll tax liabilities.

12. Issued Check No. 23 for $406.08 in payment of the liabilities for employees income taxes and FICA taxes for December.

Jan. 12. Issued Check No. 24 for $178.75 in payment of the liability for state unemployment taxes for the last quarter of the previous year.

12. Issued Check No. 25 for $210.60 in payment of the liability for federal unemployment taxes.

12. Issued Check No. 26 for $18.75 to purchase one U. S. Savings Bond for an employee.

17. Issued Check No. 36 for $515.54 in payment of the weekly payroll of $610 less deductions of $63.40 for income taxes, $19.06 for FICA taxes, and $12 for U. S. Savings Bonds deductions.

17. Recorded the employer's payroll tax liabilities.

24. Issued Check No. 49 for $457.42 in payment of the weekly payroll of $540 less a deduction of $55.20 for income taxes, $16.88 for FICA taxes, and $10.50 for U. S. Savings Bond deductions.

24. Recorded the employer's payroll tax liabilities.

31. Issued Check No. 61 for $457.42 in payment of the weekly payroll of $540 less a deduction of $55.20 for income taxes, $16.88 for FICA taxes, and $10.50 for U. S. Savings Bond deductions.

31. Recorded the employer's payroll tax liabilities.

Feb. 1. Issued Check No. 63 for $37.50 to purchase U. S. Savings Bonds (2 at $18.75) for employees.

5. Issued Check No. 70 for $380.96 in payment of the liabilities for employees income taxes and FICA taxes for January.

Chapter 24

Exercise 24-A. Calculating depreciation, recording depreciation, and finding book value

R. J. Gifford purchased the following items of equipment during the first three years that he was in business:

Fixed Asset	Date of Purchase	Initial Cost	Annual Rate of Depreciation
1	January 4, 1960	$2,400	25%
2	June 30, 1960	250	20%
3	January 6, 1961	6,000	5%
4	September 6, 1961	60	12%
5	April 1, 1962	3,300	$6\frac{2}{3}$%
6	December 3, 1962	72	$16\frac{2}{3}$%

Instructions: 1. Record the adjusting journal entry for the total depreciation expense for (a) the year ended December 31, 1960, (b) the year ended December 31, 1961, and (c) the year ended December 31, 1962.

2. Find the book value as of December 31, 1962, of each item of equipment.

Chapter 25

Exercise 25-A. Purchase and disposition of equipment

Joseph Egan, a retail shoe merchant, maintains in his general ledger accounts with Equipment, Allowance for Depreciation of Equipment, and Depreciation Expense.

Instructions: 1. Record in a combination journal the following transactions selected from those completed by Mr. Egan during the current year.

Jan. 2. Issued Check No. 3 for $410 for a new electric typewriter.

Mar. 31. Recorded the estimated depreciation of equipment for the quarter ended March 31, $162.50.

Apr. 1. Discarded two chairs for which there was no further use and which could not be sold. The chairs cost $75 and had a book value of $10 at the time they were discarded.

June 30. Recorded the estimated depreciation of equipment for the quarter ended June 30, $165.30.

July 1. Sold an old office desk to a secondhand dealer for cash, $20. The desk cost $60 and had a book value of $12 when it was sold.

Aug. 15. Issued Check No. 261 for $125 for new display shelves.

Sept. 30. Recorded the estimated depreciation of equipment for the quarter ended September 30, $164.55.

Oct. 1. Bought a new typewriter for $155 cash (Check No. 301) and an old typewriter. The old typewriter cost $145 and had a book value of $50 at the time of the trade in.

Nov. 1. Sold an old adding machine for cash, $35. The adding machine cost $180 and had a book value of $46 after depreciation was recorded on September 30. The depreciation rate was $3 a quarter. (a) Record depreciation for October. (b) Record the sale of the adding machine.

Dec. 31. Recorded the estimated depreciation of equipment for the quarter ended December 31, $164.12.

Instructions: 2. Foot, prove, and record the totals in the combination journal.

Chapter 26

Exercise 26-A. Recording transactions with bad debts expense

The Upsom Lumber Company maintains accounts with Bad Debts Expense and Allowance for Bad Debts. At the beginning of the current year the balance of the allowance for bad debts account was $216.60.

In this exercise you are given transactions taken from those completed by the Upsom Lumber Company during the current year.

Instructions: 1. Record the following transactions in a combination journal:

Feb. 13. Decided that the past-due account of Garry Fuller, $76.60, was uncollectible. Wrote off his account as a bad debt.

Mar. 27. C. W. Lee, a charge customer, became insolvent. Wrote off his account of $43 as a bad debt.

Mar. 31. (End of first quarterly fiscal period.) Increased the allowance for bad debts by making the necessary adjusting entry. The estimated bad debts expense for each quarterly fiscal period was 1¼% (.0125) of the total charge sales. The charge sales for the quarterly fiscal period ended March 31 were $11,650.

May 15. R. W. Bunker, a charge customer, became insolvent. Wrote off his account of $86.50.

June 30. The total charge sales for the second quarterly period ended June 30 were $9,990.80. Increased the allowance for bad debts 1¼% (.0125) of that amount.

Aug. 21. Decided that the past-due account of Karl Hess, $123.80, was uncollectible. Wrote off his account as a bad debt.

Sept. 30. The total charge sales for the third quarterly fiscal period ended September 30 were $10,060.75. Increased the allowance for bad debts 1¼% (.0125) of that amount.

Dec. 31. Decided that the past-due accounts of the following charge customers were uncollectible: Albert Beem $82.98; Joseph Harris, $160.30; R. B. Bough, $30. Wrote them off as bad debts in one combined entry, debiting Allowance for Bad Debts for the total.

Dec. 31. The total charge sales for the fourth quarterly fiscal period ended December 31 were $12,444.50. Increased the allowance for bad debts 1¼% (.0125) of that amount.

Instructions: 2. Foot, prove, and record the totals in the combination journal.

Chapter 27

Exercise 27-A. Proving cash

Instructions: 1. Make a daily balance slip like the one on page 397. Fill in this form and prove cash from the information given below.

At the close of business on May 2 of the current year, the count of cash in the cash register of Bette's Gift Shop was as shown in the tabulation at the left below. The detailed audit strip totals for May 2 were as shown at the right below.

Pennies	$ .35			
Nickels	1.55	– 114	$0,248.50	GT
Dimes	4.40	– 113	$0,007.75	Pd
Quarters	12.75	– 112	$0,025.00	Rc
Halves	15.50	– 111	$0,028.25	Ch
Paper money	191.00	– 110	$0,223.50	Ca
Check	15.00			

The cash register papers for May 2 were as follows:

(a) Sale on account to Mrs. C. O. Moore, $5.95.
(b) Received on account from Miss Irma Bath, $10.00.
(c) Paid out to Tom Jones for delivering orders, 60 cents.
(d) Sale on account to Mrs. David Payne, $16.50.
(e) Paid out to Mrs. A. B. Roth for merchandise returned, $4.50.
(f) Received on account from Mrs. L. D. Archer, $15.00.
(g) Sale on account to Mrs. Bessie Wilson, $5.80.
(h) Paid out to Larson Supply Co. for store supplies, $2.65.

Instructions: 2. Make a cash short and over voucher like the one on page 398. Fill in this voucher for the cash shortage for the day.

Exercise 27-B. Replenishing petty cash

On April 30 of the current year, the end of a monthly fiscal period, the petty cash fund of the Holt Haberdashery contained the following petty cash paid-out receipts and cash short and over vouchers:

	Paid-Out Receipts			Cash Short and Over Vouchers	
No.	Account	Amount	Date	Classification	Amount
26	Miscellaneous Expense	$1.45	Apr. 4	Over	$1.00
27	Supplies	3.37	10	Short	.10
28	Sales Returns and Allow.	3.95	15	Short	.30
29	Miscellaneous Expense	.35	23	Over	.20
30	Delivery Expense	1.10	29	Short	.50
31	Sales Returns and Allow.	2.75			
32	Miscellaneous Expense	4.15			
33	Delivery Expense	.25			

Instruction: 1. Classify the paid-out receipts according to the accounts to be charged and find the total amount in each group.

2. Find the net amount by which the cash is short or over.

3. Record in a combination journal the entry to replenish the petty cash fund (Check No. 129).

Exercise 27-C. Recording transactions in a combination journal

W. C. Kaston, who operates a retail store, records his transactions in a combination journal like the one on pages 402 and 403.

Instructions: 1. Record the following totals as amounts brought forward on June 27 of the current year to a new page of the combination journal:

Cash Debit, $4,265.68
Cash Credit, $2,458.90
General Debit, $394.10
General Credit, $41.50
Accounts Payable Debit, $2,677.31
Accounts Payable Credit, $3,876.29

Discount on Purchases Credit, $34.26
Accounts Receivable Debit, $348.25
Accounts Receivable Credit, $287.50
Purchases Debit, $4,315.91
Sales Credit, $5,302.80

Instructions: 2. Record in the combination journal the following transactions completed by Mr. Kaston on June 27 to 30:

June 27. Purchased merchandise on account from Meyer Mfg. Co., $115.50.
    27. The cash register totals for the day were as follows:
            Sales for cash, $214.63
            Sales on account, $21.75
            Received on account, $20.00
    28. Issued Check No. 165 for $306.23 to Henderson & Co. in payment of their invoice of June 19 for $312.48 less a 2% discount of $6.25.
    28. Received a credit memorandum for $10 from Meyer Mfg. Co. for defective merchandise.
    28. The cash register totals for the day were as follows:
            Sales for cash, $231.95
            Sales on account, $5.95
            Received on account, $14.85
    30. Issued Check No. 166 for $237.65 for the semimonthly payroll of $280 less a deduction of $33.60 for employees income taxes payable and a deduction of $8.75 for FICA taxes payable.
    30. Recorded the employer's liability of $8.75 for FICA taxes, $7.56 for state unemployment taxes, and $2.24 for federal unemployment taxes.
    30. Issued Check No. 167 for $150 to W. C. Kaston for a personal withdrawal.
    30. The cash register totals for the day were as follows:
            Sales for cash, $188.65
            Sales on account, $30.15
            Received on account, $45.25
    30. Issued Check No. 168 for $37.80 to replenish the petty cash fund. The payments from this fund were as follows:
            Sales Returns and Allowances, $12.90
            Miscellaneous Expense, $22.70
            Cash Short, $2.20

Instructions: 3. Foot, prove, and rule the combination journal.

Chapter 28

Exercise 28-A. Recording transactions in columnar special journals

Instructions: 1. Record the following transactions completed by the Billings Company during May of the current year in a sales journal and a cash receipts journal like those illustrated in Chapter 28.

May 1. Recorded the cash balance of $1,876.50 with a memorandum entry.
   1. Sold merchandise on account to R. J. Scott, $86.10; sales tax, $2.58; total invoice, $88.68 (Sale No. 53).
   3. Received a check for $153.50 from John Britt on account.
   3. Sold merchandise on account to C. Y. Young, $162; sales tax, $4.86; total invoice, $166.86. (Sale No. 54).
   3. Cash sales for May 1, 2, and 3 were $547.50; sales taxes, $16.43; total, $563.93.
   7. Sold merchandise on account to R. J. Scott, $66.60; sales tax, $2; total invoice, $68.60. (Sale No. 55).
   10. Cash sales for the week were $820.50; sales taxes $24.62; total, $845.12.
   14. Received $80.50 from James Reeves on account.
   17. Cash sales for the week were $1,090.50: sales taxes, $32.72; total, $1,123.22.
   20. Sold merchandise on account to C. Y. Young, $261.50; sales tax, $7.85; total invoice, $269.35. (Sale No. 56).
   21. Received a check for $59.84 from R. J. Scott for balance due on our invoice of May 1 less our credit memorandum No. 18 of May 13.
   24. Cash sales for the week were $1,105.20; sales taxes $33.16; total, $1,138.36.
   27. Received a check for $175 from C. Y. Young on account.
   27. Sold merchandise on account to James Reeves, $240; sales tax, $7.20; total invoice, $247.20. (Sale No. 57).
   30. Sold wrapping supplies worth $6 for cash to accommodate a customer; sales tax, 18¢; total cash received, $6.18.
   30. Cash sales for the week were $1,240.34; sales taxes, $37.21; total, $1,277.55.

Instructions: 2. Foot, prove, total, and rule the journals.

Chapter 29

Exercise 29-A. Calculating and recording interest and bank discount

Instructions: 1. Record the following selected transactions completed by Harold Perry during part of the current fiscal year. Use a cash receipts journal, a cash payments journal, and a general journal similar to those illustrated in Chapter 29.

Mar. 3. Issued our 30-day, 6% Note Payable No. 1 for $1,500 to the Diamond Lumber Co. for an extension of time on account.
   10. Received Note Receivable No. 12 for $600 at 4% for 60 days from Wilbur Carter on account.
   16. Discounted at the First National Bank our 45-day, 6% Note Payable No. 2 for $1,000. Received credit for the proceeds.
   21. Received a non-interest-bearing, 90-day Note Receivable No. 13 for $450 from Charles Cole on account.

Apr. 2. Issued Check No. 121 to the Diamond Lumber Co. in full payment of principal and interest on Note Payable No. 1, dated March 3.

20. Discounted at the First National Bank our 40-day, 6% Note Payable No. 3 for $400. Received credit for the proceeds.

30. Issued Check No. 143 to the First National Bank in full payment of our Note Payable No. 2, dated March 16 and due today.

May 9. Received a check from Wilbur Carter in full payment of principal and interest on Note Receivable No. 12, dated March 10 and due today.

10. Issued our 30-day, non-interest-bearing Note Payable No. 4 for $600 to the General Lumber Co. for an extension of time on account.

30. Issued Check No. 171 to the First National Bank in full payment of our Note Payable No. 3, dated April 20 and due today.

June 9. Issued Check No. 180 to the General Lumber Co. in full payment of our Note Payable No. 4, dated May 10 and due today.

June 19. Received notice from the bank that Charles Cole dishonored Note Receivable No. 13 when it became due today. Charged the note to the account of the maker.

Aug. 1. Decided that the past-due account of Charles Cole (see transactions of March 21 and June 19) was uncollectible. Wrote off his account as a bad debt.

Instructions: 2. Foot and prove the journals.

Chapter 30

Exercise 30-A. Adjusting and reversing entries for accrued interest and salaries

On December 31 of the current year, before reports were prepared, the salary expense account of D. E. Wenzel had a debit balance of $8,245.67 and the interest expense account had a debit balance of $68.45. At the end of this yearly fiscal period, the following expenses had accrued: interest expense, $7.15; salary expense, $125.

Instructions: 1. Open the following general ledger accounts: Interest Payable, Account No. 22; Salaries Payable, Account No. 24; Salary Expense, Account No. 68; and Interest Expense, Account No. 81. Record the balances in the expense accounts.

2. Record in a columnar general journal as of December 31 of the current year the adjusting entries for the accrued expenses. Post to the ledger accounts.

3. Record the following partial closing entry in the columnar general journal: debit Income and Expense Summary for $8,446.27; credit Salary Expense for $8,370.67; and credit Interest Expense for $75.60. Post the credits to the ledger accounts.

4. Rule the expense accounts.

5. Record in the columnar general journal, as of January 2 of the next year, the reversing entries for the accrued interest expense and the accrued salary expense. Post these entries to the ledger accounts.

6. Rule the liability accounts.

Chapter 31

Exercise 31-A. Distribution of the net income of a partnership

Ann Kling, Norma Lewis, and Ruth Martin were partners in the dress shop of Kling, Lewis & Martin. The partners had invested in the business $15,000, $10,000, and $8,000 respectively. According to the partnership agreement the net income was to be divided as follows:

(1) Each partner was to receive an amount equal to 6% of her capital.
(2) The remainder of the net income or the net loss was to be distributed among the partners equally.

At the end of the annual fiscal period on December 31 of the current year, the income statement showed that the net income for the year, after the payment of partners' salaries, amounted to $3,000.

Instructions: 1. Prepare a distribution of net income statement.

2. Prepare a capital statement. The debit balances of the partners' drawing accounts on December 31 were: Kling, $265; Lewis, $320; Martin, $120.

Exercise 31-B. Opening entries and distribution of net income of a partnership

On January 2 of the current year A. R. Mead and C. L. Post, proprietors of separate retail groceries, formed a partnership. The partnership, Mead and Post, took over the assets of the two proprietors and assumed their liabilities. Mr. Post invested enough additional cash in the partnership to make his proprietorship equal to that of Mr. Mead. The balance sheets of Mr. Mead and Mr. Post at the time the partnership was formed are shown below.

A. R. Mead
Balance Sheet
January 2, 19--

Assets			Liabilities		
Cash	2,325	60	Notes Payable	1,500	00
Notes Receivable	200	00	Accounts Payable	2,317	30
Accounts Receivable	3,312	40	Total Liabilities	3,817	30
Merchandise Inventory	7,821	80			
Supplies	157	50	Proprietorship		
Equipment	3,200	00	A. R. Mead, Capital	13,200	00
Total Assets	17,017	30	Total Liab. & Prop.	17,017	30

C. L. Post
Balance Sheet
January 2, 19--

Assets			Liabilities		
Cash	1,210	65	Accounts Payable	2,711	25
Accounts Receivable	3,279	40			
Merchandise Inventory	6,104	10	Proprietorship		
Supplies	101	10	C. L. Post, Capital	9,895	80
Prepaid Insurance	36	80			
Equipment	1,875	00			
Total Assets	12,607	05	Total Liab. and Prop.	12,607	05

Instructions: 1. Record the opening entry for each partner in a columnar general journal to show the investment of each.

According to the partnership agreement the net income was to be divided as follows:

(1) Each partner was to receive an amount equal to 6% of his capital.
(2) The remainder of the net income or the net loss was to be distributed between the partners equally.

At the end of the first year in business, the December 31 income statement showed that the net income for the year, after the payment of partners' salaries, had been $14,000.

Instructions: 2. Prepare the distribution of net income statement.

3. Prepare a capital statement. The debit balances of the partners' drawing accounts on December 31 were: Mead, $550; Post, $675.

Chapter 32

Exercise 32-A. Opening entry to incorporate a going concern

On March 1 of the current year a charter was granted to Nash & Kite, Inc., that authorized a capital stock of $50,000 consisting of 1,000 shares (par value $50). This corporation had agreed to take over the printing business owned by the partnership of Nash and Kite. On March 1 the corporation took over the assets and assumed the liabilities of the partnership shown on the following balance sheet:

Nash and Kite
Balance Sheet
February 28, 19--

Assets			Liabilities		
Cash......................	4,721	85	Notes Payable..........	1,875	00
Notes Receivable.........	900	00	Accounts Payable........	2,871	90
Accounts Receivable.......	4,621	45	Total Liabilities..........	4,746	90
Mdse. Inventory..........	6,676	80			
Supplies.................	716	40	Proprietorship		
Equipment...............	12,110	40	M. A. Nash, Capital.....	10,000	00
			J. S. Kite, Capital........	15,000	00
Total Assets..............	29,746	90	Total Liab. and Prop.....	29,746	90

On March 1, 200 shares of stock were issued to Mr. Nash and 300 shares were issued to Mr. Kite for their equities in the partnership.

Instructions: Record the opening entry in a general journal.

Exercise 32-B. Balance sheet for a corporation

The Balance Sheet columns of the work sheet of Caldwell & Co. for the fiscal year ended December 31 of the current year are shown on the next page.

Instructions: Prepare the balance sheet for Caldwell & Co. Add the net income for the current fiscal period to the retained earnings account balance.

Account Titles	Balance Sheet	
	Debit	Credit
Cash...	7,360 21	
Accounts Receivable...........................	8,187 25	
Allowance for Bad Debts.......................		106 84
Merchandise Inventory.........................	41,639 87	
Supplies.....................................	872 45	
Equipment...................................	6,750 00	
Allowance for Depreciation of Equipment.........		562 50
Accounts Payable.............................		6,123 40
Taxes Payable................................		385 60
Capital Stock.................................		50,000 00
Retained Earnings.............................		3,731 29
	64,809 78	60,909 63
Net Income..................................		3,900 15
	64,809 78	64,809 78

Exercise 32-C. Work at the end of the fiscal period

The account balances in the general ledger of The Erlanger Corporation on March 31 of the current year were as follows:

Cash, $6,819.86

Petty Cash, $100.00

Accounts Receivable, $8,112.46

Allowance for Bad Debts, $281.63

Merchandise Inventory, $22,410.50

Supplies, $381.10

Prepaid Insurance, $201.06

Equipment, $4,800.00

Allowance for Depreciation of Equipment, $560.00

Notes Payable, $2,000.00

Interest Payable, —

Accounts Payable, $6,110.45

Salaries Payable, —

Employees Income Taxes Payable, $281.40

FICA Taxes Payable, $96.88

State Unemployment Taxes Payable, $125.55

Capital Stock, $30,000.00

Retained Earnings, $3,721.01

Income and Expense Summary, —

Sales, $27,876.12

Sales Returns and Allowances, $521.30

Discount on Sales, $194.10

Purchases, $25,076.64

Purchases Returns and Allowances, $161.57

Discount on Purchases, $295.65

Bad Debts Expense, —

Delivery Expense, $610.20

Depreciation Expense, —

FICA Taxes, $48.44

Insurance Expense, —

Miscellaneous Expense, $126.45

Rent Expense, $500.00

Salary Expense, $1,550.00

State Unemployment Taxes, $41.85

Supplies Expense, —

Interest Expense, $16.30

The additional data needed at the end of the monthly fiscal period are: additional allowance for bad debts, 1% of total charge sales of $11,463.80; merchandise inventory, $24,816.33; supplies inventory, $176.30; prepaid insurance, $176.90; annual rate of estimated depreciation, 10%; accrued salary expense, $62; accrued interest expense, $7.50.

Instructions: 1. Prepare an eight-column work sheet for the monthly fiscal period ended March 31 of the current year.

2. Prepare an income statement and a balance sheet from the work sheet.

3. Record the adjusting and closing entries in the general journal.

4. Record the reversing entries for the accruals in the general journal as of April 1 of the next period.

Chapter 33

Exercise 33-A. Personal records of an individual

Charles Richards, a single man employed as a bookkeeper, maintains bookkeeping records similar to those illustrated for a family in Chapter 33. He maintains a checking account, but he pays all small bills in cash.

Mr. Richards uses the following expense classification:

Board and Room — all regular meals and rent of room.
Clothing Expense — all wearing apparel.
Donations — church and charity.
Federal Income Tax — deductions from salary for income tax.
Insurance Expense — life insurance and group insurance.
Laundry and Dry Cleaning — washing, cleaning, and pressing.
Medical Expense — drugs, dentist and doctor bills, etc.
Miscellaneous Expense — toilet and shaving articles, barber service, gifts, newspapers, magazines, books, stationery, stamps, and other unclassified expenses.
Recreation — refreshments, movies, theaters, sports, social affairs, club dues, and vacation.
Transportation — streetcar, bus, taxi, train, and airplane fares.

Mr. Richards maintains a combination journal with the following money columns:

Cash Debit	Federal Income Tax Debit
Cash Credit	Laundry and Dry Cleaning Debit
General Debit	Miscellaneous Expense Debit
General Credit	Recreation Debit
Board and Room Debit	Transportation Debit
Donations Debit	Social Security Deposits Debit

Mr. Richards carries in his pocket a notebook in which he jots down each expenditure he makes. Each night he records in his combination journal the expenditures he has made during the day. He debits the individual expense accounts for the proper amounts and credits Cash for the total amount paid out.

Instructions: **1.** Record in the combination journal the following transactions completed by Mr. Richards during May of the current year:

May 1. Cash on hand, $406.82.
     1. Paid $1.36 for stationery and stamps.
     2. Issued Check No. 37 for $30 for board and room for the week.
     3. Paid $5.95 for a shirt and a tie and $1.58 for laundry.
     4. Paid 30¢ for razor blades and 80¢ for dry cleaning.
     5. Paid $1.65 for streetcar tickets.
     6. Gave $1.50 to the church collection and paid $1.50 for dinner.
     7. Paid $2.50 for movie tickets and refreshments.
     8. Issued Check No. 38 for $6 for a doctor bill.
     9. Issued Check No. 39 for $30 for board and room for the week.
    10. Paid $1.60 for laundry and $1 for a ticket to a boxing match.
    11. Paid $1.05 for a movie ticket and refreshments.
    12. Paid $1.65 for streetcar tickets and $1.75 for toilet articles.
    13. Gave $1.50 to the church collection and paid $1.35 for dinner.
    14. Issued Check No. 40 for $7.20 for an insurance premium.
    15. Received a check for $177.62 for his semimonthly salary of $220 less a deduction of $35.50 for federal income tax and a deduction of $6.88 for social security tax.
        (Debit Cash for the amount of cash received and debit Federal Income Tax and Social Security Deposits for the amounts deducted; credit Salary for the total amount.)
    15. Deposited $25 in his savings account. (Debit Savings.)
    16. Issued Check No. 41 for $30 for board and room for the week.
    17. Paid $1.25 for a haircut, $1.44 for laundry, $5 for tickets to a dance, and $1.80 for taxi fare.
    18. Received $10 for a birthday present (credit Other Income) and paid $7.50 for a party.
    19. Paid $1.65 for streetcar tickets and 35¢ for a magazine.
    20. Gave $1.50 to the church collection and paid $1.65 for dinner.
    21. Paid $1 for dry cleaning and 78¢ for medicine.
    22. Paid $5 for Y.M.C.A. dues and 75¢ for new socks.
    23. Issued Check No. 42 for $30 for board and room for the week.
    24. Paid 70¢ for pressing and $1.15 for laundry.
    25. Paid $1.50 for bowling and $1 for magazines.
    26. Paid $1.65 for streetcar tickets and $3.50 for a sweater.
    27. Gave $1.50 to the church collection and paid $1.75 for dinner.
    28. Issued Check No. 43 for $5 for a donation to the Community Chest.
    29. Paid $1.50 for a ticket to a baseball game.
    30. Issued Check No. 44 for $30 for board and room for the week.
    31. Received a check for $177.62 for his semimonthly salary of $220 less a deduction of $35.50 for federal income tax and a deduction of $6.88 for social security tax.
    31. Deposited $25 in his savings account.
    31. Paid $1.88 for laundry, $1.25 for a haircut, and $2.40 for movie tickets and refreshments.

Instructions: 2. Foot, prove, total, and rule the combination journal. Cash on hand is $477.37.

Chapter 34

Exercise 34-A. Recording the transactions of a physician

Dr. J. H. Gordon, physician and surgeon, maintains a bookkeeping system like that used by the dentist in Chapter 34.

Instructions: 1. Open the following accounts in the ledger and record the balances indicated as of December 1 of the current year. Allow five lines for each account.

Acct. No.	(1) Assets	
11	Cash................	$ 1,361.41
12	Petty Cash............	50.00
13	Automobile..........	2,850.00
13.1	Allow. for Depr. of Automobile........	950.00
14	Medical and Surgical Equipment.........	5,533.88
14.1	Allow. for Depr. of Medical and Surgical Equipment........	608.25
15	Office Equipment.....	1,693.50
15.1	Allow. for Depr. of Office Equipment.....	214.60
	(2) Liabilities	
21	Employees Income Taxes Payable......	88.00
22	FICA Taxes Payable...	37.52
	(3) Proprietorship	
31	J. H. Gordon, Capital..	7,700.72
32	J. H. Gordon, Drawing (Dr.).............	5,500.00
33	Income and Expense Summary..........	....

Acct. No.	(4) Income	
41	Professional Fees......	$15,974.00
	(5) Expenses	
51	Automobile Expense...	903.85
52	Depr. of Automobile...	......
53	Depr. of Medical and Surgical Equip......	......
54	Depreciation of Office Equipment.........	......
55	FICA Taxes..........	103.18
56	Insurance Expense....	84.00
57	Laboratory Expense...	487.50
58	Medical Supplies Exp..	581.42
59	Miscellaneous Exp.....	276.55
510	Office Supplies Exp.....	97.80
511	Rent Expense........	2,750.00
512	Salary Expense........	3,300.00

Instructions: 2. Record the following transactions in a combination journal having amount columns for Cash Debit; Cash Credit; General Debit; General Credit; Professional Fees Credit; Automobile Expense Debit; Medical Supplies Expense Debit; Miscellaneous Expense Debit; Salary Expense Debit; Employees Income Taxes Payable Credit; FICA Taxes Payable Credit; J. H. Gordon, Drawing Debit.

All payments were made by check, the first check for December being No. 205. The transactions completed by Dr. Gordon during December of the current year were:

Dec. 1. Paid the December rent, $250.
   3. Paid Physicians' Linen Service Company for linen service, $6.75. (Charge to Miscellaneous Expense.)
   3. Paid Puro Water Company for distilled water, $5. (Charge to Medical Supplies Expense.)
   4. Paid the telephone bill, $7.25.
   5. Paid Ericson's Garage for repairs to automobile, $16.85.
   6. Deposited $367, the receipts for the past week.
   10. Withdrew $200 for personal use.
   12. Paid Johnson Drug Company for medical supplies, $31.83.
   13. Deposited $462.50, the receipts for the past week.
   15. Paid Helen Cook, nurse-secretary, her semimonthly salary of $150 less deductions of $22 for income taxes withheld and $4.69 for FICA taxes.
   15. Recorded the employer's liability of $4.69 for his share of the FICA taxes.
   17. Replenished the petty cash fund with a check for $37.73. The distribution was as follows: Automobile Expense, $15.35; Medical Supplies Expense, $12.75; Miscellaneous Expense, $4.10; Office Supplies Expense, $5.53.
   19. Paid Wilton Stationers for letterheads, $18.75. (Charge to Office Supplies Expense.)
   20. Withdrew $125 for personal use.
   20. Deposited $391.50, the receipts for the past week.
   21. Paid Lang Medical Company for medical supplies, $16.09.
   24. Paid Kramer Furniture Store for refinishing furniture, $35. (Charge to Miscellaneous Expense.)
   26. Paid Holton Laboratories, Inc. for services rendered, $41.70. (Charge to Laboratory Expense.)
   27. Deposited $275, the receipts for the past week.
   28. Replenished the petty cash fund with a check for $42.33. The distribution was as follows: Automobile Expense, $13.87; Laboratory Expense, $4.50; Medical Supplies Expense, $21.15; Miscellaneous Expense, $2.81.
   29. Withdrew $175 for personal use.
   31. Paid Helen Cook her semimonthly salary of $150 less deductions of $22 for income taxes withheld and $4.69 for FICA taxes.
   31. Recorded the employer's liability of $4.69 for his share of the FICA taxes.

Instructions: 3. Total, prove, and rule the combination journal.

4. Post the combination journal.

5. Prepare an eight-column work sheet for the annual fiscal period ended December 31, using the following data for adjustments:

> Depreciation of automobile, $950
> Depreciation of medical and surgical equipment, $275
> Depreciation of office equipment, $169.35

6. Prepare the income statement and the balance sheet.

7. Record the adjusting and closing entries and post.

8. Balance and rule the ledger accounts and take a post-closing trial balance.

Chapter 35

Exercise 35-A. Recording the transactions of a farmer

William Peters, a farmer, maintains a set of bookkeeping records similar to those illustrated in Chapter 35. His trial balance on September 30 of the current year is given below.

William Peters

Trial Balance

September 30, 19––

Cash	11	821|35	
Livestock	12	1,498|30	
Allowance for Depr. of Livestock	12.1		292|50
Livestock Purchased Cost	13	733|00	
Machinery and Equipment	14	2,337|50	
Allowance for Depreciation of Machinery and Equipment	14.1		785|75
Notes Payable	21		500|00
William Peters, Capital	31		3,644|36
William Peters, Drawing	32	1,895|50	
Income and Expense Summary	33	. . . | . .	. . . | . .
Livestock Purchased Sales	41		1,281|80
Livestock Raised Sales	42		2,476|50
Merchandise Received for Produce	43		77|15
Miscellaneous Income	44		110|00
Produce Sales	45		1,868|90
Depreciation of Livestock	51	. . . | . .	. . . | . .
Depr. of Machinery and Equipment	52	. . . | . .	. . . | . .
Feed Purchased	53	244|33	
Fertilizer and Lime	54	151|20	
Fuel and Oil (Farm Machinery)	55	91|25	
Interest Expense	56	7|50	
Machine Hire	57	61|50	
Miscellaneous Expense	58	123|10	
Rent Expense	59	2,850|00	
Repairs and Maintenance	60	108|45	
Seed, Plants, and Trees Purchased	61	113|98	
		11,036|96	11,036|96

Instructions: 1. Open ledger accounts for the accounts given in the trial balance of September 30 and enter the balances as of September 30 of the current year.

Instructions: 2. Record in a combination journal similar to the one shown on pages 502 and 503 the following transactions completed by Mr. Peters during the three-month period from October 1 to December 31. All payments were made by check, the first check for October being No. 52.

Oct.   1. Paid the fourth quarterly installment on the rent, $950.
      3. Purchased feed for the livestock, $87.50.
      4. Withdrew cash for personal use, $150.
      8. Purchased fuel and oil for the farm machines, $23.25.
    10. Received cash from the sale of livestock that had been purchased as feeders, $239.50.
    15. Exchanged eggs and vegetables worth $15 for groceries.
    16. Received cash from the sale of dairy products, $62.60.
    22. Received cash from the sale of eggs and vegetables, $39.75.
    25. Received cash from the sale of corn, $292.25.
    27. Paid cash for repairs to the tractor, $12.50.
    30. Received cash from the sale of livestock raised on the farm, $463.

Nov.   1. Received cash from the sale of corn, $151.20.
      5. Paid the note payable of $500, due today, and the interest on the note, $5.
      7. Received cash from the sale of livestock that had been purchased as feeders, $525.
      8. Withdrew cash for personal use, $125.
    11. Purchased feed for the livestock, $180.67.
    14. Purchased seed for next year, $55.70.
    18. Received cash from the sale of chickens and ducks raised on the farm, $58.05.
    21. Paid cash for repairs to the farm equipment, $10.50.
    26. Received cash from the sale of livestock raised on the farm, $174.60.
    29. Bought clothing, $29.75.

Dec.   1. Purchased a milk cow for $97.50. (Debit Livestock.)
      3. Received cash for helping a neighbor fill his silo, $15.
      5. Received cash from the sale of wheat, $245.
      6. Withdrew cash for personal use, $200.
    10. Paid cash for repairs to the barn, $75.
    15. Purchased fuel and oil for the farm machines, $19.50.
    20. Purchased seed for next year, $33.75.
    24. Received cash from the sale of livestock raised on the farm, $88.
    27. Received cash from the sale of cordwood, $30. (Miscellaneous Income.)
    30. Received $500 from the Farmers National Bank and gave the bank his 60-day, 6% note for $500.
    30. Purchased a truck for farm use, $1,050.

Instructions: 3. Total, prove, and rule the combination journal. Post to the ledger accounts.

4. Prepare an eight-column work sheet for the annual fiscal period ended December 31 of the current year. The data needed for the adjustments are:

        All livestock purchased for resale has been sold
        Depreciation of livestock, $140.35
        Depreciation of machinery and equipment, $233.75

5. Prepare an income statement and a balance sheet from the work sheet.

6. Record the adjusting and the closing entries in the General columns of the combination journal. Post to the ledger accounts.

7. Rule the ledger accounts that balance, and balance and rule each remaining account that has both debits and credits.

8. Prepare a post-closing trial balance.

Index

Footings, *defined*, 51
Form 1040, Schedule C, Internal Revenue Service, *illustrated*, 265
Form W-2, Withholding Tax Statement, 345
Four-column cash receipts journal, 181
Fundamental bookkeeping equation, 7

G

Gain, calculating, on the disposal of a fixed asset, 365; on fixed assets, *defined*, 368
General columns, 45; in journal, posting individual entries in, 65
General journal, adjusting entries in, *illustrated*, 277; cash transactions recorded in a, 44; columnar, 412; columnar, miscellaneous entries in the, 412; columnar, opening entries for partnership recorded in, 449; correcting entry in, 207; *defined*, 11, 201; entry for supplies bought on account, 205; entry for withdrawal of merchandise by proprietors, 206; four-column, 412; *illustrated*, 208; need for, 201; of Morton Supplies, 208; opening entry in the, 202; posting entry for supplies bought on account, 206; posting four-column, 413; posting totals of four-column, 413; recording total purchases invoices in, 143; recording total sales in, 175
General ledger, after all journals have been posted and the accounts have been footed, *illustrated*, 210–211; classification of accounts in, 262; closed, balanced, and ruled, *illustrated*, 283; closing the, 277; *defined*, 134; opening accounts in the, 202; proving posting of, 209; relationship between the accounts payable ledger and the accounts payable account in the, 159
Going business, purchase of a, by a corporation, 464
Gross profit on sales, 259

H

Heading, of the balance sheet, 105; of the income statement, 102; of the trial balance, 84; of the work sheet, 94

I

Immediate record, *defined*, 43; invoice, 131; of business transactions, 43; of cash payments, 47, 149; of cash receipts, 45, 181; of purchases on account, 131; of sales on account, 167
Income, accrued, 441; business, reporting on federal income tax returns, 264; calculating net, 250; *defined*, 36; net, 95, 103; other, on income statement, 370; section of income statement, 102
Income accounts, closing entry for, 112, 278; of a family, 472

Income and expense summary account, 279; closing the, 116; need for an, 111
Income and expense statement, for attorney, *illustrated*, 495; for dentist, *illustrated*, 491; for family, *illustrated*, 481
Income statement, 94, 101; bad debts expense on the, 382; *defined*, 96; depreciation expense on the, 358; discount on purchases on the, 311; discount on sales on the, 311; effect of accrued expenses on the, 437; expense section of the, 103; heading of the, 102; *illustrated*, 102, 258, 264, 312; income section of the, 102; interest on the, 428; net loss on the, 260; of a farmer, *illustrated*, 504; of a partnership, 450; of a partnership, *illustrated*, 451; other expenses on, 370; other income on, 370; Other Income and Other Expense sections of, *illustrated*, 371; purchases returns and allowances on, 311; ruling the, 103; sales returns and allowances on the, 311; steps used in preparing the, 259; use of the, 257
Income-tax data for a family, 483
Income taxes, employees, paying the liability for, 343; withheld from employees by employer, 321
Income tax reports, preparing, for a farmer, 507
Income tax return, Schedule C, Form 1040, *illustrated*, 265
Incorporation, certificate of, 460
Increase, in an account balance, 71; in assets, 32; in liabilities, 32; in proprietorship, 32; recording, in account balances, 71
Individual, beginning balance sheet of an, 2; bookkeeping for the, 483
Input, *defined*, 515; media, 515
Insurance, cash surrender value of life, 471; expense, adjustment for, 245; prepaid, *see* Prepaid insurance
Interest, accrued, 435; computing, using interest tables, 421; computing, without interest tables, 421; on income statement, 427; on notes, 421; on work sheet, 427; payment of, 441; recording collection of, 423; recording payment of, 425
Interest-bearing note, 421
Interest expense, account, need for readjusting the, 440; reporting, 427; reversing entry for accrued, 440
Interest income, reporting, 427
Interest rate, 421; *defined*, 420
Interest table, 421; analyzing the, 421
Inventory, *see also* Merchandise inventory; perpetual, *defined*, 252; physical, *defined*, 252
Inventory record sheet, 251
Investment, additional, recording in cash receipts journal, 185; cash, forming a partnership with a, 448; in a going concern, recording an, 449
Invoice, checking an, 132; *defined*, 131; *illustrated*, 131; recording an, in a purchases journal, 133; showing terms of payment, *illustrated*, 307; using, as purchases journal, 142; verifying extensions on an, 132
Items column in an account, use of, 23

562

in journal after posting, *illustrated*, 25; posting the, 22; steps in recording the, in the general journal, 12

Opening ledger, 20

Opposite position, subtraction in accounts by, 72

Other expense, accounts, closing, 372; cash short and over, 400; discount on sales as, 312; interest expense as, 428; loss on fixed assets as, 370; section on income statement, 370

Other income, cash short and over, 400; closing, accounts, 372; discount on purchases as, 312; gain on fixed assets as, 370; interest income as, 428; section on the income statement, 370

Output, 518

Outstanding check, *defined*, 223

P

Paid invoices file, 401

Paid-out receipt, *illustrated*, 395

Paid-out slips, and the petty cash fund, 398

Paper tape, punched, 457

Participation dividends, 467

Partners, *defined*, 446; division of net income or net loss among, 450

Partners' salaries, 450

Partnerships, 446; accounts, 448; adjusting entries for, 454; articles of, *illustrated*, 447; balance sheet of, 452; balance sheet of, *illustrated*, 453; capital statement of, 454; closing entries for, 454; converting single proprietorship business into, 448; *defined*, 446; forming, with cash investments, 448; income statement of, 450; income statement of, *illustrated*, 451; opening entries for, 449; organization of, 446; recording an investment in a going concern, 449; why formed, 446

Par value, 462

Passbook, bank, 218

Patient, 492

Patients record and ledger account card, analyzing the, 489; back of a, *illustrated*, 489; front of a, *illustrated*, 488

Payee, of a check, *defined*, 150; of a note, *defined*, 420

Payroll, automation for, work, 332; debits and credits required in recording the, 337; *defined*, 321; paying the, by check, 329; paying the, in cash, 330; recording the, in columnar cash payments journal, 441; recording the, in combination journal, 338; where a time clock is not used, 331

Payroll change sheet, *illustrated*, 330

Payroll check, *illustrated*, 329

Payroll receipt, *illustrated*, 331

Payroll register, 325; analyzing the, 325; *illustrated*, 325, 337

Payroll requisition form, *illustrated*, 330

Payroll taxes, 321; paying liabilities for, 343; recording employees', 338; recording employer's, 339–342

Payroll time card, 323; analyzing the, 324; *illustrated*, 323

Peg board system, 512

Perpetual inventory, *defined*, 252

Personal bookkeeping system, starting a, 1

Petty cash fund, 295; combination journal entry to replenish, 399; *defined*, 296; entries in cash payments journal, 298; entries in combination journal, 297; establishing the, 297; paid-out slips and the, 398; replenishing the, 297, 399; using the, 296

Petty cash voucher, *illustrated*, 297

Physical inventory, *defined*, 252

Post-closing trial balance, *defined*, 122, 286; *illustrated*, 123, 286

Posting, 22; columnar cash journal, 62; columnar cash payments journal, 412; columnar cash receipts journal, 411; *defined*, 22; four-column general journal, 413; from cash payments journal, 155, 157; from cash receipts journal, 188, 189; from columnar sales journal, 409; from general journal, 202; from purchases journal, 135, 137; from sales journal, 170, 173; of general ledger, proving the, 209; opening entry, 22; order of, when several journals are used, 208; steps in, 63; *see also* each journal

Posting reference column, of a general journal, 25; of a ledger account, 23

Posting reference numbers, use of, 25

Practice Set 1, Part 1, 229; Part 2, 290

Preferred stock, *defined*, 462

Prepaid insurance, adjusting, 245; adjusting entry for, 275

Prices, list, 306

Principal, of a note, 420

Proceeds, of a note, 426

Professional man, *see also* Attorney *and* Dentist; bookkeeping for, 487; need of records for a, 487

Profit, *see also* Net income; gross, on sales, 259

Profit and loss statement, *see* Income statement

Profit and loss summary account, *see* Income and expense summary account

Project No. 1, 90; No. 2, 127; No. 3, 317

Promissory note, analyzing a, 420; *defined*, 420

Proof, provided by trial balance, 85

Proprietor, cash withdrawal by the, 153; drawing account of, 153; withdrawal of merchandise by the, 206

Proprietorship, 2; accounts, balancing, 119; balance of, 25; decreases in, 33, 37; *defined*, 3; group of accounts, 263; increases in, 32, 36; of a family, 472; section of balance sheet, 105; section of corporate balance sheet, 465

Proving, cash, *defined*, 52, 187; cash, with cash register totals, 397; cash on hand, 187; cash receipts journal, 186; equality of debits and credits, 52; totals of the cash payments journal, 155

Punched card bookkeeping, 515

Punched cards, used for handling accounts receivable, 516; used for handling payroll, 518

Punched card sorter, IBM, 517

Single-entry bookkeeping, *defined*, 50
Single proprietorship, converting, into a partnership, 448
Six-column work sheet, 95
Social organization, beginning a bookkeeping system for a, 6
Social security account number, application for, *illustrated*, 322
Social security card, 322, 323; *illustrated*, 323
Social security taxes, 321; *defined*, 322
Social security wage tax table, 326
Sorter, 517; IBM punched card, *illustrated*, 517
Special columns, 44, 51; posting totals of, 67
Standard form of account, 19
Statement, distribution of net income, 452; withholding tax, 345
Statement of account, *defined*, 195; *illustrated*, 196
Statements, *see* Balance sheet *and* Income statement
State unemployment taxes, *defined*, 322; paying the liability for, 344; recording the employer's, 340
Stock, authorized capital, 462; capital, 459; common, 462; no-par-value, 462; par-value, 462; preferred, 462
Stock certificate, *defined*, 459; *illustrated*, 460
Stockholder, *defined*, 459
Stock subscriptions, 462
Subscribers, 462
Subscriptions, stock, 462
Subsidiary ledger, 134
Subtraction in accounts by opposite position, 72
Summary account, income and expense, *see* Income and expense summary account
Supplementary reports, 263
Supplies, adjusting entry for, 242, 274; purchase of, on account, 204; recording purchase of, on account, 205; used, adjustment for, 242
Supplies expense, calculating amount of, 243
Supporting schedules, 263
Surplus, earned, 465
Surrender value, cash, of life insurance, 471

T

T account, *defined*, 33
Tape, punched paper, 522
Taxes, federal unemployment, 322; FICA, 322; FICA, paying the liability for, 343; income, withheld from employees by employer, 321; payroll, 321; sales, *see* Sales taxes; social security, 321; state unemployment, 322
Tax liability accounts, 339
Tax statement, withholding, 345
Tax table, social security wage, 326
Terms of sale, *defined*, 307
Time card, payroll, 323; payroll, analyzing the, 324
Time of a note, 420
Trade discount, *defined*, 306
Transactions, analyzing, to determine debits and credits, 33; need for recording quickly, 391

Translating, 515
Trial balance, analyzing the, 93; correcting errors in the, 87; *defined*, 80; entering the, on the work sheet, 238; errors not detected by a, 85; finding errors when a, does not balance, 85; *illustrated*, 84, 209; need for interpreting the, 93; post-closing, 122; post-closing, *illustrated*, 286; preparing a, 84; proof provided by, 85; ruling a, 84

U

Uncollectible accounts, 377; entry to write off, when an allowance account is used, 384, 385; writing off, 385
Unemployment tax, federal, 322; state, 322
Updated master file, 518

V

Valuation, accounts, *defined*, 359; of accounts receivable, 378
Value, no-par, 462; par, 462
Verifying extensions on an invoice, 132
Voiding a check, 220
Voucher, cash short and over, 398; *defined*, 297; petty cash, *illustrated*, 297

W

Wage bracket withholding table, weekly, 327
Wage tax table, social security, 326
Withdrawals by proprietor, cash, 153; *defined*, 153; of merchandise, 206
Withholding table, weekly wage bracket, 327
Withholding tax statement, Form W-2, *illustrated*, 345
Work sheet, accruals on the, 436; adjustment for beginning inventory on the, 240; adjustment for bad debts on the, 380, 381; adjustment for depreciation on, 355; adjustment for ending inventory on the, 241; adjustment for prepaid insurance and insurance expense on the, 245; adjustment for supplies expense on the, 243; analyzing the, 94; balancing columns of, 95; calculating net income on, 250; completing the, 247; *defined*, 94; discount on purchases on, 310; discount on sales on, 310; eight-column, 237; eight-column, *illustrated*, 249; entering the trial balance on the, 238; finding net income from, 96; *illustrated*, 310; interest on the, 427; of a family, *illustrated*, 479; of a farmer, 504; planning the adjustments in the Adjustments column of the, 239; proving the Adjustments columns of the, 246; purchases returns and allowances on, 310; ruling and balancing columns on, 250; sales returns and allowances on, 310; showing adjustments for accrued expenses, *illustrated*, 437; showing net loss, 251; six-column, *illustrated*, 95; with Adjustments columns, *illustrated*, 249
Write-it-once principle, applied to bookkeeping machines, 512; *defined*, 512
Writing board, *illustrated*, 513; system, 512
Writing off uncollectible accounts, 384